Lecture Notes in Computer Science   11725

Commenced Publication in 1973
Founding and Former Series Editors:
Gerhard Goos, Juris Hartmanis, and Jan van Leeuwen

Advanced Research in Computing and Software Science
Subline of Lecture Notes in Computer Science

More information about this series at http://www.springer.com/series/7407

Ramin Yahyapour (Ed.)

Euro-Par 2019: Parallel Processing

25th International Conference
on Parallel and Distributed Computing
Göttingen, Germany, August 26–30, 2019
Proceedings

 Springer

Editor
Ramin Yahyapour 🆔
Gesellschaft für wissenschaftliche
Datenverarbeitung mbH Göttingen
Georg-August-Universität Göttingen
Göttingen, Germany

ISSN 0302-9743   ISSN 1611-3349 (electronic)
Lecture Notes in Computer Science
ISBN 978-3-030-29399-4   ISBN 978-3-030-29400-7 (eBook)
https://doi.org/10.1007/978-3-030-29400-7

LNCS Sublibrary: SL1 – Theoretical Computer Science and General Issues

This Springer imprint is published by the registered company Springer Nature Switzerland AG
The registered company address is: Gewerbestrasse 11, 6330 Cham, Switzerland

Preface

This volume contains the papers presented at Euro-Par 2019, the 25th International European Conference on Parallel and Distributed Computing, held during August 26–30, 2019, in Göttingen, Germany.

For 25 years, Euro-Par consistently brought together researchers in parallel and distributed computing. Founded by pioneers as a merger of the three thematically related European conference series PARLE and CONPAR-VAPP, Euro-Par started with the aim to create the main annual scientific event on parallel processing in Europe to be the primary choice of such professionals for the presentation of latest results in their fields.

A quarter of a century marks a special occasion to look back and recognize achievements and progress. Since its inception, Euro-Par has been covering all aspects of parallel and distributed computing, ranging from theory to practice, from the smallest to the largest parallel and distributed systems and infrastructures, from fundamental computational problems to full-fledged applications, from architecture, compiler, language, and interface design and implementation to tools, support infrastructures, and application performance. Euro-Par's unique organization into topics, provides an excellent forum for focused technical discussion, as well as interaction with a large, broad, and diverse audience who are researchers in academic institutions, public and private laboratories, or commercial stake-holders.

Euro-Par's topics were always oriented towards novel research issues and the current state of the art. Most topics became constant entries, while new themes emerged and were included in the conference. Euro-Par has a tradition of selecting new organizers and chairs for every edition, leading to fresh ideas and variations while staying true to the tradition. Organizers and chairs of previous editions support their successors. In this sense, Euro-Par also promotes networking across national borders, leading to the unique spirit of Euro-Par.

Previous conferences took place in Stockholm, Lyon, Passau, Southampton, Toulouse, Munich, Manchester, Paderborn, Klagenfurt, Pisa, Lisbon, Dresden, Rennes, Las Palmas, Delft, Ischia, Bordeaux, Rhodes, Aachen, Porto, Vienna, Grenoble, Santiago de Compostela, and Turin.

Thus, Euro-Par in Göttingen followed the well-established format of its predecessors. Euro-Par 2018 successfully added the Chess timer talks and the documentation of artifacts, which were carried over to Euro-Par 2019. The 25th edition of Euro-Par was organized with the support of the Georg-August-Universität Göttingen and GWDG. GWDG serves as the data center of the University and is one of the IT competence centers of the Max Planck Society. Göttingen hosts - jointly with the Konrad-Zuse-Institute in Berlin - the North-German Supercomputer (HLRN), and fosters research in and application of high performance computing. To reflect the applied aspects of parallel computing, new application oriented tracks and workshops were included in the Euro-Par 2019 program.

The topics of Euro-Par 2019 were organized into 10 tracks, where topics were merged for organizational reasons or transferred to other event types, namely:

- Support Tools and Environments
- Performance and Power Modeling, Prediction, and Evaluation
- Scheduling and Load Balancing
- Data Management, Analytics, and Deep Learning
- Cluster and Cloud Computing
- Parallel and Distributed Programming, Interfaces, and Languages
- Multicore and Manycore Parallelism
- Theory and Algorithms for Parallel Computation and Networking
- Parallel Numerical Methods and Applications
- Accelerator Computing for Advanced Applications

Overall, 142 papers were submitted from 40 countries. The number of submitted papers, the wide topic coverage, and the aim of obtaining high-quality reviews resulted in a difficult selection process involving a large number of experts. The joint effort of the members of the Scientific Committee and of the 128 external reviewers resulted in 560 reviews: 26 papers received three reviews, 97 received four reviews, and 20 received five or more, that is, on average, 3.94 reviews per paper. The accepted papers were chosen after detailed discussions and finalized during the paper selection meeting, which took place on April 30, 2019. As a result, 36 papers were selected to be presented at the conference and published in these proceedings, resulting in a 25, 3% acceptance rate.

The following two papers were nominated as 'distinguished' and presented in a plenary session: "Radio-Astronomical Imaging: FPGAs vs GPUs" and "Enhancing the Programmability and Performance Portability of GPU Tensor Operations".

In addition to the program, we had the pleasure of hosting three keynotes held by:

- Rosa M. Badia, Barcelona Supercomputing Center, Barcelona, Spain
- Michela Taufer, Tickel College of Engineering and Min H. Kao, Department of Electrical Engineering & Computer Science, Knoxville, Tennessee, USA
- Helmut Grubmüller, Max Planck Institute for Biophysical Chemistry, Theoretical and Computational Biophysics group, Göttingen, Germany

Euro-Par 2019 included a panel discussion and relaunched a poster session, which was specifically aimed at ambitious students.

The conference program started with two days of workshops and a tutorial on specialized topics. Dora Blanco Heras, Christian Boehme, and Ulrich Schwardmann ensured coordination and organization of this pre-conference event as workshop co-chairs. A selection of the papers presented at the workshops will be published in separate proceedings volumes after the conference. The workshop proceedings will also contain the contributions of the poster session.

We would like to thank the authors and chairs for contributing to the success of Euro-Par 2019. Similarly, we would like to extend our appreciation to the Euro-Par 2019 Steering Committee for its support. Last but not least, we would like to express our gratitude to the team at GWDG, whose relentless enthusiasm and effort made this event possible.

August 2019

Ramin Yahyapour
Ulrich Schwardmann
Christian Boehme

Organization

General Chair

Ramin Yahyapour   GWDG - Gesellschaft für wissenschaftliche
Datenverarbeitung mbH Göttingen,
University of Göttingen, Germany

Steering Committee

Full Members

Luc Bougé   ENS Rennes, France
Fernando Silva   University of Porto, Portugal
Marco Aldinucci   University of Turin, Italy
Dora Blanco Heras   CiTIUS, Santiago de Compostela, Spain
Emmanuel Jeannot   LaBRI-Inria Bordeaux, France
Christos Kaklamanis   Computer Technology Institute Patras, Greece
Paul Kelly   Imperial College London, UK
Thomas Ludwig   University of Hamburg, Germany
Tomàs Margalef   University Autonoma of Barcelona, Spain
Wolfgang Nagel   Technische Universität Dresden, Germany
Francisco Fernández Rivera   CiTIUS, Santiago de Compostela, Spain
Rizos Sakellariou   The University of Manchester, UK
Henk Sips   Delft University of Technology, The Netherlands
Domenico Talia   University of Calabria, Italy
Jesper Larsson Träff   Vienna University of Technology, Austria
Denis Trystram   Grenoble Institute of Technology, France
Felix Wolf   Technische Universität Darmstadt, Germany

Honorary Members

Christian Lengauer   University of Passau, Germany
Ron Perrott   Oxford e-Research Centre, UK
Karl Dieter Reinartz   University of Erlangen-Nürnberg, Germany

Observers

Krzysztof Rzadca   University of Warsaw, Poland
Ramin Yahyapour   GWDG - Gesellschaft für wissenschaftliche
Datenverarbeitung mbH Göttingen,
University of Göttingen, Germany

Workshops

Dora Blanco Heras	University of Santiago de Compostela, Spain
Christian Boehme	GWDG - Gesellschaft für wissenschaftliche Datenverarbeitung mbH Göttingen, Germany
Ulrich Schwardmann	GWDG - Gesellschaft für wissenschaftliche Datenverarbeitung mbH Göttingen, Germany

Logistics

Martina Brücher	GWDG - Gesellschaft für wissenschaftliche Datenverarbeitung mbH Göttingen, Germany
Thomas Otto	GWDG - Gesellschaft für wissenschaftliche Datenverarbeitung mbH Göttingen, Germany

Program Committee

Topic 1: Support Tools and Environments

Global Chair

João M. P. Cardoso   University of Porto, Portugal

Local Chair

Michael Gerndt   Technical University of Munich, Germany

Chairs

Giovanni Agosta	Politecnico di Milano, Italy
Mary Hall	University of Utah, USA
Sally McKee	Clemson University, USA
Bernd Mohr	Jülich Supercomputing Centre (JSC), Germany
Robert Schöne	Technische Universität Dresden, Germany
Ana Lucia Varbanescu	University of Amsterdam, The Netherlands

Topic 2: Performance and Power Modeling, Prediction and Evaluation

Global Chair

Tan Guangming   Chinese Academy of Sciences, Institute of Computing Technology, China

Local Chair

Andreas Knüpfer   Technische Universität Dresden, Germany

Chairs

Kaixi Hou	Virginia Tech, USA
Jiajia Li	Pacific Northwest National Laboratory, USA
Eric Liang	Peking University, China
Weifeng Liu	China University of Petroleum, China
Hao Wang	The Ohio State University, USA
Junmin Xiao	Chinese Academy of Sciences, Institute of Computing Technology, China
Xiaowen Xu	IAPCM Beijing, China
Liang Yuan	Chinese Academy of Sciences, Institute of Computing Technology, China
Jidong Zhai	Tsinghua University, China
Jing Zhang	Virgina Tech, USA
Xiuxia Zhang	Chinese Academy of Sciences, Institute of Computing Technology, China

Topic 3: Scheduling and Load Balancing

Global Chair

Andrei Tchernykh	CICESE Centro de Investigación Científica y de Educación Superior de Ensenada, Mexico

Local Chair

Sascha Hunold	Vienna University of Technology, Austria

Chairs

Zhihui Du	Tsinghua University, China
Fanny Dufossé	Inria Le Chesnay, France
Matthias Mnich	Universität Bonn, Germany
Risat Mahmud Pathan	Chalmers University of Technology, Sweden
Krzysztof Rzadca	University of Warsaw, Poland
Franciszek Seredynski	Cardinal Stefan Wyszyński University in Warsaw, Poland
Bertrand Simon	University of Bremen, Germany
Victor V. Toporkov	National Research University MPEI, Russia
Nodari Vakhania	Universidad Autónoma del Estado de Morelos, Mexico
Frank Werner	Otto-von-Guericke-Universität Magdeburg, Germany
Prudence W. H. Wong	University of Liverpool, UK

Topic 4: High Performance Architectures and Compilers

Global Chair

Pedro Petersen Moura Trancoso	University of Gothenburg, Sweden

Local Chair

Matthias Müller	RWTH Aachen, Germany

Chairs

Angelos Arelakis	ZeroPoint Technologies AB, Sweden
Alexandra Jimborean	Uppsala University, Sweden
Nuno Roma	Universidade de Lisboa, Portugal
Josef Weidendorfer	Technical University of Munich, Germany

Topic 5: Data Management, Analytics and Deep Learning

Global Chair

Alexandru Iosup	Vrije Universiteit Amsterdam, The Netherlands

Local Chair

Morris Riedel	Jülich Supercomputing Centre (JSC), Germany and University of Reykjavik, Iceland

Chairs

Zeynep Akata	University of Amsterdam, The Netherlands
Jorge Amaya	Katholieke Universiteit Leuven, Belgium
Ira Assent	Aarhus University, Denmark
Gabriele Cavallaro	Jülich Supercomputing Centre (JSC), Germany
Aaron Ding	Delft University of Technology, The Netherlands
Dmitry Duplyakin	University of Utah, USA
Ernir Erlingsson	University of Iceland, Iceland
Jens Henrik Goebbert	Jülich Supercomputing Centre (JSC), Germany
Markus Goetz	Karlsruhe Institute of Technology (KIT), Germany
Jenia Jitsev	Jülich Supercomputing Centre (JSC), Germany
Volodymyr Kindratenko	University of Illinois at Urbana-Champaign, USA
Kwo-Sen Kuo	Bayesics LLC, USA
Bastian Leibe	RWTH Aachen, Germany
Helmut Neukirchen	University of Iceland, Iceland
Rahul Ramachandran	NASA, USA
Tomas Runarsson	University of Iceland, Iceland
Animesh Trivedi	Vrije Universiteit Amsterdam, The Netherlands
Alexandru Uta	Vrije Universiteit Amsterdam, The Netherlands
Ana Lucia Varbanescu	University of Amsterdam, The Netherlands

Laurens Versluis   Vrije Universiteit Amsterdam, The Netherlands
Lin Wang   Vrije Universiteit Amsterdam, The Netherlands
Xiaoxiang Zhu   DLR German Aerospace Center, Technical University
                            of Munich, Germany

Topic 6: Cluster and Cloud Computing

Global Chair

Anne-Cećile Orgerie   CNRS, IRISA Rennes, France

Local Chair

Uwe Schwiegelshohn   TU Dortmund, Germany

Chairs

Alexandra Carpen-Amarie   Fraunhofer ITWM, Germany
Sebastien Lafond   Äbo Akademi University, Finland
Maciej Malawski   AGH University of Science and Technology, Poland
Maria S. Perez   Universidad Politécnica de Madrid, Spain
Rizos Sakellariou   The University of Manchester, UK

Topic 7: Distributed Systems and Algorithms

Global Chair

Dick Epema   Delft University of Technology, The Netherlands

Local Chair

Franz-Josef Pfreundt   Fraunhofer ITWM, Germany

Chairs

Gyorgy Dan   KTH Royal Institute of Technology, Sweden
Asterios Katsifodimos   Delft University of Technology, The Netherlands
Stefanie Roos   Delft University of Technology, The Netherlands
Francois Taiani   University of Rennes, CNRS, Inria, IRISA, France

Topic 8: Parallel and Distributed Programming, Interfaces, and Languages

Global Chair

Sato Mitsuhisa   RIKEN, Japan

Local Chairs

Christian Simmendinger   T-Systems Stuttgart, Germany
Vicen Beltran   Barcelona Supercomputing Center (BSC), Spain

Chairs

Olivier Aumage	Inria Le Chesnay, France
Marc Gonzalez	Universitat Politècnica de Catalunya, Spain
Changhee Jung	Virginia Tech, USA
Karla Morris	Sandia National Laboratories, USA
Alessandro Pellegrini	Sapienza University of Rome, Italy
Mirko Rahn	Fraunhofer ITWM, Germany
Miwako Tsuji	RIKEN, Japan
Tom Vander Aa	Exascience Lab at imec, Belgium
Masahiro Yasugi	Kyushu Institute of Technology, Japan

Topic 9: Multicore and Manycore Parallelism

Global Chair

Barbara Chapman · Stony Brook University, New York, USA

Local Chair

Guido Juckeland · Helmholtz-Zentrum Dresden-Rossendorf, Germany

Chairs

Sridutt Bhalachandra	Argonne National Laboratory Chicago, USA
Sunita Chandrasekaran	University of Delaware, USA
Rudolf Eigenmann	University of Delaware, USA
Oscar Hernandez	Oak Ridge National Laboratory, USA
Konstantinos Krommydas	Intel, USA
Cheng Wang	University of Houston, USA
Rengan Xu	Dell EMC, USA

Topic 10: Theory and Algorithms for Parallel Computation and Networking

Global Chair

Frédéric Vivien · Inria Le Chesnay, France

Local Chair

Henning Meyerhenke · Humboldt-Universität zu Berlin, Germany

Chairs

Kamer Kaya	Sabancı University, Turkey
Fanny Pascual	Université Pierre et Marie Curie, France
Cynthia Phillips	Sandia National Laboratories, USA
Peter Sanders	Karlsruhe Institute of Technology (KIT), Germany

Topic 11: Parallel Numerical Methods and Applications

Global Chair

Daniel Kressner   École polytechnique fédérale de Lausanne, Switzerland

Local Chair

Cornelia Grabe   DLR German Aerospace Center Göttingen, Germany

Chair

Thomas Gerhold   DLR German Aerospace Center Göttingen, Germany

Topic 12: Accelerator Computing

Global Chair

Raphael Y. de Camargo   Federal University of ABC, Brazil

Local Chair

Christian Plessl   Paderborn University, Germany

Chairs

Pedro Diniz   INESC TEC, Portugal
Holger Fröning   University of Heidelberg, Germany
Francisco Igual   Universidad Complutense de Madrid, Spain
Miriam Leeser   Northeastern University, USA
Andy Nisbet   The University of Manchester, UK

Topic 13: Algorithms and Systems for Bioinformatics

Global Chair

Folker Meyer   Argonne National Laboratory Chicago, USA

Local Chair

Alexander Sczyrba   University of Bielefeld, Germany

Chairs

Christophe Blanchet   CNRS IFB, France
Shane Canon   Lawrence Berkeley National Lab, USA
Rob Finn   EMBL-EBI, UK
Ananth Grama   Purdue University, USA

Topic 14: Algorithms and Systems for Digital Humanities

Global Chair

Iryna Gurevych   Technische Universität Darmstadt, Germany

Local Chair

Marco Büchler   Leibniz Institute of European History Mainz, Germany

Chairs

Sayeed Choudhury   Johns Hopkins University, USA
Eckart de Castilho   Technische Universität Darmstadt, Germany
Mark Hedges   King's College London, UK
Andrea Scharnhorst   DANS-KNAW, The Netherlands

Additional Reviewers

Tanwir Ahmad	Tony Curtis	Sergio Iserte
Artur Andrzejak	Alberto Antonio Del	Anshul Jindal
Eugenio Angriman	Barrio García	Jophin John
Adnan Ashraf	Alessandro Di Federico	Vasiliki Kalavri
Nikos Athanasis	Kostantinos Dogeas	Sudeep Kanur
Bartosz Balis	Manuel F. Dolz	Jeffrey Kelling
Daniel Balouek-Thomert	Fanny Dufossé	Marek Klonowski
Md Abdullah Shahneous	Tim Ehlers	Oliver Knodel
Bari	Pietro Fezzardi	Dušan Knop
Ayon Basumallik	Goran Flegar	Christian Köhler
Sergio Bernabé	Holger Fröning	Martin Kong
Anup Bhattacharya	Tobias Frust	Jan Kopanski
Akshay Bhosale	Swapnil Gaikwad	Daniel Kowalczyk
Marcus Boden	Jean-François Gibrat	Roger Kowalewski
Martin Böhm	Marcos Amarís González	David Kübel
Aurelien Bouteiller	Alexander Göke	Thomas Lambert
Lorenz Braun	Markus Götz	Sebastian Lamm
Linjin Cai	Thomas Gruber	Bo Li
Louis-Claude Canon	Loic Guegan	Lingda Li
Paris Carbone	Amina Guermouche	Key Liao
Adrián Castelló	Andrea Gussoni	Wictor Lund
Márcio Castro	Peter Györgyi	Alexander Matz
Imen Chakroun	Matthias Hauck	Jan Meizner
Stefano Cherubin	Byron Hawkins	Alok Mishra
Franz Christian Heinrich	Roman Iakymchuk	Clément Mommessin
Diego Costa	Aleksandar Ilic	Mayuri Morais
Xuewen Cui	Konstantinos Iordanou	Grégory Mounié

Stefan Mueller
Philippe Navaux
João Neto
Simon Omlor
Tim Oosterwijk
Marcus Paradies
Maciej Pawlik
Diego Perdomo
Vladimir Podolskiy
Laura Promberger
Bartlomiej Przybylski
Anna Pupykina
Issam Raïs
Carlos Reaño
Mohamad Rezaei

Crefeda Rodrigues
Javier Rojas Balderrama
Paul Saary
Amit Sabne
Danilo Carastan Santos
Günther Schindler
Scott Schneider
Malte Schwarzkopf
Rong Shi
Osman Seckin Simsek
Sebastian Starke
Athanasios Stratikopoulos
Lauritz Thamsen
Xiaonan Tian
Kim-Anh Tran

Elena Troubitsyna
Denis Trystram
Pedro Valero-Lara
Alexander van der Grinten
Pavel Veselý
Roland Vincze
Jie Wang
Tao Wang
Jianwen Wei
Minhua Wen
Chuan Wu
Jeffrey Young
Felix Zahn
Salah Zrigui
Pawel Zuk

Keynotes

Complex Workflows Development in Distributed Computing Infrastructures

Rosa Badia

Workflows and Distributed Computing Group Manager
Barcelona Supercomputing Center (BSC)
rosa.m.badia@bsc.es

Abstract. Distributed computing infrastructures are evolving from traditional models to environments that involve sensors, edge devices, instruments, etc, and, as well, high-end computing systems such as clouds and HPC clusters. A key aspect is how to describe and develop the applications to be executed in such platforms.

Very often these applications are not standalone, but involve a set of sub-applications or steps composing a workflow. The trend in these types of workflows is that the components can be of different nature, combining computationally intensive and data analytics components, for example. The scientists rely on effective environments to describe their workflows and engines and to manage them in complex infrastructures.

COMPSs is a task-based programming model that enables the development of workflows that can be executed in parallel in distributed computing platforms. The workflows that are currently supported may involve different types of tasks, such as parallel simulations (MPI) or analytics (i.e., written in Python thanks to PyCOMPSs, the Python binding for COMPSs). COMPSs, through a storage interface, makes transparent the access to persistent data stored in key-value databases (Hecuba) or object-oriented distributed storage environments (dataClay).

While COMPSs has been developed from its early times for distributed environments, we have been extending it to deal with more challenging environments, with edge devices and components in the fog, that can appear and disappear. Examples of new features that are considered in these environments are task failure management and input/output data from streams.

The talk will present an overview of the challenges on workflows' development in the mentioned environments and an overview of how it can be tackled with COMPSs.

Nanomachines at Work: Atomistic Simulations of Biomolecular Systems

Helmut Grubmüller

Director of the Theoretical and Computational Biophysics
Group at the Max Planck Institute of Biophysical Chemistry, Göttingen
hgrubmu@gwdg.de

Abstract. Without highly specialized 'nano machines' - the proteins - no organism would be able to survive. Almost all functions, e.g. photosynthesis for energy production in plants, various forms of movement, signal transmission and information processing, e.g. in the brain, sensor technology, and recognition, are performed by proteins whose perfection was already very advanced two billion years ago and often far exceeds that of our organs, not to mention our current technology.

Atomistic computer simulations of the motion and dynamics of the atoms that make up the proteins, combined with sophisticated experiments, enable a better understanding of the underlying functional mechanisms. We are beginning to realize that, already long ago, evolution 'invented' molecular electric motors, chemical factories, photocells, transformers, accumulators, 'Castor' transporters, and sensors. The lecture gives an overview of the state of the art of atomistic computer simulations, and what we can learn about how proteins are 'manufactured' by ribosomes, how antibiotics interfere with bacterial ribosomes, and how molecular recognition and specific ligand binding works.

We take a more global view on the 'universe' of protein dynamics motion patterns and demonstrate that a systematic coverage of this 'Dynasome' allows one to better predict protein function. Finally, algorithmic challenges concerning GPU implementation and scalability will be discussed.

Scientific Applications and Heterogeneous Architectures Data Analytics and the Intersection of HPC and Edge Computing

Michela Taufer and Jack Dongarra

Professor in High Performance Computing
Department of Electrical Engineering and Computer Science,
The University of Tennessee, Knoxville
taufer@utk.edu

Abstract. This talk discusses two emerging trends in computing (i.e., the convergence of data generation and analytics, and the emergence of edge computing) and how these trends can impact heterogeneous applications. Next-generation supercomputers, with their extremely heterogeneous resources and dramatically higher performance than current systems, will generate more data than we need or, even, can handle. At the same time, more and more data is generated at the edge, requiring computing and storage to move closer and closer to data sources. The coordination of data generation and analysis across the spectrum of heterogeneous systems including supercomputers, cloud computing, and edge computing adds additional layers of heterogeneity to applications workflows. More importantly, the coordination can neither rely on manual, centralized approaches as it is predominately done today in HPC nor exclusively be delegated to be just a problem for commercial Clouds. This talk presents case studies of heterogeneous applications in precision medicine and precision farming that expand scientist workflows beyond the supercomputing center and shed our reliance on large-scale simulations exclusively, for the sake of scientific discovery.

Contents

Theory and Algorithms for Parallel Computation and Networking

Parallel Numerical Methods and Applications

Accelerator Computing

Support Tools and Environments

Online Fault Classification in HPC Systems Through Machine Learning

Alessio Netti[1,2(✉)], Zeynep Kiziltan[1], Ozalp Babaoglu[1], Alina Sîrbu[3], Andrea Bartolini[4], and Andrea Borghesi[4]

[1] Department of Computer Science and Engineering, University of Bologna, Bologna, Italy
{alessio.netti,zeynep.kiziltan,ozalp.babaoglu}@unibo.it
[2] Leibniz Supercomputing Centre, Garching bei München, Germany
alessio.netti@lrz.de
[3] Department of Computer Science, University of Pisa, Pisa, Italy
alina.sirbu@unipi.it
[4] Department of Electrical, Electronic and Information Engineering, University of Bologna, Bologna, Italy
{a.bartolini,andrea.borghesi3}@unibo.it

Abstract. As *High-Performance Computing* (HPC) systems strive towards the *exascale* goal, studies suggest that they will experience excessive failure rates. For this reason, detecting and classifying faults in HPC systems as they occur and initiating corrective actions before they can transform into failures will be essential for continued operation. In this paper, we propose a fault classification method for HPC systems based on machine learning that has been designed specifically to operate with live streamed data. We cast the problem and its solution within realistic operating constraints of online use. Our results show that almost perfect classification accuracy can be reached for different fault types with low computational overhead and minimal delay. We have based our study on a local dataset, which we make publicly available, that was acquired by injecting faults to an in-house experimental HPC system.

Keywords: High-performance computing · Exascale systems · Resiliency · Monitoring · Fault detection · Machine learning

1 Introduction

Motivation. Modern scientific discovery is increasingly being driven by computation [18]. As such, HPC systems have become fundamental "instruments" for driving scientific discovery and industrial competitiveness. Exascale (10^{18} operations per second) is the moonshot for HPC systems and reaching this goal is bound to produce significant advances in science and technology. Future HPC systems will achieve exascale performance through a combination of faster processors and massive parallelism. With Moore's Law reaching its limit, the only

© Springer Nature Switzerland AG 2019
R. Yahyapour (Ed.): Euro-Par 2019, LNCS 11725, pp. 3–16, 2019.
https://doi.org/10.1007/978-3-030-29400-7_1

viable path towards higher performance has to consider switching from increased transistor density towards increased core count, thus leading to increased failure rates [6]. Exascale HPC systems not only will have many more cores, they will also use advanced low-voltage technologies that are more prone to aging effects [4] together with system-level performance and power modulation techniques, all of which tend to increase fault rates [8]. It is estimated that large parallel jobs will encounter a wide range of failures as frequently as once every 30 min on exascale platforms [16]. Consequently, exascale performance, although achieved nominally, cannot be sustained for the duration of applications running for long periods.

In the rest of the paper, we adopt the following terminology. A *fault* is defined as an anomalous behavior at the hardware or software level that can lead to illegal system states (*errors*) and, in the worst case, to service interruptions (*failures*) [10]. Future exascale HPC systems must include automated mechanisms for masking faults, or recovering from them, so that computations can continue with minimal disruptions. This in turn requires detecting and classifying faults as soon as possible since they are the root causes of errors and failures.

Contributions. We propose and evaluate a fault classification method based on supervised Machine Learning (ML) suitable for online deployment in HPC systems. Our approach relies on a collection of performance metrics that are readily available in most HPC systems. The experimental results show that our method can classify almost perfectly several types of faults, ranging from hardware malfunctions to software issues and bugs. Furthermore, classification can be achieved with little computational overhead and with minimal delay, thus meeting real time requirements. We characterize the performance of our method in a realistic context similar to online use, where live streamed data is fed to fault classifiers both for training and for detection, dealing with issues such as class imbalance and ambiguous states. Most existing studies, on the contrary, rely on extensive manipulation of data, which is not feasible in online scenarios. Moreover, we reproduce the occurrence of faults basing on real failure traces.

Our evaluation is based on a dataset that we acquired from an experimental HPC system (called Antarex) where we injected faults using FINJ, a tool we previously developed [15]. Making the Antarex dataset publicly available is another contribution of this paper. Acquiring our own dataset for this study was made necessary by the fact that commercial HPC system operators are very reluctant to share trace data containing information about faults in their systems [13].

Related Work. Automated fault detection through system performance metrics and fault injection has been the subject of numerous studies. However, ML-based methods using fine-grained monitored data (i.e., sampling once per second) are more recent. Tuncer et al. [17] propose a framework for the diagnosis of performance anomalies in HPC systems; however, they do not deal with faults that lead to errors and failures, which cause a disruption in the computation, but only with performance anomalies that result in longer runtimes for applications. Moreover, the data used to build the test dataset was not acquired continuously, but rather in small chunks related to single application runs. Thus it is not possible to determine the feasibility of this method when dealing with streamed, continuous data from an online HPC system. A similar work is proposed by Baseman et al. [2], which focuses on identifying faults in HPC systems through temperature sensors. Ferreira et al. [9] analyze the impact of CPU interference on HPC applications by using a kernel-level noise injection framework. Both works deal with specific fault types, and are therefore limited in scope.

Other authors have focused on using coarser-grained data (i.e., sampling once per minute) or on reducing the dimension of collected data, while retaining good detection accuracy. Bodik et al. [5] aggregate monitored data by using fingerprints, which are built from quantiles corresponding to different time epochs. Lan et al. [14] discuss an outlier detection framework based on principal component analysis. Guan et al. [11,12] propose works focused on finding the correlations between performance metrics and fault types through a most relevant principal components method. Wang et al. [19] propose a similar entropy-based outlier detection framework suitable for use in online systems. These frameworks, which are very similar to threshold-based methods, are not suitable for detecting the complex relationships that may exist between different performance metrics under certain faults. One notable work in threshold-based fault detection is the one proposed by Cohen et al. [7], in which probabilistic models are used to estimate threshold values for performance metrics and detect outliers. This approach requires constant human intervention to tune thresholds, and lacks flexibility.

Organization. This paper is organized as follows. In Sect. 2, we describe the Antarex dataset, and in Sect. 3, we discuss the features extracted from it. In Sect. 4, we present our experimental results, and we conclude in Sect. 5.

2   The Antarex Dataset

The Antarex dataset contains trace data collected from an HPC system located at ETH Zurich while it was subjected to fault injections. The dataset is publicly available for use by the community and all the details regarding the test environment, as well as the employed applications and faults are extensively documented.[1] Due to space limitations, here we only give a short overview.

2.1   Dataset Overview

In order to acquire data, we executed benchmark applications and at the same time injected faults in a single compute node in the HPC system. The dataset is divided into two parts: the first includes only the CPU and memory-related benchmark applications and fault programs, while the second is strictly hard drive-related. We executed each part in both single-core and multi-core settings, resulting in 4 blocks of nearly 20GB and 32 days of data in total. The dataset's

---

[1] Antarex Dataset: https://zenodo.org/record/2553224.

Table 1. A summary of the structure for the Antarex dataset.

Dataset block	Type	Parallel	Duration	Benchmark programs	Fault programs
Block I	CPU-Mem	No	12 days	DGEMM, HPCC, STREAM, HPL[a]	leak, memeater, ddot, dial, cpufreq, pagefail
Block III		Yes			
Block II	Hard Drive	No	4 days	IOZone, Bonnie++[b]	ioerr, copy
Block IV		Yes			

[a]DGEMM: https://lanl.gov/projects/crossroads/, HPCC: https://icl.cs.utk.edu/hpcc/, STREAM: https://www.cs.virginia.edu/stream/, HPL: https://software.intel.com/en-us/articles/intel-mkl-benchmarks-suite
[b]IOZone: https://iozone.org, Bonnie++: https://coker.com.au/bonnie++/

structure is summarized in Table 1. We acquired the data by continuous streaming, thus any study based on it will easily be reproducible on a real HPC system, in an online way.

2.2 Experimental Setup for Data Acquisition

The Antarex compute node used for data acquisition is equipped with two Intel Xeon E5-2630 v3 CPUs, 128 GB of RAM, a Seagate ST1000NM0055-1V4 1TB hard drive and runs the CentOS 7.3 operating system. The node has a default Tier-1 computing system configuration. The FINJ tool [15] was used to execute benchmark applications and to inject faults, in a Python 3.4 environment. To collect performance metrics, we used the Lightweight Distributed Metric Service (LDMS) framework [1]. We configured LDMS to sample a variety of metrics at each second, which come from the *meminfo, perfevent, procinterrupts, procdiskstats, procsensors, procstat* and *vmstat* plugins. This configuration resulted in a total of 2094 metrics collected each second. Some of the metrics are node-level, and describe the status of the node as a whole, others instead are core-specific and describe the status of one of the 16 available CPU cores.

2.3 Features of the Dataset

FINJ orchestrates the execution of benchmark applications and the injection of faults by means of a workload file, which contains a list of benchmark and fault-triggering tasks to be executed at certain times, on certain cores, for certain durations. For this purpose, we used several FINJ-generated workload files, one for each block of the dataset. The details regarding the internal mechanisms driving FINJ are discussed in the associated work by Netti et al. [15].

Workload Files. We used two statistical distributions in the FINJ workload generator to create the durations and inter-arrival times of the benchmark and fault-triggering tasks. The benchmark tasks are characterized by duration and inter-arrival times following normal distributions, and 75% of the dataset's duration is spent running benchmarks. Fault-triggering tasks on the other hand are

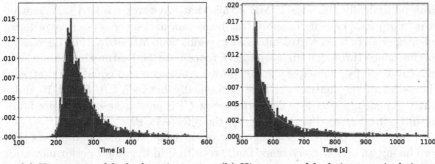

(a) Histogram of fault durations.   (b) Histogram of fault inter-arrival times.

Fig. 1. Histograms for fault durations (a) and fault inter-arrival times (b) in the Antarex dataset compared to the PDFs of the Grid5000 data, as fitted on a Johnson SU and Exponentiated Weibull distribution respectively. We define the inter-arrival time as the interval between the start of two consecutive tasks.

modeled using distributions fitted on the Grid5000 host failure trace available on the Failure Trace Archive.[2] In Fig. 1, we show the histograms for the durations (a) and inter-arrival times (b) of the fault tasks in the workload files, together with the original distributions fitted from the Grid5000 data.

FINJ generates each task in the workload by picking randomly the respective application to be executed, from those that are available. This implies that, statistically, all of the benchmark programs we selected will be subject to all of the available fault-triggering programs, given a sufficiently-long workload, with different execution overlaps depending on the starting times and durations of the specific tasks. Such a task distribution greatly mitigates overfitting issues. Finally, we do not allow fault-triggering program executions to overlap.

Benchmark Applications. We used a series of well-known benchmark applications, stressing different parts of the node and providing a diverse environment for fault injection. Since we limit our analysis to a single machine, we use versions of the benchmarks that rely on shared-memory parallelism, for example through the OpenMP library. The benchmark applications are listed in Table 1.

Fault Programs. All the fault programs used to reproduce anomalous conditions on Antarex are available at the FINJ Github repository [15]. As in [17], each program can also operate in a low-intensity mode, thus doubling the number of possible fault conditions. While we do not physically damage hardware, we closely reproduce several reversible hardware issues, such as I/O and memory allocation errors. Some of the fault programs (*ddot* and *dial*) only affect the performance of the CPU core they run on, whereas the other faults affect the entire compute node. The programs and the generated faults are as follows.

---

[2] Failure Trace Archive: http://fta.scem.uws.edu.au/.

1. *leak* periodically allocates 16 MB arrays that are never released [17] creating a *memory leak*, causing memory fragmentation and severe system slowdown;
2. *memeater* allocates, writes into and expands a 36 MB array [17], decreasing performance through a *memory interference* fault and saturating bandwidth;
3. *ddot* repeatedly calculates the dot product between two equal-size matrices. The sizes of the matrices change periodically between 0.9, 5 and 10 times the CPU cache's size [17]. This produces a *CPU and cache interference* fault, resulting in degraded performance of the affected CPU;
4. *dial* repeatedly performs floating-point operations over random numbers [17], producing an *ALU interference* fault, resulting in degraded performance for applications running on the same core as the program;
5. *cpufreq* decreases the maximum allowed CPU frequency by 50% through the Linux Intel P-State driver.[3] This simulates a *system misconfiguration* or *failing CPU* fault, resulting in degraded performance;
6. *pagefail* makes any page allocation request fail with 50% probability.[4] This simulates a *system misconfiguration* or *failing memory* fault, causing performance degradation and stalling of running applications;
7. *ioerr* fails one out of 500 hard-drive I/O operations with 20% probability, simulating a *failing hard drive* fault, and causing degraded performance for I/O-bound applications, as well as potential errors;
8. *copy* repeatedly writes and then reads back a 400 MB file from a hard drive. After such a cycle, the program sleeps for 2 s [12]. This simulates an *I/O interference* or *failing hard drive* fault by saturating I/O bandwidth, and results in degraded performance for I/O-bound applications.

3   Creation of Features

In this section, we explain how a set of features describing the state of the system for classification purposes was obtained from the metrics collected by LDMS.

Post-Processing of Data. Firstly, we removed all constant metrics (e.g., the amount of total memory in the node), which were redundant, and we replaced the raw monotonic counters captured by the *perfevent* and *procinterrupts* plug-ins with their first-order derivatives. Furthermore, we created an *allocated* metric, both at the CPU core and node level, and integrated it in the original set. This metric has a binary value, and defines whether there is a benchmark allocated on the node or not. Using such a metric is reasonable, since in any HPC system there is always knowledge of which jobs have computational resources currently allocated to them. Lastly, for each metric above, at each time point, we added its first-order derivative to the dataset as proposed by Guan et al. [11].

Feature vectors were then created by aggregating the post-processed LDMS metrics. Each feature vector corresponds to a 60-s aggregation window and is related to a specific CPU core. The step between feature vectors is of 10 s. This

---

[3] Intel P-State Driver: https://kernel.org/doc/Documentation/cpu-freq.
[4] Linux Fault Injection: https://kernel.org/doc/Documentation/fault-injection.

allows for high granularity and quick response times to faults. For each metric, we computed several indicators of the distribution of the values measured within the aggregation window [17]. These are the *average, standard deviation, median, minimum, maximum, skewness, kurtosis*, and finally the *5th, 25th, 75th* and *95th percentiles*. This results in a total of 22 statistical features, including also those related to the first-order derivatives, for each metric in the dataset. The final feature vectors contain thus a total of 3168 elements. This number does not include the metrics collected by the *procinterrupts* plugin, which were found to be irrelevant after preliminary testing. All the scripts used to process the data are available on the FINJ Github repository [15].

Labeling. In order to train classifiers to distinguish between faulty and normal states, we labeled the feature vectors either according to the fault program (i.e., one of the 8 programs presented in Sect. 2.3) running within the corresponding aggregation window, or "healthy" if no fault was running. The logs produced by the FINJ tool, which are included in the Antarex dataset, detail the fault programs running at each time-stamp. In a generic deployment scenario, if users wish to perform training using data from spontaneous faults in the system, they need to provide the labels explicitly instead of relying on fault injection.

A single aggregation window may capture multiple system states, making labeling not trivial. For example, a feature vector may contain "healthy" time points that are before and after the start of a fault, or even include two different fault types. We define these feature vectors as *ambiguous*. By using a short aggregation window of 60 s, we aim to minimize the impact of such ambiguous system states on fault detection. Since these cannot be completely removed, we experiment with two labelling methods. The first method is *mode*, where all the labels that appear in the time window are considered. Their distribution is examined and the label appearing the most is used for the feature vector. This leads to robust feature vectors, whose label is always representative of the aggregated data. The second method is *recent*, in which the label is given by the state of the system at the most recent time point in the time window. This could correspond to a fault type or could be "healthy". Such an approach may lead to a more responsive fault detection system, where what is detected is the system state at the moment, rather than the state over the last 60 s.

Detection System Architecture. For our fault detection system, we adopted an architecture based on an array of classifiers (Fig. 2). Each classifier corresponds to a specific computing resource type in the node, such as CPU cores, GPUs, MICs, etc. Each classifier is then trained with feature vectors related to all resource units of that type, and is able to perform fault diagnoses for all of them, thus detecting faults both at node level and resource level (e.g., dial and ddot). To achieve this, the feature vectors for each classifier contain all *node-level* metrics for the system, together with *resource-specific* metrics for the resource unit being considered. Since each feature vector contains data from one resource unit at most, this approach has the benefit of limiting the size of feature vectors, which improves overhead and detection accuracy. This architecture relies on the assumption that resource units of the same type behave in the same way, and

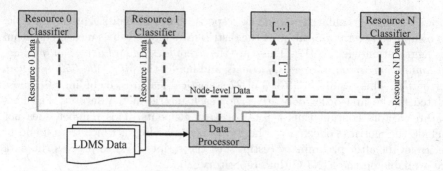

Fig. 2. Architecture of our machine learning-based fault detection system.

that the respective feature vectors can be combined in a coherent set. However, users can also opt to use separate classifiers for each resource unit of the same type, overcoming this limitation, without any alteration to the feature vectors themselves. In our case, the compute node only contains CPU cores. Therefore, we train one classifier with feature vectors that contain both node-level and core-level data, for one core at a time.

The classifiers' training can be performed offline, using labeled data resulting from normal system operation or from fault injection (as in our case). The trained classifiers can then be deployed to detect faults on new, streamed data. Due to this classifier-based architecture, we can only detect one fault at any time. This design assumption is reasonable for us, as the purpose of our study is to distinguish between different fault scenarios automatically. In a real HPC system, although as a rare occurrence, multiple faults may be affecting the same compute node at the same time. In this case, our detection system would only detect the fault whose effects on the system are deemed more relevant by the classifier.

4   Experimental Results

We tested a variety of classifiers, trying to correctly detect which of the 8 faults described in Sect. 2.3 were injected in the HPC node at any point in time of the Antarex dataset. The environment we used was Python 3.4, with the Scikit-learn package. We built the test dataset by picking the feature vector of only one randomly-selected core for each time point. Classifiers were thus trained with data from all cores, and can compute fault diagnoses for any of them.

We chose 5-fold cross-validation for evaluation of classifiers, using the average F-score as metric, which corresponds to the harmonic mean between precision and recall. When not specified, feature vectors are read in time-stamp order. In fact, while shuffling is widely used in machine learning as it can improve the quality of training data, such a technique is not well suited to our fault detection framework. Our design is tailored for online systems, where classifiers are trained using only continuous, streamed, and potentially unbalanced data as it is acquired, while ensuring robustness in training so as to detect faults in the

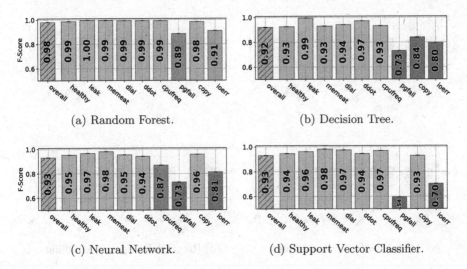

Fig. 3. The classification results on the Antarex dataset, using all feature vectors in time-stamp order, the *mode* labeling method, and different classifiers.

near future. Hence, it is very important to assess the detection accuracy without data shuffling. We reproduce this realistic, online scenario by performing cross-validation on the Antarex dataset using feature vectors in time-stamp order. Most importantly, time-stamp ordering results in cross-validation folds, each containing data from a specific time frame. Only a small subset of the tests is performed using shuffling for comparative purposes.

4.1 Comparison of Classifiers

For this experiment, we preserved the time-stamp order of the feature vectors and used the *mode* labeling method. We included in the comparison a Random Forest (RF), Decision Tree (DT), Linear Support Vector Classifier (SVC) and Neural Network (MLP) with two hidden layers, each having 1000 neurons. We choose these four classifiers because they characterize the performance of our method well, and omit results on others for space reasons. The results for each classifier and for each class are presented in Fig. 3. In addition, the overall F-score is highlighted for each classifier. It can be seen that all classifiers show very good performance, with F-scores that are well above 0.9. RF is the best classifier, with an overall F-score of 0.98, followed by MLP and SVC scoring 0.93. The critical point for all classifiers is represented by the *pagefail* and *ioerr* faults, which have substantially worse scores than the others.

We infer that a RF would be the ideal classifier for an online fault detection system, due to its 5% better detection accuracy, in terms of F-score, over the others. Additionally, random forests are computationally efficient, and therefore would be suitable for use in online environments with strict overhead requirements. It should be noted that unlike the MLP and SVC classifiers, RF and DT did not require data normalization. Normalization in an online environment is

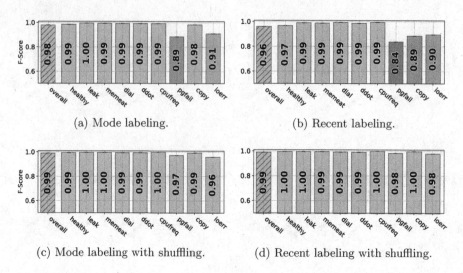

(a) Mode labeling.   (b) Recent labeling.

(c) Mode labeling with shuffling.   (d) Recent labeling with shuffling.

Fig. 4. RF classification results, using all feature vectors in time-stamp (top) or shuffled (bottom) order, with the *mode* (left) and *recent* (right) labeling methods.

hard to achieve, as many metrics do not have well-defined upper bounds. To address this issue, a rolling window-based dynamic normalization approach can be used [12]. This approach is unfeasible for ML classification, as it can lead to quickly-degrading detection accuracy and to the necessity of frequent training. Hence, in the following experiments we will use a RF classifier.

4.2 Comparison of Labeling Methods and Impact of Shuffling

Here we evaluate the two different labeling methods we implemented by using a RF classifier. The results for classification without data shuffling can be seen in Figs. 4a for *mode* and 4b for *recent*, with overall F-scores of 0.98 and 0.96 respectively, being close to the ideal values. Once again, in both cases the *ioerr* and *pagefail* faults perform substantially worse than the others. This is likely because both faults have an intermittent nature, with their effects depending on the hard drive I/O (ioerr) and memory allocation (pagefail) patterns of the underlying applications, proving more difficult to detect than the other faults.

In Figs. 4c and d, the results with data shuffling enabled are presented for the *mode* and *recent* methods, respectively. Adding data shuffling produces a sensible improvement in detection accuracy for both of the labeling methods, which show almost ideal performance for all fault programs, and overall F-scores of 0.99. Similar results were observed with the other classifiers presented in Sect. 4.1, not shown here for space reasons. It can also be seen that in this scenario, *recent* labeling performs slightly better for some fault types. This is likely due to the highly reactive nature of such labeling method, which can capture system status changes more quickly than the *mode* method. The greater accuracy (higher F-score) improvement obtained with data shuffling and *recent* labeling, compared to *mode*, indicates that the former is more sensible to temporal correlations in the data, which may lead to erroneous classifications.

4.3 Impact of Ambiguous Feature Vectors

Here we give insights on the impact of ambiguous feature vectors in the dataset on the classification process by excluding them from the training and test sets. Not all results are shown for space reasons. With the RF classifier, overall F-scores are 0.99 both with and without shuffling, leading to a slightly better classification performance compared to the entire dataset. In the Antarex dataset, around 20% of the feature vectors are ambiguous. With respect to this relatively large proportion, the performance gap described above is small, which proves the robustness of our detection method. In general, the proportion of ambiguous feature vectors in a dataset depends primarily on the length of the aggregation window, and on the frequency of state changes in the HPC system. More feature vectors will be ambiguous as the length of the aggregation window increases, leading to more pronounced adverse effects on the classification accuracy.

A more concrete example of the behavior of ambiguous feature vectors can be seen in Fig. 5, where we show the scatter plots of two important metrics (as quantified by a DT classifier) for the feature vectors related to the ddot, cpufreq and memeater fault programs, respectively. The "healthy" points, marked in blue, and the fault-affected points, marked in orange, are distinctly clustered in all cases. On the other hand, the points representing the ambiguous feature vectors, marked in green, are sparse, and often fall right between the "healthy" and faulty clusters. This is particularly evident with the cpufreq fault program in Fig. 5b.

4.4 Remarks on Overhead

Quantifying the overhead of our fault detection framework is fundamental to prove its feasibility on a real online HPC system. LDMS is proven to have a low overhead at high sampling rates [1]. We also assume that the generation of feature vectors and the classification are performed locally in each node, and that only the resulting fault diagnoses are sent externally. This implies that the hundreds of performance metrics we use do not need to be sampled and streamed at a fine granularity. We calculated that generating a set of feature vectors, one for each core in our test node, at a given time point for an aggregation window of 60 s takes on average 340 ms by using a single thread, which includes the I/O overhead of reading and parsing LDMS CSV files, and writing the output feature vectors. Performing classification for one feature vector using a RF classifier takes on average 2 ms. This results in a total overhead of 342 ms for generating and classifying feature vectors for each 60-s aggregation window, using a single thread, which is acceptable for online use. Such overhead is expected to be much lower in a real system, with direct in-memory access to streamed data, since no CSV files must be processed and therefore no file system I/O is required.

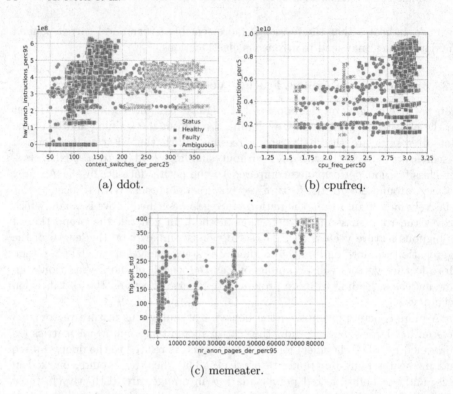

(a) ddot. (b) cpufreq.

(c) memeater.

Fig. 5. The scatter plots of two important metrics, as quantified by a DT classifier, for three fault types. The "healthy" points are marked in blue, while fault-affected points in orange, and the points related to ambiguous feature vectors in green.

Moreover, as the single statistical features are independent from each other, data processing can be parallelized on multiple threads to further reduce latency and ensure load balancing across CPU cores, which is critical to prevent slowdown for certain applications.

5   Conclusions

We have presented a fault detection and classification method based on machine learning techniques, targeted at HPC systems. Our method is designed for streamed, online data obtained from a monitoring framework, which is then processed and fed to classifiers. Due to the scarcity of public datasets containing detailed information about faults in HPC systems, we acquired the Antarex dataset and evaluated our method based on it. Results of our study show almost perfect classification accuracy for all injected fault types, with negligible computational overhead for HPC nodes. Moreover, our study reproduces the operating conditions that could be found in a real online system, in particular those related to ambiguous system states and data imbalance in the training and test sets.

As future work, we plan to deploy our fault detection framework in a large-scale real HPC system. This will involve the development of tools to aid online training of machine learning models, as well as the integration in a monitoring framework such as Examon [3]. We also need to better understand our system's behavior in an online scenario. Specifically, since training is performed before HPC nodes move into production (i.e., in a test environment) we need to characterize how often re-training is needed, and devise a procedure to perform this.

Acknowledgements. A. Netti has been supported by the *Oprecomp-Open Trans-precision Computing* project. A. Sîrbu has been partially funded by the EU project *SoBigData Research Infrastructure — Big Data and Social Mining Ecosystem* (grant agreement 654024). We thank the Integrated Systems Laboratory of ETH Zurich for granting us control of their Antarex HPC node during this study.

References

1. Agelastos, A., Allan, B., Brandt, J., Cassella, P., et al.: The lightweight distributed metric service: a scalable infrastructure for continuous monitoring of large scale computing systems and applications. In: Proceedings of SC 2014, pp. 154–165. IEEE (2014)
2. Baseman, E., Blanchard, S., DeBardeleben, N., Bonnie, A., et al.: Interpretable anomaly detection for monitoring of high performance computing systems. In: Proceedings of the ACM SIGKDD Workshops 2016 (2016)
3. Beneventi, F., Bartolini, A., Cavazzoni, C., Benini, L.: Continuous learning of HPC infrastructure models using big data analytics and in-memory processing tools. In: Proceedings of DATE 2017, pp. 1038–1043. IEEE (2017)
4. Bergman, K., Borkar, S., Campbell, D., Carlson, W., et al.: Exascale computing study: technology challenges in achieving exascale systems. DARPA IPTO, Technical Report 15 (2008)
5. Bodik, P., Goldszmidt, M., Fox, A., Woodard, D.B., et al.: Fingerprinting the datacenter: automated classification of performance crises. In: Proceedings of EuroSys 2010, pp. 111–124. ACM (2010)
6. Cappello, F., Geist, A., Gropp, W., Kale, S., et al.: Toward exascale resilience: 2014 update. Supercomput. Front. Innovations $1(1)$, 5–28 (2014)
7. Cohen, I., Chase, J.S., Goldszmidt, M., Kelly, T., et al.: Correlating instrumentation data to system states: a building block for automated diagnosis and control. OSDI **4**, 16 (2004)
8. Engelmann, C., Hukerikar, S.: Resilience design patterns: a structured approach to resilience at extreme scale. Supercomputing Front. Innovations $4(3)$, 4–42 (2017)
9. Ferreira, K.B., Bridges, P., Brightwell, R.: Characterizing application sensitivity to OS interference using kernel-level noise injection. In: Proceedings of SC 2008, p. 19. IEEE Press (2008)
10. Gainaru, A., Cappello, F.: Errors and faults. In: Herault, T., Robert, Y. (eds.) Fault-Tolerance Techniques for High-Performance Computing. CCN, pp. 89–144. Springer, Cham (2015). https://doi.org/10.1007/978-3-319-20943-2_2
11. Guan, Q., Chiu, C.C., Fu, S.: CDA: a cloud dependability analysis framework for characterizing system dependability in cloud computing infrastructures. In: Proceedings of PRDC 2012, pp. 11–20. IEEE (2012)

12. Guan, Q., Fu, S.: Adaptive anomaly identification by exploring metric subspace in cloud computing infrastructures. In: Proceedings of SRDS 2013, pp. 205–214. IEEE (2013)
13. Kondo, D., Javadi, B., Iosup, A., Epema, D.: The failure trace archive: enabling comparative analysis of failures in diverse distributed systems. In: Proceedings of CCGRID 2010, pp. 398–407. IEEE (2010)
14. Lan, Z., Zheng, Z., Li, Y.: Toward automated anomaly identification in large-scale systems. IEEE Trans. Parallel Distrib. Syst. **21**(2), 174–187 (2010)
15. Netti, A., Kiziltan, Z., Babaoglu, O., Sîrbu, A., Bartolini, A., Borghesi, A.: FINJ: a fault injection tool for HPC systems. In: Mencagli, G., et al. (eds.) Euro-Par 2018. LNCS, vol. 11339, pp. 800–812. Springer, Cham (2019). https://doi.org/10.1007/978-3-030-10549-5_62. https://github.com/AlessioNetti/fault_injector
16. Snir, M., Wisniewski, R.W., Abraham, J.A., Adve, S.V., et al.: Addressing failures in exascale computing. Int. J. High Perform. Comput. Appl. **28**(2), 129–173 (2014)
17. Tuncer, O., Ates, E., Zhang, Y., Turk, A., et al.: Online diagnosis of performance variation in HPC systems using machine learning. IEEE Trans. Parallel Distrib. Syst. **30**(4), 883–896 (2018)
18. Villa, O., Johnson, D.R., Oconnor, M., Bolotin, E., et al.: Scaling the power wall: a path to exascale. In: Proceedings of SC 2014, pp. 830–841. IEEE (2014)
19. Wang, C., Talwar, V., Schwan, K., Ranganathan, P.: Online detection of utility cloud anomalies using metric distributions. In: Proceedings of NOMS 2010, pp. 96–103. IEEE (2010)

Accelerating Data-Dependence Profiling with Static Hints

Mohammad Norouzi[1]([✉]), Qamar Ilias[1], Ali Jannesari[2], and Felix Wolf[1]

[1] Technische Universitaet Darmstadt, Darmstadt, Germany
{norouzi,wolf}@cs.tu-darmstadt.de, ilias.qamar@gmail.com
[2] Iowa State University, Ames, IA, USA
jannesari@iastate.edu

Abstract. Data-dependence profiling is a program-analysis technique to discover potential parallelism in sequential programs. Contrary to purely static dependence analysis, profiling has the advantage that it captures only those dependences that actually occur during execution. Lacking critical runtime information such as the value of pointers and array indices, purely static analysis may overestimate the amount of dependences. On the downside, dependence profiling significantly slows down the program, not seldom prolonging execution by a factor of 100. In this paper, we propose a hybrid approach that substantially reduces this overhead. First, we statically identify persistent data dependences that will appear in any execution. We then exclude the affected source-code locations from instrumentation, allowing the profiler to skip them at runtime and avoiding the associated overhead. At the end, we merge static and dynamic dependences. We evaluated our approach with 38 benchmarks from two benchmark suites and obtained a median reduction of the profiling time by 62% across all the benchmarks.

1 Introduction

Data-dependence analysis is a prerequisite for the discovery of parallelism in sequential programs. Traditionally, compilers such as PLUTO [1] perform it statically with the goal of auto-parallelizing loops. However, lacking critical runtime information such as the value of pointers and array indices, purely static dependence analysis may overestimate the amount of dependences. This is why auto-parallelization has not succeeded much beyond the confines of the polyhedral model [2], a theoretical framework for the optimization and, in particular, parallelization of loops that satisfy certain constraints.

Recently, many tools [3–7] emerged that avoid some of the limits of purely static analysis. They abandon the idea of fully automatic parallelization and instead point the user to likely parallelization opportunities, based on data dependences captured at runtime. They counter the inherent input sensitivity of such a dynamic approach by running the program with several representative inputs and by providing weaker correctness guarantees, although their suggestions more than often reproduce manual parallelization strategies. In addition,

© Springer Nature Switzerland AG 2019
R. Yahyapour (Ed.): Euro-Par 2019, LNCS 11725, pp. 17–28, 2019.
https://doi.org/10.1007/978-3-030-29400-7_2

they observed that data dependences in frequently executed code regions that are subject to parallelization do not change significantly with respect to different inputs [4–6]. Nonetheless, high runtime overhead, caused by the need to profile memory accesses during execution, makes them hard to use. Optimizations such as sampling loop iterations for profiling [8], parallelizing the data-dependence profiler itself [5,9], and skipping repeatedly executed memory operations [10] lower the overhead only to a certain degree. To reduce the overhead more substantially, we take a fundamentally different route. Leveraging the power of prior static dependence analysis, we exclude those memory accesses from profiling whose data dependences can already be determined at compile time.

Overall, we follow a hybrid approach. First, we run a static analyzer, PLUTO in our case, to identify those data dependences that every program execution must respect. We then run the dependence profiler but refrain from instrumenting all memory-access instructions that correspond to these dependences, allowing the profiler to skip them at runtime and avoid the associated overhead. Furthermore, we transform all data dependences regardless of how they have been obtained - whether statically or dynamically - into a unified representation and merge them into one output. Here, we focus on reducing the profiling overhead. How to use the acquired data dependences to identify parallelization potential is addressed in related work [4,5,7] and beyond the scope of this paper. In a nutshell, we make the following specific contributions:

- A hybrid approach to the extraction of data dependences that combines the advantages of static and dynamic techniques
- An implementation as an extension of the data-dependence profiler of DiscoPoP [7], although our approach is generic enough to it be implemented in any data-dependence profiler
- An evaluation with 38 programs from two benchmark suites, showing a median reduction of the profiling time by 62%

The remainder of the paper is organized as follows. We discuss related work in Sect. 2. Section 3 presents our approach, followed by an evaluation in Sect. 4. Finally, we review our achievements in Sect. 5.

2   Related Work

Profiling of memory accesses is a common technique to identify data dependences [4,5,7], but suffers from high runtime overhead, not seldom causing a slowdown of a factor of 100 or more. A typical method to reduce runtime overhead is sampling [8], although it does not apply well to data-dependence profiling. A data dependence is made of two distinct memory accesses and omitting only one of them is enough to miss a dependence or introduce spurious dependences.

But there are further optimizations available to lower the profiling overhead. For example, Parwiz [4], a parallelism discovery tool, coalesces contiguous memory accesses. This lowers the profiling overhead, but only for a subset of the memory accesses. Kremlin [11], another parallelization recommender system, profiles data dependences only within specific code regions. To save memory overhead, SD3 [5], a dependence profiler, compresses memory accesses with stride patterns. Moreover, it reduces the runtime overhead by parallelizing the profiler itself. DiscoPoP [7] is a parallelism discovery tool that includes a generic data-dependence profiler [9], which serves as the basis for our implementation. The original version of the profiler converts the program into its LLVM-IR representation, after which it instruments all memory access instructions. A runtime library tracks the memory accesses during execution. To reduce the memory and runtime overhead, it records memory accesses in a signature hash table. Moreover, it skips repeatedly executed memory operations. Like SD3, it runs multiple threads to reduce the runtime overhead further. Because of its favorable speed with an average slowdown of 86, we implemented our approach in DiscoPoP, although it is generic enough to improve the efficiency of any profiler. The main difference to the optimizations pursued in other tools is the hybrid combination of dynamic and static dependence analysis.

To obtain data dependences statically, we use PLUTO [1], an auto-parallelizing compiler for polyhedral loops. PLUTO annotates the beginning and end of a code section containing a polyhedral loop. The annotated area is called a SCoP (Static Control Part) and fulfills certain constraints. It has a single entry and a single exit point and contains only (perfectly-nested) loops with affine linear bounds [2]. With PLUTO extracting data dependences from SCoPs, we accelerate subsequent dependence profiling by excluding memory-access operations that appear in SCoPs from instrumentation, cutting the SCoP-related profiling overhead.

Another hybrid-analysis framework was proposed by Rus et al. [12]. It targets the automatic parallelization of loops whose parallelization is not obvious at compile time. Based on the results of static analysis, they formulate conditions and insert them into the source code. These conditions evaluate at runtime whether a loop can be parallelized or not. In contrast to their work, our contribution happens at a lower level, where we just collect data dependences, with the goal of increasing the profiling speed.

3 Approach

Below, we explain our hybrid approach to identify data dependences. Figure 1 shows the basic workflow. Dark boxes highlight our contribution in relation to the previously isolated static and dynamic dependence analyses. First, we extract data dependences statically. Based on these dependences, we identify memory-access instructions that can be eliminated from profiling. The precise elimination algorithm is explained in Sect. 3.1. The dynamic data-dependence analysis will then skip these instructions during the profiling process. Finally, we transform all data dependences we have found – whether of static or dynamic origin – into a unified representation, whose details we describe in Sect. 3.2, and merge them into a single output file. Before we proceed to the evaluation in Sect. 4, we also discuss the relation between the set of data dependences extracted by the hybrid and the purely dynamic approach in Sect. 3.3.

Algorithm 1. Exclusion of memory-access instructions from instrumentation

```
for each function f ∈ program do
    SCoPSet = PLUTO.getSCoPs(f)
    for each SCoP s ∈ SCoPSet do
        varSet = getVariables(s)
        for each variable var ∈ varSet do
            instrument(firstLoadInst(var,s))
            instrument(lastLoadInst(var,s))
            instrument(firstStoreInst(var,s))
            instrument(lastStoreInst(var,s))
```

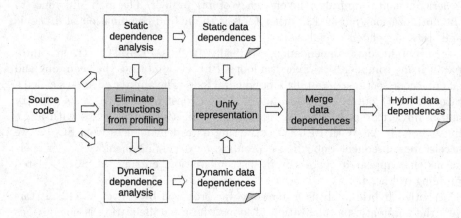

Fig. 1. The workflow of our hybrid data-dependence analysis. Dark boxes show our contributions.

3.1   Reduced Instrumentation

We exclude specific memory-access instructions from instrumentation that appear inside source code locations from which PLUTO can extract data dependences statically. Algorithm 1 shows the details and can be best understood when following the examples in Fig. 2.

We first let PLUTO annotate the target program with SCoP directives. In the example, lines 10 and 65 contain the annotations. Then, we traverse the source code and mark the variables inside a SCoP. For each variable, we determine its boundary instructions: the first and the last read and write operation. The first read and write of the array variable a appear in lines 15 and 20 and the last read and write in lines 55 and 60, respectively. We instrument only these boundary instructions and mark all other memory-access operations on a variable for exclusion. The dark box shows the section to be left out for variable a.

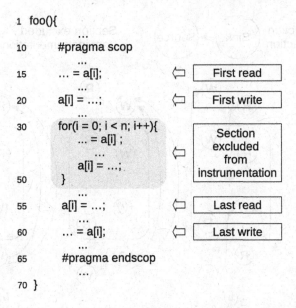

Fig. 2. A SCoP and the memory-access instructions excluded from instrumentation.

If a profiler fails to instrument one of the boundary instructions, it will report false positive and negative data dependences. False positives are data dependences that are reported but do not exist in the program. Conversely, false negatives are data dependences that exist in the program but are not reported by the profiler. False positive or negative data dependences that are reported when the boundary instructions are skipped can adversely influence parallelization recommendations that span across multiple SCoPs. The opportunities inside a SCoP, however, are not affected because PLUTO extracts all the data dependences relevant to its parallelization. We profile the boundary instructions not to miss any data dependences that a purely dynamic method would obtain. In addition, this avoids false positives and negatives and helps assess parallelization potential that stretches across SCoPs. Figures 3a and b show situations that create false negatives. If we exclude the first read in Fig. 3a, the read-after-write (RAW) dependence between the first read inside the SCoP and the last write preceding it is not reported. If the first write is eliminated, two types of false negatives will happen: on the one hand, the write-after-read (WAR) between the first write and the read before the SCoP (Fig. 3b), and the write-after-write (WAW) between the first write and the write before the SCoP on the other. Moreover, if we do not instrument the last read operation on a variable (Fig. 3a), the WAR between the last read and the write after the SCoP will be ignored. If we exclude the last write, however, dependences of two types will not be reported: the RAW between the last write and the read after the SCoP (Fig. 3b) and the WAW between the last write and the write after the SCoP. Of course, these considerations apply only to live-out loop variables that are accessed both inside and outside the loop.

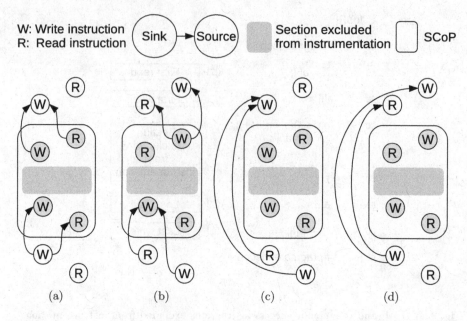

Fig. 3. Situations that create false negative (a and b) and false positive (c and d) data dependences when the first and last read and write instructions in a SCoP are not instrumented (shown in dark circles).

Figures 3c and d show situations that create false positives. Three types of false positives are reported if the boundary instructions are not instrumented. Figure 3c shows a false positive RAW between the last write preceding the SCoP and the first read succeeding it. Figure 3d shows a WAR that will be reported falsely between the last read before the SCoP and the first write after it. Finally, the write operations before and after the SCoP, in both figures, create false positive WAW dependences.

Our analysis excludes memory-access instructions that exist in polyhedral loops. In the worst case, if there are no polyhedral loops in a program, all instructions are instrumented and thus, the hybrid approach falls back to the purely dynamic approach. The overhead of the hybrid approach, in this case, is not reduced in comparison with the purely dynamic approach.

```
1        1:60 NOM {RAW 1:60|i} {WAR 1:60|i}
2        1:63 NOM {RAW 1:59|temp1} {RAW 1:67|temp1}
3        1:64 NOM {RAW 1:60|i}
4        1:65 NOM {RAW 1:59|temp1} {RAW 1:67|temp1} {WAR 1:67|temp2}
5        1:66 NOM {RAW 1:59|temp1} {RAW 1:65|temp2} {RAW 1:67|temp1}
6        1:67 NOM {RAW 1:65|temp2} {WAR 1:66|temp1}
7        1:70 NOM {RAW 1:67|temp1}
8        1:74 NOM {RAW 1:41|block}
```

Fig. 4. A fragment of unified data dependences extracted from a sequential program.

Algorithm 2. Transformation of data dependences identified by PLUTO into the unified representation.

---

for *each SCoP scop* ∈ *SCoPSet* **do**
  fileID = *findFileID*(*scop*)
  depSet = *PLUTO.getDeps*(*scop*)
  for *each dependence dep* ∈ *depSet* **do**
    varName = *getVarName*(*dep*)
    sourceLine = *findSourceLine*(*dep*)
    sinkLine = *findSinkLine*(*dep*)
    depType = *getDataType*(*dep*)
    print(*fileID* : *sinkLine depType fileID* : *sourceLine*|*varName*)

3.2 Unified Representation

A data dependence exists if the same memory location is accessed twice and at least one of the two accesses is a write. Without loss of generality, one of the accesses occurs earlier and one later during sequential execution. To store data dependences, static and dynamic tools use different representations, which we unify in this paper. A sample of unified data dependences is shown in Fig. 4. We write a data dependence as a triple <sink, type, source>. type is the dependence type (i.e., RAW, WAR, or WAW). Because they are irrelevant to parallelization and, strictly speaking, do not even constitute a dependence according to our definition above, most data-dependence profilers do not profile read-after-read (RAR) dependences, which is why we do not report them either. sink and source are the source code locations of the later and the earlier memory access, respectively. sink is specified as a pair <fileID:lineID>, while source is specified as a triple <fileID:lineID|variableName>. We assign a unique fileID to each file in a program. Existing profilers, including Parwiz, DiscoPoP, SD3, and Intel Pin [13], already display data dependences in terms of source-code files, line numbers, and variable names. Thus, transforming their output to our unified representation requires little effort.

PLUTO, in contrast, assigns a unique ID to each source-code statement in a SCoP and reports data dependences based on these IDs. We use Algorithm 2 to transform the output of PLUTO into the unified representation. First, we find the fileID of each SCoP, before we retrieve the set of data dependences in a SCoP from PLUTO. We use the IDs to identify the statements in which the source and sink of a data dependence appear. Then, we read the source code of the file to find the line number of the statements. Finally, we determine the type of the data dependence and the name of the variable involved in it. Unfortunately, PLUTO does not report data dependences for loop index variables. We apply use-def analysis to statically identify the types of data dependences for the indices appearing in SCoPs. We cannot run this analysis for an entire program because the code beyond the SCoPs may contain pointers that cannot be tracked with use-def analysis. At the end, we transform the dependences for the loop indices into the unified representation.

Once we have collected all data dependences using our portfolio of static and dynamic methods, we merge them into a joint ASCII file. To reduce the size of the output, we compress the dependence data, merging all dependences with the same sink into a single line. Finally, we sort the dependences based on the sink. The result can be used by parallelism discovery tools to find parallelization opportunities.

3.3 Hybrid vs. Dynamic Data Dependences

Now, we take a deeper look into the relationship between the set of data dependences extracted by our hybrid approach in comparison to the one produced by purely dynamic analysis, which is illustrated in Fig. 5. To better understand this relation, let us consider the listings in the figure. In Fig. 5b, both loops meet the constraints of the polyhedral model. PLUTO finds data dependences in those loops and, thus, our hybrid approach excludes the whole conditional block from profiling. Profilers might execute either the if or the else branch, depending on the condition $k < average$, and extract dependences only in the executed part. Only running the program with two different inputs, each of them causing the program to take a different branch, however, would allow a profiler to identify dependences in both parts. In general, the set of hybrid data dependences is

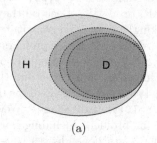

(a)

```
if ( k < average ){
    for ( i = 0; i < n; i++ ) {
        q[i] = q[i] + A[i] * p[i];
    }
} else {
    for ( j = 0; j < n; j++ ) {
        s[j] = s[j] + r[j] * A[j];
    }
}
```

```
if ( k < average ){
    for ( i = 0; i < n; i++ ) {
        w = a[f(i)];
        a[g(i)] = v;
    }
} else {
    for ( j = 0; j < n; j++ ) {
        s[j] = s[j] + r[j];
    }
}
```

```
if ( k < average ){
    for ( i = 0; i < n; i++ ) {
        w = b[f(i)];
        a[g(i)] = v;
    }
} else {
    for ( j = 0; j < n; j++ ) {
        d = d * z[colidx[j]];
    }
}
```

(b) Both loops are polyhedral

(c) Only the loop in the else part is polyhedral

(d) Neither loops are polyhedral

Fig. 5. (a): The relation between dynamic and hybrid data dependences. H includes data dependences that are identified via hybrid analysis. D contains data dependences identified via dynamic analysis with a finite set of inputs. (b) and (c): Two examples where $D \subseteq H$. (d) One example where $H = D$.

therefore a superset of the set of purely dynamic data dependences (i.e., $D \subseteq H$). Figure 5c shows a similar case where the set of hybrid dependences contains the set of dynamic dependences (i.e., $D \subseteq H$). There are two loops, but only the one in the else branch is polyhedral. Again, profilers might miss the dependences in the polyhedral loop if none of the provided inputs makes the program go through the else branch. Finally, in Fig. 5d, neither loop is polyhedral. PLUTO does not extract dependences from either loop and, thus, our approach does not exclude any instructions from instrumentation. In this case, the set of dependences identified by our approach is equal to the set of dependences detected by purely dynamic analysis (i.e., $H = D$).

In theory, H and D would be different for a program only if a polyhedral loop recognized by PLUTO was never executed. However, this condition happens rarely in practice because polyhedral loops constitute hotspots, that is, they consume major portions of the execution time. As several authors have shown [4–7], such regions are usually always visited—regardless of the specific input. Exceptions include, for example, erroneous inputs that cause the program to terminate prematurely.

4   Evaluation

We conducted a range of experiments to evaluate the effectiveness of our approach. Our test cases are the NAS Parallel Benchmarks 3.3.1 [14] (NPB), a suite of programs derived from real-world computational fluid-dynamics applications, and Polybench 3.2 [15], a test suite originally designed for polyhedral compilers. We compiled the benchmarks using clang 3.6.8, which is also used by the DiscoPoP profiler for program instrumentation. We ran the benchmarks on an Intel(R) Xeon(R) CPU E5-2650 2.00 GHz with 32Gb of main memory, running Ubuntu 14.04 (64-bit edition). To profile the benchmarks, we used the inputs the benchmark designers provided alongside the programs. Our evaluation criteria are the completeness of the data dependences in relation to purely dynamic profiling and the profiling time. We compared the set of data dependences identified by the profiler with and without prior static analysis. Because the entire source code of the benchmarks was visited during the execution with the given inputs, we observed no difference in the reported data dependences. Following the arguments of Sect. 3.3, however, we believe that higher code-coverage potential makes our approach generally less input sensitive than purely dynamic methods, a claim we want to substantiate in a follow-up study.

To measure how much our hybrid method speeds up the profiler, we ran the benchmarks first with the vanilla version of the DiscoPoP profiler. We ran each benchmark five times in isolation, recorded the median of the execution times, and declared it as our baseline. Then, we profiled the benchmarks with the enhanced version of the profiler, taking advantage of prior static analysis and reduced instrumentation. Again, we ran each benchmark fives times in isolation and calculated the median of the execution times, which we then compared with our baseline. Table 1 summarizes the relative slowdown caused by the purely dynamic vs. the hybrid approach for the two benchmark suites. Finally, Fig. 6 presents the relative overhead reduction for each benchmark.

Table 1. Relative slowdown caused by standard DiscoPoP vs. the hybrid approach.

Benchmark suites	Standard DiscoPoP			Hybrid approach		
	Min	Max	Median	Min	Max	Median
Polybench	37.57	144.98	71.67	14.26	47.84	24.42
NPB	18.60	130.50	82.67	18.11	121.09	63.18
All	18.60	144.98	72.28	14.26	121.09	27.32

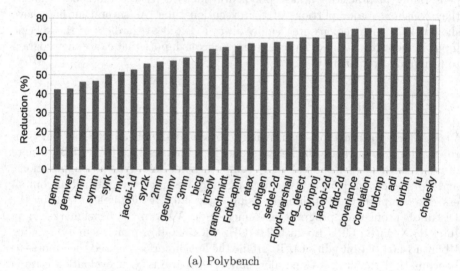

(a) Polybench

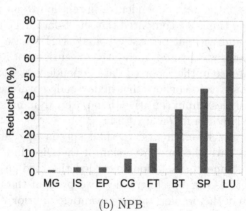

(b) NPB

Fig. 6. Profiling-time reduction relative to the standard DiscoPoP profiler.

Whether we can reduce the profiling time of a benchmark depends on its computational pattern. In theory, the more work is done in polyhedral loops, the more effective our method will be. If a program does not contain such loops, we fail to reduce the profiling overhead significantly. Notably, our method lowered the profiling time in all test cases. For four benchmarks in NPB, namely EP, IS, CG, and MG, we observed only small improvements because there we could not exclude many instructions from profiling. For all other benchmarks, our approach was highly effective. We noticed that removing write operations influences the profiling time more than removing reads; when profiling a write operation we need to look for both WAW and WAR dependences, whereas we only need to look for RAW dependence when profiling a read operation. In general, however, the number of excluded write instructions is less than the number of reads. Overall, we achieved a median profiling-time reduction by 62%. The size of the dependence files generated by the hybrid approach for these benchmarks is in the order of kBs.

5   Conclusion

Our hybrid approach to data-dependence analysis allows the profiler to skip code locations whose dependences can be extracted statically. Nevertheless, not to miss any data dependence a purely dynamic method would obtain, we still profile memory operations at the boundaries of these locations, capturing data dependences that point into and out of them. We implemented our approach in a state-of-the-art data-dependence profiler and achieved a median reduction of the profiling time by 62% across a large set of benchmarks, making it far more practical than before. Faster profiling will enable the DiscoPoP framework to identify parallelism in larger and longer running programs. However, in principle, our method can serve as frontend to any data-dependence profiler. Our specific PLUTO-based implementation focuses on polyhedral loops, which opens up two possible avenues to future work. First, we could try to expand the coverage of the static analysis, exploring dependences outside polyhedral loops. Second, since polyhedral loops can be easily parallelized statically, we could make parallelism discovery tools, whose strength lies in more unstructured parallelism outside such loops, aware of them and make them cooperate with polyhedral tools also on the level of parallelism discovery and code transformation, exploiting their advantages while filling their gaps.

Acknowledgement. This work has been funded by the Hessian LOEWE initiative within the Software-Factory 4.0 project. Additional support has been provided by the German Research Foundation (DFG) through the Program Performance Engineering for Scientific Software and the US Department of Energy under Grant No. DE-SC0015524.

References

1. Bondhugula, U.: Pluto - an automatic parallelizer and locality optimizer for affine loop nests (2015). http://pluto-compiler.sourceforge.net/. Accessed 13 June 2019

2. Benabderrahmane, M.W., Pouchet, L.N., Cohen, A., Bastoul, C.: The polyhedral model is more widely applicable than you think. In: Proceedings of the Conference on Compiler Construction. CC 2010, Paphos, Cyprus, pp. 283–303, March 2010
3. Wilhelm, A., Cakaric, F., Gerndt, M., Schuele, T.: Tool-based interactive software parallelization: a case study. In: Proceedings of the International Conference on Software Engineering. ICSE 2018, Gothenburg, Sweden, pp. 115–123, June 2018
4. Ketterlin, A., Clauss, P.: Profiling data-dependence to assist parallelization: Framework, scope, and optimization. In: Proceedings of the International Symposium on Microarchitecture. MICRO 1945, Vancouver, B.C., Canada, pp. 437–448, December 2012
5. Kim, M., Kim, H., Luk, C.K.: SD3: a scalable approach to dynamic data-dependence profiling. In: Proceedings of the International Symposium on Microarchitecture. MICRO 1943, Atlanta, GA, USA, pp. 535–546, December 2010
6. Norouzi, M., Wolf, F., Jannesari, A.: Automatic construct selection and variable classification in OpenMP. In: Proceedings of the International Conference on Supercomputing. ICS 2019, Phoenix, AZ, USA, pp. 330–342, June 2019
7. Li, Z., Atre, R., Huda, Z.U., Jannesari, A., Wolf, F.: Unveiling parallelization opportunities in sequential programs. J. Syst. Softw. 117(1), 282–295 (2016)
8. Jimborean, A., Clauss, P., Martinez, J.M., Sukumaran-Rajam, A.: Online dynamic dependence analysis for speculative polyhedral parallelization. In: Wolf, F., Mohr, B., an Mey, D. (eds.) Euro-Par 2013. LNCS, vol. 8097, pp. 191–202. Springer, Heidelberg (2013). https://doi.org/10.1007/978-3-642-40047-6_21
9. Li, Z., Jannesari, A., Wolf, F.: An efficient data-dependence profiler for sequential and parallel programs. In: Proceedings of the International Parallel and Distributed Processing Symposium. IPDPS 2015, Hyderabad, India, pp. 484–493, May 2015
10. Li, Z., Beaumont, M., Jannesari, A., Wolf, F.: Fast data-dependence profiling by skipping repeatedly executed memory operations. In: Proceedings of the International Conference on Algorithms and Architectures for Parallel Processing. ICA3PP 2015, Zhangjiajie, China, pp. 583–596, November 2015
11. Garcia, S., Jeon, D., Louie, C.M., Taylor, M.B.: Kremlin: rethinking and rebooting gprof for the multicore age. In: Proceedings of the Conference on Programming Language Design and Implementation. PLDI 2011, pp. 458–469, June 2011
12. Rus, S., Rauchwerger, L., Hoeflinger, J.: Hybrid analysis: static & dynamic memory reference analysis. Int. J. Parallel Prog. 31(4), 251–283 (2003)
13. Intel: Pin - a dynamic binary instrumentation tool (2010). https://software.intel.com/en-us/articles/pin-a-dynamic-binary-instrumentation-tool. Accessed 13 June 2019
14. Bailey, D.H., et al.: The NAS parallel benchmarks. Int. J. Supercomput. Appl. 5(3), 63–73 (1991)
15. Pouchet, L.N.: Polyhedral suite (2011). http://www.cs.ucla.edu/pouchet/software/polybench/. Accessed 13 June 2019

Multi-valued Expression Analysis
for Collective Checking

Pierre Huchant[1,2], Emmanuelle Saillard[2(✉)], Denis Barthou[1,2],
and Patrick Carribault[3]

[1] Bordeaux Institute of Technology, University of Bordeaux, LaBRI,
Bordeaux, France
[2] Inria, Bordeaux, France
emmanuelle.saillard@inria.fr
[3] CEA, DAM, DIF, 91297 Arpajon, France

Abstract. Determining if a parallel program behaves as expected on any execution is challenging due to non-deterministic executions. Static analyses help to detect all execution paths that can be executed concurrently by identifying multi-valued expressions, i.e. expressions evaluated differently among processes. This can be used to find *collective errors* in parallel programs. In this paper, we propose a new method that combines a control-flow analysis with a multi-valued expressions detection to find such errors. We implemented our method in the PARCOACH framework and successfully analyzed parallel applications using MPI, OpenMP, UPC and CUDA.

1 Introduction

Collective operations and in particular synchronizations are widely used operations in parallel programs. They are part of languages for distributed parallelism such as MPI or PGAS (collective communications), shared-memory models like OpenMP (barriers) and languages for accelerators such as CUDA (synchronization within thread blocks, cooperative groups and at warp-level). A valid use of collective operations requires at least that their sequence is the same for all threads/processes during a parallel execution. An invalid use (*collective error*) leads to deadlocks or undefined memory state that may be difficult to reproduce and debug. Indeed, these languages do not require that all processes reach the same textual collective statement (*textual alignment* property [1,2]). Finding which collective matches a given collective is needed for collective checking and requires to analyse the different concurrent execution paths of a parallel execution.

Aiken and Gay introduced the concept of *structural correctness* for synchronizations in SPMD programs, based on the notion of *multi-valued* and *single-valued* variables [3]. A variable is said multi-valued if its value is dependent on the process identifier (single-valued otherwise). A program has structurally correct synchronization if all processes have the same sequence of synchronization

© Springer Nature Switzerland AG 2019
R. Yahyapour (Ed.): Euro-Par 2019, LNCS 11725, pp. 29–43, 2019.
https://doi.org/10.1007/978-3-030-29400-7_3

operations. Thus, if a synchronization is executed conditionally, both branches of the condition have a synchronization or the condition expression is single-valued. We can extend the notion of structural correctness to collectives. In this paper, we propose a novel method to detect *collective errors* in parallel programs. It combines an inter-procedural analysis to perform collective matching and a data-flow analysis to detect multi-valued variables. The first pass finds control-flow divergence that may lead to collective deadlocks while the second one filters out the divergences that do not depend on process identifier. We show on several benchmarks and applications that this combination is more accurate than the state-of-the-art analyses and resolves some correctness issues. The analysis has been implemented in the PARallel COntrol flow Anomaly CHecker [4,5] (PARCOACH) framework and tested on benchmarks and real HPC applications, using MPI, OpenMP, UPC and CUDA.

Section 2 describes several deadlock situations in parallel programs. Section 3 presents PARCOACH analysis while Sects. 4 and 5 describe our multi-valued expression detection and its integration in PARCOACH to find collective errors. Section 6 gives related work on dependence analyses and verification tools. Section 7 shows experimental results and Sect. 8 concludes our work.

2   Motivation

This section illustrates four possible deadlock situations due to collectives in MPI, OpenMP, CUDA and UPC as presented in Fig. 1 (from a to d).

The MPI code (Fig. 1a) contains two collectives: `MPI_Barrier` and `MPI_Reduce`. The call to `MPI_Barrier` at line 17 is performed by all MPI processes, whereas the call `MPI_Reduce` in g at line 3 may deadlock. Indeed, variable n is multi-valued in the condition expression line 14. Odd-ranked processes evaluate the conditional to true and potentially execute the reduce, while even-ranked ones evaluate it to false, hanging in the `MPI_Barrier` at line 17. On the contrary, variable s is single-valued. Hence, all processes in g execute the reduce or none. The goal of our method is to statically report this situation, identifying the conditional at line 14, and only this one, as a potential cause for mismatched calls.

According to the OpenMP specification, the same explicit and implicit[1] barriers (syntactically) should be executed by all threads. In practice, the OpenMP runtimes allow the execution of syntactically different barriers, as long as all threads execute the same number of barriers. The code Fig. 1b is written in OpenMP. The `#pragma omp parallel` directive in function f defines r, containing the thread ID (l.10) and s, as private variables. The first barrier line 12 is encountered by all threads as it is in the global control flow. The barrier line 3 is either executed by all threads of the program or by none of them as s

---

[1] There is an implicit barrier at the end of all worksharing constructs, unless a `nowait` clause is specified.

is single-valued when entering function g at line 14. Because s becomes multi-valued at line 15, the barrier line 17 is conditionally executed. This leads to a deadlock situation if the number of threads is greater than 1 at runtime.

The CUDA code (Fig. 1c) manipulates multidimensional thread IDs through predefined variables such as `threadIdx`. In CUDA, synchronizations are valid if executed by all threads within the same block. Before the first synchronization, the array `tile` depends on thread IDs at line 7. As the array is shared among threads, they all share the same version after the synchronization. The synchronization at line 10 is conditionally executed depending on `tile[0]`. As this value does not depend on thread ID, there is no possible deadlock. Depending on the driver, the third synchronization at line 12 may lead to either a deadlock or an undefined memory configuration. This bug can be difficult to detect for a programmer in a real code as this is a silent synchronization error.

```
1   void g(int s) {
2     if(s > 256)
3        MPI_Reduce(com,...);
4   }
5
6   void f() {
7     int s,r,n;
8     MPI_Comm_size(com,&s);
9     MPI_Comm_rank(com,&r);
10    if (r % 2)
11       n = 1;
12    else
13       n = 2;
14    if (n == 1)
15       g(s);
16
17    MPI_Barrier(com);
18  }
```

(a) MPI example

```
1   void g(int s) {
2     if(s)
3        #pragma omp barrier
4   }
5
6   void f() {
7     int r; int s=1;
8     #pragma omp parallel private(r,s)
9     {
10       r=omp_get_thread_num();
11       ...
12       #pragma omp barrier
13       ...
14       g(s);
15       s=r%2;
16       if(s)
17          #pragma omp barrier
18    }
19  }
```

(b) OpenMP example

```
1   void f(int *data) {
2     __shared__ int tile[];
3     int tid = threadIdx.x;
4     int gid =
5        blockIdx.x*blockDim.x
                   +tid;
6
7     tile[tid] = data[gid];
8     __syncthreads();
9     if (tile[0])
10       __syncthreads();
11    if (tid)
12       __syncthreads();
13  }
```

(c) CUDA example

```
1   void f() {
2     int i=1; j=10;
3     if(MYTHREAD%2){
4        while(i<10){
5           upc_barrier; i++;
6        }
7     }else{
8        while(j<20){
9           upc_barrier; j++;
10       }
11    }
12  }
```

(d) UPC example

```
1   void f() {
2     ...
3     if(x)
4        collective
5     ...
6     if(!x)
7        collective
8
9   }
```

(e) Not verifiable

Fig. 1. Examples of collective issues and a correct program not verifiable by our analysis.

The code Fig. 1d is written in Unified Parallel C (UPC), a PGAS language. The predefined variable MYTHREAD specifies thread index. In this code, because of the multi-valued expression at line 3, threads with odd ID will call nine barriers (l.5) while the others will call ten barriers (l.9). Although structurally correct, this code leads to a deadlock. Our analysis reports all collectives in a loop as potentially deadlocking. But note that our analysis would return a false positive if the two loops had the same number of iteration.

A static analysis on the previous codes only detects situations and causes of possible deadlocks. If the codes are executed with only one process, no deadlock can happen. Also, our analysis returns a false positive for some correct but structurally incorrect codes like the example Fig. 1e. In addition to our analysis, we use PARCOACH instrumentation of programs explained in [5] to handle such situations.

3   PARCOACH Control-Flow Analysis

Our analysis first uses PARCOACH to find all conditionals (flow-divergences) that may lead to the execution of different collective sequences.

PARCOACH static analysis relies on the Parallel Program Control Flow Graph (PPCFG) representation of a program [5]. The PPCFG is a program control-flow graph (CFG) where nodes are basic blocks and edges represent the possible flow of control between nodes. To build the PPCFG, PARCOACH reduces each function control-flow graph and replaces each callsite by the callee reduced CFG. Then, with a graph traversal of the PPCFG, PARCOACH computes the possible execution order r of each collective c and the *iterated post-dominance frontier* (PDF$^+$) for collectives of the same type and order. For a set of collectives $C_{r,c}$, PDF$^+(C_{r,c})$ corresponds to the control-flow divergences that may result in the execution or non-execution of a collective in $C_{r,c}$. Note that to handle communicators in MPI programs, PARCOACH analyses the program for each communicator separately.

4   Multi-valued Expression Detection

PARCOACH finds all conditionals potentially leading to different sequences of collectives but reports false positives when conditionals do not depend on a multi-valued expression. This section presents our multi-valued expressions detection.

Enhanced SSA. Our analysis is based on the Static Single Assignment (SSA) form of the program. In SSA, variables are defined exactly once. Variables assigned in multiple statements are renamed into new instances, one per statement. This makes explicit def/use chains. When multiple control-flow paths join in the CFG, renamed variables are combined with a ϕ-function into a new variable instance. To capture control-flow dependences we compute an enhanced SSA where ϕ-functions are augmented with their predicates: $\phi(y_1, ..., y_k)$ is transformed into $\phi(y_1, ..., y_k, p_1, ..., p_k)$ with p_i the conditionals responsible for the choice of the y_i. These conditionals are determined by computing the PDF^+ of each argument y_i of the ϕ-function as in [6].

For C-like programs, variables that can be referenced with their address (*address-taken variables*), are only manipulated through pointers with load and store instructions in the SSA form. To compute def/use chains for address-taken variables, we rely on the principles exposed in flow-sensitive pointer analyses such as [7,8]: First a points-to analysis is computed to handle potential aliases among arrays and pointers. Then, each load $q = *p$ is annotated with a function $\mu(o)$ for each variable o that may be pointed-to by p to represent a potential use of o at the load. Likewise, each store $*p = q$ is annotated with $o = \chi(o)$ for each variable o that may be pointed-to by p to represent a potential def of o at the store. There is a special case to consider for shared variables. After synchronization (`#pragma omp barrier` in OpenMP, `syncthreads` in CUDA), shared variables have the same value for all threads. To create a new SSA instance that no longer depends on the value preceding the barrier, synchronizations are annotated with $o = \chi()$ for all shared variables o. Then a context-sensitive *Mod-Ref Analysis* is performed to capture inter-procedural uses and def as described in [9]. The purpose of this analysis is to capture the variables referenced and/or modified in functions through pointers. Each callsite cs is annotated with $\mu(o)$ for each variable o indirectly referenced in the called function. Similarly, each callsite is annotated with $o = \chi(o)$ to generate a new instance of o for each variable indirectly modified in the called function. For each address-taken variable referenced or modified in a function, a χ function is inserted at the beginning of the entry node of the CFG and a μ function is inserted at the end of the exit node of the CFG to represent their initial and final values. Finally, all address-taken variables are converted into an SSA form. This results in an augmented SSA with value and control dependences, and additional statements in SSA describing the effects of pointer manipulations. All possible def/use chains are built inside the SSA notation. This simplifies the construction of a dependence graph.

PDCG: Program Data- and Control-Flow Dependence Graph. A *program data- and control-flow dependence graph* (PDCG) is built from the enhanced SSA by connecting the def of each variable with its uses, following the rules presented in Fig. 2. The PDCG captures inter-procedural dependences (represented by edges between variables from different functions) but its construction only requires to analyze each function once. This graph is used to find all variables/expressions that are multi-valued. To that end, we identify the source statements that generate processes identifier and spread the dependencies following the edges of the PDCG. The first four rules (from OP to STORE) are based on the work in [7] using similar notations. Our differences are highlighted in grey.

OP and PHI rules correspond to straightforward data- and control-flow dependences. For an operation $\ell : z = x$ op y, the def of x and y at lines ℓ' and ℓ'' are connected to the def of z at line ℓ. For a ϕ statement $\ell : v_3 = \phi(v_1, v_2, ..., p_i, ..)$, the defs of the old SSA instances v_1 and v_2 at ℓ_1 and ℓ_2 are connected to the def of the new SSA instance v_3 at ℓ. For each predicate p_i, the def of p_i at ℓ_3 is connected to the def of v_3 at ℓ to handle the control-flow dependence.

LOAD and STORE rules take into account alias information for load and store statements. For a load statement $\ell : q = *p$, the def of each object o at ℓ'' pointed to by p is connected to the def of q at ℓ. We also add a link from the def of p at ℓ' to the def of q at ℓ to denote the dependence of q with the array index. Indeed, this corresponds to the case where $*p$ is in the form of $A[e]$ with e an expression. If e is multi-valued, then q is multi-valued. Similarly, for each store instruction $\ell : *p = q$ annotated with $[o_2 = \chi(o_1)]$, the defs of q and p are connected to o_2. However, we do not connect o_1 to o_2 since we assume that the old value o_1 is overwritten with o_2 (strong update).

The CALL rule handles inter-procedural dependences. At each callsite $\ell_{cs} :$ $r = f(..., p, ...)$, the def of the effective parameter p is connected to the formal parameter q in f. Furthermore, the def of the return value x in f is connected to the def of r at ℓ_{cs}. To handle indirect value-flows for address-taken variables, given a callsite annotated with $[\mu(o_1)]$ $[o_2 = \chi(o_1)]$, the def of o_1 in the calling function is connected to o_3, the first def of o in f. Similarly, the last def of o in f denoted o_4, is connected to the def of o_2 at ℓ_{cs}.

Rule	Statement (SSA form)	Edges in the PDCG
	Value Flow Dependence	
OP	$\ell : z = x@\ell'$ op $y@\ell''$	$z@\ell \hookleftarrow x@\ell' \qquad z@\ell \hookleftarrow y@\ell''$
PHI	$\ell : v_3 = \phi(v_1@\ell_1, v_2@\ell_2, ..., p@\ell_3, ...)$	$v_3@\ell \hookleftarrow v_1@\ell_1 \qquad v_3@\ell \hookleftarrow v_2@\ell_2$ $v_3@\ell \hookleftarrow p@\ell_3$
LOAD	$\ell : q = *p@\ell' \; [\mu(o@\ell'')]$	$q@\ell \hookleftarrow o@\ell'' \qquad q@\ell \hookleftarrow p@\ell'$
STORE	$\ell : *p@\ell_1 = q@\ell_2 \; [o_2 = \chi(o_1@\ell_3)]$	$o_2@\ell \hookleftarrow q@\ell_2$ ~~$o_2@\ell \hookleftarrow o1@\ell_3$~~ $\qquad o_2@\ell \hookleftarrow p@\ell_1$
CALL	$\ell_{cs} : r = f(..., p@\ell_1, ...) \; [\mu(o_1@\ell_2)]$ $[o_2 = \chi(o_1)]$ $f(..., q@\ell_3, ...) \{$ $\quad [o_3@\ell_4 = \chi()] \; ... \; [\mu(o_4@\ell_5)] \; return \; x@\ell_6 \}$	$q@\ell_3 \hookleftarrow p@\ell_1 \quad r@\ell_{cs} \hookleftarrow x@\ell_6$ $o_3@\ell_4 \hookleftarrow o_1@\ell_2$ $o_2@\ell_{cs} \hookleftarrow o_4@\ell_5$
	Optimization	
PHI ELIM	$\ell : *p@\ell_1 = q@\ell_2 \; [o_2 = \chi(o_1@\ell_3)]$ $\ell' : *p@\ell_1 = q@\ell_2 \; [o_3 = \chi(o_1@\ell_3)]$ $\ell'' : o_4 = \phi(o_2@\ell, o_3@\ell', pred@\ell_4)$	$o_4@\ell'' = \text{fuse}(o_2@\ell, o_3@\ell', o_4@\ell'')$ $\text{remove}(o_4@\ell'' \hookleftarrow pred@\ell_4)$
RESET	$\ell_{cs} : \text{reset}(buf@\ell_1, ...) \; [\mu(o_1@\ell_2)]$ $[o_2 = \chi(o_1)]$ $\text{reset}(buf@\ell_3, ...) \{$ $\quad [o_3@\ell_4 = \chi()] \; ... \; [\mu(o_4@\ell_5)] \}$	$\text{remove}(o_2@\ell_{cs} \hookleftarrow o_4@\ell_5)$
	Collective Checking	
COND	$\ell : collective(...)$ with execution order r For all $BB \in PDF^+(C_{r,collective@\ell})$ matching: ... $br \; cond@\ell'$, label1, label2	$collective@\ell \hookleftarrow cond@\ell'$

Fig. 2. Building rules for the PDCG.

PHI ELIM and RESET both correspond to edge removal optimizations. After augmenting ϕ-nodes with their predicates, false control dependences can appear if every operand of a ϕ-node denotes the same value. This occurs in particular when considering two identical function calls in two branches of an if..then..else construct. Even if these two calls use the same single-valued parameters, the returned value will still depend on the predicate of the conditional (augmented SSA). To tackle this issue, the PHIELIM rule fuses such ϕ-nodes with their operands and disconnects the predicates. In distributed memory, after a value-sharing collective such as an all-to-all collective, the communicated buffer has the same value for all processes. This implies that this buffer does not depend on processes ranks after such collective, whatever its rank-dependence before the collective. To handle this situation, the RESET rule disconnects the path from the old SSA instance of the buffer to its new SSA instance after a value-sharing collective ($o_1@\ell_2 \hookrightarrow o_3@\ell_4 \hookrightarrow o_4@\ell_5 \hookrightarrow o_2@\ell_{cs}$). The same rule applies to any value-sharing collective where all processes receive the same result such as MPI_Allreduce or MPI_Broadcast.

Finally, to detect collectives that may not be executed by all processes/ threads, we rely on PARCOACH analysis. Each collective c of execution order r is connected to all conditionals in $PDF^+(C_{r,c})$ (COND rule).

5   Collective Errors Detection

We use the PDCG to track values and nodes that depend on processes identifiers, flooding the graph from seed functions returning IDs or variables allowing tasks to identify themselves: MPI_Comm_rank and MPI_Group_rank in MPI, omp_get_thread_num for OpenMP. In UPC and CUDA, the seed is a variable: MYTHREAD and threadIdx.*. We use the dependence information from the PDCG to filter out single-valued conditionals from the PDF^+ of potentially unsafe collectives and thus reduce the number of false positives in PARCOACH. The augmented SSA takes into account value and control dependencies and the points-to analysis provides the dependencies through aliases. Note that thanks to the PDCG, our analysis can be path sensitive: An expression may be multi-valued or not, depending on the preceding calling context.

Algorithm 1 describes our whole collective errors detection. Step 1 represents PARCOACH control-flow analysis (see Sect. 3) while steps 2 and 3 respectively detect multi-valued expressions and build the PDCG (see Sect. 4). Finally, step 4 filters out single-valued conditionals and outputs warnings for potential collective errors.

Example. Figures 3a and c show the enhanced SSA for the MPI code Fig. 1a. The call to MPI_Comm_rank is annotated with a χ function to denote the indirect definition of object o'1 pointed-to by r. This generates a new SSA instance denoted o'2. Then the object o'2 pointed-to by r is loaded in reg0. Depending on whether its value is odd or even, the execution flows either to the basic block labelled if.then or the basic block labelled if.else. These two control-flow paths join at basic block if.end and a ϕ-function is inserted to combine the

// STEP 1. PARCOACH Control-flow Analysis
Input: PPCFG, **Output:** $\bigcup_{r,c} O_{r,c}$ ▷ Create the set $O_{r,c} = PDF^{+}(C_{r,c})$ for each

collective name c of execution order r

// STEP 2. Multi-Valued Expression Detection
Input: SSA, **Output:** eSSA   ▷ Build an enhanced SSA (eSSA) that captures
data- and control-flow dependencies

// STEP 3. PDCG Construction
Input: eSSA, seeds, **Output:** PDCG ▷ Build a PDCG to find all multi-valued
expressions and variables from seed functions and variables

// STEP 4. Filter-out single-valued conditionals
Input: $\bigcup_{r,c} O_{r,c}, PDCG$, **Output:** O

for c in collective names of execution order r **do**

    for each node n in $O_{r,c}$ **do**

        if n is single-valued in PDCG (there is an edge between c and n in the PDCG) **then**

            | $O_{r,c} \leftarrow O_{r,c} - n$ ▷ remove the node

    end

    $O \leftarrow O \cup (c, \{O_{r,c}\})$

end

Output nodes in O as warnings

return O

Algorithm 1. Collective error detection.

values of `reg1` and `reg2` into variable n. The predicate `cmp1` is added to the ϕ-function to indicate its value depends on `cmp1`.

Figure 3b shows the PDCG corresponding to this example. Rectangle nodes represent collectives. Diamond and circle nodes respectively represent definitions of address-taken and *top-level variables* (variables never referenced by their address). The seed function is `MPI_Comm_rank` line 7 and the first multi-valued object is o'2. All library functions have mocked-up CFGs, tagging output values as multi-valued when necessary. The graph highlights the rank-dependent path from o'2 to `MPI_Reduce` in g passing through the conditional `cmp2` in f.

In this example, the execution of `MPI_Reduce` depends on the value of `cmp` in g and the call to g depends on the value of `cmp2` in f. Hence, `MPI_Reduce@`ℓ_6 is connected to `cmp` and `cmp2`. However, there exists no path from o'2 to `cmp` as `cmp` does not depend on processes ranks. The execution of `MPI_Barrier` is not governed by any conditional. `MPI_Barrier@`ℓ_{28} is then not connected to any node in the graph and it cannot be reached from a seed statement. Since the only collective highlighted in the graph corresponds to `MPI_Reduce` in g and only one of the two conditionals governing its execution is highlighted, our new analysis only issues a warning for the multi-valued conditional line 22 in f and the call to `MPI_Reduce` in g.

```
1  define void f() {
2  entry:
3    s = alloca_o; // object o1
4    r = alloca_o';// object o'1
5    MPI_Comm_size(com, s);
        [μ(o1)]
6    [o2 = χ(o1)]
7    MPI_Comm_rank(com, r);
        [μ(o'1)]
8    [o'2 = χ(o'1)]
9    reg0 = load r [μ(o'2)]
10   rem = reg0 % 2;
11   cmp1 = rem != 0;
12   br cmp1, if.then, if.else
13 if.then:
14   reg1 = 1;
15   br label if.end
16 if.else:
17   reg2 = 2;
18   br label if.end
19 if.end:
20   n = φ(reg1, reg2, cmp1)
21   cmp2 = n == 1;
22   br cmp2, if.then2, if.end2
23 if.then2:
24   reg3 = load s; [μ(o2)]
25   g(reg3);
26   br label if.end2
27 if.end2:
28   MPI_Barrier(com);
29   ret void;
30 }
```

(a) Function f enhanced SSA.

(b) PDCG.

```
1  define void g(i32 s) {
2  entry:
3    cmp = s > 256
4    br cmp, if.then, if.end
5  if.then:
6    MPI_Reduce(com, ...);
7    br if.end
8  if.end:
9    ret void
10 }
```

(c) Function g enhanced SSA.

Fig. 3. Enhanced SSA form of the MPI code Fig. 1a and its corresponding PDCG.

6 Related Work

This section summarizes works on dependence analyses and gives an overview of existing tools for collective errors detection in parallel programs.

6.1 Dependence Analyses Techniques

Dependence analyses are the cornerstones of many optimizations/analyses in compilers. For instance, dependences are used for *Taint Analysis* [10–12] to determine how program inputs may affect the program execution and exploit security vulnerabilities, *Information Flow Tracking* [13–16] to prevent confidential information from leaking, static *Bug Detection* [17,18] or code optimization and parallelization (e.g. the polyhedral model [19]). One of the difficult issues when computing data dependences is to deal with pointers/memory aliases and non scalar variables (e.g. arrays, structures). In SVF [7] the authors annotate load and store instructions with μ and χ functions to transform address-taken variables into an SSA form. However, they do not take into account the possible dependence of the pointer itself (through an array index for instance) when they build the data dependence graph.

Many of the aforementioned analyses only consider data dependences whereas Slowinska *et al.* [20] showed that omitting control dependences can be a huge source of false negative results. In [21], the authors introduced the concept of *Strict Control Dependences* to reduce the number of false positives in *Taint Analyses* and *Lineage Tracing*. In Parfait [22] the authors propose to extend ϕ-functions with predicates in order to handle control dependences. However, address-taken variables are not transformed into an SSA form.

6.2 Collective Error Detection Techniques

Static analyses operate on the source code of an application and have the advantage of not requiring execution. They are usually based on model checking and symbolic program execution, limiting their applicability to small and moderate sized applications (the number of reachable states to consider is combinatorial). TASS [23] and CIVL [24] use this approach. They rely on symbolic execution and require source code annotations to detect collective errors in MPI programs. The OpenMP Analysis Toolkit (OAT) [25] uses the same method for OpenMP programs by exploring all program paths under symbolic values. SimGridMC [26]is a model checker for MPI applications. It uses Dynamic Partial Order Reduction and State Equality techniques to face the state space explosion problem. UPC-SPIN [27] generates finite models of UPC programs in the modeling language of the SPIN model checker. For CUDA programs, we can mention GPUVerify [28] that statically checks that all threads execute the same barriers syntactically. Unlike our analysis, the method does not give a precise feedback in case of a potential error. PARCOACH combines an inter-procedural control-flow analysis with a selective instrumentation to find MPI and OpenMP collective errors. The method is limited to control-flow information and returns many false positives. Our new analysis overcomes this limitation and extends the collective verification to other parallel programming models. The method presented by Zhang and Duesterwald in [1] is the closest to our work. It detects synchronization errors with an inter-procedural barrier matching technique for SPMD programs with textually unaligned barriers. Compared to our analysis, this method is only focused on MPI and OpenMP synchronizations and has no pointer analysis.

Unlike static tools, dynamic tools do not report false positives. However, they are dependent on the input data set and may miss errors (false negatives). PARCOACH instruments non verifiable programs to verify if processes/threads are going to call the same collective at a particular step of execution, preventing deadlocks from happening. This instrumentation is similar to what dynamic tools like MUST [29] or UPC-CHECK [30] do. However, the instrumentation starts with the first collectives that may deadlock, avoiding a full instrumentation of programs.

7   Experimental Results

Our analysis is implemented as a pass in the LLVM framework 3.9 integrated into the open source software PARCOACH[2].

Figures 4 and 5 show the impact of our multi-valued expression analysis on PARCOACH. Figure 4 displays the percentage of warnings and conditionals filtered out with our multi-valued analysis compared to the initial PARCOACH analysis on 3 HPC applications (MILC[3], Gadget[4] and MPI-PHYLIP [31]), 3 mini HPC applications (CoMD and miniAMR from the Mantevo project [32]

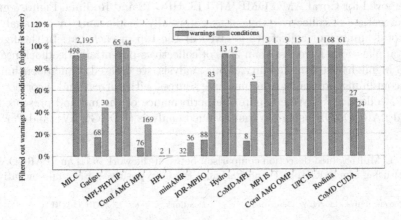

Fig. 4. Percentage of warnings and conditionals filtered by our multi-valued analysis. 100% means that the analysis proves the program is collective error free.

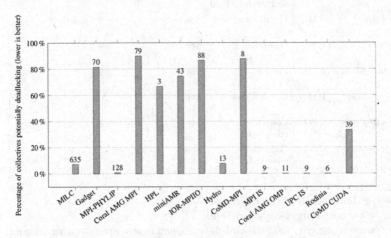

Fig. 5. Percentage of collectives potentially deadlocking.

[2] PARCOACH is available at https://github.com/parcoach/parcoach.

[3] http://www.physics.utah.edu/~detar/milc/.

[4] https://wwwmpa.mpa-garching.mpg.de/gadget/.

and Hydro[5]) and 5 widely used benchmarks (HPL[6], IOR[7], AMG[8], NAS IS[9], and the CUDA benchmarks from Rodinia[10]). In the figure, *warnings* are collectives that may lead to deadlocks, and *conditions* correspond to conditionals governing the execution of unsafe collectives. The initial number of warnings and conditionals found by PARCOACH is given at the top of each bar. 100% for a warning bar means that the application is collective error-free (all warnings are removed by our analysis, the code is proved safe), 0% means that our analysis has no impact. For MILC, 91% of the 498 warnings have been removed. PARCOACH now reports 45 warnings. As shown in the figure, about half conditionals are filtered out by our analysis for most applications and all warnings are removed for Coral AMG OMP, MPI IS, UPC IS and Rodinia. Figure 5 gives the percentage of collectives tagged as potentially deadlocking by our analysis. The total number of collectives is given at the top of each bar. In the figure, seven applications have less than 20% of collectives potentially deadlocking.

To highlight the functionality of our analysis, we created a microbenchmark suite containing programs from multiple sources with correct and incorrect use of MPI collectives[11]. We compare the performance of the method presented in [1] and PARCOACH using our multi-valued analysis (PDCG), SVF and Parfait.

Table 1. Multi-valued detection comparison between the work in [1] and PARCOACH (PAR.) using our PDCG, SVF and Parfait. FP = false positives, FN = false negative.

Program name	Origin	Description	Deadlock	Zhang et. al [1]	PARCOACH		
					PDCG	SVF	Parfait
field-sensitive	Hydro	Structure with a multi-valued field	no	FP	FP	FP	FP
index-dep	PAR	Use of an array	yes	✓	✓	FN	✓
phi-cond	PAR	Control-flow dependence	yes	✓	✓	FN	✓
pointer-instance	PAR	Fig. 1b	yes	✓	✓	✓	FP
pointer-alias	PAR	Use of aliases	yes	FN	✓	✓	FP
barrierReduce	CIVL	Collective mismatch	yes	FN	✓	✓	✓
barrierScatter	CIVL	Collective mismatch	yes	FN	✓	✓	✓

---

[5] https://github.com/HydroBench/Hydro.

[6] http://www.netlib.org/benchmark/hpl.

[7] http://www.nersc.gov/research-and-development/apex/apex-benchmarks/ior.

[8] https://asc.llnl.gov/CORAL-benchmarks/.

[9] http://www.nas.nasa.gov/software/NPB.

[10] https://www.cs.virginia.edu/~skadron/wiki/rodinia/index.php.

[11] The microbenchmark suite is available at https://gitlab.inria.fr/parcoach/microbenchmarks.

Table 1. (*continued*)

Program name	Origin	Description	Deadlock	Zhang et. al [1]	PARCOACH		
					PDCG	SVF	Parfait
BcastReduce_bad	CIVL	Collective mismatch	yes	FN	✓	✓	✓
mismatch-barrier	PAR	Collective mismatch	yes	✓	✓	✓	✓
mismatch_barrier_com	PAR	Collective mismatch	yes	✓	✓	✓	✓
mismatch_barrier_nb	PAR	Collective mismatch	yes	✓	✓	✓	✓
MPIexample	PAR	Fig. 1a	yes	FN	✓	FN	FN
noerror_barrier	PAR	Correct usage of barrier	no	✓	✓	✓	✓
not_verifiable	PAR	Fig. 1e	no	FP	FP	FP	FP
loop_barrier	PAR	Fig. 1d	yes	✓	✓	✓	✓

Table 1 shows the results. Our analysis always detect collective errors compared to the others. For the remaining false-positive results, a more precise dependence analysis is required. This is left for future work.

8   Conclusion

This article presents a new static/dynamic method to verify that a parallel program has structurally correct collectives. The analysis resorts to an inter-procedural static analysis that can prove in some cases that a program is free of collective error. The method has been applied successfully on different languages and is implemented in PARCOACH. Experiments show that our analysis leads to significant improvement over existing PARCOACH. Furthermore, through a more precise use of alias and control dependences, our static analysis outperforms existing data-flow analyses bringing additional preciseness (removing spurious dependencies) and correctness (adding missing dependencies).

References

1. Zhang, Y., Duesterwald, E.: Barrier matching for programs with textually unaligned barriers. In: PPoPP, pp. 194–204. ACM (2007)
2. Jakobsson, A., Dabrowski, F., Bousdira, W., Loulergue, F., Hains, G.: Replicated synchronization for imperative bsp programs. Procedia Comput Sci. **108**, 535–544 (2017). International Conference on Computational Science, ICCS 2017, 12–14 June 2017. Zurich, Switzerland

3. Aiken, A., Gay, D.: Barrier inference. In: Proceedings of the ACM SIGPLAN-SIGACT Symposium on Principles of Programming Languages POPL, pp. 342–354. ACM (1998)
4. Saillard, E., Carribault, P., Barthou, D.: PARCOACH: combining static and dynamic validation of MPI collective communications. IJHPCA **28**(4), 425–434 (2014)
5. Huchant, P., Saillard, E., Barthou, D., Brunie, H., Carribault, P.: PARCOACH extension for a full-interprocedural collectives verification. In: Second International Workshop on Software Correctness for HPC Applications (2018)
6. Scholz, B., Zhang, C., Cifuentes, C.: User-input dependence analysis via graph reachability (2008)
7. Sui, Y., Xue, J.: SVF: Interprocedural Static Value-flow Analysis in LLVM. CC, pp. 265–266 (2016)
8. Hardekopf, B., Lin, C.: Flow-sensitive pointer analysis for millions of lines of code. In: CGO, pp. 289–298 (2011)
9. Sui, Y., Ye, D., Xue, J.: Detecting memory leaks statically with full-sparse value-flow analysis. IEEE Trans. Softw. Eng. **40**(2), 107–122 (2014)
10. Arzt, S., et al.: FlowDroid: precise context, flow, field, object-sensitive and lifecycle-aware taint analysis for android apps. SIGPLAN Not. **49**(6), 259–269 (2014)
11. Tripp, O., Pistoia, M., Fink, S.J., Sridharan, M., Weisman, O.: TAJ: effective taint analysis of web applications. PLDI **44**, 87–97 (2009)
12. Shankar, U., Talwar, K., Foster, J.S., Wagner, D.: Detecting format string vulnerabilities with type qualifiers. In: SSYM (2001)
13. Denning, D.E., Denning, P.J.: Certification of programs for secure information flow. Commun. ACM **20**(7), 504–513 (1977)
14. Heintze, N., Riecke, J.G.: The SLam calculus: programming with secrecy and integrity. In: POPL, pp. 365–377 (1998)
15. Yin, H., Song, D., Egele, M., Kruegel, C., Kirda, E.: Panorama: capturing system-wide information flow for malware detection and analysis. In: CCS, pp. 116–127 (2007)
16. Sabelfeld, A., Myers, A.C.: Language-based information-flow security. IEEE J. Sel. A. Commun. **21**(1), 5–19 (2006)
17. Laguna, I., Schulz, M.: Pinpointing scale-dependent integer overflow bugs in large-scale parallel applications. In: SC, pp. 19:1–19:12 (2016)
18. Ye, D., Sui, Y., Xue, J.: Accelerating dynamic detection of uses of undefined values with static value-flow analysis. In: CGO, pp. 154:154–154:164 (2014)
19. Feautrier, P.: Dataflow analysis of array and scalar references. Int. J. Parallel Prog. **20**(1), 23–53 (1991)
20. Slowinska, A., Bos, H.: Pointless tainting?: evaluating the practicality of pointer tainting. In: EuroSys, pp. 61–74 (2009)
21. Bao, T., Zheng, Y., Lin, Z., Zhang, X., Xu, D.: Strict control dependence and its effect on dynamic information flow analyses. In: ISSTA, pp. 13–24 (2010)
22. Cifuentes, C., Scholz, B.: Parfait: designing a scalable bug checker. In: Proceedings of the 2008 Workshop on Static Analysis. SAW, pp. 4–11 (2008)
23. Siegel, S.F., Zirkel, T.K.: Automatic formal verification of MPI-based parallel programs. SIGPLAN Not. **46**(8), 309–310 (2011)
24. Siegel, S.F., et al.: Civl: the concurrency intermediate verification language. In: SC, pp. 1–12, November 2015
25. Ma, H., Diersen, S.R., Wang, L., Liao, C., Quinlan, D., Yang, Z.: Symbolic analysis of concurrency errors in OpenMP programs. In: PARCO. ICPP, vol. 00, pp. 510–516 (2013)

26. Pham, T.A., Jeron, T., Quinson, M.: Verifying MPI applications with SimGridMC. In: Correctness (2017)
27. Ali, E.: UPC-SPIN: a framework for the model checking of UPC programs (2011)
28. Betts, A., Chong, N., Donaldson, A., Qadeer, S., Thomson, P.: GPUVerify: a verifier for GPU Kernels. In: OOPSLA, pp. 113–132. ACM (2012)
29. Hilbrich, T., de Supinski, B.R., Hänsel, F., Müller, M.S., Schulz, M., Nagel, W.E.: Runtime MPI collective checking with tree-based overlay networks. In: EuroMPI, pp. 129–134 (2013)
30. Coyle, J., Roy, I., Kraeva, M., Luecke, G.R.: UPC-CHECK: a scalable tool for detecting run-time errors in Unified Parallel C. Comput. Sci. Res. Dev. **28**(2), 203–209 (2013)
31. Ropelewski, A.J., Nicholas Jr., H.B., Gonzalez Mendez, R.R.: MPI-PHYLIP: parallelizing computationally intensive phylogenetic analysis routines for the analysis of large protein families. PLoS ONE **5**(11), 1–8 (2010)
32. Heroux, M.A., et al.: Improving Performance via Mini-applications (2009)

Performance and Power Modeling, Prediction and Evaluation

Towards Portable Online Prediction of Network Utilization Using MPI-Level Monitoring

Shu-Mei Tseng[1]([⊠]), Bogdan Nicolae[2], George Bosilca[3], Emmanuel Jeannot[4], Aparna Chandramowlishwaran[1], and Franck Cappello[2]

[1] University of California Irvine, Irvine, USA
{shumeit,amowli}uci.edu
[2] Argonne National Laboratory, Lemont, USA
{bnicolae,cappello}@anl.gov
[3] University of Tennessee Knoxville, Knoxville, USA
bosilca@icl.utk.edu
[4] INRIA Bordeaux, Talence, France
emmanuel.jeannot@inria.fr

Abstract. Stealing network bandwidth helps a variety of HPC runtimes and services to run additional operations in the background without negatively affecting the applications. A key ingredient to make this possible is an accurate prediction of the future network utilization, enabling the runtime to plan the background operations in advance, such as to avoid competing with the application for network bandwidth. In this paper, we propose a portable deep learning predictor that only uses the information available through MPI introspection to construct a recurrent `sequence-to-sequence` neural network capable of forecasting network utilization. We leverage the fact that most HPC applications exhibit periodic behaviors to enable predictions far into the future (at least the length of a period). Our online approach does not have an initial training phase, it continuously improves itself during application execution without incurring significant computational overhead. Experimental results show better accuracy and lower computational overhead compared with the state-of-the-art on two representative applications.

1 Introduction

Network bandwidth is a precious resource on High Performance Computing (HPC) systems to the point where much of the performance of the applications depend on it [13]. However, HPC applications typically use the network bandwidth at full capacity only sporadically. This opens a *window of opportunity* for runtimes and services (that these applications depend upon) to seamlessly perform operations that require communication over the network in the background. For example, many applications need to periodically checkpoint to a parallel file system, which might be subject to I/O bottlenecks and therefore negatively impacts performance and scalability. To avoid this, runtimes stage the checkpoints first to a local storage and then flushes them in the background to the parallel file system, hiding the I/O overhead from the application.

© Springer Nature Switzerland AG 2019
R. Yahyapour (Ed.): Euro-Par 2019, LNCS 11725, pp. 47–60, 2019.
https://doi.org/10.1007/978-3-030-29400-7_4

In order to take advantage of this window of opportunity, the checkpointing runtime needs to clearly identify the time intervals when the network is underutilized by the application. Failing to do so might lead to competition for network bandwidth and could cause undesired interference that slows down the application (e.g. the flushes to the parallel file system pushed by the checkpointing runtime compete with the applications' data exchanges over the same network interfaces).

Therefore, to avoid the competition for network bandwidth, it is necessary to schedule all background operations in such a way that they finish within the window of opportunity. Unfortunately, the background operations are often non-trivial and take time to complete and/or cannot be easily suspended and resumed later (e.g. writes to the parallel file system are outside the control of the checkpointing runtime). Thus, it is important to be able to predict the network utilization sufficiently early to precisely pinpoint when and for how long the network bandwidth will stay underutilized to actually create a usable window of opportunity.

The problem of predicting network utilization is non-trivial for several reasons. First, it is tedious or impossible to obtain system-level information about the network utilization because most platforms and vendors expose it through non-standardized performance counters and APIs or do not expose it at all. Second, network utilization is challenging to reason about in an offline fashion due to the application complexity and a large number of variables (e.g. platform, input data, system noise, global resources shared with other users such as a parallel file system, etc) that influence the network utilization at runtime.

To address these challenges, we propose a solution that combines portable MPI-level monitoring of network utilization with deep learning based time series forecasting. The key novelty of our approach is two-fold: (1) we devise a mechanism to approximate network utilization using only the information available at the MPI-level (which addresses the portability challenge); (2) we introduce a periodicity-aware deep learning approach that adapts sequence-to-sequence predictors based on recurrent neural networks for adaptive online learning. This approach is capable of maintaining high prediction accuracy with low computational overhead despite variations encountered during runtime. Although the focus of this work is the prediction of network utilization, it is important to note that the basic ideas can be easily extended to predict the utilization of other resources such as CPU, I/O bandwidth, etc.

We summarize our contributions as follows: (1) we present a series of general design principles that summarize the key ideas behind our approach (Sect. 3); (2) we show how to materialize these design principles in practice by introducing an MPI-based network monitoring infrastructure (Sect. 3.2) and a framework to leverage sequence-to-sequence predictors efficiently in an online fashion (Sect. 3.4); (3) we evaluate our approach for two representative HPC applications and show significantly better prediction accuracy and lower computational overhead compared with state-of-the-art approaches (Sect. 4).

2   Related Work

MPI Monitoring. There are many different ways to monitor the network utilization of an MPI application. The most common and generic way relies on intercepting MPI API calls of interest and delivering aggregated information. PMPI is a high-level customizable profiling layer allowing tools to intercept MPI calls. Communication monitoring can be achieved by intercepting all MPI communications routines, including point-to-point, one-sided, and collectives. When such a communication routine is called, the processes involved (source and destination) as well as the amount of data involved in the transfer needs to be recorded. In addition to the overheads necessary to get information about the amount of data involved in communications, this approach cannot differentiate between point-to-point and collective data, as it is impossible to determine how the collective calls are implemented using point-to-point communications. One of the major advantages of PMPI is the existence of many stand-alone monitoring libraries, such as mpiP [27], Score-P [19], and DUMPI [3].

At a different level in the software stack, PERUSE [9, 18] allows the application to register callbacks that will be triggered at critical moments in the point-to-point request lifetime. This method provides opportunities to gather low-level information about MPI messages, including the number of unexpected messages, matching cost, payload type (i.e. point-to-point or collectives), etc. Unfortunately, this technique has failed to attract support from the MPI standardization body, and, as a result, support in widely used MPI implementations is almost non-existent.

Time Series Analysis/Forecasting. Traditional statistical models like Autoregressive Integrated Moving Average (ARIMA) have been widely used for the purpose of time series forecasting in the context of HPC applications. Prior work such as [24, 25] introduce a framework for online modeling and prediction of I/O operations to enable prefetching. Other efforts use ARIMA-based models to forecast CPU, memory, and network utilization to facilitate better resource allocation and load balancing [20].

Due to the successful application of deep learning techniques in various domains such as natural language processing [12] and language translation [17, 23] that require predictions of what elements are likely to follow in a sequence, such techniques are increasingly being considered in the context of time series forecasting. Sequence-to-sequence (seq2seq) models are particularly popular in this context. Kuznetsov and Mariet [21] provide a theoretical analysis and compare seq2seq with other classical time series models. Moreover, they also provide some quantitative guidance on how to choose different modeling approaches. One of the limitations of seq2seq is the predetermined output sequence length. Harmon and Klabjan [15] address this problem by making the network predict the dynamic length of the outputs. However, none of these approaches address the problem of efficient online learning. To the best of our knowledge, this paper is the first to address the problem of portable prediction of network utilization using online deep learning specifically tailored to the requirements of HPC applications.

3   System Design

In this section, we introduce the high-level design principles of our proposed approach, discuss the methodology, and provide a detailed description of the experimental prototype implemented to illustrate the benefits of our design on real applications.

3.1 Design Principles

Our system design is based on the following three principles.

Portable MPI-Level Monitoring. To solve the problem of portable monitoring, we propose to capture the network utilization directly from the communication library, in this context MPI. While we could get more information about the internal state of data transfers (one-sided and two-sided messages, as well as the state of all non-blocking communications) we restraint ourselves to the smallest subset of pertinent information: the number of bytes sent by each rank using MPI messages (which is of interest for HPC applications because it represents the majority of network traffic). We use this information to estimate the global network utilization imposed by the target application. However, having an accurate counting of the number of bytes sent is currently non-trivial to capture for two main reasons. (1) Messages exchanged by ranks do not necessarily go over the network (e.g., ranks co-located on the same node use shared memory). (2) Messages are not only generated by direct point-to-point communication initiated by the application but they are also generated by one-sided communications or collective operations (which often leads to complex patterns deep in the MPI library implementation). In addition, the number of bytes sent by MPI is a lower bound on the network utilization, as the network interface introduces additional overhead (headers, etc.). Section 3.2 details how we address these challenges.

Low-Overhead Online Learning. Based on the network utilization estimates obtained at the MPI-level, we propose an adaptive online learning approach that continuously refines the quality of the predictions as more monitoring information becomes available. This approach has two advantages. (1) There is no need to perform separate training offline based on the network utilization observed in the previous runs (which may be difficult to obtain and/or unavailable if it is the first run). Therefore, it is robust to inaccurate predictions due to variations in the application configuration or input data used in subsequent runs which have a significant impact on the communication pattern. (2) It facilitates more accurate predictions by dynamically adapting to the variations that are naturally occurring during the same run (e.g. system noise, shared resources with other users such as a parallel file system, etc.).

Periodicity-Aware Forecasting. A large majority of HPC applications exhibit a repetitive communication pattern, which implicitly leads to a repetitive pattern of network utilization. Given the need to predict network utilization as far as possible in the future to enable background services to schedule their operations in advance, we argue that the most useful prediction needs to cover at least the duration of one period. To this end, we propose a periodicity-aware approach that employs a recurrent neural network specifically designed for online sequence to sequence forecasting. We discuss the proposed solution in detail in Sect. 3.4.

3.2 Portable MPI-Level Monitoring

Our MPI-level monitoring is based on previous work to design a portable monitoring interface in OpenMPI [7]. We take advantage of the modular implementation of OpenMPI [5], to add support for a dynamically activated communication monitoring module. This module can be activated at runtime and distinguishes between several types of MPI traffic such as point-to-point, one-sided, and collectives and creates a global heatmap by recording, for each rank, the number of bytes and the number of messages sent to any other rank. Note that the recording is done after the collectives have been decomposed into point-to-point messages, providing a more precise picture of overall transfers. Therefore, the monitoring sees the impact of the algorithm implementing the collective.

We design a high-level abstraction called *monitoring session* that integrates the capability of the new MPI_T tools support in MPI. Once created, a monitoring session can be started, stopped, resumed, and reset. Several sessions can simultaneously coexist, allowing for independent monitoring of different parts of the code. For the purpose of our monitoring needs, and in order to guarantee timely monitoring information each MPI rank launches, on initialization, a separate background thread that starts a monitoring session. At regular intervals (e.g., every second), this thread stops the monitoring session, reads the number of bytes sent by all ranks during the previous interval and then resets and resumes the session. Using this approach, we can obtain a history of the number of bytes sent per time unit for each rank.

However, to estimate the network utilization of a node, it is not enough to count the traffic for each process located on the node but instead we need to aggregate the number of bytes sent by each rank to other ranks that are not co-located on the same node. This is necessary because, at least in OpenMPI, co-located ranks use a different low-level communication substrate, i.e. shared memory for communication. To efficiently perform this aggregation, we create a 2-level hierarchy with local and remote peers and a designated leader on each node to aggregate the information from the other co-located ranks. This is done by creating a local MPI communicator on each node that includes all ranks sharing the node. The MPI process with the lowest rank in the local communicator become the leader, and is in charge of collecting the monitoring data. An MPI reduce operation collects the information from the other co-located ranks on the leader. Then, the leader sums up the number of bytes sent to all the ranks that do not have a corresponding rank in the local communicator. This way, only the bytes that need to pass over the network (and could therefore interfere with other operations that generate network traffic) are counted. This is an approximation of the network utilization per time unit which we subsequently use for forecasting.

3.3 Sequence-to-Sequence Recurrent Neural Networks (Seq2Seq)

Recurrent neural networks (RNNs) are a type of neural networks that contain loops. Unlike convolutional neural networks (CNNs), which are feed-forward (i.e., the information only passes through the network in one direction), these loops enable RNNs to capture sequence dependencies. However, conventional RNNs [6,16] have a major limitation in the form of exploding/vanishing gradient in the training stage, which makes them unable to handle long-term dependencies accurately. To address this issue, long short term memory networks (LSTMs) [16] and gated recurrent unit networks (GRUs) [11] have been proposed. They are special types of RNNs that solve this issue by controlling what information is propagated into its internal state and what information is forgotten.

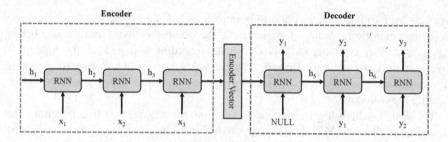

Fig. 1. Encoder-decoder diagram of the seq2seq model.

The sequence-to-sequence model (seq2seq) [23] is a particular instance of RNNs which can make use of LSTMs and GRUs as its recurrent units. Initially proposed in the context of natural language processing [23], the seq2seq model is now being used for a variety of other applications (e.g., speech recognition [10] and video captioning [26]). The model is composed of two components: an encoder and a decoder, as illustrated in Fig. 1. The input sequence is fed into the encoder one element at a time (e.g., x_1, x_2, x_3). Each recurrent unit in the encoder is a typical recurrent neural network which computes its hidden state using the hidden state of its predecessor and the current input (e.g., h_3 is computed using h_2 and x_2). The last hidden state of the input sequence is known as a *thought vector* and is used as the initial state of the decoder. It aims to encapsulate all the information from the input sequence to make the prediction of the decoder more accurate. Unlike the recurrent units in the encoder, the recurrent units of the decoder use both the previous hidden state and the last predicted output to obtain the new hidden state (e.g., h_6 is computed using h_5 and y_1).

For the purpose of our work, we leverage the same idea for network utilization prediction. We train the model with recent utilization patterns that are represented as time series. The encoder is fed one part of the time series, while the decoder is fed the other part. After training the model with multiple such time series, it learns to "translate" from a recent history of observations into a likely future evolution.

3.4 Online Periodicity-Aware Forecasting Using seq2seq RNNs

The key novelty of this paper is to adapt seq2seq for use as an online learning tool. This is a difficult problem because our model does not have a separate training phase (as is the case with traditional machine learning) and needs to learn on-the-fly as the application is progressing. This also places a strict requirement to be capable of continuously updating the model with low computational overhead.

To address this issue, we introduce the following approach, which is illustrated in Fig. 2. A history of the network utilization that is large enough to cover the most recent h repetitive patterns is kept, where h is the history size. We call the time series corresponding to a repetitive pattern an *epoch*. Using h epoch as training input helps the learning process account for potential variations between the most recent epochs. We assume the periodicity of the network utilization (and therefore the length of an epoch) is either known in advance or can be determined using an FFT-based approach (applied at key points during the application runtime when sufficient monitoring information is available, e.g., after the first checkpoint request).

The model is valid within the scope of a specific application run and starts with no initial history. After the history has accumulated two epochs, the initial training is performed by feeding the first epoch to the encoder and the second to the decoder. We perform this initial training over multiple iterations to reinforce this first pattern. At this point, we can make the first prediction of the third epoch.

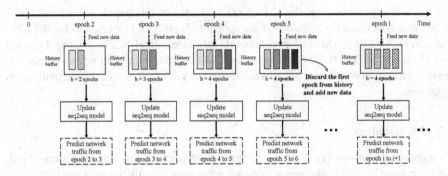

Fig. 2. Evolution of the online seq2seq predictor with the history size, $h = 4 \cdot epochs$.

Then, we wait until a new epoch is available and append this epoch to the history (which is truncated to keep only the last h epochs), as shown in Fig. 2. As the application is progressing, the model is retrained using a sliding window learning approach. Specifically, we pass over the new history in increments of one time step using a window size equal to two epochs. For each such window, the first and second epoch are fed to the encoder and decoder, respectively, in a similar way as the initial training is performed. Again, to reinforce the pattern, we repetitively pass over the history for k iterations. k is determined in an adaptive fashion based on two criteria: (1) the loss of the current iteration is smaller than the loss of each of the last p iterations (to avoid oscillation around a local optimum and to avoid unnecessary computational overhead when the loss is small); (2) a predefined number of iterations q is reached (to avoid too much overhead when convergence is slow). The entire process is then repeated whenever a new epoch is available. Independent of online learning, the model can be used at any moment during the runtime to predict the next epoch.

3.5 Implementation Details

We implemented our approach on top of OpenMPI version 4.1.0a1, which includes support for low-level monitoring of bytes sent from one rank to every other rank. We implemented the monitoring session as a library that exposes a convenient high-level API. This is then used by a separate thread spawned in each MPI rank. To create a local communicator that includes all ranks co-located on the same node, we use MPI_Comm_split_type using the MPI_COMM_TYPE_SHARED flag. To perform the aggregation on the leader, we use an in-place reduce operation on the local communicator.

To find out what ranks are remote, the leader uses MPI_Group_translate_ranks. The online predictor described in Sect. 3.4 is implemented in Python and it uses TensorFlow 1.0 as the backend.

4　Experimental Results

4.1　Experimental Setup

We ran our experiments on the Grid'5000 testbed. For this paper, we use 16 nodes of the parapluie cluster. Each node is equipped with an AMD Opteron 6164 HE CPU (12 cores), 48 GB RAM, and two network interfaces: Intel 82576 1 Gbps Ethernet and Mellanox MT25418 20 Gbps Infiniband. We use the Infiniband network interface since it's a common high-end networking technology adopted on many supercomputing machines.

4.2　Methodology

To measure the effectiveness of our approach, we perform the following steps. First, we instrument an HPC application to monitor the network utilization at the MPI-level, using the approach described in Sect. 3.2.

Second, we run the application on all 16 nodes with a representative use case that generates an inter-node communication pattern specific to the application. We log the network utilization (expressed in MB/s) at the granularity of one second, creating a time series that includes both the value reported by the MPI-level monitoring, as well as the corresponding value reported by the performance counters available through the sys\class operating system interface (henceforth referred to as system-level).

Third, we take a representative log file from one of the nodes (all nodes exhibit similar behavior for the applications we study, which are detailed below) and simulate online learning based on it. We focus on three aspects: (1) the accuracy of the MPI-level monitoring vs. system-level monitoring; (2) the accuracy of the predictions that are made by online learning using MPI-level monitoring vs. actually observed system-level values; (3) computational overhead of online learning.

This process is illustrated in Fig. 3. The log file contains the timestamp of the network utilization data, the node id, the number of bytes reported by the MPI-level monitoring approach, and the number of bytes obtained from system-level monitoring.

The accuracy is measured using two representative metrics widely used in time series analytic: *mean squared error* (MSE) and *dynamic time warping* (DTW). Both metrics quantify the distance between two time series, which in our case is the prediction vs. the actual system-level time series. For MSE, we use a standard implementation (available in the numpy library). For DTW, we use an optimized implementation (Fast-DTW) based on a linear algorithm [22].

We use two representative applications in our experiments: (1) HACC [14], a complex framework that simulates the mass evolution of the universe using particle-mesh techniques. HACC splits the force calculation into a specially designed grid-based

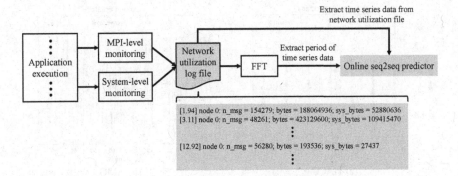

Fig. 3. Experimental methodology.

long/medium range spectral particle-mesh component that is common to all architectures, and an architecture-specific short-range solver. HACC generates a regular communication pattern, which is typical of a large class of HPC applications. (2) AMG [4], a parallel algebraic multigrid solver for linear systems arising from problems on unstructured grids. It is derived directly from the BoomerAMG solver in the hypre library, a large linear solver library that is being developed in the Center for Applied Scientific Computing (CASC) at LLNL. AMG is part of the ECP proxy application suite [2] and exhibits a highly dynamic communication pattern that is difficult to predict. For more details, please consult the artifact that accompanies this paper [1].

4.3 Monitoring Accuracy

Before being able to confidently use the data reported by the monitoring to train the RNN we need to quantify how accurate our MPI-level monitoring solution is compared to a system-level solution, in order to understand what trade-off is necessary to achieve the much desired portability that enables users to avoid implementing a custom monitoring solution specific for each platform.

To this end, we compare the time series from the log files in Figs. 4(a) and (b). As we can observe visually, for HACC (Fig. 4(a)) the difference between MPI-level and system-level is negligible. On the other hand, for AMG (Fig. 4(b)) there are slight discrepancies introduced by delays between the moment when MPI queues messages to be sent to the network interface and the moment when the network interface actually sends them. Given the high dynamicity of the communication pattern, this is expected.

Table 1. Mean squared error and fast dynamic time warping of MPI- vs. system-level network utilization (lower is better). Normalized version included for easier comparison (lower is better).

Application	MSE	FastDTW	Norm-MSE	Norm-FastDTW
HACC	36.35	376.75	0.0001	0.59
AMG	0.0074	4.57	0.07	14.23

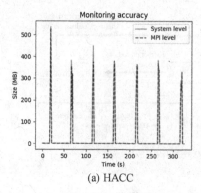 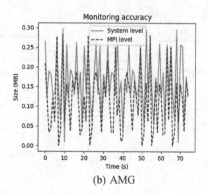

(a) HACC   (b) AMG

Fig. 4. Monitoring accuracy: MPI- vs. system-level network utilization measured every second.

Quantitatively, Table 1 details the MSE and FastDTW for both applications, both in raw and normalized form. The normalized form is calculated by scaling the values of the time series to the interval $[0, 1]$. As expected, it reveals a much better accuracy for HACC than for AMG. The raw form is interesting to note for subsequent comparison with the accuracy of the prediction, which is based on the MPI-level monitoring and thus subject to the errors introduced by it.

4.4   Prediction Accuracy

Based on the accuracy of the collected monitoring data, we can study how accurate the predictions of our proposed approach (henceforth referred to as OnlineS2S) is compared with the actual values reported at the system-level. To this end, we simulate online learning as follows. First, we determine the periodicity of the communication pattern (as discussed in Sect. 3.4). For HACC, the periodicity is 60 s, while for AMG, the periodicity is 20 s. Then, we set the *epoch* for training of our model to be equal to the periodicity. Our goal is to successfully predict one epoch in advance at every moment during the application runtime. To achieve this, we adopt the following approach: for each timestamp t in the time series, we predict the network utilization at $t + epoch$, then update the history and the model as detailed in Sect. 3.4. Then, we plot the resulting time series together with its system-level counterpart. We fix $p = 5$, $q = 100$, and $h = 5 \cdot epochs$.

We compare our approach against ARIMA [8], a popular method used in time series forecasting that combines an autoregressive (AR) with a moving average (MA) model. We also adopt the sliding window approach for ARIMA, updating the model and history as t increases. We use a standard implementation of ARIMA that is available as part of the statsmodel Python package.

The results are shown in Figs. 5(a) and (b) where the superior quality of the prediction of OnlineS2S vs. ARIMA is clearly visible. In the case of HACC (Fig. 5(a)), the spikes are accurately predicted by our approach both in terms of time and amplitude. On the other hand, ARIMA exhibits a delay in the prediction of the spikes, which means a background service relying on such predictions will incorrectly assume the

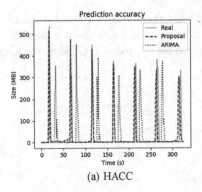 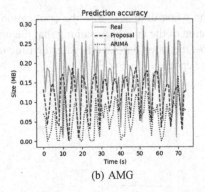

(a) HACC   (b) AMG

Fig. 5. Prediction accuracy: Estimated network utilization one epoch in the future (OnlineS2S vs. ARIMA) compared with actual system-level utilization measured at the same moment.

application will not communicate when it actually does, potentially scheduling its own network I/O at the same time and therefore causing interference. Also, the amplitude of the predictions exhibits noticeable inaccuracies. In the case of AMG (Fig. 5(b)), both predictions show a visible under-estimation of the network utilization. However, in the case of ARIMA, the under-estimation is significantly larger.

Table 2. Mean squared error and fast dynamic time warping of OnlineS2S and ARIMA predicted network utilization vs. actual system-level utilization (lower is better). Relative improvement of OnlineS2S vs. ARIMA included for easier comparison (higher is better).

HACC	MSE	FastDTW	AMG	MSE	FastDTW
OnlineS2S	6194	2737	OnlineS2S	0.00797	4.77
ARIMA	14433	4344	ARIMA	0.0168	7.14
Relative	2.3×	1.6×	Relative	2.11×	1.5×

Table 2 shows the MSE and FastDTW for both applications. In addition to the raw values, we calculate the relative improvement (values for ARIMA divided by values for OnlineS2S) for easier comparison. As we can observe, OnlineS2S has more than 2× smaller MSE and 1.5× smaller FastDTW. Thus, our approach consistently outperforms ARIMA in both typical and highly dynamic HPC network utilization scenarios.

4.5   Computational Overhead

Our last study focuses on the computational overhead required to perform the online learning during the application runtime. This is an important aspect, because online learning may cause interference with the CPU utilization of the application.

To estimate the severity of the interference, we record the time required to update the model as we pass from one epoch to another (which we refer to as sequence number).

In the worst case scenario, the application will use the CPUs at 100% for the entire duration of the epoch. Assuming that the update of the model will also use the CPUs at 100%, the worst case overhead is the time required for the update divided by the length of the epoch.

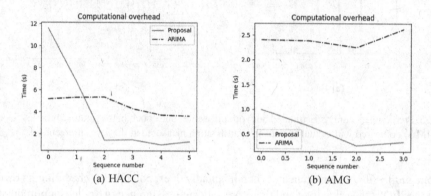

(a) HACC   (b) AMG

Fig. 6. Computational overhead: Time required to process an epoch (lower is better).

The time needed for each epoch are shown in Figs. 6(a) and (b). For HACC, OnlineS2S has a higher initial overhead but quickly stabilizes after two epochs and is consistently 2.5× faster than ARIMA. Since the epoch is 60 s in this case, this means OnlineS2S can achieve a worst-case overhead of less than 3%, whereas ARIMA is closer to 7%. In the case of AMG, OnlineS2S is much faster from the beginning and stabilizes at a point where it is at least 5× faster than ARIMA. Since the epoch is 20 s in this case, the worst-case overhead for OnlineS2S is 2.5% and more than 10% for ARIMA. With such high worst-case overhead, we conclude that ARIMA may be unfeasible to adopt for online prediction, especially for applications that exhibit small epochs.

5   Conclusions

This paper introduced an online prediction approach for network utilization specifically designed for HPC applications that exhibit periodic communication behavior. It is based on the idea of combining a mechanism to approximate network utilization at the MPI-level in a portable fashion with a deep learning approach that adapts sequence-to-sequence predictors based on recurrent neural networks for adaptive online learning.

We evaluated the accuracy and computational overhead of our approach experimentally on two representative HPC applications. We show that our approach is consistently, at least twice as accurate and at least twice as fast compared with state-of-the-art prediction approaches based on traditional time series analysis.

Encouraged by these results, we plan to broaden the scope of our work in future efforts. Specifically, there are several promising directions. First, we will run new experiments to measure the actual computational overhead of online learning when integrated with the HPC applications (as opposed to the worst case scenario we studied in this paper). Second, we will evaluate the actual benefits of leveraging predictions of network utilization to improve asynchronous checkpointing.

Acknowledgments. This research was supported by the Exascale Computing Project (17-SC-20-SC), a collaborative effort of the U.S. Department of Energy Office of Science and the National Nuclear Security Administration. This material was based upon work supported by the U.S. Department of Energy, Office of Science, under contract DE-AC02-06CH11357, and by the National Science Foundation under Grant No. #1664142. The experiments presented in this paper were carried out using the Grid'5000/ALADDIN-G5K experimental testbed, an initiative of the French Ministry of Research through the ACI GRID incentive action, INRIA, CNRS and RENATER and other contributing partners (see http://www.grid5000.fr/).

References

1. Accompanying artifact. https://doi.org/10.6084/m9.figshare.8491058
2. ECP proxy applications project. https://proxyapps.exascaleproject.org/ecp-proxy-apps-suite/
3. Adalsteinsson, H., Cranford, S., Evensky, D.A., Kenny, J.P., Mayo, J., Pinar, A., Janssen, C.L.: A simulator for large-scale parallel computer architectures. Int. J. Distrib. Syst. Technol. **1**(2), 57–73 (2010)
4. Baker, A.H., Falgout, R.D., Kolev, T.V., Yang, U.M.: Multigrid smoothers for ultraparallel computing. SIAM J. Sci. Comput. **33**(5), 2864–2887 (2011)
5. Barrett, B., Squyres, J.M., Lumsdaine, A., Graham, R.L., Bosilca, G.: Analysis of the component architecture overhead in Open MPI. In: EuroPVM/MPI 2005: 12th European Parallel Virtual Machine and Message Passing Interface Users' Group Meeting, Sorrento, Italy, pp. 175–182 (2005)
6. Bengio, Y., Simard, P., Frasconi, P., et al.: Learning long-term dependencies with gradient descent is difficult. IEEE Trans. Neural Networks **5**(2), 157–166 (1994)
7. Bosilca, G., Foyer, C., Jeannot, E., Mercier, G., Papauré, G.: Online dynamic monitoring of MPI communications. In: Rivera, F.F., Pena, T.F., Cabaleiro, J.C. (eds.) Euro-Par 2017. LNCS, vol. 10417, pp. 49–62. Springer, Cham (2017). https://doi.org/10.1007/978-3-319-64203-1_4
8. Box, G.E., Jenkins, G.M., Reinsel, G.C., Ljung, G.M.: Time Series Analysis: Forecasting and Control. Wiley, Hoboken (2015)
9. Brown, K.A., Domke, J., Matsuoka, S.: Tracing data movements within MPI collectives. In: EuroMPI 2014: Proceedings of the 21st European MPI Users' Group Meeting, Kyoto, Japan, pp. 117:117–117:118 (2014)
10. Chiu, C.C., et al.: State-of-the-art speech recognition with sequence-to-sequence models. In: ICASSP 2018: 2018 IEEE International Conference on Acoustics. Speech and Signal Processing, Calgary, AB, Canada, pp. 4774–4778 (2018)
11. Cho, K., et al.: Learning phrase representations using RNN encoder-decoder for statistical machine translation. In: EMNLP 2014: 2014 Conference on Empirical Methods in Natural Language Processing, Doha, Qatar, pp. 1724–1734 (2014)
12. Collobert, R., Weston, J., Bottou, L., Karlen, M., Kavukcuoglu, K., Kuksa, P.: Natural language processing (almost) from scratch. J. Mach. Learn. Res. **12**(Aug), 2493–2537 (2011)
13. Gerber, R., et al.: Crosscut report: exascale requirements reviews, March 9–10, 2017-tysons corner, virginia. An office of science review sponsored by: advanced scientific computing research, basic energy sciences, biological and environmental research, fusion energy sciences, high energy physics, nuclear physics. Technical report, Oak Ridge National Lab. (ORNL) (2018)

14. Habib, S., Morozov, V., Frontiere, N., Finkel, H., Pope, A., Heitmann, K.: HACC: extreme scaling and performance across diverse architectures. In: SC 2013: 2013 International Conference on High Performance Computing. Networking, Storage and Analysis, Denver, USA, pp. 1–10 (2013)

15. Harmon, M., Klabjan, D.: Dynamic prediction length for time series with sequence to sequence networks. arXiv preprint arXiv:1807.00425 (2018)

16. Hochreiter, S., Schmidhuber, J.: Long short-term memory. Neural Comput. **9**(8), 1735–1780 (1997)

17. Jean, S., Cho, K., Memisevic, R., Bengio, Y.: On using very large target vocabulary for neural machine translation. In: ACL-IJCNLP 2015: 53rd Annual Meeting of the Association for Computational Linguistics and 7th International Joint Conference on Natural Language Processing, Beijing, China, pp. 1–10 (2015)

18. Keller, R., Bosilca, G., Fagg, G., Resch, M., Dongarra, J.J.: Implementation and usage of the PERUSE-interface in Open MPI. In: EuroPVM/MPI 2006: 13th European Parallel Virtual Machine/Message Passing Interface Users' Group Meeting, Bonn, Germany, pp. 347–355 (2006)

19. Knüpfer, A., et al.: Score-P: a joint performance measurement run-time infrastructure for periscope, scalasca, TAU, and vampir. In: 5th International Workshop on Parallel Tools for High Performance Computing, Dresden, Germany, pp. 9–91 (2012)

20. Kumar, A.S., Mazumdar, S.: Forecasting HPC workload using ARMA models and SSA. In: ICIT 2016: 2016 International Conference on Information Technology, Bhubaneswar, India, pp. 294–297 (2016)

21. Kuznetsov, V., Mariet, Z.: Foundations of sequence-to-sequence modeling for time series. arXiv preprint arXiv:1805.03714 (2018)

22. Salvador, S., Chan, P.: Toward accurate dynamic time warping in linear time and space. Intell. Data Anal. **11**(5), 561–580 (2007)

23. Sutskever, I., Vinyals, O., Le, Q.V.: Sequence to sequence learning with neural networks. In: NIPS 2014: 27th Annual Conference on Neural Information Processing Systems, Montreal, Quebec, Canada, pp. 3104–3112 (2014)

24. Tran, N., Reed, D.A.: ARIMA time series modeling and forecasting for adaptive I/O prefetching. In: ICS 2001: Proceedings of the 15th International Conference on Supercomputing, Sorrento, Italy, pp. 473–485 (2001)

25. Tran, N., Reed, D.A.: Automatic ARIMA time series modeling for adaptive I/O prefetching. IEEE Trans. Parallel Distrib. Syst. **15**(4), 362–377 (2004)

26. Venugopalan, S., Rohrbach, M., Donahue, J., Mooney, R., Darrell, T., Saenko, K.: Sequence to sequence-video to text. In: ICCV 2015: 2015 IEEE International Conference on Computer Vision, Santiago, Chile, pp. 4534–4542 (2015)

27. Vetter, J.S., McCracken, M.O.: Statistical scalability analysis of communication operations in distributed applications. In: PPoPP 2001: Proceedings of the 8th ACM SIGPLAN Symposium on Principles and Practices of Parallel Programming, Snowbird, Utah, USA, pp. 123–132 (2001)

A Comparison of Random Task Graph Generation Methods for Scheduling Problems

Louis-Claude Canon[✉], Mohamad El Sayah,
and Pierre-Cyrille Héam

FEMTO-ST Institute, CNRS,
Univ. Bourgogne Franche-Comté, Besançon, France
{louis-claude.canon,mohamad.el_sayah,
pierre-cyrille.heam}@univ-fcomte.fr

Abstract. How to generate instances with relevant properties and without bias remains an open problem of critical importance to compare heuristics fairly. When scheduling with precedence constraints, the instance is a task graph that determines a partial order on task executions. To avoid selecting instances among a set populated mainly with trivial ones, we rely on properties such as the *mass*, which measures how much a task graph can be decomposed into smaller ones. This property and an in-depth analysis of existing random instance generators establish the sub-exponential generic time complexity of the studied problem.

1 Introduction

How to correctly evaluate the performance of computing systems has been a central question for a long time [15]. Among the arsenal of available evaluation methods, relying on random instances allows comparing strategies in many diverse situations. However, random generation methods are prone to bias, which prevents a fair empirical assessment. Studying the problem characteristics to constrain the uniform generation on a category of difficult instances is thus critical.

In the context of parallel systems, instances for numerous multiprocessor scheduling problems contain the description of an application to be executed on a platform [17]. This study focuses on scheduling problems requiring a Directed Acyclic Graph (DAG) as part of the input. Such a DAG represents a set of tasks to be executed in a specific order given by precedence constraints. While this work studies the DAG structure for several scheduling problems, it illustrates and analyzes existing generators in light of a specific problem with unitary costs and no communication. This simple yet difficult problem emphasizes the effect of the DAG structure on the performance of scheduling heuristics.

After exposing related works in Sect. 2, Sect. 3 lists DAG properties and covers scheduling and random generation concepts. Section 4 analyzes the proposed properties on a set of special DAGs. Section 5 provides an in-depth analysis of existing random generators supported by consistent empirical observations.

© Springer Nature Switzerland AG 2019
R. Yahyapour (Ed.): Euro-Par 2019, LNCS 11725, pp. 61–73, 2019.
https://doi.org/10.1007/978-3-030-29400-7_5

Finally, Sect. 6 studies the impact of these methods and the DAG properties on scheduling heuristics. A more detailed version of these results is also available in the extended version [4].

2   Related Work

Our approach is similar to the one followed in [6], which consists in studying the properties of randomly generated DAGs before comparing the performance of scheduling heuristics. Three properties are measured and analyzed for each studied generator: the length of the longest path, the distribution of the output degrees and the number of edges. The authors consider five random generators: two variants of the Erdős-Rényi algorithm, one layer-by-layer variant, the random orders method and the Fan-in/Fan-out method. Finally, for each generator, the paper compares the performance of four scheduling heuristics. The results are consistent with the observations done in Sect. 5 (Figs. 1, 3 and 4) for the length and the number of edges.

Many tools have been proposed in the literature to generate DAGs in the context of scheduling in parallel systems. TGFF (Task Graphs For Free) is the first tool proposed for this purpose [7]. This tool relies on a number of parameters related to the task graph structure. The task graph is constructed by creating a single-vertex graph and then incrementally augmenting it. Until the number of vertices in the graph is greater than or equal to the minimum number of vertices, this approach randomly alternates between two phases: the expansion of the graph and its contraction. The main goal of TGFF is to gain more control over the input and output degrees of the tasks.

DAGGEN was later proposed to compare heuristics for a specific problem [8]. This tool relies on a layer-by-layer approach with four parameters in addition to the number of vertices. The number of elements per layer is uniformly drawn in an interval determined by the width parameter and with a range determined by the regularity parameter. Lastly, edges are added between layers separated by a maximum number of layers determined by the jump parameter. For each vertex, the method adds a uniform number of predecessors in an interval determined by the density parameter.

GGen has been proposed to unify the generation of DAGs by integrating existing methods [6]. The tool implements two variants of the Erdős-Rényi algorithm, one layer-by-layer variant, the random orders method and the Fan-in/Fan-out method. It also generates DAGs derived from classical parallel algorithms such as the recursive Fibonacci function, the Strassen multiplication algorithm, etc.

The Pegasus workflow generator[1] can be used to generate DAGs from several scientific applications [16] such as Montage, CyberShake, Broadband, etc. XL-STaGe[2] produces layer-by-layer DAGs using a truncated normal distribution to distribute the vertices to the layers [3]. This tool inserts edges with a probability

---

[1] https://confluence.pegasus.isi.edu/display/pegasus/WorkflowGenerator.
[2] https://github.com/nizarsd/xl-stage.

that decreases as the number of layers between two vertices increases. A tool named RandomWorkflowGenerator[3] implements a layer-by-layer variant [12].

3 Background

Directed Acyclic Graphs. Let $D = (V, E)$ be a Directed Acyclic Graph (DAG), where V is a finite set of vertices and $E \subseteq V \times V$ is the set of edges, such that there is no cycle in the graph. The *length* of a DAG is defined as the maximum number of vertices in any path in this DAG and is noted len or k. The *depth* of a vertex v in a DAG is inductively defined by: if v has no predecessor, then its depth is 1; otherwise, the depth of v is one plus the maximum depth of its predecessors. The *shape decomposition* of a DAG is the tuple $(X_1, X_2, \ldots, X_k)$ where X_i is the set of vertices of depth i. The *shape* of the DAG is the tuple $(|X_1|, \ldots, |X_k|)$. The maximum (resp. minimum) value of the $|X_i|$ is called the *maximum shape* (resp. *minimum shape*) of the DAG. Computing the shape decomposition and the shape of a DAG is easy. If $|X_i| = 1$, the unique vertex of X_i is called a *bottleneck vertex*. A *block* is a subset of vertices of the form $\cup_{i < j < i+\ell} X_j$ with $\ell > 1$ where X_i is either a singleton or $i = 0$, $X_{i+\ell}$ is either a singleton or $i + \ell = k + 1$, and for each $i < j < i + \ell$, $|X_j| \neq 1$. We denote by $\mathrm{mass}^{\mathrm{abs}}(B)$ the cardinal of $B = \cup_{i < j < i+\ell} X_j$ and by $\mathrm{mass}^{\mathrm{abs}}(D) = \max\{\mathrm{mass}^{\mathrm{abs}}(B) \mid B \text{ is a block}\}$ the *absolute mass* of D. The *relative mass*, or simply the *mass*, is given by $\mathrm{mass}(D) = \frac{\mathrm{mass}^{\mathrm{abs}}(D)}{n}$.

The *transitive reduction* of a DAG D [2] is the DAG D^T for which: D^T has a directed path between u and v iff D has a directed path between u and v; there is no graph with fewer edges than D^T that satisfies the previous property. Intuitively, this operation consists in removing redundant edges.

Among dozens of DAG properties, we measure the following ones on the transitive reduction of each DAG D: the number of edges m, maximum degree $\mathrm{deg}^{\mathrm{max}}$ and degree Coefficient of Variation[4] $\mathrm{deg}^{\mathrm{CV}}$. For these properties, we specify they are measured on a transitive reduction (e.g. $m(D^T)$ for the number of edges). Moreover, we measure the length, the mean shape $\mathrm{sh}^{\mathrm{mean}}$, the shape CV $\mathrm{sh}^{\mathrm{CV}}$ and the mass. The last measured property is the number of edges in D.

Scheduling. We consider a classic problem in parallel systems noted $P|p_j = 1, prec|C_{\max}$ in Graham's notation [11]. The objective consists in scheduling a set of tasks on homogeneous processors such as to minimize the overall completion time. The dependencies between tasks are represented by a precedence DAG: before starting its execution, all the predecessors of a task must complete their executions. The execution cost p_j of task j on any processor is unitary and there are no costs on the edges (i.e. no communication). A schedule defines on which processor and at which date each task starts executing such that no processor executes more than one task at any time and all precedence constraints are met. The problem consists in finding the schedule with the minimum makespan.

---

[3] https://github.com/anubhavcho/RandomWorkflowGenerator.
[4] The CV is the ratio of the mean degree to the degree standard deviation.

This problem is strongly NP-hard [25], while it is polynomial when there are no precedence constraints, which means the difficulty comes from the dependencies. Many polynomial heuristics have been proposed for this problem (see Sect. 6). With specific instances, such heuristics may be optimal. This is the case when the width does not exceed the number of processors, which leads to a potentially large length. Any task can thus start its execution as soon as it becomes available. This paper explores how DAG properties are impacted by the generation method with the objective to control them to avoid easy instances.

Although this paper studies random DAGs with heuristics for the specific problem $P|p_j = 1, prec|C_{\max}$, generated DAGs can be used for many scheduling problems with precedence constraints. While avoiding specific instances depending on their width and length is relevant for many scheduling problems, it is not necessary the case for all of them. For instance, with non-unitary processing costs, instances with large width and small length are difficult because the problem is strongly NP-Hard even in the absence of precedence constraints $(P||C_{\max})$[10].

Mass and Scheduling. Consider a DAG $D = (V, E)$ whose minimum shape is 1; there exists a bottleneck vertex v such that the shape of the DAG is of the form $(X_1, \ldots, X_\ell, \{v\}, X_{\ell+1}, \ldots, X_k)$. The scheduling problem for D can be decomposed into two subproblems. Using recursively this decomposition, the initial problem can be decomposed into $n_c + 1$ independent scheduling problems, where n_c is the number of bottleneck vertices.

Applying a brute force algorithm for the scheduling problems computes the optimal results in a time $T \le n_c T_m$, where T_m is the maximum time required to solve the problem on a DAG with mass$^{\text{abs}}(D)$ vertices. Since exponential brute force exact approaches exist, it follows that if mass$^{\text{abs}}(D) = O(\log^k n)$ for a constant k, then an optimal solution of the scheduling problem can be computed in sub-exponential time. Consequently, scheduling heuristics are irrelevant for task graph with polylogarithmic absolute mass. Similarly, the same arguments work to claim that interesting instances for the scheduling problem must have quite a large absolute mass (not in $o(n)$). It is therefore preferable to have instances with no or few bottleneck vertices, that is a unitary mass.

The relevance of the mass property is limited to the class of scheduling problems that contains all problems for which the instance can be cut into independent subinstances.

4   Analysis of Special DAGs

To analyze the properties described in the previous section, we introduce in Table 1 a collection of special DAGs. The first three DAGs (D_{empty}, D_{complete} and D_{chain}) constitutes extreme cases in terms of precedence. The next two DAGs ($D_{\text{out-tree}}$ and D_{comb}), to which we can add the reversal of the complete binary tree ($D_{\text{in-tree}} = D^R_{\text{out-tree}}$), are examples of binary tree DAGs. The last three DAGs ($D_{\text{bipartite}}$, D_{square} and $D_{\text{triangular}}$) are denser with more edges and with a compromise between the length and the width for these last two DAGs.

Table 1. Special DAGs.

Name	description	representation
Empty (D_{empty})	no edge	
Complete (D_{complete})	maximum number of edges	
Chain (D_{chain})	transitive reduction of the complete DAG	
Complete binary tree ($D_{\text{out-tree}}$)	each non-leaf/non-root vertex has a unique predecessor and two successors	
Comb (D_{comb})	a chain where each non-leaf vertex has an additional leaf successor	
Complete bipartite ($D_{\text{bipartite}}$)	$\frac{n}{2}$ vertices connected to $\frac{n}{2}$ vertices	
Complete layer-by-layer square (D_{square})	similar to the complete bipartite with $\sqrt{n}$ layers of size $\sqrt{n}$	
Complete layer-by-layer triangular ($D_{\text{triangular}}$)	similar to the complete layer-by-layer square but the size of each new layer increases by 1	

Table 2 illustrates the properties for these special DAGs. The most extreme values are reached with the empty and complete DAGs for the length, number of edges, mass and mean shape. When considering only transitive reductions (i.e. when discarding the complete DAG), the maximum value for the maximum degree is n with a fork or a join (the bipartite DAG reaches half this value). Proposition 1 states that the maximum number of edges among all transitive reductions is $\left\lfloor \frac{n^2}{4} \right\rfloor$ (reached with the bipartite DAG).

Proposition 1. *The maximum number of edges among all transitive reductions of size n is* $\left\lfloor \frac{n^2}{4} \right\rfloor$.

Proof. Transitive reductions do not contain triangle (i.e. clique of size three), otherwise there is either a cycle or a redundant edge. By Mantel's Theorem [20], the maximum number of edges in a n-vertex triangle-free graph is $\left\lfloor \frac{n^2}{4} \right\rfloor$.

Table 2. Approximate properties of special DAGs (negligible terms are discarded for clarity). The exact properties are given in the extended version [4].

DAG	len	m	$m(D^T)$	mass	sh^{mean}	sh^{CV}	$\deg^{\max}(D^T)$	$\deg^{\text{CV}}$
D_{empty}	1	0	0	1	n	0	0	0
D_{complete}	n	$\frac{n^2}{2}$	n	0	1	0	2	$\frac{1}{\sqrt{2n}}$
D_{chain}	n	n	n	0	1	0	2	$\frac{1}{\sqrt{2n}}$
$D_{\text{out-tree}}\ D_{\text{in-tree}}$	$\log_2(n)$	n	n	1	$\frac{n}{\log_2(n)}$	$\sqrt{\frac{\log_2(n+1)}{3}}$	3	$\frac{1}{2}$
D_{comb}	$\frac{n}{2}$	n	n	1	2	$\frac{1}{\sqrt{2n}}$	3	$\frac{1}{2}$
D_{comb}^{R}	$\frac{n}{2}$	n	n	$\frac{1}{2}$	2	$\sqrt{\frac{n}{8}}$	3	$\frac{1}{2}$
$D_{\text{bipartite}}$	2	$\frac{n^2}{4}$	$\frac{n^2}{4}$	1	$\frac{n}{2}$	0	$\frac{n}{2}$	0
D_{square}	$\sqrt{n}$	$n\sqrt{n}$	$n\sqrt{n}$	1	$\sqrt{n}$	0	$2\sqrt{n}$	$\frac{1}{\sqrt{2\sqrt{n}}}$
$D_{\text{triangular}}$	$\sqrt{2n}$	$\frac{2n\sqrt{2n}}{3}$	$\frac{2n\sqrt{2n}}{3}$	1	$\sqrt{\frac{n}{2}}$	$\frac{1}{\sqrt{3}}$	$2\sqrt{2n}$	$\frac{1}{2\sqrt{2}}$

This is the case for the complete bipartite DAG because the number of edges is $\frac{n^2}{4} = \left\lfloor \frac{n^2}{4} \right\rfloor$ when n is even and $\frac{n^2-1}{4} = \left\lfloor \frac{n^2}{4} \right\rfloor$ when n is odd.

5 Analysis of Existing Generators

Random Generation of Triangular Matrices. This approach is based on the Erdős-Rényi algorithm [9] with parameter p: an upper-triangular adjacency matrix is randomly generated. For each pair of vertices (i, j) with $i < j$, there is an edge from i to j with an independent probability p. The approach is not uniform. For instance, a random generator that is uniform over all the DAGs

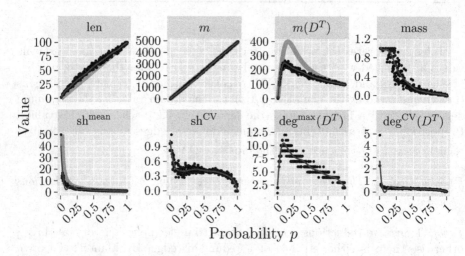

Fig. 1. Properties of 300 DAGs of size $n = 100$ generated with probability p uniformly drawn between 0 and 1 (Erdős-Rényi algorithm). Red lines correspond to formal bounds. (Color figure online)

generates the empty DAG with probability $1/25$. With $p = 0.5$, the Erdős-Rényi algorithm generates the empty DAG with probability $1/8$.

Figure 1 shows the effect of the probability parameter p on the properties of the generated DAGs. The most remarkable effect can be seen for the number of edges in the transitive reduction $m(D^T)$. This property shows that after a maximum around $p = 0.10$, adding more edges with higher probabilities leads to redundant dependencies and simplifies the structure of the DAG by making it longer. A formal result in the extended version [4, Proposition 4] confirms this effect. DAGs generated with a probability below 5% are almost empty and most edges are not redundant. These DAGs lead to a simplistic scheduling process that consists in starting each task on a critical path as soon as possible and then distributing a large number of independent tasks. Analogously, DAGs generated with probabilities p greater than 15% contain many edges that simplify the DAG structure by increasing the length and thus reducing the mean shape (recall that with a small width, the problem is easy). At the same time, the mass decreases continuously, allowing the problem to be divided into smaller problems.

The effect of probability p illustrates the compromise between the length and mean shape to avoid simplistic instances that are easily tackled.

Uniform Random Generation. One way to uniformly generate elements consists in using a classical recursive/counting approach [22] based on generating functions. This counting approach relies on recursively counting the number of DAGs with a given number of source vertices, that is vertices with no in-going edges. See [4, Section 5.2] for a complete algorithm that uniformly generates random DAGs with this approach.

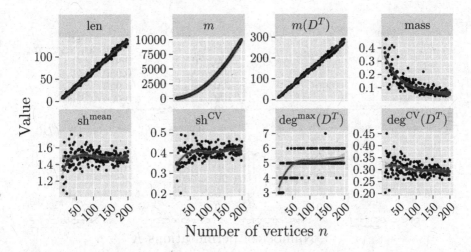

Fig. 2. Properties of DAGs generated by the recursive algorithm for each size n between 10 and 200. Red lines correspond to formal results. (Color figure online)

Figure 2 depicts the effect of the number of vertices on the selected DAG properties. The length closely follows the function $\frac{3n}{2}$. This effect is consistent with a theoretical result stating that the expected number of source vertices sh[1] in a uniform DAG is asymptotically 1.488 as $n \to \infty$ [19]. This implies that the expected value for each shape element is close to this value by construction of the shape, which makes the DAG an easy instance for scheduling problems. Moreover, the number of edges m is almost indistinguishable from the function $\frac{n^2}{4}$, which is indeed the average number of edges in a uniform DAG [21, Theorem 2]. We finally observe that the mass decreases as the size n increases. This is confirmed by the following result (proved in the extended version [4]):

Theorem 1. *Let D be a DAG uniformly and randomly generated among the labeled DAGs with n vertices. One has $\mathbb{P}(\mathrm{mass}^{\mathrm{abs}}(D) \geq \log^4(n)) \to 0$ when $n \to +\infty$.*

Therefore, the mass converges to zero as the size n tends to infinity. As shown in Sect. 3, such instances can be decomposed into independent problems and efficiently solved with a brute force strategy. This leads to a sub-exponential generic time complexity with uniform instances.

Random Orders. The random orders method derives a DAG from randomly generated orders [26]. The first step consists in building K random permutations of n vertices. Each of these permutations represents a total order on the vertices, which is also a complete DAG with a random labeling. Intersecting these complete DAGs by keeping an edge iff it appears in all DAGs with the same direction leads to the final DAG.

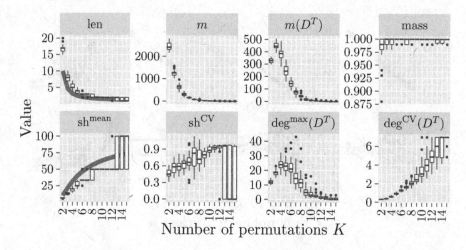

Fig. 3. Properties of 420 DAGs of size $n = 100$ generated by the random orders algorithm for each K between 2 and 15. Red lines correspond to formal results. (Color figure online)

Figure 3 shows the effect of the number of permutations K on the DAG properties with boxplots[5]. The extreme cases $K = 1$ and $K \to \infty$ are discarded from the figure for clarity. They correspond to the chain and the empty DAG, respectively. The number of permutations quickly constrains the length. For instance, the length is already between 15 and 20 when $K = 2$ and at most 5 when $K \geq 5$. A formal analysis suggests that the length is almost surely in $O(n^{1/K})$ [26, Theorem 3], which is consistent with our observation. Moreover, the mass is always close to one for $K > 1$.

Layer-by-Layer. The layer-by-layer method was first proposed by [1] but popularized later by the introduction of the STG data set [23]. This method produces DAGs in which vertices are distributed in layers and vertices belonging to the same layer are independent. This section analyzes the effect of three parameters (size n, number of layers k and connectivity probability p) using the following variant inspired from [6,12]. First, k vertices are affected to distinct layers to prevent any empty layer. Then, the remaining $n - k$ vertices are distributed to the layers using a balls into bins approach (i.e. a uniformly random layer is selected for each vertex). For each vertex not in the first layer, a random parent is selected among the vertices from the previous layer to ensure that the layer of any vertex equals its depth. Finally, random edges are added by connecting any pair of vertices from distinct layers from top to bottom with probability p.

This method always generates DAGs with a length equal to k and mean shape equal to n/k. Moreover, when all layers have the same size n/k, the expected number of edges is $\mathbb{E}(m) = n \left(1 - \frac{1}{k}\right) \left(p \left(\frac{n}{2} - 1\right) + 1\right)$ and the expected number of edges in the transitive reduction is $\mathbb{E}(m(D^T)) \geq p(k-1) \left(\frac{n}{k}\right)^2 + (1-p)n \left(1 - \frac{1}{k}\right)$.

Figure 4 represents the effect of the number of layers k. The numbers of edges in the DAG and its transitive reduction are close to the expected values for the case when all layers have the same size n/k. Finally, the mass is unitary when there are at least two balls in each bin. Since there is initially one ball per bin, this occurs when there is at least one of the $n - k$ additional balls in each of the k bin. Using a bound for the coupon collector problem [18, Proposition 2.4], this occurs with probability greater than 0.5 when $\lceil k \log(2k) \rceil + k < n$, which is the case for $k \leq 20$ when $n = 100$. This is consistent with Fig. 4 where the mass becomes non-unitary around this value.

To avoid non-unitary mass, the layer-by-layer method can be adapted to ensure that each layer has two vertices initially. For instance, we can rely on a uniform distribution between two and a maximum value, or on a balls into bins approach with two balls per bin initially.

---

[5] Each boxplot consists of a bold line for the median, a box for the quartiles, whiskers that extend at most to 1.5 times the interquartile range from the box and additional points for outliers.

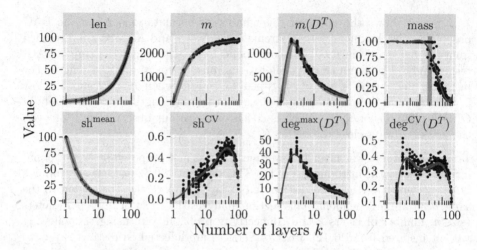

Fig. 4. Properties of 300 DAGs of size $n = 100$ generated by the layer-by-layer algorithm with probability $p = 0.5$ and a number of layers k randomly drawn between 1 and 100 (uniformly on the logarithmic scale). Red lines correspond to formal results. (Color figure online)

6   Evaluation on Scheduling Algorithms

Generating random task graphs allows the assessment of existing scheduling algorithms in different contexts. Numerous heuristics have been proposed for the problem denoted $P|p_j = 1, prec|C_{\max}$ or generalizations of this problem. Such heuristics rely on different principles. Some simple strategies, like MinMin [14, Algorithm D], execute available tasks on the processors that minimize completion time without considering precedence constraints. In contrast, many heuristics sort tasks by criticality and schedule them with the Earliest Finish Time (EFT) policy. This is the case for both HEFT [24] and HCPT [13]. HEFT first computes the upward rank of each task, which can be seen as a reverse depth, and then consider tasks by decreasing order of their upward ranks. Backfilling is performed following an insertion policy. In contract, HCPT starts by considering any task on a critical path by decreasing order of their depth. The objective is to prioritize the ancestors of such tasks and in particular when their depths are large.

Figure 5 shows the absolute difference between MinMin, HEFT and HCPT for each generator covered in Sect. 5. Despite guaranteeing an unbiased generation, instances built with the recursive algorithm fail to discriminate heuristics except when there are two processors. Recall that the mean shape is close to 1.5 for such DAGs and few processors are sufficient to obtain a makespan equal to the DAG length (i.e. an optimal schedule). In contrast, instances built with the random orders algorithm lead to different performance for each scheduling heuristics. However, this generator has no uniformity guarantee and its discrete parameter K limits the diversity of generated DAGs. Finally, the last two algorithms fail to highlight a significant difference between MinMin and HEFT even though

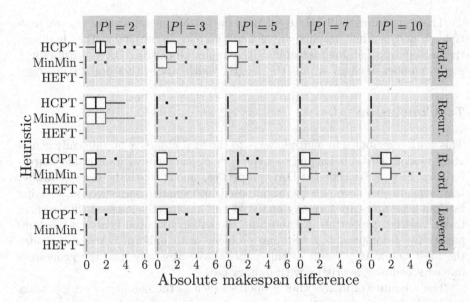

Fig. 5. Difference between the makespan obtained with any heuristic and the best value among the three heuristics for each instance. Each boxplot represents the results for 300 DAGs of size $n = 100$ built with the following algorithms: Erdős-Rényi ($p = 0.15$), recursive, random orders ($K = 3$) and layer-by-layer ($p = 0.5$ and $k = 10$). Costs are unitary and $|P|$ represents the number of processors.

the former scheduling heuristic can be expected to be inferior to the latter as it discards the DAG structure.

To support these observations, we analyze below the maximum difference between the makespan obtained with HEFT and the ones obtained with the other two heuristics. Because it lacks any backfilling mechanism, HCPT performs worse than HEFT with an instance composed of the following two elements. First, a chain of length k with $|P| - 1$ additional tasks with predecessor the $(k - 2)$th task of the chain and successor the kth task of the chain. The second element is a chain of length $k - 1$. HCPT schedules the first element and then the second one afterward, leading to a makespan of $2k - 1$ whereas the optimal one is k. With our settings, the difference from HEFT with this instance is greater than or equal to 45. Moreover, MinMin also performs worse with specific instances. Consider the ad hoc instances considered in [5] each consisting of one chain of length k and a set of $k(|P| - 1)$ independent tasks. Discarding the information about critical tasks prevents MinMin from prioritizing tasks from the chain. With $n = 100$ tasks and with $|P| \leq 10$, the worst-case absolute difference can be greater than or equal to 9. It is interesting to analyze the properties of these difficult instances for MinMin. Each DAG is characterized by a length equal to $\text{len} = \frac{n}{|P|}$ and a number of edges in the transitive reduction $m(D^T) = \text{len} - 1$. Moreover, worst-case DAGs for HCPT are characterized by a large length and width.

These experiments illustrate the need for better generators that control multiple properties while avoiding any generation bias. In particular, they highlight the need for a generator that uniformly samples all existing DAGs with a given size n, number of edges m, $m(D^T)$, length, width, and with a unitary mass.

7   Conclusion

This work contributes in multiple ways to the final objective of uniformly generating random DAGs belonging to a category of instances with desirable characteristics. First, we select eight DAG properties, among which the mass quantifies how much an instance can be decomposed into smaller ones. Second, existing random generators are formally analyzed and empirically assessed with respect to the selected properties. Establishing the sub-exponential generic time complexity for decomposable scheduling problems with uniform DAGs constitutes the most noteworthy result of this paper. Last, we study how the generators impact scheduling heuristics with unitary costs.

The relevance of many other properties such as the number of critical tasks need to be investigated further. Moreover, extending current results to instances with communications represents a challenging perspective. Finally, adapting properties to instances with non-unitary costs is left to future work.

Data Availability Statement. The datasets generated and/or analyzed during the current study are available in the Figshare repository: https://doi.org/10.6084/m9. figshare.8397623.

References

1. Adam, T.L., Chandy, K.M., Dickson, J.: A comparison of list schedules for parallel processing systems. Commun. ACM **17**(12), 685–690 (1974)
2. Aho, A.V., Garey, M.R., Ullman, J.D.: The transitive reduction of a directed graph. SIAM J. Comput. **1**(2), 131–137 (1972)
3. Campos, P., Dahir, N., Bonney, C., Trefzer, M., Tyrrell, A., Tempesti, G.: Xl-stage: a cross-layer scalable tool for graph generation, evaluation and implementation. In: 2016 International Conference on Embedded Computer Systems: Architectures, Modeling and Simulation (SAMOS), pp. 354–359. IEEE (2016)
4. Canon, L.C., El Sayah, M., Héam, P.C.: A comparison of random task graph generation methods for scheduling problems. arXiv preprint arXiv:1902.05808 (2019)
5. Canon, L.-C., Marchal, L., Simon, B., Vivien, F.: Online scheduling of task graphs on hybrid platforms. In: Aldinucci, M., Padovani, L., Torquati, M. (eds.) Euro-Par 2018. LNCS, vol. 11014, pp. 192–204. Springer, Cham (2018). https://doi.org/10. 1007/978-3-319-96983-1_14
6. Cordeiro, D., Mounié, G., Perarnau, S., Trystram, D., Vincent, J.M., Wagner, F.: Random graph generation for scheduling simulations. In: ICST, p. 60 (2010)
7. Dick, R.P., Rhodes, D.L., Wolf, W.: TGFF: task graphs for free. In: International workshop on Hardware/software codesign, pp. 97–101. IEEE (1998)

8. Dutot, P.F., N'takpé, T., Suter, F., Casanova, H.: Scheduling parallel task graphs on (almost) homogeneous multicluster platforms. IEEE TPDS **20**(7), 940–952 (2009)
9. Erdős, P., Rényi, A.: On random graphs I. Publ. Math. Debrecen **6**, 290–297 (1959)
10. Garey, M., Johnson, D.: Strong NP-completeness results: motivation, examples, and implications. J. Assoc. Comput. Mach. **25**(3), 499–508 (1978)
11. Graham, R.L., Lawler, E.L., Lenstra, J.K., Kan, A.H.G.R.: Optimization and approximation in deterministic sequencing and scheduling: a survey. Ann. Discret. Math. **5**, 287–326 (1979)
12. Gupta, I., Choudhary, A., Jana, P.K.: Generation and proliferation of random directed acyclic graphs for workflow scheduling problem. In: International Conference on Computer and Communication Technology, pp. 123–127. ACM (2017)
13. Hagras, T., Janecek, J.: A simple scheduling heuristic for heterogeneous computing environments. In: ISPDC, p. 104. IEEE (2003)
14. Ibarra, O.H., Kim, C.E.: Heuristic algorithms for scheduling independent tasks on nonidentical processors. J. ACM **24**(2), 280–289 (1977)
15. Jain, R.: The Art of Computer Systems Performance Analysis: Techniques for Experimental design, measurement, simulation, and modeling. Wiley, Hoboken (1990)
16. Juve, G., Chervenak, A., Deelman, E., Bharathi, S., Mehta, G., Vahi, K.: Characterizing and profiling scientific workflows. Future Gener. Comput. Syst. **29**(3), 682–692 (2013)
17. Leung, J.Y.: Handbook of Scheduling: Algorithms, Models, and Performance Analysis. CRC Press, Boca Raton (2004)
18. Levin, D.A., Peres, Y.: Markov Chains and Mixing Times, vol. 107. American Mathematical Society, Providence (2017)
19. Liskovets, V.: On the number of maximal vertices of a random acyclic digraph. Theory Probab. Appl. **20**(2), 401–409 (1975)
20. Mantel, W.: Problem 28. Wiskundige Opgaven **10**(60–61), 320 (1907)
21. Melançon, G., Dutour, I., Bousquet-Mélou, M.: Random generation of directed acyclic graphs. Electron. Not. Discrete Math. **10**, 202–207 (2001)
22. Robinson, R.W.: Counting labeled acyclic digraphs. In: Harray, F. (ed.) New Directions in the Theory of Graphs, pp. 239–273. Academic Press, New York (1973)
23. Tobita, T., Kasahara, H.: A standard task graph set for fair evaluation of multiprocessor scheduling algorithms. J. Sched. **5**(5), 379–394 (2002)
24. Topcuoglu, H., Hariri, S., Wu, M.Y.: Performance-effective and low-complexity task scheduling for heterogeneous computing. IEEE TPDS **13**(3), 260–274 (2002)
25. Ullman, J.: NP-complete scheduling problems. J. Comput. System Sci. **10**, 384–393 (1975)
26. Winkler, P.: Random orders. Order **1**(4), 317–331 (1985)

Hardware Counters' Space Reduction
for Code Region Characterization

Jordi Alcaraz$^{(\boxtimes)}$ (iD), Anna Sikora (iD), and Eduardo César (iD)

Universitat Autònoma de Barcelona, Cerdanyola (Barcelona), Spain
{jordi.alcaraz,anna.sikora,eduardo.cesar}@uab.cat

Abstract. This work proposes that parallel code regions in an OpenMP application can be characterized using a signature composed by the values of a set of hardware performance counters. Our proposal is aimed towards dynamic tuning and, consequently, the metrics must be collected at execution time, which limits the number of metrics that can be measured. Therefore, our main contribution is the definition of a methodology to determine a reduced set of hardware performance counters that can be measured at application's execution time and that still contains enough information to characterize a parallel region. The proposed methodology is based on principal component analysis and linear correlation analysis. Preliminary results show that it can be used to successfully reduce the number of hardware counters needed to characterize a parallel region, and that this set of counters can be measured at run time with high accuracy and low overhead using counter multiplexing.

Keywords: Performance analysis · Hardware counters ·
Parallel/distributed applications

1 Introduction

Performance analysis and tuning of parallel applications is becoming a more and more complicated task, even for expert developers, because the increasing heterogeneity and complexity of current HPC systems. Performance problems in such systems may be produced by several different, and sometimes hard to relate, causes that make it difficult to find the way to solve them. Logically, this difficulty is exacerbated when performance analysis and tuning process is done automatically and dynamically during the application execution.

Identifying performance problems requires to gather the appropriate metrics to find the causes of the bottleneck. At the processor level, the hardware performance counters are a powerful source of information. This mechanism provides metrics about the utilization of different system resources, such as access pattern to the memory hierarchy, executed instructions and their type, etc.

This work has the support of the Ministerio de Economía, Industria y Competitividad MINECO-SPAIN under contract TIN2017-84553-C2-1-R and by the Generalitat de Catalunya GenCat-DIUiE (GRR) with the project 2017-SGR-313.

R. Yahyapour (Ed.): Euro-Par 2019, LNCS 11725, pp. 74–86, 2019.
https://doi.org/10.1007/978-3-030-29400-7_6

The main hypothesis of this work is that, at the processor level, the values of the performance counters can be used to identify and characterize a parallel region during execution time. This set of values can be defined as the signature of a parallel region. This signature can be used at a later time to identify which kind of region the application is executing and to apply the appropriate tuning strategy depending on the behaviour explained by the signature.

In the case of OpenMP applications, hardware performance counters can be a good way to find which resources are being stressed and find possible solutions to improve performance [6]. We believe that hardware performance counters, such as cache misses, cycles per instruction, number of instructions executed, and others, can be used to identify and describe the execution of a parallel region.

However, current processors include an elevate number of hardware performance counters, for example, the Intel® i7 7700 includes up to 170 different counters, but only a few can be recorded simultaneously. Consequently, getting the values of all available counters for every parallel region can be costly or even unfeasible.

In this paper, we propose a method to reduce the number of hardware performance counters and characterize regions in OpenMP parallel applications at execution time with the help of counter multiplexing. This methodology will be based on (i) correlation analysis to find redundancy in the metrics provided by different counters, and (ii) principal component analysis to show that the signature composed by the values of a set of hardware performance counters can be used to characterize different parallel regions.

The remainder of this work is organized as follows. Section 2 introduces the mechanisms and techniques that are used in the proposed methodology. Next, Sect. 3 describes the methodology, which is the main contribution of this paper. Then, Sect. 4 shows the experimentation conducted to assess the methodology. Section 5 discusses relevant related work. Finally, Sect. 6 concludes this work and introduces future lines.

2   Background

This section introduces the mechanisms and techniques used in this paper to obtain the metrics to compute the signature for characterizing parallel regions and to reduce the number of hardware performance counters needed for computing this signature.

2.1   Hardware Performance Counters

Hardware performance counters are a set of special-purpose registers built into the processor to store the counts of hardware-related activities within the system, such as branch operations (branches taken or not, successfully predicted or not, etc.), memory accesses, cache misses, cycles stalled, instructions executed, and other metrics.

There are factors, such as the number of available special-purpose registers, that limit the number and groups of hardware performance counters that can be read at the same time. To overcome these limitations and collect the values of more counters, the application can be executed multiple times or counter multiplexing can be applied [3].

On the one hand, if the application is executed multiple times to measure hardware counters by groups, the measurement accuracy is high but the total execution time is multiplied by the number of executions needed. In the case of applications with long execution time, this approach is not feasible because of the required time. Moreover, this approach cannot be applied in the case of dynamic tuning as the performance problems have to be detected and solved at run-time.

On the other hand, this limitation can be overcome by multiplexing the usage of the counter registers over time (timesharing) among a large number of performance events. This approach has the advantage of executing the application once, but introduces some overhead due to counter swapping and recording. In addition, the metrics' precision is reduced because the final value of each counter is estimated using the partial values obtained in each time interval.

The most used tool to read hardware performance counters is Performance Application Programming Interface (PAPI) [5]. It grants an easy way to access hardware performance counters and allows for application profiling with counter multiplexing. In addition, it has been integrated [2], among many other tools, in MATE [11], which is a dynamic analysis and tuning environment that we are planning to use in the near future to implement a tuning strategy relaying in a counter-based application characterization.

2.2 Principal Component Analysis

In some cases, it can be difficult to obtain visual information from a set of observations of a big number of, possibly correlated, variables. Principal Component Analysis (PCA) is an analysis method that applies an orthogonal transformation that converts these observations into a set of linearly uncorrelated values called principal components. The first component explains the greatest possible fraction of the data variability, the second component the second greatest fraction, and so on and so forth. In this way, the components that explain smaller fractions of the data variability can be ignored, thus, reducing the data dimensionality [9].

Consequently, this method projects the data in a new coordinate system that highlights its variability and allows for eliminating the less informative dimensions, facilitating the exploration of this data.

2.3 Linear Correlation Analysis

Linear Correlation Analysis is a statistical evaluation to measure relationships or connections between two numerical and continuous variables.

This analysis finds a pair of linear transformations where the correlation coefficient between the variables is maximized [1].

The output of the correlation analysis is a correlation coefficient in the range $[-1, 1]$. There are three perfect scenarios depending on the value of the correlation coefficient:

- Correlated (value 1). The two variables are in a perfect increasing linear relationship.
- Not correlated (value 0). There is no linear relationship between the two variables.
- Anti-correlated (value -1). There is a perfect decreasing linear relationship.

In the case of two variables with a perfect linear relationship, be it increasing or decreasing, the value of one variable can be calculated if the appropriate linear transformation is applied to the value of the other variable.

3 Methodology

In this section, based on the mechanisms and techniques explained in Sect. 2, we propose a methodology for reducing the number of hardware performance counters used to characterize OpenMP parallel regions.

Figure 1 shows a schematic representation of this methodology, which consists of the following steps:

1. Hardware performance data collection (Sect. 3.1). In this step the data to analyze is obtained and saved in a database.
2. Data exploration (Sect. 3.2). PCA is used to check if the data can be classified visually.
3. Hardware performance counter reduction (Sect. 3.3). Correlation analysis is applied and variables with a high correlation coefficient are discarded. Then, we go back to step 2 to validate if the space reduction still allows for correctly characterizing the parallel region.

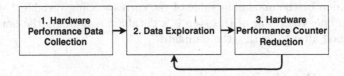

Fig. 1. Reduction of hardware performance counter space.

The advantages of eliminating redundancy and, hence, reducing the number of variables, are:

- Higher hardware counter measuring precision. If there are less hardware counters to measure, less groups are created for multiplexing, resulting in more measuring time for each group.

- Improved learning accuracy and reduced overfitting potential [12]. In machine learning and data mining, models tend to require more input data to avoid overfitting as the number of variables increases.
- Lower computational cost. Collecting less variables reduces the overhead generated by the data collection and the time required for the analysis.

3.1   Step 1: Hardware Performance Data Collection

We have decided to use PAPI's preset events because these hardware performance counters are typically available in processors for multiple platforms. Therefore, in the first place, the available preset events are obtained with the `papi_avail` command.

Next, groups of hardware counters are created taking into account the maximum number of events that can be read at the same time in one processor and if they can be accessed simultaneously. The command `papi_event_chooser` is used to check the compatibility of each group of events.

A set of code templates, representing different parallel region structures, has been developed with the objective of gathering data for a wide range of OpenMP parallel regions representative of real cases.

Each created group of hardware counters is measured for multiple executions of these templates using different combinations of compilation flags and input data sizes (template's configuration). In this way we are gathering data for different object code translations and memory access patterns associated to the same parallel region structure. The total number of executions for generating the performance database can be calculated using expression 1.

$$executions = created\_groups * data\_sizes * flag\_combinations * repetitions \quad (1)$$

Each variable in the database should be normalized before the exploration and reduction steps in order to facilitate data visualization and future usage of machine learning techniques.

We have adjusted the values of each variable in the range [0,1], dividing each recorded value by the maximum value of the corresponding variable.

Bottom line, the result of this step is a database containing the normalized data obtained after executing the templates.

3.2   Step 2: Data Exploration

We use PCA for visualizing data and validating the reduction of hardware performance counters done with correlation analysis.

PCA is applied to the normalized data resulting from step 1, which produces a new data set where variables have been transformed into principal components. With this transformation, we can check how much variance of the data is represented by each principal component and determine the minimum dimensionality needed to visualize the data without losing significant information.

With the help of PCA's dimensionality reduction we can plot the new data representation and easily check if the resulting data of the execution of each code template is visually distinguishable from the others. In addition, if a new point is inserted into the plot, it should be easy to identify to which code template and template's configuration the new point belongs to.

Moreover, PCA may also hint relationships between different hardware counters. Analyzing the weights of each variable in a principal component may indicate that some counters contribute evenly to the component (if they have similar weights), this could mean that both variables are related. Consequently, special attention shall be given to these hardware counters in the reduction step.

Summarizing, in this step we obtain a new representation of the data with fewer dimensions. The adequate visualization of this representation indicates if the available data can be used to distinguish between different parallel region templates. In addition, PCA may also hint counters that are likely to be correlated.

3.3   Step 3: Hardware Performance Counter Reduction

If two hardware performance counters (variables) are completely correlated, one of them can be considered redundant [14] and can be discarded.

Therefore, this step consists in performing a linear correlation analysis over the normalized data produced in step 1. This analysis produces a square symmetric matrix with the correlation coefficients between every pair of counters. From this matrix, we will assume that, in general, variables with a correlation coefficient close to 1 are linearly dependent and can be considered for discarding.

With the results obtained from the correlation analysis, we will check if a logical relationship can be established between counters with high correlation. We verify which hardware performance counters are accessed by the two events and analyze if they describe the same behaviour. For example, if the analysis tells us that L1 cache misses is highly correlated to branch instructions, this correlation is not logical and both counters are preserved, but if it tells us that double point operations and double point instructions are correlated, a logical relationship can be established and one of the two counters can be discarded.

Finally, if there are discarded counters the corresponding columns of the database are eliminated, generating a new database with a smaller number of variables. In this case, we go back to step 2 using the reduced database. On the contrary, if no counters have been discarded then the current database is considered to be the smallest set of data characterizing all the executions of the considered templates.

4   Experimentation

This section presents the results obtained using the proposed methodology on a specific set of templates. In addition, to show that these results effectively characterize the considered code regions, the values of the reduced set of counters are used for training a neural network for recognizing parallel region templates independently of the template's configuration.

We have used the parallel regions included in the STREAM benchmark [10] as the set of templates for our experimentation because they approximate the behaviour of multiple memory bound real OpenMP applications.

STREAM has four patterns with different number of operations and memory access pattern:

- COPY. One vector is copied into another, there are no arithmetic operations involved, just one read and one store.
- SCALE. The multiplication of the elements of a vector by a scalar is stored into another vector. There is one multiplication, one read and one store.
- SUM. The addition of two vectors is stored in a third vector. There is one addition, two reads and one store.
- TRIAD. It combines SUM and SCALE, adding a vector multiplied by a scalar to another vector. There are two operations (addition and multiplication), two reads and one store.

The hardware used in the experimentation is a DELL T7500. This machine has two Xeon E5645 processors with six multi-threaded cores per processor. Its memory hierarchy is composed by a 256KB L2 and a 12MB L3 caches in each processor, and 96GB of main memory.

Step 1 of the proposed methodology indicates that we must obtain the preset events for the target processor and determine the valid groups. PAPI reports 58 available preset events for the Xeon E5645. The measurable event types and the number of counters for each type are the following:

- Branches→7
- Cache L1→8
- Cache L2→16
- Cache L3→10
- TLB→3
- Cycles→3
- Operations→3
- Instructions→8

Next, we must execute all the combinations of the selected templates (4), created groups of counters (12), data sizes (from 3KB to 4.5GB, using 56 different sizes), compiler flags (O0 and O2), and number of repetitions (1,000); normalize the results; and build the performance database. According to expression 1, there are 1,344,000 executions for each template, which are used to build the 448,000 entries (58 columns each) of the performance database.

Then, we can proceed with step 2 of the methodology and apply PCA to the normalized database. Figure 2(b) shows the visualization of the data for the first and second principal components, which explain more than 89% of the data's variance. The different STREAM templates can be distinguished even in this two-dimensional plot, indicating that our main hypothesis is true for this set of templates.

Using the PCA's results to get hints about counters' significance, we realized that the events related to the instructions cache (18) depend more on the code generated by the compiler than on the behaviour of the application. This allows to make a first reduction of the number of columns of the performance

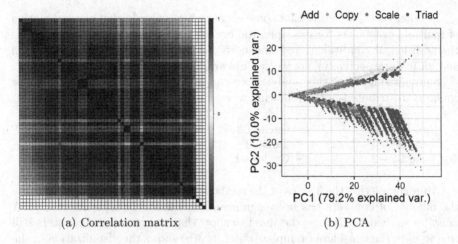

(a) Correlation matrix   (b) PCA

Fig. 2. Correlation matrix and PCA with the full list of hardware counters.

database to 40. After discarding these counters, the PCA analysis showed a small improvement in the proportion of the variance explained by the first principal components.

Table 1 shows the cumulative variance explained by the principal components for all available hardware counters (58) and the results removing those related to the instruction cache.

Table 1. Comparison of the cumulative variance before and after removing hardware counters related to instruction cache.

	PC1	PC2	PC3	PC4	PC5	PC6	PC7	PC8	PC9	PC10	PC11
All	79.17	89.14	91.73	93.73	94.94	96.01	96.87	97.63	98.21	98.72	99.22
No Inst-Cache	80.68	89.29	92.74	95.61	97.2	98.21	98.98	99.52	99.88	99.96	99.99

Next, we can go to step 3 of the methodology and perform a linear correlation analysis on the normalized database. Figure 2(a) shows the correlation matrix where darker points indicate a stronger correlation between a pair of hardware counters. Based on this matrix, we analyze the strongest correlations and decide which counters can be discarded.

For example, we discarded the hardware counter total cycles (TOT_CYC) because it is completely correlated to reference cycles (REF_CYC). We decided to keep reference cycles as it uses a reference clock instead of the clock of the CPU which can change depending on features such as Intel's turbo boost.

We also have discarded different hardware counters that access the same resource. This is the case of the single point vectorization (VEC_SP) and double point vectorization (VEC_DP) counters that read the same register, which counts the number of SIMD instructions.

In other cases, we found that some events where the addition or combination of multiple events. As for example, the branch instructions counter (BR_INS) is the addition of conditional and unconditional branch instructions ones (BR_CN and BR_UCN, respectively), so, we can discard the first one.

Summarizing, after this analysis, we end up with 20 hardware performance counters, distributed in the following way:

- Branches→4
- Cache L1→3
- Cache L2→2

- Cache L3→2
- TLB→1
- Cycles→1

- Operations→3

- Instructions→4

After completing the 3 steps of the methodology, we go back to step 2 because the number of counters has been significantly reduced. This means that PCA must be applied to the new database to show that the remaining counters still characterize the considered templates. Figure 3(b) shows the visualization of the data for the first and second principal components, which explain more than 88% of the data variance. It can be seen that the templates can still be clearly distinguished using this reduced set of counters.

Table 2 shows that the data variance explained by the first principal components is similar to the one obtained when considering the whole set of counters.

Table 2. Cumulative variance with the reduced list of hardware performance counters.

	PC1	PC2	PC3	PC4	PC5	PC6	PC7	PC8	PC9	PC10	PC11
Reduced list	76.44	88.31	92.15	95.41	97.28	98.81	99.49	99.89	99.96	99.98	99.995

Finally, we perform a new linear correlation analysis (step 3) to decide if the set of counters can be furtherly reduced.

Figure 3(a) shows the obtained correlation matrix with some dark points still indicating strong correlations between pairs of counters. However, after analyzing them, no logical relationship can be established between the corresponding counters. For example, L2 storage misses (L2_STM) is not logically related to branches taken (BR_TKN), so, both counters are kept despite they are highly correlated.

Consequently, as far as no new counters have been discarded, the performance database including 20 counters is regarded as the smallest set of data that characterizes the considered templates.

Our motivation for proposing a methodology to find a reduced number of hardware performance counters was based on the fact that current processors include a significant number of counters and measuring all of them at execution time can be costly or even unfeasible. Now, we want to illustrate this claim using the experiment described previously.

On the one hand, for several templates, multiplexing the full list of hardware performance counters lead to erroneous values (sometimes negative ones) because

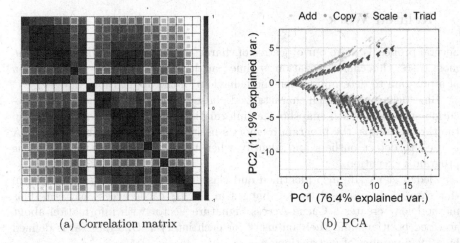

(a) Correlation matrix   (b) PCA

Fig. 3. Correlation matrix and PCA analysis with reduced list of hardware counters.

the execution time was not long enough, so, basically, it is not feasible to measure all the counters using the considered templates.

On the other hand, in the case of the reduced list of hardware counters, we were able to assess the precision of the measured metrics and the overhead for obtaining them. The overhead for regions with execution time around a few seconds is of up to 10 milliseconds, and for regions with execution time of less than a second it is of up to 4 milliseconds. This overhead includes the time for setting up the methods to count events, and the time for collecting the counters and multiplexing the groups of counters. As for the precision, in the cases of execution times of less than a second, the precision of multiplexing groups of counters is in some cases low, the accuracy is between 90% and 99%, and uncon-ditional branches are not properly estimated. For longer executions (execution time higher than one second), the accuracy increases to more than 99%.

Finally, the main hypothesis behind our work is that a parallel region can be characterized by the signature composed by the values of a set of hardware performance counters. The results of PCA seem to corroborate it, but we want to add more evidence for this claim using the results of the presented experiment.

To do so, we have trained a simple artificial neural network with one hidden layer using the database with 20 counters produced by applying the proposed methodology. This database has been divided into two subsets, one for training the network (432,000 entries) and another for validating it (the remaining 16,000 entries). The validation set is built with the entries corresponding to 2 of the 56 different input data sizes, i.e., $4(templates) \times 2(compiler flags) \times 2(datasizes) \times 1,000(repetitions)$.

After training the network for ten epochs, it gets an accuracy of up to 99.98% for the validation set. These results are relevant for two reasons, on the one hand, they provide the evidence we were looking for and, on the other hand, they hint that the signatures of parallel regions can be used in machine learning techniques.

5   Related Work

Several proposals share our objective of characterizing code regions although, in most cases, this characterization is aimed at detecting phases in the execution of a program to determine when the behaviour of the application changes.

Bhattacharyya et al. [4] characterized phases in cloud applications using execution snapshots. Each snapshot has information regarding sets of functions in the thread-dumps, the program memory's usage and the use of the CPU. PCA is used to detect outliers and identify when there is a different phase in the program's execution.

Ziedan et al. [15] also identified and classified phases in the application, in this case, their proposal tracks changes in the L2 cache access pattern. This methodology creates a Cache Access Signature Vector with information about accessed positions and their intensity for each interval. One interval is defined by a fixed number of instructions.

Fang et al. [8] generated signatures of the execution to detect phases. The signatures include information regarding cache miss rates, branch miss rates and IPC. Phases are classified using their signature and comparing it to a signature table in order to find if there is a new phase or the phase was executed before.

Chetsa et al. [7] detected application phases using execution vectors. These vectors include information about hardware performance counters, transmitted network bytes and disk usage. This methodology uses only general purpose counters to avoid redundancy (retired instructions, L3 cache references and misses, branch instructions and branch misses).

The explained methodologies sample the application in blocks of instructions to find changes in the behaviour of the application, while in our case we want to classify parallel code regions that have been identified in the code.

Another approach to generate signatures was developed by Wong et al. [13] for message passing applications. The execution of the application is divided in blocks depending on communication, instead of instructions, and the signature is generated using the communications (patterns and volume) and computational time. In this case, hardware performance counters are not used and the methodology is designed only for message passing applications.

6   Conclusion and Future Work

Considering the hypothesis that a parallel region can be characterized by the values of a set of hardware counters (region signature) as the starting point of this work, we have developed a methodology to reduce the variables (counters) of this set in order to be able to measure them at execution time with the adequate precision.

The proposed methodology, based on PCA and linear correlation analysis, has been tested using a limited set of representative OpenMP templates on a specific machine with 58 preset counters. This evaluation has shown that (i) the number counters included in the signature can be reduced following the methodology steps; (ii) that the reduced set can be measured at execution time using counter multiplexing, while measuring the full set was unfeasible; and that the resulting performance database could be used to identify the templates with high accuracy.

Currently, we are extending the set of templates with new parallel regions code patterns and also working on strategies for automatically and dynamically identifying and solving performance problems associated to these regions.

References

1. Akaho, S.: A kernel method for canonical correlation analysis. In: Proceedings of the International Meeting of the Psychometric Society. IMPS 2001. Springer-Verlag (2001)
2. Alcaraz, J., Sikora, A., Cesar, E.: Dynamic tuning of openmp memory bound applications in multisocket systems using mate. In: Proceedings of the 47th International Conference on Parallel Processing Companion. ICPP 2018, pp. 37:1–37:10. ACM (2018)
3. Azimi, R., Stumm, M., Wisniewski, R.W.: Online performance analysis by statistical sampling of microprocessor performance counters. In: Proceedings of the 19th Annual International Conference on Supercomputing. ICS 2005, pp. 101–110. ACM, New York (2005)
4. Bhattacharyya, A., Sotiriadis, S., Amza, C.: Online phase detection and characterization of cloud applications. In: 2017 IEEE International Conference on Cloud Computing Technology and Science (CloudCom), pp. 98–105, December 2017
5. Browne, S., Deane, C., Ho, G., Mucci, P.: Papi: a portable interface to hardware performance counters. In: Proceedings of Department of Defense HPCMP Users Group Conference, 06 1999
6. Caubet, J., Gimenez, J., Labarta, J., DeRose, L., Vetter, J.: A dynamic tracing mechanism for performance analysis of openmp applications. OpenMP Shared Memory Parallel Programming, p. 53 (2001)
7. Chetsa, G.L.T., Lefevre, L., Pierson, J.M., Stolf, P., da Costa, G.: A user friendly phase detection methodology for hpc systems' analysis. In: Proceedings of the 2013 IEEE International Conference on Green Computing and Communications and IEEE Internet of Things and IEEE Cyber, Physical and Social Computing, pp. 118–125. IEEE Computer Society, Washington, DC (2013)
8. Fang, Z., Li, J., Zhang, W., Li, Y., Chen, H., Zang, B.: Improving dynamic prediction accuracy through multi-level phase analysis. In: Proceedings of the 13th ACM SIGPLAN/SIGBED International Conference on Languages, Compilers, Tools and Theory for Embedded Systems, pp. 89–98. LCTES 2012, New York (2012)
9. Lovric, M. (ed.): Principal Component Analysis, pp. 1094–1096. Springer, Heidelberg (2011)
10. Mccalpin, J.: Memory bandwidth and machine balance in current high performance computers. In: IEEE Computer Society Technical Committee on Computer Architecture (TCCA) Newsletter, pp. 19–25 (1995)
11. Morajko, A., Caymes-Scutari, P., Margalef, T., Luque, E.: Mate: monitoring, analysis and tuning environment for parallel/distributed applications. Concurrency Comput. Pract. Experience 19(11), 1517–1531 (2007)
12. Tang, J., Alelyani, S., Liu, H.: Feature selection for classification: a review. Data classification: Algorithms and Applications, p. 37 (2014)

13. Wong, A., Rexachs, D., Luque, E.: Parallel application signature. In: 2009 IEEE International Conference on Cluster Computing and Workshops, pp. 1–4, August 2009
14. Yu, L., Liu, H.: Efficient feature selection via analysis of relevance and redundancy. J. Mach. Learn. Res. **5**, 1205–1224 (2004)
15. Ziedan, I., Serag, S., Shehata, H.: A run-time program phase detection technique for optimizing per-phase l2 cache demand. Egypt. Int. J. Eng. Sci. Technol. **20**, 1–9 (2016)

Combining Checkpointing and Data Compression to Accelerate Adjoint-Based Optimization Problems

Navjot Kukreja[1]($^{(\boxtimes)}$), Jan Hückelheim[1], Mathias Louboutin[2], Paul Hovland[3], and Gerard Gorman[1]

[1] Imperial College London, London, UK
nkukreja@imperial.ac.uk
[2] Georgia Institute of Technology, Atlanta, GA, USA
[3] Argonne National Laboratory, Lemont, IL, USA

Abstract. Seismic inversion and imaging are adjoint-based optimization problems that process up to terabytes of data, regularly exceeding the memory capacity of available computers. Data compression is an effective strategy to reduce this memory requirement by a certain factor, particularly if some loss in accuracy is acceptable. A popular alternative is checkpointing, where data is stored at selected points in time, and values at other times are recomputed as needed from the last stored state. This allows arbitrarily large adjoint computations with limited memory, at the cost of additional recomputations.

In this paper, we combine compression and checkpointing for the first time to compute a realistic seismic inversion. The combination of checkpointing and compression allows larger adjoint computations compared to using only compression, and reduces the recomputation overhead significantly compared to using only checkpointing.

Keywords: Checkpointing · Compression · Adjoints · Inversion · Seismic

1 Introduction

1.1 Adjoint-Based Optimization

Adjoint-based optimization problems typically consist of a simulation that is run forward in simulation time, producing data that is used in reverse order by a subsequent adjoint computation that is run backwards in simulation time. Many important numerical problems in science and engineering use adjoints and follow this pattern.

Since the data for each of the computed timestep in the forward simulation will be used later in the adjoint computation, it would be prudent to store it in memory until it is required again. However, the total size of this data can

R. Yahyapour (Ed.): Euro-Par 2019, LNCS 11725, pp. 87–100, 2019.
https://doi.org/10.1007/978-3-030-29400-7_7

often run into tens of terabytes, exceeding the memory capacity of most computer systems. Previous work has studied recomputation or data compression strategies to work around this problem. In this paper we investigate a combination of compression and recomputation.

1.2   Example Adjoint Problem: Seismic Inversion

Seismic inversion typically involves the simulation of the propagation of seismic waves through the earth's subsurface, followed by a comparison with data from field measurements. The model of the subsurface is iteratively improved by minimizing the misfit between simulated data and field measurement in an adjoint optimization problem [18]. The data collected in an offshore survey typically consists of a number of "shots" - each of these shots corresponding to different locations of sources and receivers. Often the gradient is computed for each of these shots independently on a single cluster compute node, and then collated across all the shots to form a single model update. The processing across shots is thereby easily parallelized and requires only little communication, followed by a long period of independent computation (typically around 10–100 min). Since the number of shots is typically of the order of 10^4, clusters can often be fully utilized even if individual shots are only processed on a single node.

1.3   Memory Requirements

A number of strategies have been studied to cope with the amount of data that occurs in adjoint computations - perhaps the simplest is to store all data to a disk, to be read later by the adjoint pass in reverse order. However, the computation often takes much less time than the disk read and write, hence leaving disk speed as a bottleneck.

Domain decomposition, where a single shot may be distributed across more than one node, is often used not only to distribute the computational workload across more processors, but also across more memory. While this strategy is very powerful, the number of compute nodes and therefore the amount of memory that can be used efficiently is limited, for example by communication overheads that start to dominate as the domain is split into increasingly small pieces. Secondly, this strategy can be wasteful if the need for memory causes more nodes to be used than can be completely utilized for computation. Lastly, this method is not well suited for cloud-based setups since it can complicate the setup and performance will suffer due to the slow inter-node communication.

Checkpointing is yet another strategy to reduce the memory overhead. Only a subset of the timesteps during the forward pass is stored. Other timesteps are recomputed when needed by restarting the forward pass from the last available stored state. We discuss this strategy in Sect. 3. Previous work has applied checkpointing to seismic imaging and inversion problems [9,20]. An alternative is data compression, which is discussed in Sect. 2.

In this paper, we extend the previous studies by *combining* checkpointing and compression. This is obviously useful when the data does not fit in the available memory even after compression, for example for very large adjoint problems, or for problems where the required accuracy limits the achievable compression ratios.

Compared to the use of only checkpointing without compression, this combined method often improves performance. This is a consequence of the reduced size of stored timesteps, allowing more timesteps to be stored during the forward computation. This in turn reduces the amount of recomputation that needs to be performed. On the other hand, the compression and decompression itself takes time. The answer to the question "does compression pay off?", depends on a number of factors including - available memory, the required precision, the time taken to compress and decompress, and the achieved compression factors, and various problem specific parameters like computational intensity of the kernel involved in the forward and adjoint computations, and the number of timesteps.

Hence, the answer to the compression question depends not only on the problem one is solving (within seismic inversion, there are numerous variations of the wave equation that may be solved), but also the hardware specifics of the machine on which it is being solved. In fact, as we will see in Sect. 5, the answer might even change during the solution process of an individual problem. This brings up the need to predict whether compression pays off in a given scenario, without incurring significant overheads in answering this question. To this end, we present a performance model that answers that question.

1.4 Summary of Contributions

In this paper, we study

- the use of different compression algorithms to seismic data including six lossless and a lossy compression algorithm for floating point data,
- a performance model for checkpointing alone, taking into account the time taken to read and write checkpoints, and
- an online performance model to predict whether compression would speed up an optimization problem.

2 Compression Algorithms

Data compression is increasingly used to reduce the memory footprint of scientific applications. This has been accelerated by the advent of special purpose compression algorithms for floating-point scientific data, such as ZFP or SZ [10,14].

Lossless algorithms guarantee that the exact original data can be recovered during decompression, whereas lossy algorithms introduce an error, but often guarantee that the error does not exceed certain absolute or relative error metrics. Typically, lossy compression is more effective in reducing the data size. Most popular compression packages offer various settings that allow a tradeoff between compression ratio, accuracy, and compression and decompression time.

Another difference we observed between lossless and lossy compression algorithms was that the lossless compression algorithms we evaluated tended to interpret all data as one-dimensional series only while SZ and ZFP, being designed for scientific data, take the dimensionality into account directly. This makes a difference in the case of a wavefield, for example, where the data to be compressed corresponds to a smoothly varying function in (two or) three dimensions and interpreting this three-dimensional data as one-dimensional would completely miss the smoothness and predictability of the data values.

It is worth noting that another data reduction strategy is to typecast values into a lower precision format, for example, from double precision to single precision. This can be seen as a computationally cheap lossy compression algorithm with a compression ratio of 2.

Perhaps counterintuitively, compression can not only reduce the memory footprint, but also speed up an application. Previous work has observed that the compression and decompression time can be less than the time saved from the reduction in data that needs to be communicated across MPI nodes or between a GPU and a host computer [17].

One way of using compression in adjoint-based methods is to compress all timesteps during the forward pass. If the compression ratio is sufficient to fit the compressed data in memory, compression can serve as an *alternate strategy* to checkpointing. Previous work has discussed this in the context of computational fluid dynamics [7,16] and seismic inversion using compression algorithms specifically designed for the respective applications [6,8].

Since the time spent on compressing and decompressing data is often non-negligible, this raises the question whether the computational time is better spent on this compression and decompression, or on the recomputation involved in the more traditional checkpointing approach. This question was previously answered to a limited extent for the above scenario where compression is an alternative to checkpointing, in a specific application [7]. We discuss this in more detail in Sect. 4.

2.1   Lossless Compression

Blosc is a library that provides optimized high-performance implementations of various lossless compressors, sometimes beyond their corresponding reference implementations [2]. For our experiments we use this library through its python interface. The library includes implementations for six different lossless compression algorithms, namely ZLIB, ZSTD, BLOSCLZ, LZ4, LZ4HC and Snappy. All these algorithms look at the data as a one-dimensional stream of bits and at least the blosc implementations have a limit on the size of the one-dimensional array that can be compressed in one call. Therefore we use the python package *blosc-pack*, which is a wrapper over the blosc library, to implement *chunking*, i.e. breaking up the stream into chunks of a chosen size, which are compressed one at a time.

2.2   Lossy Compression

We use the lossy compression package ZFP [14] written in C. To use ZFP from python, we developed a python wrapper for the reference implementation of ZFP[1]. ZFP supports three compression modes, namely fixed tolerance, fixed precision and fixed rate. The fixed-tolerance mode limits the absolute error, while the fixed-precision mode limits the error as a ratio of the range of values in the array to be compressed. The fixed-rate mode achieves a guaranteed compression ratio requested by the user, but does not provide any bounds on accuracy loss.

The fixed-rate mode could make our implementation more straightforward by offering a predictable size of compressed checkpoints, but the lack of error bounds makes this option less attractive. Moreover, ZFP claims to achieve the best "compression efficiency" in the fixed-tolerance mode, and we thus chose to focus on this mode.

SZ [10] is a more recently developed compression library, also focussed on lossy compression of floating-point scientific data, also developed in C. While we have also written a python wrapper for the reference implementation of SZ[2], a thorough comparison of ZFP and SZ remains future work.

3   Checkpointing Performance Model

As previously mentioned, checkpointing is a strategy to store selected timesteps, and recompute others when needed. The question which checkpoints should be stored to get the best tradeoff between recomputation time and memory footprint was answered in a provably optimal way by the Revolve checkpointing algorithm [11]. Revolve makes certain assumptions, for example that all timesteps have the same compute cost and storage size, the number of timesteps is known a priori, and there is only one level of memory (e.g. RAM) that is restricted in size, but very fast. Other authors have subsequently developed extensions to Revolve that are optimal under different conditions [4,19]. We focus in this paper on the classic Revolve algorithm, and store all checkpoints in RAM.

In this section, we build on the ideas introduced in [19] to build a performance model that predicts the runtime of an adjoint computation using Revolve checkpointing. We call the time taken by a single forward computational step C_F and correspondingly, the time taken by a single backward step C_R. For a simulation with $\mathbf{N}$ timesteps, the minimum wall time required for the full forward-adjoint evaluation is given by

$$T_N = \mathbf{C_F} \cdot \mathbf{N} + \mathbf{C_R} \cdot \mathbf{N} \tag{1}$$

If the size of a single timestep in memory is given by $\mathbf{S}$, this requires a memory of at least size $\mathbf{S} \cdot \mathbf{N}$. If sufficient memory is available, no checkpointing or compression is needed.

If the memory is smaller than $\mathbf{S} \cdot \mathbf{N}$, Revolve provides a strategy to solve for the adjoint field by storing a subset of the $\mathbf{N}$ total checkpoints and recompute

---

[1] To be released open source on publication.

[2] Also to be released open source upon publication.

the remaining ones. The overhead introduced by this method can be broken down into the recomputation overhead $\mathbf{O}_R$ and the storage overhead $\mathbf{O}_S$. The recomputation overhead is the amount of time spent in recomputation, given by

$$\mathbf{O}_R(N, M) = p(N, M) \cdot \mathbf{C_F}, \tag{2}$$

where $p(N, M)$ is the minimum number of recomputed steps from [11], given as

$$p(N, M) = \begin{cases} N(N-1)/2, & \text{if } M = 1 \\ \min_{1 <= \tilde{N} <= N} \{\tilde{N} + p(\tilde{N}, M) + p(N - \tilde{N}, M - 1)\}, & \text{if } M > 1 \end{cases} \tag{3}$$

where M is the number of checkpoints that can be stored in memory. Note that for $M \geq N$, $\mathbf{O}_R$ would be zero. For $M < N$, $\mathbf{O}_R$ grows rapidly as M is reduced relative to N.

In an ideal implementation, the storage overhead $\mathbf{O}_S$ might be zero, since the computation could be done "in-place", but in practice, checkpoints are generally stored in a separate section of memory and they need to be transferred to a "computational" section of the memory where the computation is performed, and then the results copied back to the checkpointing memory. This copying is a common feature of checkpointing implementations, and might pose a non-trivial overhead when the computation involved in a single timestep is not very large. This storage overhead is given by:

$$\mathbf{O}_{SR}(N, M) = \mathbf{W}(N, M) \cdot \frac{\mathbf{S}}{\mathbf{B}} + \mathbf{N} \cdot \frac{\mathbf{S}}{\mathbf{B}} \tag{4}$$

where $\mathbf{W}$ is the total number of times Revolve writes checkpoints for a single run, $\mathbf{N}$ is the number of times checkpoints are read, and $\mathbf{B}$ is the bandwidth at which these copies happen. The total time to solution becomes

$$T_R = \mathbf{C_F} \cdot \mathbf{N} + \mathbf{C_R} \cdot \mathbf{N} + \mathbf{O}_R(N, M) + \mathbf{O}_{SR}(N, M) \tag{5}$$

4 Performance Model Including Compression

By using compression, the size of each checkpoint is reduced and the number of checkpoints available is increased (M in Eq. 3). This reduces the recomputation overhead $\mathbf{O}_R$, while at the same time adding overheads related to compression and decompression in $\mathbf{O}_S$. To be beneficial, the reduction in $\mathbf{O}_R$ must offset the increase in $\mathbf{O}_{SR}$, leading to an overall decrease in the time to solution T.

Our performance model assumes that the compression algorithm behaves uniformly across the different time steps of the simulation, i.e. that we get the same compression ratio, compression time and decompression time, no matter which of the N possible checkpoints we try to compress/decompress. The storage overhead now becomes

$$\mathbf{O}_{SR}(N, M) = \mathbf{W}(N, M \cdot F) \cdot \left(\frac{\mathbf{S}}{\mathbf{F} \cdot \mathbf{B}} + t_c\right)$$
$$+ \mathbf{N} \cdot \left(\frac{\mathbf{S}}{\mathbf{F} \cdot \mathbf{B}} + t_d\right) \tag{6}$$

where $\mathbf{F}$ is the compression ratio (i.e. the ratio between the uncompressed and compressed checkpoint), and t_c and t_d are compression and decompression times, respectively. At the same time, the recomputation overhead decreases because $\mathbf{F}$ times more checkpoints are now available.

5 Acceptable Errors and Convergence

Our performance model is agnostic of the specific optimization problem being solved. We envision it being used in a generic checkpointing runtime that manages the checkpointed execution of an optimization problem, and accepts an acceptable error tolerance as an input parameter for each gradient evaluation and determines whether or not compression can pay off for that iteration. For this reason, we do not discuss in this paper whether or not a certain accuracy is acceptable for any given application.

We note that there is some previous work in this area, discussing for example the effect of bounded pointwise errors in a multi-dimensional field on computed numerical derivatives, for ZFP [1]. In the context of seismic inversion, other work discusses accuracy requirements in optimization loops, and notes that high accuracy is only needed when already close to a minimum [6,13]. There has been previous work on choosing the most appropriate compression algorithm under some circumstances [21]., and work that addresses convergence guarantees of trust-region based optimization methods in the presence of gradients that are only known with a probability p [5].

Despite all this previous work, for most practical adjoint optimization applications, the relationship between accuracy (whether caused by roundoff, compression or truncation errors) and convergence remains a field of ongoing research.

6 Problem and Test Case

We use Devito [15] to solve forward and adjoint wave equation problems. Devito is a domain-specific language that enables the rapid development of finite-difference solvers from a high-level description of partial differential equations. The simplest version of the seismic wave equation is the acoustic isotropic wave equation defined as:

$$m(x)\frac{\partial^2 u(t,x)}{\partial t^2} - \nabla^2 u(t,x) = q(t,x), \tag{7}$$

where $m(x) = \frac{1}{c^2(x)}$ is the squared slowness, $c(x)$ the spatially dependent speed of sound, $u(t,x)$ is the pressure wavefield, $\nabla^2 u(t,x)$ denotes the laplacian of the wavefield and $q(t,x)$ is a source term.

The solution to Eq. 7 forms the forward problem. The seismic inversion problem minimizes the misfit between simulated and observed signal given by:

$$\min_{m} \phi_s(m) = \frac{1}{2}\|d_{sim} - d_{obs}\|_2^2. \tag{8}$$

We call the kernel derived from a basic finite difference formulation of Eq. 7, the OT2 kernel because it is second-order accurate in time. We also use another formulation from [15], which is 4th-order accurate in time. We call this the OT4 kernel.

This optimization problem is usually solved using gradient based methods such as steepest descent, where the gradient is computed using the adjoint-state method.

The values of $m(x)$ used in this work are derived from the Overthrust model [3] over a grid of $287 \times 881 \times 881$ points, including an absorbing layer of 40 points on each side. The grid spacing is 25 m in space. The propagation time is 4 s that corresponds to 2526 timesteps. The wave field at the final time is shown in Fig. 2a. The uncompressed size of this single time step field is just under 900 MB. If one were to store all the timesteps, this would require 2.3 TB of memory.

To implement Revolve with Devito, we use pyRevolve [12] which is a python library to manage the execution of checkpointed adjoint computations. The performance model in Sect. 3 assumes that the implementation is similar to pyRevolve, which stores a checkpoint by copying a portion of the operator's working memory to the checkpointing memory and similarly loads a checkpoint by copying from the checkpointing memory to the operator's working memory.

For benchmarking we used a dual-socket Intel(R) Xeon(R) Platinum 8180M @ 2.50 Ghz (28 cores each) (skylake).

7   Results and Discussion

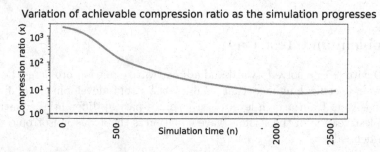

Fig. 1. Compression ratios achieved on compressing different time steps. Every timestep from 1 to 2526 was compressed and plotted.

To understand the compressibility of the data produced in a typical wave-propagation simulation, we ran a simulation as per the setup described in Sect. 6, and tried to compress every single timestep. For this we chose ZFP in fixed tolerance mode at some arbitrary tolerance level. We noted the compression ratios achieved at every timestep. As Fig. 1 shows, the initial timesteps are much easier to compress than the later ones. This is not surprising since most wave simulations start with the field at rest, i.e. filled with zeros. As the wave reaches more parts of the domain, the field becomes less compressible until it achieves a stable state when the wave has reached most of the domain.

If the simulation had started with the field already oscillating in a wave, it is likely that the compressibility curve for that simulation would be flat. This tells us that the compressibility of the last timestep of the solution is representative of the worst-case compressibility and hence we used the last timestep as our reference for comparison of compression in the rest of the analysis.

Table 1. Some results from trying out all possible compressors and settings in blosc. We selected the best compression ratio seen for each compressor. "Setting" here is the choice between speed and compression, where 0 is fastest and 9 is highest compression.

Compressor	Chunk size (bytes)	Shuffle Mode	Setting	Compression time (ms)	Decompression time (ms)	Compression Ratio
BloscLZ	1048576	SHUFFLE	6	4249.44	1288.86	1.188
LZ4	2965280	SHUFFLE	4	1371.26	920.98	1.199
LZ4HC	2097152	SHUFFLE	8	31245.16	926.69	1.265
ZLib	524288	SHUFFLE	7	30218.81	2470.04	1.291
ZStd	524288	SHUFFLE	9	117238.76	1477.34	1.312

Table 1 shows the compression ratios and times for a few different lossless compressors and their corresponding settings. As can be seen, the compression factors achieved, and the time taken to compress and decompress can vary significantly, but it is hard to say whether this compression could be used to speed up the inversion problem.

Figure 3a shows compression ratios for different tolerance settings for the fixed-tolerance mode of ZFP. The point highlighted here was the setting used to compress all timesteps in Fig. 1. Figure 2b shows the spatial distribution of the errors after compression and decompression, compared to the original field, for this setting. Table 3b shows the effect of different levels of pointwise absolute error on the overall error in the gradient evaluation. We can see that the error in the gradient evaluation does not explode.

To validate the revolve-only performance model, Fig. 4a shows the predicted runtime for a variety of peak memory constraints along with measured runtime for the same scenario. Figure 4b shows a comparison of predicted and measured runtimes for the OT2 kernel with compression enabled. Figure 4c repeats this experiment for the OT4 kernel which has a higher computational complexity. It can be seen that the model is able to predict the real performance very closely in all three cases.

We have now seen that the performance model from Sect. 4 is effective at predicting the runtime of adjoint computations. To study the performance model, we first visualize it along the axis of available memory, comparing the predicted performance of the chosen compression scheme with the predicted performance of a Revolve-only adjoint implementation. This is shown in Fig. 5 where we

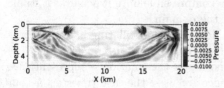

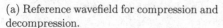

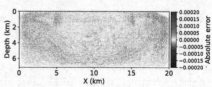

(a) Reference wavefield for compression and decompression.

(b) Errors introduced during compression and decompression using the fixed-tolerance mode.

Fig. 2. This field was formed after a Ricker wavelet source was placed at the surface of the model and the wave propagated for 2500 timesteps. This is a vertical (x-z) cross-section of a 3D field, taken at the y source location. It is interesting to note that the errors are more or less evenly distributed across the domain with only slight variations corresponding to the wave amplitude (from Figure a). A small block-like structure characteristic of ZFP can be seen.

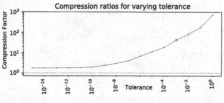

(a) Effect of tolerance on Compression Ratio

Tolerance	Gradient error
0.1	662.905
0.01	70.619
0.001	10.485
0.0001	0.763
10^{-5}	0.194
10^{-6}	0.154
10^{-7}	0.151

(b) Effect of tolerance on Gradient error

Fig. 3. Effect of tolerance settings of ZFP in fixed-tolerance mode on Compression ratio (left) and final gradient evaluation (right). We define compression ratio as the ratio between the size of the uncompressed data and the compressed data. The dashed line represents no compression. The highlighted point corresponds to the setting used for the other results here unless otherwise specified. The gradient error (right) is the 2-norm of the error tensor in the gradient, as compared with an exact computation.

can distinguish three different scenarios, depending on the amount of available memory.

1. If the memory is insufficient even with compression to store the entire trajectory, one can either use checkpointing only, or combine checkpointing with compression. This is the left section of the figure.
2. If the available memory is not sufficient to store the uncompressed trajectory, but large enough to store the entire compressed trajectory, we compare two possible strategies: Either use compression only, or use checkpointing only. This is the middle section of the figure.
3. If the available system memory is large enough to hold the entire uncompressed trajectory, neither compression nor checkpointing is necessary. This is the right section of the figure.

The second scenario was studied in previous work [7], while the combined method is also applicable to the first scenario, for which previous work has only used checkpointing without compression.

We can identify a number of factors that make compression more likely to be beneficial compared to pure checkpointing: A very small system memory size and a large number of time steps lead to a rapidly increasing recompute factor,

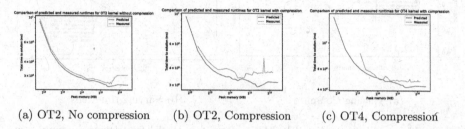

(a) OT2, No compression   (b) OT2, Compression   (c) OT4, Compression

Fig. 4. Predicted vs measured runtimes for two different kernels (OT2 and OT4), with and without compression. This shows that the performance model can predict the runtime effectively. The compression setting used was ZFP with absolute error tolerance set to 10^{-6}

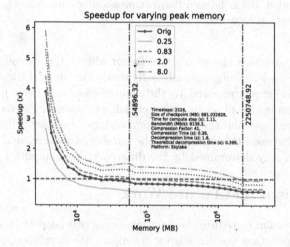

Fig. 5. The speedups predicted by the performance model for varying memory. The baseline (1.0) is the performance of a Revolve-only implementation under the same conditions. The different curves represent kernels with differing compute times (represented here as a factor of the sum of compression and decompression times). The first vertical line at 53 GB marks the spot where the compressed wavefield can completely fit in memory and Revolve is unnecessary if using compression. The second vertical line at 2.2 TB marks the spot where the entire uncompressed wavefield can fit in memory and neither Revolve nor compression is necessary. The region to the right is where these optimizations are not necessary or relevant. The middle region has been the subject of past studies using compression in adjoint problems. The region to the left is the focus of this paper.

and compression can substantially reduce this recompute factor. This can be seen in Figs. 5 and 6b.

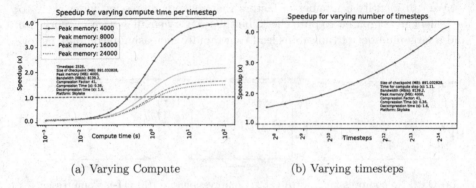

(a) Varying Compute   (b) Varying timesteps

Fig. 6. The speedups predicted by the performance model for varying compute cost (left) and number of timesteps (right). The baseline (1.0) is the performance of a Revolve-only implementation under the same conditions. The benefits of compression drop rapidly if the computational cost of the kernel that generated the data is much lower than the cost of compressing the data. For increasing computational costs, the benefits are bounded. It can be seen that compression becomes more beneficial as the number of timesteps is increased.

The extent to which the recompute factor affects the overall runtime also depends on the cost to compute each individual time step. If the compute cost per time step is large compared to the compression and decompression cost, then compression is also likely to be beneficial, as shown in Fig. 6a. As the time per time step increases and the compression cost becomes negligible, we observe that the ratio between the runtime of the combined method and that of pure checkpointing is only determined by the difference in recompute factors.

8   Conclusions and Future Work

We used compression to reduce the computational overhead of checkpointing in an adjoint computation used in seismic inversion. We developed a performance model that computes whether or not the combination of compression and check-pointing will outperform pure checkpointing or pure compression in a variety of scenarios, depending on the available memory size, computational intensity of the application, and compression ratio and throughput of the compression algorithm. In future work, we plan to extend this work by

- further exploring the relationship between pointwise error bounds in compression and the overall error of the adjoint gradient evaluation,
- extending our performance model to support non-uniform compression ratios, as would be expected for example if the initial wave field is smoother and therefore more easily compressible,

- studying strategies where different compression settings (or even no compression) is used for a subset of time steps,
- exploring compression and multi-level checkpointing, including SSD or hard drives in addition to RAM storage,
- and finally by developing checkpointing strategies that are optimal even if the size of checkpoints post-compression varies and is not known a priori.

Acknowledgments. This work was funded by the Intel Parallel Computing Centre at Imperial College London and EPSRC EP/R029423/1. This work was supported by the U.S. Department of Energy, Office of Science, Office of Advanced Scientific Computing Research, Applied Mathematics and Computer Science programs under contract number DE-AC02-06CH11357. We would also like to acknowledge the support from the SINBAD II project and the member organizations of the SINBAD Consortium.

We gratefully acknowledge the computing resources provided and operated by the Joint Laboratory for System Evaluation (JLSE) at Argonne National Laboratory.

This paper benefited from discussions with Kaiyuan Huo, Fabio Luporini, Thomas Matthews, Paul Kelly, Oana Marin.

References

1. https://computation.llnl.gov/projects/floating-point-compression/zfp-and-derivatives
2. Alted, F.: Why modern cpus are starving and what can be done about it. Comput. Sci. Eng. **12**(2), 68 (2010)
3. Aminzadeh, F., Burkhard, N., Long, J., Kunz, T., Duclos, P.: Three dimensional SEG/EAGE models–an update. Lead. Edge **15**(2), 131–134 (1996)
4. Aupy, G., Herrmann, J., Hovland, P., Robert, Y.: Optimal multistage algorithm for adjoint computation. SIAM J. Sci. Comput. **38**(3), C232–C255 (2016)
5. Blanchet, J., Cartis, C., Menickelly, M., Scheinberg, K.: Convergence rate analysis of a stochastic trust region method for nonconvex optimization. arXiv preprint arXiv:1609.07428 (2016)
6. Boehm, C., Hanzich, M., de la Puente, J., Fichtner, A.: Wavefield compression for adjoint methods in full-waveform inversion. Geophysics **81**(6), R385–R397 (2016)
7. Cyr, E.C., Shadid, J., Wildey, T.: Towards efficient backward-in-time adjoint computations using data compression techniques. Comput. Methods Appl. Mech. Eng. **288**, 24–44 (2015)
8. Dalmau, F.R., Hanzich, M., de la Puente, J., Gutiérrez, N.: Lossy data compression with DCT transforms. In: EAGE Workshop on High Performance Computing for Upstream (2014)
9. Datta, D., Appelhans, D., Evangelinos, C., Jordan, K.: An asynchronous two-level checkpointing method to solve adjoint problems on hierarchical memory spaces. Comput. Sci. Eng. **20**(4), 39–55 (2018)
10. Di, S., Tao, D., Liang, X., Cappello, F.: Efficient lossy compression for scientific data based on pointwise relative error bound. IEEE Trans. Parallel Distrib. Syst. **30**(2), 331–345 (2018)
11. Griewank, A., Walther, A.: Algorithm 799: revolve: an implementation of checkpointing for the reverse or adjoint mode of computational differentiation. ACM Trans. Math. Softw. (TOMS) **26**(1), 19–45 (2000)

12. Kukreja, N., Hückelheim, J., Lange, M., Louboutin, M., Walther, A., Funke, S.W., Gorman, G.: High-level python abstractions for optimal checkpointing in inversion problems. arXiv preprint arXiv:1802.02474 (2018)
13. van Leeuwen, T., Herrmann, F.J.: 3d frequency-domain seismic inversion with controlled sloppiness. SIAM J. Sci. Comput. **36**(5), S192–S217 (2014)
14. Lindstrom, P.: Fixed-rate compressed floating-point arrays. IEEE Trans. Visual Comput. Graphics **20**(12), 2674–2683 (2014)
15. Louboutin, M., Lange, M., Luporini, F., Kukreja, N., Witte, P.A., Herrmann, F.J., Velesko, P., Gorman, G.J.: Devito: an embedded domain-specific language for finite differences and geophysical exploration. CoRR abs/1808.01995, August 2018. https://arxiv.org/abs/1808.01995
16. Marin, O., Schanen, M., Fischer, P.: Large-scale lossy data compression based on an a priori error estimator in a spectral element code. Technical report, ANL/MCS-P6024-0616 (2016)
17. O'Neil, M.A., Burtscher, M.: Floating-point data compression at 75 gb/s on a GPU. In: Proceedings of the Fourth Workshop on General Purpose Processing on Graphics Processing Units. ACM (2011). https://doi.org/10.1145/1964179.1964189
18. Plessix, R.E.: A review of the adjoint-state method for computing the gradient of a functional with geophysical applications. Geophys. J. Int. **167**(2), 495–503 (2006)
19. Stumm, P., Walther, A.: Multistage approaches for optimal offline checkpointing. SIAM J. Sci. Comput. **31**(3), 1946–1967 (2009)
20. Symes, W.W.: Reverse time migration with optimal checkpointing. Geophysics **72**(5), SM213–SM221 (2007)
21. Tao, D., Di, S., Liang, X., Chen, Z., Cappello, F.: Optimizing lossy compression rate-distortion from automatic online selection between sz and zfp. arXiv preprint arXiv:1806.08901 (2018)

Scheduling and Load Balancing

Linear Time Algorithms for Multiple Cluster Scheduling and Multiple Strip Packing

Klaus Jansen and Malin Rau$^{(\boxtimes)}$ (ID)

Institut für Informatik, Christian-Albrechts-Universität zu Kiel, Kiel, Germany
{kj,mra}@informatik.uni-kiel.de

Abstract. We study the Multiple Cluster Scheduling problem and the Multiple Strip Packing problem. For both problems, there is no algorithm with approximation ratio better than 2 unless P = NP. In this paper, we present an algorithm with approximation ratio 2 and running time $\mathcal{O}(n)$ for both problems for $N > 2$ (and running time $\mathcal{O}(n \log(n)^2)$ for $N = 2$). While a 2 approximation was known before, the running time of the algorithm is at least $\Omega(n^{256})$ in the worst case. Therefore, an $\mathcal{O}(n)$ algorithm is surprising and the best possible.

While the above result is strong from a theoretical point of view, it might not be very practical due to a large hidden constant caused by calling an AEPTAS with a constant $\varepsilon \geq 1/8$ as subroutine. Nevertheless, we point out that the general approach of finding first a schedule on one cluster and then distributing it onto the other clusters might come in handy in practical approaches. We demonstrate this by presenting a practical algorithm with running time $\mathcal{O}(n \log(n))$, without hidden constants, that is an approximation algorithm with ratio 9/4 if the number N of clusters is dividable by 3 and bounded by $9/4 + \frac{3}{4N}$ otherwise.

1 Introduction

In the optimization problem Multiple Cluster Scheduling (MCS), we are given $n \in \mathbb{N}$ parallel jobs $\mathcal{J}$ and $N \in \mathbb{N}$ clusters. Each cluster consists of $m \in \mathbb{N}$ identical machines and each job $j \in \mathcal{J}$ has a processing time $p(j) \in \mathbb{N}$ and a machine requirement $q(j) \in \mathbb{N}_{\leq m}$. A schedule $S = (\sigma, \rho)$ of the jobs consists of two functions $\sigma : \mathcal{J} \to \mathbb{N}$ which assigns jobs to starting points and $\rho : \mathcal{J} \to \{1, \dots N\}$, which assigns jobs to the clusters. The objective is to find a feasible schedule of all the jobs, which minimizes the makespan, i.e., which minimizes $\max\{p(j) + \sigma(j) | j \in \mathcal{J}\}$. A schedule is feasible if at every time $\tau \in \mathbb{N}$ and any Cluster $i \in \mathbb{N}$ the number of used machines is bounded by m, i.e., if

$$\sum_{j \in \mathcal{J}, \sigma(j) \leq \tau < \sigma(j) + p(j), \rho(j) = i} q(j) \leq m \quad \forall i \in \{1, \dots, N\}, \tau \in \mathbb{N}.$$

Research was supported by German Research Foundation (DFG) project JA 612/20-1.

R. Yahyapour (Ed.): Euro-Par 2019, LNCS 11725, pp. 103–116, 2019.
https://doi.org/10.1007/978-3-030-29400-7_8

If the number of clusters is bounded by one, the problem is called Parallel Task Scheduling (PTS). We can assume that $n > N$ since otherwise an optimal schedule would place each job alone on one cluster and thus the problem is not hard.

The other considered problem is a closely related variant of MCS called Multiple Strip Packing (MSP). The difference is that the jobs have to be allocated on contiguous machines. We are given $n \in \mathbb{N}$ rectangular items $\mathcal{I}$ and $N \in \mathbb{N}$ strips (also called clusters). Each strip has an infinite height and the same width $W \in \mathbb{N}$. Each item $i \in \mathcal{I}$ has a width $w(i)$ and a height $h(i)$. The objective is to find a feasible packing of the items into the strips such that the packing height is minimized. A packing is feasible if all the items are placed overlapping free into the strips. If the number of strips is bounded by one, the problem is called Strip Packing (SP).

Strip Packing and Parallel Task Scheduling are classical optimization problems and the extension of these problems to multiple strips or clusters comes natural. Moreover, these problems can be motivated by real world problems. One example, as stated in [16], is the following: In operating systems, Multiple Strip Packing (MSP) arises in the computer grid and server consolidation [10]. In the system supporting server consolidation on many-core chip multi processors, multiple server applications are deployed onto virtual machines. Every virtual machine is allocated several processors and each application might require a number of processors simultaneously. Hence, a virtual machine can be regarded as a cluster and server applications can be represented as parallel tasks. Similarly, in the distributed virtual machines environment, each physical machine can be regarded as a strip while virtual machines are represented as rectangles. It is quite natural to investigate the packing algorithm by minimizing the maximum height of the strips. This is related to the problem of maximizing the throughput, which is commonly used in the area of operating systems.

In this paper, we consider approximation algorithms for MCS and MSP. We say an approximation algorithm A has an (absolute) approximation ratio α, if for each instance I of the problem it holds that $A(I) \leq \alpha \mathrm{OPT}(I)$, where $A(I)$ is the objective value obtained by the algorithm A while $\mathrm{OPT}(I)$ denotes the optimal objective value for the instance I. Note that in this paper we will denote by $\mathrm{OPT}(I)$ (or only OPT) both: the optimal objective value and an optimal solution for an instance I. A family of algorithms with approximation ratio $(1+\varepsilon)$ is called polynomial time approximation scheme (PTAS), and a PTAS whose running time is bounded by a polynomial in both the input length $\mathrm{SIZE}(I)$ and $1/\varepsilon$ is called *fully* polynomial time approximation scheme (FPTAS). If the running time of a PTAS is bounded by a function of the form $\mathrm{poly}(\mathrm{SIZE}(I)) \cdot f(1/\varepsilon)$, where f is an arbitrary function, we say the running time is *efficient* and call it an efficient PTAS or EPTAS. An algorithm A has an asymptotic approximation ratio α if there is a constant c such that $A(I) \leq \alpha \mathrm{OPT}(I) + c$ and we denote a polynomial time approximation scheme with respect to the asymptotic approximation ratio as an A(E)PTAS.

MCS and MSP cannot be approximated better than 2 unless P = NP, see [16]. On the other hand, the best algorithms so far are 2-approximations, see [2] for MSP and [9] for MCS. Both algorithms have a large worst case running time of

$\Omega(n^{256})$ since they uses an algorithm with running time $n^{\Omega(1/\varepsilon^{1/\varepsilon})}$ with constant $\varepsilon = 1/4$ as a subroutine. Because of this running time, efforts have been made to speed up the running time in expense of the approximation ratio, see for example [11] and [3]. For MCS and MSP, we present 2-approximations with a drastically improved running time with regard to the $\mathcal{O}$-notation.

Theorem 1. *There are algorithms for MCS and MSP with approximation ratio 2 and running time $\mathcal{O}(n)$ if $N > 2$, running time $\mathcal{O}(n\log(n))$ if $N \in \{1,2\}$ for MCS and running time $\mathcal{O}(n\log^2(n)/\log(\log(n)))$ if $N \in \{1,2\}$ for MSP.*

The running time of these algorithms is the best possible from a theoretical point of view with respect to the $\mathcal{O}$-notation for $N \geq 3$. Since we need to assign a start point to each job, we cannot assume that there is an algorithm for MCS with running time strictly faster than $\Omega(n)$. To achieve these results, we use an AEPTAS for the optimization problem PTS and SP as a subroutine respectively. Regarding PTS, we improved the running time of an algorithm by Jansen [6] and developed an AEPTAS. For SP, we find an AEPTAS as well. However the running time depending on $1/\varepsilon$ is worse than in the AEPTAS for PTS. Note that this algorithm is the first AEPTAS for SP that has an additive term of $h_{\max} := \max\{h(i)\,|\,i \in \mathcal{I}\}$. The best algorithm so far with additive term $h_{\max}$ is an APTAS, see [8].

Theorem 2. *There are AEPTASs for PTS and SP with running time $\mathcal{O}(n) \cdot \mathcal{O}_\varepsilon(1)$ and additive term $p_{\max} := \max\{p(j)\,|\,j \in \mathcal{J}\}$ or $h_{\max}$ respectively.*

These algorithms can be used to find an AEPTAS for MCS and MSP by cutting the solution for one cluster or strip into segments of height $(1+\varepsilon)\mathrm{OPT}$. The jobs overlapping these cuts on the top add further $p_{\max}$ to the approximation ratio resulting in an AEPTAS with additive term $p_{\max}$.

Theorem 3. *There are AEPTASs for for MCS and MSP with running time $\mathcal{O}(n) \cdot \mathcal{O}_\varepsilon(1)$ and additive term $p_{\max}$ or $h_{\max}$ respectively.*

The algorithms from Theorem 1 use the algorithms from Theorem 2 as subroutines with a constant value $\varepsilon = 1/8$ if $N = 2$, $\varepsilon = 1/5$ if $N = 5$, and $\varepsilon \in [1/4, 1/3]$ otherwise. As a result, the running time of the algorithm can be rather large, while the $\mathcal{O}$-notation suggests otherwise since it hides all the constants. Due to this fact, we have developed a truly fast algorithm where the most expensive part is sorting the jobs. However, this improved running time yields a slight loss in the approximation factor.

Theorem 4. *There is a fast $\mathcal{O}(n\log(n))$ algorithm for MCS with approximation ratio 9/4 if $N = 3i$, $(9i+5)/(4i+2) \leq 9/4 + \frac{3}{8N}$ if $N = 3i+1$, and $(9i+10)/(4i+4) \leq 9/4 + \frac{3}{4N}$ if $N = 3i + 2$ for some $i \in \mathbb{N}$.*

Note that the approximation ratio of the algorithm from Theorem 4 is worse than 7/3 for the cases that $N \in \{2,5\}$ and exactly 7/3 for the case that $N \in \{4,8\}$. However for each other N, the algorithm beats the approximation ratios of the previous fast algorithms.

Table 1. Overview of the results for MCS and MSP.

Problem	Ratio	Remarks	Source
MCS, MSP	$2 + \varepsilon$	Needs solving of Scheduling on Identical Machines with ratio $1 + \varepsilon/2$	[16]
MCS	2	Worst case running time at least $\Omega(n^{256})$; can handle clusters with different sizes	[9]
MSP	2	Worst case running time at least $\Omega(n^{256})$	[2]
MCS, MSP	AFPTAS	Additive constant in $\mathcal{O}(1/\varepsilon^2)$, and $\mathcal{O}(1)$ for large values for N	[2]
MCS	3	Fast algorithm that can handle clusters with different sizes	[11]
MCS	5/2	Fast algorithm	[3]
MCS	7/3	Fast algorithm	[3]
MCS	2	Fast algorithm; requires $\max_{j \in \mathcal{J}} q(j) \leq 1/2 \cdot m$	[3]
MCS, MSP	2	$N \geq 3$: running time $\mathcal{O}(n)$; $N = 2$: running time $\mathcal{O}(n \log(n))$ for MCS, $\mathcal{O}(n \log^2(n))$ for MSP	This paper
MCS, MSP	AEPTAS	Additive term $p_{\max}$; linear in n	This paper
MCS	9/4	If $N \bmod 3 = 0$ or if N is large	This paper
PTS, SP	AEPTAS	Additive term $p_{\max}$; linear in n	This paper

Related Work. We summarize the results for the variant of MCS and MSP studied in this paper in Table 1. Furthermore, MCS has been studied for the case that clusters do not need to have the same number of machines. It is still NP-hard to approximate this problem better than 2 [17]. Moreover, it was proven in [11] and [13] that the List Schedule cannot guarantee a constant approximation ratio for this problem. The first algorithm was presented by Tchernykh et al. [13] and has an approximation ratio of 10. This ratio was improved to a 3-approximation by Schwiegelshohn et al. [11], which is given by an online non-clairvoyant algorithm where the processing times are not known beforehand. Later, the algorithm was extended by Tchernykh et al. [14] to the case where jobs have release dates changing the approximation ratio to $2e + 1$. Bougeret et al. [1] developed an algorithm with approximation ratio 2.5 for this case. This algorithm needs the constraint that the largest machine requirement of a job is smaller than the smallest number of machines available in any given cluster. This ratio was improved by Dutot et al. [4] by presenting an algorithm with approximation ratio $(2 + \varepsilon)$. The currently best algorithm for this problem matches the lower bound of 2 [9], but has a large running time of $\Omega(n^{256})$.

Methodology. The $\mathcal{O}(n)$ algorithm consists of two steps. First, we use an AEP-TAS for MCS or MSP to find a schedule on two clusters, one with makespan at most $(1 + \varepsilon)NOPT$ and the other with makespan at most $p_{\max}$ or $h_{\max}$ respectively. This schedule on the two clusters is then distributed onto the N

clusters using a new partitioning technique. This partitioning technique is the main accomplishment of this paper and presented in Sect. 2. The AEPTASs for MCS and MSP are excluded from this extended abstract and can be found in the full version [7]. In Sect. 3, we present the algorithm from Theorem 4 that finds an approximation without the need to call the AEPTAS as a subroutine but uses the partitioning technique as well.

2 Partitioning Technique

In this section, we describe the central idea which leads to a linear running time algorithm. Indeed this technique can be used for any problem setting where there is an AEPTAS with approximation ratio $(1+\varepsilon)\mathrm{OPT}+p_{\max}$ for the single cluster version. In this context, $p_{\max}$ is the largest occurring size in the minimization dimension, e.i. it stands for $h_{\max}$ in the MSP problem.

Note that MSP can be interpreted as a scheduling problem, where the jobs have to be scheduled on contiguous machines by calling the items jobs (where the processing time corresponds to the height) and calling the strips clusters. Hence, in this section, we will speak of jobs and clusters for both problem settings MCS and MSP. In this spirit, we define the work of a job j as $\mathcal{W}(j) := p(j) \cdot q(j)$ and the work of a set of jobs $\mathcal{J}'$ as $\mathcal{W}(\mathcal{J}') := \sum_{j \in \mathcal{J}'} \mathcal{W}(j)$.

The basic idea of the algorithm can be summarized as follows. Instead of scheduling the jobs on N clusters, we first schedule them on only two clusters C_1 and C_2. In a second step, we distribute the scheduled jobs to the N clusters. In the following, let OPT be the height of an optimal schedule on N clusters for a given instance I. Hence, there exists a schedule on one cluster with makespan at most $N \cdot \mathrm{OPT}$. In the following we will assume that there is an algorithm Alg which schedules the jobs on two clusters C_1 and C_2 such that the makespan of C_1 is at most $(1 + \varepsilon)N \cdot \mathrm{OPT}$ and C_2 has a makespan of at most OPT. The algorithm mentioned in Theorem 2 is an example of such an algorithm. It has an approximation ratio of $(1 + \varepsilon)\mathrm{OPT} + p_{\max}$ since there is a set of jobs, which are added to the end of the schedule, all starting at the same time. Instead adding them on the end of the schedule, we can schedule them on cluster C_2 instead (all starting at the same time).

The case $N > 2$

The case $N > 2$ differs from the case $N = 2$ with regard to the partitioning technique and the running time.

Lemma 1. *Let C_1 and C_2 be two clusters both with m machines. Let Alg be an algorithm that schedules the jobs on two clusters C_1 and C_2 such that the makespan of C_1 is at most $(1 + \varepsilon)N\mathrm{OPT}$ and C_2 has a makespan of at most OPT with running time of $\mathcal{O}(n \cdot f(\varepsilon))$.*

We can find a schedule on $N > 2$ clusters with makespan $2\mathrm{OPT}$ in $\mathcal{O}(n + n \cdot f(\lfloor N/3 \rfloor /N)) = \mathcal{O}(n)$ operations. (Note that $\lfloor N/3 \rfloor /N \in [1/5, 1/3]$, and hence can be handled as a constant)

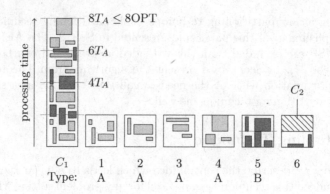

Fig. 1. An example for $N = 3i$ and $i = 2$. The schedule generated on C_1 can be seen on the left followed by its partition onto the 6 clusters. The schedule on C_1 has a height of at most $(N + \lfloor N/3 \rfloor)$OPT $\leq$ 8OPT. We get four clusters of type A, namely clusters 1 to 4, and one cluster of type B, namely cluster 5 which contains the jobs cut by the two horizontal lines at $2T_A$ and $4T_A$. Cluster 6 contains the jobs cut by the horizontal line at $6T_A$ and the jobs from cluster C_2 that remain their relative position.

In the following, we will describe how to distribute a schedule given by `Alg` to N new clusters, and which value we have to choose for ϵ in `Alg` to get the desired approximation ratio of 2. The partitioning algorithm distinguishes three cases: $N = 3i, N = 3i + 1$ and $N = 3i + 2$ for some $i \in \mathbb{N}_{\geq 1}$ and chooses the value for ε dependent on this N, such that $\varepsilon \in [1/5, 1/3]$. In the following, when speaking of a schedule the processing time is on the vertical axis while the machines are displayed on the horizontal axis, see Fig. 1.

In the following distributing algorithm, we draw horizontal lines at each multiple of $2T_A$, where $T_A \leq$ OPT is a value which depends on the makespan of the schedule defined by `Alg` and will be specified dependent on N later. We say a job j is cut by a horizontal line at $i \cdot 2T_A$ if it starts before and ends after it, i.e. if $\sigma(j) < i \cdot 2T_A < \sigma(j) + p(j)$. Let $i \in \mathbb{N}$ and consider the jobs which start at or after $2iT_A$ and end at or before $2(i+1)T_A$. We remove these jobs from C_1 and schedule them on a new cluster while maintaining their relative position. We say these new clusters have type A. Obviously the makespan of this cluster is bounded by $2T_A \leq$ 2OPT. Next, consider the set of jobs cut by the horizontal line at $2iT_A$. These jobs have a processing time of at most $p_{\max} \leq$ OPT and can be scheduled at the same time without violating any constraint, since they are already scheduled next to each other. We schedule two of these sets of jobs in a new cluster with makespan $2p_{\max} \leq$ 2OPT by letting the first set start at 0 and the second start at $p_{\max}$. We say, these clusters have type B.

Case 1: $N = 3i$.   If $N = 3i$, we choose $\varepsilon := \lfloor N/3 \rfloor / N = 1/3$. As a consequence, the schedule on C_1 given by `Alg` has a makespan of $T \leq (4/3)N$OPT $= 4i$OPT and we define $T_A := T/(4i) \leq$ OPT. We partition the given schedule as described above. Since it has a height of $4iT_A$, we get $2i$ clusters of type A each with makespan at most $2T_A \leq$ 2OPT, see Fig. 1. There are $4iT_A/(2T_A) - 1 = 2i - 1$

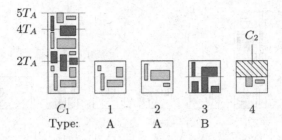

Fig. 2. An example for $N = 3i + 1$ and $i = 1$. The makespan of the schedule on C_1 is bounded by $(N + \lfloor N/3 \rfloor)\text{OPT} = 5\text{OPT}$. Hence, we get two clusters of type A, namely cluster 1 and 2, and one cluster of type B, see cluster 3. It contains the jobs cut by the horizontal lines at $2T_A$ and $4T_A$. Cluster 4 contains the jobs which are completely scheduled between $4T_A$ and $5T_A$ as well as the jobs from cluster C_2.

lines at multiples of $2T_A$ that have the possibility to cut jobs. Hence, we get $\lfloor \frac{2i-1}{2} \rfloor = i - 1$ clusters of type B since each cluster of type B contains two sets of jobs cut by such a horizontal line. The jobs intersecting the last line can be scheduled on one new cluster with makespan $p_{\max} \leq \text{OPT}$. On this last cluster after the point in time $p_{\max}$, we schedule the jobs from the cluster C_2. Remember, the schedule on C_2 has a makespan of at most OPT and, hence, the makespan of this last cluster is bounded by 2OPT as well. In total, we have partitioned the schedule into $2i + i - 1 + 1 = 3i = N$ clusters each with makespan at most 2OPT.

Case 2: $N = 3i + 1$. If $N = 3i + 1$ for some $i \in \mathbb{N}$, we choose $\varepsilon := \lfloor N/3 \rfloor / N = i/(3i + 1) \geq 1/4$. As a result, the makespan of C_1 generated by the algorithm Alg is given by $T \leq (1 + i/(3i + 1))N\text{OPT} = (4i + 1)\text{OPT}$ and we define $T_A := T/(4i + 1) \leq \text{OPT}$. There are $\lceil (4i + 1)/2 \rceil - 1 = 2i$ multiples of $2T_A$ smaller than $(4i + 1)T_A$, see Fig. 2. Above the last multiple of $2T_A$ smaller than $(4i + 1)T_A$ namely $4iT_A$, the schedule has a height of at most $T_A \leq \text{OPT}$ left. Hence using the above-described partitioning technique, we generate $2i$ clusters of type A. The jobs intersecting the $2i$ multiples of $2T_A$ can be placed into i clusters of type B. We have left the jobs above $4iT_A$, which can be scheduled in a new cluster with makespan $T_A \leq \text{OPT}$. Last, we place the jobs from cluster C_2 on top of the schedule in the new cluster, such that it has a makespan of at most $T_A + \text{OPT} \leq 2\text{OPT}$ in total. Altogether, we have distributed the given schedule on $2i + i + 1 = 3i + 1 = N$ clusters each with makespan at most 2OPT.

Case 3: $N = 3i + 2$. If $N = 3i + 2$, we choose $\varepsilon = \lfloor N/3 \rfloor / N = i/(3i+2) \geq 1/5$: As a result, the makespan on C_1 generated by Alg is bounded by $T \leq (1 + i/(3i + 2))N\text{OPT} = (4i + 2)\text{OPT}$ and we define $T_A := T/(4i + 2) \leq \text{OPT}$. Thus, there are $(4i + 2)/2 - 1 = 2i$ vertical lines at the multiples of $2T_A$, which are strictly larger than 0 and strictly smaller than $(4i + 2)T_A$, see Fig. 3. As a consequence, we construct $2i + 1$ clusters of type A and i clusters of type B. The cluster C_2 defines one additional cluster of this new schedule. In total, we have a schedule on $2i + 1 + i + 1 = N$ clusters with makespan bounded by 2OPT.

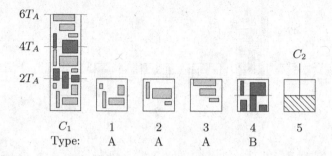

Fig. 3. An example for $N = 3i + 2$ and $i = 1$. The total height of the schedule on C_1 is bounded by $(N + \lfloor N/3 \rfloor)\text{OPT} = 6\text{OPT}$. We get three clusters of type A namely 1, 2, and 3. Furthermore, we get one cluster of type B namely cluster number 4 which contains the jobs cut by the horizontal lines at $2T_A$ and $4T_A$. The cluster C_2 builds its own cluster, see cluster 5.

This distribution can be made in $\mathcal{O}(n)$ steps since we have to relocate each job at most once. Therefore the algorithm has a running time of at most $\mathcal{O}(n + n \cdot f(\lfloor N/3 \rfloor / N)) = \mathcal{O}(n)$ since $\lfloor N/3 \rfloor / N$ is a constant of size at least $1/5$. This concludes the proof of Lemma 1.

The case $N = 2$

To find a distribution for this case, we need to make a stronger assumption to the solution of the algorithm `Alg`. Namely, we assume that the second cluster C_2 has just εm machines. As a consequence, the total work of the jobs contained on C_2 is bounded by $\varepsilon m \text{OPT}$.

Lemma 2. *Let C_1 and C_2 be two clusters with m and $\lfloor \varepsilon m \rfloor$ machines respectively. Let `Alg` be an algorithm that schedules the jobs on two clusters C_1 and C_2 such that the makespan of C_1 is at most $(1+\varepsilon)N\text{OPT}$ and C_2 has a makespan of at most OPT with running time of $\mathcal{O}(n \cdot f(\varepsilon))$. Furthermore, let `Alg2` be an algorithm that finds for the single cluster variant a schedule or packing with height at most $2 \cdot \max\{\mathcal{W}(\mathcal{J})/m, p_{\max}\}$ in $\text{Op}(\texttt{Alg2}(\mathcal{J}, m, N))$ operations.*

We can find a schedule on $N = 2$ clusters with makespan 2OPT in

$$\text{Op}(\texttt{Alg2}(\mathcal{J}, m, N)) + \mathcal{O}(n \cdot f(1/8)) = \text{Op}(\texttt{Alg2}(\mathcal{J}, m, N)) + \mathcal{O}(n)$$

operations.

Consider a schedule given by `Alg` on the clusters C_1 and C_2 for some $\varepsilon > 0$. We denote by $\mathcal{J}(C_1)$ the set of jobs scheduled on C_1 and by $\mathcal{J}(C_2)$ the set of jobs scheduled on C_2. The schedule on cluster C_1 has a makespan of $T \leq (1+\varepsilon)2\text{OPT}$. We assume that $T > 2p_{\max}$ since otherwise we have $T \leq 2\text{OPT}$ and do not need to reorder the schedule any further. We draw horizontal lines at εT and at $T - \varepsilon T$ and define two sets of jobs $\mathcal{J}_1$ and $\mathcal{J}_2$. The set $\mathcal{J}_1$ contains all jobs starting before

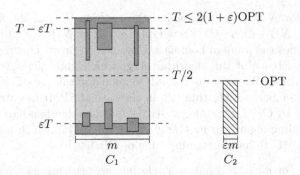

Fig. 4. An example for a schedule on C_1 and C_2 for the case that $N = 2$. The dark gray areas on the bottom represent the jobs inside the set $\mathcal{J}_1$ while the dark gray areas on the top represent the jobs contained in the set $\mathcal{J}_2$.

εT and $\mathcal{J}_2$ contains all jobs ending after $T - \varepsilon T$, see Fig. 4. Since $T \leq (1+\varepsilon)2\text{OPT}$, we have that $(1 - \varepsilon)T < 2\text{OPT}$. Furthermore, $\mathcal{J}_1$ and $\mathcal{J}_2$ are disjoint if $\varepsilon \leq 1/4$ since $p_{\max} \leq T/2$ and therefore $\varepsilon T + p_{\max} \leq T/4 + T/2 \leq {}^3\!/4T \leq (1 - \varepsilon)T$. The total work of the jobs is bounded by $2\text{OPT}m$ and, hence, $\mathcal{W}(\mathcal{J})/(2m) \leq \text{OPT}$. We distinguish two cases:

Case 1: $\mathcal{W}(\mathcal{J}_1) \leq (1 - \varepsilon)\mathcal{W}(\mathcal{J})/2$ or $\mathcal{W}(\mathcal{J}_2) \leq (1 - \varepsilon)\mathcal{W}(\mathcal{J})/2$. Let w.l.o.g $\mathcal{W}(\mathcal{J}_2) \leq (1 - \varepsilon)\mathcal{W}(\mathcal{J})/2 \leq (1 - \varepsilon)m\text{OPT}$. We remove all jobs in $\mathcal{J}_2$ from the cluster C_1. As a result this cluster has a makespan of $(1 - \varepsilon)T < 2\text{OPT}$. The total work of the jobs contained in C_2 combined with the jobs in $\mathcal{J}_2$ is at most $m\text{OPT}$, i.e. $\mathcal{W}(\mathcal{J}(C_2) \cup \mathcal{J}_2) \leq m \cdot \text{OPT}$. Therefore, we can use the algorithm **Alg2** (for example the List-Scheduling algorithm by Garay and Graham [5]) to find a schedule with makespan at most $2\max\{p_{\max}, \mathcal{W}(\mathcal{J}(C_2) \cup \mathcal{J}_2)/m\} \leq 2\text{OPT}$. Hence, we can find a schedule on two clusters in at most $\text{Op}(\text{Alg2}(\mathcal{J}, m, N)) + \mathcal{O}(n \cdot f(\varepsilon))$ for this case.

Case 2: $\mathcal{W}(\mathcal{J}_1) > (1 - \varepsilon)\mathcal{W}(\mathcal{J})/2$ and $\mathcal{W}(\mathcal{J}_2) > (1 - \varepsilon)\mathcal{W}(\mathcal{J})/2$. Consider the set of jobs $\mathcal{J}_3$ scheduled on C_1 but not contained in $\mathcal{J}_1$ or $\mathcal{J}_2$. Since the total work of the jobs is at most $\mathcal{W}(\mathcal{J}) \leq m\text{OPT}$ it holds that $\mathcal{W}(\mathcal{J}_3) \leq \mathcal{W}(\mathcal{J}) - \mathcal{W}(\mathcal{J}_1) - \mathcal{W}(\mathcal{J}_2) = \varepsilon\mathcal{W}(\mathcal{J}) \leq 2\varepsilon m\text{OPT}$. We define $\mathcal{J}_4$ as the set of jobs ending at or before εT and $\mathcal{J}_5$ as the set of jobs starting at or after $(1 - \varepsilon)T$. Both sets have a total work of at most $\varepsilon m T \leq 2(\varepsilon + \varepsilon^2)m\text{OPT}$ and therefore $\mathcal{W}(\mathcal{J}_3 \cup \mathcal{J}_4 \cup \mathcal{J}_5 \cup \mathcal{J}(C_2)) \leq (7\varepsilon + 4\varepsilon^2)m\text{OPT}$. If $\varepsilon = \frac{1}{8}$, these jobs have a total work of at most $m\text{OPT}$ and are scheduled with the algorithm **Alg2** to find a schedule on one cluster with makespan at most $2\max\{p_{\max}, \mathcal{W}(\mathcal{J}_3 \cup \mathcal{J}_4 \cup \mathcal{J}_5 \cup \mathcal{J}(C_2))/m\} \leq 2\text{OPT}$.

To this point, we have scheduled all jobs except the ones cut by the line εT and the jobs cut by the line $(1 - \varepsilon)T$. We schedule them in the second cluster by starting all the jobs cut by the first line at start point 0 and the second set of jobs at the start point $p_{\max} \leq \text{OPT}$. Note that the partition into the sets $\mathcal{J}_1, \ldots, \mathcal{J}_5$ can be done in $\mathcal{O}(n)$ and hence the partitioning step is dominated by the running time of the algorithm **Alg2**. Since we have to choose $\varepsilon = 1/8$

in both cases for $N = 2$, we can bound the running time of the algorithm by $\text{Op}(\texttt{Alg2}(\mathcal{J}, m, N)) + \mathcal{O}(n \cdot f(1/8)) = \text{Op}(\texttt{Alg2}(\mathcal{J}, m, N)) + \mathcal{O}(n)$ in this case.

This concludes the proof of Lemma 2. However, to prove Theorem 1, we need to prove the existence of the algorithm $\texttt{Alg}$, which finds the schedule on the clusters C_1 and C_2. We refer to the full version for this proof. Note that for $\texttt{Alg2}$, we use Steinbergs-Algorithm [12] in the case of SP. It has a running time that is bounded by $\mathcal{O}(n \log^2(n)/\log(\log(n)))$. On the other hand for PTS, we use the List-Scheduling algorithm by Garay and Graham [5], which was optimized by Turek et al. [15] to have a running time of $\mathcal{O}(n \log(n))$.

Corollary 1. *For all $N \geq 3$, given a schedule on two clusters C_1 and C_2 such that the makespan of C_1 is at most $(1 + \lfloor N/3 \rfloor / N) N \text{OPT}$ and C_2 has a makespan of at most OPT, we can find a schedule on N clusters with makespan at most 2OPT in at most $\mathcal{O}(n)$ additional steps.*

This corollary is a direct conclusion of the Lemma 1. As a result, instead of the AEPTAS, first, we can try to use any heuristic or other (fast) approximation algorithm: Given a schedule by any heuristic, remove all the jobs that end after the point in time where the last job starts and place them on the cluster C_2 by starting them all at the same time. The schedule on C_2 obviously has a makespan bounded by $p_{\max} \leq \text{OPT}$. Next, check whether the residual schedule on C_1 has a makespan of at most $(1 + \lfloor N/3 \rfloor / N) N \text{OPT}$. For example, compare the makespan T on C_1 to the lower bound on the optimal makespan $L :=$ $\max\{p_{\max}, \mathcal{W}(\mathcal{J})/m, p(\mathcal{J}_{>m/2})\}$, where $\mathcal{J}_{>m/2}$ is the set of all jobs with machine requirement larger than $m/2$. If the makespan T is small enough, i.e., if $T \leq (1 + \lfloor N/3 \rfloor / N) L$ use the partitioning technique to find a 2-approximation. Otherwise, use the corresponding AEPTAS presented in the full version.

3   A Faster Algorithm for a Practical Number of Jobs

In the algorithm described above, we have a running time of $\mathcal{O}(n)$, but the hidden constant can be extremely large. Hence, in practical applications it might be more beneficial to use an algorithm with running time $\mathcal{O}(n \log(n))$ or $\mathcal{O}(n^2)$, to find an $\alpha\text{OPT} + p_{\max}$ approximation for Parallel Task Scheduling (PTS), that does not have any hidden constants. For $N \in \mathbb{N} \setminus \{2, 5\}$, we use $\varepsilon \in [1/4, 1/3]$ and hence a fast poly(n) algorithm without large hidden constants and approximation ratio $(5/4)\text{OPT} + p_{\max}$ would be a significant improvement for the vast majority of cluster numbers. Even an algorithm with approximation ratio $(4/3)\text{OPT} + p_{\max}$ would speed up the algorithm for one third of all the possible instances, namely all the instances where the number of clusters is dividable by three. To this point, we did find neither of the algorithms, and leave this as an open question. Instead, we present a fast algorithm with approximation ratio $(3/2)\text{OPT} + p_{\max}$. This algorithm for PTS leads to an algorithm for MCS with approximation ratio $9/4$ for all instances where $N \bmod 3 = 0$.

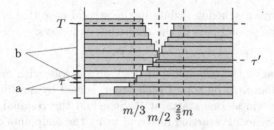

Fig. 5. A placement of the jobs with processing time larger than $m/3$. Above τ' the jobs are stacked in decreasing order of their machine requirement (width) since the algorithm places the jobs which have the largest fitting machine requirement first.

Lemma 3. *There is an algorithm for PTS with approximation guarantee of* $(3/2)\mathrm{OPT} + p_{\max}$ *and running time* $\mathcal{O}(n\log(n))$. *This schedule can be divided into two clusters* C_1 *and* C_2, *where the schedule on* C_1 *has a makespan of at most* $(3/2)\mathrm{OPT}$ *and the makespan of* C_2 *is bounded by* $p_{\max}$.

Due to space limitations, we present an overview of the algorithm, but discard the proof of correctness. We refer to the full version for the proof, see [7]. This algorithm uses the following optimized variant of List-Scheduling: Starting at time $\tau = 0$ for every endpoint of a job, schedule the widest job that can be started at this point if there is one; otherwise, go to the next endpoint and proceed as before. The first part of the algorithm can be summarized as follows:

1. For a given set of jobs $\mathcal{J}$, first consider the jobs $j \in \mathcal{J}$ with $q(j) \in [m/3, m]$ and sort them by decreasing size of the machine requirement $q(j)$.
2. We stack all the jobs $j \in \mathcal{J}$ with $q(j) > m/2$ ordered by their machine requirement such that the largest starts at time 0, see Fig. 5.
3. Look at the job with the smallest requirement of machines larger than $m/3$ and place it at the first possible point in the schedule next to the jobs with machine requirement larger than $m/2$. We call this point in time τ.
4. Schedule all the other jobs with machine requirement at least $m/3$ with the optimized List-Schedule starting at τ. The List-Schedule includes the end-points of the already scheduled jobs.

Let τ' be the point in time, where the last job j with $q(j) > m/2$ ends. Furthermore, let T' be the last point in the schedule where two jobs are processed and define $T := \max\{T', \tau'\}$. Additionally, we define τ'' to be the first point in time where both jobs scheduled at τ' have ended. We claim that $T \leq \mathrm{OPT}$ and refer to the long version for the proof. If there are no jobs with machine requirement at most $m/3$, we do not need to add further steps and have found a schedule with approximation guarantee $\mathrm{OPT} + p_{\max}$.

Let a be the total processing time before T, where only one job is scheduled, and let b be the total processing time, where exactly two jobs are scheduled. We will consider two cases: $a > b$ and $a \leq b$. In the first case, we have to dismantle the current schedule, while in the second case this is not necessary. We summarize the second part of the algorithm as follows:

5. Find a and b
6. If $a > b$, dismantle the schedule and stack all the jobs with machine requirement larger than $m/3$ on top of each other, sorted by machine requirement such that the widest one starts at 0. Schedule the residual jobs with the modified List-Schedule starting at 0 and using the endpoints of all jobs.
7. Else if $a \leq b$, determine τ'' and use the optimized List-Schedule to schedule the remaining starting at τ'' while using the endpoints of all scheduled jobs.

Last, we describe how to partition this schedule into the schedule on the clusters C_1 and C_2. In the described algorithm, the additional $p_{\max}$ is added by the last started job. To partition this schedule such that it is scheduled on the two clusters C_1 and C_2, look at the starting time ρ of the last started job. Remove this job and all the jobs which end strictly after ρ and place them into the second cluster C_2, starting at the same time. The resulting schedule on C_2 has a height of at most $p_{\max}$. Leave the residual jobs untouched and declare the cluster as C_1. The schedule up to ρ has a height of at most $(3/2)$OPT.

3.1 Proof of Theorem 4

In this section, we prove Theorem 4. We start with the schedule given by the $(3/2)$OPT $+ p_{\max}$ algorithm from Lemma 3 and its partition onto the two clusters C_1 and C_2. To partition the schedule on C_1 onto the different clusters, we differentiate the three cases $N = 3i$, $N = 3i + 1$ and $N = 3i + 2$.

Case 1: $N = 3i$ In this case, the schedule on C_1 has a height of $T \leq (9i/2)$OPT. We partition it into $2i$ parts of equal height $T/(2i) \leq (9/4)$OPT. During this partition step, we cut the schedule $2i - 1$ times. The jobs intersected by a cut have to be scheduled separately using height p_{max}. Together with the jobs in C_2, we have $2i$ sets of jobs with height bounded by p_{max} and machine requirement bounded by m. We schedule these sets pairwise on i additional clusters analogously to the clusters of type B in Sect. 2. In total, we use $3i = N$ clusters and the largest one has a height of at most $(9/4)$OPT $= 2.25$OPT.

Case 2: $N = 3i + 1$ In this case, the schedule on C_1 has a height of $T \leq (3(3i+1)/2)$OPT $= ((9i+3)/2)$OPT. We partition the schedule into $2i$ parts of equal height and one part with a smaller height. On top of this part, we schedule the jobs from C_2. Let $T_A := (2/(9i+3))T \leq$ OPT. We define the height of the $2i$ parts as $((9i+5)/(4i+2))T_A$ and the height of the last part as $((5i+3)/(4i+2))T_A$. It is easy to verify the $2i \cdot (9i + 5)/(4i + 2) \cdot T_A + (5i + 3)/(4i + 2) \cdot T_A = T$ and, hence, we have partitioned the complete schedule on C_1. By partitioning the schedule on C_1 into these parts, we have cut the schedule $2i$ times. Therefore together with the jobs on C_2, we have to schedule $2i+1$ parts of height $p_{\max}$. We schedule C_2 on the cluster with current makespan $((5i+3)/(4i+2))T_A$ resulting in a schedule of height $((5i + 3)/(4i + 2))T_A + p_{\max} \leq ((9i + 5)/(4i + 2))$OPT, (since $p_{max} \leq$ OPT). We pair the other $2i$ parts and schedule them on i distinct clusters. In total, we generate $2i+1+i = 3i+1$ cluster and the largest occurring makespan is bounded by $((9i+5)/(4i+2))$OPT.

Case 3: $N = 3i + 2$ In this case, the schedule on C_1 has a height of $T \leq (3(3i+2)/2)$OPT $= ((9i+6)/2)$OPT. We partition this schedule into $2i+1$ parts of equal height and one part with a smaller height. On top of this part, we will schedule two parts with processing time p_{max}. Let $T_A := (2/(9i+6))T \leq$ OPT. The first $2i + 1$ parts of C_1 have a height of $((9i + 10)/(4i + 4))T_A$ and the last part has a height of at most $((i+2)/(4i+4))T_A$. It is easy to verify that $(2i+1)((9i+10)/(4i+4))T_A + ((i+2)/(4i+4))T_A = ((9i+6)/2)T_A = T$ and, hence, we have scheduled all parts of C_1. Since $((i+2)/(4i+4))T_A + 2p_{max} \leq ((9i+10)/(4i+4))$OPT, we can schedule two parts with processing time at most p_{max} on this cluster. We have cut the schedule on C_1 exactly $2i+1$ times. Together, with the jobs from C_2 there are $2i + 2$ parts with processing time at most p_{max}. Since we already have scheduled two of these parts, we pair the residual $2i$ parts and generate i new clusters with makespan at most $2p_{max}$. In total, we generated $2i+2+i = 3i+2$ clusters and the largest makespan occurring on the clusters is bounded by $((9i+10)/(4i+4))$OPT.

For each of the three cases $N = 3i$, $N = 3i + 1$, and $N = 3i + 2$, we have presented a partitioning strategy which partitions the schedule from clusters C_1 and C_2 onto N clusters such that each cluster has a makespan of at most $(9/4)$OPT, $((9i+5)/(4i+2))$OPT or $((9i+10)/(4i+4))$OPT respectively. Hence, we have proven Theorem 4.

4   Conclusion

In this paper, we presented an algorithm for Multiple Cluster Scheduling (MCS) and Multiple Strip Packing (MSP) with best possible absolute approximation ratio of 2 and best possible running time $\mathcal{O}(n)$ for the case $N \geq 3$. Still open remains the question if for the case $N = 2$ the running time of $\mathcal{O}(n\log(n))$ or $\mathcal{O}(n\log^2(n)/(\log(\log(n))))$ for MCS and MSP respectively can be improved to $\mathcal{O}(n)$. Furthermore, we presented a truly fast algorithm for Multiple Cluster Scheduling (MCS) with running time $\mathcal{O}(n\log(n))$ that does not have any hidden constants. Since the running time of the $\mathcal{O}(n)$ algorithm hides large constants, it would be interesting to improve the running time of the underlying $AEPTAS$ or even to find a fast algorithm with approximation guarantee $(5/4)$OPT$+p_{max}$.

References

1. Bougeret, M., Dutot, P.-F., Jansen, K., Otte, C., Trystram, D.: A fast 5/2-approximation algorithm for hierarchical scheduling. In: D'Ambra, P., Guarracino, M., Talia, D. (eds.) Euro-Par 2010. LNCS, vol. 6271, pp. 157–167. Springer, Heidelberg (2010). https://doi.org/10.1007/978-3-642-15277-1_16

2. Bougeret, M., Dutot, P., Jansen, K., Robenek, C., Trystram, D.: Approximation algorithms for multiple strip packing and scheduling parallel jobs in platforms. Discrete Math. Alg. Appl. **3**(4), 553–586 (2011)
3. Bougeret, M., Dutot, P., Trystram, D., Jansen, K., Robenek, C.: Improved approximation algorithms for scheduling parallel jobs on identical clusters. Theor. Comput. Sci. **600**, 70–85 (2015)
4. Dutot, P., Jansen, K., Robenek, C., Trystram, D.: A $(2 + \epsilon)$-approximation for scheduling parallel jobs in platforms. In: Proceedings of the 19th Euro-Par, Aachen, Germany, August 26–30, 2013, pp. 78–89 (2013)
5. Garey, M.R., Graham, R.L.: Bounds for multiprocessor scheduling with resource constraints. SIAM J. Comput. **4**(2), 187–200 (1975)
6. Jansen, K.: A $(3/2+\varepsilon)$ approximation algorithm for scheduling moldable and non-moldable parallel tasks. In: Proceedings of the 24th ACM SPAA, Pittsburgh, PA, USA, June 25–27, pp. 224–235 (2012)
7. Jansen, K., Rau, M.: Linear time algorithms for multiple cluster scheduling and multiple strip packing. CoRR, abs/1902.03428 (2019)
8. Jansen, K., Solis-Oba, R.: Rectangle packing with one-dimensional resource augmentation. Discrete Optim. **6**(3), 310–323 (2009)
9. Jansen, K., Trystram, D.: Scheduling parallel jobs on heterogeneous platforms. Electron. Notes Discrete Math. **55**, 9–12 (2016)
10. Marty, M.R., Hill, M.D.: Virtual hierarchies to support server consolidation. In: Proceedings of the 34th ISCA, June 9–13, San Diego, California, USA, pp. 46–56 (2007)
11. Schwiegelshohn, U., Tchernykh, A., Yahyapour, R.: Online scheduling in grids. In: Proceedings of the 22nd IEEE IPDPS, Miami, Florida USA, April 14–18, 2008, pp. 1–10 (2008)
12. Steinberg, A.: A strip-packing algorithm with absolute performance bound 2. SIAM J. Comput. **26**(2), 401–409 (1997)
13. Tchernykh, A., Ramírez, J.M., Avetisyan, A., Kuzjurin, N., Grushin, D., Zhuk, S.: Two level job-scheduling strategies for a computational grid. In: Wyrzykowski, R., Dongarra, J., Meyer, N., Waśniewski, J. (eds.) PPAM 2005. LNCS, vol. 3911, pp. 774–781. Springer, Heidelberg (2006). https://doi.org/10.1007/11752578_93
14. Tchernykh, A., Schwiegelshohn, U., Yahyapour, R., Kuzjurin, N.: On-line hierarchical job scheduling on grids with admissible allocation. J. Scheduling **13**(5), 545–552 (2010)
15. Turek, J., Wolf, J.L., Yu, P.S.: Approximate algorithms scheduling parallelizable tasks. In: Proceedings of the 4th (SPAA), pp. 323–332 (1992)
16. Ye, D., Han, X., Zhang, G.: Online multiple-strip packing. Theor. Comput. Sci. **412**(3), 233–239 (2011)
17. Zhuk, S.: Approximate algorithms to pack rectangles into several strips. Discrete Math. Appl. DMA **16**(1), 73–85 (2006)

Scheduling on Two Unbounded Resources with Communication Costs

Massinissa Ait Aba[1]($\boxtimes$), Alix Munier Kordon[2], and Guillaume Pallez (Aupy)[3]

[1] CEA, LIST, Computing and Design Environment Laboratory, Palaiseau, France
Massinissa.aitaba@cea.fr
[2] Sorbonne Université, CNRS-UMR 7606 LIP6, Paris, France
Alix.Munier@lip6.fr
[3] Inria, Labri & University of Bordeaux, Talence, France
guillaume.pallez@inria.fr

Abstract. Heterogeneous computing systems are popular and powerful platforms, containing several heterogeneous computing elements (e.g. CPU+GPU). In this work, we consider a platform with two types of machines, each containing an unbounded number of elements. We want to execute an application represented as a Directed Acyclic Graph (DAG) on this platform. Each task of the application has two possible execution times, depending on the type of machine it is executed on. In addition we consider a cost to transfer data from one platform to the other between successive tasks. We aim at minimizing the execution time of the DAG (also called makespan). We show that the problem is NP-complete for graphs of depth at least three but polynomial for graphs of depth at most two. In addition, we provide polynomial-time algorithms for some usual classes of graphs (trees, series-parallel graphs).

Keywords: Scheduling · DAG · Makespan · Heterogeneous platform

1 Introduction

In this work we revisit the work by Barthou and Jeannot [1]. We consider that we have two platforms, each with an unbounded number of processors. We want to execute an application represented as a Directed Acyclic Graph (DAG) using these two platforms. Each task of the application has two possible execution times, depending on the platform it is executed on. Finally, there is a cost to transfer data from one platform to another one between successive tasks.

In their work, Barthou and Jeannot [1] considered that each task could be executed on both platforms and were able to compute in polynomial time an optimal schedule. Here we study the problem where tasks cannot be re-executed. While this problem arises more from a theoretical understanding of the process, we can envision several directions linked to the usage of parallel machines where it could be useful, in High-Performance Computing or Cloud Computing.

In High-Performance Computing, one has to deal with simulations using millions of nodes. These simulations run on machines consisting often of either

© Springer Nature Switzerland AG 2019
R. Yahyapour (Ed.): Euro-Par 2019, LNCS 11725, pp. 117–128, 2019.
https://doi.org/10.1007/978-3-030-29400-7_9

homogeneous, or of two types of nodes (e.g. CPU+GPU)[1]. These simulations generates huge volume of data, saturating access to the Parallel File System. A recent technique to deal with this data is to analyze it *in-situ* [2], that is, while it is generated. This analysis can be done both on CPUs or GPUs, with a cost to move data around. It uses fewer nodes than the simulation by many orders of magnitude, and the only constraint is not to decelerate the main simulation. Hence one will allocate as many nodes as needed to these analysis (hence almost an unbounded number).

Another motivation in the context of Big-Data Analytics is the concept of Geo-Distributed Data-centers [3]. Information for each jobs is located in different data-centers, and the main cost is to move data-around. The number of nodes in each data-center is less an issue. Furthermore in Big-Data analytics, the data-dependencies of the graph are often linked to Map-Reduce-like applications (Hadoop, Spark etc), also called Bi-Partite Graph. This is a more general version of our problem where we have k instead of 2 unbounded resources.

Related Work: Recently, the problem of scheduling jobs on hybrid parallel platforms (k types of homogeneous machines) has attracted a lot of attention. Due to lack of space we focus on those work closest to us. More details are available in the companion report of this work [4].

The most commonly studied problem is the one when $k = 2$ (typically CPU/GPU platforms) with the objective of minimizing the makespan. The problem is in NP even when the number of each resource is bounded. In this case, several families of approximation algorithms have been studied, see for example Ait Aba et al. [5] for general graphs, or Kedad-Sidhoum et al. [6] and Marchal et al. [7] for independent tasks.

In the context of an unlimited number of processors, to limit the size of the description of the problem, one needs to consider a limited number of *performance profile* (computation/communication costs). Indeed otherwise if the size of the problem is not bounded, (almost) any algorithm is polynomial in the size of the instance. If there are no communication delays, the problem is trivial, where each task is simply assigned to the fastest machine. In the case where all processors have the same processing power and there is a cost for any communication the problem remains NP-complete. Darbha and Agrawal [8] provide an optimal solution TDS (Task Duplication based Scheduling) when the communications are not too large w.r.t the computation costs. Later, Park and Choe [9] extended this work when the communications are significantly larger than computations.

The closest to our work is the work of Barthou and Jeannot [1] who studied the problem of minimizing the makespan on two unbounded hybrid platform. They provide a $\Theta(4|E| + 2|V|)$ polynomial-time algorithm when duplication of jobs is allowed (namely, each job is executed on both platforms as soon as possible). They further discuss a possible extension of their work to the case where the number of processors of each type is limited by differentiating the allocation

---

[1] See for example the supercomputers at Argonne National Laboratory https://www. alcf.anl.gov/computing-resources (Accessed 09/2018).

part (using their algorithm) and the scheduling part. While the problem with duplication makes sense when the number of processors is unbounded to reduce the makespan, it may lead to other problems, such as additional energy consumption and significant memory footprint, hence motivating our study without duplication.

Finally, there is a wide range of heuristic solutions to the problem of CPU-GPU. They can be roughly partitioned in two classes: clustering algorithms and list-scheduling algorithms. Clustering algorithms [10] usually provide good solutions for communication-intensive graphs by scheduling heavily communicating tasks onto the same processor. List-scheduling heuristics such as HEFT [11] often have no performance guarantee with communication costs, but allow to handle a limited number of processors.

Results: Our main contributions are the following. We formalize the model in Sect. 2, and show that the problem is NP-complete for graphs of depth at least three but polynomial for graphs of depth at most two. We show that the problem cannot be approximated to a factor smaller than $3/2$ unless $\mathcal{P} = \mathcal{NP}$. Then, we provide polynomial-time algorithms for several classes of graphs. Those results are presented in Sect. 3. Finally, in Sect. 4, we provide concluding remarks and future directions.

2   Model

An application is represented by a Directed Acyclic Graph (DAG) $\mathcal{G} = (V, E)$, such that for all $(v_1, v_2) \in E$, v_2 cannot start its execution before the end of the execution of v_1. We consider a parallel platform of two types of machines: machines of type $\mathcal{A}$ and machines of type $\mathcal{B}$. For each type of machine we consider that there are an unbounded number of them.

We define two cost functions: $t_{\mathcal{A}} : V \to \mathbb{R}+$ (resp. $t_{\mathcal{B}} : V \to \mathbb{R}+$) that define the time to execute a task $v \in V$ on a machine of type $\mathcal{A}$ (resp. $\mathcal{B}$).

We also define two communication cost functions: $c_{\mathcal{AB}} : E \to \mathbb{R}+$ (resp. $c_{\mathcal{BA}} : E \to \mathbb{R}+$), such that for all $(v_1, v_2) \in E$, if v_1 is scheduled on a machine of type $\mathcal{A}$ (resp. $\mathcal{B}$) and v_2 is scheduled on a machine of type $\mathcal{B}$ (resp. $\mathcal{A}$), then v_2 needs to wait $c_{\mathcal{AB}}(v_1, v_2)$ (resp. $c_{\mathcal{BA}}(v_1, v_2)$) units of time after the end of the execution of v_1 to start its execution. We assume that there is no communication cost within a platform of a given type ($c_{\mathcal{AA}} = c_{\mathcal{BB}} = 0$).

The goal is to find a schedule of each task that minimizes the execution time (or makespan). Since there is an unbounded number of processors of each type, it corresponds to finding an allocation $\sigma : V \to \{\mathcal{A}, \mathcal{B}\}$ of all tasks on each type of processors. For an allocation σ and a path $p = v_1 \to v_2 \to \cdots \to v_p$ of $\mathcal{G}$, we define the length of the path

$$\mathtt{len}(p, \sigma) = t_{\sigma(v_1)}(v_1) + c_{\sigma(v_1)\sigma(v_2)}(v_1, v_2) + t_{\sigma(v_2)}(v_2) + \cdots + t_{\sigma(v_p)}(v_p).$$

The makespan is then obtained by computing the longest path of the graph $\mathcal{G}$ including the corresponding duration of the tasks and the computations costs: $MS(\mathcal{G}, \sigma) = \max_{p \in \{\text{paths of } \mathcal{G}\}} \mathtt{len}(p, \sigma)$.

3 Results

In this section, we start by showing that the problem is strongly NP-complete for graph of depth 3, before providing some algorithms for specific graphs.

3.1 Complexity

Theorem 1. *The problem of deciding whether an instance of our main problem has a schedule of length 2 is strongly NP-complete even for graphs of depth 3.*

We perform the reduction from the 3-SATISFIABILITY (3-SAT) problem which is known to be strongly NP-complete [12,13]: given $C_1, \cdots, C_m$ be a set of disjunctive clauses where each clause contains exactly three literals over $X = \{x_1, \cdots, x_n\}$ a set of boolean variables. Is there a truth assignment to X such that each clause is satisfied?

In the following, we write each clause $C_i = \tilde{x}_{i_1} \vee \tilde{x}_{i_2} \vee \tilde{x}_{i_3}$ where $(x_{i_1}, x_{i_2}, x_{i_3}) \in X^3$, and $\tilde{x}_k = x_k$ or $\bar{x}_k$. We are looking for a truth assignment such that $\bigwedge_{i=1}^{m} C_i$ is true.

Proof. From an instance $\mathcal{I}_1$ of 3-SAT: $C_1, \cdots, C_m$ over $\{x_1, \cdots, x_n\}$, we construct the following instance $\mathcal{I}_2$ for our problem.

For all $i \in \{1, \cdots, n\}$, we define 2 tasks v_i^0 and v_i^∞, and an edge (v_i^0, v_i^∞). Then for each clause $C_i = \tilde{x}_{i_1} \vee \tilde{x}_{i_2} \vee \tilde{x}_{i_3}$, 3 tasks $v_{i_1}^i, v_{i_2}^i, v_{i_3}^i$ are created and the following set of edges: $\{(v_{i_1}^i, v_{i_2}^i), (v_{i_2}^i, v_{i_3}^i), (v_{i_1}^i, v_{i_1}^\infty), (v_{i_2}^0, v_{i_2}^i), (v_{i_3}^0, v_{i_3}^i)\}$. For any $j \in \{1, \cdots, n\}$, $v_j^\star$ denotes the set of all the instanciations of x_j in $\mathcal{G}$.

Overall, the graph $\mathcal{G} = (V, E)$ of depth 3 has $2n + 3m$ vertices and $n + 5m$ edges.

We then define the execution and communication costs that can be written in unit size: $\forall j \in \{1, \cdots, n\}$, $t_{\mathcal{A}}(v_j^\infty) = t_{\mathcal{B}}(v_j^\infty) = t_{\mathcal{A}}(v_j^0) = t_{\mathcal{B}}(v_j^0) = 0$ and $c_{\mathcal{AB}}(v_j^0, v_j^\infty) = c_{\mathcal{BA}}(v_j^0, v_j^\infty) = 3$. For all edges $(v_j^i, v_j^\infty), (v_{j'}^{i'}, v_{j'}^{i'}) \in E$, we add the communication costs $c_{\mathcal{AB}}(v_j^i, v_j^\infty) = c_{\mathcal{BA}}(v_j^i, v_j^\infty) = c_{\mathcal{AB}}(v_{j'}^0, v_{j'}^{i'}) = c_{\mathcal{BA}}(v_{j'}^0, v_{j'}^{i'}) = 3$. Then for $C_i = \tilde{x}_{i_1} \vee \tilde{x}_{i_2} \vee \tilde{x}_{i_3}$ we define the time costs:

$$t_{\mathcal{A}}(v_{i_j}^i) = 1 - t_{\mathcal{B}}(v_{i_j}^i) = \begin{cases} 1 & \text{if } \tilde{x}_{i_j} = \bar{x}_{i_j} \\ 0 & \text{if } \tilde{x}_{i_j} = x_{i_j} \end{cases} \tag{1}$$

and we set $c_{\mathcal{AB}}(v_{i_1}^i, v_{i_2}^i) = c_{\mathcal{BA}}(v_{i_1}^i, v_{i_2}^i) = c_{\mathcal{AB}}(v_{i_2}^i, v_{i_3}^i) = c_{\mathcal{BA}}(v_{i_2}^i, v_{i_3}^i) = 0$.

Finally, in the instance $\mathcal{I}_2$, we want to study whether there exists a schedule σ whose makespan is not greater than 2.

We show an example in Fig. 1 of the construction of the graph. Here, the clause $C_1 = x_1 \vee \bar{x}_4 \vee x_2$ is associated with the vertices v_1^1, v_4^1 and v_2^1 and the arcs set $\{(v_1^1, v_4^1), (v_4^1, v_2^1), (v_1^1, v_1^\infty), (v_4^0, v_4^1), (v_2^0, v_2^1)\}$. Moreover, $t_{\mathcal{A}}(v_1^1) = t_{\mathcal{A}}(v_2^1) = 0$, $t_{\mathcal{A}}(v_4^1) = 1$, $t_{\mathcal{B}}(v_1^1) = t_{\mathcal{B}}(v_2^1) = 1$ and $t_{\mathcal{B}}(v_4^1) = 0$. Note that $v_1^\star = \{v_1^0, v_1^\infty, v_1^1, v_1^2, v_1^3\}$, $v_2^\star = \{v_2^0, v_2^\infty, v_2^1, v_2^3\}$, $v_3^\star = \{v_3^0, v_3^\infty, v_3^2, v_3^3\}$ and $v_4^\star = \{v_4^0, v_4^\infty, v_4^1, v_4^2\}$.

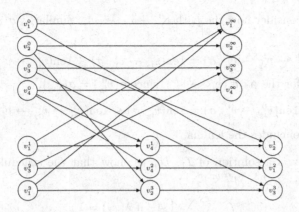

Fig. 1. Transformation of $(x_1 \vee \bar{x}_4 \vee x_2) \bigwedge (\bar{x}_3 \vee \bar{x}_4 \vee x_1) \bigwedge (x_1 \vee x_2 \vee x_3)$ ($m = 3$ clauses, $n = 4$ variables) into the associated graph $\mathcal{G} = (V, E)$.

Let S be the set of schedules such that, $\forall \sigma \in S$, all tasks from $v_j^\star$ are scheduled by the same type of machines, *i.e*, for any couple $(v_j^\alpha, v_j^\beta) \in v_j^\star \times v_j^\star$, $\sigma(v_j^\alpha) = \sigma(v_j^\beta)$. The next lemmas provide dominance properties on feasible schedules of $\mathcal{I}_2$:

Lemma 1. *Any feasible solution σ of $\mathcal{I}_2$ belongs to S.*

Proof. Let us suppose by contradiction that a feasible solution $\sigma \notin S$. Two cases must then be considered:

- If there exists $j \in \{1, \cdots, n\}$ with $\sigma(v_j^0) \neq \sigma(v_j^\infty)$, then there is a communication delay of 3 between them and $\text{len}(v_j^0 \to v_j^1, \sigma) = 3$.
- Otherwise, $\forall j \in \{1, \cdots, n\}, \sigma(v_j^0) = \sigma(v_j^\infty)$. Thus, there exists a task v_j^i with $\sigma(v_j^i) \neq \sigma(v_j^0)$. If v_j^i is associated to the first term of the clause C_i, then $(v_j^0, v_j^i) \in E$ and $\text{len}(v_j^0 \to v_j^i, \sigma) = 3$. Otherwise, $(v_j^i, v_j^\infty) \in E$ and $\text{len}(v_j^i \to v_j^\infty, \sigma) = 3$.

The makespan of σ is at least 3 in both cases, the contradiction.

Lemma 2. *For any schedule $\sigma \in S$, $MS(\mathcal{G}, \sigma) = \max_{i \in \{1, \cdots, m\}} \text{len}(v_{i_1}^i \to v_{i_2}^i \to v_{i_3}^i, \sigma)$.*

Proof. To do this, we study the length of paths of $\mathcal{G}$.

- Let $j \in \{1, \cdots, n\}$, $\text{len}(v_j^0 \to v_j^\infty, \sigma) = 0$ since $\sigma(v_j^0) = \sigma(v_j^\infty)$.
- Let $i \in \{1, \cdots, m\}$ associated with the clause $C_i = \tilde{x}_{i_1} \vee \tilde{x}_{i_2} \vee \tilde{x}_{i_3}$:

  1. Let us consider first the path $v_{i_1}^i \to v_{i_1}^\infty$. By Lemma 1, $\sigma(v_{i_1}^i) = \sigma(v_{i_1}^\infty)$ and thus $c_{\sigma(v_{i_1}^i)\sigma(v_{i_1}^\infty)}(v_{i_1}^i, v_{i_1}^\infty) = 0$. Since $\text{len}(v_{i_1}^\infty, \sigma) = 0$,

$$\text{len}(v_{i_1}^i \to v_{i_1}^\infty, \sigma) = \text{len}(v_{i_1}^i, \sigma) \leq \text{len}(v_{i_1}^i \to v_{i_2}^i \to v_{i_3}^i, \sigma).$$

2. Let us consider now the path $v_{i_2}^0 \to v_{i_2}^i \to v_{i_3}^i$. Similarly, $\sigma(v_{i_2}^0) = \sigma(v_{i_2}^i)$ hence

$$\mathrm{len}(v_{i_2}^0 \to v_{i_2}^i \to v_{i_3}^i, \sigma) = \mathrm{len}(v_{i_2}^i \to v_{i_3}^i, \sigma) \leq \mathrm{len}(v_{i_1}^i \to v_{i_2}^i \to v_{i_3}^i, \sigma).$$

3. Lastly, for the path $(v_{i_3}^0 \to v_{i_3}^i)$, since $\sigma(v_{i_3}^0) = \sigma(v_{i_3}^i)$,

$$\mathrm{len}(v_{i_3}^0 \to v_{i_3}^i, \sigma) = \mathrm{len}(v_{i_3}^i, \sigma) \leq \mathrm{len}(v_{i_1}^i \to v_{i_2}^i \to v_{i_3}^i, \sigma),$$

which concludes the lemma.

Assume that λ is a solution of $\mathcal{I}_1$, Let us show that the schedule defined as follow, $\forall j \in \{1, \cdots, n\}$, $\forall v_j^\alpha \in v_j^\star$,

$$\sigma_\lambda : v_j^\alpha \mapsto \begin{cases} \mathcal{A} & \text{if } \lambda(x_j) = 1 \\ \mathcal{B} & \text{if } \lambda(x_j) = 0 \end{cases}$$

has a makespan not greater than 2 and thus is a solution. Following Lemma 2, we must prove that $\forall i \in \{1, \cdots, n\}$, $\mathrm{len}(v_{i_1}^i \to v_{i_2}^i \to v_{i_3}^i, \sigma_\lambda) \leq 2$.

For any clause $C_i = \tilde{x}_{i_1} \vee \tilde{x}_{i_2} \vee \tilde{x}_{i_3}$, since $\lambda(C_i) = 1$, there exists $j \in \{1, 2, 3\}$ such that $\lambda(\tilde{x}_{i_j}) = 1$. Two cases must be considered:

1. If $\tilde{x}_{i_j} = x_{i_j}$, then by definition $t_\mathcal{A}(v_{i_j}^i) = 0$. Since $\lambda(x_{i_j}) = 1$, $\sigma_\lambda(v_{i_j}^i) = \mathcal{A}$ and thus $\mathrm{len}(v_{i_j}^i, \sigma_\lambda) = t_\mathcal{A}(v_{i_j}^i) = 0$.
2. Otherwise, $\tilde{x}_{i_j} = \bar{x}_{i_j}$ and $t_\mathcal{B}(v_{i_j}^i) = 0$. Now, as $\lambda(x_{i_j}) = 0$, $\sigma_\lambda(v_{i_j}^i) = \mathcal{B}$ and thus $\mathrm{len}(v_{i_j}^i, \sigma_\lambda) = t_\mathcal{B}(v_{i_j}^i) = 0$.

$\mathrm{len}(v_{i_j}^i, \sigma_\lambda) = 0$ in both cases, so $\mathrm{len}(v_{i_1}^i \to v_{i_2}^i \to v_{i_3}^i, \sigma_\lambda) \leq 2$.

Assume now that we have a solution σ of $\mathcal{I}_2$, let us show that $\lambda_\sigma(x_j) = [\sigma(v_j^\infty) = \mathcal{A}]$ is a solution to $\mathcal{I}_1$.

Following Lemma 1, $\sigma \in \mathcal{S}$. Moreover, for any clause $C_i = \tilde{x}_{i_1} \vee \tilde{x}_{i_2} \vee \tilde{x}_{i_3}$, the corresponding path of $\mathcal{G}$ verifies $\mathrm{len}(v_{i_1}^i \to v_{i_2}^i \to v_{i_3}^i, \sigma) \leq 2$. Thus, there is $j \in \{1, 2, 3\}$ with $\mathrm{len}(v_{i_j}^i, \sigma) = 0$. Two cases must be considered:

1. If $\tilde{x}_{i_j} = x_{i_j}$ then by definition $t_\mathcal{A}(v_{i_j}^i) = 0$ and $t_\mathcal{B}(v_{i_j}^i) = 1$. So, $\sigma(v_{i_j}^i) = \mathcal{A}$ and thus $\lambda_\sigma(x_{i_j}) = 1$.
2. Else, $\tilde{x}_{i_j} = \bar{x}_{i_j}$ and thus $t_\mathcal{A}(v_{i_j}^i) = 1$ and $t_\mathcal{B}(v_{i_j}^i) = 0$. So, $\sigma(v_{i_j}^i) = \mathcal{B}$ and thus $\lambda_\sigma(\bar{x}_{i_j}) = 1$.

So, at least one term of C_i is true following λ_σ, λ_σ is then a solution to $\mathcal{I}_1$.

This concludes the proof that the problem is strongly NP-complete.

Corollary 1. *There is no polynomial-time algorithm for the problem with a performance bound smaller than $\frac{3}{2}$ unless $\mathcal{P} = \mathcal{NP}$.*

Proof. By contradiction, let us suppose that there exists a polynomial-time algorithm with a performance ratio $\rho < \frac{3}{2}$. This algorithm can be used to decide the existence of a schedule a length at most 2 for any instance $\mathcal{I}$. We deduce that there exists a polynomial time algorithm to decide the existence of a schedule of length strictly less than 3, which contradicts Theorem 1.

3.2   Polynomial Algorithms

Bi-partite Graphs. We have shown that the problem is NP-hard if the graph
has depth 3. The natural question that arises is whether it is already NP-hard
for graphs of lower depth. We show that it can be solved in polynomial time for
graphs of depth 2 (bipartite graphs).

Theorem 2. BIPARTALGO($\mathcal{G}$) *described below provides an optimal solution in
polynomial time with a complexity of $\Theta(n|E|)$ when $\mathcal{G}$ has depth 2.*

Observe that in the case of a bipartite graph $\mathcal{G} = (V, E)$, the paths are
exactly the edges of $\mathcal{G}$. The intuition of the algorithm is then to compute first
the makespan of all possible allocations for all edges, and then to remove pairs
associated to forbidden allocations.

For any edge $(i, j) \in E$, 4 allocations are possible: $(\sigma(i), \sigma(j)) \in \{\mathcal{A}, \mathcal{B}\}^2 =
\{(\mathcal{A}, \mathcal{A}), (\mathcal{A}, \mathcal{B}), (\mathcal{B}, \mathcal{A}), (\mathcal{B}, \mathcal{B})\}$. We define the set of quintuplet of all these allo-
cations:

$$\texttt{WgPaths} = \Big\{(\texttt{len}(i \to j, \sigma), i, j, \sigma_i, \sigma_j)\big|$$
$$(i, j) \in V, (\sigma(i), \sigma(j)) \in \{\mathcal{A}, \mathcal{B}\}^2, \sigma(i) = \sigma_i, \sigma(j) = \sigma_j\Big\}.$$

This set can be constructed in linear time by a simple iteration through all the
edges of the graph by a procedure that we call MKWGPATHS(V, E).

Finally to minimize the makespan, we iteratively remove from `WgPaths` the
allocations that would maximize the makespan and check that there still exists
a possible schedule.

Algorithm 1. Polynomial algorithm for $\mathcal{G} = (V, E)$ a bipartite graph

---

1: **procedure** BIPARTALGO($\mathcal{G}$)
2:    WgPaths $\leftarrow$ MKWGPATHS($\mathcal{G}$)
3:    $P_{\text{alg}} \leftarrow True; P_{\text{tmp}} \leftarrow True$ /* Two clauses with n variables */

4:    **for** $(t_{\sigma_i \sigma_j}, i, j, \sigma_i, \sigma_j) \in$ WgPaths, by decreasing value of $t_{\sigma_i \sigma_j}$ **do**
5:       $P_{\text{tmp}} \leftarrow P_{\text{alg}} \wedge \big((\sigma(i) \neq \sigma_i) \vee (\sigma(j) \neq \sigma_j)\big)$
6:       **if** P_{tmp} is not satisfiable **then** Break **end if**
7:       $P_{\text{alg}} \leftarrow P_{\text{tmp}}$
8:    **end for**
9:    $\sigma(1), \cdots, \sigma(n) \leftarrow \text{Solve}(P_{\text{alg}})$ /* Using a 2-SAT solver*/

10: **end procedure**

In the rest, we use the following notation for a schedule σ and a time D:

$$\text{WP}(D) = \big\{(i, j, \sigma_i, \sigma_j) \text{ s.t. } (t_{\sigma_i \sigma_j}, i, j, \sigma_i, \sigma_j) \in \texttt{WgPaths} \quad \text{and } t_{\sigma_i \sigma_j} > D\big\}$$
$$P_D(\sigma) = \bigwedge_{(i,j,\sigma_i,\sigma_j) \in \text{WP}(D)} [(\sigma(i) \neq \sigma_i) \vee (\sigma(j) \neq \sigma_j)]$$

Intuitively, $\text{WP}(D)$ is the set of paths and allocations of length greater than D.

Lemma 3. *Let σ be a schedule of makespan D, then $P_D(\sigma)$ is satisfied.*

This result is a direct consequence of the fact that there should be no path of length greater than D. Hence for $(i, j, \sigma_i, \sigma_j) \in \mathrm{WP}(D)$, we know that we do not have simultaneously in the schedule $(\sigma(i) = \sigma_i)$ and $(\sigma(j) = \sigma_j)$. Hence,

$$\neg \bigvee_{(i,j,\sigma_i,\sigma_j)\in \mathrm{WP}(D)} [(\sigma(i) = \sigma_i) \wedge (\sigma(j) = \sigma_j)]$$

$$= \bigwedge_{(i,j,\sigma_i,\sigma_j)\in \mathrm{WP}(D)} [(\sigma(i) \neq \sigma_i) \vee (\sigma(j) \neq \sigma_j)] = P_D(\sigma) \quad (2)$$

Proof. (Proof of Theorem 2). Consider an instance $\mathcal{G}$ of the problem. Let D_{alg} be the deadline of the schedule returned by $\mathrm{BIPARTALGO}(\mathcal{G})$. Clearly, $D_{\mathrm{alg}} = \max_{(i,j)\in E}(t_{\sigma(i)}(i) + c_{\sigma(i)\sigma(j)}(i, j) + t_{\sigma(j)}(j))$. Let P_{alg} be the set of clauses computed by it (line 9). Let $W_{\mathrm{alg}} = \{(i, j, \sigma_i, \sigma_j) | (t_{\sigma_i \sigma_j}, i, j, \sigma_i, \sigma_j) \in \mathtt{WgPaths}\}$ s.t. $P_{\mathrm{alg}} = \bigwedge_{(i,j,\sigma_i,\sigma_j)\in W_{\mathrm{alg}}} [(\sigma(i) \neq \sigma_i) \vee (\sigma(j) \neq \sigma_j)]$. Then by construction of P_{alg}, we have the following properties:

1. For all $\varepsilon > 0$, $\mathrm{WP}(D_{\mathrm{alg}}) \subset W_{\mathrm{alg}} \subset \mathrm{WP}(D_{\mathrm{alg}-\varepsilon})$, because we add paths by decreasing value of makespan (line 4).
2. There exists $(D_{\mathrm{alg}}, i_0, j_0, \sigma_{i_0}, \sigma_{j_0}) \in \mathtt{WgPaths}$ such that P_{alg} is satisfiable and $P_{\mathrm{alg}} \wedge [(\sigma(i_0) \neq \sigma_{i_0}) \vee (\sigma(j_0) \neq \sigma_{j_0})]$ is not satisfiable. This is the stopping condition on line 6.

We show the optimality of Algorithm 1 by contradiction. If it is not optimal, then $D_{\mathrm{opt}} < D_{\mathrm{alg}}$, and $W_{\mathrm{alg}} \cup (i_0, j_0, \sigma_{i_0}, \sigma_{j_0}) \subset \mathrm{WP}(D_{\mathrm{opt}})$. Furthermore, according to Lemma 3, $P_{D_{\mathrm{opt}}}(\sigma_{\mathrm{opt}})$ is satisfied, hence σ_{opt} is also a solution to $P_{\mathrm{alg}} \wedge [(\sigma(i_0) \neq \sigma_{i_0}) \vee (\sigma(j_0) \neq \sigma_{j_0})]$. This contradicts the fact that it does not admit a solution hence contradicting the non-optimality.

Finally, the complexity of $\mathrm{MKWGPATHS}(V, E)$ is $\Theta(|E|)$. In Algorithm 1, we unwind the loop for (line 4) $4|E|$ times, and we verify if P_{tmp} is satisfiable in line 6 with a complexity of $\Theta(n + k)$ where k is the number of clauses is P_{tmp}. Since the number of iterations is bounded by $3|E|$, the complexity of Algorithm 1 is $\mathcal{O}(|E|^2)$.

Out-Tree Graphs. We assume now that the DAG $\mathcal{G} = (V, E)$ is an out-tree rooted by $r \in V$. For any task $u \in V$, the sub-tree rooted by u is the sub-graph $\mathcal{G}_u$ of $\mathcal{G}$ which vertices are u and the descendants of u.

For any task $u \in V$, let us denote by $D^{\mathcal{A}}(u)$ (resp. $D^{\mathcal{B}}(u)$) the lower bound of the minimal makespan of $\mathcal{G}_u$ assuming that $\sigma(u) = \mathcal{A}$ (resp. $\sigma(u) = \mathcal{B}$). Let us suppose that the arc $(u, v) \in E$. Observe that, if $D^{\mathcal{A}}(v) \leq c_{\mathcal{A}\mathcal{B}}(u, v) + D^{\mathcal{B}}(v)$, then $D^{\mathcal{A}}(u) \geq t_{\mathcal{A}}(u) + D^{\mathcal{A}}(v)$. In the opposite, $D^{\mathcal{A}}(u) \geq t_{\mathcal{A}}(u) + c_{\mathcal{A}\mathcal{B}}(u, v) + D^{\mathcal{B}}(v)$ and thus $D^{\mathcal{A}}(u) \geq t_{\mathcal{A}}(u) + \min(D^{\mathcal{A}}(v), c_{\mathcal{A}\mathcal{B}}(u, v) + D^{\mathcal{B}}(v))$. Similarly, $D^{\mathcal{B}}(u) \geq t_{\mathcal{B}}(u) + \min(D^{\mathcal{B}}(v), c_{\mathcal{B}\mathcal{A}}(u, v) + D^{\mathcal{A}}(v))$.

For any task $u \in V$, we set $\Gamma^+(u) = \{v \in V, (u, v) \in E\}$. For any allocation function σ, let $\bar{\sigma}(u) = \mathcal{A}$ if $\sigma(u) = \mathcal{B}$, $\bar{\sigma}(u) = \mathcal{B}$ otherwise. Then, for any task $u \in V$, we get $D^{\sigma(u)}(u) = t_{\sigma(u)}(u) + \max_{v\in\Gamma^+(u)} \min(D^{\sigma(u)}(v), c_{\sigma(u)\bar{\sigma}(u)} + D^{\bar{\sigma}(u)}(v))$.

Theorem 3. *For an out-tree graph $\mathcal{G} = (V, E)$ rooted by $r \in V$, an allocation σ may be built such that the corresponding schedule of length $D(r)$ verifies $D(r) = \min(D^{\mathcal{A}}(r), D^{\mathcal{B}}(r))$ and thus is optimal.*

Proof. Let us suppose that lower bounds $D^{\mathcal{A}}(u)$ and $D^{\mathcal{B}}(u)$ for $u \in V$ are given. Let us define the allocation σ as $\sigma(r) = \mathcal{A}$ if $D^{\mathcal{A}}(r) \le D^{\mathcal{B}}(r)$ and $\sigma(r) = \mathcal{B}$ in the opposite. For any task $v \ne r$ with $(u, v) \in E$, we set $\sigma(v) = \sigma(u)$ if $D^{\sigma(u)}(v) < D^{\bar{\sigma}(u)}(v) + c_{\sigma(u)\bar{\sigma}(u)}(u, v)$, and $\sigma(v) = \bar{\sigma}(u)$ otherwise.

For any task u, we prove that the length $D(u)$ of the schedule of $\mathcal{G}_u$ for the allocation σ verifies $D(u) = D^{\sigma(u)}(u)$. If u is a leaf, $D(u) = t_{\sigma(u)}(u) = D^{\sigma(u)}(u)$.

Now, let suppose that $\Gamma^+(u) \ne \emptyset$. By definition, for any arc $(u, v) \in E$, if $\sigma(u) = \sigma(v)$, $c_{\sigma(u)\sigma(v)}(u, v) = 0$. Then, if we set $\Delta^{\sigma}(u, v) = D(v) + c_{\sigma(u)\sigma(v)}(u, v)$, we get by induction $\Delta^{\sigma}(u, v) = D^{\sigma(v)}(v) + c_{\sigma(u)\sigma(v)}(u, v)$ and by definition of σ, $\Delta^{\sigma}(u, v) = \min(D^{\sigma(u)}(v), D^{\bar{\sigma}(u)}(v) + c_{\sigma(u)\bar{\sigma}(u)}(u, v))$. Now, $D(u) = t_{\sigma(u)}(u) + \max_{v \in \Gamma^+(u)} \Delta^{\sigma}(u, v)$ and thus by definition of $D^{\sigma(u)}$, $D(u) = D^{\sigma(u)}$, which concludes the proof.

A polynomial time algorithm of time complexity $\Theta(n)$ can be deduced by computing first $D^{\mathcal{A}}$, $D^{\mathcal{B}}$ and then σ.

Example 1. Let us consider as example the out-tree pictured by Fig. 2. Figure 3 shows the lower bound $D^{\mathcal{A}}$ and $D^{\mathcal{B}}$ and a corresponding optimal schedule.

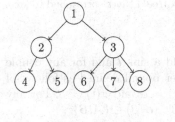

$v \in V$	$t_{\mathcal{A}}(v)$	$t_{\mathcal{B}}(v)$
1	2	3
2	3	2
3	4	2
4	5	2
5	3	3
6	5	1
7	2	5
8	3	1

$a \in E$	$c_{\mathcal{AB}}(a)$	$c_{\mathcal{BA}}(a)$
$(3, 8)$	2	3
$(3, 7)$	3	3
$(3, 6)$	3	4
$(2, 4)$	2	2
$(2, 5)$	3	2
$(1, 2)$	1	4
$(1, 3)$	4	3

Fig. 2. An out-tree $\mathcal{G}$, duration of tasks and communication costs.

Series-Parallel Graphs. Let us consider a two terminal Series Parallel digraph (2SP in short) as defined in [14,15]. Each element of this class has a unique source s and a unique sink t with $s \ne t$. It is formally defined as follows where $\mathcal{G}$ and $\mathcal{H}$ are two 2SP graphs.

- The arc $(s, t) \in 2SP$;
- The series composition of $\mathcal{G}$ and $\mathcal{H}$ is denoted by $\mathcal{G}.\mathcal{H}$ and is built by identifying the sink of $\mathcal{G}$ with the source of $\mathcal{H}$;
- The parallel composition is denoted by $\mathcal{G} + \mathcal{H}$ and identifies respectively the sinks and the sources of the two digraphs.

Figure 4 pictures a 2SP graph and its associated decomposition tree.

$v \in V$	$D^{\mathcal{A}}(u)$	$D^{\mathcal{B}}(u)$
1	10	10
2	7	5
3	8	7
4	5	2
5	3	3
6	5	1
7	2	5
8	3	1

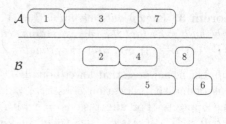

Fig. 3. Lower bounds $D^{\mathcal{A}}$ and $D^{\mathcal{B}}$. An optimal schedule is presented for the allocation $\sigma(1) = \mathcal{A}$, $\sigma(2) = \mathcal{B}$, $\sigma(3) = \mathcal{A}$, $\sigma(4) = \mathcal{B}$, $\sigma(5) = \mathcal{B}$, $\sigma(6) = \mathcal{B}$, $\sigma(7) = \mathcal{A}$ and $\sigma(8) = \mathcal{B}$.

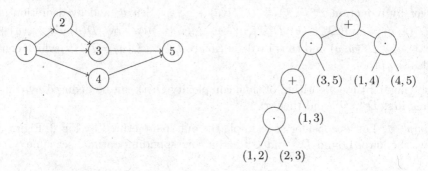

Fig. 4. A $2SP$ graph and its associated decomposition tree. Leaves correspond to arcs, while internal nodes are series or parallel compositions.

For any element $\mathcal{G} \in 2SP$ with a source s and a sink t and for any couple $(\alpha, \beta) \in \{\mathcal{A}, \mathcal{B}\}^2$, let us denote by $D^{\alpha\beta}(\mathcal{G})$ a lower bound defined as follows of the minimum length of a schedule of $\mathcal{G}$ with $\sigma(s) = \alpha$ and $\sigma(t) = \beta$. For any graph $\mathcal{G}$ with a unique arc $e = (s, t)$, for any couple $(\alpha, \beta) \in \{\mathcal{A}, \mathcal{B}\}^2$,

$$D^{\alpha\beta}(\mathcal{G}) = \begin{cases} t_\alpha(s) + t_\beta(t) + c_{\alpha\beta}(s, t) & \text{if } \alpha \neq \beta \\ t_\alpha(s) + t_\beta(t) & \text{otherwise.} \end{cases}$$

Now, if $\mathcal{G}$ and $\mathcal{H}$ are two $2SP$, then for the series composition, we set $D^{\alpha\beta}(\mathcal{G}.\mathcal{H}) = \min_{\gamma \in \{\mathcal{A}, \mathcal{B}\}}(D^{\alpha\gamma}(\mathcal{G}) + D^{\gamma\beta}(\mathcal{H}) - t_\gamma(t))$ where t is the sink of $\mathcal{G}$. Similarly, for the parallel composition, we set $D^{\alpha\beta}(\mathcal{G} + \mathcal{H}) = \max(D^{\alpha\beta}(\mathcal{G}), D^{\alpha\beta}(\mathcal{H}))$.

We define the allocation function σ associated with a $2SP$ graph $\mathcal{G}$ and the corresponding length $D(\mathcal{G})$ as follows. We set $D(\mathcal{G}) = \min_{(\alpha, \beta) \in \{\mathcal{A}, \mathcal{B}\}^2}(D^{\alpha\beta}(\mathcal{G}))$. We also set $\sigma(s)$ and $\sigma(t)$ the allocation function of the source and the sink of $\mathcal{G}$ as $D(\mathcal{G}) = D^{\sigma(s)\sigma(t)}(\mathcal{G})$. Now, for any series composition, let us suppose that s and t (resp. s' and t') are the source and the sink of $\mathcal{G}$ (resp. $\mathcal{H}$). We also suppose that $\sigma(s)$ and $\sigma(t')$ are fixed. Then, for $\mathcal{G}.\mathcal{H}$, $t = s'$ and we get $\sigma(t) = \gamma \in \{\mathcal{A}, \mathcal{B}\}$ such that $D(\mathcal{G}.\mathcal{H}) = D^{\sigma(s)\sigma(t)}(\mathcal{G}) + D^{\sigma(s')\sigma(t')}(\mathcal{H}) - t_{\sigma(t)}(t)$.

If $\mathcal{G}$ is a $2SP$ graph of source s and sink t, any vertex $v \in V - \{s, t\}$ is involved in a series composition, and thus σ is completely defined.

Theorem 4. *For any* $2SP$ *graph* $\mathcal{G}$ *of source* s *and sink* t, $D(\mathcal{G}) = D^{\sigma(s)\sigma(t)}(\mathcal{G})$.

Proof. The equality is clearly true if $\mathcal{G}$ is an arc (s,t). Indeed, we get in this case $D(\mathcal{G}) = \min_{(\alpha,\beta)\in\{A,B\}^2}(D^{\alpha\beta}(\mathcal{G})) = D^{\sigma(s)\sigma(t)}(\mathcal{G})$.

Now, let us suppose that s and t (resp. s' and t') are the source and the sink of $\mathcal{G}$ (resp. $\mathcal{H}$) and that $D(\mathcal{G}) = D^{\sigma(s)\sigma(t)}(\mathcal{G})$ and $D(\mathcal{H}) = D^{\sigma(s')\sigma(t')}(\mathcal{H})$. For a parallel composition, $D(\mathcal{G} + \mathcal{H}) = \max(D^{\sigma(s)\sigma(t)}(\mathcal{G}), D^{\sigma(s')\sigma(t')}(\mathcal{H})) = D^{\sigma(s)\sigma(t)}(\mathcal{G} + \mathcal{H})$ as $s = s'$ and $t = t'$.

For the series composition, $D(\mathcal{G}.\mathcal{H}) = D(\mathcal{G}) + D(\mathcal{H}) - t_{\sigma(t)}(t) = D^{\sigma(s)\sigma(t)}(\mathcal{G}.\mathcal{H})$, since $t = s'$, which concludes the proof.

Corollary 2. *A polynomial-time algorithm of time complexity* $\Theta(|E|)$ *can be deduced by computing lower bounds* $D^{\alpha\beta}$, $(\alpha, \beta) \in \{A, B\}^2$ *for each graph issued from the decomposition of* G *and a corresponding allocation* σ.

4   Future Directions

With this work we have studied the problem of scheduling a Directed Acyclic Graph on an unbounded hybrid platform. Specifically our platform consists of two machines, each with an unbounded number of resources. Moving data from one machine to the other one has a communication cost. We have shown the intractability of the problem by reducing this problem to the 3-satisfiability problem. We have shown that there does not exist 3/2-approximation algorithms unless P=NP. We have further provided some polynomial time algorithms for special cases of graphs. While this model seems very theoretical, we can see several applications both in High-Performance Computing (*In-Situ analysis*) and in Big Data analytics in the cloud (Geo-distributed data-Centers).

There are several extensions that we can see to this work. In the context of two unbounded platforms, it would be interesting to find some polynomial time algorithms with proven bounds to the optimal. We do not expect to be able to find one in the general case, but we hope that with some constraints between the communication costs and computation cost (as is often done in the context of scheduling DAGs with communications), one may able to find such algorithms. We plan then to evaluate these algorithms with *In-Situ* frameworks. Finally, another direction we are interested by is a version of this problem where only one machine has an unbounded number of resources, and where the data is located on the other one. For example in the context of smartphone applications, we can model the frontend/backend context where the phone (Machine 1) has a limited number of available processors, but can rely on sending some of the computation on a backend machine (cloud-based), with an unbounded number of processors. Similarly to here, the problem is a data and communication problem: given the cost to transfer data from one machine to the other one, what is the most efficient strategy.

References

1. Barthou, D., Jeannot, E.: SPAGHETtI: scheduling/placement approach for task-graphs on HETerogeneous archItecture. In: Silva, F., Dutra, I., Santos Costa, V. (eds.) Euro-Par 2014. LNCS, vol. 8632, pp. 174–185. Springer, Cham (2014). https://doi.org/10.1007/978-3-319-09873-9_15
2. Dorier, M., Dreher, M., Peterka, T., Wozniak, J.M., Antoniu, G., Raffin, B.: Lessons learned from building in situ coupling frameworks. In: Proceedings of the First Workshop on In Situ Infrastructures for Enabling Extreme-Scale Analysis and Visualization, pp. 19–24. ACM (2015)
3. Zhou, A.C., Ibrahim, S., He, B.: On achieving efficient data transfer for graph processing in geo-distributed datacenters. In: 2017 IEEE 37th International Conference on Distributed Computing Systems (ICDCS), pp. 1397–1407 (2017)
4. Ait Aba, M., Aupy, G., Munier-Kordon, A.: Scheduling on two unbounded resources with communication costs. Inria, Research Report RR-9264, Mar 2019. https://hal.inria.fr/hal-02076473
5. Ait Aba, M., Zaourar, L., Munier, A.: Approximation algorithm for scheduling applications on hybrid multi-core machines with communications delays. In: IPDPSW. IEEE (2018)
6. Kedad-Sidhoum, S., Monna, F., Mounié, G., Trystram, D.: A family of scheduling algorithms for hybrid parallel platforms. Int. J. Found. Comput. Sci. 29(01), 63–90 (2018)
7. Marchal, L., Canon, L.-C., Vivien, F.: Low-cost approximation algorithms for scheduling independent tasks on hybrid platforms. Ph.D. dissertation, Inria-Research Centre Grenoble-Rhône-Alpes (2017)
8. Darbha, S., Agrawal, D.P.: Optimal scheduling algorithm for distributed-memory machines. IEEE Trans. Parallel Distrib. Syst. 9(1), 87–95 (1998)
9. Park, C.-I., Choe, T.-Y.: An optimal scheduling algorithm based on task duplication. In: 2001 Proceedings, Eighth International Conference on Parallel and Distributed Systems, ICPADS 2001, pp. 9–14. IEEE (2001)
10. Boeres, C., Rebello, V.E., et al.: A cluster-based strategy for scheduling task on heterogeneous processors. In: 2004 16th Symposium on Computer Architecture and High Performance Computing, SBAC-PAD 2004, pp. 214–221. IEEE (2004)
11. Topcuoglu, H., Hariri, S., Wu, M.-Y.: Performance-effective and low-complexity task scheduling for heterogeneous computing. IEEE Trans. Parallel Distrib. Syst. 13(3), 260–274 (2002)
12. Garey, M.R., Johnson, D.S.: Complexity results for multiprocessor scheduling under resource constraints. SIAM J. Comput. 4(4), 397–411 (1975)
13. Karp, R.M.: Reducibility among combinatorial problems. Complexity of Computer Computations, pp. 85–103. Springer, Boston (1972). https://doi.org/10.1007/978-1-4684-2001-2_9
14. Valdes, J., Tarjan, R., Lawler, E.: The recognition of series parallel digraphs. SIAM J. Comput. 11(2), 298–313 (1982). https://doi.org/10.1137/0211023
15. Schoenmakers, B.: A new algorithm for the recognition of series parallel graphs, series, CWI report. CS-R, CWI (1995)

Improving Fairness in a Large Scale HTC System Through Workload Analysis and Simulation

Frédéric Azevedo[1], Dalibor Klusáček[2(✉)], and Frédéric Suter[1]

[1] IN2P3 Computing Center / CNRS,
Lyon-Villeurbanne, France
{frederic.azevedo,frederic.suter}@cc.in2p3.fr
[2] CESNET a.l.e., Prague, Czech Republic
klusacek@cesnet.cz

Abstract. Monitoring and analyzing the execution of a workload is at the core of the operation of data centers. It allows operators to verify that the operational objectives are satisfied or detect and react to any unexpected and unwanted behavior. However, the scale and complexity of large workloads composed of millions of jobs executed each month on several thousands of cores, often limit the depth of such an analysis. This may lead to overlook some phenomena that, while not harmful at a global scale, can be detrimental to a specific class of users.

In this paper, we illustrate such a situation by analyzing a large High Throughput Computing (HTC) workload trace coming from one of the largest academic computing centers in France. The *Fair-Share* algorithm at the core of the batch scheduler ensures that all user groups are fairly provided with an amount of computing resources commensurate to their expressed needs. However, a deeper analysis of the produced schedule, especially of the job waiting times, shows a certain degree of unfairness between user groups. We identify the configuration of the quotas and scheduling queues as the main root causes of this unfairness. We thus propose a drastic reconfiguration of the system that aims at being more suited to the characteristics of the workload and at better balancing the waiting time among user groups. We evaluate the impact of this reconfiguration through detailed simulations. The obtained results show that it still satisfies the main operational objectives while significantly improving the quality of service experienced by formerly unfavored users.

1 Introduction

The analysis of workload traces is a common approach to understand and optimize the behavior of the system that manages the access to resources and the execution of jobs in a data center, i.e., the batch scheduling system. Most of the historical workload traces available in the Parallel Workload Archive (PWA)[6] were originally studied with such an objective in mind. More recently, a methodology to characterize HPC workloads and assess their heterogeneity based on the analysis of the workloads executed over a year on three systems deployed at NERSC was proposed in [12]. This study not only helps to understand the

R. Yahyapour (Ed.): Euro-Par 2019, LNCS 11725, pp. 129–141, 2019.
https://doi.org/10.1007/978-3-030-29400-7_10

behavior of current HPC systems but can also be used to develop new scheduling strategies for the forthcoming exascale systems. Similar studies mixing the characterization, modeling, and prediction of HPC workloads have been proposed in [5,17]. In [8], the authors proposed a complete reconfiguration of their batch scheduling systems, including the definition of the scheduling queues, based on a thorough analysis of the workload characteristics and detailed simulations. The effects of this reconfiguration have then been analyzed in [9].

The common point of all the aforementioned studies is to consider HPC workloads that are composed of parallel jobs spanning over multiple cores and multiple nodes. In this paper we study a large High Throughput Computing (HTC) workload trace coming from the Computing Center of the National Institute of Nuclear Physics and Particle Physics (CC-IN2P3)[14] which is one of the largest academic computing centers in France. One of the main characteristics of this workload trace is that it is composed of a vast majority of jobs running on only one core, i.e., Monte-Carlo simulations and analyzes made on experimental data. This trace is also much larger than HPC traces with nearly 3,000,000 jobs executed every month on 33,500 cores. Finally, this workload captures a mix of two different types of submissions. As one of the twelve Tier-1 centers engaged in the processing of the data produced by the Large Hadron Collider (LHC) at CERN, half of job submissions come from an international computing grid through a complex middleware stack. The other half is directly submitted to the batch scheduling system by users belonging to more than 70 scientific collaborations.

In a previous work, we described the process of simplification of the operation of this infrastructure by reducing the "human-in-the-loop" component in scheduling decisions [2]. The main contribution of this paper is that we conduct a thorough analysis of the workload processed at a real large scale HTC system to show that the current system configuration tends to favor the jobs coming through the grid. The fair-share algorithm implemented by the scheduler is thus not as fair as it seems. Indeed, jobs submitted by local users suffer from a significantly higher waiting time. Based on our observations, we propose and evaluate through simulation a drastic modification of the quotas and the configuration of the scheduling queues that aims at further improving the fairness of the produced schedule. The obtained results show that it still guarantees the satisfaction of the main operational objectives while significantly improving the quality of service experienced by the formerly unfavored users. To ensure the reproduction and further investigation of the presented results, and thus favor Open Science, we made our large workload trace available to the scientific community [3].

This paper is organized as follows. Section 2 describes the computing infrastructure operated at CC-IN2P3 with details about the hardware, configuration of the batch scheduling systems, and operational constraints. In Sect. 3 we present and discuss the main characteristics of the workload executed on this infrastructure. Section 4 details the proposed modification of the system configuration and evaluates its impact on the quality of service and fairness experienced by the submitted jobs. Section 5 briefly explains how we produce and make available the workload trace used in this work. Finally, we conclude this paper and detail future work directions in Sect. 6.

Table 1. Characteristics of the nodes in the CC-IN2P3's HTC computing farm.

Model	Nodes	Cores/Node	Memory/Node	Cores
Xeon E5-2650 v4 2.20GHz	232	48	144 GB	11,136
Xeon Silver 4114 2.20GHz	240	40	128 GB	9,600
Xeon E5-2680 v2 2.80GHz	149	40	128 GB	5,960
Xeon E5-2680 v3 2.50GHz	124	48	144 GB	5,952
Xeon E5-2670 0 2.60GHz	24	32	96 GB	768
Xeon Silver 4114 2.20GHz	1	40	1,512 GB	40
Total	**770**			**33,456**

2   System Description

The IN2P3 Computing Center [14] is one of the largest academic computing centers in France. At the time of writing of this article, the CC-IN2P3 provides its users with about 33,500 *virtual* cores (i.e., hyper-threading is activated) on 770 physical nodes, whose characteristics are given in Table 1. In addition to this HTC computing farm, the CC-IN2P3 also offers resources for parallel, GPU-based, large memory, and interactive jobs that we ignored in this study.

These resources are managed by Univa Grid Engine (UGE v8.4.4)[16] which implements the *Fair Share Scheduler* first described in [7] and thus assigns priorities to all the unscheduled jobs to determine their order of execution. These priorities directly derive from the resources pledges expressed by the different user groups. As detailed in [2], each group has to provide an estimation of its computing needs as an amount of work, expressed in *Normalized HS06.hours*[11], to be done during each quarter of the following year. Once arbitration has been done with regard to the total available computing power, the respective share that has to be allocated to each group is converted into a consumption objective used by UGE to determine a fair-share schedule. This algorithm addresses one of the two main operational objectives of the CC-IN2P3: ensure that each user group is served according to its expressed resource request for the year.

In addition to this central scheduling algorithm, resources are organized in queues whose characteristics are given in Table 2. These queues are listed in the order in which they are considered by the job scheduler. They mainly differ by maximum allowed duration, both in terms of wallclock and CPU times, available memory and scratch disk space per job, and the type of jobs allowed to enter the queue, i.e., sequential or multi-core (denoted by the mc- prefix).

The *long* queues can both access the entire infrastructure. As it will be shown in Sect. 3, these two queues have to absorb the bulk of the workload. However, jobs are not really distinguished by their execution time in this configuration, with a minimal limit on execution time set to 48 CPU hours (or 58 hours) for all jobs. The *huge* queues are intended to jobs that need more memory or disk space while the access to the *longlasting* queues is limited to certain user groups.

Table 2. Names and upper limits (per job) of the queues. Queues are listed in the order in which they are considered by the job scheduler.

Queue name	CPU time	Time	Memory	File size	Pool size (in cores)
mc-long	48 h	58 h	3.6 GB	30 GB	33,456 (100%)
mc-huge	72 h	86 h	8 GB	30 GB	9,040 (27%)
mc-longlasting	202 h	226 h	3 GB	30 GB	19,800 (59%)
long	48 h	58 h	4 GB	30 GB	33,456 (100%)
huge	72 h	86 h	10 GB	110 GB	10,418 (31%)
longlasting	168 h	192 h	4 GB	30 GB	3,931 (12%)

We also see that all queues combined could virtually access more than three times the actual number of available cores. This configuration aims at achieving the highest possible utilization of the resources which is the second main operational objective of the center. Indeed, this ensures that load variations in the different scheduling queues cannot lead to leaving some cores idle.

Another important operational constraint of this system is related to the access to storage subsystems. High Energy Physics is a data-driven science, hence most of the jobs rely on locally stored data. Some user groups exhibit heavy I/O patterns that may become harmful to the storage subsystems in the worst case scenario where many jobs from these groups are executed concurrently. To prevent an overload of the storage subsystem, the number of concurrent jobs can be limited to a safe number for some groups by setting *Resource Quota Sets* (RQSs). The downside of this method is that it may increase the number of waiting jobs when this limit is reached. In such a case, operators can dynamically and temporarily modify the RQSs if the storage subsystems can cope with the extra load.

3   Workload Analysis

In this section we describe the main characteristics of the workload processed in November 2018 at CC-IN2P3. Over this month, 2,669,401 jobs were executed on the 33,456 available cores (or slots in the UGE vocabulary). We distinguish two sub-workloads depending on whether jobs are submitted to the batch system by *Local* users (1,174,078 jobs) or through a *Grid* middleware (1,495,323 jobs).

Figure 1 shows how many slots are simultaneously used. The dashed line indicates the total number of available slots while solid lines respectively show the overall utilization and which part of it comes from Grid and Local jobs.

This figure show that the main operational objective of the CC-IN2P3 is achieved with a global utilization well over 90%. We also see that this utilization is dominated by Grid jobs that use 3.45 times more slots than Local jobs while there are only 1.27 times more jobs coming through the grid than submitted by local users. About 28% of Grid jobs are multi-core, while 98% of Local jobs

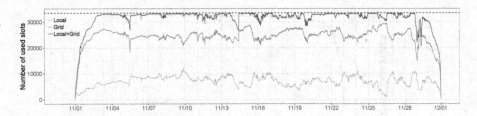

Fig. 1. Utilization of the resources, in terms of slots, over the considered period. The dashed line indicates the number of available slots, the other lines show the global utilization and the respective contributions of Local and Grid jobs.

request only one core for their execution. There were less than 17,000 multi-core Local jobs submitted over the considered 1-month period which required at most 16 cores. Most of multi-core Grid jobs fall in two categories. First, production jobs submitted by two LHC experiments (ATLAS and CMS) always require 8 cores. Second, two-core short-lived probe jobs are periodically submitted to check for site availability. They represent about 5% of the multi-core Grid jobs.

These two sub-workloads show several additional differences. The first one pertains to the expressed job duration. Figure 2 (left) shows a cumulative distribution function of the requested CPU time for Local and Grid jobs. There are only three values for the Grid jobs which correspond to the queue upper limits on CPU time (i.e., 48, 72, and 192 CPU hours). These predefined requirements are automatically added at the level of the Computing Element, i.e., the interface to the resources of a Grid site. The rationale is that most of the user groups that submit their jobs through the Grid manage their own workloads with pilot jobs [15]. Local jobs show a larger diversity in their CPU time requirements, even though about 35% of the jobs either require the upper limits of the queues or do not express any requirements. We also observe that a large fraction of Local jobs expresses requirements that are much lower than the queues upper limits. Nearly 40% of the jobs explicitly announce that they run for less than 12 hours but fall in the same queue as jobs potentially running for two days.

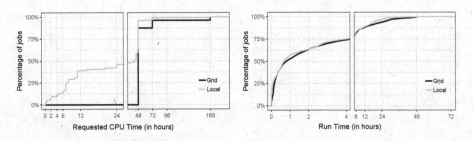

Fig. 2. Cumulative distribution functions of local and Grid jobs requested (left) and consumed (right) run times.

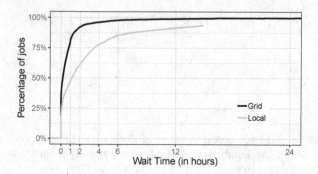

Fig. 3. Cumulative distribution functions of local and Grid jobs wait time.

Figure 2 (right) shows the cumulative distribution functions of the actual run times of Local and Grid jobs. We can see that the distribution of job duration is very similar for both sub-workloads with a large proportion of jobs running for less than four hours. There is thus an important discrepancy between the characteristics of the jobs in terms of execution time and both the expression of requirements and the configuration of the scheduling queues.

Another important difference between the two sub-workloads is about how fast jobs can start their execution, i.e., how much time jobs have to wait in queues before starting. Figure 3 shows the cumulative distribution function of this waiting time for Local and Grid Jobs. We can see that while 99% of the jobs wait for less than a day, Local jobs tend to wait much more than Grid jobs. Indeed, more than 75% of the Grid jobs but only 50% of the Local wait for less than one hour. To understand the origin of such a discrepancy, we analyze the evolution of the number of jobs waiting in the queues over the considered period. Figure 4 shows this evolution which confirms that there are much more Local jobs waiting than Grid Jobs. On average, there are about 1,650 waiting Grid jobs but nearly 5,600 waiting Local jobs. More importantly, while the maximum number of waiting Grid jobs is always less than 4,000, there can be more than 40,000 Local jobs waiting in queues. Several factors can explain this difference.

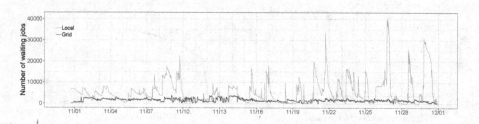

Fig. 4. Evolution of the number of waiting local and Grid jobs.

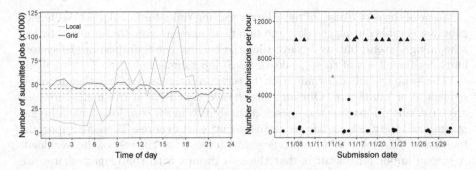

Fig. 5. Daily arrival rate for local and Grid jobs on week days (left). Dashed lines depict the average number of submissions per hour. Submission pattern of a specific user group (right). Triangles correspond to submission bursts.

First, they clearly differ by their submission patterns. Figure 5 (left) shows the daily arrival rates for Local and Grid jobs. The dashed lines depict the average number of submissions per hour which is quite similar for the two sub-workloads (respectively 40,666 and 45,695 jobs per hour). However, we clearly observe two different submission patterns. Local jobs follow a traditional "working hours" pattern, while Grid jobs are submitted at an almost constant rate.

Figure 5 (right) shows the submission pattern of a specific user group that leverages the "array job" feature of UGE that enables the submission of up to 10,000 related jobs in a single command. Then we clearly observe burst submissions which are typical and correspond to "production" periods. They are usually followed by "result analysis" periods of lower activity. The combination of these general and specific submission patterns amplifies the difference in the number of waiting jobs with Grid submissions that are controlled upstream by monitoring and the use of pilot jobs.

The other factors that contribute to the observed discrepancy are that the groups submitting jobs through the Grid have the highest priorities in the fairshare computation, they are the main source of multi-core jobs that benefit of higher priorities on the mc-* queues, and more stringent RQSs are set for Local users thus limiting the number of concurrent running jobs.

4 Revisiting the Configuration of the Batch System

The analysis conducted in the previous section confirmed that the main operational objectives, i.e., a maximal utilization of the computing resources and the respect of a fair sharing of resources derived from the pledges made by the different user groups, were achieved. However, we also observed that the overall fairness provided by the scheduling algorithm hides a more unfair behavior that has been overlooked by operators. We showed in Fig. 3 that jobs submitted by Local users wait much more than Grid jobs.

Some of the root causes of these larger waiting times for Local jobs, i.e., higher submission rates during the day, and burst submissions, can not be solved by the scheduling system, but we believe that the current configuration of the system amplifies the effects of these peaks in Local job submission.

The primary job discrimination factor currently used is whether a job is sequential or multi-core. Our analysis showed that 96% of the multi-core jobs are Grid jobs. Moreover, the queues dedicated to multi-core jobs have a higher priority and the mc-long has access to the entire set of cores. Then, an important fraction of Grid jobs (27%) is privileged with regard to the rest of the workload. A second important factor is that the user groups with the biggest shares are the main source of grid jobs, hence increasing the priority gap with Local jobs. Finally, while local jobs express an estimation of their execution time, the current configuration of scheduling queues does not leverage this information.

To better reflect the respective characteristics of the two identified sub-workloads and increase fairness by better balancing the waiting times across jobs, we propose a new configuration of the scheduling queues described in Table 3.

The first three queues are dedicated to Local jobs and are considered in increasing order of expressed job duration. Moreover, the shorter the jobs are in a queue, the more resources the corresponding queue can access. Indeed, short jobs will quickly release resources, and thus can use more slots at a given time without harming the overall throughput. Then, all the Grid jobs are now placed in a single dedicated grid queue. By considering this queue *after* those for Local jobs, we give a higher priority to Local jobs and then reduce their waiting times. Finally, we merged the queues for jobs with special requirements to remove the sequential/multi-core distinction. The number of slots a queue can access has been empirically chosen based on the utilization shown in Fig. 1. We aim at having a good tradeoff between preventing queue overload and ensuring a maximal utilization even under load variations within the sub-workloads.

To assess the impact of these modifications on the overall utilization and the waiting times experienced by jobs, we implemented a simulator using the *Alea job scheduling simulator*[1,10] which is based on the GridSim toolkit [13]. Alea allows for detailed simulations, supports several mainstream scheduling

Table 3. Names and upper limits (per job) of the queues in the new configuration. Queues are listed in the order in which they are considered by the job scheduler.

Queue name	CPU time	Time	Memory	File size	Pool size (in cores)
local-short	6 h	7 h	4 G	30 G	20,000 (59.8%)
local-medium	24 h	28 h	4 G	30 G	15,000 (44.8%)
local-long	48 h	58 h	4 G	30 G	10,000 (29.9%)
grid	48 h	58 h	3.6 G	30 G	25,000 (74.7%)
huge	72 h	86 h	10 G	110 G	10,000 (29.9%)
longlasting	202 h	226 h	3 G	30 G	5,000 (14.9%)

Table 4. Distribution of job waiting times.

Workload	Scenario	Average	Percentiles			Maximum
			50th	75th	90th	
Grid	Baseline	1 h 10 m	0 s	8 m 18 s	1 h 18 m	15 d 21 h 54 m
	Modified	1 h 45 m	0 s	14 m	2 h 2 m	14 d 4 h 33 m
Local	Baseline	2 h 3 m	4 m 30 s	1 h 40 m	6 h 40 m	11 d 21 h 41 m
	Modified	1 h 58 m	8 s	1 h 10 m	6 h 20 m	4 d 19 h 6 m

algorithms (e.g., FCFS, variants of Backfilling, Fair-Share) and commonly used system restrictions such as queue limits and quotas. We implemented two variants of the scheduling system. The first one constitutes a *baseline* and aims at reproducing the current configuration of the system. It uses the same queue definitions, shares, and RQSs as those used by UGE. Moreover the simulation starts with a set of "dummy" jobs running to mimic the state of the system on Nov. 1, 2018 at 12 am. The *modified* variant only differs by the definitions of the scheduling queues to use those presented in Table 3. We compare in Table 4 the distribution of waiting times in the two sub-workloads in the *baseline* and *modified* simulated schedules.

The proposed modification achieves its objectives. The average waiting time which was almost two times shorter for Grid jobs than for Local jobs is now more balanced, yet still shorter for Grid jobs. The median and third quartile values show that for a large fraction of Grid jobs, the impact of our modification is negligible, i.e., an increase of 6 min only, while the waiting times of Local jobs is reduced by half an hour. At the 90th percentile, the waiting of Grid jobs almost doubles, but remains three times less than that of the Local jobs. Finally, our modification reduces the maximum waiting time for both sub-workloads with a noticeable reduction of one week for the most waiting Local job.

Then we verify in Fig. 6 that both variants of the simulator can reproduce the main trends of the original schedule for each sub-workload, even though it

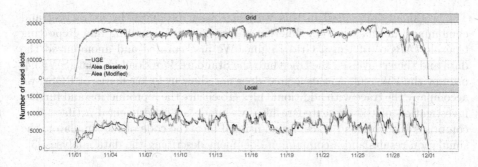

Fig. 6. Actual (UGE) and simulated (Alea) resource utilization, in slots, for Grid (top) and Local (bottom) jobs.

Table 5. Impact of RQS relaxation on job waiting times.

Workload	Scenario	Average	Percentiles			Maximum
			50th	75th	90th	
Grid	Conservative	1 h 53 m	0 s	16 m	2 h 21 m	13 d 15 h 21 m
	Extreme	1 h 57 m	4 s	17 m 41 s	2 h 47 m	14 d 4 h 41 m
Local	Conservative	1 h 39 m	2 s	45 m 40 s	5 h 8 m	3 d 16 h 58 m
	Extreme	1 h 14 m	1 s	21 m 55 s	2 h 30 m	3 d 23 h 11 m

does not capture all the configuration parameters of the real system. We can see that the *baseline* version can be used to evaluate the impact of the proposed modification and that the proposed modification achieves a very similar overall utilization and thus does not compromise the main operational objective.

We also propose to investigate the impact of a relaxation of the RQSs that are applied to local user groups and limit their access to resources. We make the assumption that the bigger is the original RQS, the bigger an acceptable increase can be. Indeed, a group constrained to use very few resources is more likely to cause I/O issues than a group allowed to use a large number of slots. We thus classify local user groups in three categories (i.e., 0–5%, 5–10%, and 10+%) according to the fraction of resources they can use. We propose two scenarios: a *conservative* one in which RQSs are respectively increased by 5%, 10% and 20%, and an *extreme* scenario in which increases are of 100%, 200%, and 300%. Table 5 shows a further reduction of the waiting time of Local jobs with a moderate impact on Grid Jobs. The *extreme* relaxation leads to the fairest schedule with similar waiting times up to the 90th percentile. However, it may be too extreme to be accepted by the system administrators. From these experiments, we can conclude that the new scheduling queues in Table 3. combined with a conservative relaxation of the RQSs is a good candidate for production.

5   Workload Trace Production and Availability

The workload trace used in this work has been produced by extracting and combining information from different tables of the Accounting and Reporting Console (ARCo) of Univa Grid Engine. We first curated and anonymized the data and then converted the trace into the Standard Workload Format (SWF)[4] used by the PWA [6]. As this format does not allow us to log shares or RQSs, we accompany the trace with additional files. To ensure the reproduction and further investigation of the presented results, we made an experimental artifact that comprises the workload trace, its additional files, the code of the simulator, the simulation results and a companion document describing the data analyses [3].

6   Conclusion and Future Work

The operation of a large data center is a complex task which is usually driven by a few selected operational objectives. In the case of the IN2P3 Computing Center, these objectives are to ensure a maximal utilization of the computing farm and the respect of a sharing of the resources proportional to the requests expressed for the year by the different user groups. To meet these objectives, operators rely on the implementation of the Fair-Share algorithm proposed by the Univa Grid Engine batch scheduling system and benefit from the main characteristic of the processed workload to be composed of a vast majority of sequential jobs.

Thanks to the batch scheduling system, the objective of an overall fairness across user groups, in terms of resource utilization, is achieved. However, the deeper analysis of the workload and its processing that we proposed in this paper showed that the current configuration of the system leads to a significant unfairness, in terms of job waiting time. We identified the root causes of this unfairness and proposed a pragmatic reconfiguration of the scheduling queues and quotas to address this issue. Detailed simulations of the original and modified configurations show that the proposed modifications better balance the waiting times across jobs without hindering the overall utilization of the system. The main operational objective is thus still achieved and the quality of service is improved for local users. Jobs submitted through the grid, which were previously favored now experience waiting times on par with those of the local jobs.

.We are aware that the presented analysis and proposed optimizations are tightly coupled to the very specific use case of the CC-IN2P3. The applicability of our findings to other systems can thus be legitimately questioned. However, we believe that two important and more general lessons can be drawn from this study. First, the behavior and performance of a job and resource management system are not only driven by the sole scheduling algorithm. This central component is the most studied in the job scheduling literature, but we shown that other components such as the scheduling queues and resource quotas can be key factors too and have to be included in performance studies. Second, the configuration of a batch system is a slowly evolving process and decisions made at a given time may last beyond an important evolution of the workload and impede the operation. Regular analyses of the workload and revisits of the system configuration should thus be seen as good operation practices.

As future work, we would like to improve the simulator to better mimic the behavior of the system in production. A faithful replay of the original workload will allow us to better measure the impact of potential modifications of the system, and thus ensure that these modifications can be safely applied in production. We also plan to refine the configurations of the queues and investigate which parameters could be further tuned, e.g., handle array jobs more specifically, to improve the quality of service experienced by CC-IN2P3's users.

Acknowledgements. We kindly acknowledge the support provided by Meta-Centrum under the program LM2015042 and the project Reg. No. CZ.02.1.01/ 0.0/0.0/16_013/0001797 co-funded by the Ministry of Education, Youth and Sports of the Czech Republic. We also thank L. Gombert, N. Lajili, and O. Aidel for their kind help.

References

1. ALEA 4: Job scheduling simulator, Feb 2019. https://github.com/aleasimulator
2. Azevedo, F., Gombert, L., Suter, F.: Reducing the human-in-the-loop component of the scheduling of large HTC workloads. Job Scheduling Strategies for Parallel Processing. Lecture Notes in Computer Science, vol. 11332. Springer, Cham (2019). https://doi.org/10.1007/978-3-030-10632-4_3
3. Azevedo, F., Klusáček, D., Suter, F.: Companion of the improving fairness in a large scale HTC system through workload analysis and simulation article (2019). https://doi.org/10.6084/m9.figshare.8427785
4. Chapin, S.J., et al.: Benchmarks and standards for the evaluation of parallel job schedulers. In: Feitelson, D.G., Rudolph, L. (eds.) JSSPP 1999. LNCS, vol. 1659, pp. 67–90. Springer, Heidelberg (1999). https://doi.org/10.1007/3-540-47954-6_4
5. Emeras, J., Varrette, S., Guzek, M., Bouvry, P.: EVALIX: classification and prediction of job resource consumption on HPC platforms. In: Desai, N., Cirne, W. (eds.) JSSPP 2015-2016. LNCS, vol. 10353, pp. 102–122. Springer, Cham (2017). https://doi.org/10.1007/978-3-319-61756-5_6
6. Feitelson, D., Tsafrir, D., Krakov, D.: Experience with using the parallel workloads archive. J. Parallel Distrib. Comput. **74**(10), 2967–2982 (2014)
7. Kay, J., Lauder, P.: A fair share scheduler. Commun. ACM **31**(1), 44–55 (1988)
8. Klusáček, D., Tóth, Š.: On interactions among scheduling policies: finding efficient queue setup using high-resolution simulations. In: Silva, F., Dutra, I., Santos Costa, V. (eds.) Euro-Par 2014. LNCS, vol. 8632, pp. 138–149. Springer, Cham (2014). https://doi.org/10.1007/978-3-319-09873-9_12
9. Klusáček, D., Tóth, Š., Podolníková, G.: Real-life experience with major reconfiguration of job scheduling system. In: Desai, N., Cirne, W. (eds.) JSSPP 2015-2016. LNCS, vol. 10353, pp. 83–101. Springer, Cham (2017). https://doi.org/10.1007/978-3-319-61756-5_5
10. Klusáček, D., Tóth, V., Podolníková, G.: Complex job scheduling simulations with ALEA 4. In: Proceedings of the 9th EAI International Conference on Simulation Tools and Techniques (Simutools 2016). pp. 124–129. ICST, Prague, Czech Republic (2016)
11. Michelotto, M., et al.: A comparison of HEP code with SPEC 1 benchmarks on multi-core worker nodes. J. Phys.: Conf. Ser. **219**(5), 052009 (2010)
12. Rodrigo, G., Östberg, P., Elmroth, E., Antypas, K., Gerber, R., Ramakrishnan, L.: Towards understanding HPC users and systems: a NERSC case study. J. Parallel Distrib. Comput. **111**, 206–221 (2018)
13. Sulistio, A., Cibej, U., Venugopal, S., Robic, B., Buyya, R.: A toolkit for modelling and simulating data grids: an extension to GridSim. Concurrency Comput.: Pract. Experience **20**(13), 1591–1609 (2008)
14. The IN2P3 /CNRS Computing Center. http://cc.in2p3.fr/en/
15. Turilli, M., Santcroos, M., Jha, S.: A comprehensive perspective on pilot-job systems. ACM Comput. Surv. **51**(2), 43:1–43:32 (2018)

16. Univa Corporation: Grid Engine. http://www.univa.com/products/
17. You, H., Zhang, H.: Comprehensive workload analysis and modeling of a petascale supercomputer. In: Cirne, W., Desai, N., Frachtenberg, E., Schwiegelshohn, U. (eds.) JSSPP 2012. LNCS, vol. 7698, pp. 253–271. Springer, Heidelberg (2013). https://doi.org/10.1007/978-3-642-35867-8_14

Toggle: Contention-Aware Task Scheduler for Concurrent Hierarchical Operations

Saurabh Kalikar$^{(\boxtimes)}$ and Rupesh Nasre

CSE, IIT Madras, Chennai, India
{saurabhk,rupesh}@cse.iitm.ac.in

Abstract. Rooted hierarchies are efficiently operated on using hierarchical tasks. Effective synchronization for hierarchies therefore demands hierarchical locks. State-of-the-art approaches for hierarchical locking are unaware of how tasks are scheduled. We propose a lock-contention aware task scheduler which considers the locking request while assigning tasks to threads. We present the design and implementation of Toggle, which exploits nested intervals and work-stealing to maximize throughput. Using widely used STMBench7 benchmark, a real-world XML hierarchy, and a state-of-the-art hierarchical locking protocol, we illustrate that Toggle considerably improves the overall application throughput.

1 Introduction

Managing concurrent data structures efficiently is challenging as well as error-prone. Due to *irregular* memory accesses, the access pattern cannot be precisely captured at compile time. Such a data-driven behavior necessitates runtime thread-coordination. For synchronizing across threads, logical locks continue to be prevalent for concurrent data structures.

We work with hierarchies; a hierarchy is a rooted directed graph wherein nodes at a level control or contain all the reachable nodes at the levels below. Such hierarchies are quite useful in modeling relations such as manager-employee. Our motivation arises from the use of hierarchies to store data in relational databases. For instance, Oracle *database* is composed of several *tablespaces*, each of which contains several *datafiles*. Each datafile, in turn, may host several *tables*, and each table may contain multiple *rows* where data is stored [12]. Similarly, Sybase database uses the hierarchy of database, extents, tables, datapages and rows [14]. The hierarchy is layered according to the *containment* property. Thus, a table is completely contained into an extent. Concurrent updates to part of the database requires thread synchronization. For instance, for answering *range queries* [11], the concurrency mechanism in the database server acquires locks on multiple rows. Two transactions accessing overlapping ranges (e.g., rows 10..20 and rows 15..25) may be allowed concurrent execution if their accesses are *compatible* (both are reads, for instance).

Existing hierarchical locking protocols such as *intention locks* [3] exploit this containment property for detection of conflicting lock-requests.

© Springer Nature Switzerland AG 2019
R. Yahyapour (Ed.): Euro-Par 2019, LNCS 11725, pp. 142–155, 2019.
https://doi.org/10.1007/978-3-030-29400-7_11

However, due to the requirement of multiple traversals (from root to the nodes being locked), intention locks are expensive for non-tree structures (such as DAGs). The state-of-the-art approaches [6,8] improve upon intention locks by making use of *interval numbering*. These approaches assign numeric intervals to nodes while respecting their hierarchical placement. The intervals can be quickly consulted for locking requests, leading to fast conflict-detection and improved throughput.

Unfortunately, the state-of-the-art approaches do not coordinate with the task scheduler. Thus, the task scheduler does not know how threads process hierarchical lock requests, and the threads do not know how various tasks (involving lock requests) get assigned to them by the scheduler. Such a lack of coordination forces the task scheduler to use uniform schemes across threads – for instance, using round-robin scheduling for assigning tasks to threads. While round-robin mechanism is fair, it is oblivious to locking requests and works well only when the requests are spread uniformly across the hierarchy. In practice, however, some parts of the hierarchy are more frequently accessed while several parts witness infrequent accesses. This gives rise to skewed access pattern, which also evolves over time (that is, different data records get more frequently accessed over time). To cater to these changes, it is crucial to marry lock management with task scheduling. Thus, the worker threads can provide information on how the locking requests are spread in the hierarchy, and how loaded each thread is. On the other hand, the task scheduler can distribute tasks to threads based on the feedback received from the worker threads – to improve overall throughput.

Making the lock manager talk to the task scheduler is challenging and involves several design changes to a traditional scheduler. Our primary contribution in this work is to motivate the need for those design decisions and to illustrate how those can be efficiently implemented. In particular,

- We propose Toggle, a novel hashing-based task-scheduling policy for hierarchies. Built upon the interval numbering, such a policy allows the task scheduler to quickly assign a task to a thread.
- We design and implement a communication protocol for threads using a lightweight concurrent data structure.
- We illustrate the effectiveness of our proposal by incorporating the design into STMBench7. Our proposal improves the overall throughput by 22%.

2   Background and Motivation

Hierarchy is a special linked data-structure where each child node exhibits a containment relationship with its parents. For instance, in a hierarchy of employees within an organization, an edge from a project-manager to its team-member indicates a containment relationship. Hierarchical structures are often operated on using hierarchical operations which work on sub-hierarchies. For instance, an operation "bulk updates to *a particular department* in an organization" accesses the sub-hierarchy rooted at the department. Traditional fine-grained locking necessitates locking each node in this sub-hierarchy that gets accessed by the

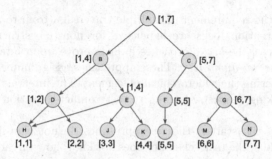

Fig. 1. Sample hierarchy. Numbers at nodes represent subsuming intervals.

bulk operation. As the hierarchy size grows, fine-grained locking is prohibitive from efficiency perspective. Therefore, hierarchical or multi-granularity locking (MGL) have been proposed. MGL at a node semantically allows the whole sub-hierarchy rooted at that node to be locked. In the extreme case, locking the root of the hierarchy locks the whole hierarchy. For instance, Fig. 1 represents a sample hierarchy wherein locking the node E locks nodes E, H, J and K. MGL is an efficient way to ensure race-free access for hierarchical operations. Various approaches towards implementing multiple-granularity locking have been proposed in the literature [2,3,6,8].

Existing MGL techniques lack coordination between thread scheduling and lock management. For instance, consider two threads operating on nodes B and D in Fig. 1. Due to MGL protocol, they both semantically try to lock the common node H. If the accesses are non-compatible (e.g., both are writes) then only one thread should be able to succeed in acquiring the lock, while the other must wait. As an aftereffect, the two operations get executed sequentially. If this is known to the scheduler, it may decide to assign the two operations to the same thread, reducing the contention and improving the throughput. In absence of such a knowledge, the scheduler may make suboptimal decisions while assigning tasks to threads. In fact, as we illustrate in our experimental evaluation, round-robin scheduling, which is fair and achieves good load balance, does not perform very well for hierarchical operations. This is because the load balance is achieved with respect to the *number of tasks* executed by a thread, rather than the *amount of work* done, which is dependent on both the sub-hierarchy size as well as the amount of contention.

3   Toggle: Contention-Aware Scheduler

In this section, we describe the design of our task scheduler. A *task*, denoted as $X : (Op, L)$ which consists of a set of operations (Op) to be performed atomically on the shared hierarchy and a set of lock objects L to be acquired at the beginning of the task. The execution of tasks follows standard 2-phase locking protocol in which all the required locks are acquired at the beginning and released at the end of the operation. Every hierarchical lock object $l_i \in L$ can be represented by its reachable leaf level locks. For instance, in Fig. 1, node B represents a set of nodes H, I, J and K. We define a set of leaf level locks for set L as,

$$Leaf(L) = \bigcup_{l_i \in L} \{x \mid x \text{ is leaf node and reachable from } l_i \}$$

Any pair of tasks say, $X_1 : (Op_1, L_1)$ and $X_2 : (Op_2, L_2)$, are classified into two types: *independent* tasks and *conflicting* tasks. Two tasks are independent iff $Leaf(L_1) \cap Leaf(L_2) = \phi$, i.e., they do not access any common node in the hierarchy; otherwise they conflict. Scheduling two conflicting tasks to different threads may degrade performance due to the overhead of lock contention.

3.1 Representing Hierarchy as a System of Nested Intervals

Traversing lock hierarchy to compute the set of leaf level locks using reachability information is costly. To avoid such traversals, the hierarchies are pre-processed to compute and store the reachability information. One of the techniques for encoding reachability is using nested intervals where each node in the hierarchy keeps track of their leaf level descendents as an interval [6,7]. For example, in Fig. 1, nodes H, I, J, K are reachable from B. Initially each leaf node is assigned with a unique interval range H: [1, 1], I: [2, 2] and so on. Each internal node maintains its interval range such that the range subsumes the interval range of every reachable leaf node (e.g. D: [1, 2]). We build upon these intervals to compute leaf lock set L for quick classification and scheduling of tasks.

3.2 Concurrent Data Structure for Task Classification and Scheduling

A global task pool maintains a list of pending tasks to be executed. A worker thread picks one task at a time from the global task pool and executes it on the physical core. In absence of a proper scheduler, the allocation of a task to a thread happens arbitrarily depending on the order in which worker threads extract the next available tasks. Therefore, multiple threads can get blocked simultaneously based on the locking requests.

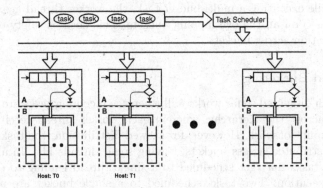

Fig. 2. Scheduler design: A and B represent outer and inner buckets resp.

Our proposed scheduler assigns a task to appropriate worker thread to avoid lock contention. Figure 2 shows the data structure used for task organization. The data structure contains a list of hash buckets. The size of the list is equal to the number of worker threads in the system. Every leaf node in the hierarchy is hashed to a specific bucket in the list. Consider there are 100 leaf node in the hierarchy indexed from 0 to 99 (during pre-processing) and there are 5 hash buckets in the list. Therefore, each bucket represents a range of 20 hierarchical nodes ([0–19], [20–39], ...). The scheduler, after extracting a task from the common task pool, analyzes the task by its set of lock objects. The scheduler inserts the task into one of the buckets as follows: if all the leaf level lock objects of the task fall into the range of a single bucket then insert the task in that bucket. Otherwise (request spans multiple buckets), insert the task into the bucket having the smallest bucket id. For instance, the hierarchy in Fig. 1 has 7 leaf nodes and say there are 2 hash buckets in the list, i.e., bucket 0 with range [0, 3] and bucket 1 with range [4, 6]. A task with lock set containing node D falls into bucket 0 as the leaf level locks H [1, 1] and I [2, 2], both fall into the range of bucket 0. On the other hand, if a locking request contains nodes J and G, then the leaf locks span both the buckets. In this case, the task gets inserted into the bucket with the least bucket id, i.e., bucket 0 (to ensure deterministic behavior). In the case of a task spanning multiple buckets, we maintain a bit mask of size equal to the total number of buckets with a bit set for each overlapping bucket. As the probability of two tasks within a bucket being conflicting is high, we assign one host thread to each bucket and mark it as primary responsible thread for executing the tasks. This imposes a sequential ordering among the tasks within a bucket which helps us minimizing the unnecessary lock contention.

3.3   Modified Locking Policy

Tasks are spread across buckets, and each bucket is served by a thread. The invariant the scheduler tries to maintain is that tasks in different buckets are independent. This invariant can allow a thread to operate on the nodes within its bucket without taking locks, since the conflicting requests are now spaced temporally. Unfortunately, this is violated by the locking requests that span buckets. While executing a multi-bucket task, the worker thread acquires locks (using bitmask) on all the overlapping buckets. This ensures safety of the concurrent operation across buckets.

3.4   Nested Bucketing

The approach discussed so far works well when the incoming tasks are uniformly distributed across the hierarchy, wherein each worker thread receives almost the same amount of work. However, for skewed distribution, the tasks are non-uniformly distributed across buckets, leaving some threads idle. In an extreme case, all the tasks may get scheduled to a single thread leading to completely sequential execution. Two tasks scheduled to a single bucket are not always conflicting and they can be run in parallel. To mitigate such effects, Toggle

Algorithm 1. Toggle Protocol

Input: Bucket B

1 count ← 0
2 **while** *there are tasks to execute* **do**
3   **if** *B.OuterBucket is not empty* **then**
4   Task t ← ExtractTaskFromOuterBucket()
5   **if** *t spans single inner bucket* **then**
6   call InnerBucket.insert(t)
7   **if** *InnerBucket.size() ≥ Threshold* **then**
8   call SwitchToInnerBucket()
9   **else**
            /* Task spans multiple inner buckets   */
10   call Execute(t)
11   count ← count + 1
12   **if** *count ≥ DelayThreshold* **then**
13   call SwitchToInnerBucket()
14   count ← 0
15   **else**
16   **if** *InnerBucket is not empty* **then** call SwitchToInnerBucket()
17   **else** call StealRemoteTask()
18

---

divides each bucket into two sub-parts: outer bucket A and inner bucket B, as shown in Fig. 2. Algorithm 1 presents the detailed protocol to be followed by each worker thread. While executing the tasks from the outer part of bucket, the host thread checks whether the task can be moved into one of the inner buckets (according to the hash range of inner buckets – line 12). If yes, the host thread removes the task from the outer bucket, and schedules its execution from the inner bucket. After every few cycles of tasks (line 7), the host toggles the mode of execution from outer to inner buckets. An invariant strictly enforced is that the inner bucket tasks are single-bucket tasks. Therefore, two tasks from two inner-buckets never overlap. Once the host thread changes its execution mode to inner bucket (line 8, 13, 16), it also allows other non-host threads to steal tasks from the inner bucket. Note that, no two threads execute tasks from the same inner bucket. This achieves good load balancing in the case of skewed distributions, and no thread remains idle for long.

3.5 Task Stealing

Worker threads can execute tasks from the inner buckets of remote threads if the worker thread is idle. In Algorithm 1, each worker thread starts stealing (line 17) if both outer and inner buckets are empty. While stealing, the worker thread iterates over remote buckets and checks whether any of the host threads are operating on inner bucket. If yes, it coordinates with the host thread to finish its task from inner bucket by picking one inner bucket at a time. However, while stealing, we need a proper thread synchronization for checking the status of the host thread and picking inner buckets.

3.6   Thread Communication

Every host thread maintains a *flag* indicating one of the execution states, namely, outer or inner. The worker, by default, executes tasks from the outer bucket. According to the protocol mentioned in Algorithm 1, whenever the host changes its state from the outer-bucket to the inner-bucket by reseting the flag, it broadcasts the message to all the threads. Any remote thread trying to steal the work, has to wait till the host thread toggles its state to inner bucket and is disallowed from stealing from the inner bucket when the host thread is operating on the outer bucket. Maintaining this protocol ensures that there are no conflicts between the remote thread and the host thread. Once the first condition of the toggle state is satisfied, remote threads are allowed to pick any one of the inner buckets and start executing the tasks one-by-one. However, as multiple threads steal in parallel, Toggle enforces (using atomic instructions) that one bucket gets picked by maximum one thread.

Algorithm 2 presents our lock-free implementation of communication mechanism and the task execution at the inner buckets. Variables ToggleFlag and Atomic_Counter are associated with each hash bucket, and are shared across threads. Host thread initializes these variables while switching the execution mode (lines 2, 3). All the remote threads check the state of these variables at the entry point and enter only when the state of the host thread has changed to inner and there is at least one inner bucket available for stealing (line 8). Instead of using heavyweight locks, we use relatively lightweight memory-fence instructions and atomic increment instructions at lines 4, 5, 7. The calls to memory_fence(release) and memory_fence(acquire) ensure that the values of the atomic counter and the ToggleFlag are written/read directly to/from the main memory (and not from the caches with stale data). Remote as well as host threads atomically and repetitively pick one inner bucket at a time (by incrementing the Atomic_Counter) till all the inner buckets become empty. Finally, the host thread resets the shared variables and returns to the execution of the outer bucket.

4   Experimental Evaluation

All our experiments are carried out on an Intel Xeon E5-2650 v2 machine with 32 cores clocked at 2.6 GHz having 100 GB RAM running CentOS 6.5 and 2.6.32-431 kernel. We implement our scheduler as part of STMBench7 [4], a widely used benchmark for the evaluation of synchronization mechanisms for hierarchical structures. STMBench7 represents an application operating on a complex real-world hierarchy consisting of various types of hierarchical nodes, such as *modules→assemblies→complex assemblies→composite-parts* and finally *atomic parts*

Algorithm 2. Thread communication in Toggle

Input: Bucket B, Thread T

1   **if** $T == B.HostThreadId$ **then**
2 | B.Atomic_Counter $\leftarrow$ 0
3 | B.ToggleFlag $\leftarrow$ inner
4 | MyInnerBucketId $\leftarrow$ atomic_increment(Atomic_Counter)
5 | memory_fence(release)

6   **else**
7 | memory_fence(acquire)
8 | **if** $B.ToggleFlag == outer$ OR $B.Atomic\_Counter > MaxInnerBucketId$ **then**
9 | | return
10 | MyInnerBucketId $\leftarrow$ atomic_increment(B.Atomic_Counter)

11 **while** $MyInnerBucketId \leq MaxInnerBucketId$ **do**
12 | **while** $MyInnerBucket$ *is not empty* **do**
13 | | Task t $\leftarrow$ ExtractTask()
14 | | call Execute(t)
15 | MyInnerBucketId $\leftarrow$ atomic_increment(B.Atomic_Counter)

16 **if** $T == B.HostThreadId$ **then**
17 | wait till all remote threads finish their respective tasks
18 | B.ToggleFlag $\leftarrow$ outer
19 | memory_fence(release)

---

at the leaf level. The operations accessing different parts of the hierarchy are defined to evaluate various synchronization aspects. We evaluate Toggle against four different locking mechanisms: two from STMBench7 (namely, coarse-grained and medium-grained), and two MGL-based techniques: DomLock [6] and Num-Lock [8].

We also use a real-world hierarchical dataset, *tree-bank* [15], (available in XML format) having 2.4 million nodes. For stress-testing our approach, we use a synthetically generated hierarchy having k-ary tree structure of 1 million nodes to study the effect of various parameters. A command-line argument *skewness* controls the probability of an operation accessing certain parts of the hierarchy.

4.1 STMBench7

Figure 3(a) shows the overall throughput achieved on STMBench7 by different locking mechanisms. In STMBench7, each parallel thread iteratively picks one operation at a time from a common pool. This mimics a fair round-robin task scheduling policy. Our scheduler operates on top of the worker threads and assigns tasks at runtime. In Fig. 3(a), x-axis shows the number of parallel threads and y-axis is the throughput (tasks/second) across all threads. We primarily compare with DomLock and NumLock, and extend them with our scheduler. Across all threads, Toggle achieves maximum throughput compared to coarse-grained, medium-grained, DomLock, and NumLock. This is primarily due to reduced lock contention. NumLock is an improved version of DomLock with optimal locking choices. We plug Toggle with NumLock; Toggle improves overall throughput with NumLock as well. We observe that the STMBench7 operations access certain part of hierarchy frequently. Every operation accessing such a subset of nodes gets sequentialized irrespective of the thread performing the operation. The scheduler dynamically detects such sequential bottleneck among the tasks and assigns them to only few threads letting other threads remain idle. In our experiments, the maximum throughput is achieved with the configuration of only four parallel threads. Overall, Toggle achieves 44%, 22% and 10% more throughput compared to coarse-grained, medium-grained and DomLock respectively.

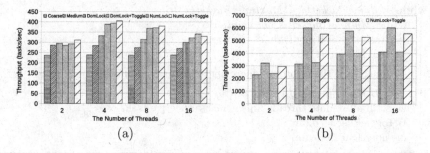

Fig. 3. (a) Comparison with STMBench7 (b) Effect on XML hierarchy

4.2 XML Hierarchy

We also evaluate our technique on *tree-bank*, a real-world hierarchical dataset available in XML format [15]. The hierarchy represents a non-uniform structure consisting of 2,437,666 nodes with maximum depth of 36 and average depth of 7.87 levels. We perform parallel tasks on the hierarchy where tasks access hierarchical nodes with equal probability. The tasks are diverse in nature: Some tasks exhibit skewed access whereas others are equally distributed. Tasks also vary with respect to the size of critical sections, i.e., some tasks spend less time in critical sections representing short transactions and while some are long transactions. We maintain the ratio of read:write operations as 7:3. Figure 3(b) shows the throughput gain of our scheduler with a fair round-robin scheduler. We observe that, our scheduler yields 16% more throughput and scales well with the number of threads whereas round-robin fails to scale due to lock-contention.

4.3 Effect of Skewness

We use our stress-test implementation to evaluate the effect of various parameters on the performance of Toggle. Figure 4 shows the overall throughput with 16 parallel threads with different levels of skewness. The x-axis shows the skewness index; *skewness = 1* indicates uniform random distribution. As we increase the

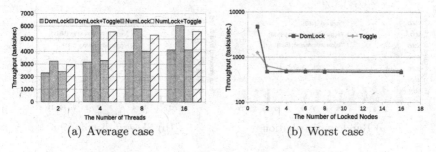

Fig. 4. Throughput improvement with Toggle

skewness index on x-axis, the access pattern becomes more localized to certain part of the hierarchy. For instance, skewness = 2 indicates two disjoint sub-sets of hierarchy nodes and any task can access nodes within only one subset. Figure 4(a) shows that the maximum throughput improvement is obtained with the most skewed and localized access pattern. Toggle achieves more through-put than round-robin scheduling because the conflicting tasks gets assigned to particular buckets according to the hash ranges of buckets.

It is crucial to handle the worst-case scenario for the task scheduling. As Toggle assigns tasks according to the bucket range and the host thread executes them sequentially, it is possible that every task falls into a single bucket leaving all other buckets empty. Note that, the tasks from one bucket may not conflict and may exhibit concurrency. We evaluate this scenario by forcing tasks to access multiple nodes from one particular range. In Fig. 4(b), x-axis shows the num-ber of nodes a task is operating on and y-axis shows throughput (log-scale) for round-robin and Toggle. As we keep on increasing the value on x-axis, the prob-ability of conflicts becomes very high. The throughput obtained using Toggle is consistently better than round-robin because of two reasons. First, even though the tasks get assigned to single bucket, the host thread allows other threads to steal tasks from the inner-buckets, utilizing available parallelism. Second, indi-vidual threads do not execute conflicting tasks, therefore they do not introduce extra lock contention. However, for tasks accessing only one node, (i.e., at x-axis value = 1), every task is guaranteed to be independent except the two tasks accessing exactly the same node. In this case, even though Toggle assigns all the tasks to a single thread and internally allows other threads to steal tasks, it fails to achieve better throughput because of synchronization cost involved in stealing. This is the only case where round-robin scheduling performs better than Toggle (although round-robin is also suboptimal for this scenario). Figure 4 shows the throughput with DomLock. The results with NumLock are omitted from Fig. 4(b) as both plots coincide due to the logscale.

4.4 Effect of Task Stealing

In this section, we compare the effect of scheduling in terms of resource utiliza-tion. As we discussed in the previous section, round-robin and Toggle achieve

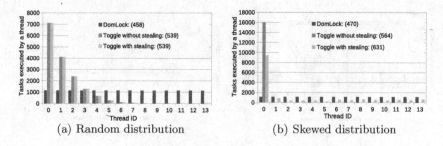

(a) Random distribution   (b) Skewed distribution

Fig. 5. Effect of task-stealing

similar throughput for random distribution. Figure 5(a) shows the work-load distribution across worker threads (threadIDs 0..13) for round-robin, Toggle without and with task stealing. Out of total 16 threads, remaining two threads are reserved: threadID 14 is a task-generator and threadID 15 is Toggle task-scheduler. x-axis represents different thread IDs and the y-axis represents the number of tasks executed by each thread. The obtained throughput with each scheduling policy is shown along with the legends. We observe that, in round-robin scheduling, every thread execute nearly equal number of tasks. However, for Toggle, threads with smaller IDs execute more tasks than the other. In fact, half of the threads remain idle. Despite this, the obtained throughput is better than round-robin. Note that the work-load distribution gradually decreases with the higher thread IDs. This happens because the tasks accessing nodes from a random distribution generally span multiple buckets, but our scheduler assigns such multi-bucket tasks to smaller thread IDs. Moreover, there is almost no scope for task stealing in the case of random distribution, as Toggle with and without stealing executes a similar number of tasks and achieves equal throughput.

Unlike this, for a skewed distribution, task stealing plays important role in performance improvement. Figure 5(b) shows tasks distribution across threads for the configuration of the worst-case scenario with every task accessing exactly 2 nodes. In absence of task stealing, each task gets assigned to a single bucket and each of them is executed sequentially, still achieving better throughput than round-robin scheduling. However, permitting other threads to steal tasks from remote buckets, we achieve further improvement in the overall throughput (shown with the legends). This shows the importance of task stealing in skewed distributions, which is prevalent in real-world scenarios. Our scheduler dynamically enables and disables task stealing based on the run-time load distribution.

4.5   Effect of Hierarchy Size

Figure 6(a) shows the throughput against different hierarchy sizes, from 100 to 1 million nodes. As we see, parallel operations on a smaller hierarchy are likely to get blocked. Toggle achieves throughput gain even in high-contention scenario. As we increase the hierarchy size, Toggle consistently outperforms DomLock.

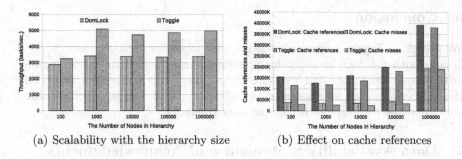

(a) Scalability with the hierarchy size   (b) Effect on cache references

Fig. 6. Effect of hierarchy size on throughput and cache misses

We also see the benefit of scheduling in terms of caching. A worker thread primarily executes operations within its bucket. Tasks within a bucket are mostly conflicting, i.e., access same nodes, therefore it avoids extra cache misses as the data would be available in processors private cache. As we increase the hierarchy size, the bucket ranges become wider. The tasks in such a wider bucket are less likely to be conflicting, therefore for every task, accessing new nodes leads to cache miss. In Fig. 6(b), this effect is visible for large sized hierarchies.

5   Related Work

Hierarchical locking is imposed in many ways. Traditionally, in database context, hierarchical locking is implemented as multiple granularity locks using intention locks [3] at ancestor nodes. However, in multi-threads applications, threads get contended while acquiring these intention locks. DomLock [6] solves this problem by dominator locking using nested intervals. NumLock [8] further improves by generating optimal hierarchical locking combination. Our task scheduler can be used with any of these hierarchical locking protocols. Similar to the idea of interval locking, key-range locking [9,10] is in databases locks a range of records satisfying certain predicates. In this case, key-range lock guards not only the keys present in the databases but also any phantom insertions. However, it is not a hierarchical locking technique. Although Toggle works with hierarchical locking, it can be tuned to work with key-range locking as well.

Task scheduling has been the topic of interest in many domains. Hugo Rito et al. proposed PrOPS [13], a fine-grained pessimistic scheduling policy for STMs. ProPS also used STMBench7 for evaluating different STM implementations. We use it for evaluating Toggle over locking techniques. Several techniques have been proposed for scheduling *task DAGs* where nodes represent tasks and directed edges are precedence relation. Zhao et al. [5] proposed a policy for scheduling multiple task DAGs on heterogeneous systems. Cui et al. [1] present a lock-contention-aware scheduler at the kernel level. However, none of the schedulers addresses the challenges with lock-contention for hierarchical locks.

6   Conclusion

We presented Toggle, a contention-aware task scheduler for hierarchies. It coordinates with the lock manager for scheduling tasks to maximize throughput, using nested bucketing and work-stealing. Using large hierarchies and STM-Bench7 benchmarks, we illustrated the effectiveness of Toggle, which considerably improves the average throughput over DomLock.

7   Data Availability Statement and Acknowledgments

We thank all the reviewers whose comments improved the quality of the paper substantially. The artifacts of the work have been successfully evaluated and are available at: https://doi.org/10.6084/m9.figshare.8496464.

References

1. Cui, Y., Wang, Y., Chen, Y., Shi, Y.: Lock-contention-aware scheduler: a scalable and energy-efficient method for addressing scalability collapse on multicore systems. ACM Trans. Archit. Code Optim. **9**(4), 44:1–44:25 (2013). https://doi.org/10.1145/2400682.2400703
2. Ganesh, K., Kalikar, S., Nasre, R.: Multi-granularity locking in hierarchies with synergistic hierarchical and fine-grained locks. In: Aldinucci, M., Padovani, L., Torquati, M. (eds.) Euro-Par 2018. LNCS, vol. 11014, pp. 546–559. Springer, Cham (2018). https://doi.org/10.1007/978-3-319-96983-1_39
3. Gray, J.N., Lorie, R.A., Putzolu, G.R.: Granularity of locks in a shared data base. In: VLDB. pp. 428–451. ACM, New York (1975)
4. Guerraoui, R., Kapalka, M., Vitek, J.: STMBench7: a benchmark for software transactional memory. In: Proceedings of the 2Nd ACM SIGOPS/EuroSys European Conference on Computer Systems 2007, pp. 315–324. EuroSys 2007, ACM, New York (2007). https://doi.org/10.1145/1272996.1273029
5. Zhao, H., Sakellariou, R.: Scheduling multiple dags onto heterogeneous systems. In: Proceedings 20th IEEE International Parallel Distributed Processing Symposium, p. 14. April 2006
6. Kalikar, S., Nasre, R.: Domlock: a new multi-granularity locking technique for hierarchies. In: Proceedings of the 21st ACM SIGPLAN Symposium on Principles and Practice of Parallel Programming, pp. 23:1–23:12. PPoPP 2016, ACM, New York (2016). https://doi.org/10.1145/2851141.2851164
7. Kalikar, S., Nasre, R.: DomLock: a new multi-granularity locking technique for hierarchies. ACM Trans. Parallel Comput. **4**(2), 7:1–7:29 (2017)
8. Kalikar, S., Nasre, R.: NumLock: towards optimal multi-granularity locking in hierarchies. In: Proceedings of the 47th International Conference on Parallel Processing, pp. 75:1–75:10. ICPP 2018, ACM, New York (2018). https://doi.org/10.1145/3225058.3225141
9. Lomet, D., Mokbel, M.F.: Locking key ranges with unbundled transaction services. Proc. VLDB Endow. **2**(1), 265–276 (2009)
10. Lomet, D.B.: Key range locking strategies for improved concurrency. In: Proceedings of the 19th International Conference on Very Large Data Bases, pp. 655–664. VLDB 1993, Morgan Kaufmann Publishers Inc., San Francisco (1993)

11. MSDN: Sql server 2016 database engine (2015). https://msdn.microsoft.com/en-us/library/ms187875.aspx
12. Oracle: Oracle database 10g r2 (2015). http://docs.oracle.com/cd/B19306_01/index.htm
13. Rito, H., Cachopo, J.: ProPS: a progressively pessimistic scheduler for software transactional memory. In: Silva, F., Dutra, I., Santos Costa, V. (eds.) Euro-Par 2014. LNCS, vol. 8632, pp. 150–161. Springer, Cham (2014). https://doi.org/10.1007/978-3-319-09873-9_13
14. Sybase: Adaptive server enterprise: Performance tuning and locking (2003). http://infocenter.sybase.com/help/topic/com.sybase.help.ase_12.5.1/title.htm
15. Treebank: Xml data repository (2002). http://aiweb.cs.washington.edu/research/projects/xmltk/xmldata/www/repository.html

Load-Balancing for Parallel Delaunay Triangulations

Daniel Funke[✉], Peter Sanders, and Vincent Winkler

Karlsruhe Institute of Technolgy, Karlsruhe, Germany
{funke,sanders}@kit.edu, vincent.winkler@student.kit.edu

Abstract. Computing the Delaunay triangulation (DT) of a given point set in $\mathbb{R}^D$ is one of the fundamental operations in computational geometry. Recently, Funke and Sanders [11] presented a divide-and-conquer DT algorithm that merges two partial triangulations by re-triangulating a small subset of their vertices – the *border* vertices – and combining the three triangulations efficiently via parallel hash table lookups. The input point division should therefore yield roughly equal-sized partitions for good load-balancing and also result in a small number of border vertices for fast merging. In this paper, we present a novel divide-step based on partitioning the triangulation of a small sample of the input points. In experiments on synthetic and real-world data sets, we achieve nearly perfectly balanced partitions and small border triangulations. This almost cuts running time in half compared to non-data-sensitive division schemes on inputs exhibiting an exploitable underlying structure.

1 Introduction

The Delaunay triangulation (DT) of a given point set in $\mathbb{R}^D$ has numerous applications in computer graphics, data visualization, terrain modeling, pattern recognition and finite element methods [15]. Computing the DT is thus one of the fundamental operations in geometric computing. Therefore, many algorithms to efficiently compute the DT have been proposed (see survey in [23]) and well implemented codes exist [13,20]. With ever increasing input sizes, research interest has shifted from sequential algorithms towards parallel ones.

Recently, we presented a novel divide-and-conquer (D&C) DT algorithm for arbitrary dimension [11] that lends itself equally well to shared and distributed memory parallelism and thus hybrid parallelization. While previous D&C DT algorithms suffer from a complex – often sequential – divide or merge step [8,17], our algorithm reduces the merging of two partial triangulations to re-triangulating a small subset of their vertices – the *border* vertices – using the same parallel algorithm and combining the three triangulations efficiently via hash table lookups. All steps required for the merging – identification of relevant vertices, triangulation and combining the partial DTs – are performed in parallel.

© Springer Nature Switzerland AG 2019
R. Yahyapour (Ed.): Euro-Par 2019, LNCS 11725, pp. 156–169, 2019.
https://doi.org/10.1007/978-3-030-29400-7_12

The division of the input points in the divide-step needs to address a twofold sensitivity to the point distribution: the partitions need to be approximately equal-sized for good load-balancing, while the number of *border vertices* needs to be minimized for fast merging. This requires partitions that have many internal Delaunay edges but only few external ones, i.e. a graph partitioning of the DT graph. In this paper we propose a novel divide-step that approximates this graph partitioning by triangulating and partitioning a small sample of the input points, and divides the input point set accordingly.

The paper is structured as follows: we review the problem definition, related work on partitioning for DT algorithms and our D&C DT algorithm from [11] in Sect. 2. Subsequently, our proposed divide-step is described in Sect. 3, along with a description of fast intersection tests for the more complexly shaped partition borders and implementation notes. We evaluate our algorithms in Sect. 4 and close the paper with conclusions and an outlook on future work in Sect. 5.

2 Preliminaries

2.1 Delaunay Triangulations

Given a D-dimensional point set $\mathbf{P} = \{p_1, p_2, \ldots, p_n\} \subset \mathbb{R}^D$ for all $i \in \{1, \ldots, n\}$, a triangulation $T(\mathbf{P})$ is a subdivision of the convex hull of $\mathbf{P}$ into D-simplices such that the set of vertices of $T(\mathbf{P})$ coincides with $\mathbf{P}$ and any two simplices of T intersect in a common $D - 1$ facet or not at all. The union of all simplices in $T(\mathbf{P})$ is the convex hull of point set $\mathbf{P}$. A Delaunay triangulation $DT(\mathbf{P})$ is a triangulation of $\mathbf{P}$ such that no point of $\mathbf{P}$ is inside the circumhypersphere of any simplex in $DT(\mathbf{P})$. The DT of n points can be computed in $\mathcal{O}(n \log n)$ time for $D = 2$ and $\mathcal{O}(n^{\lceil \frac{D}{2} \rceil})$ time for $D \geq 3$.

2.2 Related Work

Many algorithms for the parallel construction of the DT of a given point set have been proposed in the literature. They generally fall into one of two categories: parallel incremental insertion and D&C approaches. We will focus on a review of the divide-step of the latter. A more comprehensive discussion of both algorithm types is given in [11].

Aggarwal et al. [1] propose the first parallel D&C DT algorithm. They partition the input points along a vertical line into blocks, which are triangulated in parallel and then merged sequentially. The authors do not prescribe how to determine the location of the splitting line. Cignoni et al. [8] partition the input along cutting (hyper)planes and firstly construct the simplices of the triangulation crossing those planes before recursing on the two partitions. The remaining simplices can be created in parallel in the divided regions without further merging. The authors mention that the regions should be of roughly equal cardinality, but do not go into the details of the partitioning. Chen [5] and Lee et al. [17] explicitly require splitting along the median of the input points. Whereas the former uses classical splitting planes, the latter traces the splitting line with Delaunay edges, thus eliminating the need for later merging.

The subject of input partitioning has received more attention in the meshing community. A *mesh* of a point set **P** is a triangulation of every point in **P** and possibly more – so called *Steiner points* – to refine the triangulation. Chrisochoides [6] surveys algorithms for parallel mesh generation and differentiates between continuous domain decomposition – using quad- or oct-trees – and discrete domain decomposition using an initial coarse mesh that is partitioned into submeshes, trying to minimize the surface-to-volume ratio of the submeshes.Chrisochoides and Nave [7] propose an algorithm that meshes the subproblems via incremental insertion using the Bowyer-Watson algorithm.

2.3   Parallel Divide-and-Conquer DT Algorithm

Recently, we presented a parallel D&C algorithm for computing the DT of a given point set [11]. Our algorithm recursively divides the input into two partitions which are triangulated in parallel. The contribution lies in a novel merging step for the two partial triangulations which re-triangulates a small subset of their vertices and combines the three triangulations via parallel hash table lookups. For each partial triangulation the *border* is determined, i.e. the simplices whose circumhypersphere intersects the bounding box of the other triangulation. The vertices of those border simplices are then re-triangulated to obtain the border triangulation. The merging proceeds by combining the two partial triangulations, stripping the original border simplices and adding simplices from the border triangulation iff (i) they span multiple partitions; or (ii) are contained within one partition but exist in the same form in the original triangulation.

The algorithm's sensitivity to the input point distribution is twofold: the partitions need to be of equal size for good load-balancing between the available cores and the number of simplices in the border needs to be minimized in order to reduce merging overhead. As presented in [11], the algorithm splits the input into two partitions along a hyperplane. Three strategies to choose the splitting dimension are proposed: (i) constant, predetermined splitting dimension; (ii) cyclic choice of the splitting dimension – similar to k-D trees; or (iii) dimension with largest extend. This can lead to imbalance in the presence of non-homogeneously structured inputs, motivating the need for more sophisticated partitioning schemes.

3   Sample-Based Partitioning

In this paper, we propose more advanced strategies for partitioning the input points than originally presented in [11]. The desired partitioning addresses both data sensitivities of our algorithm. The underlying idea is derived from sample sort: gain insight into the input distribution from a (small) sample of the input. Algorithm 1 describes our partitioning procedure. A sample $\mathbf{P}_S$ of $\eta(n)$ points is taken from the input point set **P** of size n and triangulated to obtain $DT(\mathbf{P}_S)$. A similar approach can be found in Delaunay hierarchies, where the sample triangulation is used to speed up point location queries [10].

Algorithm 1. partitionPoints($\mathbf{P}, k$): partition input into k partitions.

Input: points $\mathbf{P} = \{p_1, \ldots, p_n\}$ with $p_i \in \mathbb{R}^D$, number of partitions k
Output: partitioning $(\mathbf{P}_1 \ldots \mathbf{P}_k)$
  1: $\mathbf{P}_S \leftarrow$ choose $\eta(n)$ from $\mathbf{P}$ uniformly at random $\triangleright \eta(n)$ sample size
  2: $T \leftarrow$ Delaunay($\mathbf{P}_S$)
  3: $G = (V, E, \omega)$ with $V = \mathbf{P}_S$, $E = T$ and weight function ω
  4: $(V_1 \ldots V_k) \leftarrow$ partition(G) $\triangleright$ partition graph
  5: $(\mathbf{P}_1 \ldots \mathbf{P}_k) \leftarrow (\varnothing \ldots \varnothing)$
  6: **parfor** $p \in \mathbf{P}$ **do**
  7:     $v_n \leftarrow \arg\min_{v \in \mathbf{P}_S} \|p - v\|$ $\triangleright$ find nearest sample point to p
  8:     $\mathbf{P}_i \cup= p$ with $i \in [1 \ldots k] : v_n \in V_i$ $\triangleright$ assign p to v_n's partition
  9: **return** $(\mathbf{P}_1 \ldots \mathbf{P}_k)$

Instead, we transform the DT into a graph $G = (V, E, \omega)$, with V being equal to the sample point set $\mathbf{P}_S$ and E containing all edges of $DT(\mathbf{P}_S)$. The resulting graph is then partitioned into k blocks using a graph partitioning tool.

The choice of the weight function ω influences the quality of the resulting partitioning. As mentioned in Sect. 2.3, the D&C algorithm is sensitive to the balance of the blocks as well as the size of the border triangulation. The former is ensured by the imbalance parameter ϵ of the graph partitioning, which guarantees that for all partitions i: $|V_i| \leq (1+\epsilon)\lceil \frac{|V|}{k} \rceil$. The latter needs to be addressed by the edge weight function ω of the graph. In order to minimize the size of the border triangulation, dense regions of the input points should not be cut by the partitioning. Sparse regions of the input points result in long Delaunay edges in the sample triangulation. As graph partitioning tries to minimize the weight of the cut edges, edge weights need to be inversely related to the Euclidean length of the edge. In Sect. 4.1 we evaluate several suitable edge weight functions.

Given the partitions of the sample vertices $(V_1 \ldots V_k)$, the partitioning needs to be extended to the entire input point set. The dual of the Delaunay triangulation of the sample point set – its Voronoi diagram – defines a partitioning of the Euclidean space $\mathbb{R}^D$ in the following sense: each point $p_{S,i}$ of the sample is assigned to a partition $j \in [1 \ldots k]$. Accordingly, its Voronoi cell with respect to $\mathbf{P}_S$ defines the sub-space of $\mathbb{R}^D$ associated with partition j. In order to extend the partitioning to the entire input point set, each point $p \in \mathbf{P}$ is assigned to the partition of its containing Voronoi cell.

All steps in Algorithm 1 can be efficiently parallelized. Sanders et al. [18] present an efficient parallel random sampling algorithm. The triangulation of the sample point set $\mathbf{P}_S$ could be computed in parallel using our DT algorithm recursively. However, as the sample is small, a fast sequential algorithm is typically more efficient. Graph conversion is trivially done in parallel and Akhremtsev et al. [2] present a state-of-the-art parallel graph partitioning algorithm. The parallelization of the assignment of input points to their respective partitions is explicitly given in Algorithm 1.

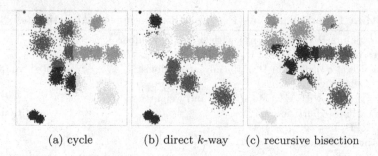

(a) cycle   (b) direct k-way   (c) recursive bisection

Fig. 1. Example of a two-dimensional partitioning with four partitions for 10000 points and a sample size of 1000.

3.1 Recursive Bisection and Direct k-way Partitioning

Two possible strategies exist to obtain k partitions from a graph: direct k-way partitioning and recursive bisection. For the latter, the graph is recursively partitioned into $k' = 2$ partitions $\log k$ times. In the graph partitioning community, Simon and Teng [22] prove that recursive bisection can lead to arbitrarily bad partitions and Kernighan and Lin [14] confirm the superiority of direct k-way partitioning experimentally. However, recursive bisection is still widely – and successfully – used in practice (e. g. for initial partitioning in KaHIP [19]). We therefore consider both strategies to obtain k partitions for our DT algorithm.

The partitioning schemes originally proposed in [11] can be seen as recursive bisection: the input is recursively split along the median. The splitting dimension is chosen in a cyclic fashion, similiar to k-D trees. Figure 1a shows an example.

Similarly, our new partitioning algorithm can be applied $\log k$ times, at each step i drawing a new sample point set $\mathbf{P}_{S,i}$, triangulating and partitioning $\mathbf{P}_{S,i}$, and assigning the remaining input points to their respective partition. As in the original scheme, this leads to $k - 1$ merge steps, entailing $k - 1$ border triangulations. In the sample-based approach however, the partitioning avoids cutting dense regions of the input, which would otherwise lead to large and expensive border triangulations; refer to Fig. 1c.

Using direct k-way partitioning, only one partitioning and one merge step is required. The single border point set will be larger, with points spread throughout the entire input area. This however, allows for efficient parallelization of the border triangulation step using our DT algorithm recursively. Figure 1b depicts an example partitioning.

For a fair comparison, we also implemented a variant of the original cyclic partitioning scheme, where all leaf nodes of the recursive bisection tree are merged in a single k-way merge step. This allows us to determine, whether any runtime gains are due to the k-way merging or due to our more sophisticated data-sensitive partitioning.

3.2   Geometric Primitives

Our D&C algorithm [11] mostly relies on combinatorial computations on hash values except for the base case computations and the detection of the border simplices. The original partitioning schemes always result in partitions defined by axis-aligned bounding boxes. Therefore, the test whether the circumhypersphere of a simplex intersects another partition can be performed using the fast box-sphere overlap test of Larsson et al. [16]. However, using the more advanced partitioning algorithms presented in this paper, this is no longer true. Therefore the geometric primitives to determine the border simplices need to be adapted to the more complexly shaped partitions. The primitives need to balance the computational cost of the intersection test itself with the associated cost for including non-essential points in the border triangulation.

We propose three intersection tests:[1] (i) each partition is crudely approximated with an axis-aligned *bounding box* and the fast intersection test of Larsson et al. [16] is used to determine the simplices that belong to the border of a partition. While computationally cheap, the bounding box can overestimate the extent of a partition. (ii) for each partition it is determined which cells of a *uniform grid* are occupied by points from that partition. This allows for a more accurate test whether a given simplex s of partition i intersects with partition j by determining whether any of j's occupied grid cells are intersected by the circumhypersphere of s, again using the box-sphere intersection test [16]. To further accelerate the intersection test we build an AABB tree [4] on top of the grid data structure. (iii) to *exactly* determine the necessary points for the border triangulation we use the previous test to find the grid cells of partition j intersected by the circumhypersphere of s and then use an adaptive precision *inSphere*-test [21] for all points contained in these cells to test whether s violates the Delaunay property and thus its vertices need to be added to the border triangulation.

4   Evaluation

Batista et al. [3] propose three input point distributions to evaluate the performance of their DT algorithm: n points distributed uniformly (a) in the unit cube; (b) on the surface of an ellipsoid; and (c) on skewed lines. Furthermore, Lee et al. [17] suggest normally distributed input points around (d) the center of the unit cube; and (e) several "bubble" centers, distributed uniformly at random within the unit cube. We furthermore test our algorithm with a real world dataset from astronomy. The Gaia DR2 catalog [9] contains celestial positions and the apparent brightness for approximately 1.7 billion stars. Additionally, for 1.3 billion of those stars, parallaxes and proper motions are available, enabling the computation of three-dimensional coordinates. As the image next to Table 1 shows, the data exhibits clear structure, which can be exploited by our partitioning strategy. We use a random sample of the stars to evaluate our algorithm. All experiments

---

[1] For a more detailed description of the primitives we refer to the technical report [12].

Table 1. Input point sets and their resulting triangulations. Running times are reported for $k = t = 16$, parallel KaHIP, $\eta(n) = \sqrt{n}$, grid-based intersection test with $c_{\mathcal{G}} = 1$ and logarithmic edge weights. The image on the right shows an Aitoff projection of a random sample of 25000 sources from the Gaia DR2 dataset.

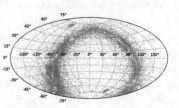

Dataset	Points	Simplices	$\frac{\text{simplices}}{\text{point}}$	Runtime
uniform	50 000 000	386 662 755	7.73	164.6 s
normal	50 000 000	390 705 843	7.81	162.6 s
ellipsoid	500 000	23 725 276	4.74	88.6 s
lines	10 000	71 540 362	7154.04	213.3 s
bubbles	50 000 000	340 201 778	6.80	65.9 s
Gaia DR2	50 000 000	359 151 427	7.18	206.9 s

Table 2. Parameters of our algorithm (top) and conducted experiments (bottom).

Parameter	Values
Sample size $\eta(n)$	1%, 2%, $\log n$, $\sqrt{n}$
KaHIP configuration	STRONG, ECO, FAST, PARALLEL
Edge weight $\omega(e)$	constant, inverse, log, linear
Geometric primitive	bbox, exact, grid with cell sizes $c_{\mathcal{G}} = [\frac{1}{2}, 1, 2]$
Partitions k	$1, 2, 4, \ldots, 64$
Threads t	$t = k$
Points n	$[1, 5, 10, 25, 50] \cdot 10^6$ [a]
Distribution	see Table 1

[a] Unless otherwise stated in Table 1

are performed in three-dimensional space ($D = 3$). Table 1 gives an overview of all input point sets, along with the size of their resulting triangulation.

The algorithm was evaluated on a machine with dual Intel Xeon E5-2683 16-core processors and 512 GiB of main memory. The machine is running Ubuntu 18.04, with GCC version 7.2 and CGAL version 4.11.

Implementation Notes: We integrated our divide-step into the implementation of [11], which is available as open source.[2] We use KaHIP [19] and its parallel version [2] as graph partitioning tool. The triangulation of the sample point set is computed sequentially using CGAL [13] with exact predicates.[3]

4.1 Parameter Studies

The parameters listed in Table 2 can be distinguished into configuration parameters of our algorithm and parameter choices for our experiments. In our parameter study we examine the configuration parameters of our algorithm and

---

[2] https://git.scc.kit.edu/dfunke/DelaunayTriangulation.
[3] `CGAL::Exact_predicates_inexact_constructions_kernel`.

determine robust choices for all inputs. The parameter choice influences the quality of the partitioning with respect to partition size deviation and number of points in the border triangulation. As inferior partitioning quality will result in higher execution times, we use it as indicator for our parameter tuning. We use the uniform, normal, ellipsoid and random bubble distribution for our parameter tuning and compare against the originally proposed cyclic partitioning scheme for reference. Due to space constrains we refer to the technical report [12] for an in-depth discussion of each parameter individually and only present a short summary here.

Our experiments show, that a sample size of $\eta(n) = \sqrt{n}$ balances the approximation quality of a partitioning of the final triangulation with the runtime for the sample triangulation. Considering edge weights, dense regions of the input point set are reflected by *many* short edges in the sample triangulation. Therefore, even constant edge weights result in a sensible partitioning. However, logarithmic edge weights[4] are better when there is an exploitable structure in the input points. For KaHIP we chose the parallel configuration as default as it requires a similar runtime to the ECO configuration while achieving a cut only slightly worse then STRONG. The grid-based intersection test with a cell size of $c_g = 1$ shows the best trade-off between accuracy – i.e. only essential simplices are included in the border triangulation – and runtime for the geometric primitive itself.

4.2 Partitioning Quality

Given a graph partitioning $(V_1 \ldots V_k)$, its quality is defined by the weight of its cut, $\sum_{e \in C} \omega(e)$ for $C := \{e = (u,v), e \in E$ and $u \in V_i, v \in V_j$ with $i \neq j\}$. As mentioned in Sect. 3, the balance of the graph partitioning is ensured by the imbalance parameter ϵ, $|V_i| \leq (1+\epsilon)\lceil \frac{|V|}{k} \rceil$ for all $i \leq k$. When the partitioning of the sample triangulation is extended to the entire input set, this guarantee no longer holds. We therefore study two quality measures: (i) the deviation from the ideal partition size and (ii) the coefficient of variation of the partition sizes. Due to space constraints we only discuss the latter measure for two of our input distributions here. We refer to the technical report [12] for the full discussion.

The coefficient of variation c_v of the partition sizes p_i, $i \leq k$, is given by

$$c_v = \frac{\sigma}{\mu} = \frac{\sqrt{\frac{\sum_{i \leq k}(p_i - \mu)^2}{k-1}}}{\frac{\sum_{i \leq k} p_i}{k}}.$$

Figure 2 shows c_v for two different sample sizes and two of our input distributions.. For all distributions, our sample-based partitioning scheme robustly achieves a c_v of $\approx 6\%$ and $\approx 12\%$ for sample sizes $\sqrt{n}$ and $0.01n$, respectively. Both lie above the chosen imbalance of the graph partitioning of $\epsilon = 5\%$, as expected. The larger sample size not only decreases the average imbalance but also its spread for various random seeds. Moreover, the deficits of the original

---

[4] $\omega(e = (v,w)) = -\log d(v,w)$ width $d(\cdot)$ denoting the Euclidean distance.

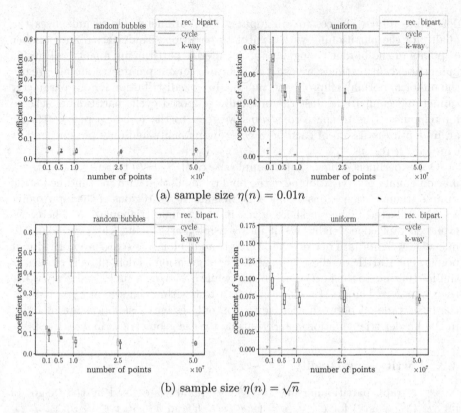

(a) sample size $\eta(n) = 0.01n$

(b) sample size $\eta(n) = \sqrt{n}$

Fig. 2. Coefficient of variation of the partition sizes for $k = t = 16$, parallel KaHIP, logarithmic edge weights and grid-based intersection test with $c_G = 1$.

cyclic partitioning scheme become apparent: whereas it works exceptionally well for uniformly distributed points, it produces inferior partitions in the presence of an underlying structure in the input, as found for instance in the random bubble distribution.

In total, our recursive algorithm triangulates more than the number of input points due to the triangulation of the sample points, and the triangulation(s) of the border point set(s). We quantify this in the overtriangulation factor o_{DT}, given by

$$o_{DT} := \frac{|\mathbf{P}| + \sum |\mathbf{P}_S| + \sum |\,\text{vertices}(\mathbf{B})|}{|\mathbf{P}|}.$$

$\mathbf{B}$ is the set of border simplices determined by our D&C algorithm. For direct k-way partitioning, only one sample and one border triangulation are necessary; for recursive bisectitioning there are a total of $k - 1$ of each. Figure 3 shows the overtriangulation factor a fixed choice of KaHIP configuration, edge weight and two different sample sizes and two of our input distributions. For all distributions, the larger sample size reduces the oversampling factor. As the partitioning of the larger sample DT more closely resembles the partitioning of the full DT,

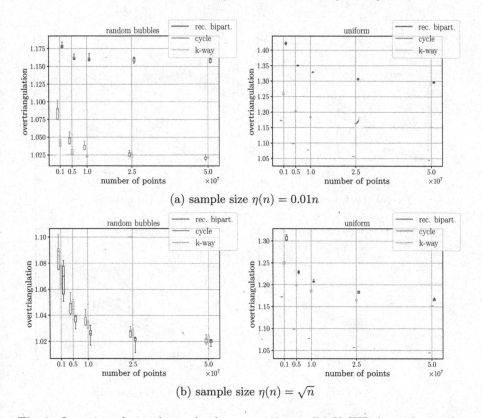

(a) sample size $\eta(n) = 0.01n$

(b) sample size $\eta(n) = \sqrt{n}$

Fig. 3. Overtriangulation factor for $k = t = 16$, parallel KaHIP, logarithmic edge weights and grid-based intersection test with $c_{\mathcal{G}} = 1$.

the number of points in the border triangulation is reduced. For the random bubble distribution, the overtriangulation factor is on par or below that of the original cyclic partitioning scheme. For the uniform distribution, our new divide-step suffers from the jagged border between the partitions compared to the smooth cut produced by the cyclic partitioning scheme. This results in more circumhyperspheres intersecting another partition and thus the inclusion of more points in the border triangulation. Our experiments with the exact intersection test primitive confirm this notion.

4.3   Runtime Evaluation

We conclude our experiments with a study of the runtime of our D&C algorithm with the new sample-based divide step against the originally proposed cyclic division strategy, its k-way variant – called "flat cycle" – as well as the parallel incremental insertion algorithm of CGAL. Figure 4 shows the total triangulation time for our fixed choice of configuration parameters.

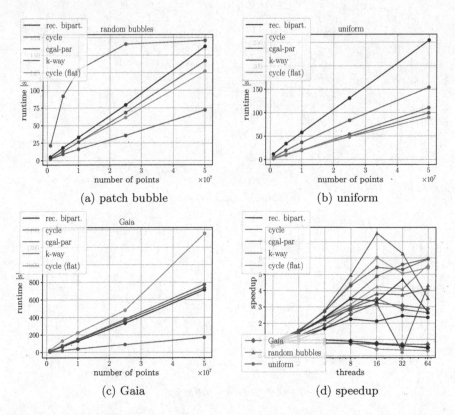

Fig. 4. Runtime evaluation for $k = t = 16$, parallel KaHIP, $\eta(n) = \sqrt{n}$, grid-based intersection test with $c_g = 1$ and logarithmic edge weights. Absolute speedup over sequential CGAL for $k = t$ and all distributions tested with 50×10^6 points.

Direct k-way partitioning performs best on the random bubbles distribution, with a speedup of up to 50% over the cyclic partitioning scheme. Considering the flattened cycle partitioner, a small fraction of this speedup can be attributed to the k-way merging, however the larger fraction is due to the data sensitivity of the sample-based scheme. CGAL's parallel incremental insertion algorithm requires locking to avoid race conditions. It therefore suffers from high contention in the bubble centers, resulting in a high variance of its runtime and a 350% speedup for our approach. For uniformly distributed points, our new divide-step falls behind the cyclic partitioning scheme as there is no structure to exploit in the input data and due to the higher overtriangulation factor of $o_{DT} = 1.15$ for k-way partitioning compared to $o_{DT} = 1.05$ for cyclic partitioning. As discussed in the previous section, the higher overtriangulation factor is caused by the jagged border between the partitions, resulting in a larger border triangulation and consequently also in higher merging times, as seen in Fig. 5b.

Of particular interest is the scaling behavior of our algorithm with an increasing number of threads. Figure 4d shows a strong scaling experiment.

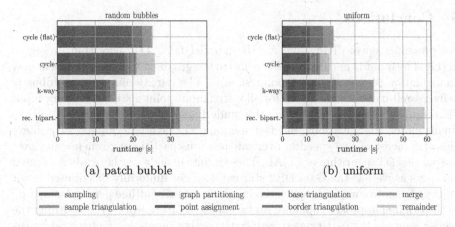

Fig. 5. Runtime breakdown for $k = t = 16$, parallel KaHIP, $\eta(n) = \sqrt{n}$, grid-based intersection test with $c_g = 1$ and logarithmic edge weights.

The absolute speedup of an algorithm A over the sequential CGAL algorithm is given by $\mathrm{Speedup}_A(t) := \frac{T_{\mathrm{CGAL}}}{T_A(t)}$ for t threads.

In the presence of exploitable input structure – such as for the random bubble distribution – direct k-way partitioning scales well on one physical processor (up to 16 cores). It clearly outperforms the original cyclic partitioning scheme and the parallel DT algorithm of CGAL. Nevertheless, it does not scale well to two sockets ($t > 16$ threads) and hyper-threading ($t > 32$ threads). The overtriangulation factor of 1.19 for 64 threads compared to 1.015 for 16 suggests that the size of the input is not sufficient to be efficiently split into 64 partitions.

Considering our real world dataset, the direct k-way partitioning scheme also exhibits the best scaling behavior. As illustrated in the image next to Table 1, the dataset comprises a large dense ring accompanied by several smaller isolated regions. This can be exploited to reduce border triangulation sizes and achieve a speedup, compared to the slowdown for the cyclic partitioning scheme and CGAL's parallel algorithm. The former is due to large border triangulations in the central ring, whereas the latter suffers from contention in the central region.

Clearly, direct k-way partitioning outperforms recursive bisection in every configuration. Following the theoretical considerations in Sect. 3.1 regarding the number of merge-steps required, this is to be expected. A measure to level the playing field would be to only allow for $\eta(n)$ *total* number of sample points on all levels, i.e. adjust the sample size on each level of the recursion according the expected halving of the input size.

Figure 5 shows a breakdown of the algorithm runtime for our fixed choice of configuration parameters. The sample-based partitioning requires 30% to 50% more runtime than the cyclic scheme. For favorable inputs with an exploitable structure, this additional runtime is more than mitigated by faster merging.

5   Conclusions

We present a novel divide-step for the parallel D&C DT algorithm presented in [11]. The input is partitioned according to the graph partitioning of a Delaunay triangulation of a small input point sample. The partitioning scheme robustly delivers well-balanced partitions for all tested input point distributions. For input distributions exhibiting an exploitable underlying structure, it further leads to small border triangulations and fast merging. On favorable inputs, we achieve almost a factor of two speedup over our previous partitioning scheme and over the parallel DT algorithm of CGAL. These inputs include synthetically generated data sets as well as the Gaia DR2 star catalog. For uniformly distributed input points, the more complex divide-step incurs an overall runtime penalty compared to the original approach, opening up two lanes of future work: (i) smoothing the border between the partitions to reduce the overtriangulation factor, and/or (ii) an adaptive strategy that chooses between the classical partitioning scheme and our new approach based on easily computed properties of the chosen sample point set, before computing its DT. The sample-based divide step can also be integrated into our distributed memory algorithm presented in [11], where the improved load-balancing and border size reduces the required communication volume for favorable inputs.

Acknowledgments. The authors gratefully acknowledge the Deutsche Forschungs-gemeinschaft (DFG) who partially supported this work under grants SA 933/10-2 and SA 933/11-1.

References

1. Aggarwal, A., Chazelle, B., Guibas, L.: Parallel computational geometry. Algorithmica **3**(1), 293–327 (1988)
2. Akhremtsev, Y., Sanders, P., Schulz, C.: High-quality shared-memory graph partitioning. In: Aldinucci, M., Padovani, L., Torquati, M. (eds.) Euro-Par 2018. LNCS, vol. 11014, pp. 659–671. Springer, Cham (2018). https://doi.org/10.1007/978-3-319-96983-1_47
3. Batista, V.H., Millman, D.L., Pion, S., Singler, J.: Parallel geometric algorithms for multi-core computers. Comp. Geom. **43**(8), 663–677 (2010)
4. van den Bergen, G.: Efficient collision detection of complex deformable models using aabb trees. J. Graph. Tools **2**(4), 1–13 (1997)
5. Chen, M.B.: The merge phase of parallel divide-and-conquer scheme for 3D Delaunay triangulation. In: International Symposium on Parallel and Distributed Processing with Applications (ISPA), pp. 224–230, IEEE (2010)
6. Chrisochoides, N.: Parallel mesh generation. Numerical Solution of Partial Differential Equations on Parallel Computers. LNCS, vol. 51, pp. 237–264. Springer, Berlin (2006). https://doi.org/10.1007/3-540-31619-1_7
7. Chrisochoides, N., Nave, D.: Simultaneous mesh generation and partitioning for Delaunay meshes. Math. Comput. Sim. **54**(4), 321–339 (2000)
8. Cignoni, P., Montani, C., Scopigno, R.: DeWall: a fast divide and conquer Delaunay triangulation algorithm in E^d. CAD **30**(5), 333–341 (1998)

9. Collaboration, G.: Gaia data release 2. summary of the contents and survey properties. arXiv (abs/1804.09365) (2018)
10. Devillers, O.: The Delaunay hierarchy. Int. J. Found. Comput. Sci. **13**(02), 163–180 (2002)
11. Funke, D., Sanders, P.: Parallel d-d Delaunay triangulations in shared and distributed memory. In: ALENEX, pp. 207–217, SIAM (2017)
12. Funke, D., Sanders, P., Winkler, V.: Load-Balancing for Parallel Delaunay Triangulations. arXiv (abs/1902.07554) (2019)
13. Hert, S., Seel, M.: dD convex hulls and delaunay triangulations. In: CGAL User and Reference Manual, CGAL Editorial Board, 4.7 edn. (2015)
14. Kernighan, B.W., Lin, S.: An efficient heuristic procedure for partitioning graphs. Bell Syst. Techn. J. **49**(2), 291–307 (1970)
15. Kohout, J., Kolingerová, I., Žára, J.: Parallel Delaunay triangulation in E2 and E3 for computers with shared memory. Par. Comp. **31**(5), 491–522 (2005)
16. Larsson, T., Akenine-Möller, T., Lengyel, E.: On faster sphere-box overlap testing. J. Graph., GPU, Game Tools **12**(1), 3–8 (2007)
17. Lee, S., Park, C.I., Park, C.M.: An improved parallel algorithm for Delaunay triangulation on distributed memory parallel computers. Parallel Process. Lett. **11**, 341–352 (2001)
18. Sanders, P., Lamm, S., Hübschle-Schneider, L., Schrade, E., Dachsbacher, C.: Efficient parallel random sampling - vectorized, cache-efficient, and online. ACM Trans. Math. Softw. **44**(3), 29:1–29:14 (2018)
19. Sanders, P., Schulz, C.: Think locally, act globally: highly balanced graph partitioning. In: Bonifaci, V., Demetrescu, C., Marchetti-Spaccamela, A. (eds.) SEA 2013. LNCS, vol. 7933, pp. 164–175. Springer, Heidelberg (2013). https://doi.org/10.1007/978-3-642-38527-8_16
20. Shewchuk, J.: Triangle: engineering a 2D quality mesh generator and Delaunay triangulator. Appl. Comp. Geom. Towards Geom. Eng. **1148**, 203–222 (1996)
21. Shewchuk, J.: Adaptive precision floating-point arithmetic and fast robust geometric predicates. Disc. Comp. Geom. **18**(3), 305–363 (1997)
22. Simon, H.D., Teng, S.H.: How good is recursive bisection? J. Sci. Comput. **18**(5), 1436–1445 (1997)
23. Su, P., Drysdale, R.L.S.: A comparison of sequential delaunay triangulation algorithms. In: Symposium on Computing Geometry (SCG), pp. 61–70, ACM (1995)

Design-Space Exploration
with Multi-Objective Resource-Aware
Modulo Scheduling

Julian Oppermann[1]($\boxtimes$) (ID), Patrick Sittel[2](ID), Martin Kumm[3](ID),
Melanie Reuter-Oppermann[4](ID), Andreas Koch[1](ID), and Oliver Sinnen[5]

[1] Embedded Systems and Applications Group, Technische Universität Darmstadt,
Darmstadt, Germany
{oppermann,koch}@esa.tu-darmstadt.de
[2] Circuits and Systems Group, Imperial College London, London, UK
psittel@ic.ac.uk
[3] Faculty of Applied Computer Science, University of Applied Sciences Fulda,
Fulda, Germany
martin.kumm@cs.hs-fulda.de
[4] Discrete Optimization and Logistics Group, Karlsruhe Institute of Technology,
Karlsruhe, Germany
melanie.reuter@kit.edu
[5] Parallel and Reconfigurable Computing Lab, University of Auckland,
Auckland, New Zealand
o.sinnen@auckland.ac.nz

Abstract. Many of today's applications in parallel and concurrent computing are deployed using reconfigurable hardware, in particular field-
programmable gate arrays (FPGAs). Due to the complexity of modern
applications and the wide spectsrum of possible implementations, manual
design of modern custom hardware is not feasible. Computer-aided design
tools enable the automated transformation of high-level descriptions into
hardware. However, the efficient identification of Pareto-optimal solutions to trade-off between resource utilisation and throughput is still an
open research topic. Combining resource allocation and modulo scheduling, we propose a new approach for design-space exploration of custom hardware implementations. Using problem-specific rules, we are able
to exclude obviously dominated solutions from the design space before
scheduling and synthesis. Compared to a standard, multi-criteria optimisation method, we show the benefits of our approach regarding runtime
at the design level.

1 Introduction

The use of reconfigurable platforms including field-programmable gate arrays
(FPGAs) is common for hardware acceleration in the area of applied and
high-performance embedded computing. Compared to costly and inflexible

© Springer Nature Switzerland AG 2019
R. Yahyapour (Ed.): Euro-Par 2019, LNCS 11725, pp. 170–183, 2019.
https://doi.org/10.1007/978-3-030-29400-7_13

application-specific integrated circuits, FPGAs provide relatively high throughput and low power implementations while enabling rapid-prototyping [4]. Due to the exponential rise of complexity of digital systems and FPGA capacity, the process of manually implementing specifications in hardware is inefficient regarding design time and quality [5]. To overcome this, high-level synthesis (HLS) can be applied to automatically transform behavioural descriptions into hardware. The three main steps of HLS are resource allocation, operation scheduling and binding [9]. In the allocation step, physical resources are determined. Using only the allocated resources, the scheduling step assigns execution times, usually in clock cycles, to every operation such that no data dependency is violated. Next, the operations are bound to specific functional units in hardware. Finally, the high-level input description is transformed into a hardware description language (HDL) representation that implements the operations, memory interfacing and data flow control at the register-transfer level.

The scheduling phase is crucial for the accelerator's performance, and is therefore typically the most time-consuming step in this process. Using conventional scheduling algorithms, the achievable throughput is reciprocally proportional to the determined schedule length (latency). The throughput can be increased by using *modulo scheduling*, which interleaves successive schedules [15]. Usually allocation, scheduling and binding are performed sequentially in order to reduce design time. This limits the number and quality of trade-off points in the design space. Detaching resource allocation from scheduling, state-of-the-art modulo schedulers only determine a single solution without providing any information about trade-offs or resource saving opportunities [3,12]. The research question of how to use resource allocation and scheduling efficiently to obtain Pareto-optimal trade-off points, remains open. Enumerating all possible allocations and scheduling each of them typically leads to prohibitively long runtimes. Fan et al. proposed cost-sensitive modulo scheduling [8] to synthesise the smallest (in terms of resource use) accelerator for a loop at a given, externally specified initiation interval. While their goal is similar to ours, they compute the number of functional units before scheduling using heuristic rules, whereas we can minimise the allocation as part of an exact scheduling formulation. We can thus handle the situation where the trivial resource allocation is infeasible for a given interval. The only published formulation that includes the minimisation of allocated resources in a modulo scheduling formulation is the one proposed by Šůcha and Hanzálek [18]. The above works did not address design-space exploration (DSE), however.

In this work, we make the following contributions. Firstly, we establish a formal definition and a framework for resource-aware modulo schedulers, discussing the necessary changes required to make existing, exact formulations suitable for multi-objective, resource-aware optimisation. Secondly, we discuss how to apply a standard method from multi-criteria optimisation, and propose a novel problem-specific approach compatible with our extended formulations. Our evaluation shows that the problem-specific approach outperforms the standard method in terms of both overall runtime and number of trade-off points.

2   Scheduling Framework

At the beginning of an HLS flow, an intermediate data flow graph (DFG) representation is constructed from the input loop description, modelling the *operations* that constitute the computation as vertices, and the data flow and other precedence relationships between the operations as edges. In contrast to general-purpose processors, HLS tools employ a spatial approach to computation, meaning that in the extreme case, an individual *operator* is instantiated for each operation. However, as each operator occupies a certain amount of an FPGA device's finite number of *resources*, an HLS compiler can choose to *share* operators among several operations in different time steps.

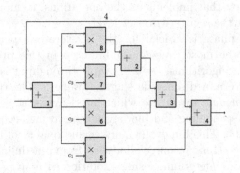

Fig. 1. Data flow graph of example.

Figure 1 shows an example DFG which we use to further illustrate the problem and introduce our notation. The DFG contains four multiplications and four additions which are represented as vertices. The result of operation 3 is delayed by four iterations (edge marked with '4') and fed back into the input of operation 1. There are different ways to schedule the execution of the operations, as illustrated in Fig. 2. Figure 2(a) shows one extreme where a separate operator is instantiated for each operation. It takes five time steps to compute one iteration, i.e. the result of operation 4, due to the data dependencies illustrated by the non-shaded parts. However, with modulo scheduling, each operator can accept new operands in each time step such that up to five iterations are processed concurrently as represented by the different colours. Since a new iteration can be initiated at operation 1 at every time step, the *initiation interval* (II) is equal to one. Figure 2(b) shows the other extreme where only one instance is used per operator type. Here, it takes eight time steps to compute one result value, but new iterations can be initiated every II = 4 time steps. Usually, several solutions exist between these extremes providing trade-offs between throughput and resource utilisation.

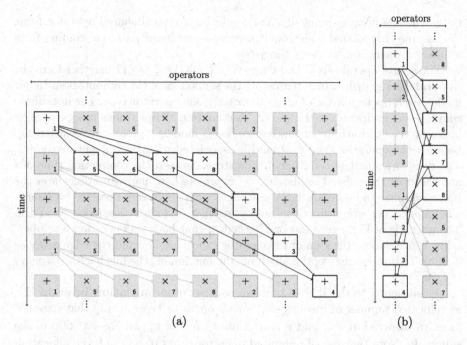

Fig. 2. Two example schedules of DFG in Fig. 1 with (a) eight parallel operators and II = 1 and (b) two parallel operators and II = 4

2.1   Formal Definitions

We now introduce the necessary terms and notations used throughout the paper, starting with the definition of the *resource-aware modulo scheduling* (**RAMS**) problem. The **target device** is abstracted to the different types of low-level resources R, and the number of elements N_r available of each resource $r \in R$. Typical resources include lookup tables (LUTs), digital signal-processing blocks (DSPs), and memory elements such as flip-flops and on-chip block RAM. The set of **operator types** Q is derived from the HLS tool's library, which usually provides modules for the basic arithmetic/logic functionality, as well as ports to random-access memories. Each instance of operator type $\mathbf{q}$ performs a single function that takes $l_\mathbf{q}$ time steps to complete, and has an associated demand $n_{\mathbf{q},r} \in \mathbb{N}_0$ in terms of the device's resources $r \in R$. Most operator types are simple enough to implement on FPGAs to have $n_{\mathbf{q},r} \ll N_r$ regarding all resources. Therefore, it is reasonable for the HLS tool to treat them as practically unlimited, i.e. instantiate as many operators as needed. In contrast, operators whose resource demands exceed a certain threshold are candidates to be time-multiplexed by the HLS tool. Their types constitute the set of **shared operator types** $\hat{Q} \subseteq Q$. While the concrete threshold is tool-dependent, we assume that the resource demand of the multiplexing logic required for sharing is negligible in comparison to the resource demands of shared operators. Accordingly, integer addition is the canonical example for an unlimited operator type, whereas floating-point division would be a typical shared operator type. We assume that shared operators can accept new input data, i.e. coming from a different operation, at every time step.

The sets of operations O and edges $E = \{(i \rightarrow j)\} \subseteq O \times O$ together form the **dependence graph**, which represents the semantics of the computation. In our model, each operation $i \in O$ maps to exactly one operator type. For notational convenience, we introduce the sets $O_\mathbf{q}$ that contain all operations using a specific operator type $\mathbf{q}$. Each dependence edge $(i \rightarrow j)$ models a precedence relationship between the operations $i, j \in O$, and is associated with two integer attributes. The delay δ_{ij} mandates additional time steps between the completion time of i and the start time of j. The distance β_{ij} expresses how many iterations later the precedence has to be satisfied. We call edges with a non-zero-distance *backedges*. The dependence graph may contain cycles that include at least one backedge. The example of Fig. 1 contains one backedge: that between operation 3 to operation 1. We denote the sum of i's operator type's latency and the edge delay as d_{ij}. In addition, we may optionally limit the maximum schedule length (latency) $U \in \mathbb{N}_0$.

A solution S to the RAMS problem consists of an **initiation interval** II^S, an allocated number of instances $a_\mathbf{q}^S$ for all operator types $\mathbf{q} \in Q$ that together form an **allocation** A^S, and a start time t_i^S for all operations $i \in O$, i.e. the **schedule**. Note that for all unlimited operator types $\mathbf{q}' \in Q \setminus \hat{Q}$, the allocation is fixed to $a_{\mathbf{q}'}^S = |O_{\mathbf{q}'}|$. We define the solution's utilisation of resource $\mathbf{r}$ as:

$$\eta_\mathbf{r}(A^S) = \sum_{\mathbf{q} \in Q} a_\mathbf{q}^S \cdot n_{\mathbf{q},\mathbf{r}} \tag{1}$$

Any **feasible** solution S must satisfy the following constraints

$$t_i^S + d_{ij} \le t_j^S + \beta_{ij} \cdot \mathrm{II}^S \quad \forall (i \rightarrow j) \in E \tag{2}$$

$$|\{i \in O_\mathbf{q} : t_i^S \bmod \mathrm{II}^S = m\}| \le a_\mathbf{q}^S \quad \forall \mathbf{q} \in \hat{Q} \text{ and } m \in [0, \mathrm{II}^S - 1] \tag{3}$$

$$\eta_\mathbf{r}(A^S) \le N_\mathbf{r} \quad \forall \mathbf{r} \in R \tag{4}$$

where constraints (2) assert that all dependence edges are honoured, (3) state that no operator type shall be oversubscribed and (4) ensure that the allocation does not exceed the target device's limits.

In our setting, two **competing objectives** exist, i.e. the minimisation of the initiation interval (II), and the minimisation of the resource utilisation (RU):

$$f_{\mathrm{II}}(S) = \mathrm{II}^S \qquad f_{\mathrm{RU}}(S) = \frac{1}{|R|} \sum_{\mathbf{r} \in R} \frac{\eta_\mathbf{r}(A^S)}{N_\mathbf{r}} \tag{5}$$

As no universally applicable weighting exists, we seek to compute a set $\mathcal{S}$ of Pareto-optimal solutions with different trade-offs between the two objectives, and refer to this endeavour as the *multi-objective resource-aware modulo scheduling* (**MORAMS**) problem. A solution $S \in \mathcal{S}$ is Pareto-optimal if it is not *dominated* by any other solution, i.e. $\nexists S' \in \mathcal{S}$ with $(f_{\mathrm{II}}(S'), f_{\mathrm{RU}}(S')) < (f_{\mathrm{II}}(S), f_{\mathrm{RU}}(S))$.

2.2 Bounds

The solution space for the MORAMS problem can be confined by simple bounds derived from the problem instance.

We define the minimum allocation $A^\perp$ to contain $a_{\mathbf{q}}^\perp = 1$ instances for each shared operator type $\mathbf{q} \in Q$, and $a_{\mathbf{q}'}^\perp = |O_{\mathbf{q}'}|$ instances for each unlimited type $\mathbf{q}' \in Q \setminus \hat{Q}$. Note that the minimum allocation may be infeasible for any II if a MORAMS instance contains backedges, or an additional latency constraint is given. We assume that $\eta_r(A^\perp) \leq N_r$, regarding all resources r, as otherwise the problem instance is trivially infeasible.

---

minimise $f_{\mathrm{RU}}(X)$

subject to formulation-specific dependence constraints $\hspace{2cm}$ ($\rightarrow$ 2)

$\hspace{1cm}$ formulation-specific constraints that ensure at most $a_{\mathbf{q}}^X$ operations using operator type $\mathbf{q}$ are started in each congruence class modulo II^X ($\rightarrow$ 3)

$\hspace{1cm}$ $\eta_r(A^X) \leq N_r \quad \forall r \in R$ $\hspace{3cm}$ ($\rightarrow$ 4)

$\hspace{1cm}$ $a_{\mathbf{q}}^X \in \mathbb{N}_0$, and $a_{\mathbf{q}}^\perp \leq a_{\mathbf{q}}^X \leq a_{\mathbf{q}}^\top \quad \forall \mathbf{q} \in Q$

Fig. 3. Template model for resource-aware modulo scheduling

The maximum allocation $A^\top$ models how many operators of a particular type would fit on the device if all other operator types were fixed at their minimum allocation. Formally, we define, for each $\mathbf{q} \in \hat{Q}$:

$$a_{\mathbf{q}}^\top = \min \left\{ \underbrace{1}_{(a)} + \underbrace{\min_{r \in R : n_{\mathbf{q},r} > 0} \left\lfloor \frac{N_r - \eta_r(A^\perp)}{n_{\mathbf{q},r}} \right\rfloor}_{(b)}, \underbrace{|O_{\mathbf{q}}|}_{(c)} \right\} \qquad (6)$$

Here, (a) represents the one $\mathbf{q}$-instance already considered in the minimum allocation, (b) models how many extra $\mathbf{q}$-instances would fit using the remaining elements of resource r, i.e. when subtracting the r-utilisation of the minimum allocation. Lastly, (c) limits the allocation to its trivial upper bound, i.e. the number of operations that use $\mathbf{q}$. For completeness, we set $a_{\mathbf{q}'}^\top = |O_{\mathbf{q}'}|$ for the remaining, unlimited operator types $\mathbf{q}' \in Q \setminus \hat{Q}$.

The minimum initiation interval $\mathrm{II}^\perp$ is usually defined (e.g. in [15]) as $\mathrm{II}^\perp = \max\{\mathrm{II}_{\mathrm{rec}}^\perp, \mathrm{II}_{\mathrm{res}}^\perp\}$, i.e. the maximum of the recurrence-constrained minimum II and the resource-constrained minimum II. $\mathrm{II}_{\mathrm{rec}}^\perp$ is induced by (2) and the recurrences (cycles) in the dependence graph, while $\mathrm{II}_{\mathrm{res}}^\perp$ follows from (3):

$$\mathrm{II}_{\mathrm{res}}^\perp = \max_{\mathbf{q} \in \hat{Q}} \left\lceil \frac{|O_{\mathbf{q}}|}{a_{\mathbf{q}}^\top} \right\rceil \qquad (7)$$

The upper bound for the initiation interval $\mathrm{II}^\top$ is obtained by scheduling the instance with a non-modulo scheduler that uses heuristic resource constraints according to the minimum allocation.

3   ILP Formulations for the RAMS Problem

The template formulation in Fig. 3 illustrates how ILP-based modulo scheduling formulations can be made resource-aware with small changes. In principle, it suffices to replace formerly constant limits in the base formulation with integer decision variables modelling the allocation. For notational convenience, we consider these variables to be part of an intermediate solution X. Then, one would minimise the ILP according to the objective function $f_{RU}(X)$. The specific changes required to extend state-of-the-art schedulers are described in the following.

Formulation by Eichenberger and Davidson. The formulation by Eichenberger and Davidson (abbreviated here as *ED*) limits the use of an operator (M_q, in their notation) per modulo slot only on the right-hand sides of constraints (5) [7]. Replacing M_q by the appropriate allocation variables and the objective are thus the only changes required to their model.

Formulation by Šůcha and Hanzálek. The formulation by Šůcha and Hanzálek (*SH*), is the only formulation for which a resource-aware extension was already proposed [18]. We reimplemented their unit-processing time formulation to be used in our MORAMS approach. Note though that we needed to use the weaker form of their constraints (9), i.e. before applying their Lemma 1, as otherwise the number of constraints would need to be adapted according to the dynamic values of the allocation decision variables (m_1 in their notation), which is not possible in ILPs.

Formulation by Oppermann et al. The Moovac formulation (*MV*) by Oppermann et al. was presented in two variants: Moovac-S, which is a single-II scheduler, and Moovac-I, which models the initiation interval as a decision variable [12]. The changes needed to make them resource-aware are the same for both, however. Note that the formulation, as presented in [12], does compute a *binding*, i.e. mapping of operations to concrete operators, in contrast to the ED and SH formulations, which only ensure that no more than the allocated number of operators are used in each modulo congruence class. For a fairer comparison, we adapted Šůcha and Hanzálek's idea of counting the modulo slot conflicts among the operations competing for the same shared operator type. To this end, we drop the variables r_i (in their notation) and the constraints (M3-M5), (M9) and (M11) from the formulation, and instead add the following constraints (again, in their notation):

$$\sum_{j \in L_k, i \neq j} 1 - \mu_{ij} - \mu_{ji} \leq a_k - 1 \; \forall i \in L_k \tag{8}$$

The binary variables μ_{ij} and μ_{ji} are both zero iff operations i and j occupy the same congruence class. The formulation can be made resource-aware by replacing the parameter a_k with the appropriate allocation variable.

4   Approaches for the MORAMS Problem

In the following, we discuss two different approaches to solve the MORAMS problem, i.e. computing a set S of Pareto-optimal solutions regarding $f_{\mathrm{II}}(X)$ and $f_{\mathrm{RU}}(X)$, with the help of the RAMS formulations described above.

4.1 ε-Approach

The ε-approach is a standard method from the multi-criteria optimisation field [6]. Its core idea, given two objectives, is to optimise for only one objective and add a constraint for the other. In order to apply the method for solving the MORAMS problem, we need to employ a RAMS formulation where *all* components of a solution are decision variables, such as the Moovac-I formulation with the extensions discussed above. The approach starts with determining an extreme point by one objective, $f_{\mathrm{II}}(X)$ in our case, and determining the value for the other, i.e. the resource utilisation $f_{\mathrm{RU}}(X)$. For the next iteration, a constraint forcing the resource utilisation to be less than current value *minus an* ε, is added, and the model is again solved with the II minimisation objective. We use $\varepsilon = \min_{r \in R} \frac{1}{N_r \cdot |R|}$, i.e. the smallest possible decrease in the objective value according to the device resources. This algorithm is iterated until the successively stronger ε-constraints prevent any new feasible solution to be discovered. We deviate slightly from the standard method by lexicographically minimising both the II and the resource utilisation, to ensure that we obtain the smallest possible allocation for each interval. As a bonus, we know that the II will increase in each iteration, and encode this insight in the form of a second, nonstandard ε-constraint regarding $f_{\mathrm{II}}(X)$. We only accept ILP solutions that were proven to be optimal by the solver, as suboptimal solutions could yield dominated MORAMS solutions and interfere with the convergence of the algorithm. Conversely, the returned set of solutions S is guaranteed to only contain Pareto-optimal solutions, thus no post-filtering is needed.

4.2   Iterative Approach

As an alternative to the ε-approach that requires the II to be a decision variable, we propose an iterative approach, in which the II is a constant for each iteration, to tackle the MORAMS problem. This approach is outlined in Algorithm 1. We choose successively larger candidate IIs from the range of possible intervals (Line 3), construct the ILP parameterised to that II, solve it with the resource utilisation objective (Line 6) and, given that the ILP solver has proven optimality, retrieve and record the solution (lines 11–13). We stop the exploration if the solver returns either no solution, or a suboptimal one, due to a violated time limit. Note that the resulting set of solutions can contain dominated solutions. While filtering out these solutions after scheduling (Line 16) is easy, significant time may be wasted in computing them. To this end, we propose two heuristic rules to skip scheduling attempts that would result in obviously dominated solutions.

Algorithm 1. Iterative approach to the RAMS problem

1: Let `ILP` be an exact modulo scheduling formulation with a candidate interval II^X (a parameter), and decision variables $a_{\mathbf{q}}^X \; \forall \mathbf{q} \in Q$ and $t_i^X \; \forall i \in O$. Consider the candidate II and the decision variables as part of an intermediate solution X.

2: $\mathcal{S} \leftarrow \emptyset$; $S^{-1} \leftarrow$ null

3: **for** $\text{II}^X \in [\text{II}^\perp, \text{II}^\top]$ **do**   ▷ Iterate in ascending order

4:     **if** $S^{-1} \neq$ null and $\forall \mathbf{q} \in \hat{Q} : a_{\mathbf{q}}^{S^{-1}} = \left\lceil \frac{|O_{\mathbf{q}}|}{\text{II}^X} \right\rceil$ **then**

5:         **continue** with next candidate II to skip obviously dominated solutions

6:     `ILP.construct(` II^X `)` ; `ILP.solveWithObjective(` $f_{\text{RU}}(X)$ `)`

7:     **if** solver status is "infeasible" **then**

8:         $S^{-1} \leftarrow$ null ; **continue** with next candidate II

9:     **else if** solver status is not "optimal" **then**

10:        **stop** exploration

11:    $S \leftarrow$ new solution

12:    $\text{II}^S \leftarrow \text{II}^X$; $a_{\mathbf{q}}^S \leftarrow$ `ILP.value(` $a_{\mathbf{q}}^X$ `)` $\forall \mathbf{q} \in Q$; $t_i^S \leftarrow$ `ILP.value(` t_i^X `)` $\forall i \in O$

13:    $\mathcal{S} \leftarrow \mathcal{S} \cup \{S\}$; $S^{-1} \leftarrow S$

14:    **if** $A^S = A^\perp$ **then**

15:        **stop** exploration, as minimal allocation is achieved

16: **return** FilterDominatedSolutions($\mathcal{S}$)

The first rule is shown in lines 4–5. We already used the feasibility constraint in (3) to establish a static lower bound for the II. However, with knowledge of the current interval II^X, we can also use it to derive a lower bound for the allocation of each shared operator type $\mathbf{q} \in \hat{Q}$. Recall that each $\mathbf{q}$-instance can only accommodate II^X operations, which yields:

$$a_{\mathbf{q}}^X \geq \left\lceil \frac{|O_{\mathbf{q}}|}{\text{II}^X} \right\rceil \tag{9}$$

We call an allocation A^X *trivial* for an II^X if all $a_{\mathbf{q}}^X$ are equal to the right-hand side of (9).

Now, we can skip the current candidate II if the previously computed allocation $A^{S^{-1}}$ is equivalent to the trivial allocation for II^X, because it cannot be improved with respect to the previous solution. Li et al. used a similar rule to filter candidate IIs' based on the respective trivial allocations [11]. However, their definition disregards the possibility that these allocations may be infeasible, and therefore can lead to incorrectly excluded candidate IIs.

The second rule (lines 14–15) stops the exploration if the minimum allocation $A^\perp$ is achieved. All remaining solutions would be dominated by the current solution because the allocation cannot be improved further, and those solutions would have larger IIs. Note that both rules can only be applied if the respective minimal allocations are feasible, which may not be the case in the presence of deadlines imposed by either backedges or latency constraints.

Table 1. Complexity of problem instances

	Min	Median	Mean	Max
# operations	14	49	104	1374
# shared operations	0	4	16	416
# edges	17	81	237	4441
# backedges	0	3	23	1155

4.3 Dynamic Lower Bound for the Allocation

In order to make it easier for the ILP solver to prove that it has reached the optimal allocation for the current II, we propose to include bound (9) in the models. When using the iterative approach, we can simply add it as a linear constraint to the formulation, since II^X is a constant. For the ε-approach, (9) would be a quadratic constraint. To linearise it, we introduce binary variables II_π^X with $II_\pi^X = 1 \Leftrightarrow II^X = \pi$ for $\pi \in [II^\perp, II^\top]$, adding the following linear constraints to the formulation:

$$a_{\mathbf{q}}^X \geq \left\lceil \frac{|O_{\mathbf{q}}|}{\pi} \right\rceil \cdot II_\pi^X \quad \forall \pi \in [II^\perp, II^\top] \tag{10}$$

5 Evaluation

We evaluated the presented MORAMS approaches on a set of **204** realistic test instances. These modulo scheduling problems were extracted from two different HLS environments: 16 instances originate from Simulink models compiled by the Origami HLS project [2], whereas 188 instances represent loops from the well-known C-based HLS benchmark suites CHStone [10] and MachSuite [16]. The latter were compiled by the Nymble C-to-hardware compiler as described in [13], using an operator library from the Bambu HLS framework [14]. Table 1 summarises the instances' complexity. Our target device was the Xilinx Zynq XC7Z020, a popular low-cost FPGA found on several evaluation boards. As resources, we model its number of lookup tables (53200), DSP slices (220), and, specifically for the C-based benchmark instances, assume the availability of up to 16 memory ports that can be used to either read from or write to an address space shared with the ARM CPU-based host system of the Zynq device.

We performed the proposed design-space exploration using Gurobi 8.1 as ILP solver on 2×12-core Intel Xeon E5-2680 v3 systems running at 2.8 GHz with 64 GiB RAM. The schedulers were allowed to use up to 8 threads, 6 hours wall-clock time and 16 GiB of memory *per instance*. We report each instance's *best* result from two runs, considering first the number of solutions, and then the accumulated runtime of the exploration.

In modulo schedulers, the II can be much lower than its latency. However, the latency should not be unbounded and there exist latency critical applications (like in closed control loops) where a low latency is important in addition to a low II. Hence, we consider the latency as a separate user constraint. As this can significantly influence the results, we scheduled our test instances subject to three different latency constraints that cover the whole spectrum of cases: The strongest constraint is to limit the schedule length U to the length of the critical path U_{CP}. Using $\mathrm{II}^{\top}$, i.e. the length of a non-modulo schedule with heuristic resource constraints, relaxes the operations' deadlines slightly. Lastly, we adapt the loose but conservative bound U_{Im} from [12] to the maximum allocation, which by construction does not exclude any modulo schedule with minimal length.

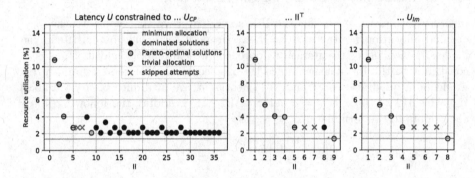

Fig. 4. Trade-off points for instance splin_pf, computed with the iterative approach

Let $\mathcal{S}_C$ be the set of solutions computed by a particular approach. We distinguish the set of Pareto-optimal solutions $\mathcal{S}$ and dominated solutions $\mathcal{S}_D$ with $\mathcal{S}_C = \mathcal{S} \cup \mathcal{S}_D$. Additionally, we define the set $\mathcal{S}_T \subseteq \mathcal{S}$ of trivial solutions, i.e. solutions with the trivial allocation for their respective II.

Figure 4 illustrates these metrics and the shape of the solution space resulting from the exploration with our iterative approach for the instance representing the Simulink model splin_pf. We picked this particular instance because it behaves differently under the three latency constraints, and showcases the effects of our heuristic rules. In the case $U = U_{\mathrm{CP}}$, many dominated solutions were computed because the minimal allocation $A^{\perp}$ was not feasible, and consequently, the early-termination rule (Lines 14–15) in Algorithm 1 was not applicable. Also, the candidate-skipping rule (Lines 4–5) was only able to skip candidate IIs 6–7. For $U = \mathrm{II}^{\top}$, the situation was significantly relaxed, as we only computed one dominated solution at $\mathrm{II} = 8$, and were able stop the exploration at $\mathrm{II} = 9$. Lastly, with $U = U_{\mathrm{Im}}$, all solutions were trivial, and no extra dominated solutions were computed. The equivalent plots for the ε-approach, which we omit here for brevity, only contain the orange-coloured Pareto-optimal solutions by construction. All approaches completed the exploration for splin_pf within three seconds of runtime.

The results of the exploration across all 204 test instances are summarised in Table 2 for the ε-approach of Sect. 4.1, as well as the iterative approach of Sect. 4.2 together with the ED, SH or MV formulations. The scheduler runtimes are accumulated in the columns "RT [h]" to give intuition into the computational effort required by the different approaches. Note that in practice, one would not need to schedule a set of instances sequentially. We then count the number of solutions in the aforementioned categories.

According to the complete exploration, the clear winner is the resource-aware ED formulation within our problem-specific, iterative approach, as it computes the most Pareto-optimal solutions (columns "$|\mathcal{S}|$") in the least amount of time (columns "RT [h]"), across all latency constraints, by a large margin. The SH formulation performs slightly better than the Moovac formulation in the MORAMS setting. We observe that for the tightest latency constraint U_{CP}, fewer trivial allocations are feasible than for the other bounds, which causes the iterative approaches to compute $|\mathcal{S}_C| \gg |\mathcal{S}|$, due to the non-applicability of the heuristic tweaks in Algorithm 1. On the other hand, the fact that $|\mathcal{S}| > |\mathcal{S}_T|$ demonstrates that only considering solutions with the trivial allocation for the respective II (e.g. as suggested in [8]) would, in general, not be sufficient to perform a complete exploration.

Table 2. Design-space exploration results for 204 instances

Method	$U \leq U_{\mathrm{CP}}$				$U \leq \mathrm{II}^T$				$U \leq U_{\mathrm{Im}}$			
	RT [h]	$|\mathcal{S}_C|$	$|\mathcal{S}|$	$|\mathcal{S}_T|$	RT [h]	$|\mathcal{S}_C|$	$|\mathcal{S}|$	$|\mathcal{S}_T|$	RT [h]	$|\mathcal{S}_C|$	$|\mathcal{S}|$	$|\mathcal{S}_T|$
ε-app	12.2	285	285	168	48.4	372	372	302	70.6	321	321	290
ED (iter)	2.4	1510	290	170	26.4	498	453	381	34.9	441	422	382
SH (iter)	16.2	1502	289	170	48.1	448	412	341	47.7	416	408	371
MV (iter)	16.0	1492	289	170	48.2	422	379	308	54.3	353	346	312

RT [h] = "total runtime in hours". $\mathcal{S}_C$, $\mathcal{S}$, $\mathcal{S}_T$ = "computed, Pareto-optimal, trivial solutions".

By design, the ε-approach computes only the Pareto-optimal solutions, regardless of the latency constraint (columns "$|\mathcal{S}_C|$" $\equiv$ "$|\mathcal{S}|$"). However, this benefit is apparently outweighed by the additional complexity introduced by modelling the II as a decision variable in the Moovac-I formulation, causing the ε-approach to be outperformed by the ED formulation.

6   Conclusion and Outlook

We presented a framework to perform a scheduler-driven design-space exploration in the context of high-level synthesis. Despite of leveraging ILP-based modulo scheduling formulations, the MORAMS problem can be tackled in a reasonable amount of time, and yields a variety of throughput vs. resource utilisation trade-off points. An open-source implementation of the proposed iterative

MORAMS approach, as well as the test instances used in the evaluation, are available as part of the HatScheT scheduling library [1].

We believe that this work can serve as the foundation for the development of heuristic approaches, as well as an environment to investigate *binding-aware* objective functions, such as register minimisation [17], or balancing the workload of the allocated operators for interconnect optimisation.

It could also be investigated, if the formulation by Eichenberger and Davidson, which already yielded the best results with our proposed, iterative approach, can be sped up further by applying a problem-reduction technique [13].

Acknowledgements. The authors would like to thank James J. Davis for providing detailed feedback regarding the clarity of this paper. The experiments for this research were conducted on the Lichtenberg high-performance computing cluster at TU Darmstadt.

References

1. HatScheT - Project Website (2019). http://www.uni-kassel.de/go/hatschet
2. Origami HLS - Project Website (2019). http://www.uni-kassel.de/go/origami
3. Canis, A., Brown, S.D., Anderson, J.H.: Modulo SDC scheduling with recurrence minimization in high-level synthesis. In: 24th International Conference on Field Programmable Logic and Applications (2014)
4. Chen, F., et al.: Enabling FPGAs in the Cloud. In: Proceedings of the 11th ACM Conference on Computing Frontiers (2014)
5. De Michell, G., Gupta, R.K.: Hardware/software co-design. Proc. IEEE **85**, 3 (1997)
6. Ehrgott, M.: Multicriteria Optimization, 2nd edn, p. 323. Springer, Berlin (2005). https://doi.org/10.1007/3-540-27659-9
7. Eichenberger, A.E., Davidson, E.S.: Efficient formulation for optimal modulo schedulers. In: Proceedings of the ACM SIGPLAN 1997 Conference on Programming Language Design and Implementation, Las Vegas, USA (1997)
8. Fan, K., Kudlur, M., Park, H., Mahlke, S.A.: Cost sensitive modulo scheduling in a loop accelerator synthesis system. In: 38th Annual IEEE/ACM International Symposium on Microarchitecture, Barcelona, Spain (2005)
9. Gajski, D.D., Dutt, N.D., Wu, A.C., Lin, S.Y.: High-level synthesis: Introduction to Chip and System Design (2012)
10. Hara, Y., Tomiyama, H., Honda, S., Takada, H.: Proposal and quantitative analysis of the chstone benchmark program suite for practical c-based high-level synthesis. JIP **17**, 242–254 (2009)
11. Li, P., Zhang, P., Pouchet, L., Cong, J.: Resource-aware throughput optimization for high-level synthesis. In: Proceedings of the 2015 ACM/SIGDA International Symposium on Field-Programmable Gate Arrays, Monterey, CA, USA (2015)
12. Oppermann, J., Reuter-Oppermann, M., Sommer, L., Koch, A., Sinnen, O.: Exact and practical modulo scheduling for high-level synthesis. ACM Trans. Reconfigurable Technol. Syst. **12**(2), 1–26 (2019)
13. Oppermann, J., Reuter-Oppermann, M., Sommer, L., Sinnen, O., Koch, A.: Dependence graph preprocessing for faster exact modulo scheduling in high-level synthesis. In: 28th International Conference on Field Programmable Logic and Applications, Dublin, Ireland (2018)

14. Pilato, C., Ferrandi, F.: Bambu: a modular framework for the high level synthesis of memory-intensive applications. In: 23rd International Conference on Field programmable Logic and Applications, Porto, Portugal (2013)

15. Rau, B.R.: Iterative modulo scheduling. Int. J. Parallel Program. **24**(1), 3–64 (1996)

16. Reagen, B., Adolf, R., Shao, Y.S., Wei, G., Brooks, D.M.: MachSuite: benchmarks for accelerator design and customized architectures. In: IEEE International Symposium on Workload Characterization, Raleigh, USA (2014)

17. Sittel, P., Kumm, M., Oppermann, J., Möller, K., Zipf, P., Koch, A.: ILP-based modulo scheduling and binding for register minimization. In: 28th International Conference on Field Programmable Logic and Applications, Dublin, Ireland (2018)

18. Sucha, P., Hanzalek, Z.: A cyclic scheduling problem with an undetermined number of parallel identical processors. Comp. Opt. Appl. **48**(1), 71–90 (2011)

Implementing YewPar: A Framework for Parallel Tree Search

Blair Archibald[1]($\boxtimes$)(iD), Patrick Maier[3](iD), Robert Stewart[2](iD),
and Phil Trinder[1](iD)

[1] School of Computing Science, University of Glasgow, Glasgow G12 8QQ, UK
{Blair.Archibald,Phil.Trinder}@Glasgow.ac.uk
[2] Mathematical and Computer Sciences, Heriot-Watt University, Edinburgh, UK
[3] Department of Computing, Sheffield Hallam University, Sheffield, UK

Abstract. Combinatorial search is central to many applications yet hard to parallelise. We argue for improving the reuse of parallel searches, and present the design and implementation of a new parallel search framework. YewPar generalises search by abstracting search tree generation, and by providing algorithmic skeletons that support three search types, together with a set of search coordination strategies. The evaluation shows that the cost of YewPar generality is low (6.1%); global knowledge is inexpensively shared between workers; irregular tasks are effectively distributed; and YewPar delivers good runtimes, speedups and efficiency with up to 255 workers on 17 localities.

Keywords: Exact combinatorial search · Parallel search · HPX

1 Introduction

Exact combinatorial search is essential to a wide range of applications including constraint programming, graph matching, and computer algebra. Combinatorial problems are solved by systematically exploring a search space, and doing so is computationally hard both in theory and in practice, encouraging the use of approximate algorithms.

Alternatively, exact search can be parallelised to reduce execution time. Parallel search is, however, extremely challenging due to huge and highly irregular search trees, and the need to preserve search heuristics. The state of the art is parallel searches that (1) are single purpose, i.e. for a specific search application, e.g. Embarrassingly Parallel Search [12] supports constraint programming only; and (2) use hand crafted parallelism, e.g parallel MaxClique [13], with almost no reuse of parallelism between search applications. Hence typically an application is parallelised just once in an heroic effort.

We provide a high-level approach to parallel search that allows non-expert users to benefit from increasing CPU core counts. Specifically YewPar supports *algorithmic skeletons* that provide reusable implementations of common parallel search patterns.

© Springer Nature Switzerland AG 2019
R. Yahyapour (Ed.): Euro-Par 2019, LNCS 11725, pp. 184–196, 2019.
https://doi.org/10.1007/978-3-030-29400-7_14

Contributions. We present for the first time the design (Sect. 3) and implementation (Sect. 4) of YewPar, a new C++ parallel search framework. YewPar provides both high-level skeletons and low-level search specific schedulers and utilities to deal with the irregularity of search and knowledge exchange between workers. YewPar uses the HPX library for distributed task-parallelism [11], allowing search on multi-cores, clusters, HPC etc.

A novel element of YewPar is the *depth-pool*, a search-specific distributed workpool that aims to preserve search heuristics. We describe the depth-pool and show average runtime performance very similar to the widely-used deque, yet dramatically reduced variance for some searches (Sect. 5).

We evaluate YewPar using around 15 instances of two search applications covering two search types. The applications are evaluated on standard challenge instances, e.g. the DIMACS benchmark suite [10]. We investigate how YewPar shares knowledge between search threads (workers), and how effectively it scales from 15 to 255 workers, on a Beowulf cluster. The sequential YewPar overheads are low, with a mean 6.1% slowdown compared to a hand-coded sequential implementation.

2 Existing Search Approaches

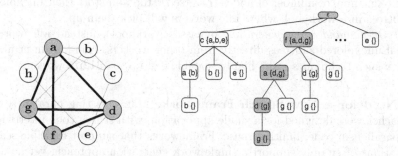

Fig. 1. MaxClique: graph with maximum clique $\{a, d, f, g\}$ and search tree

Conceptually exact combinatorial search proceeds by generating and traversing a tree representing alternative options. In practice the trees are huge and grow exponentially, e.g. 378×10^{12} nodes at depth 67 with a growth rate of 1.62 in [9], and as such are not materialised fully during search.

There are three main *search types*: *enumeration*, which searches for all solutions matching some property, e.g. all maximal cliques in a graph; *decision*, which looks for a specific solution, e.g. a clique of size k; or *optimisation*, which finds a solution that minimises/maximises an objective function, e.g. finding a maximum clique. To illustrate, Fig. 1 shows a small graph, and a fragment of the search tree generated during a maximum clique search. The search proceeds depth-first, repeatedly adding nodes to extend the current clique. After exploring the subtree rooted at c it backtracks to explore the subtree rooted at f, which comes heuristically after c.

Although decades of algorithmic research have developed search heuristics that minimise search time, the scale of the search trees mean that many can take days to solve [9]. Alongside algorithmic improvements, parallel search is often used to increase the range of problems that can be practically solved.

Parallel search comes in three main variants: *parallel node processing*, where children of a node are generated in parallel; *portfolio methods*, where multiple sequential searches (with differing strategies) race to find an optimal solution; and *space-splitting*, where distinct areas of the search tree are searched in parallel. Space-splitting search follows a task parallel approach, where a task searches a given subtree. We focus on space-splitting techniques as they are application independent and scalable, making them ideal for general purpose frameworks such as YewPar.

There are three main work generation approaches for tree search:

(1) Static work generation, as in embarrassingly parallel search [12], creates all tasks at startup and stores them in a (global) workpool, where they are picked up by idle workers. To balance load these approaches need to generate vastly more tasks than the number of workers, which increases startup cost.

(2) Periodic work generation intersperses search with work generation. In `mts` [4], for example, workers that do not complete a task within a given budget (e.g. time, or number of nodes traversed) stop and store their unexplored subtrees in a workpool, where idle workers will pick them up.

(3) On-demand work generation bypasses workpools; instead idle workers steal unexplored subtrees directly from other workers. Abu-khzam et al. [1] show such techniques to be highly scalable e.g. up to 131,072 workers.

The Need for a New Search Framework. Many existing parallel search approaches were designed for a single application, with search code intertwined with parallelism code, limiting reuse. Frameworks that support multiple search applications often only support a single work generation approach, yet no approach works *best* for all applications, making it difficult to choose an appropriate framework [2].

YewPar solves this by providing a more general, i.e. more *reusable* approach for parallel search, supporting all of the above work generation approaches, i.e. static, periodic and on-demand. A user writes their application *once* and has access to a library of parallel skeletons that realise common parallel search patterns. Importantly, the user never writes code for parallelisation, making it easy to port existing sequential search applications and experiment with the different parallelism configurations that YewPar provides.

While existing task-parallel frameworks such as Cilk [8] appear to provide suitable parallelism, key aspects of their implementations are entirely inappropriate for search. For example, deque-based work-stealing can break heuristic search orderings [13], and the common assumption that the number of tasks in a workpool is a good measure of load is invalid when learned knowledge during

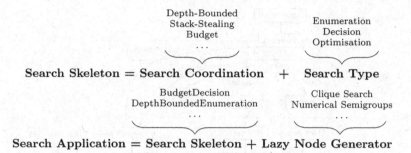

Fig. 2. Creating search skeletons and applications

search is globally distributed, pruning search tasks. YewPar instead provides parallel coordinations and a workpool that are all specialised for search.

3   YewPar Design

YewPar parallelises tree search using distributed task parallelism that adapts to the dynamic and irregular nature of search, and enables scaling on common distributed-memory platforms.

Users construct search applications by combining a YewPar search skeleton with a lazy node generator that they implement to characterise their search problem, as shown in Fig. 2. The lazy node generator specifies how to generate the search tree on demand and in which order to traverse the tree. Each skeleton comprises a search coordination, e.g. *Depth-Bounded* (Sect. 3.1), and a search type, e.g *Decision*. For example, YewPar's *DepthBoundedEnumeration* skeleton statically generates work and enumerates the search space. The skeleton library is extensible, allowing new search coordination methods to be added.

3.1   Search Coordination Methods

During a search potentially **any** node in the search tree may be converted to a task, but to minimise search time it is critical to choose heuristically a *good* node. We follow existing work e.g. [14], using search heuristics, as encoded in the lazy node generator, and select subtrees close to the root as we expect these to be large; minimising scheduling overheads.

YewPar provides a range of standard search coordinations. A novel parallel operational semantics for each coordination is provided in Chapter 4 of [2]. *Sequential* coordination is provided for reference and simply searches the tree without generating any tasks.

Depth-Bounded coordination implements semi-static work generation by converting all nodes below a user-defined cut-off depth (d_{cutoff}) into tasks and placing them in a workpool. New tasks are generated throughout the computation as subtrees with nodes below d_{cutoff} are stolen rather than being generated upfront.

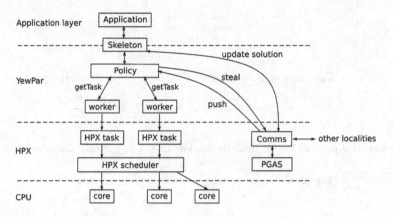

Fig. 3. YewPar system stack

Budget coordination uses periodic work generation. On stealing a new task, a worker is given a user-defined *backtrack budget*. If the worker reaches the backtracking limit before completing the task, it offloads all unexplored subtrees at the lowest depth, i.e. closest to the root, into a workpool, before resetting the budget and continuing to search the remaining subtrees.

Stack-Stealing coordination provides on-demand work generation, triggered by work-stealing, similar to [1]. On receiving a steal request, the victim ships the lowest unexplored subtree from its own stack to the thief. Victim selection is random but biased to favour local over remote steals in order to minimise steal latency. YewPar combines work-stealing with work-pushing on startup in order to distribute tasks quickly.

4   YewPar Implementation

YewPar[1] is C++ parallel search framework. It supports the parallel algorithmic skeletons of Sect. 3 and provides low-level components such as schedulers, workpools, and global knowledge management so that new skeletons can be created. For efficiency and type safety, YewPar uses C++ templates to compile search applications. This specialises code to the specific application types, e.g. the node type, and enables type directed optimisations.

For distributed-memory parallelism YewPar uses HPX [11], a library designed for Exascale computing (10^{18} FLOPS). Figure 3 shows the YewPar system stack. The implementation achieves scalability using asynchronous task-parallelism and lightweight, user-space threads (HPX-threads). Distributed load management has been implemented directly in YewPar as HPX does not provide it. Crucially the load management aims to maintain search order heuristics (Sect. 5).

HPX is selected as the distributed task library as it does not require a bespoke compiler and provides APIs for user-level access to tasks, futures, schedulers etc.

---

[1] https://github.com/BlairArchibald/YewPar.

Alternatively, parallel languages with distributed tasks could also be used, such as Chapel [6] or X10 [7].

Application-Level Scheduling: YewPar divides operating system threads, one per physical core, into two types: (1) **worker** threads that run the scheduling loop until they are terminated, and (2) **HPX manager** threads. YewPar has one HPX manager thread per locality for processing of active messages, synchronisation, and PGAS updates. In order to minimise latency, YewPar also reserves one CPU core for this manager thread.

Distributed Scheduling Policies. Conceptually, idle workers request new tasks from a scheduling *policy*, that is determined by the coordination method, for example Depth-Bounded relies on a workpool whereas Stack-Stealing does not. Policies communicate directly with HPX to either push work to remote localities, or receive stolen tasks from other localities. Two scheduling policies are currently available, more could be added.

1. The **distributed workpool** policy, used by Depth-Bounded and Budget, features one workpool per locality that stores all locally generated tasks. Steals, both local and remote, are directed to the workpool, which aims to serve thiefs tasks in heuristic order (Sect. 5).
2. The **pickpocket** policy, used by Stack-Stealing, has no workpools as Stack-Stealing generates tasks only on demand. Instead, there is a special component per locality, the *pickpocket*. Steals, both local and remote, are directed to the pickpocket, which requests an unexplored subtree from a busy local worker and serves it to the thief. Like the workpool, the pickpocket aims to pick unexplored subtrees in heuristic order.

Both policies follow the same victim selection strategy when stealing. Victims are chosen at random, with two provisos: (1) Local steals take priority; remote steals are attempted only if there is no work locally. (2) Remote steals are biased towards the victim of the most recent successful steal, in the hope that it still has more work.

Global Knowledge Management. Current search results are shared between workers. YewPar provides each locality with a registry that shares search specific variables – for example current bounds and skeleton parameters – between all workers of a locality. Although primary access to this state is local, it supports global updates via active messages, e.g. when receiving improved bounds.

The global incumbent object, e.g. the current solution for a decision/ optimisation problem, is stored in HPX's Partitioned Global Address Space (PGAS) making it accessible to any worker. On receiving an update message the incumbent checks that no better solution has been found and, if so, updates the stored solution and *broadcasts* the new bound to all localities. Section 6.2 shows that one global object suffices due to the infrequent and irregular access patterns.

5 Depth-Pool: A Workpool that Respects Search Heuristics

The performance of many tree searches depends heavily on a search heuristic that prescribes the order the search tree is traversed, aiming to find good solution(s) quickly and to minimise the search space through pruning. Failure to follow a good heuristic can cause detrimental search anomalies where large parts of the search tree are traversed that could have been pruned [5].

Workpool choice is key to ensuring search heuristics are maintained. Most work-stealing workpools use *deques*, where local steals pick the youngest tasks from one end, and remote steals pick the oldest tasks from the other. This works well for divide-and-conquer workloads, as Cilk [8] has shown, but not for tree searches that depend on heuristics [13]. The reason is that deque-based workpools do not maintain heuristic orderings; worse still the steal policy selects tasks that are heuristically unfavourable.

Fully respecting heuristic orderings entirely eliminates search anomalies but centralises task selection, severely limiting scalability [3]. At larger scale, a distributed workpool is needed that (1) preserves heuristic ordering as far as possible, (2) biases remote steals towards big tasks (i.e. subtrees close to the root), and (3) has low steal latency. Low steal latency is crucial since standard latency hiding techniques such as task pre-fetching disrupt the heuristic ordering. To this end, we propose a new workpool, the *depth-pool*, illustrated in Fig. 4.

The central data structure is an array of first-in-first-out (FIFO) queues. The array is indexed by the depth in the search tree, i.e. the i-th queue holds tasks spawned at depth i. The depth-pool biases remote steals towards the root of the tree, where tasks are likely bigger, while biasing local steals to the deepest depth, thereby improving locality. By using FIFO queues the heuristic ordering is maintained at each depth, which avoids the heuristically poor choices made by deque-based scheduling. Steal latency is low as a HPX manager thread is available to handle steals.

As the depth-pool is more complex than a deque, one might expect higher overheads, but maintaining the search heuristics should reduce runtime variance. All of the results in the following section use the depthpool, and show good performance. Moreover, a direct comparison of depth-pools and deques for 7 instances of two search applications shows very similar performance, with depth-pool delivering dramatically lower variance in at least one instance (Figure 6.6 of [2]).

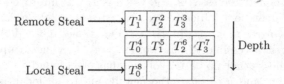

Fig. 4. Depth-pool structure. T_0^1 is a task with id 1 and heuristic position 0. Lower implies better heuristic position.

6   Evaluation

We evaluate YewPar performance on a cluster of 17 localities each with dual 8-core Intel Xeon E5-2640v2 CPUs (2 Ghz; no hyper-threading), 64 GB of RAM and running Ubuntu 14.04.3 LTS. Datasets underpinning the experiments are available online[2].

Input datasets, e.g. particular graphs, to search applications are known as instances. YewPar is evaluated in [2] with 25 instances across seven search applications that cover all three search types. Here we report results for a selection of instances of the following two state-of-the-art search applications covering two search types.

MaxClique searches a graph for the largest set of vertices (optimisation search) where each vertex is adjacent to all other vertices in the set. We implement Prosser's MCSa1 algorithm [15], as sketched in Fig. 1. The instances are drawn from the DIMACS benchmark suite [10].

Numerical Semigroups (NS) enumerates the numerical semigroups with a genus $\leq g$. A numerical semigroup is defined over the set of natural numbers with a set of numbers removed (*holes*) such that the remaining set still forms a semigroup under addition. The genus of a numerical semigroup is the number of holes. The implementation is closely based on, and uses the efficient bit representation for semigroups, of [9]. Each step in the search removes a number from the group generator and adds additional elements to maintain the group property.

Section 6.1 compares YewPar sequential performance with a state-of-the-art MaxClique solver. However parallel performance comparisons are made only with other YewPar implementations as no other parallel comparator is available. That is, there is no other system that allows both MaxClique and Numerical Semigroups to be implemented, nor is there another distributed-memory parallel version of the MCSa1 algorithm [3].

6.1   Skeleton Overheads

The generality of the YewPar skeletons incurs performance overheads compared with search specific implementations. For example lazy node generation requires that nodes are duplicated rather than updated in place. Compared with hand written sequential clique search, YewPar shows low overheads with a geometric mean overhead of only 6.1% across 21 DIMACS MaxClique instances (Table 6.1 of [2]).

6.2   Global Knowledge Exchange

Searches share global knowledge, e.g. the current incumbent in an optimisation search, and YewPar uses HPX's broadcasts and PGAS to do so. We evaluate the performance implications using MaxClique instances on 255 workers (17 localities) with Depth-Bounded coordination and $d_{cutoff} = 2$.

---

[2] https://doi.org/10.5281/zenodo.3240291.

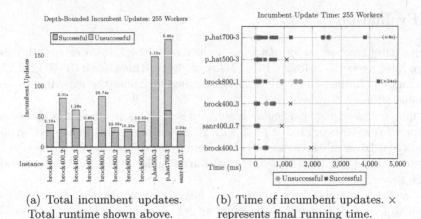

(a) Total incumbent updates.   (b) Time of incumbent updates. ×
Total runtime shown above.   represents final running time.

Fig. 5. Incumbent updates.

Figure 5a shows the mean number of attempted incumbent updates (to the nearest integer) for each instance. Failure to update occurs when a better solution was found before the update message arrived. For most instances, regardless of their runtime, the total number of updates is small: often less than 50. In instances with more updates, a greater proportion are unsuccessful. Moreover Fig. 5b shows how most updates occur early in the search.

While the number of successful updates is bounded by the size of the maximum clique, the variation in the number of successful and unsuccessful steals is instance specific and depends, for example, on how many branches near the start of the search report similar incumbent values (before·bound propagation occurs). This non-predictability is a key challenge in parallel search.

Given the small amount of global knowledge exchanged, YewPar's approach combining PGAS and broadcast is appropriate and likely scales beyond the current architecture. Crucially, although message delays may reduce performance, they do not affect the correctness of the search.

6.3   Work-Stealing Performance

Effective work-stealing is crucial to obtaining good performance in task parallel search. We investigate this using three representative MaxClique instances, brock400_1, brock800_4 and brock400_3, to show that performance portability is achievable. We report results from a single execution on 8 localities with Depthbounded, Stack-Stealing, and Budget search coordinations.

Figure 6a shows the number of spawns, and local/distributed steals per locality for brock400_1 with Depth-Bounded coordination. A uniform distribution of tasks across localities is unlikely given the huge variance in task runtime. Rather, YewPar effectively ensures that all localities have work, i.e. almost all localities have 2000+ tasks.

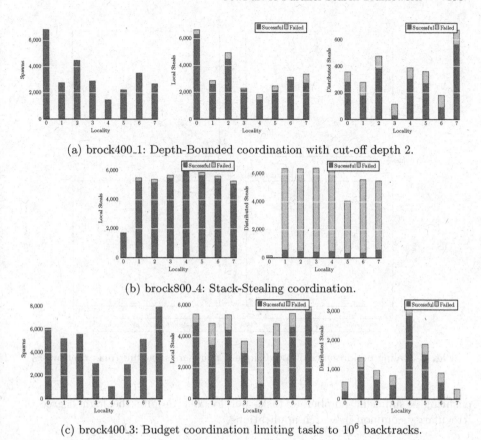

(a) brock400_1: Depth-Bounded coordination with cut-off depth 2.

(b) brock800_4: Stack-Stealing coordination.

(c) brock400_3: Budget coordination limiting tasks to 10^6 backtracks.

Fig. 6. Sample per-locality work generation and stealing statistics.

Tasks are well distributed across the localities as they are spawned during the search rather than upfront. A large proportion of the steals occur locally as there are many localities with < 500 distributed steals. YewPar handles the large numbers of tasks efficiently, scheduling and running 26924 tasks in 3.5s (7692 tasks per second). .

Figure 6b summarises the work-stealing statistics for brock800_4 with Stack-Stealing coordination. As work is generated on demand, there is no spawn count. As steals can occur at any depth in the search tree many local steals are successful. Locality 0 steals little, probably because it holds the largest tasks.

Figure 6c summarises work-stealing statistics for brock800_4 with Budget coordination. Like Depth-Bounded the work is well spread across the localities, with almost all having 2000+ tasks. Locality 4 has relatively few tasks despite stealing successfully, and we infer that most of the tasks stolen are small.

In summary, YewPar efficiently handles searches with thousands of tasks spread over 120 workers. All search coordinations work well with MaxClique

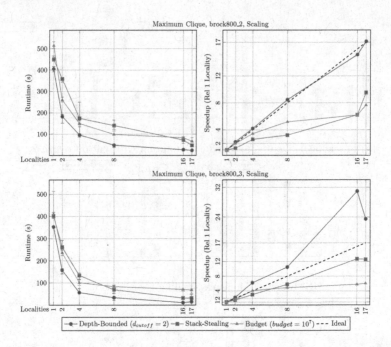

Fig. 7.. Scaling performance of MaxClique. Error bars show min/max runtimes.

ensuring a sufficient number of tasks per locality despite the high degree of irregularity common in search applications.

6.4   Scalability of YewPar

To investigate scalability we evaluate the runtimes and relative speedups of large instances of both MaxClique instances and Numerical Semigroups on 255 workers across 17 localities. Speedup is relative to a single locality with 15 workers as one worker runs take a significant time, i.e. around 2–3 hours per instance.

Figure 7 shows the runtime and relative speedup for the three search coordinations on two MaxClique instances. Depth-Bounded is best with a super-linear speedup, caused by subtree pruning, of 31.0 on 16 localities. We deduce that tasks searching subtrees at d_{cutoff} are generally long running. In comparison, Stack-Stealing and Budget are slower as they interrupt search more frequently.

Parameter values like d_{cutoff} and $budget$ can have a large impact of parallel performance (see 6.5 and 6.7 of [2]). Techniques that guide users to chose good, or low-risk, values remains an open problem.

Figure 8 shows the runtime and relative speedups of Numerical Semigroups. Budget is best with a maximum speedup of 15.4 on 17 localities. Depth-Bounded performs worst, timing out after 30 min regardless of the number of workers. This illustrates the need for a search framework like YewPar to provide multiple search coordinations that are suitable for different search applications; allowing

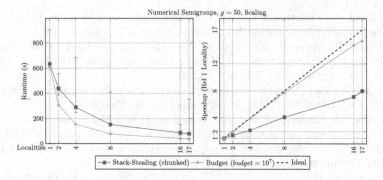

Fig. 8. Scaling performance of Numerical Semigroups. Error bars show min/max runtimes.

it to often achieve an average efficiency of $>50\%$ even for these highly irregular computations.

7   Conclusion

Parallel combinatorial search is challenging and we argue for improving the reuse of parallel searches. For this purpose we present the design and implementation a new parallel search framework. YewPar generalises search by abstracting the search tree generation, and by providing algorithmic skeletons that support three search types, and a set of standard search coordination strategies. A novel feature is the *depth-pool*, a new distributed workpool that preserves search heuristics to minimise runtime variance.

Evaluating YewPar on around 15 instances of two search applications (Max-Clique and Numerical Semigroups) demonstrates its generality and effectiveness. The cost of YewPar generality is low: averaging 6.1% compared with a specific implementation. Moreover global knowledge is inexpensively shared between search tasks; the irregular tasks are effectively distributed; and YewPar delivers good runtimes, speedups and efficiency with up to 255 workers on 17 locations.

Acknowledgments. Work supported by UK EPSRC Grants: S4: Science of Sensor Systems Software (EP/N007565/1); Border Patrol: Improving Smart Device Security through Type-Aware Systems Design (EP/N028201/1); AJITPar: Adaptive Just-In-Time Parallelisation (EP/L000687/1); and CoDiMa (EP/M022641). We also thank Greg Michaelson and the anonymous reviewers for their helpful comments.

References

1. Abu-Khzam, F.N., Daudjee, K., Mouawad, A.E., Nishimura, N.: On scalable parallel recursive backtracking. J. Parallel Distrib. Comput. **84**, 65–75 (2015). https://doi.org/10.1016/j.jpdc.2015.07.006

2. Archibald, B.: Skeletons for Exact Combinatorial Search at Scale. Ph.D. thesis, University of Glasgow (2018). http://theses.gla.ac.uk/id/eprint/31000
3. Archibald, B., Maier, P., McCreesh, C., Stewart, R.J., Trinder, P.: Replicable parallel branch and bound search. J. Parallel Distrib. Comput. **113**, 92–114 (2018). https://doi.org/10.1016/j.jpdc.2017.10.010
4. Avis, D., Jordan, C.: MTS: a light framework for parallelizing tree search codes. CoRR abs/1709.07605 (2017). http://arxiv.org/abs/1709.07605
5. de Bruin, A., Kindervater, G.A.P., Trienekens, H.W.J.M.: Asynchronous parallel branch and bound and anomalies. In: Ferreira, A., Rolim, J. (eds.) IRREGULAR 1995. LNCS, vol. 980, pp. 363–377. Springer, Heidelberg (1995). https://doi.org/10.1007/3-540-60321-2_29
6. Chamberlain, B.L., Callahan, D., Zima, H.P.: Parallel programmability and the chapel language. IJHPCA **21**(3), 291–312 (2007). https://doi.org/10.1177/1094342007078442
7. Charles, P., et al.: X10: an object-oriented approach to non-uniform cluster computing. In: Proceedings of the 20th Annual ACM SIGPLAN Conference on Object-Oriented Programming, Systems, Languages, and Applications, OOPSLA 2005, 16–20 October 2005, San Diego, CA, USA. pp. 519–538. https://doi.org/10.1145/1094811.1094852
8. Frigo, M., Leiserson, C.E., Randall, K.H.: The implementation of the cilk-5 multi-threaded language. In: PLDI. pp. 212–223 (1998). https://doi.org/10.1145/277650.277725
9. Fromentin, J., Hivert, F.: Exploring the tree of numerical semigroups. Math. Comp. **85**(301), 2553–2568 (2016). https://doi.org/10.1090/mcom/3075
10. Johnson, D.J., Trick, M.A. (eds.): Cliques, Coloring, and Satisfiability: Second DIMACS Implementation Challenge, Workshop, 11–13 October 1993. AMS (1996)
11. Kaiser, H., Heller, T., Adelstein-Lelbach, B., Serio, A., Fey, D.: HPX: a task based programming model in a global address space. In: PGAS. pp. 6:1–6:11 (2014). https://doi.org/10.1145/2676870.2676883
12. Malapert, A., Régin, J.C., Rezgui, M.: Embarrassingly parallel search in constraint programming. J. Artif. Intell. Res. **57**, 421–464 (2016)
13. McCreesh, C., Prosser, P.: The shape of the search tree for the maximum clique problem and the implications for parallel branch and bound. TOPC **2**(1), 8:1–8:27 (2015). https://doi.org/10.1145/2742359
14. Pietracaprina, A., Pucci, G., Silvestri, F., Vandin, F.: Space-Efficient Parallel Algorithms for Combinatorial Search Problems. CoRR abs/1306.2552 (2013). http://arxiv.org/abs/1306.2552
15. Prosser, P.: Exact algorithms for maximum clique: a computational study. Algorithms **5**(4), 545–587 (2012). https://doi.org/10.3390/a5040545

PLB-HAC: Dynamic Load-Balancing for Heterogeneous Accelerator Clusters

Luis Sant'Ana[1], Daniel Cordeiro[2], and Raphael Y. de Camargo[1(✉)]

[1] Federal University of ABC, Santo André, Brazil
[2] University of São Paulo, São Paulo, Brazil
raphael.camargo@ufabc.edu.br

Abstract. Efficient usage of Heterogeneous clusters containing combinations of CPUs and accelerators, such as GPUs and Xeon Phi boards requires balancing the computational load among them. Their relative processing speed for each target application is not available in advance and must be computed at runtime. Also, dynamic changes in the environment may cause these processing speeds to change during execution. We propose a Profile-based Load-Balancing algorithm for Heterogeneous Accelerator Clusters (PLB-HAC), which constructs a performance curve model for each resource at runtime and continuously adapt it to changing conditions. It dispatches execution blocks asynchronously, preventing synchronization overheads and other idleness periods due to imbalances. We evaluated the algorithm using data clustering, matrix multiplication, and bioinformatics applications and compared with existing load-balancing algorithms. PLB-HAC obtained the highest performance gains with more heterogeneous clusters and larger problems sizes, where a more refined load-distribution is required.

1 Introduction

Heterogeneous clusters, containing different combinations of CPUs and accelerators, such as GPUs and Intel MIC boards, are becoming increasingly widespread. In order to achieve the best performance offered by these clusters, scientific applications must take into account the relative processing speed of each processor unit and balance the computational load accordingly.

For data-parallel applications, it is necessary to determine an appropriate data (task) division among the CPUs and accelerators. A division of the load based on simple heuristics, such as the number of cores in the GPU is usually ineffective [5]. Another solution is to use simple algorithms for task dispatching, such as greedy algorithms, where tasks are dispatched to the devices as soon as the devices become available. Such heuristics are fast and straightforward, but result in suboptimal distributions.

A more elaborate and precise load-balancing algorithm causes a higher overhead, but a better task distribution can compensate for the overhead. For instance, it is possible to determine the performance profiles for each GPU type

© Springer Nature Switzerland AG 2019
R. Yahyapour (Ed.): Euro-Par 2019, LNCS 11725, pp. 197–209, 2019.
https://doi.org/10.1007/978-3-030-29400-7_15

and application task and use it to determine the amount of work given to each GPU. This profiling can be statically computed, before the execution of the application [5], or dynamically computed at runtime [1,3,10].

We present a Profile-based Load-Balancing algorithm for Heterogeneous Accelerator Clusters (PLB-HAC), which improves PLB-HeC [10] by removing synchronization phases, enhancing the rebalancing mechanism, and including support for Xeon Phi accelerators. The algorithm uses performance information gathered at runtime in order to devise a performance model customized for each processing device. The algorithm is implemented inside the StarPU framework [2], easing its use both on legacy applications and novel ones.

2   Related Work

In this work, we focus on the development of a dynamic algorithm with adaptability, through the use of performance models based on the processing capacity. Acosta et al. [1] proposed an algorithm for GPUs where processors record their individual execution time on periodic synchronization, to asymptotically generate the RP (Relative Power) of the processors. The main drawbacks are that asymptotic convergence causes suboptimal load distributions during several iterations and frequent synchronizations further slow down application execution.

In another work, Zhong et al. [11] use the concept of logical processors to model GPU-CPU hybrid systems. The workload is split using an FPM (Functional Performance Model) that provides a detailed performance model. The approach is limited because it requires prior information about the problem to set up the model parameters.

Heterogeneous Dynamic Self-Scheduler (HDSS) [3] is a dynamic load-balancing algorithm for heterogeneous GPU clusters. In an adaptive phase, it determines weights that reflect the speed of each GPU, which it uses to divide the work among GPUs in the remaining iterations. The performance model is specific to GPUs and the use of a simple weight per GPU limits the data distribution. Finally, it does not adjust the data distribution during the execution phase and synchronizations in the adaptive phase slow down application execution.

Kaleen et al. [8] proposed the *naive algorithm*, which executes in two phases: profiling and execution. In the profiling phase, the algorithm determines the processing rate Gr of GPUs and Cr of CPUs, which are used for data distribution in the execution phase. A second algorithm, called *asymmetric algorithm*, reduces the overhead of the initial phase by sharing a pool of work between CPU and GPU. Their approach is suited for CPUs and GPUs and reduces synchronizations, but the obtained performance can degrade in case of changes during the execution phase.

PLB-HeC [10] performs dynamic load-balancing in two phases for clusters with CPUs and GPUs. The first phase constructs the performance model using profiling, while in the second blocks of the selected sizes are dispatched to the processing units. It differs from previous approaches in that it models the processors (CPUs and GPUs) using a system of nonlinear equations to improve the

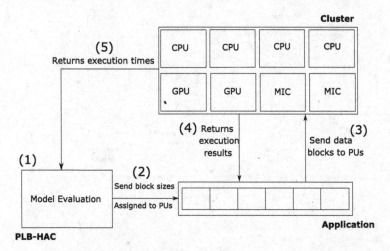

Fig. 1. Overview of the load-balancing algorithm, including the performance model evaluation, block distribution, and task execution.

accuracy of block size distributions. However, it still contains several synchronization steps, which slowdowns application execution.

Our proposed algorithm addresses the limitations of previous dynamic load-balancing algorithms. It uses the same approach of solving a system of nonlinear equations from PLB-HeC, but it has no explicit or implicit synchronization between processors within the training and execution phases. Moreover, it performs a progressive refinement of the performance models for the processors during the entire execution, which allows it to adapt to changes in the execution environment. Idle periods that could still result from imperfect load-balancing are filled with smaller blocks of the correct size. Finally, it supports several classes of processing devices, including CPUs, GPUs, and Xeon Phi boards.

3   Proposed Algorithm

In a typical data-parallel application, data is divided into blocks that can be concurrently processed by multiple threads, in a process called domain decomposition [6]. The results are then merged, and the application can proceed to its next phase. The goal of the PLB-HAC algorithm is to find a near-optimal distribution of the size of data blocks assigned to threads located on each CPU and accelerator in the system. We use the term Processing Unit (PU) to refer to both CPUs, GPUs and Xeon Phi coprocessors.

PLB-HAC generates and evaluates performance models of PUs and determine the optimal block size distribution, which is shown in the "Model Evaluation" box in Fig. 1. The list of block sizes is sent (2) to the application, which sends the data blocks for execution in the assigned PUs (3), together with the execution code for that PU. The PUs process the data blocks and return the results to the

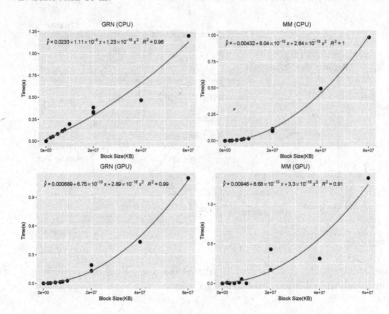

Fig. 2. Execution times and performance models for the GPU and CPU implementations of the k-means and matrix multiplication applications.

application (4) and the execution time of the block to PLB-HAC (5), which are used to improve the performance model.

The mechanics of data and code migration can be managed by a framework such as StarPU and Charm++, where a user is presumed to implement only the task code. The remaining of this section discuss the implementation of the "Model Evaluation" from Fig. 1 in PLB-HAC in a framework-agnostic way and the next section show how the algorithm can be integrated to StarPU.

3.1   Processing Unit Performance Modeling

The algorithm devises a performance model for each processing unit based on execution time measurements. The algorithm constructs two functions $F_p[x]$ and $G_p[x]$, representing the amount of time a processing unit p spends processing and transmitting a block of size x, respectively. These functions are generated in a training phase, where the algorithm first assigns a block of size x_{init}—initially defined by the user—to be processed by each PU. The unit that finishes first receives a second block of size $2 * x_{init}$, while each other PU p receives a block of size equal to $2 * x_{init} * R$, where R is the ratio between the time spent by the fastest unit and the time spent by unit p. The idea is to balance the load better, preventing a long delay between the finish times of the different processing units.

The measured execution and data transfer times for each new block and PU are used to create the performance model. The algorithm performs a linear regression to determine the execution time functions $F_p[x]$ that better fit the existing pairs (x, t_x) using the least squares method. The same is done for $G_p[x]$, but using the data transfer times. The curve is initially fitted using two points and after each new iteration, another point is added to the model, resulting in better models. This calculation is done in the first CPU that finishes the execution of its assigned block. The algorithm performs a linear regression of the form:

$$F_p[x] = a_1 f_1(x) + a_2 f_2(x) + ... + a_n f_n(x) \qquad (1)$$

where $f_i(x)$ are functions from the set x, x^2, x^3, e^x, $\ln x$, and the combinations $x \cdot e^x$ and $x \cdot \ln x$. This set should contemplate the vast majority of applications, but other functions can be included if necessary. Figure 2 shows sample processing time measurements and model fittings for a GPU and a CPU for different block sizes on two different applications. For the $G_p[x]$ function, we used an equation of the form:

$$G_p[x] = a_1 x + a_2 \qquad (2)$$

where the linear coefficient a_1 represents the network and PCIe bandwidths, and a_2 the network and system latency. We assume that the data transfer delay increases linearly with data size, which should be a valid approximation for compute-bound applications.

3.2   Block Size Selection

The proposed algorithm determines the block size assigned to each processing unit with the objective that all PUs have the same execution time. Consider that we have n processing units and input data of size normalized to 1. The algorithm assigns a data chunk of size $x_p \in [0, 1]$ for each processing unit $p = 1, ..., n$, corresponding to a fraction of the input data, such that $\sum_{p=1}^{n} x_p = 1$. We denote as $E_p(x_p)$ the execution time of task E in the processing unit p, for input of size x_p. To distribute the work among the processing units, we find a set of values $(x_p)_{i=1}^n$ that minimizes the system of fitted curves for all processing units, determined in the training phase, while keeping the same execution time for all units. The full set of equations are given by:

$$\begin{cases} E_1(x_1) = F_1(x_1) + G_1(x_1) \\ E_2(x_2) = F_2(x_2) + G_2(x_2) \\ \cdots \\ E_n(x_n) = F_n(x_n) + G_n(x_n) \\ E_1(x_1) = E_2(x_2) = \cdots = E_n(x_n) \\ \sum_{p=1}^{n} x_p = 1 \end{cases} \qquad (3)$$

The equation system is solved applying an interior point line search filter method [9], which finds the minimum solution of a convex equation set, subject to a set of constraints, by traversing the interior of its feasible region. The solution of the equation system results in a block size x_p for each processing unit p. The block size is rounded to the closest valid application data block size, so that all units will spend approximately the same processing time executing their blocks. We also use a minimum block size that does not underutilize the GPUs.

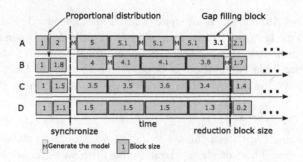

Fig. 3. PLB-HAC execution example. The number inside boxes represents the block sizes assigned to units, M represents model evaluation to determine block sizes. Shaded boxes are regular assigned blocks and white boxes are gap filling blocks.

3.3 Execution Phase

The execution phase is asynchronous. Tasks of size x_p, determined at the training phase, are sent to each PU p. When a PU notifies the scheduler that it finished executing a task, the measured performance is added to the set of points of the performance model and another task of size x_p is sent to the PU.

The task size x_p is updated at the end of each "virtual step", which occurs when all PUs finish the execution of their assigned blocks. During the update, the first CPU to become idle solves the equation system (3)—using all the execution time measurements collected from each unit—to determine the block size x_p for each processing unit p. No synchronization is required since the scheduler uses the most recent already available x_p when assigning a block size to PU p.

Two other mechanisms improve the load-balancing process. The first one is a gap-filling mechanism, used if a processing unit finishes the execution of its assigned block earlier than expected. The algorithm provides a new block to fill the gap between the predicted and actual execution time that a unit needed to process its last block. We used a default threshold of 400 ms, which can be changed by the user. The second mechanism is a gradual decrease in block sizes after 70% of the application data was processed, with the goal of reducing possible unbalances at the end of the execution. The decrease is by a constant factor $\alpha = 0.1$, and the user can adjust this factor to suit the application better.

Figure 3 shows an execution example of four heterogeneous PUs (A, B, C, and D). At the left of the first vertical dashed line is the training phase, where blocks of size 1 are sent to each PU. Machine A finishes processing its block first and receives a new block of size 2, while others receive smaller blocks. A synchronization then takes place and the first complete model is generated. This is the only synchronization step in the entire execution. Between the dashed lines is the execution phase, with several virtual steps. At the beginning of each virtual step, the first unit to finish the last step evaluates a new model. Unit A also receives a gap-filling block. Near the end of the execution, the blocks are progressively reduced in size until there is no more data to process.

3.4   Complete Algorithm

Algorithm 1 shows the pseudocode of the PLB-HAC algorithm. The function `FinishedTaskExecution` is a callback function, invoked when a processing unit finishes a task. It receives the finish time ($finishTime$) and the processing unit identifier ($proc$). If there is still data left to be processed, it first checks if the finish time of the application was smaller than the $gapThreshold$, in which case it sends a new block to fill the gap between the predicted and finished time. Otherwise, it calls `PLB-HAC` to determine the next block size.

Algorithm 1. Compute the performance model for each processing unit

---

X : global vector
function PLB-HAC($proc$)
$firstProc \leftarrow$ firstProcessVirtualStep($proc$);
if $proc == firstProc$ **then**
   $fitValues \leftarrow$ determineModel()
   $X \leftarrow$ solveEquationSystem($fitValues$);
   if $assignedData \geq 0.7 * totalData$ **then**
      $X \leftarrow X * k$;
   end if
   $assignedData \leftarrow assignedData +$ sum(X);
end if
distributeTask($X[proc]$, $proc$);

function FinishedTaskExecution($proc$, $finishTime$)
if $assignedData \leq totalData$ **then**
   if $finishedTime / predictedTime \leq gapThreshold$ **then**
      $assignedData \leftarrow assignedData +$ determineGapBlockSize();
      distributeTask(X, $proc$);
   else
      PLB-HAC();
   end if
end if

Function `PLB-HAC` first calls `firstProcessVirtualStep`, which keeps track of the PU's current virtual step and returns the identifier $firstProc$ of the first unit to enter the current virtual step. If the calling unit is $firstProc$, it first determines a new performance model for all units using the `determineModel` function, which returns a structure $fitValues$ containing the model. Function `solveEquationSystem` then solves the system of equations (3) and returns the best distribution of block sizes for each PU in X. Finally, if 70% of all data was already processed, the algorithm decreases the block size by multiplying it by k, a constant that defines the rate of block size reduction. At the end of the function, function `distributeTask` is called, which sends the data block of the determined size to the unit.

4   Implementation

The PLB-HAC algorithm was implemented in C++ over StarPU [2], a frame-work for parallel programming that supports hybrid architectures. StarPU is based on the concept of codelets, which describe computational kernels that can be implemented on multiple architectures.

For comparison sake, we also implemented two other load-balancing algorithms: *greedy* and HDSS [3]. The greedy algorithm divides the input set in pieces and assigns each piece to the first available processing unit. HDSS was implemented using minimum square estimation to determine the weights and divided into two phases: adaptation and completion phase. We used the IPOPT [9] (Interior Point OPTimizer) library to solve the equations systems produced by Eq. (3).

4.1   Applications

We used three applications to evaluate the PLB-HAC algorithm: a *matrix multiplication* (MM) application, a gene regulatory network (GRN) inference [4] application, and a clustering algorithm, the K-Means. Each application was implemented as a pair of *codelets*, containing optimized GPU and CPU implementations.

The MM application distributes a copy of the matrix A to all PUs and divides matrix B among the PUs according to the load-balancing scheme. We used an optimized version from the CUBLAS 4.0 library. Multiplication of two $n \times n$ matrices has complexity $O(n^3)$.

Gene Regulatory Network (GRN) inference [4] is a bioinformatics problem in which gene interactions must be deduced from gene expression data. It depends on an exhaustive search of the gene subset with a given cardinality that best predicts a target gene. The division of work consisted of distributing the gene sets that are evaluated by each processor. The complexity of the algorithm is known to be $O(n^3)$, where n is the number of genes.

K-means clustering is a popular method for cluster analysis which partitions n observations into k clusters. The problem can be exactly solved in time $O(n^{dk+1})$, where n is the number of entities to be clustered and d is the input dimensionality [7].

5   Results

We used five machines with different PU configurations (Table 1). We considered five scenarios: one machine (A); two machines (A, B); three machines (A, B, and C); four machines (A, B, C, and D) and five machines (A, B, C, D, and E). For GPUs, we launched kernels with 1 thread block per Stream Multiprocessors (SMs). For the CPUs and Xeon Phi, we created one thread per (virtual) core.

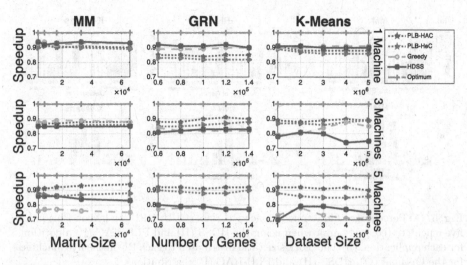

Fig. 4. Speedup (compared to the optimum execution) for the Matrix Multiplication (MM), Gene Regulatory Network (GRN) inference application and K-Means algorithm, using different number of machines and input sizes.

Table 1. Machine configurations

Machines	Description				
	PU type	Model	Core count	Cache/throughput	Memory
A	CPU	Intel i7 - 5930K	6 cores @ 3.5 GHz	15 MB cache	32 GB
	GPU	Quadro K5200	2304 cores	192 GB/s	8 GB
B	CPU	Intel i7 - 5930K	6 cores @ 3.5 GHz	15 MB cache	32 GB
	GPU	GTX 970	1667 cores	224 GB/s	4 GB
	Xeon Phi	3120 series	57 cores	240 GB/s	6 GB
C	CPU	Intel Xeon E-2620	6 cores @ 2.10 GHz	15 MB cache	32 GB
	GPU	Quadro K620	384 cores	29 GB/s	2 GB
D	CPU	Intel i7-4930k	6 cores @ 3.40 GHz	12 MB cache	32 GB
	GPU	GPU Titan	2688 cores	288.4 GB/s	6 GB
E	CPU	Intel Xeon E-2620	6 cores @ 2.10 GHz	15 MB cache	32 GB
	GPU	Quadro K620	384 cores	29 GB/s	2 GB
	Xeon Phi	3120 series	57 cores	240 GB/s	6 GB

5.1 Application Speedup

Figure 4 shows the average of 10 runs of each algorithm. Lines labeled "Optimum" show results for the optimal load balancing, obtained empirically by brute force searching. We used the same initial block size for both PLB-HAC, PLB-HeC, and HDSS, with 1024 elements.

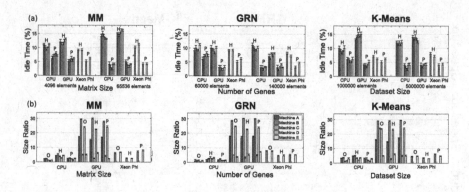

Fig. 5. (a) Percentage of idle time for each PU class (CPU, GPU, and Xeon Phi) in the five machines (colored bars), when using the HDSS (H) and PLB-HAC (P) algorithms for each application. (b) The block size ratio distributed to each PU in the five machines for the Optimal (O), HDSS (H) and PLB-HAC (P) distributions.

With three or more machines, PLB-HAC algorithm approximates the optimal curve and exceeds the performance of the compared algorithms. The cost involved in the calculation of the block size distribution (about 100 ms per iteration), is mitigated by the better distribution of blocks. The behavior is similar for all three applications evaluated, with PLB-HAC performing better in more heterogeneous environments.

With one machine, PLB-HAC exhibited lower performance than HDSS and Greedy. For HDSS, the overhead from the model generation occurs only once, at the end of the adaptive phase. Note that PLB-HAC has a better performance than PLB-HeC due to the removal of the synchronization steps.

5.2   Block Size Distribution

We compared the distribution of block sizes among the PUs. Figure 5b shows the results for a matrix of 65,536 elements for matrix multiplication, 140,000 genes for GRN and 500,000 points for k-means. We used the five machines A, B, C, D, and E. The values represent the ratio of the total data allocated on a single step to each CPU/GPU processor, normalized so that total size is equal to 100. We considered the block sizes generated at the end of the training phase for the algorithm PLB-HAC, and at the end of phase 1 for the HDSS algorithm. We performed 10 executions and present the average values and standard deviations. The standard deviation values are small, showing that all algorithms are stable through different executions.

The PLB-HAC algorithm produced a distribution that was qualitatively more similar to the optimum algorithm than HDSS, with proportionally smaller blocks allocated to CPUs and larger blocks to GPUs. We attribute this difference to the use of a performance curve model by PLB-HAC, in contrast to the use of the simpler linear weighted means from a set of performance coefficients done by HDSS.

5.3   Processing Unit Idleness

We also measured the percentage of time that each CPU and GPU was idle during application execution, using the same experimental setup from the block size distribution experiment. At each task submission round, we recorded the time intervals where each processing unit remained idle. We executed each application with each load-balancing algorithm 10 times.

Figure 5a shows that HDSS produced larger processing unit idleness than PLB-HAC in all scenarios. This idleness occurred mainly in the first phase of HDSS, where non-optimal block sizes are used to estimate the computational capabilities of each processing unit. PLB-HAC prevents these idleness periods in the initial phase by starting to adjust the block sizes after the submission of the first block, significantly reducing the idleness generated on this phase.

Another measured effect is that with larger input sizes—which are the most representative when considering GPU clusters—the percentage of idleness time was smaller. This occurred mainly because the time spent in the initial phase, where most of the idleness time occurs, was proportionally smaller when compared to the total execution time. This effect is evident when comparing the idle times of the matrix multiplication application with 4,096 and 65,536 elements for the PLB-HAC algorithm.

Incorrect block size estimations also produce idleness in the execution phase of the algorithms, especially in the final part, since some processing units may finish their tasks earlier than others. HDSS and PLB-HAC prevent part of this idleness using decreasing block size values during the execution.

5.4   Adaptability

We evaluated the adaptability of PLB-HAC to situations where the resource state changes during application execution. For instance, an external application could be started in some of the machines where the PLB-HAC managed application is executing.

We used two machines (A and B), with one CPU and GPU on each. They are initially idle, and we start the execution of the MM application. After 142 s, we start the execution of a CUDA-based GRN application at machine A, which competes for GPU resources. PLB-HAC detects that executions at GPU A are taking longer and reduces the block size for this GPU, as shown in Fig. 6a. Conversely, the block size for GPU B is increased, compensating the reduction in GPU A. Figure 6b shows a scenario where we start a render application in GPU A after 142 s. Note that the PLB-HAC reduces the block size to GPU A to near zero while increasing the block size of GPU B.

It is important to note that the adaptation was fast, with the block size falling from 2500 KB to 1188 KB within 38 s in the first case (a) and from 2500 KB to

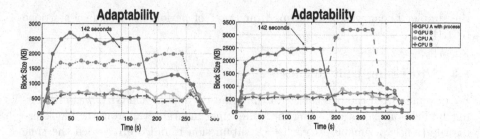

Fig. 6. Evolution of the block size distribution for two machines (A and B) in the presence of a competing process, which is started at GPU A at instant 142 s, denoted by the vertical line.

320 KB in 43 s in the second case (b). Also note the decrease of block sizes at the end of the execution, which is a result of PLB-HAC policy of distributing smaller blocks at the end of the execution, avoiding possible load unbalances that could occur at this phase.

6   Conclusions

In this paper, we presented PLB-HAC, a novel algorithm for dynamic load-balancing of domain decomposition applications executing on clusters of heterogeneous CPUs, GPUs and Xeon-Phi. It performs a profile-based online estimation of the performance curve for each processing unit and selects the block size distribution among processing units solving a non-linear system of equations. We used three real-world applications in the fields of linear algebra, bioinformatics, and data clustering and showed that our approach decreased the application execution time when compared to other dynamic algorithms.

Experiments showed that PLB-HAC performed better for higher degrees of heterogeneity and larger problem sizes, where a more refined load-distribution is required. The PLB-HAC was implemented on top of the well-known StarPU framework, which allows its immediate use for several existing applications and an easier development cycle for new applications.

As future work, we need to evaluate the scalability of PLB-HAC by executing experiments with applications that require hundreds or thousands of processing units. Another point is to extend the method to work with applications that have multiple kernels.

Acknowledgment. The authors would like to thank UFABC and FAPESP (Proc. n. 2013/26644-1) for the financial support, Fabrizio Borelli for providing the GRN application and Samuel Thibalt for helping with StarPU. This research is part of the INCT of the Future Internet for Smart Cities funded by CNPq proc. 465446/2014-0, Coordenação de Aperfeiçoamento de Pessoal de Nível Superior – Brasil (CAPES) – Finance Code 001, FAPESP proc. 14/50937-1, and FAPESP proc. 15/24485-9.

References

1. Acosta, A., Blanco, V., Almeida, F.: Towards the dynamic load balancing on heterogeneous multi-GPU systems. In: 2012 IEEE 10th International Symposium on Parallel and Distributed Processing with Applications (ISPA), pp. 646–653 (2012)
2. Augonnet, C., Thibault, S., Namyst, R.: StarPU: a runtime system for scheduling tasks over accelerator-based multicore machines. Technical report RR-7240, INRIA, March 2010
3. Belviranli, M.E., Bhuyan, L.N., Gupta, R.: A dynamic self-scheduling scheme for heterogeneous multiprocessor architectures. ACM Trans. Arch. Code Optim. **9**(4), 57:1–57:20 (2013)
4. Borelli, F.F., de Camargo, R.Y., Martins Jr., D.C., Rozante, L.C.: Gene regulatory networks inference using a multi-GPU exhaustive search algorithm. BMC Bioinform. **14**(18), 1–12 (2013)
5. de Camargo, R.: A load distribution algorithm based on profiling for heterogeneous GPU clusters. In: 2012 Third Workshop on Applications for Multi-Core Architectures (WAMCA), pp. 1–6 (2012)
6. Gropp, W.D.: Parallel computing and domain decomposition. In: Fifth International Symposium on Domain Decomposition Methods for Partial Differential Equations, Philadelphia, PA (1992)
7. Inaba, M., Katoh, N., Imai, H.: Applications of weighted Voronoi diagrams and randomization to variance-based k-clustering. In: Proceedings of the Tenth Annual Symposium on Computational Geometry, pp. 332–339. ACM (1994)
8. Kaleem, R., Barik, R., Shpeisman, T., Lewis, B.T., Hu, C., Pingali, K.: Adaptive heterogeneous scheduling for integrated GPUs. In: Proceedings of the 23rd International Conference on Parallel Architectures and Compilation, PACT 2014, pp. 151–162. ACM, New York (2014). https://doi.org/10.1145/2628071.2628088
9. Nocedal, J., Wächter, A., Waltz, R.: Adaptive barrier update strategies for nonlinear interior methods. SIAM J. Optim. **19**(4), 1674–1693 (2009). https://doi.org/10.1137/060649513
10. Sant'Ana, L., Cordeiro, D., Camargo, R.: PLB-HeC: a profile-based load-balancing algorithm for heterogeneous CPU-GPU clusters. In: 2015 IEEE International Conference on Cluster Computing, pp. 96–105, September 2015. https://doi.org/10.1109/CLUSTER.2015.24
11. Zhong, Z., Rychkov, V., Lastovetsky, A.: Data partitioning on heterogeneous multicore and multi-GPU systems using functional performance models of data-parallel applications. In: 2012 IEEE International Conference on Cluster Computing (CLUSTER), pp. 191–199, September 2012. https://doi.org/10.1109/CLUSTER.2012.34

Data Management, Analytics and Deep Learning

Enhancing the Programmability and Performance Portability of GPU Tensor Operations

Arya Mazaheri[1]([✉]), Johannes Schulte[1], Matthew W. Moskewicz[2], Felix Wolf[1], and Ali Jannesari[3]

[1] Technische Universität Darmstadt,
Darmstadt, Germany
{mazaheri,wolf}@cs.tu-darmstadt.de,
j_schulte@outlook.com
[2] Deepscale Inc., Mountain View, CA, USA
moskewcz@deepscale.ai
[3] Iowa State University, Ames, IA, USA
jannesari@iastate.edu

Abstract. Deep-learning models with convolutional networks are widely used for many artificial-intelligence tasks, thanks to the increasing adoption of high-throughput GPUs, even in mobile phones. CUDA and OpenCL are the two largely used programming interfaces for accessing the computing power of GPUs. However, attaining code portability has always been a challenge, until the introduction of the Vulkan API. Still, performance portability is not necessarily provided. In this paper, we investigate the unique characteristics of CUDA, OpenCL, and Vulkan kernels and propose a method for abstracting away syntactic differences. Such abstraction creates a single-source kernel which we use for generating code for each GPU programming interface. In addition, we expose auto-tuning parameters to further enhance performance portability. We implemented a selection of convolution operations, covering the core operations needed for deploying three common image-processing neural networks, and tuned them for NVIDIA, AMD, and ARM Mali GPUs. Our experiments show that we can generate deep-learning kernels with minimal effort for new platforms and achieve reasonable performance. Specifically, our Vulkan backend is able to provide competitive performance compared to vendor deep-learning libraries.

Keywords: GPU · Deep learning · Performance portability

1 Introduction

Differences across GPU architectures and programming interfaces, such as CUDA and OpenCL, make the efficient execution of tensor operations, the constituents of convolutional neural networks (CNN), a challenging task. While CUDA works only on NVIDIA devices, the latter has been designed with portability in mind to run on any OpenCL compatible device. Nonetheless,

© Springer Nature Switzerland AG 2019
R. Yahyapour (Ed.): Euro-Par 2019, LNCS 11725, pp. 213–226, 2019.
https://doi.org/10.1007/978-3-030-29400-7_16

performance is not necessarily portable [4]. Furthermore, some vendors, such as NVIDIA, are reluctant to fully support OpenCL as they see it as a rival to their own standard. This becomes even worse on a number of mobile GPUs for which there is no official support.

The Khronos group released a new programming API called Vulkan [19] along with an intermediate language named SPIR-V [18] to address the portability of GPU programs. Vulkan is inherently a low-level graphics and compute API, much closer to the behavior of the hardware, and claims to be cross-platform yet efficient on modern GPUs. Unlike others, Vulkan is supported by all major mobile and desktop GPUs. This single feature makes Vulkan a more attractive programming interface compared with OpenCL, not to mention its unique low-level optimizations. However, such worthwhile features come at a price, as it requires significantly higher programming effort. Particularly for newcomers, rewriting their code with Vulkan is a cumbersome task.

CNN inference frameworks such as TVM [1], PlaidML [7], and Tensor Comprehensions [20], which provide support for coding new tensor operations, have been optimized in many ways that allow a more efficient use of the underlying hardware. Important steps in that regard were the use of compiler techniques [7,20] as well as device-specialized kernels written in shader assembly instead of high-level programming languages [2] or platform-independent intermediate representations. However, implementations that work on multiple platforms are often optimized for certain architectures or vendors. This reduces the portability and performance predictability of CNN execution on server-/desktop-grade GPUs and mobile GPUs alike.

In this paper, we conduct a comparative analysis of CUDA, OpenCL, and Vulkan, which we call *target APIs* in the rest of the paper. We then use the outcome to extend Boda [13], a CNN inference framework, and propose an abstraction layer that enables GPU tensor code generation using any of the target APIs. Equipped with meta-programming and auto-tuning, our code generator can create multiple implementations and select the best performing version on a given GPU. Therefore, we enhance programmability and provide better performance portability with code auto-tuning. Our experiments show that our approach eases the overall burden of targeting NVIDIA, AMD and Mali GPUs while achieving modest performance. We also achieve competitive performance using Vulkan in comparison to existing deep-learning vendor libraries. In some cases, our method achieved higher speedups, by up to 1.46× and 2.28× relative to cuDNN and AMD's MIOpen libraries. In essence, this paper makes the following major contributions:

- Programmability comparison of CUDA, OpenCL, and Vulkan code
- CUDA, OpenCL, and Vulkan code generation using an abstract single-source approach, which reduces the required programming effort by up to 98%
- Acceleration of convolution layers using Vulkan's new features such as kernel batching
- Performance portability analysis of our code generator for each of the three programming interfaces on latest architectures, including mobile GPUs

In the remainder of the paper, we first provide a comparative code analysis for the target APIs. Then, in Sect. 3 our code generation method will be introduced, followed by an evaluation in Sect. 4. A concise review of related works is presented in Sect. 5. Finally, we conclude the paper in Sect. 6.

2   Comparison of CUDA, OpenCL, and Vulkan

CUDA and OpenCL share a range of core concepts, such as the platform, memory, execution, and programming model. Furthermore, their syntax and built-in functions are fairly similar to each other. Thus, it is relatively straightforward to convert a CUDA to an OpenCL program, and vice versa [5,9]. On the other hand, Vulkan does not fully conform to CUDA and OpenCL standards, as it is geared both towards general-purpose computation and graphics while being portable and efficient. Various OpenCL offline compilers exist for converting C code to an intermediate language, from which later platform-specific assembly code can be easily generated. In contrast, Vulkan is able to target different platforms using a single input code and SPIR-V, a new platform-independent intermediate representation for defining shaders and compute kernels. Currently, SPIR-V code can be generated from HLSL, GLSL and C with OpenCL.

Vulkan has been designed from scratch with asynchronous multi-threading support [10,16]. Moreover, each Vulkan-capable device exposes one or more queues that can also process work asynchronously to each other. Each queue carries a set of *commands* and acts as a gateway to the execution engine of a device. These commands can represent many actions, from data transfer and compute-shader execution to draw commands. Each command specifies the requested action along with input/output data. The information about the available actions and the corresponding data is encapsulated in a so-called *pipeline*. This pipeline is then bound to a *command buffer*, which represents a sequence of commands that should be sent in batches to the GPU. These buffers are created prior to execution and, to save in time, can be submitted to a queue for execution as many times as required. Creating command buffers is a time-consuming task. Therefore, the host code often employs multiple threads, working asynchronously, to construct command buffers in parallel. Once finished, a thread may submit these command buffers to a queue for execution. Right after the submission, the commands within a command buffer execute without any interruption in order or out of order—depending on the ordering constraints.

Despite these conceptual design differences, we prepared a mapping for the key concepts within each API in terms of memory regions and execution models in Table 1. The table shows that the memory hierarchy abstractions of the three interfaces are quite similar. Figure 1 illustrates the kernel execution space of the target APIs in more detail. Each point in the space is occupied by a thread/work-item/invocation. Each item is an execution instance of the kernel, with multiple of them combined into a thread block or group. The whole execution space is called grid or NDRange. Note that this mapping only covers the concepts shared among these APIs and does not fully cover the features of Vulkan.

Table 1. A comparison of the terminology used in CUDA, OpenCL, and Vulkan

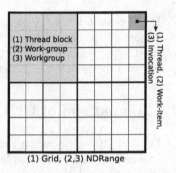

	CUDA	OpenCL	Vulkan (SPIR-V)
Memory region	Global mem.	Global mem.	CrossWorkGroup, Uniform
	Constant mem.	Constant mem.	UniformConstant
	Texture mem.	Constant mem.	PushConstant
	Shared mem.	Local mem.	Workgroup
	Registers	Private memory	Private memory
Execution model	Thread	Work-item	Invocation
	Thread block	Work-group	Workgroup
	Grid	NDRange	NDRange

Fig. 1. Kernel execution space for (1) CUDA, (2) OpenCL, and (3) Vulkan

Further comparison shows that Vulkan is more explicit in nature rather than depending on hidden heuristics in the driver. Vulkan provides a more fine-grained control over the GPU on a much lower level. This enables programmers to enhance performance across many platforms. Even though such privilege comes with an extra programming effort, this feature can immensely increase the overall performance. Operations such as resource tracking, synchronization, memory allocation, and work submission internals benefit from being exposed to the user, which makes the application behavior more predictable and easier to control. Similarly, unnecessary background tasks such as error checking, hazard tracking, state validation, and shader compilation are removed from the runtime and instead can be done in the development phase, resulting in lower driver overhead and less CPU usage [10] compared with other APIs.

Particularly, synchronization mechanisms require the developer to be explicit about the semantics of the application but in return save a significant amount of overhead. While other APIs tend to insert implicit synchronization primitives between invocations and constructs, such as kernel executions and buffer reads, Vulkan is by default asynchronous. All synchronization between kernels or buffer I/O must be added explicitly to their respective command buffer via built-in synchronization primitives, including fences, barriers, semaphores, and events. Therefore, if no synchronization is required, we can strictly avoid the overhead of such operations.

Another difference is how Vulkan allocates memory, both on the host and the device. While CUDA and OpenCL often provide a single device buffer type and primitive functions for copying data between the host and device buffers, Vulkan puts the programmer in full control of memory management, including buffer creation, buffer type selection, memory allocation, and buffer binding. Furthermore, by making an explicit distinction between host-transparent device buffers and device-local buffers, we can implement explicit staging buffers or decide if they are not necessary—either because the amount of I/O to the buffer is negligible or because host memory and device memory are actually shared, as

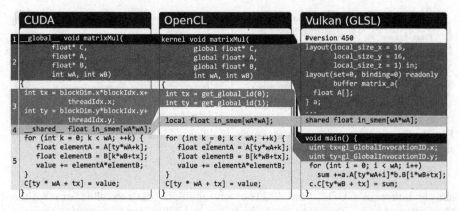

Fig. 2. A SGEMM kernel implemented with CUDA, OpenCL, and Vulkan (GLSL). Numbers on the left denote: (1) function declaration, (2) kernel arguments and data layout, (3) API-specific keywords, (4) shared-memory allocation.

it is the case on many mobile platforms. Such explicit querying and handling of the underlying hardware can reduce unnecessary work and utilize the hardware more efficiently.

Programming Conventions. In contrast to other APIs, Vulkan has its own programming conventions. Therefore, code similarities might not seem obvious at the first glance. Figure 2 shows a naïve matrix-multiplication kernel implemented using each programming interface. For Vulkan, we chose GLSL as our kernel language because of its better compatibility. We trimmed off some parts of the code for brevity. Regions with the same color and number share the same functionality. Syntactically, GLSL is similar to OpenCL and CUDA. However, GLSL is more restricted in certain ways, which requires rewriting some parts of the code. The biggest three differences are:

- Arguments to a kernel are not declared in the function header. Instead, they are declared in the global scope as so-called bindings, which can then be set with Vulkan. The compiler expects the entry function for the kernel to take no arguments. However, accessing the arguments within the kernel is the same as in other APIs.
- Workgroup dimensions have to be defined in the kernel and not in the host code. Each workgroup contains many work items or compute-shader invocations.
- GLSL does not provide explicit support for pointer objects. Instead, all pointers are represented as arrays of undefined length.
- Shared-memory objects are not declared within the kernel body. Instead, they are defined in the bindings.

Due to the conceptual discrepancies between Vulkan and the other APIs, the host code of Vulkan is radically different. For example, we can create a

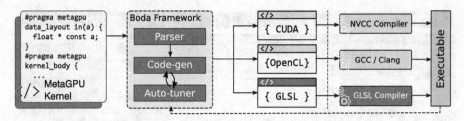

Fig. 3. The workflow behind our approach. Highlighted (dark) boxes denote the extensions in the Boda framework.

simple buffer in CUDA (`cudaMalloc`) or OpenCL (`clCreateBuffer`) with a single line of code. To create the same buffer in Vulkan, we have to: (1) create a buffer object, (2) get the memory requirements for that object, (3) decide which memory heap to use, (4) allocate memory on the selected heap, and (5) bind the buffer object to the allocated memory. This requires more than 40 lines of code. Clearly, host code programming in Vulkan is proportionally more complex, which stems from its explicit nature. Such code verbosity not only increases the programming effort but also makes the code more error-prone.

3 Code Generation

To generate tensor kernels, we use Boda [13] as the main engine. Boda is a CNN inference framework that uses template meta-programming to generate efficient GPU tensor code. Relying only on meta-programming made Boda a lightweight framework with minimal external software dependencies. The major required software packages comprise a C++ compiler, Python for building Boda itself, and a compatible GPU backend compiler, such as NVCC, Clang with OpenCL enabled, or GLSL to compile GPU tensor codes. We extended this framework by adding new components to provide Vulkan backend support as well as a kernel-abstraction layer to generate GPU code for each target API. Figure 3 depicts a high-level overview of our method. In the following, we will explain the key components.

MetaGPU Abstraction Layer. Considering the code discrepancies among the target APIs (see Fig. 2), we propose MetaGPU, a compatibility layer over our target APIs. It abstracts away the syntactic differences for the basic GPU programming concepts shared by our target APIs. We did not want to invent a new language because it creates additional learning overhead for programmers. Instead, we keep the coding convention very similar to CUDA and OpenCL and simply ask the user to separate the code into three regions using `#pragma` directives, similar to OpenMP. Figure 4 shows a MetaGPU code sample.

1. *Tuning parameters:* The first region defines tuning parameters. We can either access them in the kernel code or in the host program.

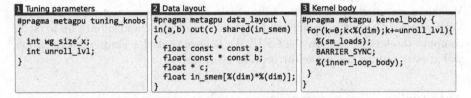

Fig. 4. A trivial sample of MetaGPU code.

Table 2. The list of pre-defined keywords in the kernel body alongside their corresponding value within each target API.

	CUDA	OpenCL	Vulkan
GLOB_ID_1D	blockDim.x*blockIdx.x+threadIdx.x	get_global_id(0)	gl_GlobalInvocationID.x
LOC_ID_1D	threadIdx.x	get_local_id(0)	gl_LocalInvocationID.x
GRP_ID_1D	blockIdx.x	get_group_id(0)	gl_WorkGroupID.x
LOC_SZ_1D	blockDim.x	get_local_size(0)	gl_WorkGroupSize.x
BARRIER_SYNC	__syncthreads()	barrier(CLK_LOCAL_MEM_FENCE)	barrier()

2. *Data layout:* The kernel arguments and required memories which need to be allocated in the shared memory are defined within this region. Additionally, the scope of each argument should be defined with any of **in**, **out** or **smem** keywords.

3. *Kernel body:* As the name suggests, this region contains the actual kernel logic. A subtle difference is that using pointers is not allowed. Furthermore, the user has to use pre-defined keywords for accessing the GPU threads, workgroups and synchronization barriers. Table 2 shows the list of keywords and their corresponding string in each target API. MetaGPU also supports template meta-programming to generate adaptive code. Template placeholders are defined by %(placeholder_name)% and, using Boda, the user can populate them with C instructions or any desired string. Such a feature can help dynamically generate code and unroll loops to further improve performance.

Code Generation. We first parse the input MetaGPU code and extract the three regions. The tuning parameters can later be used for auto-tuning. Then, the data layout of the kernel is parsed to find out the kernel arguments for CUDA/OpenCL code and the bindings for Vulkan GLSL code. Based on the target programming interface, we can then generate the kernel by generating corresponding argument declarations and merging them with the kernel body. All those template placeholders and abstract keywords will be replaced by their values as well.

We also added Vulkan support to Boda by creating a new backend to support host programming. All the required buffers, synchronizations, and timings will be handled by the Vulkan backend within Boda. Therefore, the end user does not have to write any host code using Vulkan. Since the programming effort of

Vulkan is very high, this feature will greatly enhance programmer productivity. Furthermore, we use the kernel batching feature in Vulkan and submit up to eight compute shaders at once to the GPU. We believe that this simple optimization will greatly reduce the kernel-invocation overhead.

Auto-tuning. Tensor operations have a wide range of possible input sizes and parameters. It is generally difficult, even with meta-programming, to write code that runs well across more than a limited range of input sizes. Such tuning parameters might control thread blocking, memory access patterns, or load/store/compute vector widths. Thus, the auto-tuner automatically searches the tuning space to find the right values for the given tuning knobs in the MetaGPU code and even across different implementation variants. This is an important step towards higher performance portability.

The key feature of our autotuning method is automatic per-platform variant selection and automated sweeping over tuning parameters. Currently, we apply a simple brute-force search over a fixed set of configurations, combined with a heuristic parameter selection method, to reduce the search space to a tractable size.

4   Experimental Results

To evaluate the programmability and performance portability of our approach, we selected a range of convolution operations and generated the corresponding GPU code for each of the target APIs. We extracted 43 unique convolutions from AlexNet, Network-in-Network, and the InceptionV1 networks, which have (1) a batch size of five, and (2) more than $1e8$ FLOPS. The rationale behind this selection is that we wanted these convolutions to model a streaming deployment scenario with high computational load but some latency tolerance. The exact specifications for each of these 43 convolutions can be found in Table 3.

For the sake of precision, we measured the execution times using GPU timers. Furthermore, to counter run-to-run variation, we executed each kernel five times and reported the average of the runtimes we obtained. Because Vulkan GPU timers were not supported on our mobile platform, we had to use its CPU timers instead. All the average speedups reported across the convolutions are computed using the geometric mean. Our evaluation artifacts, including source code and instructions on how to rerun the experiments, are available on Figshare [11].

Experimental Setup. We chose NVIDIA GTX 1080 Ti and AMD Radeon RX 580, two recent desktop GPUs. We also used a mobile platform based on the Hikey 960 development kit, which contains an ARM Mali-G71 MP8 GPU. Table 4 summarizes the configuration details of the target platforms.

Table 3. KSZ, S, OC and B are the kernel size, stride, number of output channels, and batch size of each convolution operation. *in* and *out* are the sizes of input and output, specified as $y \times x \times chan$; FLOPs is the per-operation FLOP count.

KSZ	S	OC	B	in	out	FLOPs
5	1	32	5	$28 \times 28 \times 16$	$28 \times 28 \times 32$	1.00352e+08
5	1	64	5	$14 \times 14 \times 32$	$14 \times 14 \times 64$	1.00352e+08
1	1	256	5	$7 \times 7 \times 832$	$7 \times 7 \times 256$	1.04366e+08
1	1	112	5	$14 \times 14 \times 512$	$14 \times 14 \times 112$	1.12394e+08
1	1	128	5	$14 \times 14 \times 512$	$14 \times 14 \times 128$	1.28451e+08
1	1	64	5	$28 \times 28 \times 256$	$28 \times 28 \times 64$	1.28451e+08
1	1	64	5	$56 \times 56 \times 64$	$56 \times 56 \times 64$	1.28451e+08
1	1	128	5	$14 \times 14 \times 528$	$14 \times 14 \times 128$	1.32465e+08
1	1	144	5	$14 \times 14 \times 512$	$14 \times 14 \times 144$	1.44507e+08
1	1	96	5	$28 \times 28 \times 192$	$28 \times 28 \times 96$	1.44507e+08
1	1	384	5	$7 \times 7 \times 832$	$7 \times 7 \times 384$	1.56549e+08
1	1	160	5	$14 \times 14 \times 512$	$14 \times 14 \times 160$	1.60563e+08
1	1	160	5	$14 \times 14 \times 528$	$14 \times 14 \times 160$	1.65581e+08
1	1	4096	5	$1 \times 1 \times 4096$	$1 \times 1 \times 4096$	1.67772e+08
1	1	192	5	$14 \times 14 \times 480$	$14 \times 14 \times 192$	1.80634e+08
5	1	128	5	$14 \times 14 \times 32$	$14 \times 14 \times 128$	2.00704e+08
3	1	320	5	$7 \times 7 \times 160$	$7 \times 7 \times 320$	2.25792e+08
1	1	384	5	$13 \times 13 \times 384$	$13 \times 13 \times 384$	2.49201e+08
1	1	128	5	$28 \times 28 \times 256$	$28 \times 28 \times 128$	2.56901e+08
1	1	256	5	$14 \times 14 \times 528$	$14 \times 14 \times 256$	2.64929e+08
1	1	96	5	$54 \times 54 \times 96$	$54 \times 54 \times 96$	2.68739e+08
3	1	384	5	$7 \times 7 \times 192$	$7 \times 7 \times 384$	3.2514e+08
3	1	208	5	$14 \times 14 \times 96$	$14 \times 14 \times 208$	3.52236e+08
1	1	1000	5	$6 \times 6 \times 1024$	$6 \times 6 \times 1000$	3.6864e+08
1	1	1024	5	$6 \times 6 \times 1024$	$6 \times 6 \times 1024$	3.77487e+08
6	1	4096	5	$6 \times 6 \times 256$	$1 \times 1 \times 4096$	3.77487e+08
3	1	224	5	$14 \times 14 \times 112$	$14 \times 14 \times 224$	4.42552e+08
1	1	256	5	$27 \times 27 \times 256$	$27 \times 27 \times 256$	4.77757e+08
3	1	256	5	$14 \times 14 \times 128$	$14 \times 14 \times 256$	5.78028e+08
5	1	96	5	$28 \times 28 \times 32$	$28 \times 28 \times 96$	6.02112e+08
3	1	288	5	$14 \times 14 \times 144$	$14 \times 14 \times 288$	7.31566e+08
3	1	128	5	$28 \times 28 \times 96$	$28 \times 28 \times 128$	8.67041e+08
3	1	320	5	$14 \times 14 \times 160$	$14 \times 14 \times 320$	9.03168e+08
11	4	96	5	$224 \times 224 \times 3$	$54 \times 54 \times 96$	1.01617e+09
11	4	96	5	$227 \times 227 \times 3$	$55 \times 55 \times 96$	1.05415e+09
7	2	64	5	$224 \times 224 \times 3$	$112 \times 112 \times 64$	1.18014e+09
3	1	1024	5	$6 \times 6 \times 384$	$6 \times 6 \times 1024$	1.27402e+09
3	1	256	5	$13 \times 13 \times 384$	$13 \times 13 \times 256$	1.4952e+09
3	1	384	5	$13 \times 13 \times 256$	$13 \times 13 \times 384$	1.4952e+09
3	1	192	5	$28 \times 28 \times 128$	$28 \times 28 \times 192$	1.73408e+09
3	1	384	5	$13 \times 13 \times 384$	$13 \times 13 \times 384$	2.24281e+09
3	1	192	5	$56 \times 56 \times 64$	$56 \times 56 \times 192$	3.46817e+09
5	1	256	5	$27 \times 27 \times 96$	$27 \times 27 \times 256$	4.47898e+09

Table 4. Experimental setup.

	Nvidia GTX 1080Ti	AMD RX 580	ARM Mali G71 MP8
OS	Ubuntu 16.04 64-bit		Android 7.0
CPU	Intel Xeon Gold 6126, 12 Core @ 2.6 GHz		4 Cortex A73 + 4 Cortex A53
Host Memory	64 GB		3 GB LPDDR4 SDRAM
GPU Memory	11 GB GDDR5X	8 GB GDDR5	-
Driver	Linux Display Driver 410.66	AMDGPU-PRO Driver 17.40	Native driver
CUDA	CUDA 10.0	-	-
OpenCL	OpenCL 1.2	OpenCL 2.0	OpenCL 2.0
Vulkan SDK	Vulkan 1.1.97	Vulkan 1.1.97	Vulkan 1.1.97

Table 5. Lines-of-code comparison for different convolution implementations alongside computed effort metric.

	$LOC_{MetaGPU}$	LOC_{CUDA}	LOC_{OpenCL}	LOC_{Vulkan}	$LOC_{TotalUniqueLines}$	Effort
Direct convolution	113	562	631	1137	2330	4.84
Tiled convolution	115	548	618	1119	2285	5.03
GEMM convolution	89	1103	1172	1666	3941	2.25
1x1 convolution	160	1190	1259	1761	4210	3.80

Programmability Analysis. Our method offers performance portability while easing the burden of rewriting the program for each API. However, to quantitatively evaluate the programming effort required to generate efficient deep-learning kernels, we propose a metric based on total lines of code. Inspired by Memeti et al. [12], we use clock to determine the lines of MetaGPU code $LOC_{MetaGPU}$ and the total unique lines of code $LOC_{TotalUniqueLines}$ needed to be written for our target APIs to provide code portability. We then define the programming effort as follows.

$$\text{Effort}[\%] = (LOC_{MetaGPU}/LOC_{TotalUniqueLines}) \times 100 \qquad (1)$$

In most CNN frameworks, including Boda, multiple convolution variants exist, each specialized for a specific case. For instance, Boda provides direct, tiled, GEMM, and 1×1 convolution variants. We counted the LOCs for each variant and target API. The results are shown in Table 5. For a fair programming effort analysis, we used total unique lines between all the target APIs. The results indicate that using our method requires on average 8% of the total effort needed to implement the code with all of the target APIs.

Performance Portability Analysis. We now present per-convolution-operation runtime results across hardware targets and programming interfaces to illustrate the performance portability of our method. We sorted the operations by FLOP count, a reasonable proxy for the difficulty of the operations.

A runtime comparison of CUDA, OpenCL, and Vulkan on our benchmark set of operations is given in Fig. 5. All runtimes are for running each operation using the best function generated by our method for that operation, selected by auto-tuning. The implementations are the same and only the backend API is different. We also added cuDNN runtimes as the baseline to show the performance of our method relative to the highly-tuned vendor CNN library. The results clearly show that our Vulkan backend often yields lower runtime in comparison to the other two, and closer to cuDNN's performance. We believe that this is owed to kernel batching and the optimizations provided by Vulkan. Note that we are slower especially in cases with 3×3 kernel sizes, where cuDNN is using Winograd convolution, which we have not yet implemented. On average, Vulkan outperformed CUDA and OpenCL kernels by a factor of 1.54 and 1.86, respectively. Although cuDNN was able to operate 1.38× faster than Vulkan, we noticed that in some cases, Vulkan can be up to 1.46× faster than cuDNN.

Figure 6 compares the runtimes of our benchmark using OpenCL and Vulkan on the AMD GPU. We also show MIOpen runtimes as the baseline to show the performance of our method relative to the optimized AMD CNN library. Again, we notice that Vulkan outperforms OpenCL by a factor of 1.51 on average. Presumably benefiting from Winograd convolutions and a highly-optimized MIOpenGEMM, MIOpen performs better than our Vulkan implementation for

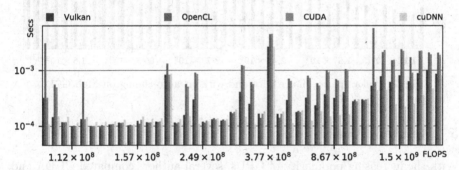

Fig. 5. The runtime comparison of kernels generated by our method and cuDNN vendor library on Nvidia GTX 1080 Ti.

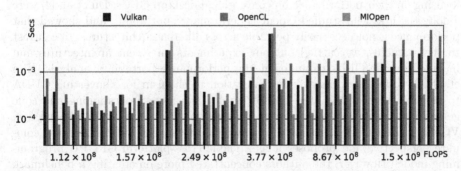

Fig. 6. The runtime comparison of kernels generated by our method and the MIOpen vendor library on AMD Radeon RX 580.

25 out of 43 operations. For the 18 remaining operations, however our Vulkan version runs up to 2.28× faster than MIOpen.

Together, Figs. 5 and 6 illustrate that we were able to achieve competitive performance compared to the vendor libraries on two different platforms. This observation confirms that our method achieves good performance portability. To further validate the effect of auto-tuning on performance portability, we executed the Vulkan code generated by our backend with and without auto-tuning. The final results after selecting the right variant and tuning parameters are shown in Fig. 7. Note that runtimes are reported using CPU timers, because Vulkan GPU timestamps are not supported on Mali G71. Auto-tuning requires much less effort than manual tuning and improves performance significantly—on average by a factor of 3.11.

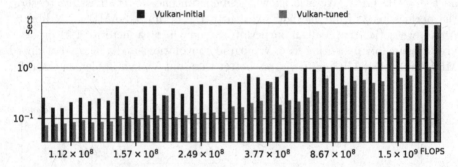

Fig. 7. Vulkan performance with and without auto-tuning on Mali G71.

5   Related Work

With the increasing popularity of GPUs, several authors compared CUDA and OpenCL programming models [3–5,8,9,12,15,17], but none of them studied Vulkan. Karimi et al. [8] and Fang et al. [5] compared CUDA with OpenCL, focusing on their performance on conventional desktop GPUs. Du et al. [4] were among the first who studied OpenCL performance portability and showed that performance is not necessarily portable across different architectures. In contrast to these studies, we carried out our experiments on recent architectures and included mobile GPUs to augment the performance portability analysis. Kim et al. [9] proposed a one-to-one translation mechanism for converting CUDA to OpenCL kernels, but they do not employ any meta-programming and code generation to achieve higher efficiency as we do. To the best of our knowledge, VComputeBench [10] is the only work which investigates Vulkan from the compute perspective and proposes it as a viable cross-platform GPGPU programming model. However, the authors concentrated more on creating a benchmark suite and did not provide a method for code translation and enhancing performance portability.

The amount of work published on the portable execution of CNNs as well as the use of Vulkan in this context is very limited. In recent years, a number of tensor compilers and frameworks, such as PlaidML [7], Tensor Comprehensions [20], TVM [1], DeepMon [6], and Boda [13,14] have been introduced to address the portability issue of deep-learning frameworks using code generation and compiler optimizations. However, none of them are able to generate code for our target APIs using a single-source approach for the kernel definition. PlaidML and Tensor Comprehension do not support Vulkan at all. TVM and DeepMon are able to generate Vulkan code, but they require different input code for each programming model, demanding extra programming effort to introduce new tensor operations. Boda, on the other hand, has a compatibility layer on top of OpenCL and CUDA. Its approach is based on writing lowest-common-denominator code that is compatible between the two and uses macro definitions to abstract away syntactic differences. However, because of its larger code divergence such an approach is definitely not extendable to include Vulkan as well.

6 Conclusion and Outlook

This paper presents a comparative analysis of the GPU programming interfaces CUDA, OpenCL, and Vulkan. We let this comparison guide us in developing a method for generating tensor GPU kernels coded in any of those APIs from a single source that abstracts away the syntactic differences between these APIs. We implemented our approach in a state-of-the-art CNN inference framework called Boda and analyzed the programmability and performance portability of the generated kernels. Based on our experiments, our method reduces the programming effort by 98% when code portability between different APIs is demanded. Furthermore, we showed that Vulkan offers better performance compared with other APIs on our convolution benchmarks and sometimes performs better than CNN vendor libraries.

Acknowledgment. This research has been supported by the Klaus Tschira Foundation, the Hessian LOEWE initiative within the Software-Factory 4.0 project, and the German Research Foundation (DFG) through the Program Performance Engineering for Scientific Software.

References

1. Chen, T., et al.: TVM: an automated end-to-end optimizing compiler for deep learning. In: 13th USENIX Symposium on Operating Systems Design and Implementation, OSDI 2018, pp. 578–594 (2018)
2. Chetlur, S., et al.: cuDNN: efficient primitives for deep learning. arXiv preprint arXiv:1410.0759 (2014)
3. Da Silva, H.C., Pisani, F., Borin, E.: A comparative study of SYCL, OpenCL, and OpenMP. In: Proceedings of International Symposium on Computer Architecture and High-Performance Computing Workshops, SBAC-PADW 2016, pp. 61–66. IEEE (2016)

4. Du, P., Weber, R., Luszczek, P., Tomov, S., Peterson, G., Dongarra, J.: From CUDA to OpenCL: towards a performance-portable solution for multi-platform GPU programming. Parallel Comput. **38**(8), 391–407 (2012)
5. Fang, J., Varbanescu, A.L., Sips, H.: A comprehensive performance comparison of CUDA and OpenCL. In: Proceedings of International Conference on Parallel Processing (ICPP), pp. 216–225. IEEE (2011)
6. Huynh, L.N., Lee, Y., Balan, R.K.: DeepMon: mobile GPU-based deep learning framework for continuous vision applications. In: Proceedings of 15th Annual International Conference on Mobile Systems, Applications, and Services, MobiSys 2017, pp. 82–95. ACM (2017)
7. Intel: PlaidML (2019). https://www.intel.ai/plaidml
8. Karimi, K., Dickson, N.G., Hamze, F.: A performance comparison of CUDA and OpenCL. arXiv preprint arXiv:1005.2581 (2010)
9. Kim, J., Dao, T.T., Jung, J., Joo, J., Lee, J.: Bridging OpenCL and CUDA: a comparative analysis and translation. In: Proceedings of International Conference for High Performance Computing, Networking, Storage and Analysis, SC 2015, pp. 1–12. ACM (2015)
10. Mammeri, N., Juurlink, B.: VComputeBench: a Vulkan benchmark suite for GPGPU on mobile and embedded GPUs. In: Proceedings of International Symposium on Workload Characterization, IISWC 2018, pp. 25–35. IEEE (2018)
11. Mazaheri, A., Schulte, J., Moskewicz, M., Wolf, F., Jannesari, A.: Artifact Evaluation (2019). https://doi.org/10.6084/m9.figshare.8490146
12. Memeti, S., Li, L., Pllana, S., Kołodziej, J., Kessler, C.: Benchmarking OpenCL, OpenACC, OpenMP, and CUDA: programming productivity, performance, and energy consumption. In: Proceedings of Workshop on Adaptive Resource Management and Scheduling for Cloud Computing, pp. 1–6. ACM (2017)
13. Moskewicz, M.W., Jannesari, A., Keutzer, K.: A metaprogramming and auto-tuning framework for deploying deep learning applications. arXiv preprint arXiv:1611.06945 (2016)
14. Moskewicz, M.W., Jannesari, A., Keutzer, K.: Boda: a holistic approach for implementing neural network computations. In: Proceedings of International Conference on Computing Frontier, CF 2017, pp. 53–62. ACM (2017)
15. Sachetto Oliveira, R., et al.: Comparing CUDA, OpenCL and OpenGL implementations of the cardiac monodomain equations. In: Wyrzykowski, R., Dongarra, J., Karczewski, K., Waśniewski, J. (eds.) PPAM 2011. LNCS, vol. 7204, pp. 111–120. Springer, Heidelberg (2012). https://doi.org/10.1007/978-3-642-31500-8_12
16. Sampson, A.: Let's fix OpenGL. In: Leibniz International Proceedings in Informatics, LIPIcs 2017, vol. 71. Schloss Dagstuhl, Leibniz-Zentrum füer Informatik (2017)
17. Su, C.L., Chen, P.Y., Lan, C.C., Huang, L.S., Wu, K.H.: Overview and comparison of OpenCL and CUDA technology for GPGPU. In: Proceedings of Asia Pacific Conference on Circuits and Systems, APCCAS 2012, pp. 448–451. IEEE (2012)
18. The Khronos Group: Khronos SPIR-V registry (2019). https://www.khronos.org/registry/spir-v
19. The Khronos Group: Khronos Vulkan registry (2019). https://www.khronos.org/registry/vulkan
20. Vasilache, N., et al.: Tensor comprehensions: framework-agnostic high-performance machine learning abstractions. arXiv preprint arXiv:1802.04730 (2018)

Unified and Scalable Incremental Recommenders with Consumed Item Packs

Rachid Guerraoui[1], Erwan Le Merrer[2(✉)], Rhicheek Patra[3],
and Jean-Ronan Vigouroux[4]

[1] EPFL, Lausanne, Switzerland
Rachid.Guerraoui@epfl.ch
[2] Univ Rennes, Inria, CNRS, IRISA, Rennes, France
erwan.le-merrer@inria.fr
[3] Oracle Labs, Zurich, Switzerland
rhicheek.patra@oracle.com
[4] Technicolor, Rennes, France
jean-ronan.vigouroux@technicolor.com

Abstract. Recommenders personalize the web content using collaborative filtering to relate users (or items). This work proposes to unify *user-based*, *item-based* and *neural word embeddings* types of recommenders under a single abstraction for their input, we name Consumed Item Packs (CIPs). In addition to genericity, we show this abstraction to be compatible with incremental processing, which is at the core of low latency recommendation to users. We propose three such algorithms using CIPs, analyze them, and describe their implementation and scalability for the Spark platform. We demonstrate that all three provide a recommendation quality that is competitive with three algorithms from the state-of-the-art.

Keywords: Implicit recommenders · Incremental updates ·
Parallelism · Spark

1 Introduction

Recent recommender systems exploit implicit feedback [1–3] (*i.e.*, they do not leverage *ratings* collected from users), and show competitive results with Singular Value Decomposition (SVD) based recommenders [4]. They aim at uncovering high-order relations between consumed items. Each paper proposes a specific algorithm, with an arbitrary definition of sequences of consumed items. Our motivation is to investigate the existence of a higher level abstraction for sequences of consumed items, and algorithms for dealing with it. Such an abstraction, we name a *Consumed Item Pack* (CIP), allows to reason about and to propose sequence-aware algorithms within the same framework, capable of addressing implicit recommendation.

The challenges are threefold. *(i)* We first have to highlight that the notion of CIP captures the analogous consumption pattern of users (*e.g.*, the one exposed

© Springer Nature Switzerland AG 2019
R. Yahyapour (Ed.): Euro-Par 2019, LNCS 11725, pp. 227–240, 2019.
https://doi.org/10.1007/978-3-030-29400-7_17

in [1]). *(ii)* The second challenge is the computational complexity of the proposed algorithms in the CIP framework. Leveraging CIPs for building implicit recommenders is not immediate, for the computation time can easily become prohibitive given the size of user consumption logs in production systems. This is for instance the case in the previously introduced sequential approach HOSLIM [1], where algorithmic tractability is at stake. Section 2 presents three CIP based algorithms. Concerning memory-based Collaborative Filtering (CF), we show in Subsect. 2.1 (resp. Subsect. 2.2) how to build a CIP based similarity metric that is *incremental*, which helps in designing an implicit user-based (resp. item-based) recommender that *scales* while providing good recommendation quality. Moreover, we also present a model-based CF technique incorporating CIPs in Subsect. 2.3, which leverages neural word embeddings [5]. We demonstrate that our techniques scale with an increasing number of computing nodes while achieving a speedup comparable to Spark's Alternating Least Squares (ALS) recommender from the MLLIB library. *(iii)* These proposed implicit algorithms have to provide an accuracy that is at least comparable with classic CF recommenders, in order to be adopted in practice. For assessing their performance, we then conduct a comparison with an explicit SVD-based recommender [4], with an implicit one [6], as well as with a recent state-of-the-art algorithm [7] incorporating both implicit and explicit techniques.

Consumed Item Packs. Our CIPs relate to high order relations between items enjoyed by a user. Some previous works such as HOSLIM [1], considered the consumption of items by the same user as the basis for implicit recommendation. HOSLIM places the so called *user-itemsets* (implicit feedback) in a matrix, and then computes the similarity of jointly consumed items over the whole user history (that leads to the optimal recommendation quality). High-order relations are sought in principle, but due to the tractability issue of this approach (for m items and order k: $O(m^k)$ combinations of the items are enumerated and tested for relevance), authors limit computations only to pairs of items. Recently, Barkan et al. proposed to consider item-item relations using the model of word embeddings in their technical report [2]. Our work generalizes the notion of implicit item relations, based on consumption patterns.

To get access to useful information from service logs, we define the CIP data structure. CIPs are extracted from users' consumption patterns, and allow us to compute the similarity between those users (or items consumed by them). A user's profile is composed of multiple CIPs. The notion of CIP is then instantiated in three different algorithms: in a user-based algorithm (Subsect. 2.1), in an item-based one (Subsect. 2.2) and in a word embedding based one (Subsect. 2.3).

To make things more precise, consider a set of m users $\mathcal{U} = \{u_1, u_2, ..., u_m\}$ and a set of n items from a product catalog $\mathcal{I} = \{i_1, i_2, ..., i_n\}$. The transaction history of a user u, consists of a set of pairs of the form $\langle i, t_{ui}\rangle$ (where u consumed an item i at a time $t_{u,i}$), extracted from service logs. We denote u's profile as P_u, which consists of the time-ordered items in the log. CIPs are composed of items: each CIP $\in \mathcal{I}^*$. The order of the items in a given user's CIP represents their relative appearance in time, the leftmost symbol being the oldest one: $\text{CIP}_u = [i_1, i_2, i_3, ..., i_k]$ such that $t_{u,i_1} < t_{u,i_2} < ... < t_{u,i_k}$.

A CIP then represents the items consumed by a user over a predefined period of time. Using such a data structure, one can devise a *similarity* measure *sim* : $\mathcal{I}^* \times \mathcal{I}^* \to \mathbb{R}^+$ between two CIPs, that captures the proximity between users (or items) as we explain it in the next section.

2 CIP Based Algorithms

The core claim of this paper is that the notion of CIP is general enough to capture different types of algorithms that rely on sequences of items. In the next three subsections, we present novel algorithms that determine CIP based similarities and leverage sequence of items for recommendation. To illustrate the generality of CIPs, the last subsection shows how a previously introduced algorithm (FISM [3]) is captured by the CIP framework.

2.1 CIP-U: A User-Based Recommender

CIP-U is an incremental algorithm that maintains a user-user network where each user is connected to the most similar K other users. CIP-U exploits users' CIPs, and accepts batches of items freshly consumed by users (*i.e.*, last logged transactions on the service) to update this network.

P_u^l denotes the profile of a user u till the lth update of her consumed items, while CIP_u^{l+1} denotes the batch of new items consumed by her since the last batch update. Assuming $P_u^l = i_1 i_2 ... i_k$ and $\text{CIP}_u^{l+1} = i_{k+1} i_{k+2} ... i_n$, we can denote the profile of a user u after the $(l+1)^{th}$ iteration as $P_u^{l+1} = P_u^l \cup \text{CIP}_u^{l+1}$. Note that $\cup$ is an order preserving union here.

Before we provide the similarity measure to compare users, we introduce some preliminary definitions. We first introduce the notion of *hammock distance* between a pair of items in the profile of a given user u.

Definition 1 (HAMMOCK DISTANCE). *The hammock distance between a pair of items (i, j) in P_u, denoted by $\mathcal{H}_u(i, j)$, is the number of hops between them.*

For instance, in $P_u = [i_{14}, i_3, i_{20}, i_{99}, i_{53}, i_{10}, i_{25}]$, $\mathcal{H}_u(i_{14}, i_{99}) = 3$.

Definition 2 (HAMMOCK PAIRS). *Given two users u and v, their hammock pairs $\mathcal{HP}_{u,v}$ are the set of distinct item pairs both present in P_u and in P_v, under the constraint that the number of hops between pairs is at most δ_H.*

$$\mathcal{HP}_{u,v} = \{(i,j) \mid \mathcal{H}_u(i,j) \leq \delta_H \ \wedge \ \mathcal{H}_v(i,j) \leq \delta_H \ \wedge \ i \neq j\}$$

Hyper-parameter δ_H denotes the *hammock threshold* and serves the purpose of tuning the CIP based latent feature considered between related items.

Let $[]$ denote the Iverson bracket: $[P] = 1$ if P is True, 0 otherwise. From hammock pairs, we derive the similarity of two users with regards to their CIPs:

Definition 3 (SIMILARITY MEASURE FOR USER-BASED CIP). *The simi-larity between two users u and v is defined as a function of the cardinality of the set of hammock pairs between them:*

$$sim_{\text{CIP-U}}(u,v) = 1 - (1 - [P_u = P_v]) \cdot e^{-|\mathcal{HP}_{u,v}|} \qquad (1)$$

We obtain $sim_{\text{CIP-U}} \in [0,1]$, with the boundary conditions, $sim_{\text{CIP-U}} = 0$ if the two users have no pair in common ($|\mathcal{HP}_{u,v}| = 0$ and $[P_u = P_v] = 0$), while $sim_{\text{CIP-U}} = 1$ if their CIPs are identical ($[P_u = P_v] = 1$).

Incremental Updates. CIP-U enables incremental updates, in order to conve-niently reflect the latest users' consumption in recommendations without requir-ing a prohibitive computation time. CIP-U processes batches of events (con-sumed items) at regular intervals and updates the similarity measure for pairs of users. $C_{u,v}$ denotes the set of items common in the profiles of two users u and v. More precisely, after the lth iteration, we obtain: $C_{u,v}^l = P_u^l \cap P_v^l$. Then, at the $(l+1)^{th}$ iteration, we get:
$C_{u,v}^{l+1} = P_u^{l+1} \cap P_v^{l+1} = (P_u^l \cup \text{CIP}_u^{l+1}) \cap (P_v^l \cup \text{CIP}_v^{l+1}) = (P_u^l \cap P_v^l) \cup (P_u^l \cap \text{CIP}_v^{l+1}) \cup (P_v^l \cap \text{CIP}_u^{l+1}) \cup (\text{CIP}_u^{l+1} \cap \text{CIP}_v^{l+1}) = C_{u,v}^l \cup \Delta C_{u,v}^{l+1}$, where $\Delta C_{u,v}^{l+1} = (P_u^l \cap \text{CIP}_v^{l+1}) \cup (P_v^l \cap \text{CIP}_u^{l+1}) \cup (\text{CIP}_u^{l+1} \cap \text{CIP}_v^{l+1})$. Note that the time complexity of this step is $O((|P_u^l| + |\text{CIP}_v^{l+1}|) + (|P_v^l| + |\text{CIP}_u^{l+1}|))$, where $|\text{CIP}_u^{l+1}|$, $|\text{CIP}_v^{l+1}|$ are bounded by the number of events, say Q, after which the batch update will take place. Hence, the time complexity is $O(n + Q) = O(n)$, where n denotes the total number of items, and when Q is a constant (and $Q << n$ as expected in a system built for incremental computation).

We next incrementally compute the new hammock pairs. $\Delta\mathcal{HP}_{u,v}$ denotes the set of new hammock pairs for users u and v. Computation is performed as follows: $\Delta\mathcal{HP}_{u,v} = \{(i,j) \mid (i \in C_{u,v}^l, j \in \Delta C_{u,v}^{l+1}) \land (i \in \Delta C_{u,v}^{l+1}, j \in \Delta C_{u,v}^{l+1}) \land \mathcal{H}_u(i,j) \leq \delta_H \land \mathcal{H}_v(i,j) \leq \delta_H\}$.

The time complexity of this step is $O(|C_{u,v}^l| \cdot |\Delta C_{u,v}^{l+1}|)$, where $|\Delta C_{u,v}^{l+1}|$ is bounded by the number of events after which the batch update takes place (Q). Hence, the time complexity is also of $O(n \cdot Q) = O(n)$.

Finally, the similarities are computed leveraging the cardinality of the com-puted incremental hammock pairs. More precisely, we compute the updated sim-ilarity on-the-fly between a pair of users u and v after the $(l+1)^{th}$ iteration as follows: $sim_{u,v}^{l+1} = 1 - (1 - [P_u^{l+1} = P_v^{l+1}]) \cdot e^{-|\mathcal{HP}_{u,v}^l + \Delta\mathcal{HP}_{u,v}|}$.

Hence, the similarity computation between one user and all m others is $O(nm)$. In CIP-U, we retain a small number K of the most similar users (where $K << m$) per given user. Selecting the top-K similar users for collaborative fil-tering based on their similarity requires sorting, which induces an additional $O(m \log m)$. The total complexity is $O(nm) + O(m \log m) = O(nm)$ (since $n >> \log m$). Note that classic explicit collaborative filtering algorithms (user or item-based) have same time complexity for periodically updating their recom-mendation models. Note that complexity for the top-K neighbors can be reduced further to $O(n)$ by using biased sampling and iteratively updating neighbors [8].

2.2   CIP-I: An Item-Based Recommender

CIP-I is also an incremental algorithm that processes user consumption events in CIPs, to update its item-item network. Similar to CIP-U, we also leverage the notion of user *profiles*: a profile of a user u is noted P_u, and is composed of one or more disjoint CIPs. We use multiple CIPs in a user profile to model her consumption pattern. CIPs are separated based on the timestamps associated with the consumed items: two consecutive CIPs are disjoint if the former's last and latter's first items are separated in time by a given interval δ.

Definition 4 (CIP PARTITIONS IN A USER PROFILE). *Let i_k and i_{k+1} denote two consecutive consumption events of a user u, with consumption timestamps t_{u,i_k} and $t_{u,i_{k+1}}$, such that $t_{u,i_k} \leq t_{u,i_{k+1}}$. Given i_k belongs to CIP_u^l, item i_{k+1} is added to CIP_u^l if $t_{u,i_{k+1}} \leq t_{u,i_k} + \delta$. Otherwise i_{k+1} is added as the first element in a new CIP_u^{l+1}.*

These CIPs are defined as δ-distant. The rationale behind the creation of user profiles composed of CIPs is that each CIP is intended to capture the semantic taste of a user within a consistent consumption period.

With $i <_{\mathrm{CIP}} j$ denoting the prior occurrence of i before j in a given CIP, and the inverse hammock distance $\epsilon_u(i,j)$ being a penalty function for distant items in a CIP_u (*e.g.*, $\epsilon_u(i,j) = \frac{1}{\mathcal{H}_u(i,j)}$), we express a similarity measure for items, based on those partitioned user profiles, as follows.

Definition 5 (SIMILARITY MEASURE FOR ITEM-BASED CIP). *Given a pair of items (i,j), their similarity is:*

$$sim_{\mathrm{CIP\text{-}I}}(i,j) = \frac{\sum_u \sum_{l=1}^{|l|_u}[(i,j) \in \mathrm{CIP}_u^l \wedge i <_{\mathrm{CIP}} j](1 + \epsilon_u(i,j))}{2 \cdot \max\{\sum_u \sum_{l=1}^{|l|_u}[i \in \mathrm{CIP}_u^l], \sum_u \sum_{l=1}^{|l|_u}[j \in \mathrm{CIP}_u^l]\}} \qquad (2)$$

$$= \frac{score_{\mathrm{CIP\text{-}I}}(i,j)}{2 \cdot max\{cardV(i), cardV(j)\}},$$

with $|l|_u$ the number of CIPs in u's profile, and $[]$ the Iverson bracket.

This reflects the number of close and ordered co-occurrences of items i and j over the total number of occurrences of both items independently: $sim_{\mathrm{CIP\text{-}I}}(i,j) = 1$ if each appearance of i is immediately followed by j in the current CIP. Contrarily, $sim_{\mathrm{CIP\text{-}I}}(i,j) = 0$ if there is no co-occurrence of those items in any CIP. Furthermore, we denote the numerator term as $score_{\mathrm{CIP\text{-}I}}(i,j)$ and the denominator term as a function of $cardV(i)$ and $cardV(j)$ sub-terms for Eq. 2, where $cardV(i) = \sum_u \sum_{l=1}^{|l|_u}[i \in \mathrm{CIP}_u^l]$. As shown in Algorithm 1, we can update $score_{\mathrm{CIP\text{-}I}}(i,j)$ and $cardV(i)$ terms incrementally. Finally, we compute the similarity on-the-fly with the $score_{\mathrm{CIP\text{-}I}}(i,j)$ and $cardV(i)$ terms.

Incremental Updates. CIP-I processes users' recent CIPs scanned from users' consumption logs. Score values ($score_{\mathrm{CIP\text{-}I}}$) are updated (Algorithm 1). We require an item-item matrix to maintain the *score* values, as well as a n-dimensional vector that maintains the current number of occurrences of each item.

After the update of the *score* values, the algorithm terminates by updating a data structure containing the top-K closest items for each given item, leveraging the *score* matrix and the cardinality terms for computing the similarities on-the-fly.

Algorithm 1. *Incremental Updates for Item Pairs.*

Require: CIP_u ▷ last δ-distant CIP received for user u
1: $score_{\text{CIP-I}}[\,][\,]$ ▷ item-item *score* matrix, initialized to 0
2: $cardV$ ▷n-dim. vector of appearance cardinality of items
3: **for** item i in CIP_u **do**
4:     $cardV(i) = cardV(i) + 1$
5:     **for** item j in CIP_u **do**
6:       **if** $i \neq j$ **then**
7:         $\epsilon(i,j) = \epsilon(j,i) = \frac{1}{\mathcal{H}_u(i,j)}$
8:       **if** $i <_{\text{CIP}} j$ **then**
9:         $score_{\text{CIP-I}}[i][j] \mathrel{+}= (1 + \epsilon(i,j))$
10:       **else**
11:         $score_{\text{CIP-I}}[j][i] \mathrel{+}= (1 + \epsilon(j,i))$

The complexity of Algorithm 1 depends on the maximum tolerated size of incoming CIPs. As one expects an incremental algorithm to receive relatively small inputs as compared to the total dataset size, the final complexity is compatible with online computation: *e.g.*, if the largest CIP allowed has cardinality $|CIP| = O(\log n)$, then run-time complexity is poly-logarithmic.

2.3 DEEPCIP: An Embedding-Based Recommender

In this subsection, we present an approach based on machine learning, inspired by WORD2VEC [2,5]. This approach relies on word embedding, transposed to items. We specifically adapt this concept to our CIP data structure.

Neural word embeddings, introduced in [5,9], are learned vector representations for each word from a text corpus. These neural word embeddings are useful for predicting the surrounding words in a sentence. A common approach is to use a multi-layer Skip-gram model with negative sampling. The objective function minimizes the distance of each word with its surrounding words within a sentence while maximizing the distances to randomly chosen set of words (*negative samples*) that are not expected to be close to the target. This is an objective quite similar to ours as it enables to compute proximity between items in the same CIP. With DEEPCIP, we feed a Skip-gram model with item-pairs in CIPs where each CIP is as usual an ordered set of items (similar to the instantiation in CIP-I). More precisely, CIPs are δ-distant as instantiated in Subsect. 2.2.

DEEPCIP trains the neural network with pairs of items at a distance less than a given *window size* within a CIP. This window size corresponds to the notion of hammock distance (defined in Subsect. 2.1) where the distance hyper-parameter δ_H is defined by the *window size*. More formally, given a sequence of T training items' vectors $i_1, i_2, i_3, ..., i_T$, and a maximum hammock distance of k, the objective of the DEEPCIP model is to maximize the average log probability:

$$\frac{1}{T} \sum_{t=k}^{T-k} log\ P(i_t | i_{t-k}, ..., i_{t-1}, i_{t+1}, ..., i_{t+k}). \tag{3}$$

The Skip-gram model is employed to solve the optimization objective 3, where the weights of the model are learned using back-propagation and stochastic gradient descent. We implement DEEPCIP using asynchronous stochastic gradient descent (DOWNPOUR-SGD [10]). DOWNPOUR-SGD enables distributed training for the Skip-gram model on multiple machines by leveraging asynchronous updates from them. We use a publicly-available deep learning framework [11] which implements DOWNPOUR-SGD in a distributed setting. More precisely, DEEPCIP trains the model using DOWNPOUR-SGD on the recent CIPs thereby updating the model incrementally.

DEEPCIP uses a *most_similar* functionality to select items to recommend to a user, using as input recently consumed items (the current CIP). We compute a CIP vector using the items in the given CIP and then use this vector to find most similar other items. More precisely, the *most_similar* method uses the cosine similarity between a simple mean of the projection weight vectors of the recently consumed items (i.e., items in a user's most recent CIP) and the vectors for each item in the database.

Incremental Updates. Online machine learning is performed to update a model when data becomes available. The DEEPCIP model training is performed in an online manner [12], in which the model is updated using the recent CIPs. Online machine learning is crucial for recommendation systems, as it is necessary for the algorithm to dynamically adapt to new temporal patterns [13] in the data. Hence, the complexity of the model update is dependent on the number of new CIPs received along with the hyper-parameters for the learning algorithm (primarily: the Skip-gram model parameters, the dimensionality of item vectors, the number of training iterations, and the hammock distance).

2.4 The FISM Algorithm Under CIPs

We now demonstrate that the CIP framework can incorporate the state-of-art sequence-based algorithm FISM [3] (standing for Factored Item Similarity Models), in order to illustrate the generality of the CIP notion. In FISM, the item-item similarity is computed as a product of two low-ranked matrices $\mathbf{P} \in \mathcal{R}^{m \times k}$ and $\mathbf{Q} \in \mathcal{R}^{m \times k}$ where $k << m$. More precisely, the item-item similarity between any two items is defined as $sim(i, j) = \mathbf{p}_j \mathbf{q}_i^T$ where $\mathbf{p}_j \in \mathbf{P}$ and $\mathbf{q}_i \in \mathbf{Q}$.

Finally, the recommendation score for a user u on an unrated item i (denoted by $\bar{r}_{ui}$) is calculated as an aggregation of the items that have been rated by u:

$$\bar{r}_{ui} = b_u + b_i + (n_u^+)^{-\alpha} \sum_{j \in \mathcal{R}_u^+} \mathbf{p}_j \mathbf{q}_i^T, \tag{4}$$

where $\mathcal{R}_u^+$ is the set of items rated by user u (note that FISM do not leverage ratings, but only the fact that a rated item has been consumed by definition), b_u and b_i are the user and item biases, $\mathbf{p}_j$ and $\mathbf{q}_i$ are the learnt item latent factors, n_u^+ is the number of items rated by u, and α is a user specified parameter between 0 and 1. Moreover, term $(n_u^+)^{-\alpha}$ in Eq. 4 is used to control the degree of agreement between the items rated by the user with respect to their similarity to the item whose rating is being estimated (*i.e.*, item i).

We now present how Eq. 4 is adapted to fit into the CIP notion. For a user u, her profile (P_u) consists of $|l|_u$ different CIPs (similar to the notations introduced for Eq. 4). Equation 4 is rewritten with CIPs as:

$$\bar{r}_{ui} = b_u + b_i + (|\cup_{k=1}^{|l|_u} \mathrm{CIP}_u^k|)^{-\alpha} \sum_{k=1}^{|l|_u} \sum_{j \in \mathrm{CIP}_u^k} \mathbf{p}_j \mathbf{q}_i^T, \tag{5}$$

where $|\cdot|$ denotes the cardinality. We substitute consumed items by CIP structures; this last transformation shows that indeed CIPs incorporates the FISM definition of item sequences. We also note that due to the CIPs, the terms in Eq. 5 could be incrementally updated, similarly to CIP-U and CIP-I, by incorporating the latest CIP of user u.

3   Implementation with Spark and Evaluation

We first note that we open sourced our algorithms on GitHub [14]. We consider Apache Spark [15] as our framework for the computation of recommendations. Spark is a cluster computing framework for large-scale data processing; it provides several core abstractions, namely Resilient Distributed Datasets (RDDs), parallel operations and shared variables. We now introduce the RDDs adapted to our CIP-based algorithms.

RDDs for CIP-U. We store the collected information into three primary RDDs as follows. USERSRDD stores the information about the user profiles. USER-SIMRDD stores the hammock pairs between all pairs of users. The pairwise user similarities are computed using a transformation operation over this RDD. USERTOPKRDD stores the K most similar users.

During each update step in CIP-U, after Q consumption events, the new events are stored into a DELTAPROFILES RDD, which is broadcast to all the executors using the *broadcast* abstraction of Spark. Then, the hammock pairs between users are updated (in USERSIMRDD) and consequently transformed to pairwise user similarities using Eq. 1. Finally, CIP-U updates the top-K neighbors (USERTOPKRDD) based on the updated similarities.

RDDs for CIP-I Two Primary RDDs Are Used. ITEMSIMRDD stores *score* values between items. The pairwise item similarities are computed using a transformation operation over this RDD. ITEMTOPKRDD stores the K most similar items for each item based on the updated similarities.

During each update step in CIP-I, the item scores are updated incorporating the received CIP using Algorithm 1 in the ITEMSIMRDD, and consequently the pairwise item similarities are also revised using Eq. 2. CIP-I computes the top-K similar items and updates the ITEMTOPKRDD at regular intervals.

RDDs for DEEPCIP. We implement the DEEPCIP using the DeepDist deep learning framework [11] which accelerates model training by providing asynchronous stochastic gradient descent (DOWNPOUR-SGD) for Spark data. DEEP-CIP implements a standard master-workers parameter server model [10]. On the master node, the CIPsRDD stores the recent CIPs aggregated from the user transaction logs preserving the consumption order. Worker nodes fetch the model from the master before processing each partition, and send back the gradient updates. The master node performs the stochastic gradient descent asynchronously using the updates sent by the worker nodes. Finally, DEEPCIP predicts the most similar items to a given user, based on its most recent CIP.

3.1 Experimental Setup

For our experiments, we use a deployment of the Spark large-scale processing framework [15]. We launch Spark as Standalone, with 19 executors each with 5 cores for a total of 96 cores in the cluster.

We then use the Grid5000 testbed to launch a Spark cluster consisting of 20 machines on Hadoop YARN, for the scalability experiments. Machines host an Intel Xeon CPU E5520@ 2.26 GHz.

Datasets and Evaluation Scheme. We use real-world traces from the Movielens movie recommendation website (ML-100K, ML-1M) [16], as well as from the Ciao [17] product review website. Those traces contain users' ratings for movies they enjoyed (ratings vary from 1 to 5). Note that the ratings are only leveraged for the explicit (rating-based) SVD recommender we use as a competitor.

The dataset is sorted based on the Unix timestamps associated with the rating events. Then, the sorted dataset is replayed to simulate the temporal behavior of users. We measure the recommendation quality as follows: we divide the sorted dataset into a *training set*, a *validation set* and a *test set*. The training set is used to train our CIP based models, whereas the validation set is used to tune the hyper-parameters of the models. For each event in the test set (or rating when applied to the explicit recommender), a set of top recommendations is selected as the *recommendation set* with size denoted as N.

Competitors. We compare the recommendation quality of our three algorithms with the following three competitors:

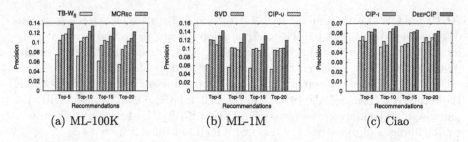

Fig. 1. Result quality (precision) for CIP-based algorithms and competitors.

Matrix factorization (SVD). Matrix factorization techniques map both users and items to a joint latent factor space, such that ratings are modeled as inner products in that space. We use a publicly available library (Python-recsys [18]) for evaluations.

Implicit time-based recommender (TB-W_5). A popular time-based recommender is providing recommendations without the need for explicit feedback [6]. Pseudo ratings are built from the collected implicit feedback based on temporal information (*user purchase-time* and *item launch-time*). We use the best performing variant: W_5 (fine-grained function with five launch-time groups and five purchase-time groups).

Markov chain-based recommender (MCREC). We compare with a recent recommender which combines matrix factorization and Markov-chains [7] to model personalized sequential behavior. We use a publicly available library [19] for the evaluation. We do not compare with FISM [3], as it is empirically shown to be outperformed by the Markov-chain based algorithm [7].

3.2 Comparison with Competitors

We refer to our technical report [20] for an in-depth exploration of parameters for our three CIP based algorithms. We obtained the following optimal setting for the hyper-parameters of those algorithms. For CIP-U: we set $\delta_H = 10$ for ML-100K, $\delta_H = 30$ for ML-1M, and $\delta_H = 10$ for Ciao to attain the best possible quality; model size is set to $K = 50$. For CIP-I we set $\delta = 1\,\mathrm{min}$ for ML-100K, $\delta = 1\,\mathrm{min}$ for ML-1M, and $\delta = 100\,\mathrm{min}$ for Ciao; model size is set to $K = 30$. Finally for DEEPCIP we set $\delta = 1\,\mathrm{min}$ for ML-100K, $\delta = 1\,\mathrm{min}$ for ML-1M, and $\delta = 100\,\mathrm{min}$ for Ciao. We set the window size (W) to 5 for all three datasets.

The recommendation quality of all six evaluated algorithms in terms of precision ($N = 10$) is shown in Fig. 1. We draw the following observations:

(a) Regarding our three algorithms, DEEPCIP always outperforms CIP-I, which in turn is always outperforming CIP-U (except on the Top-5 result on the Ciao dataset, which is due to the relatively limited number of recommendations).

(b) The CIP based algorithms outperform TB-W$_5$ on all three datasets. For example, consider the top-10 recommendations in the ML-1M dataset: CIP-U provides around 1.82× improvement in the precision, CIP-I provides around 2.1× improvement, and DEEPCIP provides around 2.4× improvement.

(c) The CIP-U algorithm performs on par with MCREC, as well as with the SVD technique. CIP-I overcomes MCREC on all three scenarios, sometimes only by a short margin (ML-1M). Most notably, DEEPCIP outperforms all other approaches significantly. For example, consider the top-10 recommendations in the ML-1M dataset: DEEPCIP provides 2.4× improvement over TB-W$_5$, 1.29× improvement over MCREC, and 1.31× improvement over the matrix factorization algorithm. The reason behind this improvement is that DEEPCIP considers, for any given item, the *packs* of items at a distance dependent on the defined window size, whereas MCREC only considers item pairs in the sequence of chain states (*i.e.*, has a more constrained learning). Note that the precision of the SVD algorithm on Movielens (11% to 12%) is consistent with other standard quality evaluation benchmarks for state-of-the-art recommenders [21].

These results show the existence of the latent information contained in closely consumed items, accurately captured by the CIP structure. It is consistent for DEEPCIP to perform well in this setting: the original WORD2VEC concept captures relations among words w.r.t. their proximity in a given context. DEEPCIP captures item proximity w.r.t. their consumption time.

3.3 Scalability of the CIP Based Algorithms

We evaluate the scalability of our algorithms while increasing the Spark cluster size from one machine to a maximum of 20 machines. Furthermore, we also compare the speedup achieved by a matrix factorization technique (ALS)

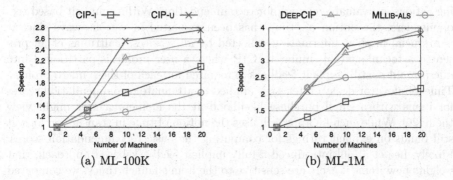

(a) ML-100K   (b) ML-1M

Fig. 2. Spark cluster size effects on computation speedup.

implemented in the publicly available MLLIB library for Spark. We use 50 Spark partitions.[1]

Figure 2 depicts a sublinear increase in speedup while increasing the number of machines, on both datasets. The sublinearity in the speedup is due to communication overheads in Spark with the increasing number of machines. The speedup on ML-1M is higher due to more computations being required for larger datasets and higher utilization of the cluster. The speedup for CIP-I is similar for both datasets as its time complexity depends on the CIP size (Algorithm 1). DEEPCIP scales well due to the distributed asynchronous stochastic gradient descent (DOWNPOUR-SGD) for training the Skip-gram model, where more gradient computations are executed asynchronously in parallel with the increasing number of nodes. CIP-U and DEEPCIP scale better than ALS.

4   Related Work

CIP-based algorithms belong to the category of recommenders using implicit feedback from users. HOSLIM [1] proposes to compute higher order relations between items in consumed itemsets; those relations are the ones that maximize the recommendation quality, but without notions of temporality in item consumption. The proposed algorithm is time-agnostic, and does not scale for orders superior to pairs of items. Moreover, it is not designed to efficiently incorporate freshly consumed items and faces computational intractability. Barkan et al. present ITEM2VEC in their technical report [2], that also uses skip-gram with negative sampling to retrieve items' relations w.r.t their context in time. Besides the fact that their implementation does not scale on multiple machines due to the use of synchronous stochastic gradient descent, the technical report evaluates algorithms on private datasets. Implicit feedback has been used for multiple applications: *e.g.*, in search engines, where clicks are tracked [22]. SPrank [23] leverages semantic descriptions of items, gathered in a knowledge base available on the web. Koren et al. [24] have shown that implicit TV switching actions are valuable enough for recommendation. Within implicit based recommenders, the notion of "time" has been exploited in various ways since it is a crucial implicit information collected by all services. Baltrunas et al. presented a technique [25] similar to CIP where a user profile is partitioned into micro-profiles; still, explicit feedback is required for each of these micro-profiles. Time window (or decay) filtering is applied to attenuate recommendation scores for items with a small purchase likelihood at the moment a user might view them [26]. While such an approach uses the notion of time in transaction logs, it still builds on explicit ratings for computing the basic recommendation scores. Finally, Lee et al. [6] introduced a fully implicit feedback based approach, that weights new items if users are sensitive to the item's launch times; we compared to [6] and demonstrated a better performance.

---

[1] Please refer to our technical report [20] for a detailed study of the scalability of CIP based algorithms facing a varying number of partitions.

5   Conclusion

In an effort for a detailed and scalable proposal for generalizing such a direction, we presented two memory-based and one model-based recommendation algorithms exploiting the implicit notion of *consumed item packs*. We made them available on GitHub [14]. We have shown this framework to incorporate a state-of-the-art approach. In our experiments, CIP based algorithms provided a better recommendation quality than the widespread SVD-based approach [4], as well as implicit ones leveraging consumption times [6] or consumption sequences [7]. Importantly for deployments, those fits the incremental nature of collected data, to leverage freshly consumed items.

References

1. Christakopoulou, E., Karypis, G.: HOSLIM: higher-order sparse linear method for top-n recommender systems. In: PAKDD (2014)
2. Barkan, O., Koenigstein, N.: Item2vec: neural item embedding for collaborative filtering. CoRR abs/1603.04259 (2016)
3. Kabbur, S., Ning, X., Karypis, G.: FISM: factored item similarity models for top-n recommender systems. In: KDD (2013)
4. Koren, Y., Bell, R., Volinsky, C.: Matrix factorization techniques for recommender systems. Computer **42**(8), 30–37 (2009)
5. Mikolov, T., Chen, K., Corrado, G., Dean, J.: Efficient estimation of word representations in vector space. CoRR abs/1301.3781 (2013)
6. Lee, T.Q., Park, Y., Park, Y.-T.: An empirical study on effectiveness of temporal information as implicit ratings. Expert. Syst. Appl. **36**(2), 1315–1321 (2009)
7. McAuley, J., Ruining, H.: Fusing similarity models with Markov chains for sparse sequential recommendation. In: ICDM (2016)
8. Boutet, A., Frey, D., Guerraoui, R., Kermarrec, A.-M., Patra, R.: HyRec: leveraging browsers for scalable recommenders. In: Middleware (2014)
9. Bengio, Y., Ducharme, R., Vincent, P., Janvin, C.: A neural probabilistic language model. J. Mach. Learn. Res. **3**, 1137–1155 (2003)
10. Dean, J., et al.: Large scale distributed deep networks. In: NIPS (2012)
11. DeepDist: lightning-fast deep learning on spark. http://deepdist.com/
12. Fontenla-Romero, Ó., Guijarro-Berdiñas, B., Martinez-Rego, D., Pérez-Sánchez, B., Peteiro-Barral, D.: Online machine learning. In: Efficiency and Scalability Methods for Computational Intellect, p. 27 (2013)
13. Chen, C., Yin, H., Yao, J., Cui, B.: TeRec: a temporal recommender system over tweet stream. In: VLDB (2013)
14. CIP-based implicit recommenders: GitHub code repo. https://github.com/rpatra/CIP
15. Apache spark. https://spark.apache.org/
16. Movielens. http://grouplens.org/datasets/movielens/
17. Ciao. http://www.ciao.com/
18. Python recsys. https://pypi.python.org/pypi/python-recsys/0.2
19. Sequence-based recommendations: GitHub code repo. https://github.com/rdevooght/sequence-based-recommendations
20. Guerraoui, R., Le Merrer, E., Patra, R., Vigouroux, J.: Sequences, items and latent links: recommendation with consumed item packs. CoRR abs/1711.06100 (2017)

21. Cremonesi, P., Koren, Y., Turrin, R.: Performance of recommender algorithms on top-n recommendation tasks. In: RecSys (2010)
22. Craswell, N., Szummer, M.: Random walks on the click graph. In: SIGIR (2007)
23. Ostuni, V.C., Di Noia, T., Di Sciascio, E., Mirizzi, R.: Top-n recommendations from implicit feedback leveraging linked open data. In: RecSys (2013)
24. Hu, Y., Koren, Y., Volinsky, C.: Collaborative filtering for implicit feedback datasets. In: ICDM (2008)
25. Baltrunas, L., Amatriain, X.: Towards time-dependant recommendation based on implicit feedback. In: CARS (2009)
26. Gordea, S., Zanker, M.: Time filtering for better recommendations with small and sparse rating matrices. In: Benatallah, B., Casati, F., Georgakopoulos, D., Bartolini, C., Sadiq, W., Godart, C. (eds.) WISE 2007. LNCS, vol. 4831, pp. 171–183. Springer, Heidelberg (2007). https://doi.org/10.1007/978-3-540-76993-4_15

Declarative Big Data Analysis for High-Energy Physics: TOTEM Use Case

Valentina Avati[1], Milosz Blaszkiewicz[1], Enrico Bocchi[2], Luca Canali[2],
Diogo Castro[2], Javier Cervantes[2], Leszek Grzanka[1], Enrico Guiraud[2],
Jan Kaspar[2], Prasanth Kothuri[2], Massimo Lamanna[2], Maciej Malawski[1(✉)],
Aleksandra Mnich[1], Jakub Moscicki[2], Shravan Murali[2], Danilo Piparo[2],
and Enric Tejedor[2]

[1] AGH Universtity of Science and Technology, Krakow, Poland
{grzanka,malawski}@agh.edu.pl
[2] CERN, 1211 Geneva 23, Switzerland
{enrico.bocchi,luca.canali,diogo.castro,javier.cervantes,enrico.guiraud,
jan.kaspar,prasanth.kothuri,massimo.lamanna,jakub.moscicki,
shravan.murali,danilo.piparo,enric.tejedor}@cern.ch

Abstract. The High-Energy Physics community faces new data processing challenges caused by the expected growth of data resulting from the upgrade of LHC accelerator. These challenges drive the demand for exploring new approaches for data analysis. In this paper, we present a new declarative programming model extending the popular ROOT data analysis framework, and its distributed processing capability based on Apache Spark. The developed framework enables high-level operations on the data, known from other big data toolkits, while preserving compatibility with existing HEP data files and software. In our experiments with a real analysis of TOTEM experiment data, we evaluate the scalability of this approach and its prospects for interactive processing of such large data sets. Moreover, we show that the analysis code developed with the new model is portable between a production cluster at CERN and an external cluster hosted in the Helix Nebula Science Cloud thanks to the bundle of services of Science Box.

Keywords: High-Energy Physics · Distributed data analysis ·
Apache Spark · Scalability

1 Introduction

The High-Energy Physics (HEP) community of thousands of researchers around the world processing massive amounts of data has always been renown for driving the development of distributed processing tools and infrastructures. Regarding the tools, the predominant software toolkit for data analysis is ROOT [6]. ROOT provides all the functionalities required to deal with big data processing, statistical analysis, visualisation and storage. To give an idea of its importance,

© Springer Nature Switzerland AG 2019
R. Yahyapour (Ed.): Euro-Par 2019, LNCS 11725, pp. 241–255, 2019.
https://doi.org/10.1007/978-3-030-29400-7_18

all the data collected so far by the Large Hadron Collider (LHC), the particle accelerator hosted at CERN, is stored in ROOT format (around 1 EB). Regarding the infrastructures, batch processing on clusters and grid technologies are the typical means of operations on HEP data.

On the other hand, recent developments in commercial big data processing tools and infrastructures, which include toolkits such as Apache Spark [19] and cloud computing, show the importance of high-level interfaces and user-friendly APIs to exploit the full potential of new data analysis infrastructures. This becomes even more apparent with the upgrades of the LHC experiments foreseen for Run III [2] and High-Luminosity LHC (HL-LHC) [3] and the consequent increase in the amount and complexity of data to be collected and processed. Specifically, the HL-LHC will operate at at least 10 times higher data rate than the current machine. With such an increased demand for data storage and processing, together with the need for more user-friendly analysis tools, investigating new approaches for big data analysis, become an important research problem.

To address this challenge, we present, in this paper, a new declarative programming model of ROOT, called RDataFrame, and its distributed processing backend based on Apache Spark. The developed framework enables high-level operations on the data, while preserving performance, scalability and compatibility with existing HEP data files and software. Specifically, while using the parallel processing of Spark, optimized C++ code runs on the backend, reading ROOT files directly, and uses the wide set of existing ROOT tools for creating high quality histograms, plots and statistical analysis calculations.

In order to evaluate the developed framework, we present our experience with porting a real production analysis of 4.7 TB data from the TOTEM [8] experiment at LHC. With dedicated experiments on the Helix Nebula Cloud and a production Spark cluster at CERN, we show the (1) correctness of the results, (2) scalability of this approach, (3) prospects for interactivity with the use of ScienceBox [7], and (4) portability of the high-level code across infrastructures.

2   Related Work

Apache Spark [19] is probably the most popular, open-source framework for distributed analysis on clusters, providing scalability and fault tolerance capacity. Its Directed Acyclic Graph (DAG) and task schedulers features allow for the deployment of data transformation operations such as filtering and reductions in a scalable way on large clusters. In this work, we leverage these features to parallelize and scale ROOT jobs across a cluster.

Several approaches to usage of big data tools in HEP have been proposed. The main challenges come from the fact that ROOT is based on C++ and relies heavily on its native objects for data serialization into its specific data format, while tools such as Spark are Java based.

One of the approaches [18] is thus to transform the ROOT input data to HDF5 format before porting the analysis code from ROOT C++ to Spark operations. This has the advantage of allowing usage of standard HDF5 libraries and

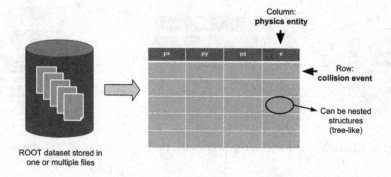

Fig. 1. Layout of a columnar ROOT dataset.

common Spark operations. Limitations come from the fact that data need to be converted first, and then stored for processing, however our approach allows unmodified input ROOT files to be used.

A different approach consists of reading ROOT files into the native Spark structures. It can be done using the Spark-Root connector developed by the CMS Big Data project [10]. This approach requires data processing jobs to be written using native Spark Dataframe APIs, which has the advantage of being compatible with popular big data toolkits, at the cost of the effort needed to re-implement all the code in a new programming language. Moreover, performance overheads of the code running in Java Virtual Machine may become non-negligible in comparison to direct usage of C++ as we propose.

In addition to Java-based frameworks, other toolkits such as Python's Dask [1] could be used. The framework allows running the same analysis at the local machine as well as at the cluster with minimal changes to the code. Unfortunately, those benefits come at a certain price. Dask requires the developer to go very deep into the technical details of the parallelization, adding another responsibility for the developer, in this case the physicist.

We should also mention here earlier approaches [12] of using Hadoop for implementing HEP data analysis using MapReduce model. Their experience shows that using HDFS for data storage can reduce network I/O thanks to using data locality. In our approach, we directly use EOS, a standard storage at CERN, which does not take advantage of data locality as with HDFS, but still provides a good scalability.

3   Declarative Data Analysis with ROOT RDataFrame

3.1   From Imperative to Declarative: RDataFrame

A ROOT file can contain multiple properties of every collision event, arranging them in a columnar format. A typical ROOT dataset is therefore similar to a table whose column values – the event properties – can vary from floating point numbers to arbitrarily complex objects and nested structures (Fig. 1).

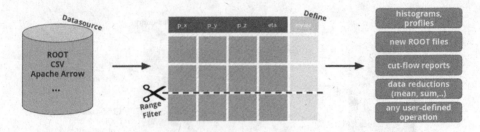

Fig. 2. RDataFrame design integration with the processing of ROOT datasets.

Traditionally, HEP analysis programs have been based on an loop over a ROOT dataset, where the properties of an event are read at every iteration and information is aggregated in some way for later analysis (e.g. filling histograms with some physics quantities). This corresponds to a more imperative programming approach, where users explicitly manage the reading and processing of a dataset via interfaces offered by ROOT. Such interfaces provide more control over the whole process but, at the same time, they can make programs more error-prone, since the user deals with lower-level details in longer programs, which can hinder their programming productivity.

More recently, ROOT has proposed a new interface for data analysis, called **RDataFrame** (formerly known as TDataFrame) [13], whose objective is twofold:

- Providing a *high-level interface for data analysis* that overcomes the productivity issues mentioned above, making it simpler for physicists to express their analyses, and to focus on physics rather than on implementation.
- Opening the door to runtime optimisations, such as parallelisation, thanks to a *declarative* expressing the analysis, stating *what* to do but not *how*.

Therefore, in a similar vein to other modern data analysis frameworks such as Apache Spark's DataFrames [19] and Python's data analysis library pandas [15], RDataFrame exposes a declarative API designed to be easy to use correctly and hard to use incorrectly. Novel elements introduced by RDataFrame are the choice of programming language (C++, although it provides a Python interface too), the integration of just-in-time compilation of user-defined expressions to make analysis definition concise and a tight integration with the rest of the ROOT.

An RDataFrame program basically expresses a set of operations to be applied on a dataset. At runtime, the implementation reads from a columnar data format via a data source, applies the required operations to the data (i.e. selects rows and/or defines new columns) and produces results (i.e. data reductions like histograms, new ROOT files, or any other user-defined object). Figure 2 illustrates this process, while Fig. 3 shows an example of an RDataFrame program.

3.2 Local Parallelisation

The abstraction provided by the RDataFrame programming model paves the way for crucial run time optimisations that can potentially lead physicists to their results faster. Indeed, the future requirements of the LHC, introduced in Sect. 1, make it necessary not only to simplify the programming of analyses, but also to exploit the underlying resources in the most efficient way possible.

```
ROOT::EnableImplicitMT();  ·························  Run a parallel analysis
ROOT::RDataFrame df(dataset);  ·················  on this (ROOT, CSV, ...) dataset
auto df2 = df.Filter("x > 0")  ·······················  only accept events for which x > 0
           .Define("r2", "x*x + y*y");  ··············  define r2 = x² + y²
auto rHist = df2.Histo1D("r2");  ················  plot r2 for events that pass the cut
df2.Snapshot("newtree", "out.root");  ··········  write the skimmed data and r2
                                                   to a new ROOT file
```

Fig. 3. Example of a simple RDataFrame application. The first line, which is optional, enables the implicit parallelisation of the program, as explained in Sect. 3.2.

User-transparent task-based parallelism has been a goal of RDataFrame since its inception, as detailed by [13]. A sequential RDataFrame program can be easily parallelised just by adding one line, as shown in Fig. 3. When the implicit multi-threading mode is activated, RDataFrame concurrently reads chunks of data from the source and spreads the work among multiple threads, which will apply the required operations to their fragment. Moreover, a reduction step to obtain the final results is also performed under the hood at the end.

3.3 Distributed Parallelisation

This paper presents a new python library built on top of ROOT RDataFrame that extends its parallelisation scheme, allowing not only local cores but also a set of distributed resources to be exploited. Moreover, in order to go from local to distributed, no changes are required to the application, since the library offers the same API as the RDataFrame Python interface. The extension to C++ will be investigated in the future.

The modular design of the distributed RDataFrame is presented in Fig. 4, where the application generates a computation graph that reflects the set of operations applied on the input dataset. Underneath, multiple backends can be implemented for either local or distributed execution. Regarding the latter, a Spark backend has been developed to be able to exploit Spark clusters.

When starting an RDataFrame application, the Spark backend inspects the metadata of the input dataset to know about its total number of rows (or entries). This dataset can correspond to one or more ROOT files, which are typically stored on CERN's mass storage system, EOS [16]. With the information about the number of entries and the available resources, the Spark backend creates

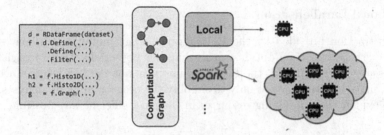

Fig. 4. Applications that use RDataFrame can run both on local and distributed resources thanks to its multiple backends.

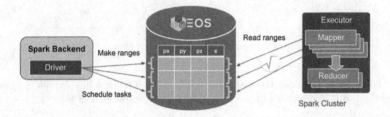

Fig. 5. The Spark backend of RDataFrame launches a map-reduce computation, where mapper tasks read ranges of entries and apply the computation graph to them, before a reduce phase aggregates the final results.

logical ranges of entries, which represent the partitioning of the data. After that, it launches a map-reduce computation where every mapper task will process a given range of entries. Thus, the mapper code receives the lower and upper boundaries of its range and uses the ROOT I/O libraries to read the entries of that particular range (e.g. remotely from EOS). Then, it applies the RDataFrame computation graph to its entries and generates partial results, which are finally merged during a reduce phase. This whole process is illustrated in Fig. 5.

It is worth pointing out that, even if the RDataFrame program is written in Python, most of the computation happens in C++, which is the language in which RDataFrame is implemented. The Python interface of ROOT just provides a thin layer on top of its C++ libraries (for I/O, histogramming, etc.).

3.4 Data Management

Moreover, our framework does not need any interface between Java and C++ code since the Spark runtime does not manage the input data but instead it is the ROOT C++ library that reads remotely that data. As a result, no reading is involved in the Java layer. On this approach, Spark is only used as a task scheduler: creation of the map-reduce tasks to be run on the remote workers and the coordination the tasks. At runtime, each worker spawns its own Python subprocess, which in turn uses C++ code to run the actual processing.

Furthermore, the implementation of RDataFrame has been optimised to be as efficient as possible when reading the input data in the mapper tasks: only the entries of the assigned range are considered and only the columns that are actually used in the RDataFrame computation graph are read and internally cached.

4   TOTEM Analysis Use Case

The physics analysis we used in the evaluation is the analysis of the elastic scattering data gathered by the TOTEM experiment in 2015 during a special LHC run. The dataset comprises 1153 files totalling 4.7 TB of data in ROOT Ntuple format, and stores 2.8 Billion events representing proton-proton collisions. The choice of TOTEM data was in part motivated by the fact that TOTEM is a relatively small experiment: the test dataset was fully available on EOS (not distributed on the grid). Moreover, a small collaboration facilitated the direct interactions between physicists doing analysis, software engineers and students supporting their work, data administrators granting access rights, and ROOT team developing RDataFrame, as well as CERN IT team responsible for cloud and Spark setup.

4.1   Original Analysis

The original analysis was written using the ROOT framework and includes 2 stages: (1) data reduction, and (2) filtering based on physics cuts. It followed a traditional approach of implementing an imperative processing loop. The first stage is a simple filtering which rejects a majority of input entries. The remaining set is subject to more complex computations. The output is a set of one and two dimensional histograms representing distributions of interesting trends.

4.2   Porting of Analysis to RDataFrame

The conversion from ROOT C++ code to the new RDataFrame interface is a required preparation step before running the analysis on Spark. Unlike [18], the input data for this analysis can keep the original format and still be run on Spark, as the RDataFrame interface delegates every I/O operations to the ROOT internals. While the original code has to be adapted to the new programming paradigm offered by RDataFrame, all operations can be reused since RDataFrame is part of ROOT. Consequently, all C++ headers, data structures and custom functions defined by users can be adopted from the original analysis with minimal changes on the new version. As a result, the migration of the existing analysis to the new interface requires significantly less effort than using e.g. Scala language (native for Spark) where everything needs to be rewritten.

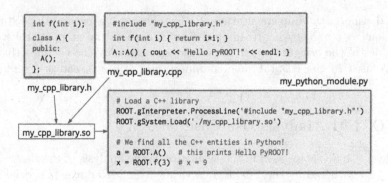

Fig. 6. Dynamic library loading mechanism with ROOT

Dealing with C++ Code from Python. As stated in Sect. 3.1, RDataFrame exposes a Python interface with support for all methods available in C++. Therefore, every line of the original C++ code can be expressed with an equivalent Python syntax keeping the same functionality. Besides, manipulating C++ code from Python benefits from a simpler and quicker interface while still getting a level of performance closer to C++ than raw Python. These advantages do not come for free as all C++ expressions on the Python interface will be *just-in-time* compiled to C++, leading to a known overhead which may vary depending on the use-case. On the other hand, this Python interface lowers the hurdles to run C++ code on Spark clusters. Libraries and C++ headers defined on the original code can be reused as shown in Listing 1.1.

```
1  ROOT.gInterpreter.Declare('#include "common_algorithms.h"')
2  ...
3  f1 = rdf.Filter("!SkipTime(time)")
```

Listing 1.1. Equivalent example of Listing 1.2 with RDataFrame

SkipTime is defined in the common_algorithms.h which is written in C++. Before starting the computation, the string !SkipTime(time) is compiled by the ROOT C++ Interpreter and ready to be called during the execution.

This process can be slightly improved by providing compiled libraries rather than just headers, thereby saving one step to the interpreter. In this regard, all headers ought to be modified to keep only structs and function definitions while real implementations go to a different source file. These two files can be later compiled into a shared library and injected to Python. Figure 6 illustrates an example of this mechanism.

From an Imperative to a Declarative Model. Following a declarative programming model rapidly reduce the verbosity of the code compared to the imperative version where half of the lines are boilerplate. Listings 1.2 and 1.3 show a simplified example of filling a histogram written in both ways. The first listing requires the creation of temporal variables (rp_L_1_N, rp_L_2_N, rp_L_2_F) to store the values read from the dataset (lines 9–14) using manual memory assignments. Then, the iteration over all the dataset entries needs to be specified in form of a `for` loop. Finally, a histogram, previously created, is filled with the valid entries, which are filtered by a `IsValidEntry` function. In contrast, the RDataFrame version (Listing 1.3) just specifies the required actions rather than the real implementation, hence it circumvents the necessity of temporal variables, explicit loops and manual memory assignments.

```
1   // Input data with all events
2   TChain data = new TChain(TotemData);
3
4   // Custom object with Totem data structure
5   rp_L_1_N = new TotemDataStructure();
6   rp_L_2_N = new TotemDataStructure();
7   rp_L_2_F = new TotemDataStructure();
8
9   // Read three columns
10  data->SetBranchStatus("track_rp_5.*", 1);
11  data->SetBranchAddress("track_rp_5.", &rp_L_1_N);
12  ...
13  data->SetBranchStatus("track_rp_25.*", 1);
14  data->SetBranchAddress("track_rp_25.", &rp_L_2_F);
15
16  // Loop over all entries
17  long int ev_index = 0;
18  for (; ev_index < data->GetEntries() ; ev_index++){
19      // Assigns entry values to corresponding custom objects
20      data->GetEvent(ev_index);
21      if (IsValidEntry(rp_L_1_N, rp_L_1_N, rp_L_2_F...)
22          histogram->Fill(rp_L_1_N);
23  }
```

Listing 1.2. Reading from file, selection of branches and filtering in the original analysis

```
1   rdf = ROOT.ROOT.RDataFrame(TotemData)
2   histo = rdf.Filter(IsValidEntry, {"track_rp_5",
3                                     "track_rp_21",
4                                     "track_rp_26"})
5              .Histo1D("track_rp_5");
```

Listing 1.3. Equivalent example of Listing 1.2 with RDataFrame

The original analysis codebase written in ROOT C++ has around 4000 lines of code. Approximately 60% of this code describes the main process of the analysis, so-called the event-loop, while the remaining 40% defines data structures, algorithms and global parameters on headers files.

The code corresponding to the main process was completely rewritten with the new RDataFrame interface, leading to a 76% reduction of the code length, applying similar changes to the ones describes in Listings 1.2 and 1.3. The 40% of the code corresponding to header files can be reused by RDataFrame without any conversion, since it can be loaded by the ROOT C++ Interpreter and used from RDataFrame at runtime.

Besides decreasing the amount of code, local executions of the analysis expressed in RDataFrame Python code on a single core showed that it performs three times faster than the original version. Although it has not been properly analysed, one possible reason for this difference in performance may be the presence of inefficiencies on the original code that are repeated on every event loop. This demonstrates that the fact of using a high-level interface based on Python does not add any major overhead for this analysis since underneath the real computation runs on C++.

5   Evaluation – Interactive Data Analysis in the Cloud

The main objective of our evaluation was to verify that the proposed RDataFrame framework can handle the workload of real physics data analysis. We used the TOTEM experiment dataset as described in Sect. 4. Our experiments were designed to demonstrate (1) the correctness of obtained results, (2) the scalability of parallel processing along with the increasing number of cores, (3) the interactivity provided by the user interface and the reduced computing times, and (4) the code portability between clusters located at CERN and on the Open Telekom Cloud (T-Systems), the latter being provided exclusively for our experiments thanks to the Helix Nebula initiative [11] (referred to as HNSciCloud).

5.1   Science Box Software Bundle

To achieve portability and interactivity, we used the Science Box software bundle [7]. As described in [4], the main components are:

- EOS [16], the distributed storage system used to host all physics data at CERN. A dedicated EOS instance hosting a subset of the TOTEM experiment data is deployed on the HNSciCloud.
- SWAN [17], a web-based platform to perform interactive data analysis. It builds on top of Jupyter notebooks by integrating the ROOT analysis framework and the computational power of Spark clusters.
- A dedicated Spark cluster accessible from the SWAN notebook interface.
- CERNBox [14], the synchronization and sharing service for personal and scientific files that uses EOS as storage backend.

All the Science Box services run in containers orchestrated by Kubernetes with the only exception of Spark, which runs on VMs with Cloudera Manager.

5.2   Testbed Details

The testbed used for the physics analysis consisted of two independent clusters:

- Analytix, a general purpose Hadoop and Spark cluster located at CERN that is used as a shared resource for various analytics jobs.
- the Spark cluster deployed on the HNSciCloud.

All the performance and scalability experiments were executed on the cluster on the HNSciCloud. It consists of 57 nodes of 32 cores and 128 GiB each, giving a total of 1,824 vCPUs and 7296 GiB of memory. The cluster was equipped with 21.5 TiB of storage, out of which 16.4 TiB were available to EOS (the actual space available is 8.2 TiB due to the `replica` 2 layout of stored files). Network connectivity among the different Science Box containers and the Spark cluster was provided by general purpose 10 Gigabit Ethernet interfaces.

5.3   Correctness

One of the most important requirements for physicists was to make sure that the analysis re-implemented in RDataFrame produces the same results as the original one. First, all the output histograms and their main statistics (mean and standard deviation) have been compared with the help of physicists and ROOT experts. Second, a set of scripts was developed to automate the comparison of resulting outputs [9]. These checks confirmed that the results are correct. We also observed that the way ROOT displays the number of entries in weighted histograms may be misleading, since it depends on the number of partitions, but it is a known issue and does not influence the other physics results. For more details, we refer to the report [5].

5.4   Scalability

The main goal of these experiments was to measure the performance and parallel scalability of the analysis running on Spark depending on the number of CPU cores. We conducted multiple experiments in order to identify the bottlenecks and tune the Spark configuration, e.g. the number of partitions, executors per node and worker reuse policy. From these experiments it turned out that the best configuration is to use one Spark executor per node and the number of partitions data is divided into should be equal to the number of cores allocated.

   Here we report on the results of the largest run, when we allocated up to 1470 cores total and we varied the number of partitions, which limited the number of cores actually used. In order to measure the effect of Python worker restart policy in Spark, which may affect the performance for larger deployments, we include two series of data contrasting the results obtained when using a fixed number of Python workers that do not `fork()` a process for every task (i.e., `spark.python.worker.reuse = True`) against the ones obtained when forking (i.e., `spark.python.worker.reuse = False`).

The results are shown in Fig. 7. As we can see, the policy of reusing workers gives better results for larger number of cores. The best computing time achieved was 1 min 43 s at 736 cores, while on 16 cores it was 34 min 15 s and on 1 core 8 h 15 min 20 s. It results in a best speedup of about 280x compared to single core execution, but we observe that beyond 800 cores the execution time begins to grow. This shows that we reached the limits of parallelism for this particular analysis application. The scalability limits can be attributed to: (a) overheads during start-up time and work distribution, (b) not ideal load balancing of computing tasks, and (c) possible memory leaks in the current implementation of the framework. We expect that two former issues may become less pronounced when dealing with larger data sets, while the latter will be investigated in further development.

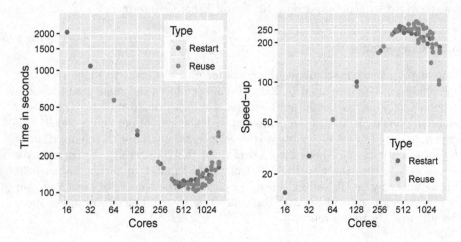

Fig. 7. Execution time and speedup versus the number of CPU cores used for the two configuration options of `spark.python.worker.reuse`.

5.5   Interactivity

One of the challenges we addressed is to examine whether it is possible to perform an *interactive* data analysis of the full 4.7 TB dataset at a large scale. We consider two relevant aspects: (1) the provisioning of user interfaces to run code and visualize the results interactively, and (2) the reduction of the computing time to consider the waiting time acceptable. According to the collected results, we argue that we have shown interactivity in both aspects. (1) was achieved by using the SWAN interface so that the whole analysis was implemented and executed via Jupyter notebook (see repo: [9]). SWAN together with ScienceBox builds on top of Jupyter, providing such additional features as notebook sharing between users of CERNBox, integration with Spark provides interactive monitoring of job progress directly in the notebook, and direct access to CERN resources (Spark clusters, EOS). (2) was achieved by reducing the computing time below 2 min, as discussed in Sect. 5.4. While interactivity is not simple to quantify, we are convinced that our approach is a big step towards interactivity compared to traditional batch processing, which takes hours or even days and requires the use of multiple command-line tools and intermediate copies of data.

5.6 Portability

Implementing the analysis in the RDataFrame model and the components described in Sect. 5.1 allowed us to achieve transparent portability of the code across two infrastructures, namely the Analytix cluster at CERN and the Spark cluster at HNSciCloud. In particular, the whole dataset was replicated on the EOS instance at HN with the same directory structure, so that the same paths to data files could be used in both clusters. Next, the same version of SWAN was deployed on both clusters and local files could be synchronized via CERN-Box. Thanks to this setup, the same Jupyter Notebook [9] could be executed on both clusters. We emphasize that our solution is not specific to the HNSci-Cloud but it can be used on any public cloud infrastructures or private Open-Stack clouds. Specifically, services provided through Science Box can be deployed on any Kubernetes cluster or Kubernetes-based container orchestration engine, while the Spark cluster can be deployed on commodity virtual machines.

6 Conclusions

In this paper, we presented recent developments in the data analysis frameworks for HEP community. The declarative RDataFrame extension to the popular ROOT toolkit allowed us to transparently parallelize the data analysis process using Apache Spark, while still preserving compatibility with the existing ecosystem of tools. Moreover, by the usage of Science Box Tools we were able to perform the whole analysis interactively with modern Web-based notebooks.

We consider the results of our evaluation very promising to the HEP community planning their data analysis for the future experiments expecting higher data volumes. We have shown that the framework works correctly on a real analysis of 4.7 TB of data from the TOTEM experiment, and that thanks to distributed processing we can reduce the computing time to less than 2 min. The analysis we used for evaluation was not simplified by any means, and we can consider it as representative for typical data processing in HEP. Other, more complex analysis programs sometimes use external numerical libraries (e.g. for integration, approximation, etc.), but as they are available for use with Python or C++, we foresee no major issues with their integration in our framework.

Our results are important also to other scientific or commercial data analysis applications. We have shown that it is possible to combine efficient widespread High-Energy Physics C++ libraries with a Java- and Python-based Apache Spark platform. Moreover, a combination of open source tools that comprise the Science Box environment can be dynamically deployed in an external cloud, providing additional resources for similar big data science and engineering projects.

Future work includes studies on performance with the larger data sets or the multi-user and multi-application workloads, including comparisons with other solutions described in Sect. 2. We also plan to investigate other emerging frameworks and infrastructures, such as serverless or containerized clouds.

Acknowledgments. This work was supported in part by the Polish Ministry of Science and Higher Education, grant DIR/WK/2018/13.

References

1. Python Dask. http://docs.dask.org/en/latest/why.html
2. Alves Jr., A.A., et al.: A roadmap for HEP software and computing R&D for the 2020s. Technical report HSF-CWP-2017-001, December 2017. http://cds.cern.ch/record/2298968
3. Apollinari, G., et al.: High-Luminosity Large Hadron Collider (HL-LHC): Technical Design Report V. 0.1. CERN Yellow Reports: Monographs. CERN, Geneva (2017). https://cds.cern.ch/record/2284929
4. Avati, V., et al.: Big data tools and cloud services for high energy physics analysis in TOTEM experiment. In: 2018 IEEE/ACM International Conference on Utility and Cloud Computing Companion, Zurich, Switzerland, 17–20 December 2018, pp. 5–6 (2018). https://doi.org/10.1109/UCC-Companion.2018.00018
5. Blaszkiewicz, M., Mnich, A.: Interactive data analysis of data from high energy physics experiments using Apache Spark. Technical report (2019). http://cds.cern.ch/record/2655457. BSc Thesis Presented 2019
6. CERN: ROOT a data analysis framework (2018). https://root.cern.ch
7. CERN: Science Box (2018). https://sciencebox.web.cern.ch
8. CERN: The TOTEM Experiment (2018). https://totem.web.cern.ch
9. Cervantes, J.: Rdataframe-totem repository (2018). https://github.com/JavierCVilla/RDataFrame-Totem/
10. Cremonesi, M., et al.: Using big data technologies for HEP analysis. https://indico.cern.ch/event/587955/contributions/2937521/attachments/1684310/2707721/chep_bigdata.pdf
11. Gasthuber, M., Meinhard, H., Jones, R.: HNSciCloud - overview and technical challenges. J. Phys. Conf. Ser. **898**(5), 052040 (2017). 5 p. http://cds.cern.ch/record/2297173
12. Glaser, F., Neukirchen, H., Rings, T., Grabowski, J.: Using MapReduce for high energy physics data analysis. In: 2013 IEEE 16th International Conference on Computational Science and Engineering, pp. 1271–1278 (2013). https://doi.org/10.1109/CSE.2013.189
13. Guiraud, E., Naumann, A., Piparo, D.: TDataFrame: functional chains for ROOT data analyses (2017). https://doi.org/10.5281/zenodo.260230
14. Mascetti, L., Labrador, H.G., Lamanna, M., Moscicki, J., Peters, A.: CERNBox + EOS: end-user storage for science. J. Phys. Conf. Ser. **664**(6), 062037 (2015). 6 p
15. McKinney, W., et al.: Data structures for statistical computing in Python. In: Proceedings of the 9th Python in Science Conference, Austin, TX, vol. 445, pp. 51–56 (2010)
16. Peters, A., Sindrilaru, E., Adde, G.: EOS as the present and future solution for data storage at CERN. J. Phys. Conf. Ser. **664**(4), 042042 (2015). 7 p. http://cds.cern.ch/record/2134573

17. Piparo, D., Tejedor, E., Mato, P., Mascetti, L., Moscicki, J., Lamanna, M.: SWAN: a service for interactive analysis in the cloud. Future Gener. Comput. Syst. **78**(CERN–OPEN–2016–005), 1071–1078 (2016). 17p. http://cds.cern.ch/record/2158559

18. Sehrish, S., Kowalkowski, J., Paterno, M.: Spark and HPC for high energy physics data analyses. In: Proceedings, 31st IEEE International Parallel and Distributed Processing Symposium Workshops (IPDPSW), Orlando, Florida, USA, 29 May–2 June 2017, pp. 1048–1057 (2017). https://doi.org/10.1109/IPDPSW.2017.112

19. The Apache Software Foundation: Apache Spark (2018). https://spark.apache.org/

Clustering as Approximation Method to Optimize Hydrological Simulations

Elnaz Azmi[1]([⊠])[iD], Uwe Ehret[2][iD], Jörg Meyer[1][iD], Rik van Pruijssen[2][iD], Achim Streit[1][iD], and Marcus Strobl[1][iD]

[1] Steinbuch Centre for Computing, Karlsruhe Institute of Technology, Karlsruhe, Germany
{elnaz.azmi,joerg.meyer2,achim.streit,marcus.strobl}@kit.edu
[2] Institute of Water and River Basin Management, Karlsruhe Institute of Technology, Karlsruhe, Germany
{uwe.ehret,rik.pruijssen}@kit.edu

Abstract. Accurate water-related predictions and decision-making require a simulation of hydrological systems in high spatio-temporal resolution. However, the simulation of such a large-scale dynamical system is compute-intensive. One approach to circumvent this issue, is to use landscape properties to reduce model redundancies and computation complexities. In this paper, we extend this approach by applying machine learning methods to cluster functionally similar model units and by running the model only on a small yet representative subset of each cluster. Our proposed approach consists of several steps, in particular the reduction of dimensionality of the hydrological time series, application of clustering methods, choice of a cluster representative, and study of the balance between the uncertainty of the simulation output of the representative model unit and the computational effort. For this purpose, three different clustering methods namely, K-Means, K-Medoids and DBSCAN are applied to the data set. For our test application, the K-means clustering achieved the best trade-off between decreasing computation time and increasing simulation uncertainty.

Keywords: Clustering · Time series analysis · K-Means · K-Medoids · DBSCAN · Simulation optimization

1 Introduction

The simulation of hydrological systems and their interactions needs an advanced modeling of water-, energy- and mass cycles in high spatio-temporal resolution [20]. This kind of modeling is used to support water-related predictions and decision making. Such a high-resolution, distributed and physically based modeling demands high performance computing (HPC) and parallel processing of the model units to function fast and efficiently [10,13,14]. However, parallel running of such models is challenging for domain scientists, since the interactions among the model units are not strictly independent. Either one can run

© Springer Nature Switzerland AG 2019
R. Yahyapour (Ed.): Euro-Par 2019, LNCS 11725, pp. 256–269, 2019.
https://doi.org/10.1007/978-3-030-29400-7_19

the processes parallel e.g by using a Message Passing Interface (MPI) for communication and exchange of data between processes, or one can run processes of independent model units in parallel and the processes of dependent model units sequentially. Furthermore, development, testing, execution and update of such a model on HPC Clusters involve potentially a large configuration overhead and require advanced programming expertise of domain scientists. The main aim of this work is to reduce the computational effort of the model, and in addition, to discover underlying patterns of the hydrological systems [5]. The remainder of this paper is structured as follows: Sect. 2 provides further information about the study background, Sect. 3 is a survey of related work, the proposed approach is explained in Sect. 4. In Sect. 5, the processing results are presented, Sect. 6 is about the implementation environment and the conclusions are drawn in Sect. 7.

2   Background

2.1   Hydrological Model

In this paper we apply our methods on the CAOS (Catchment as Organized Systems) model proposed by Zehe et al. [20]. This model simulates water related dynamics in the lower mesoscale catchments (few tens to few hundreds of square kilometers). The CAOS model provides a high-resolution and distributed process based simulation of water- and energy fluxes in the near surface atmosphere, the earth's surface and subsurface. These simulations are generally applicable in the field of hydrological research, agricultural water demand estimation and erosion protection or flood forecasting. The landscape is represented by model elements organized in three major hierarchy levels (Fig. 1). The smallest model elements are soil columns referred to as Elementary Functional Units (EFUs). Each EFU is composed of Soilsurface, Soillayers, Macropores (vertical cracks) and Vegetation. In an EFU, all vertical water movements (infiltration, vertical soil water flow, and evapotranspiration) are modelled. On the second hierarchy level, Hillslope model elements contain and connect all EFUs along the downhill path from a

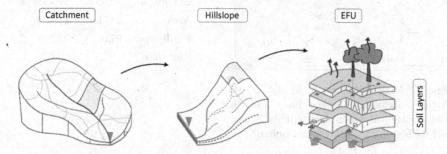

Fig. 1. Simplified hierarchy of the CAOS model units (modified after [20]). (Color figure online)

ridge line to a river. In a Hillslope, all lateral, downhill flow processes (surface flow and groundwater flow) are modelled in network-like flow structures called rills on the surface and pipes in the subsurface (blue lines in Fig. 1, middle and right sketch). A catchment model element finally contains all Hillslopes, i.e. the drainage area up to a point of interest at a river. In a catchment, all processes of lateral water transport in a river are modelled. EFUs within the same Hillslope may interact due to backwater effects. Hillslopes act completely independent of each other. Before executing the hydrologic simulation, the catchment is divided into Hillslopes based on the flow network derived from a Digital Elevation Model (DEM). Hillslopes are then subdivided in laterally connected EFUs (Fig. 1). The hierarchy of model elements can be abstracted into a network model [5] to profit the advantages of such a representation of objects and their relationships.

2.2   Study Case

The study area used to develop and test the hydrological model is the Attert catchment in the Grand Duchy of Luxembourg. Since the computation of the hydrological model is time consuming, a representative subset of the Attert catchment, the Wollefsbach catchment, is used for the initial development (Fig. 2). To give an insight into the required simulation time, we executed the CAOS model of the Wollefsbach catchment for January 2014 in 5-min resolution on a single core system. The properties, main structure statistics, and execution time are presented in Table 1. The simulation execution time of the whole Attert catchment has not been determined yet.

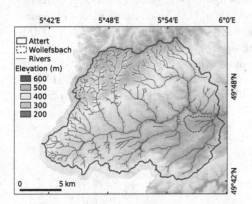

Fig. 2. Digital Elevation Model of the Attert catchment (brown line) and the Wollefsbach catchment (current study case, red dashed line). (Color figure online)

Table 1. Case study properties.

Catchment	Attert	Wollefsbach
Area	247 km^2	4.5 km^2
# Hillslopes	9716	232
Run time	-	50.6 h

3   Related Work

Environmental scientists mostly use classification and clustering methods in order to detect patterns in data sets, make decisions and extract the required information by using similarity measurements [3,15,18,19]. [19] studied K-means, Clara, HClust and Fuzzy clustering algorithms to analyze the uncertainty of weather situations. The proposed method reduced the RMSE of point forecasts by up to 10%. In order to predict the minimum and maximum of weather parameters like temperature and humidity, [17] compared the application of K-means and Hierarchical clustering using internal validation measures. [18] used spectral clustering to determine regions of coherent precipitation regime. They obtained spatial patterns of the precipitation regions that provide a new hydro-climatological insight to understand the hydrological systems. Furthermore, time series is one of the main input data types in environmental science [6] and dealing with these data requires additional preprocessing like dimensionality reduction and distance measurement [1].

4   Methodology

In order to speed up the simulation, we introduce a two-step approach. The first step is to apply an elementary parallelization on the independent model elements level (Hillslopes) and execute the simulation on multi-core processors [5]. The simulation has been run for the Wollefsbach catchment for the duration of one month (January, 2014). The model time resolution of the Hillslope outputs (flux drainage to River) is set to five minutes. Since the simulation code is being developed in MathWorks Matlab, for the elementary parallelization, we have used its *parfor* functionality. The average execution time of the parallel simulation with a 16-cores processor is 5.4 h, which is a 9.4 times speedup in comparison to the sequential run. The second step of our method can be categorized into Model Order Reduction techniques [8] which is the focus of this paper. Such techniques aim to reduce the computational costs by dimensionality reduction and by computing an approximation of the original model. We exploit the hydrological similarity [9] to reduce the model complexity and computation efforts as a result. The underlying idea of our approach is that similar model units function similarly if departing from similar initial states and being exposed to similar forcing (rainfall or radiation). To realize that we apply clustering algorithms to cluster functionally similar model units. The studied model units are Hillslopes (the model units without exchange between individuals). Then we run the simulation only on the representative of each cluster and map the output to the other members of every cluster. The uncertainty of the approximation can be controlled by the number of clusters and the corresponding computation time.

5   Processing Results

In this work, the initial clustering which defines the initial state of the simulation model units is introduced. We use the time series of discharge from Hillslope model elements obtained from a drainage test (Fig. 3). In the drainage test, the simulation model is executed for all of the Hillslopes initiated with full storage of water. In other words, at the beginning of the test, the Hillslopes are full of water up to·their maximum capacity and drain over time. The test is applied on the Wollefsbach catchment and starts from an arbitrary time (in this case, January; Fig. 3) and lasts until the drainage of Hillslopes reaches a predefined boundary (Equilibrium). This time duration is called *Time to Equilibrium (TE)* of the Hillslopes. During the test no forcing factor is being applied. These time series are integral signatures of Hillslope size, slope, soil (Hillslope structure) and drainage properties, which we then express by two key features that are *TE* and *Active Storage (AS)*. The second feature, *AS* extracted from drainage test is the accumulated volume of water flowing out of a Hillslope at each time step normalized to the initial Total Storage of that Hillslope. The time series are used as the input data of our approach (Fig. 4).

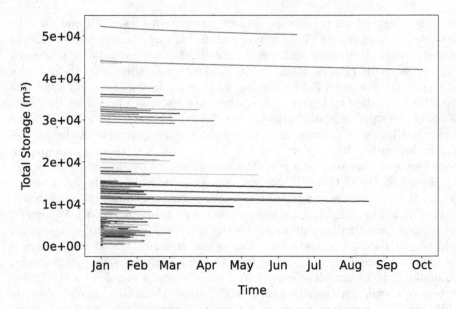

Fig. 3. Time series of Total Storage (total water volume) of Hillslopes at each time step; Each line represents a single Hillslope.

5.1   Dimensionality Reduction

Considering the input time series shown in Fig. 4, we extract the features describing their characteristics. The hydrologically meaningful features are *AS* of each Hillslope at the *TE* and the gradient of the first time step of the time series called

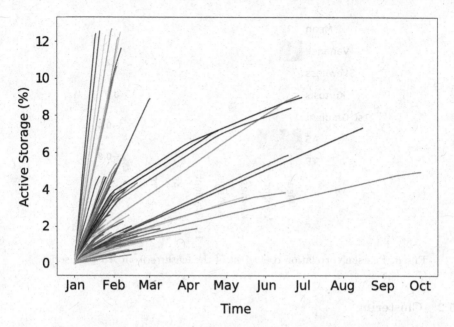

Fig. 4. Time series of AS; Each line represents a single Hillslope.

1st-Gradient, because the speed of drainage especially at the first steps of the test, characterizes the Hillslopes. Other features describing the time series are mathematical moments that express the shape of the distribution. We extracted the four moments *Mean*, *Variance*, *Skewness* and *Kurtosis*. Thus initially, we have overall a seven-dimensional feature set. Then, each feature set of all Hillslopes are normalized to standard deviation (σ) of that feature set. Dimensionality reduction is an important method to reduce computation complexity. For further dimensionality reduction, we filter highly correlated, i.e. redundant features. Principally, highly correlated features carry similar information so we can reduce them to only one feature. Here, the Pearson correlation coefficient was calculated for each pair of the extracted features (Fig. 5). The Pearson value ranges from -1 to 1 where 1 defines the total positive linear correlation, 0 is the no linear correlation and -1 is for total negative linear correlation [16]. Our extracted features are mostly non or positively correlated. Since AS and TE are our hydrological key features, we filter the features that are highly correlated with these two. Regarding Fig. 5, *Mean*, *Variance* and AS fit to our exclusion criteria. Therefore, we filter *Mean* and *Variance* from our feature set and keep AS. There is no pair of features with highly negative correlation. Finally, we have a five-dimensional feature set consisting of *Skewness*, *Kurtosis*, *1st-Gradient*, AS and TE.

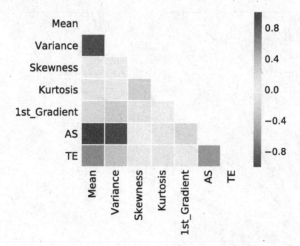

Fig. 5. Pearson correlation coefficient of the features from AS time series.

5.2 Clustering

Having a feature set as input data, we continue our approach with the application of popular conventional clustering methods namely K-means, K-medoid and DBSCAN and present their efficiency in our use case.

Application of K-Means Clustering. The only required parameter for the K-means algorithm is the number of clusters (K). In order to determine K, there exists the conventional elbow method to define the optimal number of K using the total within-cluster sum of squares (WSS) or the average distance to centroid [11]. This method is useful in cases where K should be determined only based on the location of the points to be clustered. However, there might be additional constraints suggesting K. In this work, we propose an approach that considers the uncertainty of the simulation introduced by the clustering approach. There is a balance between the number of clusters, K, and the hydrological model uncertainty, based on the RMSE and the simulation computation time of Hillslopes. We determine K with a small yet representative catchment (Wollefsbach) to apply it to the bigger catchment (Attert). Thus, the K parameter can be selected according to the criteria of the hydrologist. Initially, we apply the K-means clustering with varying number of K. Then the RMSE is calculated within each cluster between the cluster members and the representative of that cluster. We define the cluster representative as the Medoid data point whose average dissimilarity to other points in the cluster is minimal. Formally, the Medoid of $x_1, x_2, \cdots, x_n$ as members of each cluster is defined as [12]:

$$x_{\text{medoid}} = \text{argmin}_{y \in \{x_1, x_2, \cdots, x_n\}} \sum_{i=1}^{n} d(y, x_i), \tag{1}$$

where $d(y, x_i)$ is the distance function between y and the ist x. RMSE is the standard deviation of the prediction errors. Formally, RMSE is [7]:

$$\text{RMSE} = \sqrt{\sum_{i=1}^{N}(z_{f_i} - z_{o_i})^2/N},\qquad(2)$$

where N is the sample size, z_{f_i} are the predicted values and z_{o_i} are the observed values. According to this, the RMSE measure was calculated between the AS time series of the cluster members and the representative of that cluster. Thus, there is one RMSE measurement per Hillslope for each K variation. Finally, the total RMSE measure of all Hillslopse is calculated and plotted in Fig. 6 using the following equation:

$$\sigma_{\text{totalRMSE}} = \sqrt{\sum_{i=1}^{P}(\text{RMSE}_i)^2},\qquad(3)$$

where P is the number of data points in the feature set. In order to find the optimal number of K, we use the trade-off between the RMSE measurement and sum of the computation time of representative Hillslopes of each cluster. According to our methodology, the simulation is applied only on the representative Hillslopes and sum of their computation time is calculated for each

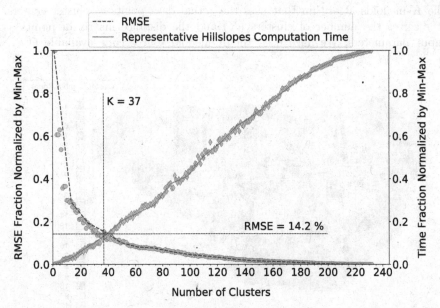

Fig. 6. RMSE and representative Hillslopes computation time for varying Ks using K-means clustering. The gray markers show the original values and the curves in red and green represent their smoothed trend. (Color figure online)

number of K. The results of this experiment are shown in Fig. 6, where the horizontal axis represents the number of clusters and the vertical axis, the RMSE measurement and sum of the computation time of representative Hillslopes of each cluster normalized by Min-Max normalization. Evidently, as the number of clusters raises, the corresponding RMSE decreases while the computation time increases (Fig. 6). The main goal of our approach is to achieve the best trade-off between computation time and simulation uncertainty. In Fig. 6, a range of the intended compromise between RMSE and computation time is recognizable where the curves intersect. As K-means places the initial centeroids randomly, the output of its executions with the same number of K differs slightly. Thus, the intended compromise occurs where $32 < K < 42$, $11.8\% < RMSE < 14.2\%$ of the maximum $RMSE = 39.2$ and the computation time ranges from 10.3% to 16.2% of total computation time (31.8 days). As an example, the spatial distribution of the K-means clustering at $K = 37$ which corresponds to the best compromise between RMSE and computation time in Wollefsbach catchment is shown in Fig. 7. Each color indicates a cluster and the number of its members can be found in the legend of map. All the single member clusters are shown in blue, which are single Hillslopes that do not fit into the other clusters. The map shows a valid Hillslopes clustering, considering the hydrological parameters like the structure, size and location of the Hillslopes. Generally, the overhead of running such a clustering during the simulation is negligible.

Application of K-Medoids Clustering. Another variant of K-means is the K-medoids algorithm that uses the actual data points as cluster centers. It receives the number of clusters (K) and the distance matrix of points as input parameters. We have used the K-medoid source code available at [2].

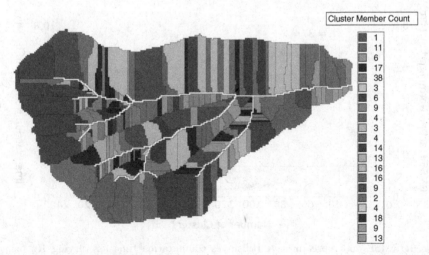

Fig. 7. Spatial distribution of K-means clusters at $K = 37$ applied on Wollefsbach catchment. All single member clusters are shown in dark blue. (Color figure online)

The algorithm was run for variable number of K and the results are shown in Fig. 8. The plot indicates that the intended compromise range between RMSE and computation time occurs where $58 < K < 78$, $16.8\% < RMSE < 34.7\%$ of the maximum $RMSE = 31.8$ and the related computation time is between 22.7% and 33.8% of the maximum computation time (31.8 days).

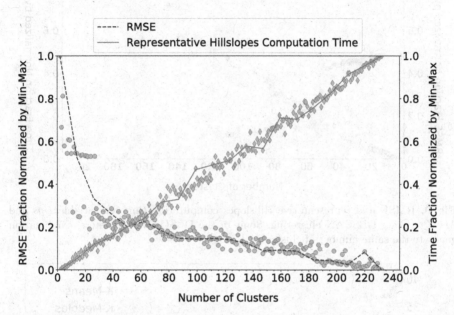

Fig. 8. RMSE and representative Hillslopes computation time for varying Ks using K-medoids clustering. The gray markers show the original values and the curves in red and green represent the smoothed trend. (Color figure online)

Application of DBSCAN Clustering. DBSCAN clustering requires two main parameters as input, namely Eps and $MinPts$. In order to find a set of optimal parameters, DBSCAN clustering is applied on a different range of Eps and $MinPts$. The same method of determining and visualizing RMSE with the computation time described in Sect. 5.2 is used with DBSCAN clustering. For each set of parameters, the number of clusters is calculated. Noise clusters are considered as one cluster in the whole number of clusters. The results shown in Fig. 9 indicate that the intended compromise range between RMSE and computation time is achieved where the number of clusters ranges between $51-62$, $0.3 < Eps < 0.7$, $1 < MinPts < 21$, the RMSE is between 14.5% and 31.4% of maximum RMSE (38.6) and the computation time is in range of 17.9% and 23% of the maximum computation time (31.8 days). The direct comparison of the three applied methods is illustrated in Fig. 10, which clearly shows that the K-means clustering performs better for the studied case and features the lowest RMSE for up to 18 days of computation. A summary of all results are available in Table 2.

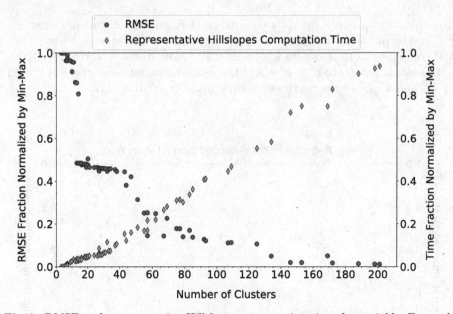

Fig. 9. RMSE and representative Hillslopes computation time for variable *Eps* and *MinPts* using DBSCAN clustering. Some of the DBSCAN parameters' combination generate the same number of clusters.

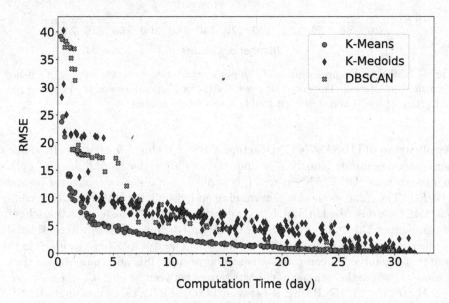

Fig. 10. Comparison of the RMSE and computation time of all analyses.

Table 2. Parameters and achievements of different clustering methods

Parameters	K-Means	K-Medoids	DBSCAN
K (# clusters)	32–42	58–78	51–62
Eps	-	-	0.3–0.7
MinPts	-	-	1–21
RMSE (%)	11.8–14.2	16.8–34.7	14.5–31.4
Max RMSE	39.2	31.8	38.6
Computation time (%)	10.3–16.2	22.7–33.8	17.9–23
Max computation time (d)	31.8	31.8	31.8

6   Implementation Environment

All the analysis methods are implemented in Python and executed on a computer with Ubuntu 16.04.4 LTS operating system running the Linux kernel 4.4.0-127-generic and a four-core 64-bit Intel(R) Core(TM) i5-6300U CPU @ 2.40 GHz processor. The benchmarking of simulation model parallelization has been done on a computer with Red Hat Enterprise Linux Server release 7.4 running the linux kernel 3.10.0-693.11.6.el7.x86_64 and a 16-core Intel(R) Xeon(R) CPU E5-2640 v2 @ 2.00 GHz processor. All scripts, data files and requirements of the analyses are available as a gitlab repository named "hyda" [4].

7   Conclusions and Future Work

In this work we introduced an approach to make use of landscape properties to reduce computational redundancies in hydrological model simulations. We applied three different clustering methods namely, K-Means, K-Medoids and DBSCAN on the time series data from a study case in hydrology. According to the results, the K-means clustering functions better than the other applied clustering methods. It achieves the intended compromise between RMSE and Hillslopes computation time in a range of $11.8\% < RMSE < 14.2\%$ and $10.3\% < computation\ time < 16.2\%$. The K-means clustering requires a smaller number of clusters and consequently lower representative Hillslopes computation time in comparison to the other studied clustering methods. Considering the $16.8\% < RMSE < 34.7\%$ and $22.7\% < computation\ time < 33.8\%$, K-medoids clustering shows worse performance than the other two methods. DBSCAN clustering has promising results also not pleasing as the K-means method. The main challenge of applying DBSCAN is to find an intended balance of both Eps and $MinPts$ parameters. As a future work, the methods will be applied on the whole Attert catchment simulations and as a forward step the clustering approach will be extended to consider also forcing in the simulation model.

References

1. Aghabozorgi, S., Shirkhorshidi, A.S., Wah, T.Y.: Time-series clustering-a decade review. Inf. Syst. 16–38 (2015). https://doi.org/10.1016/j.is.2015.04.007
2. Alspaugh, S.: k-medoids clustering, May 2018. https://github.com/salspaugh/machine_learning/blob/master/clustering/kmedoids.py
3. Arroyo, Á., Tricio, V., Corchado, E., Herrero, Á.: A comparison of clustering techniques for meteorological analysis. In: 10th International Conference on Soft Computing Models in Industrial and Environmental Applications, pp. 117–130 (2015)
4. Azmi, E.: Hydrological data analysis, August 2018. https://gitlab.com/elnazazmi/hyda
5. Azmi, E.: On using clustering for the optimization of hydrological simulations. In: 2018 IEEE International Conference on Data Mining Workshops (ICDMW), pp. 1495–1496 (2018). https://doi.org/10.1109/ICDMW.2018.00215
6. Bărbulescu, A.: Studies on Time Series Applications in Environmental Sciences, vol. 103. Springer, Cham (2016). https://doi.org/10.1007/978-3-319-30436-6
7. Barnston, A.G.: Correspondence among the correlation, RMSE, and Heidke forecast verification measures; refinement of the Heidke score. Weather Forecast. **7**, 699–709 (1992)
8. Benner, P., Faßbender, H.: Model order reduction: techniques and tools. In: Baillieul, J., Samad, T. (eds.) Encyclopedia of Systems and Control, pp. 1–10. Springer, London (2013). https://doi.org/10.1007/978-1-4471-5058-9
9. Ehret, U., Zehe, E., Scherer, U., Westhoff, M.: Dynamical grouping and representative computation: a new approach to reduce computational efforts in distributed, physically based modeling on the lower mesoscale. Presented at the AGU Chapman Conference, 23–26 September 2014 (Abstract 2093) (2014)
10. Jones, J.E., Woodward, C.S.: Newton-Krylov-multigrid solvers for large-scale, highly heterogeneous, variably saturated flow problems. Adv. Water Resour. 763–774 (2001). https://doi.org/10.1016/S0309-1708(00)00075-0
11. Kassambara, A.: Practical Guide to Cluster Analysis in R: Unsupervised Machine Learning, vol. 1 (2017)
12. Kaufman, L., Rousseeuw, P.: Clustering by means of Medoids. In: Statistical Data Analysis Based on the L1-Norm and Related Methods (1987)
13. Kollet, S.J., et al.: Proof of concept of regional scale hydrologic simulations at hydrologic resolution utilizing massively parallel computer resources. Water Resour. Res. (4) (2010). https://doi.org/10.1029/2009WR008730
14. Maxwell, R., Condon, L., Kollet, S.: A high-resolution simulation of groundwater and surface water over most of the continental US with the integrated hydrologic model ParFlow V3. Geosci. Model Dev. 923 (2015). https://doi.org/10.5194/gmd-8-923-2015
15. Netzel, P., Stepinski, T.: On using a clustering approach for global climate classification? J. Climate 3387–3401 (2016). https://doi.org/10.1175/JCLI-D-15-0640.1
16. Pearson, K.: VII. Mathematical contributions to the theory of evolution. III. Regression, heredity, and panmixia. Philos. Trans. R. Soc. A 253–318 (1896). https://doi.org/10.1098/rsta.1896.0007
17. Shobha, N., Asha, T.: Monitoring weather based meteorological data: clustering approach for analysis. In: 2017 International Conference on Innovative Mechanisms for Industry Applications (ICIMIA), pp. 75–81 (2017). https://doi.org/10.1109/ICIMIA.2017.7975575

18. Türkeş, M., Tatlı, H.: Use of the spectral clustering to determine coherent precipitation regions in Turkey for the period 1929–2007. Int. J. Climatol. 2055–2067 (2011). https://doi.org/10.1002/joc.2212
19. Zarnani, A., Musilek, P., Heckenbergerova, J.: Clustering numerical weather forecasts to obtain statistical prediction intervals. Meteorol. Appl. 605–618 (2014). https://doi.org/10.1002/met.1383
20. Zehe, E., et al.: HESS opinions: from response units to functional units: a thermodynamic reinterpretation of the HRU concept to link spatial organization and functioning of intermediate scale catchments. Hydrol. Earth Syst. Sci. 4635–4655 (2014). https://doi.org/10.5194/hess-18-4635-2014

Cluster and Cloud Computing

YOLO: Speeding Up VM and Docker Boot Time by Reducing I/O Operations

Thuy Linh Nguyen[1], Ramon Nou[2(✉)], and Adrien Lebre[1(✉)]

[1] IMT Atlantique, Inria, LS2N, Nantes, France
{thuy-linh.nguyen,adrien.lebre}@inria.fr
[2] Barcelona Supercomputing Center (BSC), Barcelona, Spain
ramon.nou@bsc.es

Abstract. Although this comes as a surprise, the time to boot a Docker-based container can last as long as a virtual machine in high consolidated cloud scenarios. Because this time is critical as boot duration defines how an application can react w.r.t. demands' fluctuations (horizontal elasticity), we present in this paper the *YOLO* mechanism (*You Only Load Once*). *YOLO* reduces the number of I/O operations generated during a boot process by relying on a *boot image* abstraction, a subset of the VM/container image that contains data blocks necessary to complete the boot operation. Whenever a VM or a container is booted, *YOLO* intercepts all read accesses and serves them directly from the boot image, which has been locally stored on fast access storage devices (*e.g.*, memory, SSD, etc.). In addition to *YOLO*, we show that another mechanism is required to ensure that files related to VM/container management systems remain in the cache of the host OS. Our results show that the use of these two techniques can speed up the boot duration 2–13 times for VMs and 2 times for containers. The benefit on containers is limited due to internal choices of the docker design. We underline that our proposal can be easily applied to other types of virtualization (*e.g.*, Xen) and containerization because it does not require intrusive modifications on the virtualization/container management system nor the base image structure.

Keywords: Virtualization · Containerization · Boot duration

1 Introduction

The promise of the elasticity of cloud computing brings the benefits for clients of adding and removing new VMs in a manner of seconds. However, in reality, users may have to wait several minutes to get a new environment in public IaaS clouds [10] such as Amazon EC2, Microsoft Azure or RackSpace. Such long startup duration has a strong negative impact on services deployed in a cloud system. For instance, when an application (*e.g.*, a web service) faces peak demands, it is important to provide additional resources as fast as possible to

R. Yahyapour (Ed.): Euro-Par 2019, LNCS 11725, pp. 273–287, 2019.
https://doi.org/10.1007/978-3-030-29400-7_20

prevent loss of revenue for this service. DevOps expects that the use of container technologies such as Docker [11] would tackle such issues. However as discussed in this article, provisioning a container can last as long as a VM under high consolidated scenarios. Therefore, the startup time of VMs or containers plays an essential role in provisioning resources in a cloud infrastructure.

Two parts should be considered for the startup: (i) the time to transfer the VM/container image from the repository to the selected compute node and (ii) the time to perform the boot process. While a lot of efforts focused on mitigating the penalty of the image transferring time for VMs [7,16,17] as well as Docker [6,12], only a few works addressed the boot duration challenge for VMs [8,18,23] and to the best of our knowledge, none for containers. The process to boot a VM (or a container) leads to I/O and CPU operations that should be handled by the compute node. As a consequence, the duration of the boot process depends on the effective system load, in particular, the interference on the I/O path [13,14,21].

To deal with the aforementioned limitation, we investigated in this article the use of cache strategies that allow us to mitigate the number of I/O operations and thus to reduce the boot time. Concretely, we consolidated previous observations which have shown that only a small portion of the image is required to complete the VM boot process [15,17,23]. More precisely, we analyzed the I/O operations that occur during a boot process of a VM and a container. This analysis enabled us to conclude that (i) like VMs, containers only require to access a small part of the image to complete the boot process and (ii) unlike VMs, the amount of manipulated data for a container is much smaller in comparison to the I/O operations performed by the container management system itself.

Leveraging these results, we designed *YOLO* (*You Only Load Once*) as an agnostic mechanism to cache the data of a VM/container image that are mandatory to complete the boot operation: For each VM/container image, we construct a *boot image, i.e.*, a subset of the image that contains the mandatory data needed for booting the environment, and store it on a fast access storage device (memory, SSD, etc.) on each compute node. When a VM/container boot process starts, *YOLO* transparently loads the corresponding boot image into the memory and serves all I/O requests directly. In terms of storage requirements, the size of a boot image is in the average of 50 MB and 350 MB for respectively Linux and Windows VMs (storing boot images for the 900+ VM images from the Google Cloud platform would represent 40 GB, which is acceptable to be locally stored on each compute node). Regarding container technologies, the size of a boot image is much smaller with an average of 5 MB. For the I/O operations that are related to the VM/container management system, we simply use the vmtouch [4] program that enables to lock specific pages in the Linux system. We underline that using vmtouch for boot images is not relevant as it will be not acceptable to populate the cache with all possible boot images.

By mitigating the I/O operations that are mandatory to boot a VM or a container, *YOLO* can reduce the boot duration 2–10 times for VM and 2 times for containers according to the system load conditions.

The rest of this paper is organized as follows. Section 2 gives background elements regarding VM/container boot operations. Section 3 introduces *YOLO*. Section 4 describes the setup for all of our experiments. Sections 5 and 6 discuss the results we obtained. Section 7 deals with related works. Finally, Sect. 8 concludes the article and highlights future works.

2   Background

In this section, we give the background about QEMU-KVM and Docker that we used to perform our analysis, we choose these two virtualization solutions because of their wide used. For each technique, we first describe the boot process so that readers can understand clearly different steps of the boot operation. Second, we discuss the types of virtual disks that can be used in a QEMU/KVM-based or a Docker environment. Finally, we give details regarding access patterns and amount of manipulated data that a VM or a container performed during a boot operation.

2.1   QEMU-KVM Virtual Machine

Boot Process. The boot operation of a VM is managed by the QEMU-KVM hypervisor that is in charge of creating the virtual abstraction of the machine (*e.g.*, CPU, memory, disks, etc.) and launching the boot process. The boot process follows the usual workflow: first, the BIOS of the VM checks all devices and tests the system, then it loads the boot loader into memory and gives it the control. The boot loader (GRUB, LILO, etc.) is responsible for loading the guest kernel. Finally, the guest kernel invokes the `init` script that starts major services such as SSH. A QEMU-KVM VM can rely on two different VM Disk as discussed in the following.

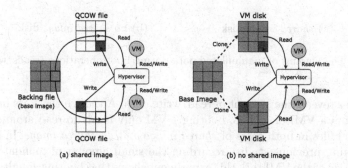

(a) shared image   (b) no shared image

Fig. 1. Two types of VM disk

VM Images. QEMU offers two strategies to create a VM disk image from the VMI (*a.k.a.* the VM base image). For the sake of simplicity, we call them *shared image* and *no shared image* strategies. Figure 1 illustrates these two strategies. In the *shared image* strategy, the VM disk is built on top of two files: the backing and the QCOW (QEMU Copy-On-Write) files. The backing file is the base image that can be shared between several VMs while the QCOW file is related to a single VM and contains all write operations that have been previously performed. When a VM performs read requests, the hypervisor first tries to retrieve the requested data from the QCOW and if not it forwards the access to the backing file. In the *no shared image* strategy, the VM disk image is cloned fully from the base image and all read/writes operations executed from the VM will be performed on this standalone disk.

Amount of Manipulated Data. To identify the amount of data that is manipulated during VM boot operations, we performed a first experiment that consisted in booting up to 16 VMs simultaneously on the same compute node. We used QEMU/KVM (QEMU-2.1.2) as the hypervisor, VMs are created from the 1.2 GB Debian image (Debian 7, Linux-3.2) with *writethrough* cache mode (*i.e.*, each write operation is reported as completed only when the data has been committed to the storage device).

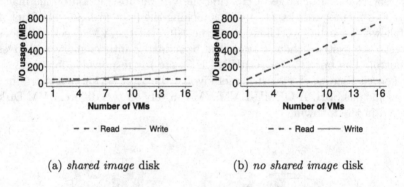

(a) *shared image* disk   (b) *no shared image* disk

Fig. 2. The amount of manipulated data during boot operations (reads/writes)

Figure 2 reveals the amount of read/write data. Although the VMs have been created from a VMI of 1.2 GB, booting 1 VM only needs to read around 50 MB from kernel files in both cases of *shared image* and *no shared image*. In addition to confirming previous studies regarding the small amount of mandatory data w.r.t. the size of the VMI [17], this experiment shows that booting simultaneously several instances of the same VM leads to the different amount of manipulated data according to the disk strategy. When the VMs share the same backing file (Fig. 2a), the different boot process benefit from the cache and the total amount of read data stays approximately around 50 MB whatever the number of VMs started (the mandatory data has to be loaded only once and stays into the cache for later accesses). When the VMs rely on different VM disks (Fig. 2b), the amount of read data grows linearly since each VM has to load 50 MB data for its own boot process. Regarding write accesses, both curves follow the same increasing trend. However, the amount of manipulated data differs: the *shared image* strategy writes 10 MB data when booting one VM and 160 MB for booting 16 VMs while the *no shared image* strategy slightly rises from 2 MB to 32 MB. The reason why the *shared image* strategy writes 5 times more data is due to the *"copy-on-write"* mechanism: when a VM writes less than cluster size of the QCOW file (generally 64 kB), the missing blocks should be read from the backing file, modified with the new data and written into that QCOW file [5].

In addition to reading from the base image, the QEMU-KVM process (*i.e.*, the daemon in charge of handling the boot request) has to load into the memory a total of 23 MB. This amount of data correspond to host libraries and the QEMU binary file. The write operations performed by the QEMU-KVM process are negligible (a few KBytes).

2.2   Docker Container

Boot Process. Although we use the words *Docker boot process* in comparison with the virtualization system terminology, it is noteworthy that a Docker container does not technically boot, but rather start. Booting a docker starts when the *dockerd* daemon receives the container starting request from the client. After verifying that the associated image is available, *dockerd* prepares the container layer structure, initializes the network settings, performs several tasks related to the specification of the container and finally gives the control to the *containerd* daemon. *containerd* is in charge of starting the container and managing its life cycle.

Docker Images. From the storage viewpoint a docker container is composed of two layers: the image layer and the container layer (*a.k.a.* the *lowerdir* and *uppperdir* files). These two layers can be seen as the backing and COW files in the VM terminology. The image layer is a read-only file that can be shared between multiple containers. The container layer contains differences w.r.t. the base image for each container. The unified view of the two directories is exposed as the *merged* union mount that is mounted into the container thanks to the *overlayfs* file system. This file system implements the copy-on-write strategy.

Amount of Manipulated Data. Although the order of magnitude differs, the amount of manipulated data when booting several times the same container follows the same trend of VMs sharing the same backing file: thanks to the cache, the amount of read data is constant. However, at the opposite of VMs, we observed that the significant part of read accesses when booting one container is related to the host directories and not the docker image. In other words, loading the docker binaries (*docker*, *docker-containerd-shim* and *docker-runc*), their associated libraries and configuration files represent much more Bytes than the I/O accesses that are performed on the docker image. Table 1 gives the details for different kinds of containers. Regarding the write operations, they are related to the creation of the container layer and the union mount. Although this amount is not significant w.r.t read operations, we noticed that the creation of the merge union mount point is a synchronous process: the docker daemon has to wait the completion of this action before progressing in the boot process. This is an important point as the more competition we will have on the I/O path, the longer will be the time to start the container.

Table 1. The amount of read data during a docker boot process

	Host OS	Docker image
debian	62.9 MB	3.7 MB
ubuntu	62.6 MB	4.1 MB
redis	61.8 MB	8.2 MB
postgres	60.1 MB	24.4 MB

3 YOLO Overview

Booting a VM or a container leads to a significant number of I/O operations. Because these operations can interfere with each other, in particular, in high consolidated scenarios, it is critical to mitigate them as much as possible. For such a purpose, we implement *YOLO* as a first mechanism to limit the impact of I/O operations related to the VM or container image on the boot duration. In the following, we give an overview of *YOLO* foundations and its implementation. First, we explain how boot images are created. Second, we introduce how *yolofs*, our custom file system, intercepts I/O requests to speed up a boot process.

3.1 *YOLO* Boot Image

YOLO relies on the boot image abstraction, *i.e.*, a subset of the VM (or container) image that corresponds to the data mandatory to complete the boot operation. To create a boot image, we capture all read requests generated when we boot completely a VM (or respectively a container). Each read request has: (i) a *file_descriptor* with *file_path* and *file_name*, (ii) an *offset* which is the beginning logical address to read from, and (iii) a *length* that is the total length of the data to read. For each read request, we calculate the list of all *block_id* to be read by using the *offset* and *length* information and we record the *block_id* along with the data of that block. In the end, a boot image contains a dictionary of key-value pairs in which the key is the pair (*file_name*, *block_id*) and the value is the content of that block. Therefore, with every read request on the VM (or container) image, we can use the pair (*file_name*, *block_id*) to retrieve the corresponding data of that block.

To avoid generating I/O contention with other operations, boot images should be stored on dedicated devices for *yolofs*, which can be either local storage devices (preferably SSD), remote attached volumes or even memory. To give an order of magnitude, we created the boot images for 900+ available VMIs from Google Cloud and the result depicts that the space needed to store all these boot images is around 40 GB, which is less than 3% of the original size of all VMIs (1.34 TB). Storing such an amount on each compute node looks to us an acceptable tradeoff.

3.2 *yolofs*

To serve all the read requests from the boot image instead of the VM or container image, we developed a new FUSE file system, entitled *yolofs*. In addition to not being intrusive, recent analysis [19] confirmed that the small overhead of FUSE for read requests is acceptable.

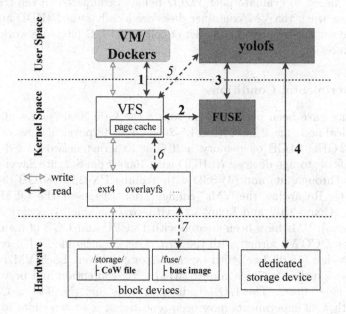

Fig. 3. yolofs read/write data flow

Figure 3 depicts the workflow of *yolofs* along with the read/write data flow for a QEMU-KVM VM or a Docker container. *yolofs* is executed as a daemon on each compute node (that is before any boot operation). When a VM/container issues read operations on its base image, which is linked to our mounted *yolofs* file system, the VFS routes the operation to the FUSE's kernel module, and *yolofs* will process it (*i.e.*, Step 1, 2, 3 of the read flow). *yolofs* then returns the data directly from the boot image (Step 4). If the boot image is not already into the memory, *yolofs* will load it from its dedicated storage device to the memory. Whenever the VM/docker wants to access data that is not available in the boot image, *yolofs* redirects the request to the kernel-based file system to read the data from the disk (Step 5, 6, and 7 of the read flow). Regarding write operations, they are not handled by *yolofs* and are forwarded normally to the corresponding COW file (the write flow in Fig. 3).

4   Experimental Protocol

In this section, we discuss our experiment setup and scenarios. The code of *YOLO* as well as the set of scripts we used to conduct the experiments are available on public git repositories[1]. We underline that all experiments have been made in a software-defined manner so that it is possible to reproduce them on other testbeds (with slight adaptations in order to remove the dependency to Grid'5000). We have two sets of experiments for both VMs and containers. The first set is aimed to evaluate how *YOLO* behaves compared to the traditional boot process when the VM/container disks are locally stored (HDD and SSD). The second set investigates the impact of collocated I/O intensive workloads on the boot duration.

4.1   Experimental Conditions

Experiments have been performed on top of the Grid'5000 Nantes cluster [1]. Each physical node has 2 Intel Xeon E5-2660 CPUs (8 physical cores each) running at 2.2 GHz; 64 GB of memory, a 10 Gbit Ethernet network card and one of two kinds of storage devices: (i) HDD with 10000 rpm Seagate Savvio 200 GB (150 MB/s throughput) and (ii) SSD with Toshiba PX02SS 186 GB (346 MB/s throughput). Regarding the VMs' configuration, we used the QEMU-KVM hypervisor (Qemu-2.1.2 and Linux-3.2) with *virtio* enabled (network and disk device drivers). VMs have been created with 1 vCPU and 1 GB of memory and a disk using QCOW2 format with the *writethrough* cache mode. For container, we used Docker (18.06.3-ce) with overlay2 storage driver. Each VM/container has been assigned to a single core to avoid CPU contention and prevent non-controlled side effects. The I/O scheduler of VMs and the host is CFQ. We underline that all experiments have been repeated at least ten times to get statistically significant results.

VM boot time: we assumed that a VM is ready to be used when it is possible to log into it using SSH. This information can be retrieved by reading the system log, and it is measured in milliseconds. To avoid side effect due to the starting of other applications, SSH has been configured as the first service to be started.

Docker container boot time: the main idea behind a container is running applications in isolation from each other. For this reason, docker boot duration is measured as the time to get a service runs inside a docker.

---

[1] https://github.com/ntlinh16/vm5k.

4.2   Boot Time Methodologies

We considered three boot policies as depicted as follow:

- *all at once:* using a normal boot process we boot all VMs/dockers at the same time (the time we report is the maximum boot time among all VMs/dockers).
- *YOLO:* All VMs/dockers have been started at the same time, and when a VM/docker needs to access the boot data, *YOLO* will serve them. We underline that boot images have been preloaded into the *YOLO* memory before starting a boot process. This way enables us to emulate a non volatile device. While we agree that there might be a small overhead to copy from the non-volatile device to the *YOLO* memory, we believe that doing so is acceptable as (i) the amount of manipulated boot images in our experiments is just 50 MB for a VM or 5 MB for a container and (ii) the overhead to load simultaneously 16 boot images from a dedicated SSD is less than 1%, as depicted in Fig. 4.
- *YOLO + vmtouch:* we use *vmtouch* to enforce QEMU and Docker daemon data to stay in the cache before we boot VMs/dockers by using *YOLO*.

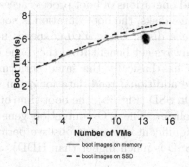

Fig. 4. Overhead of serving boot's I/O requests from the memory *vs.* a dedicated SSD

5   VM Boot Time Analysis

5.1   Booting Multiple VMs Simultaneously

For the first experiment, we investigated the time to boot up to 16 VMs in parallel using three boot policies mentioned above. With *all at once* policy, we used two different VM disk strategies: *shared image* and *no shared image* (see Sect. 2). There is no different between these VM disk strategies for *YOLO* because all necessary data for the boot process is already served by *YOLO*. Our goal was to observe multiple VMs deployment scenarios from the boot operation viewpoint.

Figure 5 shows the time to boot up to 16 VMs on a cold environment (*i.e.*, there is no other VMs running on the compute node). On HDD (Fig. 5a), the

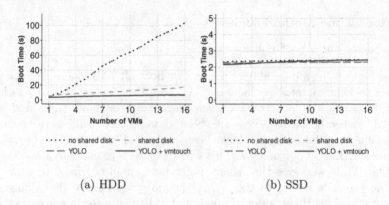

(a) HDD   (b) SSD

Fig. 5. Time to boot multiple VMs with shared and no shared disks

all at once boot policy with *no shared image* disk has the longest boot duration because VMs perform read and write I/O operations at the same time for their boot processes on different VM disks. This behavior leads to I/O contentions: the more VMs started simultaneously, the less I/O throughput can be allocated to each VM. Because read operations of boot process access the same backing file for VMs with *shared image* disks, the boot duration is noticeably faster than the VMs with *no shared image* disks. Using *YOLO* speeds up the boot time (from 4–13 times) since VMs always get benefit from the cache for reading mandatory data. *YOLO + vmtouch* has basically the same performance as *YOLO* alone because time to load the additional read data for qemu beside boot data from VMI is not significant. On SSD (Fig. 5b), the boot time of several VMs is mostly constant for all boot policies. The I/O contention generated during the boot process on SSD is not significant enough to observe performance penalties (the I/O throughput of the SSD is much higher than HDD).

5.2   Booting One VM Under I/O Contention

This experiment aims to understand the effect of booting a VM in a high-consolidated environment. We defined two kinds of VMs:

- *eVM* (*experimenting* VM), which is used to measure the boot time;
- *coVM* (*collocated* VM), which is collocated on the same compute node to run competitive workloads.

We measured the boot time of one *eVM* while the n *coVMs* ($n \in [0, 15]$) are running the I/O workloads by using the command **stress**[2]. Each *coVM* utilises a separate physical core to avoid CPU contention with the *eVM* while running the *Stress* benchmark. The I/O capacity is gradually used up when we increase the number of *coVMs*. There is no difference between VMs with *no*

---

[2] http://people.seas.harvard.edu/apw/stress/.

shared image and *shared image* disks because we measure the boot time of only one *eVM*. Hence, we simply started one *eVM* with the *normal* boot process.

Figure 6 shows the boot time of one eVM under an I/O-intensive scenario. *YOLO* delivers significant improvements in all cases. On HDD, booting only one eVM lasts up to 2 min by using the *normal* boot policy. Obviously, *YOLO* speeds up boot duration much more than the *normal* one because the data is loaded into the cache in a more efficient way. *YOLO + vmtouch* can further improves the boot time by preloading the data for the VM management system.

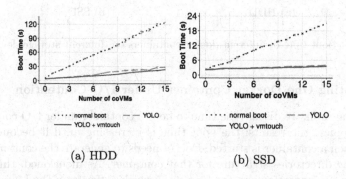

(a) HDD   (b) SSD

Fig. 6. Boot time of 1 VM (with *shared image* disk, *write through* cache mode) under I/O contention environment

The same trend can be found on SSD in Fig. 6b where the time to boot the eVM increased from 3 to 20 s for the *normal* strategy, and from 3 to 4 s for *YOLO*. *YOLO* is up to 4 times faster than *all at once* policy under I/O contention of 15 coVMs.

6   Docker Container Boot Time Analysis

6.1   Booting Multiple Distinct Containers Simultaneously

Similarly to VMs, we discuss in this paragraph the time to boot several different containers simultaneously. Figure 7 presents the results. Although *YOLO* reduces the time to boot containers, the time increases more significantly in comparison to VMs. This is due to the write operations that need to be completed as explained in Sect. 2.2. Understanding how such writes can be handled more efficiently is let as future works. Overall, *YOLO* enables the improvement of the boot time by a factor 2 in case of HDD (Fig. 7a). The trend for SSD is similar to the VM one: there is not enough competition on the I/O path to see an improvement.

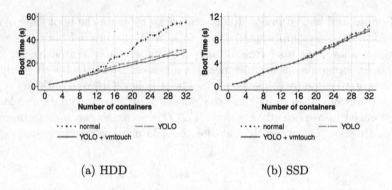

(a) HDD   (b) SSD

Fig. 7. Boot time of different docker containers on different storage devices

6.2 Booting One Docker Container Under I/O Contention

In this paragraph, we discuss the time to boot a container under I/O contention. Figure 8 depicts the results: the boot time is increasing until it becomes quite stable. When a container is started, Docker needs to generate the container layer with all the directories structure for that container. As mentioned, this action generates write operations on the host disk, which suffer from the I/O competition. Although *YOLO* and *YOLO + vmtouch* help mitigate the read operations, Docker still waits for the finalization of the container layer to continue its boot process. Therefore, the gain of *YOLO* is much smaller than for VMs.

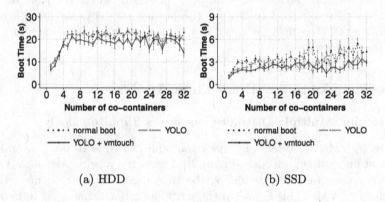

(a) HDD   (b) SSD

Fig. 8. Boot time of one debian docker container under I/O contention

7   Related Work

To improve Docker startup time, most works only tackle the image pulling challenge of Docker because they assume that the container boot time is negligible. However, improving the docker image pulling is out of scope of this article.

To the extent of our knowledge, our work is the first one to take into account the boot duration of a Docker container. Meanwhile, there are some solutions that improved the VM boot time, which utilize two main methods: cloning techniques or suspend/resume capabilities of VMs.

Kaleidoscope [2], SnowFlock [9] and Potemkin [20] are similar systems that can start stateful VMs by cloning them from a parent VM. While Potemkin marks a parent VM memory pages as copy-on-write and shares these states to all child VMs, SnowFlock utilises lazy state replication to fork child VMs and Kaleidoscope has introduced a novel VM state replication technique that can speed up VM cloning process by identifying semantically related regions of states. These systems clone new VMs from a live VM so that they have to keep many VMs alive for the cloning process. Another downside is that the cloned VMs have to be reconfigured because they are the exact replica of the original VM so they have the same configuration parameters like MAC address as the original one.

Other works [3,8,22] attempt to speed up VM boot time by suspending the entire state of a VM and resuming when necessary, which leads to a storage challenge. VMThunder+ [23] boots a VM then hibernates it to generate the persistent storage of VM memory data and then use this to quickly resume a VM to the running state. The authors use hot plug technique to re-assign the resource of VM. However, they have to keep the hibernate file in the SSD devices to accelerate the resume process. Razavi et al. [18] introduce prebaked μVMs, a solution based on lazy resuming technique to start a VM efficiently. To boot a new VM, they restore a snapshot of a booted VM with minimal resources configuration and use their hot-plugging service to add more resources for VMs based on client requirements. However, The authors only evaluated their solution by booting one VM with μVMs on a SSD device.

8   Conclusion

Starting a new VM or container in a cloud infrastructure depends on the time to transfer the base image to the compute node and the time to perform the boot process itself. According to the consolidation rate on the compute node, the time to boot a VM (or a container) can reach up to one minute and more. In this work, we investigate how the duration of a boot process can be reduced. Preliminary studies showed that booting a VM (or container) generates a large amount of I/O operations. To mitigate the overhead of these operations, we proposed *YOLO*. *YOLO* relies on the boot image abstraction which contains all the necessary data from a base image to boot a VM/container. Boot images are stored on a dedicated fast efficient storage device and a dedicated FUSE-based file system is used to load them into memory to serve boot I/O read requests. We discussed several evaluations that show the benefit of *YOLO* in most cases. In particular, we showed that booting a VM with *YOLO* is at least 2 times and in the best case 13 times faster than booting a VM in the normal way. Regarding containers, *YOLO* improvements are limited to 2 times in the best case. Although such a gain is interesting, we claim that there is space for more improvements. More precisely, we are investigating how the creation of the container layer can be performed in a more efficient manner in order to mitigate the dependencies of the write requests with respect to the storage layer.

Acknowledgment. All experiments presented in this paper were carried out using the Grid'5000 testbed, supported by a scientific interest group hosted by Inria and including CNRS, RENATER and several Universities as well as other organizations (see https:// www.grid5000.fr). This work is also a part of the BigStorage project, *H2020-MSCA-ITN-2014-642963*, funded by the European Commission within the Marie Sklodowska-Curie Actions framework. This work was partially supported by the Spanish Ministry of Science and Innovation under the TIN2015-65316 grant, the Generalitat de Catalunya undercontract 2014-SGR-1051.

References

1. Balouek, D., et al.: Adding virtualization capabilities to the Grid'5000 testbed. In: Ivanov, I.I., van Sinderen, M., Leymann, F., Shan, T. (eds.) CLOSER 2012. CCIS, vol. 367, pp. 3–20. Springer, Cham (2013). https://doi.org/10.1007/978-3-319-04519-1_1
2. Bryant, R., et al.: Kaleidoscope: cloud micro-elasticity via VM state coloring. In: EuroSys 2011, pp. 273–286. ACM (2011)
3. De, P., Gupta, M., Soni, M., Thatte, A.: Caching VM instances for fast VM provisioning: a comparative evaluation. In: Kaklamanis, C., Papatheodorou, T., Spirakis, P.G. (eds.) Euro-Par 2012. LNCS, vol. 7484, pp. 325–336. Springer, Heidelberg (2012). https://doi.org/10.1007/978-3-642-32820-6_33
4. Doug, H.: vmtouch: the Virtual Memory Toucher. https://hoytech.com/vmtouch/
5. Garcia, A.: Improving the performance of the QCOW2 format. https://events.static.linuxfound.org/sites/events/files/slides/kvm-forum-2017-slides.pdf
6. Harter, T., et al.: Slacker: fast distribution with lazy docker containers. In: FAST 2016, pp. 181–195 (2016)
7. Jeswani, D., Gupta, M., De, P., Malani, A., Bellur, U.: Minimizing latency in serving requests through differential template caching in a cloud. In: IEEE CLOUD 2012, pp. 269–276. IEEE (2012)
8. Knauth, T., Fetzer, C.: DreamServer: truly on-demand cloud services. In: ACM SYSTOR 2014. ACM (2014)
9. Lagar-Cavilla, H.A., et al.: SnowFlock: rapid virtual machine cloning for cloud computing. In: EuroSys 2009, pp. 1–12. ACM (2009)
10. Mao, M., Humphrey, M.: A performance study on the VM startup time in the cloud. In: IEEE CLOUD 2012, pp. 423–430. IEEE (2012)
11. Merkel, D.: Docker: lightweight Linux containers for consistent development and deployment. Linux J. **2014**(239), 2 (2014)
12. Nathan, S., Ghosh, R., Mukherjee, T., Narayanan, K.: CoMICon: a co-operative management system for docker container images. In: IEEE IC2E 2017, pp. 116–126 (2017)
13. Nguyen, T.L., Lèbre, A.: Virtual machine boot time model. In: IEEE PDP 2017, pp. 430–437. IEEE (2017)
14. Nguyen, T.L., Lèbre, A.: Conducting thousands of experiments to analyze VMs, dockers and nested dockers boot time. Technical report (2018)

15. Nicolae, B., Cappello, F., Antoniu, G.: Optimizing multi-deployment on clouds by means of self-adaptive prefetching. In: Jeannot, E., Namyst, R., Roman, J. (eds.) Euro-Par 2011. LNCS, vol. 6852, pp. 503–513. Springer, Heidelberg (2011). https://doi.org/10.1007/978-3-642-23400-2_46

16. Nicolae, B., Rafique, M.M.: Leveraging collaborative content exchange for on-demand VM multi-deployments in IaaS clouds. In: Wolf, F., Mohr, B., an Mey, D. (eds.) Euro-Par 2013. LNCS, vol. 8097, pp. 305–316. Springer, Heidelberg (2013). https://doi.org/10.1007/978-3-642-40047-6_32

17. Razavi, K., Kielmann, T.: Scalable virtual machine deployment using VM image caches. In: SC 2013, p. 65. ACM (2013)

18. Razavi, K., Van Der Kolk, G., Kielmann, T.: Prebaked μVMs: scalable, instant VM startup for IAAS clouds. In: IEEE ICDCS 2015, pp. 245–255. IEEE (2015)

19. Vangoor, B.K.R., Tarasov, V., Zadok, E.: To FUSE or not to FUSE: performance of user-space file systems. FAST **2017**, 59–72 (2017)

20. Vrable, M., et al.: Scalability, fidelity, and containment in the Potemkin virtual honeyfarm. In: ACM SOSP 2005, vol. 39, pp. 148–162. ACM (2005)

21. Wu, R., et al.: A reference model for virtual machine launching overhead. IEEE Trans. Cloud Comput. **4**(3), 250–264 (2016)

22. Zhang, I., Denniston, T., Baskakov, Y., Garthwaite, A.: Optimizing VM check-pointing for restore performance in VMware ESXi. In: USENIX Annual Technical Conference, pp. 1–12 (2013)

23. Zhang, Z., Li, D., Wu, K.: Large-scale virtual machines provisioning in clouds: challenges and approaches. Front. Comput. Sci. **10**(1), 2–18 (2016)

Parallel and Distributed Programming, Interfaces, and Languages

Celerity: High-Level C++ for Accelerator Clusters

Peter Thoman[1]([✉]), Philip Salzmann[1], Biagio Cosenza[2],
and Thomas Fahringer[1]

[1] University of Innsbruck, 6020 Innsbruck, Austria
{petert,psalz,tf}@dps.uibk.ac.at
[2] Technical University of Berlin, 10623 Berlin, Germany
cosenza@tu-berlin.de

Abstract. In the face of ever-slowing single-thread performance growth for CPUs, the scientific and engineering communities increasingly turn to accelerator parallelization to tackle growing application workloads. Existing means of targeting distributed memory accelerator clusters impose severe programmability barriers and maintenance burdens.

The Celerity programming environment seeks to enable developers to scale C++ applications to accelerator clusters with relative ease, while leveraging and extending the SYCL domain-specific embedded language. By having users provide minimal information about how data is accessed within compute kernels, Celerity automatically distributes work and data.

We introduce the Celerity C++ API as well as a prototype implementation, demonstrating that existing SYCL code can be brought to distributed memory clusters with only a small set of changes that follow established idioms. The Celerity prototype runtime implementation is shown to have comparable performance to more traditional approaches to distributed memory accelerator programming, such as MPI+OpenCL, with significantly lower implementation complexity.

1 Introduction

As Moore's Law is dying [5], end-users in many computational domains are turning to increasingly sophisticated parallelization methods in order to see speedups in their workloads. One particularly promising avenue is GPU computing, which leverages the high peak performance and energy efficiency of GPUs – or, more generally, *accelerators* – to implement suitable algorithms. To achieve even better performance and to tackle larger workloads, targeting a compute cluster of accelerators can be highly beneficial.

While these considerations seem straightforward from a hardware-centric, parallelism expert perspective, in practical use the *programmability* of such systems is a significant hindrance to their broader adoption in domain sciences [9]. Targeting accelerators requires an accelerator-specific API and programming model, and the most widespread vendor-agnostic option, OpenCL [12], assumes

© Springer Nature Switzerland AG 2019
R. Yahyapour (Ed.): Euro-Par 2019, LNCS 11725, pp. 291–303, 2019.
https://doi.org/10.1007/978-3-030-29400-7_21

familiarity with low-level hardware details and imposes significant implementation effort and maintenance overhead. When targeting clusters, these issues are compounded by the additional requirement of managing distributed-memory semantics, usually by leveraging MPI [10] for explicit message passing.

Not only does this type of software stack impose programmability and maintenance challenges, it also greatly reduces flexibility in optimizing and adapting a given program for current and future hardware architectures by hard-coding data and work distribution strategies.

Celerity aims to address these shortcomings, while keeping the barrier of adoption for users at a minimum. To this end, the basis of Celerity is SYCL [13], an open industry standard for programming arbitrary OpenCL devices using modern high-level C++. Celerity automates the parallelization of SYCL programs across heterogeneous computing clusters, opting to provide reasonable defaults and performance for domain scientists, while leaving room for manual tuning on a per-application basis. In this work we focus specifically on the programmability goals of Celerity, with our central contributions comprising:

- The *Celerity API* extending industry-standard SYCL programs to distributed memory with minimal programmer overhead, by introducing the concept of *custom data requirement functors* and a *virtual global queue*.
- A *prototype runtime implementation* based on a *multi-level task graph*, which is implicitly generated and distributed during the execution of a Celerity program.
- An *evaluation* of this API and prototype runtime implementation from *both programmability and performance perspectives*, compared to traditional MPI+OpenCL and state-of-the-art MPI+SYCL implementations.

2   Related Work

The increasing prevalence of parallelism in all application domains has warranted significant research into how the scheduling and partitioning of parallel codes can be automated [14]. In this section we summarize a number of languages and libraries which relate to the goals of Celerity.

Charm++ [7] is a task-based distributed runtime system and C++ language extension. Its global shared address space execution model allows executing asynchronous functions on distributed objects called *chares*, which may reside on a local or remote processor and which are transparently invoked through internally passed messages. Charm++ supports GPUs with a GPU Manager component, but is not natively designed for accelerator clusters. Furthermore, somewhat reducing programmability, a so-called *interface definition file* has to be provided for user-defined classes.

StarPU [2] is a task-based runtime system that provides data management facilities and sophisticated task scheduling algorithms for heterogeneous platforms, with the ability to easily implement custom schedulers. Its API is however still relatively low-level, and does not provide multi-node distributed memory parallelism out of the box. While it does feature facilities to integrate with

MPI, even automatically transferring data between nodes based on specified task requirements [1], the splitting and distribution of work still remains the responsibility of the user.

OmpSs [6], another task-based runtime system and compiler extension, builds on top of the well-established OpenMP standard. Using extended OpenMP #pragma directives to express data dependencies between tasks allows for asynchronous task parallelism. The ability to provide different implementations depending on the target device enables OmpSs to also support heterogeneous hardware. By annotating functions that wrap MPI communications with information about their data dependencies, effectively turning them into tasks as well, OmpSs can integrate them into the task graph and interleave OpenMP computations with MPI data transfers. However, the runtime itself has no explicit notion of MPI and thus again all work splitting and distribution decisions are offloaded to the user.

PHAST [11] is a heterogeneous high-level C++ library for programming multi- and many-core architectures. It features data containers for different dimensionalities and provides various STL-like parallel algorithms that can operate on said containers. Additionally, custom kernel functors are supported through a set of macros that wrap function headers and bodies. It does not feature any facilities for targeting distributed memory systems.

The Kokkos C++ library [4] allows thread parallel execution on many-core devices and attempts to provide performance portability by automatically adjusting data layouts of multidimensional arrays to fit the access patterns of a target device. It does not provide any facilities for distributed memory parallelism (i.e., everything has to be done manually), and it is again a rather low-level approach.

Legion [3] allows for even more flexibility by describing data accessed by tasks in terms of *logical regions*, while delegating decisions about how to lay them out in physical memory, alongside the decision of where to run tasks, to a (potentially user-provided) *mapper*. Logical regions and associated tasks can be partitioned and executed across heterogeneous clusters, with Legion taking care of ensuring data coherence between nodes. Again, partitioning decisions as well as the mapping of tasks to devices are delegated to the user.

While each of these approaches is well-suited to particular use cases, none of them with the exception of Legion and PHAST were natively designed for accelerator computing. Crucially, they all operate on a lower level of abstraction and thus require higher implementation effort compared to Celerity when targeting distributed memory accelerator clusters.

3   The Celerity System

Figure 1 gives a high-level overview of the entire Celerity system. At its core, the project extends the ease of use of the SYCL domain-specific embedded language to distributed clusters. While execution of shared memory parallel kernels is still handled by the SYCL runtime on each individual worker node, the Celerity

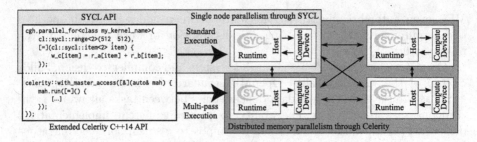

Fig. 1. A bird's-eye view of the Celerity system.

runtime acts as a wrapper around each compute process, handling inter-node communication and scheduling.

The central components making this possible are Celerity's user-facing *API*, and its *multi-pass execution* process at runtime. The latter allows the distributed system to gain a shared understanding of the program being executed and automatically distribute kernel executions while ensuring that their data requirements are fulfilled.

3.1   The Programming Interface

```
1    sycl::queue queue;
2
3    sycl::buffer<float, 2> buf_a(hst_a.data(), sycl::range<2>(512, 512));
4    sycl::buffer<float, 2> buf_b(hst_b.data(), sycl::range<2>(512, 512));
5    sycl::buffer<float, 2> buf_c(sycl::range<2>(512, 512));
6
7    queue.submit([&](sycl::handler& cgh) {
8        auto r_a = buf_a.get_access<acc::read>(cgh);
9        auto r_b = buf_b.get_access<acc::read>(cgh);
10       auto w_c = buf_c.get_access<acc::write>(cgh);
11       cgh.parallel_for<class my_kernel_name>(sycl::range<2>(512, 512),
12           [=](sycl::item<2> itm) {
13               w_c[itm] = r_a[itm] + r_b[itm];
14           });
15   });
```

Listing 1. A simple SYCL program that adds up two buffers.

Listing 1 illustrates the main portions of a simple SYCL program. Note that SYCL-related types are marked in orange, and that we assume a prologue of namespace sycl = cl::sycl and using acc = sycl::access::mode in all our examples for brevity. At its core, a SYCL program consists of a *queue* used to submit commands to a compute device, as well as data structures such as *buffers*, and the *kernels* which operate on them.

Lines 3 through 5 define three two-dimensional float buffers of size 512 × 512, the first two of which are being initialized using existing host data. On line 7, a so-called *command group* is submitted to the execution queue. Command groups serve as wrappers for device kernel calls, allowing the specification of data access requirements as well as the kernel code that operates on said data in one place, tied together by the *command group handler* `cgh`. This handler is passed as an argument into the C++ lambda expression constituting the command group, and is used to request *device accessors* on lines 8 through 10. Accessors concisely express the intent of the subsequent operation (reading, writing, or both), allowing the SYCL runtime to determine dependencies between subsequent kernel invocations and schedule data transfers required to ensure data coherence between the host and device.

In this particular command group, read access to buffers `buf_a` and `buf_b` is requested over their entire range. Conversely, write access is requested for buffer `buf_c`. Finally, on lines 11 through 15 the actual kernel is specified: A simple sum of the two read-buffers is computed. Note that each kernel has to be invoked using a template method such as `parallel_for<class kernel_name>` which uses a unique *tag-type* to allow linking of the intermediate representation of a kernel – which potentially is generated in a separate, implementation-defined compilation step – to the kernel invocation in the host program.

```
1   celerity::distr_queue queue;
2
3   celerity::buffer<float, 2> buf_a(hst_a.data(),sycl::range<2>(512, 512));
4   celerity::buffer<float, 2> buf_b(hst_b.data(),sycl::range<2>(512, 512));
5   celerity::buffer<float, 2> buf_c(sycl::range<2>(512, 512));
6
7   queue.submit([=](celerity::handler& cgh) {
8       auto one_to_one = celerity::access::one_to_one<2>();
9       auto r_a = buf_a.get_access<acc::read>(cgh, one_to_one);
10      auto r_b = buf_b.get_access<acc::read>(cgh, one_to_one);
11      auto w_c = buf_c.get_access<acc::write>(cgh, one_to_one);
12      cgh.parallel_for<class my_kernel_name>(sycl::range<2>(512, 512),
13          [=](sycl::item<2> itm) {
14              w_c[itm] = r_a[itm] + r_b[itm];
15          });
16  });
```

Listing 2. The same program as shown in Listing 1, now using the Celerity API.

Listing 2 shows the Celerity version of the program previously seen in Listing 1. The first observation of note is that the overall structure of the two programs is quite similar. While some objects now live under the `celerity` namespace, we still have buffers, a queue and a command group containing buffer accessors as well as a kernel invocation. In fact, whenever possible, the original objects from the `sycl` namespace are used, allowing for code to be migrated to Celerity with minimal effort. Since unlike SYCL, Celerity may call command groups multiple times during a user program's execution – as will be discussed in Sect. 3.2 – it is recommended to capture all required buffers by value rather than reference, as can be seen on line 7.

Notice the lack of typical indicators of a distributed memory parallel program, such as the notion of a local *rank* and the total number of nodes running. Nonetheless, given this program, the Celerity runtime is able to distribute the workload associated with kernel `my_kernel_name` to any number of workers dynamically at runtime.

This is made possible in large parts by one of Celerity's most significant API additions: So-called *range mappers* specify the data access behavior of each kernel and are provided as the final parameter to Celerity's get_access() calls on lines 9 through 11.

Specifying Data Requirements. When Celerity workers execute disjunct parts of the same logical kernel in parallel, they typically each require different portions of some input data. Distributing full buffers to each node and compute device is theoretically valid, but clearly untenable in terms of performance due to potentially redundant data transfers. Furthermore, a different part of the result is produced on each worker, a fact that needs to be taken into consideration when deciding on how to use their output in subsequent computations.

What is required is a flexible and minimally invasive method of specifying exactly what data requirements a kernel has, in a way that is independent of data distribution and work scheduling. In Celerity this is accomplished by *range mappers*, which are arbitrary functors with the following signature:

```
(celerity::chunk<KD>) -> celerity::subrange<BD>
```

Here, a celerity::chunk<KD> specifies an N-dimensional chunk of a kernel, containing an offset, a range, and a global size. The offset and range of a chunk depend on how the Celerity runtime decides to distribute a kernel across worker nodes, i.e., each chunk represents a portion of the execution of a kernel, each assigned to a particular worker node. A chunk is then mapped to a celerity::subrange<BD>, which specifies the offset and range of a data buffer the kernel chunk will operate on. KD and BD can differ: a 2D kernel may for example access data stored in a 1D buffer.

```
1   queue.submit([=](celerity::handler& cgh) {
2       auto i_r = input.get_access<acc::read>(cgh, celerity::access::
            one_to_one<2>());
3       auto o_w = output.get_access<acc::write>(cgh,
4           [](celerity::chunk<2> chnk) -> celerity::subrange<2> {
5               return { { chnk.offset[1], chnk.offset[0] },
6                       { chnk.range[1],  chnk.range[0] } };
7           });
8       cgh.parallel_for<class transpose>(sycl::range<2>(128, 256),
9           [=](sycl::item<2> itm) {
10              auto idx = sycl::id<2>(itm[1], itm[0]);
11              o_w[idx] = i_r[itm];
12          });
13  });
```

Listing 3. Range mapper for computing a matrix transpose.

Listing 3 shows how a range mapper can be used to specify data requirements for a simple matrix transpose. Implemented on lines 4 through 7, this range mapper specifies that for any input matrix of size $n \times m$, the kernel will write to an output matrix of size $m \times n$. Crucially, it also specifies that for any given submatrix of size $p \times q$ at location (i, j) with $i + p \leq n, j + q \leq m$, it will write to the corresponding output submatrix of size $q \times p$ at location (j, i).

Note that the range mapper merely acts as a contract of how data is going to be accessed, and does not affect the actual kernel in any way. The index-reversal and subsequent assignment on lines 10 and 11 is where the actual transpose is computed. Given this range mapper, regardless of the number of workers executing the kernel (i.e., the number of chunks the kernel is split into), it is always clear where which parts of the resulting matrix are computed. Likewise, the Celerity runtime also knows exactly what parts of the input matrix each worker node requires in order to produce the transpose. While in Listing 3 a matrix of size 128×256 is transposed to a 256×128 matrix, notice how this size is not relevant to the range mapper definition itself. This allows both users and library authors to write mappers in a generic and reusable way.

Built-in Range Mappers. The Celerity API provides several built-in range mappers for common data access patterns. One that is very frequently used, `celerity::access::one_to_one`, can be seen in both Listings 2 and 3. This range mapper specifies that a kernel, for every individual work item, will access a buffer only at that same global index. In Listing 3 this means that to compute the "result" for work item (i, j), the kernel will access the input matrix at index (i, j) as well – while writing to the output matrix at index (j, i), as specified by the custom mapper described previously.

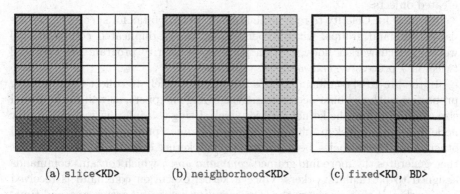

(a) `slice<KD>`   (b) `neighborhood<KD>`   (c) `fixed<KD, BD>`

Fig. 2. Example inputs and outputs for three built-in range mappers, in this case applied to 2-dimensional kernels and buffers.

Figure 2 illustrates three additional range mappers currently provided by the Celerity API. Thick lines indicate the input chunk, colored areas the associated output subrange (i.e., the accessed portion of a buffer). Each color corresponds to a different configuration of a range mapper. The `slice` range mapper allows extending the range of a chunk along one dimension indefinitely, thus selecting an entire slice of a buffer in that dimension. A common use case for this is matrix multiplication. The `neighborhood` range mapper allows selecting a given border around a chunk, a pattern that is commonly encountered in stencil codes. Finally, the `fixed` range mapper always returns a given, fixed subrange of a buffer, regardless of the input chunk. This can be useful when each worker needs to read the same input buffer, e.g. a mask when applying a discrete convolution.

3.2   The Prototype Runtime System

The Celerity runtime system is a multi-threaded application built on top of SYCL and MPI that runs in concert with a user-defined program in a *single program multiple data* (SPMD) fashion. It uses a master/worker execution model, where the master node is responsible for scheduling all the distributed work. Worker nodes encapsulate the available accelerator hardware (i.e., one worker is spawned per accelerator). They asynchronously receive *commands* from the master node and execute them as soon as possible.

Commands are lightweight asynchronous operations such as the execution of a certain chunk of a kernel, or initiating a data transfer with another worker. The master node generates commands as part of a graph and includes dependency information within the directives sent to each worker. This allows workers to execute commands as soon as all of their dependencies are satisfied. The resources that they operate on, i.e. kernels and buffers, are identified by unique numerical IDs within the lightweight command data structure. To enable this, each worker, as well as the master node, has an implicit shared understanding of what any particular ID refers to. This is possible because each Celerity process executes the exact same user code, deterministically assigning IDs to newly created objects.

To allow for Celerity to retain the familiar SYCL syntax for specifying kernels using command groups, without performing lots of duplicated computational work on each worker node, certain parts of a Celerity program are executed twice, in a process we call *multi-pass execution.*

In the *pre-pass*, command groups are executed solely to collect their defining properties, such as buffer accesses and their range mappers, as well as the global size of a kernel and the kernel function itself. Using this information, the master node constructs a task graph that respects consumer/producer relationships and other data dependencies between subsequent kernel executions. From this, it then generates the more fine grained *command graph* which contains commands assigned to particular workers. Once a kernel execution command is received by a worker, it then executes the corresponding command group a second time. During this *live-pass*, the actual computation on the device takes place. However, instead of using the global size provided by the user, it is transparently executed on the chunk assigned by the master node.

While the pre-pass is performed immediately upon first encounter of a command group within a user program, the Celerity runtime needs to be able to defer the live-pass to a later point in time in order to schedule additional work ahead. If that were not the case, each command group would act as an implicit global barrier, which is highly undesirable. This in turn means that Celerity has to retain command groups internally to be able to execute the live-pass at a later point in time, independently of the user program's execution flow. As the combination of C++11 lambda closures and this deferred execution can cause hard to diagnose lifetime bugs, we recommend to only capture parameters by value. While this is currently being enforced through static assertions, more sophisticated diagnostics enabled by compiler extensions might be explored in the future.

It is crucial to note that pre-pass and live-pass execution, as well as task and command graph generation all occur asynchronously – and, in fact, at the same time in any non-trivial program. Most importantly, this means that worker nodes can execute their local command graphs, performing computations and peer-to-peer data transfers, completely independently of the main task generation process. In practice, this system ensures that Celerity imposes no bandwidth overhead compared to a fully decentralized approach, and no latency overhead outside of a startup phase during which the initial commands are generated.

4   Evaluation

This section evaluates Celerity as a framework for writing distributed memory accelerator applications. To this end, we compare the Celerity implementation of three programs with more traditional implementations.

The example programs highlighted in this chapter are: (i) *MatMul*, a sequence of dense matrix-matrix multiplications, (ii) *Pendulum*, which simulates the behavior of a pendulum swinging across a board with an arrangement of magnets, and (iii) *WaveSim*, a simulation of the 2D wave equation. For each of these programs, we compare a Celerity version with a MPI+SYCL version representing the current state of the art. For *MatMul*, we additionally consider a traditional MPI+OpenCL variant, to verify that SYCL performs equally to this baseline.

4.1   Programmability

To estimate and compare the differences of each implementation from a programmer's point of view, we present two different metrics. First, the widely employed *cyclomatic complexity* [8] measures code complexity in terms of the number of linearly independent paths of execution a program could take. It is computed using the pmccabe command-line utility, which is available for many Linux distributions. As a somewhat simpler – but perhaps more immediately apprehensible – metric, the number of non-comment lines of code (NLOC) is provided. Note that all non-essential code, such as selection of compute devices, instrumentation, and result verification is excluded from these metrics. The former two need to be performed manually for the classical implementations while they are included in Celerity, and the latter is the same across all versions.

Figure 3 summarizes the programmability metrics for all three applications. Note that across all programs and both metrics, there is a very significant decrease in implementation complexity of about factor 2 going from MPI+SYCL to Celerity. This is primarily caused by eliminating the need for most traditional trappings associated with distributed memory programming, including manual work and data distribution as well as data synchronization. The smallest difference is observed in NLOC for *Pendulum*, which is due to the fact that there is

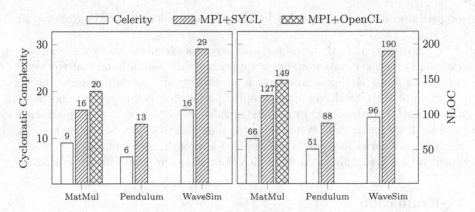

Fig. 3. Comparison of programmability metrics.

no data redistribution required in this algorithm outside of the initial conditions and final aggregation.

When considering the MPI+OpenCL version for *MatMul*, we see that there is a further increase in implementation effort associated with the lower-level OpenCL API compared to the high-level SYCL, although a less significant one than what is required for distributed memory.

4.2 Performance

While Sect. 4.1 demonstrates the significant programmability advantages conferred by Celerity compared to state-of-the-art methods, these advantages would be relatively meaningless if they came at a large general loss in performance potential. Therefore, although the current Celerity runtime implementation is still only a prototype, we provide some initial benchmarks in this section which demonstrate its performance.

Table 1. Per-node specification for the benchmarking system.

Host	AMD Ryzen Threadripper 2920X 12-Core, 32 GB DDR4 RAM
GPUs	4x Nvidia RTX 2070
Interconnect	10 Gigabit Ethernet
Software	Ubuntu 18.04; OpenMPI 4.0.0; GPU driver 410.79; hipSYCL 0.7.9

All benchmarks were executed on a small cluster comprised of 8 GPUs, situated in two distinct but otherwise identical machines with 4 GPUs each. Thus, all runs using 4 GPUs or less are on a single machine, while runs with 8 GPUs utilize both. Table 1 summarizes the hardware of each machine, as well as the software stack used for this evaluation. For each benchmark, the workload is statically distributed in a uniform fashion, i.e., no load-balancing strategies are employed. Figure 4 illustrates the speedup achieved by each application scaling from 1 to 8 GPUs (corresponding to 2304 to 18432 CUDA cores). The results presented are based on the median of 5 benchmark runs for each configuration.

Before discussing the individual results, note that we do not include the MPI+OpenCL version of *MatMul* in this chart. Its performance is exactly equivalent to the MPI+SYCL version and is therefore omitted for clarity.

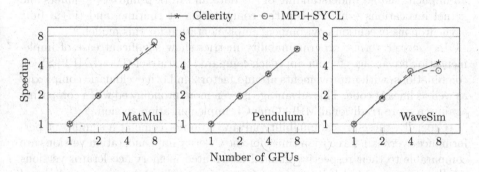

Fig. 4. Speedup for 1 to 8 GPUs of Celerity compared to manual MPI+SYCL.

Evidently, Celerity offers performance comparable to the manual distributed memory accelerator implementation in all three applications benchmarked. This is most apparent in *Pendulum*, which shows the exact same speedup for both variants. This is a result of the absence of intermediate data transfers resulting in a relative lack of network transmission impact on the overall execution time.

For *MatMul*, Celerity shows equivalent behavior up to 4 GPUs, but slightly worse scaling to 8 GPUs. We have examined this drop in efficiency and determined that it is due to the manual MPI version leveraging collective communication for data transfers in between individual matrix multiplications, while the Celerity prototype currently performs point-to-point communication. This is a quality-of-implementation issue rather than an inherent feature of our approach, and we intend to improve on this behavior in future work.

Finally, *WaveSim* actually demonstrates better scaling from 4 to 8 GPUs in its Celerity variant than it does in MPI+SYCL. This stencil-like code is relatively latency-sensitive, as ghost cells need to be exchanged after every time step. The Celerity version benefits from the fact that all (automatic) data distribution is inherently implemented asynchronously in our runtime system. While the MPI+SYCL version could also be made entirely asynchronous, likely resulting in similar performance, this would further increase its implementation complexity in the metrics discussed in Sect. 4.1.

5 Conclusion

In this work we have introduced the Celerity API for programming distributed memory accelerator clusters. It builds on the SYCL industry standard, and allows extending existing single-GPU programs to GPU clusters with a minimal set of changes, while shielding the user from much of the complexity associated with work and data distribution on clusters.

This is achieved by (i) a concise API extension focusing on flexible, reusable *range mapper* functors, (ii) a multi-pass runtime execution model which builds an implicit, shared understanding of the data and work primitives – buffers and kernel invocations – involved in the computation at runtime, and (iii) a fully asynchronous execution environment implementation for this model.

In concrete terms, programmability metrics show significant ease of implementation advantages for our approach compared to state-of-the-art MPI+SYCL combinations, with improvements around factor 2 in both cyclomatic complexity as well as lines of code. This advantage is even more pronounced when comparing against a more traditional MPI+OpenCL implementation version.

Crucially, these programmability advances do not come at a significant performance overhead. Execution times for the Celerity implementation versions are comparable to their respective manual distributed memory accelerator versions in all programs tested, with minor advantages and disadvantages in individual benchmarks.

The approach introduced in Celerity enables a broad spectrum of future research. On the API level, even more concise or domain-specific abstractions can be introduced to further improve ease of use for domain scientists. Independently – and without requiring any change to the input programs – the efficiency of the runtime system can be increased, by e.g. introducing command graph optimizations which gather individual transfers into collective operations, or by improving scheduling for kernels with non-uniform workloads.

Acknowledgments. This research has been partially funded by the FWF (I 3388) and DFG (CO 1544/1-1, project number 360291326) as part of the CELERITY project.

References

1. Agullo, E., et al.: Achieving high performance on supercomputers with a sequential task-based programming mode. IIEEE Trans. Parallel Distrib. Syst. (2017)
2. Augonnet, C., Thibault, S., Namyst, R., Wacrenier, P.A.: StarPU: a unified platform for task scheduling on heterogeneous multicore architectures. Concurr. Comput. Pract. Exp. **23**(2), 187–198 (2011)
3. Bauer, M., Treichler, S., Slaugther, E., Aiken, A.: Legion: expressing locality and independence with logical regions. In: 2012 International Conference for High Performance Computing, Networking, Storage and Analysis (SC). IEEE (2012)
4. Carter Edwards, H., Trott, C.R., Sunderland, D.: Kokkos: enabling manycore performance portability through polymorphic memory access patterns. J. Parallel Distrib. Comput. **74**(12), 3202–3216 (2014)

5. Courtland, R.: Gordon Moore: The Man Whose Name Means Progress (2015). https://spectrum.ieee.org/computing/hardware/gordon-moore-the-man-whose-name-means-progress
6. Duran, A., et al.: OmpSs: a proposal for programming heterogeneous multi-core architectures. Parallel Process. Lett. **21**(02), 173–193 (2011)
7. Kale, L.V., Krishnan, S.: CHARM++: a portable concurrent object oriented system based on C++. In: Proceedings of the Eighth Annual Conference on Object-Oriented Programming Systems, Languages, and Applications, vol. 10, pp. 91–108 (1993)
8. McCabe, T.J.: A complexity measure. IEEE Trans. Softw. Eng. **SE-2**(4), 308–320 (1976)
9. Meade, A., Deeptimahanti, D.K., Buckley, J., Collins, J.J.: An empirical study of data decomposition for software parallelization. J. Syst. Softw. **125**, 401–416 (2017)
10. Message Passing Interface Forum: MPI: A Message-Passing Interface Standard, Version 3.1 (2015). https://www.mpi-forum.org/docs/mpi-3.1/mpi31-report.pdf
11. Peccerillo, B., Bartolini, S.: PHAST library – enabling single-source and high performance code for GPUs and multi-cores. In: Smari, W.W. (ed.) 2017 International Conference on High Performance Computing and Simulation, pp. 715–718. IEEE, Piscataway (2017)
12. The Khronos Group: The OpenCL Specification, Version 1.2 Revision 19 (2012). https://www.khronos.org/registry/OpenCL/specs/opencl-1.2.pdf
13. The Khronos Group: SYCL Specification, Version 1.2.1 Revision 3 (2018). https://www.khronos.org/registry/SYCL/specs/sycl-1.2.1.pdf
14. Thoman, P., et al.: A taxonomy of task-based parallel programming technologies for high-performance computing. J. Supercomput. **74**(4), 1422–1434 (2018)

Dataflow Execution of Hierarchically Tiled Arrays

Chih-Chieh Yang[1]([⊠]), Juan C. Pichel[2], and David A. Padua[3]

[1] IBM Thomas J. Watson Research Center, Yorktown Heights, NY 10598, USA
chih.chieh.yang@ibm.com
[2] CiTIUS, Universidade de Santiago de Compostela, Santiago de Compostela, Spain
juancarlos.pichel@usc.es
[3] University of Illinois at Urbana-Champaign, Urbana, IL 61801, USA
padua@illinois.edu

Abstract. As the parallelism in high-performance supercomputers continues to grow, new programming models become necessary to maintain programmer productivity at today's levels. Dataflow is a promising execution model because it can represent parallelism at different granularity levels and to dynamically adapt for efficient execution. The downside is the low-level programming interface inherent to dataflow. We present a strategy to translate programs written in Hierarchically Tiled Arrays (HTA) to the dataflow API of Open Community Runtime (OCR) system. The goal is to enable program development in a convenient notation and at the same time take advantage of the benefits of a dataflow runtime system. Using HTA produces more comprehensive codes than those written using the dataflow runtime programming interface. Moreover, the experiments show that, for applications with high asynchrony and sparse data dependences, our implementation delivers superior performance than OpenMP using parallel for loops.

Keywords: Parallel programming · Dataflow ·
High-level programming abstraction · Parallel algorithm

1 Introduction

Over the last decade, the pursuit of system performance has moved from increasing processor frequency to increasing the number of processing cores so that today's supercomputers can contain millions of cores [24]. This number is likely to increase significantly as we move to exascale systems. New notations will be

This material is based upon work supported by the Department of Energy [Office of Science] under awards DE-SC0008716 and DE-SC0008717, the National Science Foundation under award 1533912, MINECO under award RTI2018-093336-B-C21, the Xunta de Galicia under award ED431C 2018/19, and the European Regional Development Fund.

© Springer Nature Switzerland AG 2019
R. Yahyapour (Ed.): Euro-Par 2019, LNCS 11725, pp. 304–316, 2019.
https://doi.org/10.1007/978-3-030-29400-7_22

necessary for these future systems to keep the complexity of parallel programming at a manageable level. Such notations will rely on runtime systems [10] that create a simplified machine model and can better deal with applications whose performances depend on various dynamic decisions, such as scheduling and data movements.

Dataflow is a promising model for runtime systems. In a conceptually simple notation, it captures multiple levels of parallelism needed for efficient execution on exascale systems. It uses task graphs where tasks (i.e. sequential code segments) are represented by nodes and can be scheduled to execute as soon as their incoming data dependences (represented by the graph edges) are satisfied. Compared with conventional models which rely on programmers use of control dependences, a dataflow model utilizes inherent parallelism in programs naturally. Although implementations of such model [2,4,6,15–17,20] have shown great potential for exploiting parallelism, many of them lack high-level programming abstractions to attract programmers. To program using a native dataflow notation is a daunting task, because its programming style is unfamiliar and the learning curve is steep. Moreover, even when one learns to program in this way, the resulting codes could contain numerous dependence edges and lack structure, making these codes difficult to debug and maintain.

In this paper, we propose using Hierarchically Tiled Arrays (HTA) [1,5,11,12] as high-level abstractions to exploit the benefits provided by dataflow runtime systems, while helping productivity with a familiar programming interface for those trained to program in conventional notations. We implemented a fully functional HTA library on top of the dataflow-based Open Community Runtime (OCR) [8,17], and show through experiments that our design preserves the benefits of OCR while removing the need to program in the task graph notation.

The remainder is organized as follows. Section 2 gives an overview of the programming model HTA and OCR, the dataflow runtime system of our choice. Section 3 describes the design and implementation of HTA as a library on top of OCR (HTA-OCR). Section 4 presents the performance evaluation of our HTA implementation using various benchmark applications. The related work is described in Sect. 5. Finally, the conclusions are presented in Sect. 6.

2 Background

2.1 Overview of Hierarchically Tiled Arrays

An HTA program can be conceived as a sequential program containing operations on tiled arrays or sub-arrays. With HTA, programmers express parallel computations as tiled array operations. Because tiles are a first class object, the HTA notation facilitates the control of locality, which is of great importance today and will be even more so for future exascale systems.

By expressing computations in terms of high-level tiled array operations, programmers can focus on designing algorithms for maximal parallelism and better data locality and leave the mapping to the target machine and runtime system,

```
1 HTA A(2,                /*dimension*/
2      2,                /*levels*/
3         Tuple(N, N),   /*flat array size*/
4         Tuple(X, X));  /*tiling        */
5 HTA B(A.shape()), C(A.shape());
6 A.init(RANDOM); B.init(RANDOM); C.init(RANDOM);
7 for(k = 0; k < X; k++) {
8   for(i = 0; i < X; i++) {
9   C(i,{0:X-1}) += A(i,k) * B(k,{0:X-1}); }}
```

Listing 1. Example of tiled matrix-matrix multiplication in HTA.

including synchronization operations, to the HTA implementation which, for the one reported here, took the form of a library.

In HTA, programmers explicitly express parallelism by choosing the *tiling* (i.e. partitioning a flat array into tiles) of arrays. Multilevel tiling can be used, and each level can be tiled for different purposes. For example, there can be a top-level tiling for coarse-grain parallelism, a second-level tiling for fine-grain parallelism, and a third level for data locality in the cache.

An example of an HTA program in C++-like syntax is given in Listing 1. The code first constructs three HTAs, A, B and C. Each of them is an $N \times N$ array partitioned into $X \times X$ tiles. A, B and C are initialized, and then a two-level nested **for** loop performs tiled matrix-matrix multiplication. The parenthesis operator represent tile accesses and the curly braces represent array range selections. For instance, C(i,{0:X-1}) selects the ith row of tiles in C. The operator * performs a matrix multiplication of two tiles. In this code segment, the creation, initialization, multiplication and addition assignment are HTA operations, and the control loops are sequential statements. There are plenty of parallelization opportunities, but the exact way is hidden from the user in the HTA library implementation of operations and memory access.

It has been shown [5] that HTA programs are expressive and concise. It is particularly convenient to parallelize an existing sequential program by replacing parallelizable computations such as for loops with operations on tiled arrays. Even without existing sequential code, using HTA facilitates building parallel applications from scratch. HTA programs are also more portable, since they are written in high-level abstractions without machine dependent details.

2.2 Overview of Open Community Runtime

Open Community Runtime (OCR) is a product of the X-Stack Traleika Glacier project [18] funded by Department of Energy of the US government. Its goal is to provide a task-based execution model for future exascale machines through software and hardware co-design.

In OCR, computations are represented as directed acyclic graphs where nodes are event driven tasks (EDTs, called simply *tasks* hereafter) that operate on relocatable data. The OCR API provides functions to create *objects* including *tasks*, *events*, and *data blocks*. Tasks represent computation, data blocks represent data used or produced in the computation, and events are used to describe either data or control dependences between tasks.

The execution of OCR tasks is dictated by events. Tasks are not scheduled for execution immediately after their creation. Instead, at creation, an OCR task is placed in a queue, and the runtime system keeps track of its incoming dependences. When all the incoming dependences of an OCR task are satisfied, the task becomes *ready* and the runtime system can schedule it for execution. Tasks run to completion without ever being blocked, since all the data needed for the computation is available when they are scheduled.

Since task execution depends only on data blocks passed to tasks and not on data in the call stack or global heap objects, OCR runtime system can freely relocate tasks, as long as the data blocks needed can be accessed at the place of execution. The fact that both tasks and data blocks are relocatable makes it possible for the runtime system to make dynamic scheduling decisions for workload distribution, energy saving, and various other optimizations. This saves application programmers from having to optimize application code with machine specific details. However, to program directly using the OCR programming interface, one has to formulate computations as a dataflow task graph. It is a verbose way of programming since every task and dependence have to be explicitly specified. It is also difficult to maintain and debug code written in such fashion. In the next section, we explain how this weakness can be overcome by bridging the gap with HTA.

3 Design and Implementation of HTA-OCR

In this section, we describe the main ideas behind our HTA library implemented on top of OCR. We call this library HTA-OCR. Our goal is to take advantage of both the programmability of HTA and the performance benefits of OCR's dependence-driven execution. Interested readers can find more details in [26].

3.1 Program Execution

An HTA-OCR program starts with a master task which executes the program sequentially except for HTA operations that are typically executed in parallel. The library routine implementing an HTA operation analyzes the operands (HTA tiles) and determines the data dependences (if any) of the subtasks performing operation. Then, the routine invokes OCR routines to create the subtasks and specifies their dependences in the form of OCR events. If it does not depend on the results of the subtasks, the master task then continues executing subsequent statements of the HTA program without waiting for the subtasks to complete, possibly overlapping execution with the subtasks.

Figure 1 shows a two-statement code segment and its dataflow task execution. The program operates on three 1-D HTAs, each containing tiles. The first statement assigns the content of B tiles to the corresponding tiles of A. The second performs another assignment from the tiles of A to those of C. Obviously, there

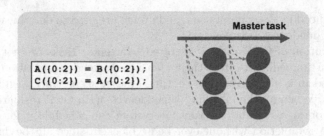

Fig. 1. HTA-OCR task graphs of assignment operations. The thick blue arrow represents the master task execution; The blue circles represent subtasks; The dotted blue thin arrows represent subtask creations; The orange thin arrows represent the data dependences between tasks. (Color figure online)

are flow dependences between the two statements. The right-hand side of the figure, shows the dynamically constructed task graph. The master task is represented as a thick blue arrow to show that its execution typically spans longer than other subtasks, represented as circles. The dotted blue thin arrows represent subtask creations, and the orange thin arrows represent the data dependences between tasks. When the master task executes the first statement, three subtasks are spawned and each copies one tile of **B** to the corresponding tile of **A**. Next, three more subtasks are spawned for the second statement. The second group of subtasks have incoming data dependences (the continuous arrows) from the first group due to the flow dependences on the tiles of **A**.

OCR shared memory implementation manages multiple worker threads upon which tasks can be scheduled. As soon as the incoming dependences of a subtask are satisfied, it is ready and can be scheduled for execution. The worker threads use a work-stealing scheduling algorithm so that tasks can be stolen by other threads for load balancing. To best utilize computing resources, the program should generate abundant subtasks that have sparse dependence edges among them, so that there is a higher probability of having numerous ready tasks to be scheduled at any given time.

3.2   Data Dependences

In the execution style described above, parallel tasks spawn dynamically with their dependences discovered by the master task examining and updating access record of HTA tiles. *Non-HTA variables* of global scope are always assigned in the master task. On the other hand, *HTAs* are only assigned in subtasks. Considering the two types of variables, data dependences exist whenever, in program order, a location is first written and then read or written, or is first read and then written. Four different cases exist:

1. The assignment to an HTA tile depends on some non-HTA variable accessed previously by the master task.
2. The assignment to a non-HTA variable depends on some non-HTA variable accessed previously by the master task.

3. The assignment to a non-HTA variable depends on some HTA accessed by a previous HTA operation.
4. The assignment to an HTA tile depends on some HTA accessed by a previous HTA operation.

In Case 1, the data dependence is resolved automatically, since the master task would have evaluated the non-HTA variable at the spawning point of the subtask to compute the HTA. Thus, the variable can be passed by value into the subtask. Similarly, in Case 2, the data dependence is guaranteed to be resolved because non-HTA variables are always evaluated by the master task in program order. In Case 3, the non-HTA variable assignment has data dependence on the completion of subtasks. Since in OCR, block-waiting for tasks is not supported, we implemented a split-phase continuation mechanism, explained in 3.3. In Case 4, the new subtasks must wait for the results of previous subtasks, and therefore data dependence arcs must be created. For this case, we developed a tile-based dependence tracking mechanism which utilizes access record of HTA tiles to ensure that tasks using the same HTAs always access them in the correct order respecting the data dependences.

3.3 Split-Phase Continuation

During program execution, the master task sometimes must wait for the results of a subtask. When it discovers incoming dependences from subtasks, it creates a new *continuation* task which is a clone of itself, and passes the original program context (including the program stack, the register file, and the program counter) to the clone, along with a list of new dependence events. As a result, the runtime system will only schedule the continuation task after both the original master task completes and the new incoming data dependences are satisfied. When it starts, it restores the program context and then continues the execution with new inputs.

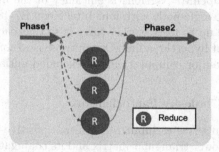

Fig. 2. Split-phase continuation. The thick blue arrow representing the master task execution which splits into two phases due to the new dependences on the reduction results. The continuation resumes executing the main program when it receives the reduction results. (Color figure online)

Consider a reduction on a 1-D HTA of three tiles, illustrated in Fig. 2. The master task (Phase 1) spawns three subtasks and each sequentially performs reduction on its assigned tile to get a single scalar value. Since the number of subtasks is small, the three scalar values are sent directly to the continuation task (Phase 2) to be reduced to the final result. If the number of leaf tiles are large, a parallel tree reduction can be used.

4   Experiments

Table 1. List of benchmarks.

Source	Benchmark
Hand-coded	Cholesky
Teraflux [9]	Sparse LU
NAS parallel benchmarks [3]	EP, IS, LU, FT, MG, CG

We evaluate our HTA-OCR shared memory implementation using several benchmarks listed in Table 1. The baseline are OpenMP versions of these programs that use parallel loops *as the only parallel construct*. We use this baseline in two ways. First, for the first two benchmarks in Table 1, the baseline implementation helps us assess the benefit of overlapping subtasks from different vector assignments which are implemented as separate parallel loops in the OpenMP versions. Since OpenMP parallel loops execute a barrier at the end, this overlap is not possible in OpenMP and therefore the overlap is the reason for performance advantage of the HTA version. Second, for the NAS Parallel Benchmarks, the OpenMP implementation helps us evaluate the efficiency of our implementation. Because in the NAS Parallel Benchmarks the overlapping of subtasks from different array operations is very limited, and therefore differences in performance between the HTA-OCR and the OpenMP versions is efficiency of the implementation. The experiments are on a single-node with four Intel Xeon E7-4860 processors, each has ten cores. We use up to forty worker threads so that each thread binds to a dedicated core without hyperthreading. Our purpose is to compare the execution models, so we timed major computation and excluded initial setup.

4.1   Tiled Dense Cholesky Factorization

Cholesky factorization takes as input a Hermitian positive-definite matrix and decomposes it into a lower triangular matrix and its conjugate transpose. We use a tiled Cholesky fan-out algorithm. Intel MKL sequential kernels are used for tile-by-tile multiplication and tile triangular decomposition. The OpenMP version (Listing 2) factorizes a diagonal tile (Line 3), and uses the result to update the tiles of the same column in the lower triangular matrix (Line 5–6). The submatrix tiles in the lower triangular matrix are then updated using the results of the

```
1  for(int k = 0; k < n; k++) {
2      int numGEMMS = (n-k)*(n-k-1)/2;
3      POTRF(&A[k*n+k]);
4      #pragma omp parallel for schedule(dynamic, 1)
5      for(int i = k+1; i < n; i++)
6          TRSM(&A[i*n+k], &A[k*n+k]);
7      #pragma omp parallel for schedule(dynamic, 1)
8      for(int x = 0; x < numGEMMS; x++) {
9          int i, j;
10         GET_I_J(x, k+1, n, &i, &j);
11         if(i == j) SYRK(&A[j*n+j], &A[j*n+k]);
12         else       GEMM(&A[i*n+j], &A[i*n+k], &A[j*n+k]);}}
```

Listing 2. Tiled dense Cholesky factorization in OpenMP.

```
1  for(int k = 0; k < n; k++) {
2      map(POTRF, A(k, k));
3      map(TRSM, A({k+1:n-1}, k), A(k, k));
4      for(int j = k+1; j < n; j++) {
5          map(SYRK, A(j, j), A(j, k));
6          map(GEMM, A({j+1:n-1},j),A({j+1:n-1},k),A(j,k));}}
```

Listing 3. Tiled dense Cholesky factorization in HTA-OCR.

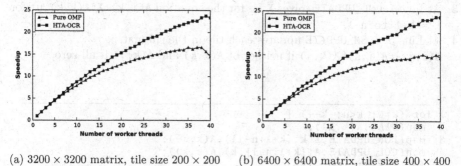

(a) 3200 × 3200 matrix, tile size 200 × 200   (b) 6400 × 6400 matrix, tile size 400 × 400

Fig. 3. Tiled dense Cholesky factorization results.

column tiles as input (Line 9–12). The updates in different parallel for loops have an implicit barrier in-between, and a k loop iteration blocks before all updates of the previous loop iteration complete. The HTA-OCR version (Listing 3) has a similar program structure, but it replaces the parallel for loops with the map() operations and array range selection, resulting in more concise code. During execution, the master task discovers dependences and constructs task graphs dynamically. No implicit global synchronization barriers are necessary.

In Fig. 3, we use two different problem sizes with the same partition of 16×16 tiles and plot the speedup over sequential execution under various number of worker threads. In both settings, the task granularity is large, and the curves are similar. The HTA-OCR version has better speedup overall and scales better. It is about 1.5× faster at higher thread counts. As mentioned above, its advantage comes from eliminating the barriers which allows not only the tasks in the two different inner loops but also in the different outermost loop iterations to overlap. In contrast, implicit global synchronization barriers in the OpenMP version prevent task executions from overlapping even when required input data is ready, resulting in lower compute resource utilization.

4.2 Tiled Sparse LU Factorization

LU factorization converts a matrix A into the product of a lower triangular matrix L and an upper triangular matrix U. Adapted from the sparse LU code in Teraflux project [9], Listing 4 shows the HTA-OCR implementation. An outer k loop contains four steps:

1. At Line 2, `DIAG` factors the diagonal tile `A(k,k)` into the lower triangular part `A(k,k).lt` and the upper triangular part `A(k,k).ut`.
2. At Line 3, `ROW_UPDATE` solves X for the equation `A(k,j)=A(k,k).lt*X` for `j = k+1 to n-1`.
3. At Line 4, `COL_UPDATE` solves X for for the equation `A(i,k)=X*A(k,k).ut` for `i = k+1 to n-1`.
4. At Line 5–8, `SM_UPDATE` updates each tile in the submatrix `A(i,j)-=A(i,k)*A(k,j)` if neither of `A(i,k)` and `A(k,j)` is all-zero.

```
1  for (k=0; k<n; k++) {
2    map(DIAG,A(k,k));
3    map(ROW_UPDATE,A(k,{k+1:n-1}),A(k,k));
4    map(COL_UPDATE,A({k+1:n-1},k),A(k,k));
5    for(i=k+1; i<n; i++)
6      if (A(i,k) != NULL)
7        for (j=k+1; j<n; j++)
8          if (A(k,j)!= NULL) map(SM_UPDATE,A(i,j),A(i,k),A(k,j));}
```

Listing 4. Parallel tiled sparse LU factorization in HTA-OCR.

The operations within a step are fully independent, but data dependences exist between different steps. There are also dependences across iterations of the k loop. The HTA-OCR library can dynamically construct a dataflow task graph by discovering the data dependences without user explicitly stating the dependences. Compared with Cholesky factorization in Sect. 4.1, the computation graph of LU factorization can be more complex, but the sparseness eliminates some nodes and dependence edges that would exist for the dense case. The OpenMP version uses a parallel for loop for each step and relies on implicit global barriers for the correctness.

The results of two problem sizes are shown in Fig. 4, both with 16 × 16 tiles and tile sizes are 100 × 100 and 200 × 200 respectively. Similar to the results

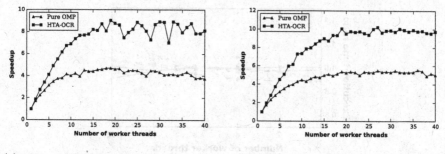

(a) 1600×1600 matrix, tile size 100×100 (b) 3200×3200 matrix, tile size 200×200

Fig. 4. Tiled sparse LU factorization results.

of tiled Cholesky factorization in Sect. 4.1, the HTA-OCR version shows greater scalability. It is close to $2\times$ faster under forty threads. The advantages come from having no global barriers that may over-restrict task overlapping, just as in Cholesky factorization.

4.3 NAS Parallel Benchmarks

NAS (Numerical Aerodynamic Simulation) Parallel Benchmarks [3] are created by NASA for evaluating the performance of parallel supercomputers. We implemented six of them in HTA-OCR and observed the strong scaling results of class C as shown in Fig. 5. We plot the ratio of the HTA-OCR execution time over the OpenMP counterpart under the same number of threads. Most of them have a workload consists of regular computations that can be evenly divided easily and use global synchronizations. Because there is little opportunity for overlapping the execution of subtasks from different HTA statements, the main difference in performance between the HTA-OCR implementations and their OpenMP counterparts is overhead of execution. As can be seen in Fig. 5, in practically all cases there is less than 20% difference in performance and in some cases the HTA-OCR version is faster. We conclude that the performance of our experimental HTA-OCR implementation is competitive with that of the mature (an likely highly optimized) OpenMP library [13].

4.4 Summary of Experiments

For dense Cholesky factorization and sparse LU factorization, HTA-OCR shows superior performance than OpenMP. While HTA-OCR program complexity is similar to OpenMP, the dataflow runtime system can utilize CPUs effectively for the abundant asynchronous subtasks and their sparse data dependences. In contrast, OpenMP implicit barriers restrict task overlapping and this results in bad performance. Note that, if OpenMP Tasking is used instead of parallel loops, it

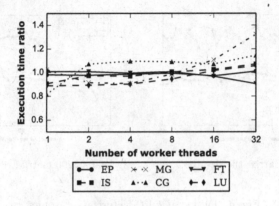

Fig. 5. NAS Parallel Benchmark results (Class C).

is possible to express the dataflow graph and execute in a data driven fashion. It would have comparable performance as HTA-OCR, but its code would be more cumbersome, since explicit data dependence annotations are needed. For the NAS Parallel Benchmarks, HTA-OCR shows decent results close to OpenMP. In most cases, the performance difference is within 20%. The HTA-OCR performance does not always surpass OpenMP, because the benchmarks mostly have easily-balanced workloads and bulk-synchronous execution which are ideal for OpenMP.

In all of our experiments, we present strong scaling results. The task management overhead (spawning, event satisfaction, scheduling, ..., etc) in OCR is significantly larger than the that of parallel loops in OpenMP. This makes HTA-OCR performance more sensitive to task granularity. To achieve good parallel efficiency, the task granularity has to be large enough to amortize the overhead. However, in strong scaling, as we use more threads, we partition a fixed-sized problem into more tiles and thus increasing task management overhead while decreasing task granularity. Devoting more future efforts into improving task overhead is crucial for the success of the dataflow runtime systems.

5   Related Work

OCR is based on the codelet model [14,27]. This model incorporates some of the ideas and advantages of the macro-dataflow models [23], where the granularity is defined not at the instruction level but a coarser grain one, and also of the hybrid dataflow/Von Neumman EARTH system [25]. Similarly, PaRSEC [6] is another runtime system that adopts dataflow model for coarse-grain task executions.

The Concurrent Collection (CnC) model [7] is a high-level programming model implemented upon both Habanero [21] and Intel Threading Building Blocks [22], and it is inspired by dynamic dataflow.

Charm++ [15] is a programming paradigm that also adapts the dataflow execution model for its runtime system design. Charm++ provides an object oriented programming interface, thus it might be more suitable for application programmers to develop large parallel applications than OCR.

Based on the encouraging results of SMPSs [19], OpenMP Tasking was extended to support data dependent tasks. The expressible data dependences are limited to tasks within the same parallel section. In comparison, HTA-OCR tasks are not confined within parallel sections.

Legion [4] lets user write programs by decomposing application data into *logical regions* and explicitly spawning asynchronous tasks that operate on the regions. A software out-of-order processor dynamically infer data dependences. In terms of programming abstraction, Legion is lower-level than HTA, as parallel tasks are implicitly created in HTA.

6   Conclusions

This paper presents the design and implementation of the HTA programming model for execution on top of a dataflow runtime. Our work is among the first attempts to provide high-level programming abstractions upon dataflow runtime systems. We propose a strategy to map HTA programs onto dataflow task graphs, and we implemented the design as a fully functional HTA-OCR library whose important mechanisms were also discussed in detail. While our work describes data dependences in parallel programs among array tiles, we believe that our strategy can be extended to support other data structures, such as parallel sets, to provide a general-purpose programming paradigm. For performance evaluation, a variety of benchmarks were implemented using the HTA-OCR API and the experiments were conducted. The results show great promises of using HTA as programming abstractions upon dataflow runtime systems for its programmability and its ability to preserve the benefits from dataflow execution.

References

1. Andrade, D., Fraguela, B.B., Brodman, J., Padua, D.: Task-parallel versus data-parallel library-based programming in multicore systems. In: 17th Euromicro International Conference on Parallel, Distributed and Network-based Processing, pp. 101–110 (2009)
2. Augonnet, C., Thibault, S., Namyst, R., Wacrenier, P.A.: Starpu: a unified platform for task scheduling on heterogeneous multicore architectures. Concurr. Comput. Pract. Exp. **23**(2), 187–198 (2011)
3. Bailey, D., et al.: The NAS parallel benchmarks. Int. J. High Perform. Comput. Appl. **5**(3), 63–73 (1991)
4. Bauer, M., Treichler, S., Slaughter, E., Aiken, A.: Legion: expressing locality and independence with logical regions. In: International Conference on High Performance Computing, Networking, Storage and Analysis, p. 66 (2012)
5. Bikshandi, G., et al.: Programming for parallelism and locality with hierarchically tiled arrays. In: 11th ACM SIGPLAN Symposium on Principles and Practice of Parallel Programming, pp. 48–57 (2006)
6. Bosilca, G., et al.: Parsec: exploiting heterogeneity to enhance scalability. Comput. Sci. Eng. **15**(6), 36–45 (2013)

7. Budimlic, Z., et al.: Concurrent collections. Sci. Prog. **18**(3–4), 203–217 (2010)
8. Budimlic, Z., et al.: Characterizing application execution using the open community runtime. In: International Workshop on Runtime Systems for Extreme Scale Programming Models and Architectures, in conjunction with SC15 (2015)
9. Consortium, T.: Teraflux applications (2017). https://svn.teraflux.eu/svnpub/apps/, Accessed 04 June 2017
10. Da Costa, G., et al.: Exascale machines require new programming paradigms and runtimes. Supercomput. front. Innovations **2**(2), 6–27 (2015)
11. Fraguela, B., et al.: The hierarchically tiled arrays programming approach. In: 7th Workshop on Languages, Compilers, and Run-time Support for Scalable Systems, pp. 1–12 (2004)
12. Fraguela, B., et al.: Optimization techniques for efficient HTA programs. Parallel Comput. **38**(9), 465–484 (2012)
13. Free Software Foundation: Gomp - an openmp implementation for GCC. https://www.gnu.org/software/gcc/projects/gomp/, Accessed 01 Feb 2019
14. Gao, G.R., Zuckerman, S., Suetterlein, J.: Toward an execution model for extreme-scale systems - runnemede and beyond, May 2011
15. Kale, L.V., Krishnan, S.: Charm++: a portable concurrent object oriented system based on c++. In: Proceedings of the Conference on Object Oriented Programming Systems, Languages and Applications, pp. 91–108 (1993)
16. Lauderdale, C., et al.: Swarm: A Unified Framework for Parallel-for, Task Dataflow, and Distributed Graph Traversal. ET International Inc., Newark (2013)
17. Mattson, T., et al.: The open community runtime: a runtime system for extreme scale computing. In: High Performance Extreme Computing Conference, pp. 1–7 (2016)
18. Modelado Foundation: Traleika glacier project (2018). https://wiki.modelado.org/Traleika_Glacier, Accessed 01 Oct 2018
19. Perez, J.M., Badia, R.M., Labarta, J.: A dependency-aware task-based programming environment for multi-core architectures. In: International Conference on Cluster Computing, pp. 142–151 (2008)
20. Planas, J., Badia, R.M., Ayguadé, E., Labarta, J.: Hierarchical task-based programming with starss. Int. J. High Perf. Comput. Appl. **23**(3), 284–299 (2009)
21. Barik, R., et al.: The Habanero multicore software research project. In: Proceedings of the 24th ACM SIGPLAN Conference Companion on Object Oriented Programming Systems Languages and Applications. pp. 735–736 (2009)
22. Reinders, J.: Intel Threading Building Blocks, 1st edn. O'Reilly & Associates Inc, Sebastopol (2007)
23. Sarkar, V., Hennessy, J.: Partitioning parallel programs for macro-dataflow. In: ACM Conference on LISP and Functional Programming, pp. 202–211 (1986)
24. Strohmaier, E., Dongarra, J., Simon, H., Meuer, M.: Top500 list (2008). https://www.top500.org/, Accessed 01 Oct 2018
25. Theobald, K.B.: EARTH: and effcient architecture for running threads. Ph.D. thesis, McGill University, Montreal, Canada (1999)
26. Yang, C.C.: Hierarchically Tiled Arrays as High-Level Programming Abstractions for Dataflow Runtime Systems. Ph.D. thesis, University of Illinois at Urbana-Champaign (2017)
27. Zuckerman, S., Suetterlein, J., Knauerhase, R., Gao, G.R.: Using a codelet program execution model for exascale machines: position paper. In: 1st International Workshop on Adaptive Self-Tuning Computing Systems for the Exaflop Era, pp. 64–69 (2011)

Scalable FIFO Channels for Programming via Communicating Sequential Processes

Nikita Koval[1,2(✉)], Dan Alistarh[1], and Roman Elizarov[2]

[1] IST Austria, Klosterneuburg, Austria
dan.alistarh@ist.ac.at
[2] JetBrains, Saint Petersburg, Russia
ndkoval@ya.ru, elizarov@gmail.com

Abstract. Traditional concurrent programming involves manipulating shared mutable state. Alternatives to this programming style are communicating sequential processes (CSP) and actor models, which share data via explicit communication. These models have been known for almost half a century, and have recently had started to gain significant traction among modern programming languages. The common abstraction for communication between several processes is the *channel*. Although channels are similar to producer-consumer data structures, they have different semantics and support additional operations, such as the select expression. Despite their growing popularity, most known implementations of channels use lock-based data structures and can be rather inefficient.

In this paper, we present the first efficient lock-free algorithm for implementing a communication channel for CSP programming. We provide implementations and experimental results in the Kotlin and Go programming languages. Our new algorithm outperforms existing implementations on many workloads, while providing non-blocking progress guarantee. Our design can serve as an example of how to construct general communication data structures for CSP and actor models.

Keywords: Concurrency · Synchronous queue · Rendezvous channel · Lock-freedom · Scalability

1 Introduction

Programming via communicating sequential processes (CSP) was introduced by Hoare [18] almost half a century ago, and has had significant research and practical impact [10]. In particular, many modern programming languages, such as Go [8], Kotlin [4], Scala [25], and Rust [9] provide support for this programming paradigm, as an alternative, or complement, to synchronization via shared memory.

Very roughly, programs in CSP can be seen as a parallel composition of sequential processes, communicating with each other via synchronous message-passing.[1] The CSP paradigm is built around *channels*, which provide the basic communication and synchronization mechanisms between the computational processes.

---

[1] CSP is broadly similar to the actor model [12], with key distinctions in terms of the basic assumptions regarding process identities and synchronization.

© Springer Nature Switzerland AG 2019
R. Yahyapour (Ed.): Euro-Par 2019, LNCS 11725, pp. 317–333, 2019.
https://doi.org/10.1007/978-3-030-29400-7_23

To efficiently support CSP programming on modern multi-threaded multi-processors, it is critical to be able to implement *fast, scalable* channels, supporting the CSP semantics. Naively, concurrent channels can be seen as a classic instance of first-in-first-out (FIFO) queues, which have been extensively studied in shared-memory programming [17]. Yet, CSP channels typically require additional, non-trivial semantics, which are not easy to pigeonhole in the classic producer-consumer data structure definitions, and their usage scenarios can vary broadly. One such example is commonly-used the `select` expression, by which a process can register operations in a set of channels, returning on the first operation that succeeds.

Different programming language implementations fill this implementation gap by "brewing" their own FIFO channel implementations, either independently, or adapting ideas present in the concurrency literature. Most implementations, including Go [8] and Rust [9], rely on *lock-based* designs. In particular, they rely on careful combinations of fine-grained and coarse-grained synchronization to implement the complex channel semantics. One notable exception is the Kotlin coroutines library [4], which implements a complex producer-consumer data structure, based on a doubly-linked list design [31]. Unfortunately, this implementation is known to allow for live-lock in certain corner cases [5]. Another one exception is `SynchronousQueue` in Java [27], which is based on Michael-Scott queue [23]; however, it does not support the `select` expression.

Contribution. In this work, we revisit the question of implementing an efficient channel with CSP semantics. We provide the first linearizable, lock-free implementation of a rendezvous channel supporting `send`, `receive`, and `select` operations, that is fast in both contended and uncontended scenarios, and can be extended to implement CSP semantics as specified by various programming languages.

Our design builds on ideas from previous work on lock-free FIFO queues, e.g. [11,23,27]. Our base data structure is similar to the Michael-Scott queue, but where nodes are *segments*, which can accommodate multiple waiting operations of either `send` or `receive` type.

We non-trivially extend this blueprint to support extended semantics in a wide range of contended and uncontended scenarios. Specifically, we add efficient support for `select` operations, which can wait on operation in a *set* of channels, via a customized implementation of descriptors [14]. A novel feature of our mechanism is that it permits physical removal of elements from the middle of a queue-like structure in $O(1)$ amortized operations, which is required for an implementation of the `select` expression. The proposed algorithm is quite general, in that it can be adapted to other synchronization primitives for CSP programming, such as buffered channels, mutexes, and semaphores.

We validate our algorithm with efficient implementations of our channel in Go and Kotlin. Our algorithm can provide comparable performance relative to the lock-based Go implementation in a range of scenarios, and outperforms it by up to 2× in terms of average time per operation. Our Kotlin implementation significantly outperforms the existing library implementation [4], especially the `select` expression. It speeds up the `send` and `receive` operations by up to 2× for the most part, and by a couple of magnitude in certain scenarios; the `select` expression is faster by up to 10×.

2 Channel Semantics

The rendezvous channel is the main abstraction for message passing protocols used in both CSP and actor programming models. Intuitively, in this abstraction, there are two types of processes, producers and consumers, which perform a rendezvous handshake as a part of their protocol. This section describes the channel semantics and its API, which is shown in Listing 1. In the following, we assume that threads are either *producers*, which perform send requests, or *consumers*, which perform receive requests.

```
1  class Channel {
2      fun send(element: Any)
3      fun receive(): Any
4  }
5
6  fun select(alternatives: SelectAlt[])

7  class SelectAlt(
8      val channel: Channel,
9      val element: Any?, // null for receive
10     val action: fun(Any?)
11 )
```

Listing 1. Rendezvous channel API

Send and Receive Semantics. In order for a producer to "send" an element, it has to perform a rendezvous handshake with a consumer, to which it passes this element. The consumer semantics are symmetric. At the same time, we assume *first-in-first-out (FIFO)* guarantees, meaning that all requests in a channel should be processed in the order of arrival.

At the operational level, the rendezvous channel is essentially a queue of waiting processes, where each request atomically checks if the queue has processes of the opposite type, and either removes the first one and resumes it, or·adds itself to the queue and suspends. Practical systems offer an efficient way to suspend a process waiting for a request, and resume it after that. This mechanism is described in Sect. 4.

The select Expression. Channels in the CSP programming model usually support selection among several alternates. This expression is usually called select and it makes possible to await multiple send or receive invocations on different channels, and select the first one which becomes available. At the same time, the chosen process should be removed from the other waiting queues. The classic select expression checks the alternatives in the enumeration order, while the unbiased version uses a random order [4,8]. For simplicity, we assume an arbitrary order on alternatives, but the proposed algorithm does not rely on this restriction and can be easily modified to support any ordering strategy.

Programming languages take different approaches for defining the select expression. For example, Go supports it as a built-in feature [8], while Kotlin implements it in the Kotlin Coroutines library providing a domain specific language (DSL) for the select declaration [4]. For this paper we use a DSL-based API, which can be used for built-in expression implementation as well.

To describe alternatives, we use the SelectAlt class, which specifies a channel, an element to be sent (null is used for receiving), and an action to be executed with the received element (null is passed when sending) in case this alternative is selected. The selection algorithm can be implemented as an external select function taking an array of alternatives. Listing 2 shows an example usage of this API.

```
1 ch1 := Channel(), ch2 := Channel()
2 select(
3   SelectAlt(ch1, 42,   { _ -> println("Sent 42") }),
4   SelectAlt(ch2, null, { res -> println("Received $res") })
5 )
```

Listing 2. Example of the select expression usage. This code either sends "42" to the first channel or receives an element from the second one.

3 Related Work

3.1 Coroutines and Actors

Two basic parallel programming models use message passing for synchronization: actors [12] and coroutines [20]. The second one is also known as green threads and fibers. Roughly, an actor can be represented as a coroutine associated with a channel, to which other actors can send messages, and from which this actor can receive them. In contrast to actors, coroutines use channels directly and can perform the select expression on them.

Several modern programming languages and libraries use one of these models. For example, Go [8], Kotlin [4], Clojure [7], Rust [9], and project Loom for Java [6] use coroutines, while Erlang [3] and Akka [2] use the actor model; all of them have their own channel implementations. Almost all solutions we are aware of use *locks* in order to support a waiting queue, and perform the select expression using fine-grained synchronization on these locks. These approaches are fundamentally blocking.

To our knowledge, the only *non-blocking* channel implementation is a part of the Kotlin coroutines library [4], which is *lock-free*. Here, the waiting queue is implemented using a modified instance of the doubly-linked list designed by Sundell and Tsigas [31], and Harris descriptors [14] to ensure the atomicity. The resulting implementation is extremely complex, and shows significant overhead, as we show in the experimental section. Moreover, it is known that Kotlin's lock-free algorithm for a correctness bug, and can get into a livelock [5]. This makes our solution for the select expression the first lock-free implementation to support such semantics.

3.2 Producer-Consumer Data Structures

Fair Synchronous Queues. Among classic data structures, *synchronous queues* are probably closest to channels in terms of semantics. They support send and receive operations, which wait for a rendezvous. The main difference is that they do not support the select expression. Hanson suggested an algorithm based on three semaphores [13], which was improved in Java 5 using a global lock and wait-notify mechanism in order to make a rendezvous.

Java 6 implements a lock-free algorithm suggested by Scherer, Lea, and Scott [27]. Their solution is based on Michael-Scott lock-free queue [23]; we use a similar technique for maintaining the waiting queue.

Reference [19] presents an improved general scheme for implementing non-blocking dual containers. Their approach leverages the LCRQ non-blocking queue design [24] in a clever way, to implement a rendezvous mechanism. While this approach is quite interesting and efficient in practice, it requires access to double-width atomic primitives, which are only supported by Intel CPUs. This makes the code non-portable: for instance, it would prevent implementation in both Java/Kotlin and Go. Therefore, we cannot apply it in our setting.

Unfair Synchronous Queues. Scherer, Lea, and Scott also propose *unfair* but scalable synchronous queue, which is based on a stack instead of a queue [27]. However, this approach still induces a sequential bottleneck on the stack. To work around a single point of synchronization, Afek, Korland, Natanzon, and Shavit introduced *elimination-diffraction trees* [11]. In this solution, each request goes through a binary tree, in which internal nodes are *balancer objects* [30], and leaves are synchronous queues.

Another approach to reducing contention is *flat combining* [15], which was applied to unfair synchronous queue problem by Hendler et al. [16].

Elimination. One more way to reduce contention is using elimination, which was firstly applied for stacks [29] by Shavit and Touitou. They observed that concurrent push and pop operations can be *eliminated* preserving atomicity by having the push operation pass directly to pop, without modifying the stack. Scherer, Lea, and Scott use elimination in their exchanger algorithm [26], where there is only one type of request and so a rendezvous happens between any two threads that show up. In case of channels, not all pairings are allowed, so their approach is not applicable for our problem.

4   Preliminaries

Coroutines Management. To implement send and receive operations, we need to have an ability to store the current coroutine somewhere and suspend it, after what an opposite operation can resume it. It is worth noting that some libraries use another approach and store continuation, which has the required information for resuming. Nevertheless, both approaches are equivalent for our purpose and should provide the described above functionality.

The algorithm presented in the paper uses definitions from Listing 3. The Coroutine class represents a coroutine and new fields can be inserted into it for synchronization. To get the current coroutine, we use the curCor function. The park and unpark methods are used for suspending and resuming the coroutine respectively. As well as in the native thread park mechanism, we assume that park returns without suspension if unpark has been called before. However, in case of suspension, park does not block the current thread, but schedules to another waiting coroutine.

Not all environments provide such contracts. For example, in Go language gopark (park) invocation should always *happen before* goready (unpark) invocation. This solution is sufficient for the lock-based algorithm, but can be also easily extended to support the required contract by providing an appropriate implementation of park on top of gopark.

In order to send an element to a suspended coroutine, we suggest adding a special field into Coroutine class, which stores the result. This way, in case of resuming a coroutine, we use resume method which stores the result in this field and unparks the coroutine. From the other side, to suspend and return this result we use suspendAndGetResult, which parks the current coroutine and returns the previously stored result right after it was unparked.

```
1  class Coroutine {                    11  fun resume(c: Coroutine, res: Any?) {
2    ...                                12    c.result = res
3    var result: Any?                   13    unpark(c)
4  }                                     14  }
5                                        15
6  fun curCor(): Coroutine              16  fun suspendAndGetResult(): Any? {
7                                        17    c := curCor()
8  fun park()                            18    park(c)
9  fun unpark(c: Coroutine)             19    return c.result
10                                       20  }
```

Listing 3. Coroutines management primitives

Lock-Freedom. When discussing progress guarantees, we assume that the provided park, unpark, and curCor functions are lock-free. In case of park, this means that the current thread parks the current coroutine and schedules another one in a lock-free way.

Taking into account that the channel is a blocking data structure by design (sender waits for a receiver and vice versa), it is possible to guarantee lock-freedom for a part of the algorithm only. Similar to the dual data structures formalism [28], we split every operation into two parts. At first, it atomically checks for an opposite coroutine in the waiting queue and either removes it or adds the current one. Secondly, in case of adding to the waiting queue (or adding to all waiting queues in select statement), it parks the current coroutine and waits for an unpark invocation. Thus, we guarantee lock-freedom for the first part only, which essentially does all the synchronization.

Memory Model and Atomic Primitives. For simplicity of exposition, we assume a sequentially-consistent memory model, although our implementations work under the practical, weaker models. The presented algorithm requires only *compare-and-set* (CAS) primitive in addition to the standard read and write. It is denoted as **CAS**(&p, old, new), and atomically checks that the value located by address p equals to old and changes it to new. It returns false if the check fails and true otherwise.

Memory Reclamation. We assume that run-time environment supports garbage collection, which is true for Kotlin and Go. However, this assumption is mostly for simplicity of exposition. Reclamation techniques like hazard pointers [22] can be used in other environments.

5   Algorithm Description

Overview. Similarly to the rendezvous channel specification, our algorithm maintains a waiting queue, which is loosely based on the Michael-Scott [23] queue design. However, our waiting queue stores several waiters in each node, and supports a more complex channel contracts, including the select expression. This section describes the proposed algorithm iteratively. At first, the basic algorithm for send and receive operations is discussed; after that, we extend the algorithm in order to support the select expression.

5.1   Channel Structure Overview

Essentially, our algorithm implements a fair synchronous queue, which stores several waiting processes in each node, and supports the select expression. The data structure corresponding to the proposed algorithm is shown in Listing 4.

The overall structure of the channel is represented as a Michael-Scott lock-free queue [23], using head and tail pointers to Node instances. However, instead of dynamically creating a new Node for each operation to be waited on, our Node has a fixed-size waiters array of NODE_SIZE structures of Waiter type. The Waiter structure represents either a waiting receiver (if its el field is a special marker element RECEIVE_EL) or a waiting sender (when el field is the element that is being sent which is neither the marker nor null), together with the reference to the corresponding coroutine in the cor field. Initially, all items in the waiters array are filled with null values (both el and cor fields). Every instance of Node has a unique integer id that is equal to zero for the first node. When a new node is added to the next pointer, the invariant is maintained that node.next.id = node.id + 1.

In contrast to the synchronous queue algorithm by Scherer et al. [27], our channel has global enqIdx and deqIdx which indicate the current position to enqueue a new waiter and to dequeue the oldest one correspondingly. These positions are monotonically increasing 64-bit integer counters, their value modulo SEGMENT_SIZE indicate an offset in waiters array, while the remainder modulo SEGMENT_SIZE corresponds to the id of the corresponding Node.

While updating these indices, we maintain the invariant that deqIdx $\leq$ enqIdx, and these indices are equal when the channel is empty. An additional invariant is that the first waiter slot in waiters array of a node is always occupied when this node is added to the queue. To maintain this invariant, the initial values of deqIdx and enqIdx start with one. In practical applications, 64-bit counters are big enough as to never overflow. In effect, with a linked list of Node structures we are modelling an array-based queue of unbounded size, where each node is a *segment* of this array.

Similarly to the LCRQ algorithm [24], and unlike the synchronous queue [27] and Michael-Scott [23] algorithms, both send and receive operations are linearized on the writes of the el field to the corresponding Waiter slot in the node. Lock-freedom is guaranteed in a similar way to LCRQ.

5.2   The **send** and **receive** Operations

Send and receive operations follow almost identical algorithm steps. They both
look for a potential rendezvous with a waiter of the opposite type (send
rendezvous-es with `receive`, and vice versa) or add themselves as a new waiter.
This complex operation has to be performed atomically with respect to other
operations, maintaining the invariant that the queue contains waiters of one
type only (either senders or receivers), or is empty. The only difference between
send and receive is that on rendezvous `send` transfers its element to the waiting
`receive`, while `receive` does the opposite. So, in the following explanation
we consider algorithm for the `send` operation only.

```
1  class Node {                               10  class Channel {
2    val id: Long // initialized on creation  11    var enqIdx: Long = 1 // enqueue index
3    val waiters: Waiter[SEGMENT_SIZE]         12    var deqIdx: Long = 1 // dequeue index
4    var next: Node? = null                    13    var head, tail: Node
5  }                                           14
6  struct Waiter {                             15    Channel() {
7    var cor: Coroutine? = null                16      head = tail = Node{ id: 0 }
8    var el: Any? = null // element            17    }
9  }                                           18  }
```

Listing 4. Data structures for the channel

High-Level Overview. The pseudo-code for `send` operation is presented in
Listing 5. Without interference from other threads, the `send` algorithm proceeds
as follows. First, it reads both `enqIdx` and `deqIdx` (in this order) and checks if
the queue is empty, adding itself to the queue in this case. If the queue contains
waiters, it reads the first element and checks if it has the opposite type (if it is
a `send` operation—the opposite type is `receive`). If a rendezvous is possible,
it removes the first waiter from the queue and makes the rendezvous, resuming
the corresponding coroutine with the specified element, terminating after that.
Otherwise, the queue contains waiters of the same send type and the current
coroutine is added to the queue as a new waiter. The whole `send` operation
is enclosed in an infinite loop to retry when interference from other threads is
detected.

Adding to the Waiting Queue. The algorithm to add to the waiting queue
is presented in function `addToQueue`. The `enqIdx` for this operation has been
already read in the beginning of the algorithm, and references the slot to which
the waiter information is going to be written to. At first, the algorithm reads the
`tail` pointer of the waiting queue, which references the last `Node` in it. There
are two cases here: if a slot is in this last node then `storeWaiter` function is
used, otherwise a new node is created using the `addNewNode` function.

When storing the waiter information to the last node, we increment the
global `enqIdx` first, then write the current coroutine, then write the element.
The storing of the element is the linearization point of the operation.

```
 1  fun send(el: Any) = while (true) {
 2    enqIdx := this.enqIdx;
 3    deqIdx := this.deqIdx
 4    // Are enqIdx and deqidx consistent?
 5    if (enqIdx < deqIdx) continue
 6    // Is the queue empty?
 7    if (deqIdx == enqIdx) {
 8      if (addToQueue(enqIdx, element)) {
 9        park()
10        return
11      } else continue
12    }
13    head := this.head // read head
14    // Is the state consistent?
15    if (deqIdx / SEGMENT_SIZE < head.id)
16      // deqIdx is inconsistent
17      // with head
18      continue
19    if (deqIdx / SEGMENT_SIZE > head.id) {
20      // head is outdated,
21      // move it forward
22      CAS(&this.head, head, head.next)
23      continue
24    }
25    // Read the first element
26    idxInNode := deqIdx % SEGMENT_SIZE
27    firstEl := readEl(head, idxInNode)
28    if (firstEl == BROKEN) {
29      // The slot is broken, skip it
30      CAS(&this.deqIdx, deqIdx, deqIdx + 1)
31      continue
32    }
33    if (firstEl == RECEIVE_EL) {
34      // Try to make a rendezvous
35      if (resumeWaiter(head, deqIdx, elem))
36        return
37    } else {
38      // Try to add to the queue
39      if (addToQueue(enqIdx, element)) {
40        park()
41        return
42      }
43    }
44  }
45
46  fun resumeWaiter(head: Node, i: Int,
47                   el: Any): Bool {
48    if (!CAS(&this.deqIdx, i, i + 1))
49      return false
50    w := head.waiters[i] // read slot
51    head.waiters[i] = null // clear
52    resume(w.cor, el)
53    return true
54  }
```

```
55  fun addToQueue(i: Int, el: Any): Bool {
56    tail := this.tail // read tail
57    // Is the state consistent?
58    if (tail.id > i / SEGMENT_SIZE)
59      return false
60    if (tail.id == i / SEGMENT_SIZE &&
61        i % SEGMENT_SIZE == 0)
62      CAS(&this.enqIdx, i, i + 1)
63    // Either store to the tail
64    // or create a new node
65    if (i % SEGMENT_SIZE != 0)
66      return storeWaiter(tail, enqIdx, el)
67    else
68      return addNewNode(tail, enqIdx, el)
69  }
70
71  fun addNewNode(tail: Node, i: Int,
72                 el: Any): Bool {
73    while (true) {
74      tailNext := tail.next
75      if (tailNext != null) {
76        // Help another thread
77        CAS(&this.tail, tail, tailNext)
78        CAS(&this.enqIdx, i, i + 1)
79        return false
80      }
81      newTail := Node {id: tail.id + 1}
82      newTail.waiters[0].el = el
83      newTail.waiters[0].cor = curCor()
84      if (CAS(&tail.next, null, newTail) {
85        // Others can help us
86        CAS(&this.tail, tail, newTail)
87        CAS(&this.enqIdx, i, i + 1)
88        return true
89      } else continue
90    }
91  }
92
93  fun storeWaiter(tail: Node, i: Int,
94                  el: Any): Bool {
95    if (CAS(&this.enqIdx, i, i + 1))
96      return false
97    tail.waiters[enqIdx].cor = curCor()
98    if (CAS(&tail.waiters[i].el, null, el))
99      return true
100   tail.waiters[i].cor = null
101   return false
102 }
103
104 fun readEl(n: Node, i: Int): Any? {
105   el := n.waiters[i].el
106   if (el != null) return el
107   if (CAS(&n.waiters[i].el, null, BROKEN)
108     return
109   else return n.waiters[i].el
110 }
```

Listing 5. Algorithm for send, without the select expression support

When a new node is created, our algorithm uses the same logic as the Michael-Scott queue: it creates a new node with the current coroutine and element as the first waiter, changes the next field of the current tail, and updates the tail field. The linearization point here is update of the next field, as in Michael-Scott queue. Subsequent updates of the tail only maintain queue consistency, and other concurrent operations can help updating it. In our algorithm, we also maintain the global enqIdx similarly to how the tail pointer is maintained in the Michael-Scott queue. We update the enqIdx after the tail is updated. In case of concurrent execution, other operations can help with this update as well.

Rendezvous. The algorithm for rendezvous is presented as function resumeWaiter. In this case, the first element is already read, and we only need to increment the deqIdx to remove it from the queue. The successful CAS of deqIdx linearizes this operation.

Reading an Element. When a new waiter is added to the queue, enqIdx is incremented, which signals that the queue is non-empty. After that, another thread can try to remove a waiter from this slot in waiters array, while the element was not written there yet. We cannot wait for the writer to write an element in a lock-free algorithm, so if the thread reads the null element, it does a CAS from null to a special BROKEN marker to "poison" this slot (see readEl function). On the other hand, the writer attempts to CAS from null to the element, and aborts the operation on encountering a broken slot. This solution is similar to LCRQ [24]. Two threads can repeatedly interfere with each other, which would render this algorithm obstruction-free if the waiters array were unbounded. However, the waiters array is bounded, and will be ultimately be filled with broken slots, triggering the creation of a new node with the already stored waiter, which proceeds as in the Michael-Scott algorithm and guarantees lock-freedom.

Concurrency. In order to preserve consistency of the data structure, all modifications before linearization points are performed using CAS, restarting on failures. Modifications after linearization points also use CAS, but do not retry on failures, as other threads can detect such inconsistencies and help fix them.

To check that the state is consistent, after reading the enqIdx and deqIdx fields, we check that enqIdx ≥ deqIdx. If this condition does not hold, it means that indices were updated by concurrent operations in between reading of enqIdx and deqIdx. In this case, we retry the operation immediately, to re-read a consistent pair of indices. However, a consistent pair of indices can still point to wrong slots by the time we come to reading or writing them, due to concurrent operations.

We first consider the case when the send operation decides to add itself as a waiter to the queue, invoking addToQueue. This invocation succeeds and returns true only if enqIdx is not updated concurrently. Because enqIdx read is the very first action in the send algorithm, concurrent operations could only have removed elements from the waiting queue, incrementing deqIdx. However, removing elements from the queue does not invalidate the decision to add a new waiter to the queue: a new waiter is added when the queue either contains waiters of the same type, or is empty.

In the case when send decides to make a rendezvous and invokes resumeWaiter, the first action of it is to increment deqIdx using CAS, to ensure it is not updated by concurrent operations. The first resumeWaiter to successfully perform this CAS claims this slot. This successful CAS is a linearization point for send operation in this case.

5.3   The **select** Expression

A high-level algorithm for the select expression is presented in Listing 6 and
proceeds in several phases. Each select instance is internally represented by
SelectOp class, which contains the current coroutine (cor field) and the current state of this select instance (state field). In the first *registration* phase
the select instance is added to all the corresponding channels as a waiter, similarly to the plain send and receive operations. During this phase, it can make
a rendezvous with another waiter, become selected, and jump to the *removing*
phase. If the registration phase completes without rendezvous, then this select
is in the waiting phase until another coroutine makes a rendezvous with it by
performing an opposite operation. After that the *removing* phase starts, during
which all the registered waiters for this select instance are removed from the
corresponding channels to avoid memory leaks.

Registration. In the *registration* phase, the select instance is registered in
each channel sequentially, using regSelect function in Listing 6. It uses a similar algorithm as for the simple send and receive operations, but instead
of adding the current coroutine to the waiting queue, the reference to the
SelectOp object is stored. If it makes a rendezvous with an opposite operation, we should change the state of this SelectOp object from PENDING to
the corresponding channel atomically, via CAS, as shown on Fig. 1. This CAS
can fail if another coroutine has already made a rendezvous with this select,
due to a possibility that this select instance is already stored as a waiter in
other channels. Due to this fact, we also cannot linearize on deqIdx increment:
this increment claims the slot, but the select instance can fail on doing a rendezvous if it is already selected. Therefore, we change the el waiter field life-cycle
(see Fig. 2) and linearize on performing a successful CAS from Element state to
DONE. This change allows updating deqIdx lazily. However, with this change
we have to update two fields atomically: the state of this select instance and
the corresponding el field; this successful update is a linearization point of performed by this select rendezvous. For this, we use descriptors (SelectDesc
state in Fig. 2) similarly to the Harris lock-free multi-word CAS [14]. Like in the
Harris algorithm, concurrent operations that encounter a descriptor in the el
field help to complete the operation it describes.

Rendezvous with select. Simple send and receive operations should
atomically change the select instance state from PENDING to the corresponding channel, what is a linearization point of successful rendezvous with select.

A rendezvous between two select-s is more complicated, it requires updating both their states from PENDING to the corresponding channels, as well as
the update in el field. Like in the registration phase we use descriptors, and
update states to a SelectDesc at the beginning of the possible rendezvous
(see Fig. 1), processing the descriptor after that. It is known by the Harris paper
that we have to always set descriptors in the same order to avoid livelocks. For
this, we introduce an unique id field in SelectOp, and order select instances
using it.

```
1  class SelectOp {
2    val id: Long // unique
3    val cor: Coroutine
4    var state: Any?
5  }
6
7  fun select(alternatives: SelectAlt[]) {
8    s := SelectOp {cor: curCor(); state: REG}
9    // Registration phase
10   regInfos := emptyList<RegInfo>()
11   for (alt in alternatives) {
12     regInfo := alt.regSelect(s, alt.element)
13     if (regInfo == null)
14       // This select is done, the corresponding
15       // channel is stored in the state field,
16       // the result -- in the coroutine.
17       break
18     regInfos.add(regInfo)
19   }
20   // Waiting phase
21   result := suspendAndGetResult() // does not suspend
22                                   // if was selected
23   // Removing phase
24   for (regInfo in regInfos)
25     regInfo.segment.clean(regInfo.index)
26   // Invoke the of the selected alternative
27   alternatives.find{alt -> alt.channel == channel}
28             .action(result)
29 }
30 class RegInfo { val node: Node; val index: Int }
```

Listing 6. High-level algorithm for select

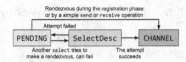

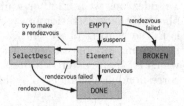

Fig. 1. Life-cycle of the state in select instance (see SelectOp).

Fig. 2. Life-cycle of the el field in waiter slot. Broken slot is represented as a waiter with a special BROKEN token in el field.

The Removing Phase. During the *removing* phase, we clean the corresponding waiter fields and remove a node if it is full of processed waiter cells; the number of cleaned waiters is maintained via an atomic counter, separately for each node. When this counter reaches SEGMENT_SIZE, we consider the node to be cleaned and logically removed from the queue. We physically remove the node from the Michael-Scott queue using remove function presented in Listing 7.

To perform removing in constant time, we add a new prev field into Node, which references the previous node and is initialized to the current tail when it is added to the queue. That helps us to remove nodes from the middle of the queue; however, we forbid removing head and tail. If the node to be removed is head, it is going to be removed after the constant number of increments due to the head moving forward in the Michael-Scott algorithm. At the same time, if the tail is fully cleaned, it is not considered as logically removed; it is going to be removed from the queue right after a new tail node is added.

When remove operations do not interfere, we first get the previous and next nodes, and then change their next (for the previous node) and prev (for the next one) links to each other. Our construction guarantees that neither of these prev and next links are not null when the node is neither head nor tail.

However, remove operations on neighbour nodes can interfere with each other and head or tail updates. In order to ensure correctness, we update prev field to the closest node of lower id that has not yet been cleaned, and the next field to the closest non-cleaned node of larger id. This way, concurrent operations cannot break linked list invariants and effectively help each other to move the prev and next references after logical removal, moving them to the left and to the right respectively (methods movePrevToLeft and moveNextToRight in Listing 7, they update prev and next pointers if the passed node has lower or greater id respectively), to physically remove all cleaned nodes from the list.

```
1  fun remove(n: Node) {                 10     // Link next and prev
2    next := n.next;                      11     prev.moveNextToRight(next)
3    prev := n.prev                       12     next.movePrevToLeft(prev)
4    // check if this segment is not tail 13     // Help other threads
5    if (next == null)                    14     if (prev.cleaned == SEGMENT_SIZE)
6      return                             15       prev.remove()
7    // check if this segment is not head 16     if (next.cleaned == SEGMENT_SIZE)
8    if (prev == null)                    17       next.remove()
9      return                             18  }
```

Listing 7. Removing empty node from the queue

We also need to ensure that these previous and next nodes are not logically removed, so we check this invariant after the re-linking and help with removing these previous and next nodes if needed.

6 Evaluation

We implemented the proposed rendezvous channel algorithm in Kotlin and Go [21]. As a comparison point, we use the optimized implementations provided by the languages; for Kotlin, we also implement and compare against the fair synchronous queue algorithm by Scherer et al. [27].

Go synchronizes channel operations via a coarse lock, and implements a fine-grained locking algorithm for the select expression. In Kotlin, all channel operations are lock-free, and use a concurrent doubly linked list, alongside with a descriptor for each operation, which is stored into the list head field and therefore forces other threads to help with the operation first. This way, all operations on a given channel are executing almost sequentially. The fair synchronous queue presented of Scherer et al. [27] is based on the classic Michael-Scott queue algorithm [23]. It is lock-free, but does not support the select expression.

Benchmarks. Our initial set of experiments consider a single channel to which coroutines apply a series of send and receive operations. To increase the parallelism level, we increase the maximum number of threads for the coroutines scheduler. We use the following three benchmarks to evaluate the performance:

- *Multiple-producer single-consumer:* This scenario simulates a channel associated with an actor, and shows the potential of using the proposed algorithms in actor-like scenarios. We have the same number of coroutines as the number of threads.
- *Multiple-producer multiple-consumer:* This is a standard benchmark for queue-like data structures. We again have the same number of coroutines as the number of threads.
- *Multiple-producer multiple-consumer with a thousand coroutines.* In CSP programming, it is often the case that one has significantly more coroutines than the number of cores ("oversubscription"). We therefore examine this scenario as well.

To benchmark the select expression, we use the same benchmarks, but where all operations inside the select expression receive from an empty coroutine-local channel at the same time. This benchmark simulates checking if the coroutine should be cancelled or not by trying to receive a special token from a specific additional channel. This is a widely used pattern in producer-consumer scenarios [1].

Methodology. To avoid artificial *long run scenarios* [23], we simulate some amount of work between operations. Specifically, we have threads consume 100 CPU cycles in an non-contended local loop, which decreases the contention on the channel. Result trends are similar for higher values of this "backoff" term, but tend to have high variance, induced by contention, for much smaller values. We measure the time it takes to send 10^6 elements over each channel implementation, averaged over 10 runs. This time is then divided by the number of operations, to obtain the results shown. In our algorithm, we have chosen a NODE_SIZE size of 32, based on some minimal tuning.

Platform. We used a server with 4 Intel Xeon Gold 6150 (Skylake) sockets, each socket has 18 2.70 GHz cores, each of which multiplexes 2 hardware threads, for a total of 144 hardware threads.

6.1   Experimental Results

Figure 3 shows the experimental results on different benchmarks. We compare our algorithm with Go (top) and Kotlin coroutines (bottom). In addition, we compare with the fair synchronous queue of Scherer et al. [27], implemented in Kotlin, the results of which are presented on the bottom-side graphs as well. We split the analysis of the results into two parts, considering the performance of plain send and receive operations, and the select expression.

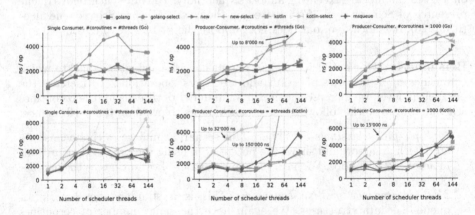

Fig. 3. Performance of the proposed channel algorithm compared against Go and Kotlin rendezvous channels, and the FIFO synchronous queue algorithm by Scherer et al. The results of the select expression are shown on the same plots, but with the suffix *select* in line titles and using dimmed colors.

Send and receive Performance. Our algorithm outperforms the Go implementation in all benchmarks and shows similar performance in the single thread case. A little loss of performance at more than 64 scheduler threads in multi-producer multi-consumer benchmarks is explained by the fact that our algorithm is more complicated to ensure lock-freedom, and therefore suffers in terms of cache performance under high contention.

Kotlin Coroutines implementation of send and receive works similarly in the single-consumer scenario and is outperformed by our algorithm in all other benchmarks, especially at high thread count. This happens because Kotlin uses a considerably more complex doubly-linked list with descriptors under the hood. Our benchmarks do not show the garbage collection overhead, which should also be decreased significantly with our algorithm.

We found that the baseline Kotlin implementation performed particularly badly for large number of coroutines (see Fig. 3, bottom middle). We believe these bad results are due to the recursive helping mechanism employed by this implementation.

Our algorithm for send and receive improves on the fair synchronous queue by Scherer et al., and shows superior results for all benchmarks. One main difference comes from the fact that we are using a node for several items, which decreases the number of allocations and possible cache misses.

The select Expression Performance. Go's implementation uses a lock-based algorithm. In our setup, compared with simple send and receive operations, the 'select' operation needs to acquire an extra lock for another channel without contention. In contrast, our algorithm needs to create a descriptor for each such operation, and perform an additional CAS operations to update the SelectOp.state field. Our algorithm also requires a concurrent version of park/unpark primitives, which also does an additional CAS and degrades the performance. This explains a bit higher cost of our algorithm in low-contended scenarios (≤ 4 threads). However, because of no other difference compared with the plain 'send' and 'receive' operations, our algorithm shows the same performance trend with increasing the number of threads, and outperforms Go's implementation by up to $2\times$.

Our algorithm outperforms the lock-free Kotlin baseline implementation in all scenarios. It does so significantly at large thread counts and shows a bit better results on smaller thread counts. Similarly to the simple send and receive operations analysis, we believe, that so bad Kotlin's implementation behavior on large number of threads is a consequence of a lot of helping.

7   Discussion and Future Work

We have presented the first lock-free implementation of a channel supporting complete CSP semantics. Our design is built on several good ideas introduced in the context of lock-free ordered data structures, and introduces some new techniques to handle CSP semantics, in particular, the select expression and removing from the middle of a queue-like structure as a part of it. Our implementations [21] in Kotlin and Go outperform the existing baselines and show much better scalability, especially for the select expression. We also believe that it is possible to achieve better performance since our implementations are not as good optimized as Go and Kotlin Coroutines ones. In future work, we aim to study further optimizations for our algorithm in the high-contention case, and extend support for additional semantics, such as operation cancellation and channel closing.

References

1. Go Concurrency Patterns: Pipelines and cancellation - The Go Blog (2014). https://blog.golang.org/pipelines
2. Akka (2018). https://akka.io/
3. Erlang Programming Language (2018). http://www.erlang.org/
4. Kotlin Coroutines (2018). https://github.com/Kotlin/kotlin-coroutines
5. Livelock bug in the Kotling Coroutine Implementation (2018). https://github.com/Kotlin/kotlinx.coroutines/issues/504
6. OpenJDK: Loom (2018). http://openjdk.java.net/projects/loom/
7. The Clojure Programming Language (2018). https://clojure.org/
8. The Go Programming Language (2018). https://golang.org/
9. The Rust Programming Language (2018). https://www.rust-lang.org/
10. Abdallah, A.E.: Communicating Sequential Processes. The First 25 Years. Symposium on the Occasion of 25 Years of CSP, London, UK, 7–8 July 2004. Revised Invited Papers, vol. 3525. Springer, Heidelberg (2005). https://doi.org/10.1007/b136154
11. Afek, Y., Korland, G., Natanzon, M., Shavit, N.: Scalable producer-consumer pools based on elimination-diffraction trees. In: D'Ambra, P., Guarracino, M., Talia, D. (eds.) Euro-Par 2010. LNCS, vol. 6272, pp. 151–162. Springer, Heidelberg (2010). https://doi.org/10.1007/978-3-642-15291-7_16
12. Agha, G.A.: Actors: a model of concurrent computation in distributed systems. Technical report, Massachusetts Inst of Tech Cambridge Artificial Intelligence Lab (1985)
13. Hanson, D.R.: C Interfaces and Implementations: Techniques for Creating Reusable Software. Addison-Wesley Longman Publishing Co., Inc., Boston (1996)
14. Harris, T.L., Fraser, K., Pratt, I.A.: A practical multi-word compare-and-swap operation. In: Malkhi, D. (ed.) DISC 2002. LNCS, vol. 2508, pp. 265–279. Springer, Heidelberg (2002). https://doi.org/10.1007/3-540-36108-1_18
15. Hendler, D., Incze, I., Shavit, N., Tzafrir, M.: Flat combining and the synchronization-parallelism tradeoff. In: Proceedings of the Twenty-Second Annual ACM Symposium on Parallelism in Algorithms and Architectures, pp. 355–364. ACM (2010)
16. Hendler, D., Incze, I., Shavit, N., Tzafrir, M.: Scalable flat-combining based synchronous queues. In: Lynch, N.A., Shvartsman, A.A. (eds.) DISC 2010. LNCS, vol. 6343, pp. 79–93. Springer, Heidelberg (2010). https://doi.org/10.1007/978-3-642-15763-9_8
17. Herlihy, M., Shavit, N.: The Art of Multiprocessor Programming. Morgan Kaufmann, San Francisco (2011)
18. Hoare, C.A.R.: Communicating sequential processes. Commun. ACM **21**(8), 666–677 (1978)
19. Izraelevitz, J., Scott, M.L.: Generality and speed in nonblocking dual containers. ACM Trans. Parallel Comput. **3**(4), 22:1–22:37 (2017). https://doi.org/10.1145/3040220. http://doi.acm.org/10.1145/3040220
20. Kahn, G., MacQueen, D.: Coroutines and networks of parallel processes (1976)
21. Koval, N., Alistarh, D., Elizarov, R.: Channel implementations in go and kotlin. https://doi.org/10.6084/m9.figshare.8586311
22. Michael, M.M.: Hazard pointers: safe memory reclamation for lock-free objects. IEEE Trans. Parallel Distrib. Syst. **6**, 491–504 (2004)

23. Michael, M.M., Scott, M.L.: Simple, fast, and practical non-blocking and blocking concurrent queue algorithms. In: Proceedings of the Fifteenth Annual ACM Symposium on Principles of Distributed Computing, pp. 267–275. ACM (1996)
24. Morrison, A., Afek, Y.: Fast concurrent queues for x86 processors. In: ACM SIGPLAN Notices, vol. 48, pp. 103–112. ACM (2013)
25. Odersky, M., et al.: The scala language specification (2007)
26. Scherer III, W.N., Lea, D., Scott, M.L.: A scalable elimination-based exchange channel. In: SCOOL 2005, p. 83 (2005)
27. Scherer III, W.N., Lea, D., Scott, M.L.: Scalable synchronous queues. In: Proceedings of the Eleventh ACM SIGPLAN Symposium on Principles and Practice of Parallel Programming, pp. 147–156. ACM (2006)
28. Scherer III, W., Scott, M.: Nonblocking concurrent objects with condition synchronization. In: Proceedings of the 18th International Symposium on Distributed Computing (2004)
29. Shavit, N., Touitou, D.: Elimination trees and the construction of pools and stacks: preliminary version. In: Proceedings of the Seventh Annual ACM Symposium on Parallel Algorithms and Architectures, pp. 54–63. ACM (1995)
30. Shavit, N., Zemach, A.: Combining funnels: a dynamic approach to software combining. J. Parallel Distrib. Comput. **60**(11), 1355–1387 (2000)
31. Sundell, H., Tsigas, P.: Lock-free and practical doubly linked list-based deques using single-word compare-and-swap. In: Higashino, T. (ed.) OPODIS 2004. LNCS, vol. 3544, pp. 240–255. Springer, Heidelberg (2005). https://doi.org/10.1007/11516798_18

TWA – Ticket Locks Augmented with a Waiting Array

Dave Dice$^{(\boxtimes)}$ (iD) and Alex Kogan (iD)

Oracle Labs, Burlington, MA, USA
{dave.dice,alex.kogan}@oracle.com

Abstract. The classic *ticket lock* is simple and compact, consisting of `ticket` and `grant` fields. Arriving threads atomically fetch-and-increment `ticket` to obtain an assigned ticket value, and then wait for `grant` to become equal to that value, at which point the thread holds the lock. The corresponding unlock operation simply increments `grant`. This simple design has short code paths and fast handover (transfer of ownership) under light contention, but may suffer degraded scalability under high contention when multiple threads busy wait on the `grant` field – so-called *global spinning*.

We propose a variation on ticket locks where long-term waiting threads – those with an assigned `ticket` value far larger than `grant` – wait on locations in a *waiting array* instead of busy waiting on the `grant` field. The single waiting array is shared among all locks. Short-term waiting is accomplished in the usual manner on the `grant` field. The resulting algorithm, <u>TWA</u>, improves on ticket locks by limiting the number of threads spinning on the `grant` field at any given time, reducing the number of remote caches requiring invalidation from the store that releases the lock. In turn, this accelerates handover, and since the lock is held throughout the handover operation, scalability improves. Under light or no contention, TWA yields performance comparable to the classic ticket lock. Under high contention, TWA is substantially more scalable than the classic ticket lock, and provides performance on par or beyond that of scalable queue-based locks such as MCS by avoiding the complexity and additional accesses incurred by the MCS handover operation while also obviating the need for maintaining queue elements.

We provide an empirical evaluation, comparing TWA against ticket locks and MCS for various user-space applications, and within the Linux kernel.

Keywords: Locks · Mutexes · Mutual exclusion · Synchronization · Concurrency control

1 Introduction

The classic ticket lock [16,17] is compact and has a very simple design. The acquisition path requires only one atomic operation – a fetch-and-add to increment the ticket – and the unlock path requires no atomics. Under light or no

© Springer Nature Switzerland AG 2019
R. Yahyapour (Ed.): Euro-Par 2019, LNCS 11725, pp. 334–345, 2019.
https://doi.org/10.1007/978-3-030-29400-7_24

contention, the handover latency, defined as the time between the call to unlock and the time a successor is enabled to enter the critical section, is low. Handover time impacts the scalability as the lock is held throughout handover, increasing the effective length of the critical section [11]. A ticket lock is in *unlocked* state when `ticket` and `grant` are equal. Otherwise the lock is held, and the number of waiters is given by `ticket - grant - 1`. Ignoring numeric rollover, `grant` always lags or is equal to `ticket`. The increment operation in unlock either passes ownership to the immediate successor, if any, and otherwise sets the state to unlocked.

Ticket locks suffer, however, from a key scalability impediment. All threads waiting for a particular lock will busy wait on that lock's `grant` field. An unlock operation, when it increments `grant`, invalidates the cache line underlying `grant` for all remote caches where waiting threads are scheduled. In turn, this negatively impacts scalability by retarding the handover step. Ticket locks use global spinning, as all waiting threads monitor the central lock-specific `grant` variable.

In Fig. 1 we show the impact of readers on a single writer. We refer to the number of participating caches as the *invalidation diameter* [8]. The `Invalidation Diameter` benchmark spawns T concurrent threads, with T shown on the X-axis. A single writer thread loops, using an atomic fetch-and-add primitive to update a shared location. The other $T - 1$ threads are readers. They loop, fetching the value of that location. The shared variable is sequestered to avoid false sharing and

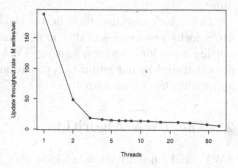

Fig. 1. Invalidation diameter

is the sole occupant of its underlying cache sector. We present the throughput rate of the writer on the Y-axis. As we increase the number of concurrent readers, the writer's progress is slowed. This scenario models the situation in ticket locks where multiple waiting threads monitor the `grant` field, which is updated by the current owner during handover. The benchmark reports the writer's throughput at the end of a 10 s measurement interval. The data exhibited high variance due to the NUMA placement vagaries of the threads and the home node of the variable. As such, for each data point show, we took the median of 100 individual runs, reflecting a realistic set of samples. The system-under-test is described in detail in Sect. 4.

The *MCS lock* [16] is the usual alternative to ticket locks, performing better under high contention, but also having a more complex path and often lagging behind ticket locks under no or light contention. In MCS, arriving threads use an atomic operation to append an element to a queue of waiting threads, and then busy wait on a field in that element. The lock's tail variable is explicit and the head – the current owner – is implicit. When the owner releases the lock it reclaims the element it originally enqueued and sets the flag in the next element, passing ownership. Specifically, to convey ownership, the MCS unlock operator must identify the successor, if any, and then store to the location where the successor busy waits. The handover path is longer than that of ticket locks and accesses more distinct shared locations. MCS uses so-called local waiting where at most one thread is waiting on a given location at any one time. As such, an unlock operation will normally need to invalidate just one location – the flag where the successor busy waits. Under contention, the unlock operator must fetch the address of the successor node from its own element, and then store into the flag in the successor's element, accessing two distinct cache lines, and incurring a dependent access to reach the successor. In the case of no contention, the unlock operator must use an atomic compare-and-swap operator to detach the owner's element.

Ticket locks and TWA require no such indirection or dependent accesses in the unlock path and also avoid the need for queue elements and the management thereof. The queue of waiting threads is implicit in ticket locks and TWA, and explicit in MCS. MCS, ticket locks and TWA all provide strict FIFO admission order.

Ticket locks are usually a better choice under light or no contention, while MCS locks are more suitable under heavy contention [2,3]. By employing a waiting array for long-term waiting, TWA achieves the best of the two worlds, as demonstrated by our empirical evaluation with multiple user-space applications and within the Linux kernel.

2   The TWA Algorithm

TWA builds directly on ticket locks. We add a new *waiting array* for long-term waiting. The array is shared amongst all threads and TWA locks in an address space. Arriving threads use an atomic fetch-and-increment instruction to advance the `ticket` value, yielding the lock request's assigned ticket value, and then fetch `grant`. If the difference is 0 then we have uncontended acquisition and the thread may enter the critical section immediately. (This case is sometimes referred to as the lock acquisition *fast-path*). Otherwise TWA compares the difference to the `LongTermThreshold` parameter. If the difference exceeds `LongTermThreshold` then the thread enters the long-term waiting phase. Otherwise control proceeds to the short-term waiting phase, which is identical to that of normal ticket locks; the waiting thread simply waits for `grant` to become equal to the ticket value assigned to the thread. While `LongTermThreshold` is a tunable parameter in our implementation, we found a value of 1 to be suitable for all environments, ensuring that only the immediate successor waits in short-term mode. All data reported below uses a value of 1.

A thread entering the long-term waiting phase first hashes its assigned ticket value to form an index into the waiting array. Using this index, it then fetches the value from the array and then recheck the value of `grant`. If the observed `grant` value changed, it rechecks the difference between that new value and its assigned ticket value, and decides once again on short-term versus long-term waiting. If `grant` was unchanged, the thread then busy waits for the waiting array value to change, at which point it reevaluates grant. When grant is found to be sufficiently near the assigned ticket value, the thread reverts to normal short-term waiting. The values found in the waiting array have no particular meaning, except to conservatively indicate that a grant value that maps to that index has changed, and rechecking of grant is required for waiters on that index.

The TWA unlock operator increments grant as usual from U to $U + 1$ and then uses an atomic operator to increment the location in the waiting array that corresponds to threads waiting on ticket value $U + 1 + LongTermThreshold$, notifying long-term threads, if any, that they should recheck grant. An atomic operation is necessary as the location may be subject to hash collisions. We observe that this change increases the path length in the unlock operator, but crucially the store that effects handover, which is accomplished by a non-atomic increment of grant, happens first. Given a LongTermThreshold value of 1, we expect at most one thread, the immediate successor, to be waiting on grant. Updating the waiting array occurs *after* handover and outside the critical section.

All our experiments use a waiting array with 4096 elements, although ideally, we believe the waiting array should be sized as a function of the number of CPUs in the system. Hash collisions in the table are benign, at worst causing unnecessary rechecking of the grant field. Our hash function is cache-aware and intentionally designed to map adjacent ticket values to different 128-byte cache sectors underlying the waiting array, to reduce false sharing among long-term waiters. We multiply the ticket value by 127, EXCLUSIVE-OR that result with the address of the lock, and then mask with $4096 - 1$ to form an index into the waiting array. We selected a small prime $P = 127$ to provide the equidistribution properties of a *Weyl sequence* [15]. We include the lock address into our deterministic hash to avoid the situation where two locks might operate in an entrained fashion, with ticket and grant values moving in near unison, and thus suffer from excessive inter-lock collisions. A given lock address and ticket value pair always hashes to the same index.

TWA leaves the structure of the ticket lock unchanged, allowing for easy adoption. As the instance size remains the same, the only additional space cost for TWA is the waiting array, which is shared over all locks, reflecting a one-time space cost.

The TWA fast-path for acquisition remains unchanged relative to ticket locks. The unlock path adds an increment of the waiting array, to notify long-term waiters, if any. that they should transition from long-term to short-term waiting. We note that TWA doesn't reduce overall coherence traffic, but does act to reduce coherence traffic in the critical handover path, constraining the invalidation diameter of the store in unlock that accomplishes handover. TWA thus captures the desirable performance aspects of both MCS locks and ticket locks.

Listing 1.1 depicts a pseudo-code implementation of the TWA algorithm. Lines 7 through 16 reflect the classic ticket lock algorithm and lines 20 through 71 show TWA. TWA extends the existing ticket lock algorithm by adding lines 41 through 57 for long-term waiting, and line 71 to notify long-term waiters to shift to classic short-term waiting.

Listing 1.1: Simplified Python-like Implementation of TWA

```
1   ## Classic Ticket Lock
2
3   class TicketLock :
4     int Ticket = 0        ## Next ticket to be assigned
5     int Grant  = 0        ## "Now Serving"
6
7   TicketAcquire (TicketLock * L) :
8     ## Atomic fetch-and-add on L.Ticket
9     auto tx = FetchAdd (L.Ticket, 1)
10    while tx != L.Grant :
11      Pause()
12
13  TicketRelease (TicketLock * L) :
14    ## succession via direct handoff ...
15    ## Increment does not require atomic instructions
16    L.Grant += 1
17
18  ## ======================================================
19
20  ## TWA : Ticket lock augmented with waiting array
21
22  ## tunable parameters
23  ## short-term vs long-term proximity threshold
24  LongTermThreshold = 1                              |
25  ArraySize         = 4096                           |
26
27  ## Global variables :
28  ## Long-term waiting array, initially all 0
29  ## Shared by all locks and threads in the address space
30
31
32  uint64_t WaitArray [ArraySize]                     |
33
34  TWAAcquire (TWA * L) :
35    auto tx = FetchAdd (L.Ticket, 1)
36    auto dx = tx - L.Grant
37    if dx == 0 :
38      ## fast-path return - uncontended case
39      return
40
41    ## slow path with contention -- need to wait       /
42    ## Select long-term vs short-term based on the number /
43    ## of threads waiting in front of us               /
44    if dx > LongTermThreshold :                        |
45      ## long-term waiting via WaitArray               /
46      auto at = Hash(L, tx)                            |
47      for                                              |
48        auto u = WaitArray[at]                         |
49        dx = tx - L.Grant                              |
50        assert dx >= 0                                 |
51        if dx <= LongTermThreshold : break             |
52        while WaitArray[at] == u :                      |
53          Pause()                                      |
54      ## This waiting thread is now "near" the front of /
55      ## the logical queue of waiting threads           /
56      ## Transition from long-term waiting to           /
57      ## short-term waiting                             /
58
59    ## classic short-term waiting on L.Grant field
60    while L.Grant != tx :
61      Pause()
62
63  TWARelease (TWA * L) :
64    ## Notify immediate successor, if any
65    ## such threads will be in short-term waiting phase
66    ## non-atomic increment
67    auto k = ++ L.Grant
68
69    ## Notify long-term waiters                        /
70    ## atomic increment required                       /
71    FetchAdd (WaitArray[Hash(L,k + LongTermThreshold)], 1)|
```

2.1 Example Scenario – TWA in Action

① Initially the lock is in *unlocked* state with `Ticket` and `Grant` both 0.

② Thread *T1* arrives at Listing 1.1 line 34 attempting to acquire the lock. *T1* increments `Ticket` from 0 to 1, and the atomic `FetchAdd` operator returns the original value of 0 into the local variable `tx`, which holds the assigned ticket value for the locking request. At line 36 *T1* then fetches `Grant` observing a value of 0. Since `tx` equals that fetched value, we have uncontended lock acquisition. *T1* now holds the lock and can enter the critical section immediately, without waiting, via the fast path at line 39.

③ Thread *T2* now arrives and tries to acquire the lock. The `FetchAdd` operator advances `Ticket` from 1 to 2 and returns 1, the assigned ticket, into `tx` at line 35. *T2* fetches `Grant` and notes that `tx` differs from that value by 1. The `dx` variable holds that computed difference, which reflects the number of threads between the requester and the head of the logical queue, which is the owner. *T2* has encountered contention and must wait. The difference is only 1, and *T2* will be the immediate successor, so *T2* proceeds to line 60 for short-term waiting similar to that used in classic ticket locks shown at line 10. *T2* waits for the `Grant` field to become 1.

④ Thread *T3* arrives and advances `Ticket` from 2 to 3, with the `FetchAdd` operator returning 2 as the assigned ticket. The difference between that value (2) and the value of `Grant`(0) fetched at line 64 exceeds the `LongTermThreshold` (1), so *T3* enters the path for long-term waiting at line 49. *T3* hashes its observed ticket value of 2 into an index `at`, say 100, in the long-term waiting array and then fetches from `WaitArray[at]` observing *U*. To recover from potential races with threads in the unlock path, *T3* rechecks that the `Grant` variable remains unchanged (0) at line 49 and that the thread should continue with long-term waiting. Thread *T3* busy waits at lines 52–53 on the `WaitArray` value.

⑤ Thread *T4* arrives, advances `Ticket` from 3 to 4, obtaining a value in its `tx` variable of 3. Similar to *T3*, *T4* enters the long-term. *T4* hashes its assigned ticket value of 3 yielding an index of, say, 207, and fetches `WaitArray[207]` observing *V*. *T4* then busy waits, waiting for `WaitArray[207]` to change from *V* to any other value.

⑥ Thread *T1* now releases the lock, calling `TWARelease` at line 63. *T1* increments `Grant` from 0 to 1 at line 67, passing ownership to *T2* and sets local variable `k` to the new value (1).

⑦ Thread *T2* waiting at lines 60–61 notices that `Grant` changed to match its `tx` value. *T2* is now the owner and may enter the critical section.

⑧ Thread *T1*, still in `TWARelease` at line 71 then hashes $k + LongTermThreshold$ (the sum is 2) to yield index 100 and then increments `WaitArray[100]` from *U* to $U + 1$.

⑨ Thread *T3* waiting at lines 52–53 observes that change, rechecks `Grant`, sees that it is close to being granted ownership, exits the long-term waiting loop and switches to classic short-term waiting at lines 60–61. *T1* has promoted *T3* from long-term to short-term waiting in anticipation of the next unlock operation, to eventually be performed by *T2*.

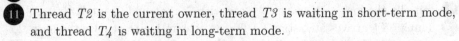

Thread *T1* now exits the `TWARelease` operator.

Thread *T2* is the current owner, thread *T3* is waiting in short-term mode, and thread *T4* is waiting in long-term mode.

3 Related Work

Mellor-Crummey and Scott [16] proposed ticket locks with *proportional backoff*. Waiting threads compare the value of their ticket against the `grant` field. The difference reflects the number of intervening threads waiting. That value is then multiplied by some tunable constant, and the thread delays for that period before rechecking `grant`. The constant is platform- and load-dependent, and requires tuning. While this approach may decrease the futile polling rate on `grant`, it does not decrease the invalidation diameter. TWA and ticket locks with proportional backoff both make a distinction among waiting threads based on their relative position in the queue.

Partitioned Ticket Locks [9] augment each ticket lock with a constant-length private array of `grant` fields, allowing for *semi-local waiting*. Critically, the array is not shared between locks, and to avoid false sharing within the array, the memory footprint of each lock instance is significantly increased. Anderson's array-based queueing lock [1] is also based on ticket locks. It employs a waiting array for each lock instance, sized to ensure there is at least one array element for each potentially waiting thread, yielding a potentially large footprint. The maximum number of participating threads must be known in advance when initializing the array. Such dynamic sizing also makes static allocation of Anderson's locks more difficult than would be the case for a lock with a fixed size, such as TWA.

Various authors [2,12] have suggested switching adaptively between MCS and ticket locks depending on the contention level. While workable, this adds considerable algorithmic complexity, particularly for the changeover phase, and requires tuning. Lim [13] suggested a more general framework for switching locks at runtime.

4 Empirical Evaluation

Unless otherwise noted, all data was collected on an Oracle X5-2 system. The system has 2 sockets, each populated with an Intel Xeon E5-2699 v3 CPU running at 2.30 GHz. Each socket has 18 cores, and each core is 2-way hyperthreaded, yielding 72 logical CPUs in total. The system was running Ubuntu 18.04 with a stock Linux version 4.15 kernel, and all software was compiled using the provided GCC version 7.3 toolchain at optimization level "-O3". 64-bit C or C++ code was used for all experiments. Factory-provided system defaults were used in all cases, and Turbo mode [18] was left enabled. In all cases default free-range unbound threads were used. TWA is trivial to implement in C++ with `std::atomic<>` primitives.

We implemented all user-mode locks within LD_PRELOAD interposition libraries that expose the standard POSIX `pthread_mutex_t` programming interface. The framework was made available by Dice et al. [10]. This allows us to change lock implementations by varying the LD_PRELOAD environment variable and without modifying the application code that uses locks. The C++ `std::mutex` construct maps directly to `pthread_mutex` primitives, so interposition works for both C and C++ code. All busy-wait loops used the Intel `PAUSE` instruction for polite waiting.

We use a 128 byte sector size on Intel processors for alignment to avoid false sharing. The unit of coherence is 64 bytes throughout the cache hierarchy, but 128 bytes is required because of the adjacent cache line prefetch facility where pairs of lines are automatically fetched together.

4.1 MutexBench

The MutexBench benchmark spawns T concurrent threads. Each thread loops as follows: acquire a central lock L; execute a critical section; release L; execute a non-critical section. At the end of a 10 s measurement interval the benchmark reports the total number of aggregate iterations completed by all the threads. We show the median of 5 independent runs in Fig. 2. The critical section advances a C++ `std::mt19937` pseudo-random generator (PRNG) 4 steps. The non-critical section uses that same PRNG to compute a value distributed uniformly in $[0, 200)$ and then advances the PRNG that many steps. To facilitate comparison of the algorithms, the X-axis is logarithmic and the Y-axis is offset to the minimum score.

As seen in the figure, ticket locks performs the best up to 6 threads, with TWA lagging slightly behind. As we further increase the thread count, however, ticket locks fail to scale. MCS provides stable asymptotic performance that surpasses ticket locks at 24 threads. TWA manages to always outperform MCS, freeing the developer from making a choice between MCS locks and ticket locks.

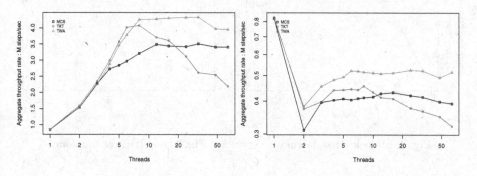

Fig. 2. MutexBench   **Fig. 3.** throw

4.2   throw

The "throw" benchmark launches T threads, each of which loop, executing the following line of C++ code:

$$\texttt{try \{ throw 20 ;\} catch (int e) \{\}.}$$

Naively, this construct would be expected to scale linearly, but the C++ run-time implementation acquires mutexes that protect the list of dynamically loaded modules and their exception tables. The problem is long-standing and has proven difficult to fix given the concern that some applications might have come to depend on the serialization[1]. At the end of a 10 s measurement interval the benchmark reports the aggregate number of loops executed by all threads. Throw-catch operations are performed back-to-back with no intervening delay. In Fig. 3 we observe that performance drops significantly between 1 and 2 threads. There is little or no benefit from multiple threads, given that execution is largely serialized, but coherent communication costs are incurred. As we increase beyond two threads performance improves slightly, but never exceeds that observed at one thread. Beyond 2 threads, the shape of the graph recapitulates that seen in MutexBench.

4.3   libslock stress_latency

Figure 4 shows the performance of the "stress latency" benchmark from [7][2]. The benchmark spawns the specified number of threads, which all run concurrently during a 10 s measurement interval. Each thread iterates as follows: acquire a central lock; execute 200 loops of a delay loop; release the lock; execute 5000 iterations of the same delay loop. The benchmark reports the total number of iterations of the outer loop.

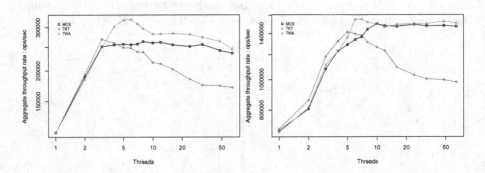

Fig. 4. libslock stress_latency   **Fig. 5.** LevelDB readrandom

---

[1] https://patchwork.ozlabs.org/patch/652301/.

[2] We use the following command line: ./stress_latency -l 1 -d 10000 -a 200 -n *threads* -w 1 -c 1 -p 5000.

4.4   LevelDB readrandom

In Fig. 5 we used the "readrandom" benchmark in LevelDB version 1.20 database[3] varying the number of threads and reporting throughput from the median of 5 runs of 50 s each. Each thread loops, generating random keys and then trying to read the associated value from the database. We first populated a database[4] and then collected data[5]. We made a slight modification to the db_bench benchmarking harness to allow runs with a fixed duration that reported aggregate throughput. Ticket locks exhibit a very slight advantage over MCS and TWA at low threads count after which ticket locks fade and TWA matches or exceeds the performance of MCS. LevelDB uses coarse-grained locking, protecting the database with a single central mutex: DBImpl::Mutex. Profiling indicates contention on that lock via leveldb::DBImpl::Get().

4.5   RocksDB readwhilewriting

We next present results in Fig. 6 from the RocksDB[6] version 5.14.2 database running the "readwhitewriting" benchmark which has one fixed writer thread and a variable number of readers. The benchmark is similar to the form found in LevelDB, above, but the underlying database allows more concurrency and avoids the use of a single central lock. We intentionally use a command-line configured to stress the locks that protect the sharded LRU cache, causing contention in LRUShard::lookup()[7].

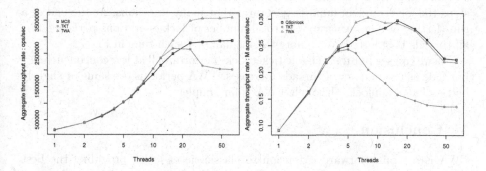

Fig. 6. RocksDB readwhilewriting   **Fig. 7.** LockTorture

---

[3] leveldb.org.
[4] db_bench —threads=1 —benchmarks=fillseq —db=/tmp/db/.
[5] db_bench —threads=*threads* —benchmarks=readrandom
    —use_existing_db=1 —db=/tmp/db/ —duration=50.
[6] rocksdb.org.
[7] db_bench —duration=200 —threads=*threads*
    —benchmarks=readwhilewriting —compression_type=none
    —mmap_read=1 —mmap_write=1 —cache_size=100000
    —cache_numshardbits=0 —sync=0 —verify_checksum=0.

4.6 Linux Kernel `locktorture`

We ported TWA into the Linux kernel environment and evaluated its performance with the `locktorture` benchmark[8]. `Locktorture` is distributed as a part
of the Linux kernel and is implemented as a loadable kernel module. The benchmark spawns a specified number of threads, each of which loops, contending for
a central lock. We used locktorture to compare TWA, classic ticket locks, and
the default kernel qspinlock.

The Linux *qspinlock* construct [4,5,14] is a compact 32-bit lock, even on
64-bit architectures. The low-order bits of the lock word constititue a simple
test-and-set lock while the upper bits encode the tail of an MCS chain. In order
to fit into a 32-bit work – a critical requirement – the chain is formed by logical
CPU identifiers instead of traditional MCS queue node pointers. The result is a
hybrid of MCS and test-and-set[9]. We note that qspinlocks replaced classic ticket
locks as the kernel's primary low-level spin lock mechanism in 2014, and ticket
locks replaced test-and-set locks, which are unfair and allow unbounded bypass,
in 2008 [6].

The average critical section duration used by `locktorture` is a function
of the number of concurrent threads. In order to use the benchmark to measure and report scalability, we augmented it to parameterize the critical and
non-critical section durations, which are expressed as steps of the thread-local
pseudo-random number generator provided in the `locktorture` infrastructure.
We used 20 steps for the critical section. Each execution of the non-critical
section computes a uniformly random distributed number in $[0 - 400)$ and then
steps the local random number generator that many iterations. At the end of a
run (lasting 30 s in our case), the total number of lock operations performed by
all threads is reported. We report the median of 7 such runs in Fig. 7.

As we can see in Fig. 7, classic ticket locks perform well at low conconcurrency
but fade as the number of threads increases. TWA performs the same or slightly
better than qspinlock, although TWA is far simpler[10].

5 Conclusion

TWA is a straightforward extension to classic ticket locks, providing the best
performance properties of ticket locks and MCS locks. Like ticket locks, it is
simple, compact, and has a fixed memory footprint. The key benefit conferred
by TWA arises from improved transfer of ownership (handover) in the unlock
path, by reducing the number of threads spinning on the **grant** field at any given
time. Even though TWA increases the overall path length in the unlock operation,
adding an atomic fetch-and-increment operation compared to the classic ticket
lock, it decreases the effective critical path duration for contended handover.

---

[8] https://www.kernel.org/doc/Documentation/locking/locktorture.txt.

[9] https://github.com/torvalds/linux/blob/master/kernel/locking/qspinlock.c.

[10] An extended version of this paper is available at https://arxiv.org/abs/1810.01573,
   where we apply various complexity measures to compare ticket locks, qspinlock, and
   TWA.

References

1. Anderson, T.E.: The performance of spin lock alternatives for shared-money multiprocessors. IEEE Trans. Parallel Distrib. Syst. (1990). https://doi.org/10.1109/71.80120
2. Antić, J., Chatzopoulos, G., Guerraoui, R., Trigonakis, V.: Locking made easy. In: Proceedings of the 17th International Middleware Conference, Middleware 2016. ACM (2016). http://doi.acm.org/10.1145/2988336.2988357
3. Boyd-Wickizer, S., Kaashoek, M.F., Morris, R., Zeldovich, N.: Non-scalable locks are dangerous. In: Ottawa Linux Symposium (OLS) (2012). https://www.kernel.org/doc/ols/2012/ols2012-zeldovich.pdf
4. Corbet, J.: Cramming more into struct page, 28 August 2013. https://lwn.net/Articles/565097. Accessed 01 Oct 2018
5. Corbet, J.: MCS locks and qspinlocks, 11 March 2014. https://lwn.net/Articles/590243. Accessed 12 Sept 2018
6. Corbet, J.: Ticket spinlocks, 6 February 2008. https://lwn.net/Articles/267968. Accessed 12 Sept 2018
7. David, T., Guerraoui, R., Trigonakis, V.: Everything you always wanted to know about synchronization but were afraid to ask. In: SOSP (2013). http://doi.acm.org/10.1145/2517349.2522714
8. Dice, D.: Malthusian locks. In: Proceedings of the Twelfth European Conference on Computer Systems, EuroSys 2017 (2017). http://doi.acm.org/10.1145/3064176.3064203
9. Dice, D.: Brief announcement: a partitioned ticket lock. In: Proceedings of the Twenty-third Annual ACM Symposium on Parallelism in Algorithms and Architectures, SPAA 2011 (2011). http://doi.acm.org/10.1145/1989493.1989543
10. Dice, D., Marathe, V.J., Shavit, N.: Lock cohorting: a general technique for designing NUMA locks. ACM Trans. Parallel Comput. (2015). http://doi.acm.org/10.1145/2686884
11. Eyerman, S., Eeckhout, L.: Modeling critical sections in Amdahl's law and its implications for multicore design. In: ISCA. ACM (2010). http://doi.acm.org/10.1145/1815961.1816011
12. Ha, P.H., Papatriantafilou, M., Tsigas, P.: Reactive spin-locks: a self-tuning approach. In: 8th International Symposium on Parallel Architectures, Algorithms and Networks, ISPAN 2005 (2005). https://doi.org/10.1109/ISPAN.2005.73
13. Lim, B.H., Agarwal, A.: Reactive synchronization algorithms for multiprocessors. In: Proceedings of the Sixth International Conference on Architectural Support for Programming Languages and Operating Systems, ASPLOS VI. ACM (1994). http://doi.acm.org/10.1145/195473.195490
14. Long, W.: qspinlock: introducing a 4-byte queue spinlock implementation, 31 July 2013. https://lwn.net/Articles/561775. Accessed 19 Sept 2018
15. Marsaglia, G.: Xorshift RNGs. J. Stat. Softw. (2003). https://doi.org/10.18637/jss.v008.i14. https://www.jstatsoft.org/v008/i14
16. Mellor-Crummey, J.M., Scott, M.L.: Algorithms for scalable synchronization on shared-memory multiprocessors. ACM Trans. Comput. Syst. (1991). http://doi.acm.org/10.1145/103727.103729
17. Reed, D.P., Kanodia, R.K.: Synchronization with eventcounts and sequencers. Commun. ACM (1979). http://doi.acm.org/10.1145/359060.359076
18. Verner, U., Mendelson, A., Schuster, A.: Extending Amdahl's law for multicores with turbo boost. IEEE Comput. Arch. Lett. (2017). https://doi.org/10.1109/LCA.2015.2512982

Enabling Resilience in Asynchronous Many-Task Programming Models

Sri Raj Paul[1]([⊠]), Akihiro Hayashi[2],
Nicole Slattengren[3], Hemanth Kolla[3],
Matthew Whitlock[3], Seonmyeong Bak[1],
Keita Teranishi[3], Jackson Mayo[3],
and Vivek Sarkar[1]

[1] Georgia Institute of Technology, Atlanta, GA, USA
{sriraj,sbak5,vsarkar}@gatech.edu
[2] Rice University, Houston, TX, USA
ahayashi@rice.edu
[3] Sandia National Laboratories, Livermore, CA, USA
{nlslatt,hnkolla,mwhitlo,knteran,jmayo}@sandia.gov

Abstract. Resilience is an imminent issue for next-generation platforms due to projected increases in soft/transient failures as part of the inherent trade-offs among performance, energy, and costs in system design. In this paper, we introduce a comprehensive approach to enabling application-level resilience in Asynchronous Many-Task (AMT) programming models with a focus on remedying Silent Data Corruption (SDC) that can often go undetected by the hardware and OS. Our approach makes it possible for the application programmer to declaratively express resilience attributes with minimal code changes, and to delegate the complexity of efficiently supporting resilience to our runtime system. We have created a prototype implementation of our approach as an extension to the Habanero C/C++ library (HClib), where different resilience techniques including task replay, task replication, algorithm-based fault tolerance (ABFT), and checkpointing are available. Our experimental results show that task replay incurs lower overhead than task replication when an appropriate error checking function is provided. Further, task replay matches the low overhead of ABFT. Our results also demonstrate the ability to combine different resilience schemes. To evaluate the effectiveness of our resilience mechanisms in the presence of errors, we injected synthetic errors at different error rates (1.0%, and 10.0%) and found modest increase in execution times. In summary, the results show that our approach supports efficient and scalable recovery, and that our

Sandia National Laboratories is a multimission laboratory managed and operated by National Technology & Engineering Solutions of Sandia, LLC, a wholly owned subsidiary of Honeywell International Inc., for the U.S. Department of Energy's National Nuclear Security Administration (NNSA) under contract DE-NA0003525. This work was funded by NNSA's Advanced Simulation and Computing (ASC) Program. This paper describes objective technical results and analysis. Any subjective views or opinions that might be expressed in the paper do not necessarily represent the views of the U.S. Department of Energy or the United States Government.

© Springer Nature Switzerland AG 2019
R. Yahyapour (Ed.): Euro-Par 2019, LNCS 11725, pp. 346–360, 2019.
https://doi.org/10.1007/978-3-030-29400-7_25

approach can be used to influence the design of future AMT programming models and runtime systems that aim to integrate first-class support for user-level resilience.

Keywords: Resilience · AMT runtimes · Habanero C/C++

1 Introduction

High performance computing plays a critical role in the advancement of science and engineering through simulations of large complex systems. Due to the insatiable demand for increased computing capability, multiple nations have committed to the development of exascale supercomputers. One of the major new challenges in exascale computing is the projected increases in silent data corruptions (SDC) [7], which are unexpected alterations in computation or data that can occur undetected. In such cases, application and software level mechanisms can play an essential role in improving application resilience.

The most popular resilience technique for application users today is coordinated checkpoint and restart (C/R) typically with bulk-synchronous parallel programming models [21], which involves global coordination of processing elements (PEs) for identifying a consistent global application state. However, this global recovery model is better suited for hard failures, and suffers from excessive performance overheads when global recovery is triggered for transient local failures. However, a majority of application failures are attributed to local node/process failure as reported by [21], with the recognition that recovery can potentially be applied only to the corrupted processes and data without requiring global coordination. Another example of local recovery is Containment Domains (CDs) [8], which provide an abstraction of error detection and correction to a local boundary intended for efficient and transparent recovery of HPC applications.

Asynchronous many-task (AMT) programming models [2–5,9,17,20] are intended for managing the increasing complexity of node architectures and heterogeneity. These frameworks decompose an application program into small, transferable units of work (many tasks) with associated inputs (dependencies or data blocks) rather than simply decomposing the application at the process level (MPI ranks). The term, 'many-task', encompasses the idea that the application is decomposed into many transferable or migratable units of data/work, to enable the overlap of communication and computation as well as asynchronous load balancing strategies. We believe that the AMT foundations of transferable units and dynamic load balancing are also conducive to supporting fault tolerance. Specifically, we claim that AMT models are better suited to enabling local error recovery in next-generation platforms than bulk-synchronous models, since AMT models provide explicit abstractions of data and tasks, i.e., (1) a task represents a small piece of program execution, (2) failures are manifested as failed or lost tasks, and (3) failures can typically be remediated using lightweight mechanisms such as task replay.

In this paper, we introduce a comprehensive approach to enabling resilience in AMT programming models. While some of the prior approaches discuss different resilience techniques including task replay, task replication, algorithm-based fault tolerance (ABFT [15]), and checkpoint/restart for different AMT programming models such as OmpSs [24] and PaRSEC [6], they are usually limited to a specific technique or to a specific application domain. Our approach complements existing checkpoint/restart mechanisms with reusable APIs to enable abstraction of data and program execution to map to multiple resilience patterns, and compositions thereof. To the best of our knowledge, this is the first work to discuss the design, implementation, and evaluation of a unified programming model that supports multiple resilience techniques.

Specifically, this paper makes the following contributions:

1. Programming model extensions to enable resilience techniques from past work (replay, replication, ABFT, checkpoint/restart) for AMT applications.
2. Support for arbitrary compositions of the extensions in 1.
3. Unified execution of resilient and non-resilient tasks in a single framework.
4. Implementation of our approach as extensions to the Habanero-C/C++ library for many-task parallelism.
5. Comprehensive performance evaluation of our implementation with synthetic error rates, and analysis of the results.

2   Design

A key question for any resilience design is to identify a program location at which we can perform error checking and recovery. For AMT programming models, the task boundary provides an ideal location around which resilience can be implemented. The task constructs that are of our interest do not involve internal synchronization, i.e., once a task is started, it runs to completion without blocking or waiting for other tasks or data. This implies that a task can start only after it acquires all its inputs, and that we can publish the results once it is finished; therefore, the task boundary provides a natural fit as the location around which resilience can be implemented, without worrying about internal task states or the global application state.

Once the program location around which resilience can be implemented is identified, the next step is to identify the data that needs to be checked to ensure correctness. A trivial choice is to ensure the integrity of the entire data used in the program, but this could be very expensive to implement and also unnecessary. The next obvious choice is to look at data that is going to be used past the task boundary, i.e. the task outputs. It is common for task-based runtimes to discourage the use of global variables for communicating data between tasks, and instead use built-in constructs for task inputs and outputs. For example, Legion [3] uses Logical regions, and Open-Community-Runtime (OCR) [20] uses Data-blocks to share data between tasks. C++11 includes **promise** and **future** constructs to enable transfer of data between tasks along with synchronization to avoid data races. A **promise** is a thread-safe container that uses single-assignment semantics to fill its value. The filled value can be read using a read-only handle called a `future`. `promise` and `future` together enable point-to-point synchronization between one source task to many sink tasks. Thus, if the application programmer uses only `promise-future` pairs to perform communication between tasks, then the data in the `promise` objects becomes the live data at the task boundaries. Thus, we have identified both the program location and data that needs to be checked to enable resilience for applications based on AMT runtimes. Errors in the global state can be handled by other global recovery approaches; our approach is still beneficial in such cases because its support for local recovery for tasks enables more scalable and efficient resilience relative to the use of global recovery everywhere.

We assume, that for the same inputs, the task generates promises with data that is within some known range. Tasks do not need to be entirely deterministic - random numbers, etc. can be used within tasks so long as errors within the margin of the randomization's effect are permissible.

2.1 Resilient API Specifications

To reiterate, the key components of our approach to enable resilience in AMT runtimes are tasks and promise/futures. This section discusses our resilient API design. In short, we identified appropriate software abstractions that allow programmers to easily enable/disable different resilience techniques while keeping the original program mostly unchanged. In the following listings, we use `async` as a generic construct that creates an asynchronous task with a user-provided lambda expression, and `async_await` is a variant of `async` that can wait on one or more futures.

First, as a baseline implementation without resilience, Listing 1.1 shows a code example where the function `operation_val()` in Line 17 creates an asynchronous task waiting on the completion of two tasks, namely `read_first_val()` and `read_second_val()`. As shown in Lines 8 and 14, a `future` is satisfied by performing a `put` operation on the corresponding `promise`. Once the promises are satisfied, the `operation_val()` task which depends on the two promises is scheduled for execution. After the completion of the task, the result (`res`) is printed in the `print_result()` task.

Listing 1.1. A baseline non-resilient AMT program to perform an operation on two asynchronously generated values.

```
 1  auto val1_dep = new promise();
 2  auto val2_dep = new promise();
 3  auto res_dep = new promise();
 4
 5  void read_first_val() {
 6    async([=] {
 7      val1 = new value(get_val_from_src());
 8      val1_dep->put(val1);
 9    }); // async
10
11  void read_second_val() {
12    async ([=] {
13      val2 = new value(get_val_from_src());
14      val2_dep->put(val2);
15    }); // async
16
17  void operation_val() {
18    async_await ([=] {
19      val1 = get_value(val1_dep);
20      val2 = get_value(val2_dep);
21      res = new value(op(val1, val2));
22      res_dep->put(res);
23    },  val1_dep->get_future()
24    ,  val2_dep->get_future()  );//async
25  }
26
27  void print_result() {
28    async_await ([=] {
29      res = get_value(res_dep);
30      print(res);
31    },  res_dep->get_future()  ); // async
32  }
```

Task Creation
Satisfying a promise
Waiting on a promise

Replication. Task replication is aimed at proactive reliability enhancement by executing the same task multiple times, assuming that the majority of the replicas produce the same output for determining correctness. The obvious drawback is the increase in computational cost, but it is still effective in situations where a few tasks in a critical path of the task graph may leave the computing system underutilized. The replication overhead can be reduced by selective replication to control the trade-offs between reliability and performance penalties.

Since task replication is based on equality checking of the outputs of the replica tasks, the runtime can internally take care of performing the replication and equality checking. There is no need for the user to provide any additional information other than the equality checking operator for each data type used. Also, the task APIs should include a mechanism to communicate the result of equality checking. This can be done using a promise that will have a value of 1 for success and 0 for failure. The replication version of the `operation_val()` task from Listing 1.1 is shown Listing 1.2. We can see that the only modification required in user code is to change the name of the task creation API and add a parameter, the `err_dep` promise which tells whether a majority of the replicas produced the same output.

The only data that gets propagated to dependent tasks are those that are `put` to a `promise`. With non-resilient tasks, dependent tasks get scheduled for execution once the necessary `put` operations have been performed. In order to prevent errors discovered in replication from propagating to dependent tasks, we do not publish any `put` operations from a replicated task until the equality checking of the replicas succeed.

Listing 1.2. Resilient AMT program based on replication to perform an operation on two asynchronously generated values.

```
1  auto err_dep = new promise();
2
3  void operation_val() {
4      replication::async_await_check ([=] {
5          val1 = get_value(val1_dep);
6          val2 = get_value(val2_dep);
7          res = new value(op(val1, val2));
8          res_dep->put(res)
9      }, err_dep ,
10         val1_dep->get_future(),
11         val2_dep->get_future());//async
12 .}
13
14 void print_result() {
15     async_await([=] {
16         recoverable = get_value( err_dep );
17         if (recoverable == 0) exit(1);
18         res = get_value(res_dep);
19         print(res);
20     }, res_dep->get_future(),
21        err_dep->get_future()); // async
22 }
```

The task replication construct
A promise with a failure status

Listing 1.3. Resilient AMT program based on replay to perform an operation on two asynchronously generated values.

```
1  bool  err_chk_func   (void *data) {
2      if (data is good) return true;
3      else return false;
4  }
5
6  auto err_dep = new promise();
7  void *chk_data = nullptr;
8
9  void operation_val() {
10     replay::async_await_check ([=]{
11         val1 = get_value(val1_dep);
12         val2 = get_value(val2_dep);
13         res = new value(op(val1, val2));
14         res_dep->put(res);
15         chk_data  = res;
16     }, err_dep,  err_chk_func ,  chk_data ,
17        val1_dep->get_future(),
18        val2_dep->get_future()); // async
19 }
```

The task replay construct
User-defined error checking function
Arguments to the error checking

Replay. Task replay is a natural extension of Checkpoint/Restart for the conventional execution models. Instead of applying a rollback of the entire program, as few as one tasks are replayed when an error is detected. Task replay is more sophisticated than replication but has much less overhead. In this form of resilience, the task is replayed (up to N times) on the original input if its execution resulted in some errors. Compared to replication, the application programmer needs to provide an error checking function so that the runtime can use it to check for errors. User-visible abstraction for a replay task is to extend the task creation API to include an error checking function and data on which that function operates. The application programmer needs to fill the data (`chk_data`) that needs to be checked for errors using the error checking function (`err_chk_func`). The replay version of the `operation_val()` task from Listing 1.2 is shown Listing 1.3. Similar to Replication tasks, Replay tasks also do not publish the output until error checking succeeds.

Algorithm-Based Fault Tolerance (ABFT). Algorithm-based fault tolerance (ABFT) mitigates failures using algorithm or application specific knowledge to correct data corruptions and computation errors. One of the seminal papers [15] introduced checksums that are embedded into the matrix and vector operators in parallel dense matrix computations to enable runtime error detection and correction. By using the numerical properties of the algorithm, ABFT uses checksums or provides alternative formulations to recover from an error thus ensuring forward progress without redoing the whole computation. Thus the API designed for an ABFT task should provide a facility to check for errors and if there is an error, a way to recover from it. Therefore, the user level abstraction to include ABFT is to extend the replay task API with a recovery facility as shown in Listing 1.4.

Listing 1.4. Resilient ABFT task signature containing the error correction mechanism.

```
1    abft::async_await_check ([=] {
2       actual computation
3    }, err_dep, err_chk_func, chk_data,
4       err_correction_func  , futures);

The ABFT construct
User-defined error correction function
```

Checkpoint/Restart (C/R). Checkpointing involves the saving of intermediate program state/outputs on to secure storage so that in case of failure, the application can be restarted from the point when the checkpoint was taken rather than from the beginning of the program's execution. From the context of task-based runtimes, once the error/equality checking succeeds at the boundary of a task, the output data can be checkpointed. Later in some following task, if all other resilience techniques fail, it can re-fetch the input data from the checkpoint and execute again.

Checkpointing can be added to any of the resilient tasks listed above. A proposed user level abstraction for a checkpoint task created by extending the replay task is shown in Listing 1.5. The only addition is to specify where to store the checkpoint data using the `set_archive_store` API as shown in Line 13. In our current preliminary implementation, we keep a copy of the checkpoint in the memory itself, as in diskless checkpointing [22]. Efficiently performing these checkpoints and their performance evaluation is a topic for future work.

Listing 1.5. Resilient AMT program based on replay to perform an operation on two asynchronously generated values and also checkpoints the results.

```
 1  void operation_val() {
 2      checkpoint::async_await_check  ([=] {
 3      val1 = get_value(val1_dep);
 4      val2 = get_value(val2_dep);
 5      res = new value(op(val1, val2));
 6      res_dep->put(res);
 7      chk_data = res;
 8  }, err_dep, err_chk_func, chk_data,
 9      val1_dep->get_future(),
10      val2_dep->get_future()); // async
11  }
12
13  set_archive_store(storage object);
```

The checkpoint/restart construct
The checkpoint API that specifies where to store the checkpoint data
(invoked just once, before async_await_check)

2.2 Memory Management

C++ requires the user to perform memory management; i.e., the application programmer needs to explicitly free any data that is allocated in the heap memory. This could be reasonable to manage in normal AMT programs, but when we introduce resilience techniques manual deallocation poses certain challenges.

Many resilience techniques involve multiple executions of the task to get the correct results. This would mean that the user needs to keep track of the good or bad executions of the task. For the good runs, the data generated by a task would be used later in some consumer tasks; therefore, they need to be deallocated only after the consumption of the data. For bad runs, there is no need for the data created in the task and, therefore, they need to be deallocated at the end of the producer task itself. Keeping track of good or bad runs and selectively deallocating memory would create unnecessary complexity in the application code.

Therefore, to reduce the user's burden of manual memory management, we decided to add the reference counting capability that deallocates the data automatically once its use is over. Since data is being transferred between tasks using promise and future, reference counting is added by extending the promise to include the reference count. Ideally, the reference count specifies the number of tasks dependent on the future associated with the promise. The reference count is passed on to a promise when it is created. In other words, a reference count N specifies that only N tasks consume data from the given promise, and therefore the promise and the associated data can be freed once N tasks have used it.

3 Implementation

In this section, we discuss the implementation of our resilient-AMT prototype [1], extended from the Habanero C++ library (HClib) [11]. An overview of HClib and its runtime capability are discussed in Sect. 3.1 followed by efforts for the extension of HClib.

3.1 HClib

HClib [11] is a lightweight, work-stealing, task-based programming model and runtime that focuses on offering simple tasking APIs with low overhead [13] task creation. HClib is entirely library-based (i.e. does not require a custom compiler) and supports both a C and C++ API. HClib's runtime consists of a persistent thread pool, across which tasks are load balanced using lock-free concurrent dequeues. At the user-visible API level, HClib exposes several useful programming constructs. A brief summary of the relevant APIs is as follows. The `hclib::launch()` API initializes the HClib runtime, including spawning runtime threads. The `async([] { body; })` API creates a dynamic task executing `body` provided as a C++ lambda expression; this API optionally allows the inclusion of parameters that specify precondition events thereby supporting event-driven execution for tasks when so desired (i.e., the `async_await()`). The `finish([] { body; })` API waits for all tasks created in `body`, including transitively spawned tasks, before returning.

3.2 Enabling Resilience in HClib

We extended HClib to include the resilience constructs (Sect. 2.1), and the reference counting capability (Sect. 2.2).

As mentioned in Sect. 2.1, to hold the `put` operations until equality checking succeeds, we need additional space within the `promise`. The normal `promise` can hold only one value that had been added to it using the `put` operation. For replication, however, all replicas perform the `put` operation and, therefore, we need N locations within the `promise` rather than one. To accommodate this, we extended the reference counting `promise` with an array to store N values so that we can perform majority voting among them. During a `put` operation inside a replication task, the ith replica stores the value in the ith location of the array. Similarly for replay or ABFT tasks, to hold the output inside the `promise` until it is published, we extended the reference counting `promise` to include a temporary storage. Unlike replication, which requires an array of temporary storage, a replay and ABFT `promise` needs only one temporary storage space since the replay happens sequentially.

We need to collect all the `put` operations within the resilient tasks so that they can be checked for errors after all replicas finish. For this purpose, we extended HClib with task-local storage. Each `put` operation in the replica with index zero (we assume all replicas perform the same `put` operations) adds the associated `promise` to the task-local storage. Finally, while merging the results from the replicas, we fetch the promises from the task-local storage and check for equality on the data attached to those promises using an equivalence operator the user provides.

4   Evaluation

This section presents the results of an empirical evaluation of our runtime system, mostly on a single-node platform with a few experiments on a multi-node platform to show its viability in a distributed environment.

Machine: We present the results on the Cori supercomputer located at NERSC, in which each node has two sockets, each of which has 16-core Intel Xeon E5-2698 v3 CPUs at 2.30 GHz. Cori uses Cray Aries interconnect with Dragonfly topology having a global peak bisection bandwidth is 45.0 TB/s. We used GCC 7.3.0 compiler for building the library and most benchmarks and Intel Compiler 18.0.1 for benchmarks that require MKL support.

Benchmarks: Our first benchmark is the stencil 1D benchmark that solves linear advection (a hyperbolic PDE). We implemented this using the Lax-Wendroff 3-point stencil. In this benchmark, we use 128 tiles of size 16,000 doubles, 128 time steps per iteration (each task advances its assigned tile 128 time steps), and 8,192 iterations. For our next benchmark, we solve heat diffusion (a parabolic PDE) on a 3D domain with periodic boundary conditions using a 7-point stencil. Here we use 16^3 cubes, each representing a subdomain of size 32^3, and run for 1,024 iterations. Our next benchmark is a tiled version of Conjugate Gradient (CG), which is an iterative method for solving sparse systems of linear equations. A square matrix from the "SuiteSparse" collection (52,804 rows/columns, 5,333,507 non-zeros) was set up with the CG method with 128 tiles and 500 iterations. Our fourth benchmark is the Smith-Waterman algorithm that performs local sequence alignment, which is widely used for determining similar regions between two strings of nucleic acid sequences. We use two input strings of sizes 185,600 and 192,000, divided among 4,096 tiles arranged as 64×64. Our last benchmark is the Cholesky decomposition algorithm, which is used primarily to find the numerical solution of linear equations. Here we decompose a matrix of size $24,000 \times 24,000$ into tiles of size 400×400. We report the average of five runs for each experiment.

For the stencil benchmarks, we can detect corruption anywhere on a subdomain using physics-based checksums because conservation requires that the sum of values over the subdomain only changes by the flux through the subdomain boundary. For the Conjugate gradient and Smith-waterman benchmarks, there are not any sophisticated error detection mechanisms, so we simply return true, implying no error occurred. In the case when we want to inject faults, we pick a few instances of the error checking function to return false. Error-checking functions are expected to be domain/application dependent and are not the subject of this paper, and we emulate the scenario arising from a prescribed fault rate. The design of checksums for Cholesky decomposition is based on the work by Cao [6].

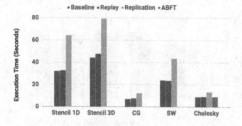

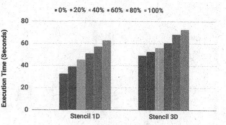

Fig. 1. Comparison of execution times of different resilience schemes on the five benchmarks without faults.

Fig. 2. Comparison of execution times of the stencil benchmarks while mixing replay and replication with percent of replication shown.

4.1 Performance Numbers Without Failures

Single Resilience Technique. To show the overhead of the resilient runtime, the execution time of the five benchmarks using various resilience techniques without failures is shown in Fig. 1. For all the benchmarks, we used replay and replication to enable resilience. For the Cholesky benchmark, in addition to replay and replication, we included ABFT. From the figure, we can see that for the stencil benchmarks, some additional time is required for the replay variant compared to the baseline. For the stencil 1D benchmark, this accounts for less than 5% overhead whereas in stencil 3D the overhead is around 8%. A close examination reveals the overhead includes both the computation of the checksum and additional overhead from the replay runtime. For the Conjugate gradient benchmark, the replay runtime incurs an overhead of less than 10%. For the Smith-Waterman and Cholesky benchmarks, we did not notice any significant overhead while using replay. For the Cholesky benchmark, we also enabled ABFT and found that the time required for ABFT is comparable to that of replay.

When replication is used, we can see that the execution time increases for all the benchmarks. We expected the time to double because, in the absence of faults, duplication of the tasks occurs. However, for a few benchmarks, the execution time was significantly less than double primarily due to L3 cache reuse.

Mixing Resilience Techniques. To illustrate that the various resilience techniques can be seamlessly combined, we also tried to mix replay and replication in the stencil benchmarks. On one end, the application only uses replay, and on the other end, it uses just replication. In between, the amount of replication is increased in increments of 20%. Figure 2 shows that the execution time increases linearly while mixing replay and replication. This implies that the increase directly corresponds to the additional cost for running replication and thus no additional overhead is involved.

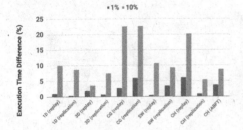

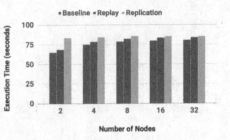

Fig. 3. Comparison of percentage of change in execution times w.r.t baseline of different resilience schemes with faults injected at 1% and 10% rate.

Fig. 4. Weak scaling of Stencil 1D with different number of nodes and resilience schemes with no fault injection

4.2 Performance Numbers with Failures

To check the effectiveness of our resilience mechanisms in the presence of soft errors, we ran all the benchmarks while introducing errors. We injected errors at a rate of 1% and 10%. Here, 10% implies that an error is injected into 10% of the total tasks. Figure 3 shows the execution time for various benchmarks and resilience techniques in the presence of faults. Here, also, we can see that the increase in execution time closely follows the amount of failure occurred. For the 10% failure rate, in most cases, the increase in execution time is also around 10%. Failures do not cause much time increase in case of ABFT because the ABFT error correction is very lightweight compared to others.

4.3 Performance Numbers on Multiple Nodes

We run some preliminary experiments using stencil 1D with multiple nodes using MPI to measure the overhead of our implementation in multi-node environments[1]. We ran weak scaling of Stencil 1D by only increasing the number of tiles while keeping the same configuration of other parameters as the experiment on a single node. In Fig. 4, we can see some performance degradation because of internode communication during a two-node run. However, the replication scheme worked well without degrading performance significantly because the communication incurred by MPI routines is overlapped with the replicated execution of tasks. For runs without resilience or with replay, MPI routines are called only when the original task or replayed task generates correct results, which causes a delay because it cannot be overlapped with other tasks. Thus, the execution time of such runs increases with more nodes.

---

[1] There is no resilience across nodes. We provide only single-node resilience and use MPI for communication. Resilience across nodes is part of future work.

5 Related Work

Task Replication: Subasi *et al.* [25] study a combination of task replication and checkpoint/restart for a task-parallel runtime, OmpSs [9]. Their checkpoint API is integrated with the input data parameters of OmpSs directives to protect the task input. They also suggested deferring launch of the third replica until duplicated tasks report a failure. However, the mixing with other resilience techniques and analysis of the performance penalties are yet to be studied.

Task Replay: Subasi *et al.* [24] also study a combination of task replay and checkpoint/restart for OmpSs. As with task replication, checkpoint/restart is utilized for preserving the input of tasks. During the execution of a task, errors notified by the operating system trigger a replay of the task using the input data stored in the checkpoint. Cao *et al.* [6] has a similar replay model. However, the drawback of these approaches is a lack of mitigation for failure propagation, as they assume *reliable* failure detection support, e.g., by the operating system, which is not always available. Our approach provides a general interface that allows user-level failure detection.

ABFT: Cao *et al.* [6] also discuss an algorithm-based fault tolerance for tiled Cholesky factorization [16] in the PaRSEC runtime. However, they do not discuss their user-visible APIs in terms of general applicability, while our approach provides a general support for ABFT.

6 Conclusions and Future Work

The traditional checkpoint/restart (C/R) approach for resilience was designed to support the bulk-synchronous MPI programming model under the assumption that failure is a rare event. However, C/R is not well suited for supporting higher-frequency soft errors or unexpected performance anomalies. The resilient-AMT idea for applications mitigates the shortcoming of traditional C/R, so as to support scalable failure mitigation. Task decomposition allows localization and isolation of failures in the resilient-AMT framework, and thus keeps the recovery inexpensive. Our work realizes the four resilience programming concepts suggested by Heroux [14]. Task boundary helps to perform **Local Failure Local Recovery** for scalable application recovery. The task replication and replay APIs allow **selective reliability**; the use of replication and replay on individual tasks can be at the user's discretion. The task replay and ABFT APIs enable **skeptical programming**, which can incorporate inexpensive user-defined error detection. The response to an error is either task replay (rollback) or recovery (application-specific correction). The AMT execution model **relaxes the assumption of bulk-synchrony** of conventional parallel programs.

In the future, we would like to extend our resilient-AMT approach to support both intra-node and inter-node resilience (MPI based communication). Another direction is to combine both replication and replay mechanisms in an "eager replay" approach. During eager replay, if extra resources are available, the replay task can run multiple copies instead of waiting for the task to finish and select the correct output from the replicas using a `selection` function. Our current approach also depends on the use of a user-provided `equals` function to check for equivalence of data which could be automated using a compiler. Although we support the use of nested non-resilient tasks within a resilient task, nesting of resilient tasks is a topic of future research. Also the restriction of side-effect free tasks can be relaxed by using idempotent regions as task boundaries [19]. Our current approach only supports one level of checkpointing, with access to checkpoints of parent tasks. If that execution fails again, we may need to recover from checkpoints of further ancestors (multi-level checkpointing), as part of our future work. Another direction is to study the characteristics of faults [18,23] and perform fault injection [10,12] to efficiently and extensively cover them.

Data Availability Statement. The datasets and code generated during and/or analysed during the current study are available through the Figshare repository: https://doi.org/10.6084/m9.figshare.8485994.

References

1. HClib Resilience Branch. https://github.com/srirajpaul/hclib/tree/feature/resilience. Accessed 14 June 2019
2. Augonnet, C., et al.: StarPU: a unified platform for task scheduling on heterogeneous multicore architectures. Concurr. Comput. Pract. Exp. **23**(2), 187–198 (2011). https://doi.org/10.1002/cpe.1631
3. Bauer, M., et al.: Legion: expressing locality and independence with logical regions. In: Proceedings of the International Conference on High Performance Computing, Networking, Storage and Analysis, SC 2012, pp. 66:1–66:11 (2012). https://doi.org/10.1109/SC.2012.71
4. Bennett, J., et al.: ASC ATDM level 2 milestone #5325: asynchronous many-task runtime system analysis and assessment for next generation platform. Technical report SAND2015-8312, Sandia National Laboratories, September 2015
5. Bosilca, G., et al.: PaRSEC: exploiting heterogeneity to enhance scalability. Comput. Sci. Eng. **15**(6), 36–45 (2013). https://doi.org/10.1109/MCSE.2013.98
6. Cao, C., et al.: Design for a soft error resilient dynamic task-based runtime. In: 2015 IEEE International Parallel and Distributed Processing Symposium, pp. 765–774, May 2015. https://doi.org/10.1109/IPDPS.2015.81
7. Cappello, F., et al.: Toward exascale resilience: 2014 update. Supercomput. Front. Innov. Int. J. **1**(1), 5–28 (2014). https://doi.org/10.14529/jsfi140101
8. Chung, J., et al.: Containment domains: a scalable, efficient, and flexible resilience scheme for exascale systems. In: Proceedings of the International Conference on High Performance Computing, Networking, Storage and Analysis, SC 2012, pp. 58:1–58:11 (2012). https://doi.org/10.1109/SC.2012.36
9. Fernández, A., Beltran, V., Martorell, X., Badia, R.M., Ayguadé, E., Labarta, J.: Task-based programming with OmpSs and its application. In: Lopes, L., et al. (eds.) Euro-Par 2014. LNCS, vol. 8806, pp. 601–612. Springer, Cham (2014). https://doi.org/10.1007/978-3-319-14313-2_51

10. Georgakoudis, G., et al.: Refine: realistic fault injection via compiler-based instrumentation for accuracy, portability and speed. In: Proceedings of the International Conference for High Performance Computing, Networking, Storage and Analysis, SC 2017, pp. 29:1–29:14 (2017). https://doi.org/10.1145/3126908.3126972
11. Grossman, M., et al.: A pluggable framework for composable HPC scheduling libraries. In: 2017 IEEE International Parallel and Distributed Processing Symposium Workshops (IPDPSW), pp. 723–732 (2017). https://doi.org/10.1109/IPDPSW.2017.13
12. Guan, Q., et al.: F-sefi: a fine-grained soft error fault injection tool for profiling application vulnerability. In: 2014 IEEE 28th International Parallel and Distributed Processing Symposium, pp. 1245–1254 (2014). https://doi.org/10.1109/IPDPS.2014.128
13. Hayashi, A., et al.: Chapel-on-X: exploring tasking runtimes for PGAS languages. In: ESPM2 2017, pp. 5:1–5:8. ACM, New York (2017). https://doi.org/10.1145/3152041.3152086
14. Heroux, M.A.: Toward Resilient Algorithms and Applications (2014). http://arxiv.org/abs/1402.3809
15. Huang, K.H., Abraham, J.A.: Algorithm-based fault tolerance for matrix operations. IEEE Trans. Comput. C-33(6), 518–528 (1984). https://doi.org/10.1109/TC.1984.1676475
16. Jeannot, E.: Performance analysis and optimization of the tiled Cholesky factorization on NUMA machines. In: Proceedings of the 2012 Fifth International Symposium on Parallel Architectures, Algorithms and Programming, PAAP 2012, pp. 210–217 (2012). https://doi.org/10.1109/PAAP.2012.38
17. Kaiser, H., et al.: Parallex an advanced parallel execution model for scaling-impaired applications. In: 2009 International Conference on Parallel Processing Workshops, pp. 394–401 (2009). https://doi.org/10.1109/ICPPW.2009.14
18. Li, D., et al.: Classifying soft error vulnerabilities in extreme-scale scientific applications using a binary instrumentation tool. In: Proceedings of the International Conference on High Performance Computing, Networking, Storage and Analysis, SC 2012, pp. 57:1–57:11 (2012). https://doi.org/10.1109/SC.2012.29
19. Liu, Q., et al.: Compiler-directed lightweight checkpointing for fine-grained guaranteed soft error recovery. In: Proceedings of the International Conference for High Performance Computing, Networking, Storage and Analysis, SC 2016, pp. 20:1–20:12 (2016). https://doi.org/10.1109/SC.2016.19
20. Mattson, T.G., et al.: The open community runtime: a runtime system for extreme scale computing. In: 2016 IEEE High Performance Extreme Computing Conference (HPEC), pp. 1–7, September 2016. https://doi.org/10.1109/HPEC.2016.7761580
21. Moody, A., et al.: Design, modeling, and evaluation of a scalable multi-level checkpointing system. In: Proceedings of the 2010 ACM/IEEE International Conference for High Performance Computing, Networking, Storage and Analysis, SC 2010, pp. 1–11 (2010). https://doi.org/10.1109/SC.2010.18
22. Plank, J.S., Li, K., Puening, M.A.: Diskless checkpointing. IEEE Trans. Parallel Distrib. Syst. 9(10), 972–986 (1998). https://doi.org/10.1109/71.730527
23. Shantharam, M., et al.: Characterizing the impact of soft errors on iterative methods in scientific computing. In: Proceedings of the International Conference on Supercomputing, ICS 2011, pp. 152–161 (2011). https://doi.org/10.1145/1995896.1995922

24. Subasi, O., et al.: NanoCheckpoints: a task-based asynchronous dataflow framework for efficient and scalable checkpoint/restart. In: 2015 23rd Euromicro International Conference on Parallel, Distributed, and Network-Based Processing, pp. 99–102. https://doi.org/10.1109/PDP.2015.17
25. Subasi, O., et al.: Designing and modelling selective replication for fault-tolerant HPC applications. In: 2017 17th IEEE/ACM International Symposium on Cluster, Cloud and Grid Computing (CCGRID), pp. 452–457, May 2017. https://doi.org/10.1109/CCGRID.2017.40

Multicore and Manycore Parallelism

Avoiding Scalability Collapse
by Restricting Concurrency

Dave Dice[(✉)] ⓘ and Alex Kogan[(✉)] ⓘ

Oracle Labs, Burlington, MA, USA
{dave.dice,alex.kogan}@oracle.com

Abstract. Saturated locks often degrade the performance of a multithreaded application, leading to a so-called scalability collapse problem. This problem arises when a growing number of threads circulating through a saturated lock causes the overall application performance to fade or even drop abruptly. This problem is particularly (but not solely) acute on oversubscribed systems (systems with more threads than available hardware cores).

In this paper, we introduce GCR (generic concurrency restriction), a mechanism that aims to avoid the scalability collapse. GCR, designed as a generic, lock-agnostic wrapper, intercepts lock acquisition calls, and decides when threads would be allowed to proceed with the acquisition of the underlying lock. Furthermore, we present GCR-NUMA, a non-uniform memory access (NUMA)-aware extension of GCR, that strives to ensure that threads allowed to acquire the lock are those that run on the same socket.

The extensive evaluation that includes more than two dozen locks, three machines and three benchmarks shows that GCR brings substantial speedup (in many cases, up to three orders of magnitude) in case of contention and growing thread counts, while introducing nearly negligible slowdown when the underlying lock is not contended. GCR-NUMA brings even larger performance gains starting at even lighter lock contention.

Keywords: Locks · Scalability · Concurrency restriction · NUMA

1 Introduction

The performance of applications on multi-core systems is often harmed by *saturated* locks, where at least one thread is waiting for the lock. Prior work has observed that as the number of threads circulating through a saturated lock grows, the overall application performance often fades or even drops abruptly [2,7,16,17], a behavior called *scalability collapse* [7]. This happens because threads compete over shared system resources, such as computing cores and last-level cache (LLC). For instance, the increase in the number of distinct threads circulating through the lock typically leads to increased cache pressure,

© Springer Nature Switzerland AG 2019
R. Yahyapour (Ed.): Euro-Par 2019, LNCS 11725, pp. 363–376, 2019.
https://doi.org/10.1007/978-3-030-29400-7_26

resulting in cache misses. At the same time, threads waiting for the lock consume valuable resources and might preempt the lock holder from making progress with its execution under lock, exacerbating the contention on the lock even further.

An example for scalability collapse can be seen in Fig. 1 that depicts the performance of a key-value map microbenchmark with three popular locks on a 2-socket x86 machine featuring 40 logical CPUs in total (full details of the microbenchmark and the machine are provided later). The shape and the exact point of the performance decline differ between the locks, yet all of them are unable to sustain peak throughput. With the Test-Test-Set lock, for instance, the performance

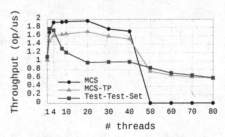

Fig. 1. Microbenchmark performance with different locks on a 2-socket machine with 20 hyper-threads per socket.

drops abruptly when more than just a few threads are used, while with the MCS lock [21] the performance is relatively stable up to the capacity of the machine and collapses once the system gets oversubscribed (i.e., has more threads available than the number of cores). Note that one of the locks, MCS-TP, was designed specifically to handle oversubscription [14], yet its performance falls short of the peak.

It might be tempting to argue that one should never create a workload where the underlying machine is oversubscribed, pre-tuning the maximum number of threads and using a lock, such as MCS, to keep the performance stable. We note that in modern component-based software, the total number of threads is often out of the hands of the developer. A good example would be applications that use thread pools, or even have multiple mutually unaware thread pools. Furthermore, in multi-tenant and/or cloud-based deployments, where the resources of a physical machine (including cores and caches) are often shared between applications running inside virtual machines or containers, applications can run concurrently with one another without even being aware that they share the same machine. Thus, limiting the maximum number of threads by the number of cores does not help much. Finally, even when a saturated lock delivers a seemingly stable performance, threads spinning and waiting for the lock consume energy and take resources (such as CPU time) from other, unrelated tasks[1].

In this paper we introduce *generic concurrency restriction* (GCR) to deal with the scalability collapse. GCR operates as a wrapper around any existing lock (including POSIX pthread mutexes, and specialized locks provided by an application). GCR intercepts calls for a lock acquisition and decides which threads would proceed with the acquisition of the underlying lock (those threads are called *active*) and which threads would be blocked (those threads are called *passive*). Reducing the number of threads circulating through the locks improves cache performance, while blocking passive threads reduces competition over CPU

---

[1] We also discuss other waiting policies and their limitations later in the paper.

time, leading to better system performance and energy efficiency. To avoid starvation and achieve long-term fairness, active and passive threads are shuffled periodically. We note that the admission policy remains fully work conserving with GCR. That is, when a lock holder exits, one of the waiting threads will be able to acquire the lock immediately and enter its critical section.

In this paper we also show how GCR can be extended into a non-uniform access memory (NUMA) setting of multi-socket machines. In those settings, accessing data residing in a local cache is far cheaper than accessing data in a cache located on a remote socket. Previous research on locks tackled this issue by trying to keep the lock ownership on the same socket [3,9,10,23], thus increasing the chance that the data accessed by a thread holding the lock (and the lock data as well) would be cached locally to that thread. The NUMA extension of GCR, called simply GCR-NUMA, takes advantage of that same idea by trying to keep the set of active threads composed of threads running on the same socket. As a by-product of this construction, GCR-NUMA can convert any lock into a NUMA-aware one.

We have implemented GCR (and GCR-NUMA) in the context of the LiTL library [13,20], which provides the implementation of over two dozen various locks. We have evaluated GCR with all those locks using a microbenchmark as well as two well-known database systems (namely, Kyoto Cabinet [12] and LevelDB [18]), on three different systems (two x86 machines and one SPARC). The results show that GCR avoids the scalability collapse, which translates to substantial speedup (up to three orders of magnitude) in case of high lock contention for virtually every evaluated lock, workload and machine. Furthermore, we show empirically that GCR does not harm the fairness of underlying locks (in fact, in many cases GCR makes the fairness better). GCR-NUMA brings even larger performance gains starting at even lighter lock contention.

2   Related Work

Prior work has explored adapting the number of active threads based on lock contention [7,17]. However, that work customized certain types of locks, exploiting their specific features, such as the fact that waiting threads are organized in a queue [7], or that lock acquisition can be aborted [17]. Those requirements limit the ability to adapt those techniques into other locks and use them in practice. For instance, very few locks allow waiting threads to abandon an acquisition attempt, and many spin locks, such as a simple Test-Test-Set lock, do not maintain a queue of waiting threads. Furthermore, the lock implementation is often opaque to the application, e.g., when POSIX pthread mutexes are used. At the same time, prior research has shown that every lock has its own "15 min of fame", i.e., there is no lock that always outperforms others and the choice of the optimal lock depends on the given application, platform and workload [6,13]. Thus, in order to be practical, a mechanism to control the number of active threads has to be lock-agnostic, like the one provided by GCR.

Other work in different, but related contexts has observed that controlling the number of threads used by an application is an effective approach for meeting certain performance goals. For instance, Raman et al. [24] demonstrate that with a run-time system that monitors application execution to dynamically adapt the number of worker threads executing parallel loop nests. In another example, Pusukuri et al. [22] propose a system that runs an application multiple times for short durations while varying the number of threads, and determines the optimal number of threads to create based on the observed performance. Chadha et al. [4] identified cache-level thrashing as a scalability impediment and proposed system-wide concurrency throttling. Heirman et al. [15] suggested intentional undersubscription of threads as a response to competition for shared caches. Hardware and software transactional memory systems use contention managers to throttle concurrency in order to optimize throughput [25]. The issue is particularly acute in the context of transactional memory as failed optimistic transactions are wasteful of resources.

Trading off between throughput and short-term fairness has been extensively explored in the context of NUMA-aware locks [3,9,10,23]. Those locks do not feature a concurrency restriction mechanism, and in particular, do not avoid contention on the intra-socket level and the issues resulting from that.

3   Background

Contending threads must wait for the lock when it is not available. There are several common waiting policies. The most simple one is unbounded spinning, also known as busy-waiting or polling. There, the waiting threads spin on a global or local memory location and wait until the value in that location changes. Spinning consumes resources and contributes to preemption when the system is oversubscribed, i.e., has more ready threads than the number of available logical CPUs. Yet, absent preemption, it is simple and provides fast lock handover times, and for those reasons used by many popular locks, e.g., Test-Test-Set.

An alternative waiting policy is parking, where a waiting thread voluntarily releases its CPU and passively waits (by blocking) for another thread to unpark it when the lock becomes available. Parking is attractive when the system is oversubscribed, as it releases CPU resources for threads ready to run, including the lock holder. However, the cost of the voluntary context switching imposed by parking is high, which translates to longer lock handover times when the next owner of the lock has to be unparked.

To mitigate the overhead of parking and unparking on the one hand, and limit the shortcomings of unlimited spinning on the other hand, lock designers proposed a hybrid spin-then-park policy. There, threads spin for a brief period, and park if the lock is still not available by the end of that time. While tuning the optimal time for spinning is challenging [16,19], it is typically set to the length of the context-switch round trip [7].

4   Generic Concurrency Restriction

GCR "wraps" a lock API, i.e., calls to Lock/Unlock methods go through the corresponding methods of GCR. In our implementation, we interpose on the standard POSIX pthreads_mutex_lock and pthreads_mutex_unlock methods. Thus, using the standard LD_PRELOAD mechanism on Linux and Unix, GCR can be made immediately available to any application that uses the standard POSIX API, even without recompiling the application or its locks.

The pseudo-code implementation is provided in Fig. 2[2], where FAA, SWAP and CAS stand for atomic fetch-and-add, swap and compare-and-swap instructions, respectively. In the following description, we distinguish between *active* threads, that is, threads allowed by GCR to invoke the API of the underlying lock, and *passive* threads, which are not allowed to do so. Note that this distinction is unrelated to the running state of the corresponding threads. That is, active threads may actually be blocked (parked) if the underlying lock decides doing so, while passive threads may be spinning, waiting for their turn to join the set of active threads. In addition, given that GCR by itself does not provide lock semantics (even though it implements the lock API), we will refer to the underlying lock simply as *the lock*.

The auxiliary data structures used by GCR include Node and LockType (cf. Fig. 2). The Node structure represents a node in the queue of passive threads. In addition to the successor and predecessor nodes in the queue, the Node structure contains the event flag. This flag is used to signal a thread when its node moves to the head in the queue.

The LockType structure contains the internal lock metadata (passed to the Lock and Unlock functions of that lock) and a number of additional fields:

- top and tail are the pointers to the first and the last nodes in the queue of passive threads, respectively.
- topApproved is a flag used to signal the passive thread at the top of the queue that it can join the set of active threads.
- numActive is the counter for the number of active threads.
- numAcqs is a counter for the number of lock acquisitions. It is used to move threads from the passive set to the active set, as explained below.

In addition to LockType structure, GCR uses nextLock (nextUnlock) function pointer, which is initialized to the Lock (Unlock, respectively) function of the underlying lock. The initialization code is straightforward (on Linux it can use the dlsym system call), and thus is not shown.

GCR keeps track of the number of active threads per lock. When a thread invokes the Lock method wrapped by GCR, GCR checks whether the number of active threads is larger than a preconfigured threshold (cf. Line 3, where we use a threshold of 1). If not, the thread proceeds by calling the lock's Lock

---

[2] For the clarity of exposition, we assume sequential consistency. Our actual implementation uses memory fences as well as volatile keywords and padding (to avoid false sharing) where necessarily.

```
     typedef struct _Node {
       struct _Node * next;
       struct _Node * prev;
       int event;
     } Node;

     typedef struct {
       lock_t internalMutex;

       Node * top;
       Node * tail;
       int topApproved;

       int numActive;

       int numAcqs;
     } LockType ;

     static int (*nextLock)(lock_t *);
     static int (*nextUnlock)(lock_t *);

1    int Lock(LockType *m) {
2      /* if there is at most one active thread */
3      if (m->numActive <= 1) {
4        /* go to the fast path */
5        FAA(&m->numActive, 1);
6        goto FastPath;
7      }

8    SlowPath:
9      /* enter the queue of passive threads */
10     Node *myNode = pushSelfToQueue(m);

11     /* wait (by spin - then - park) for my
12        node to get to the top */
13     if (!myNode->event)
14       Wait(myNode->event);

15     /* wait (by spinning ) for a signal to join
16        the set of active threads */
17     while (!m->topApproved) {
18       Pause();
19       /* stop waiting if no active
20          threads left */
21       if (m->numActive == 0) break;
22     }

23     if (m->topApproved != 0)
24       m->topApproved = 0;
25     FAA(&m->numActive, 1);

26     popSelfFromQueue(m, myNode);

27   FastPath:
28     return nextLock(&m->internalMutex);
29   }
```

```
31   int Unlock (LockType * m) {
32     /* check if it is time to bring someone from
33        the passive to active set */
34     if (((m->numAcqs++ % THRESHOLD) == 0)
35          && m->top != NULL) {
36       /* signal the selected thread that it can go */
37       m->topApproved = 1;
38     }

39     FAA(&m->numActive, -1);

40     /* call underlying lock */
41     return nextUnlock(&m->internalMutex);
42   }

43   Node *pushSelfToQueue(LockType * m) {
44     Node * n = (Node *)malloc(sizeof(Node));
45     n->next = NULL;
46     n->event = 0;
47     Node * prv = SWAP (&m->tail, n);
48     if (prv != NULL) {
49       prv->next = n;
50     } else {
51       m->top = n;
52       n->event = 1;
53     }

54     return n;
55   }

56   void popSelfFromQueue(LockType * m, Node * n) {
57     Node * succ = n->next;
58     if (succ == NULL) {
59       /* my node is the last in the queue */
60       if (CAS (&m->tail, n, NULL)) {
61         CAS (&m->top, n, NULL);
62         free(n);
63         return;
64       }
65       for (;;) {
66         succ = n->next ;
67         if (succ != NULL) break;
68         Pause();
69       }
70     }

71     m->top = succ;
72     /* unpark successor if it is parked in Wait */
73     succ->event = 1;

74     free(n);
75   }
```

Fig. 2. GCR pseudo-code implementation.

method after incrementing (atomically) the (per-lock) counter of active threads (numActive) in Line 5. This constitutes the fast path of the lock acquisition. We note that the check in Line 3 and the increment in Line 5 are not mutually atomic, that is, multiple threads can reach Line 5 and thus increment the counter stored in numActive concurrently. However, the lack of atomicity may only impact performance (as the underlying lock will become more contended), and not correctness. Besides, this should be rare when the system is in the steady state.

If the condition in Line 3 does not hold, GCR detects that the lock is saturated, and places the (passive) thread into a (lock-specific) queue where that thread waits for its turn to join the set of active threads. This queue is based on a linked list; each node is associated with a different thread. Every thread in the queue but the first can wait by spinning on a local flag (event) in its respective node, yield the CPU and park, or any combination of thereof. (The thread at the head of the queue has to spin as explained below.) In practice, we choose the spin-then-park policy for all passive threads in the queue but the first, to limit the use of system resources by those threads.

The thread at the top of the queue monitors the signal from active threads to join the active set. It does so by spinning on the `topApproved` flag (Line 17). In addition, this thread monitors the number of active threads by reading the `numActive` counter (Line 21). Note that unlike the `topApproved` flag, this counter changes on every lock acquisition and release. Thus, reading it on every iteration of the spinning loop would create unnecessary coherence traffic and slow down active threads when they attempt to modify this counter. In the longer version of this paper [8], we describe a simple optimization that allows to read this counter less frequently while still monitoring the active set effectively. Once the passive thread at the top of the queue breaks out of the spinning loop, it leaves the queue, notifying the next thread t (if exists) that the head of the queue has changed (by setting a flag in t's node and unparking t if necessarily), and proceeds by calling the lock's `Lock` method.

When a thread invokes GCR's `Unlock` method, it checks whether it is time to signal the (passive) thread at the head of the queue to join the set of active threads (cf. Lines 34–38). This is done to achieve a long-term fairness, preventing starvation of passive threads. To this end, GCR keeps a simple counter for the number of lock acquisitions (`numAcqs`), which is incremented with a simple store, as it is done under the lock. (Other alternatives, such as timer-based approaches, are possible.) Following that, GCR atomically decrements the counter of active threads and calls the lock's `Unlock` method.

In the longer version of the paper [8], we describe a number of optimizations intended to reduce the overhead of GCR when the underlying lock is not saturated. For instance, we show how to avoid atomic operations on the counter of active threads (`numActive`) by dynamically enabling and disabling GCR based on the actual contention on the lock.

5   NUMA-Aware GCR

As GCR controls which threads would join the active set, it may well do so in a NUMA-aware way. In practice, this means that it should strive to maintain the active set composed of threads running on the same socket (or, more precisely, on the same NUMA node). Note that this does not place any additional restrictions on the underlying lock, which might be a NUMA-aware lock by itself or not. Naturally, if the underlying lock is NUMA-oblivious, the benefit of such an optimization would be higher.

Introducing NUMA-awareness into GCR requires relatively few changes. On a high level, instead of keeping just one queue of passive threads per lock, we keep a number of queues, one per socket. Thus, a passive thread joins the queue corresponding to the socket it is running on. In addition, we introduce a notion of a preferred socket, which is a socket that gets preference in decisions which threads should join the active set. In our case, we set the preferred socket solely based on the number of lock acquisitions (i.e., the preferred socket is changed in a round-robin fashion every certain number of lock acquisitions), but other refined (e.g., time-based) schemes are possible.

We say that a (passive) thread is eligible (to check whether it can join the active set) if it is running on the preferred socket *or* the queue (of passive threads) of the preferred socket is empty. When a thread calls the Lock function, we check whether it is eligible and let it proceed with examining the size of the active set (i.e., read the numActive counter) only if it is. Otherwise, it immediately goes into the slow path, joining the queue according to its socket. This means that once the designation of the preferred socket changes (when threads running on that socket acquire and release the lock "enough" times), active threads from the now not-preferred socket will become passive when they attempt to acquire the lock again.

Having only eligible threads monitor the size of the active set has two desired consequences. First, only the passive thread at the top of the queue corresponding to the preferred socket will be the next thread (out of all passive threads) to join the set of active threads. This keeps the set of active threads composed of threads running on the same (preferred) socket and ensures long-term fairness. Second, non-eligible threads (running on other, non-preferred sockets) do not access the counter of active threads (but rather wait until they become eligible), reducing contention on that counter.

6   Evaluation

We implemented GCR as a stand-alone library conforming to the pthread mutex lock API defined by the POSIX standard. We integrated GCR into LiTL [20], an open-source project providing an implementation of dozens of various locks, including well-known established locks, such as MCS [21] and CLH [5], as well as more recent ones, such as NUMA-aware Cohort [10] and HMCS locks [3]. The LiTL library also includes the implementation of a related Malthusian lock [7], which introduces a concurrency restriction mechanism into the MCS lock. Furthermore, the LiTL library allows specifying various waiting policies (e.g., spin or spin-then-park) for locks that support that (such as MCS, CLH or Cohort locks). Overall, we experimented with 24 different lock+waiting policy combinations in LiTL (for brevity, we will refer to each lock+waiting policy combination simply as a lock).

We run experiments on three different platforms. For this paper, we focus on a dual-socket x86-based system with 40 logical CPUs in total. The qualitative results from other two systems (a four-socket x86-based system with 144 logical CPUs in total and a dual-socket SPARC-based system with 512 logical CPUs in total) were similar, and are included in the longer version of the paper [8].

In all experiments, we vary the number of threads up to twice the capacity of each machine. We do not pin threads to cores, relying on the OS to make its choices. In all experiments, we employ a scalable memory allocator [1].

We disable the turbo mode to avoid the effect of that mode, which varies with the number of threads, on the results. Each reported experiment has been run 3 times in exactly the same configuration. Presented results are the average of results reported by each of those 3 runs.

6.1   AVL Tree Microbenchmark

The microbenchmark uses a sequential AVL tree implementation protected by a single lock. The tree supports the API of a key-value map, including operations for inserting, removing and looking up keys (and associated values) stored in the tree. After initial warmup, not included in the measurement interval, all threads are synchronized to start running at the same time, and apply tree operations chosen uniformly and at random from the given distribution, with keys chosen uniformly and at random from the given range. At the end of this time period (lasting 10 s), the total number of operations is calculated, and the throughput is reported. The reported results are for the key range of 4096 and threads performing 80% lookup operations, while the rest is split evenly between inserts and removes. The tree is pre-initialized to contain roughly half of the key range. Finally, the microbenchmark allows to control the amount of the external work, i.e., the duration of a non-critical section (simulated by a pseudo-random number calculation loop). In this experiment, we use a non-critical section duration that allows scalability up to a small number of threads.

The absolute performance of the AVL tree benchmark (in terms of the total throughput) with several locks is shown in Fig. 3. Figure 3(a) and (b) show how the popular MCS lock [21] performs without GCR, with GCR and with GCR-NUMA, and how those locks compare to the recent Malthusian lock [7], which implements a concurrency restriction mechanism directly into the MCS lock. Locks in Fig. 3(a) employ the spinning waiting policy, while those in Fig. 3(b) employ the spin-then-park policy. In addition, Fig. 3(c) and (d) compare the performance achieved with the simple Test-Test-Set (TTAS) lock and the POSIX pthread mutex lock, respectively, when used without GCR, with GCR and with GCR-NUMA. The concurrency restriction mechanism of a Malthusian lock cannot be applied directly into the simple TTAS or POSIX pthread mutex locks, so we do not include a Malthusian variant in those two cases.

With the spinning policy (Fig. 3(a)), GCR has a small detrimental effect (2% slowdown for a single thread, and in general, at most 12% slowdown) on the performance of MCS as long as the machine is not oversubscribed. This is because all threads remain running on their logical CPUs and the lock hand-off is fast at the time that GCR introduces certain (albeit, small) overhead. The Malthusian lock performs similarly to (but worse than) GCR. MCS with GCR-NUMA, however, tops the performance chart as it limits the amount of cross-socket communication incurred by all other locks when the lock is handed off between threads running on different sockets. The performance of the MCS and Malthusian locks plummets once the number of running threads exceeds the capacity of the machine. At the same time, GCR (and GCR-NUMA) are not

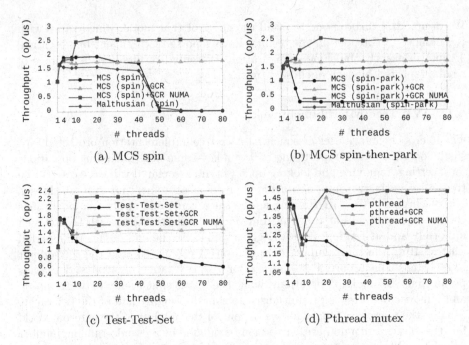

Fig. 3. Throughput results for several popular locks (AVL tree).

sensitive to that as they park excessive threads, preserving the overall performance. In case of GCR-NUMA, for instance, this performance is close to the peak achieved with 10 threads.

The MCS and Malthusian locks with the spin-then-park policy exhibit a different performance pattern (Fig. 3(b)). Specifically, the former shows poor performance at the relatively low number of threads. This is because as the number of threads grows, the waiting threads start quitting spinning and park, adding the overhead of unparking for each lock handoff. The Malthusian lock with its concurrency restriction mechanism avoids that. Yet, its performance is slightly worse than that of MCS with GCR. Once again, MCS with GCR-NUMA easily beats all other contenders.

In summary, the results in Fig. 3(a) and (b) show that despite being generic, the concurrency restriction mechanism of GCR performs superiorly to that of the specialized Malthusian lock. Besides, unlike the Malthusian lock, the choice of a waiting policy for the underlying lock becomes much less crucial when GCR (or GCR-NUMA) is used.

The TTAS and pthread mutex locks exhibit yet another performance pattern (Fig. 3(c) and (d)). Similarly to the MCS spin-then-park variant, their performance drops at low thread counts, however they manage to maintain reasonable throughput even as the number of threads grows. Along with that, both GCR and GCR-NUMA variants mitigate the drop in the performance.

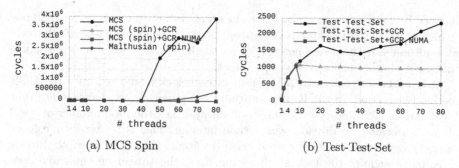

Fig. 4. Handoff time for the MCS (spin) and Test-Test-Set locks (AVL tree).

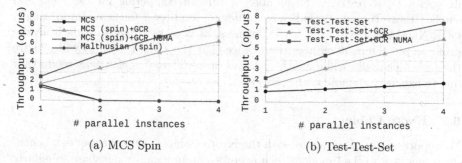

Fig. 5. Total throughput measured with multiple instances of the microbenchmark, each run with 40 threads.

We also run experiments in which we measured the handoff time for each of the locks presented in Figure 3, that is the interval between a timestamp taken right before the current lock holder calls `Unlock()` and right after the next lock holder returns from `Lock()`. Previous work has shown that the performance of a parallel system is dictated by the length of its critical sections [11], which is composed of the time required to acquire and release the lock (captured by the handoff data), and the time a lock holder spends in the critical section. Indeed, the data in Fig. 4 shows correlation between the throughput achieved and the handoff time. That is, in all cases where the throughput of a lock degraded in Fig. 3, the handoff time has increased. At the same time, GCR (and GCR-NUMA) manages to maintains a constant handoff time across virtually all thread counts.

In a different experiment, we run multiple instances of the microbenchmark, each configured to use the number of threads equal to the number of logical CPUs (40). This illustrates the case where an application with a configurable number of threads chooses to set that number based on the machine capacity (as it typically happens by default, for instance, in OpenMP framework implementations). Figure 5 presents the results for two of the locks. Both GCR and GCR-NUMA scale well up to 4 instances for all tested locks. Except for pthread mutex (not shown), all locks without GCR (or GCR-NUMA) exhibit greatly reduced performance, especially when the number of instances is larger than one (which is when the machine is oversubscribed). Pthread mutex fares relatively well, although it should be noted that its single instance performance is worse than several other locks in this experiment.

It is natural to ask how the fairness of each lock is affected once the GCR mechanism is used. In the longer version of the paper [8], we demonstrate that GCR can, in fact, improve the long-term fairness, i.e., the total number of operations performed by threads over a time interval. This is because some locks can be grossly unfair mainly due to caching effects. That is, if multiple threads attempt to acquire the lock at the same time, the thread on the same core or socket as a previous lock holder is likely to win as it has the lock word in its cache. GCR restricts the number of threads competing for the lock, and shuffles those threads periodically, achieving long-term fairness. Interestingly, GCR-NUMA achieves even better fairness, as it picks active threads from the same socket. Thus, it reduces the chance that the same thread(s) will acquire the lock repeatedly while another thread on a different socket fails to do that due to expensive remote cache misses.

6.2 Kyoto Cabinet

We report on our experiments with the Kyoto Cabinet [12] `kccachetest` benchmark run in a `wicked` mode, which exercises an in-memory database. Similarly to [7], we modified the benchmark to use the standard POSIX pthread mutex locks, which we interpose with locks from the LiTL library. We also modified the benchmark to run for a fixed time and report the aggregated work completed. Finally, we fixed the key range at a constant (10M) elements. (Originally, the benchmark set the key range dependent on the number of threads). All those changes were also applied to Kyoto in [7] to allow fair comparison of performance across different thread counts. The length of each run was 60 s.

Kyoto employs multiple locks, each protecting a slot comprising of a number of buckets in a hash table; the latter is used to implement a database [12]. Given that the `wicked` mode exercises a database with random operations and random keys, one should expect a lower load on each of the multiple slot locks compared to the load on the central lock used to protect the access to the AVL tree in the microbenchmark above. Yet, Kyoto provides a view on how GCR behaves in a real application setting.

The results are presented in Fig. 6, where we run GCR and GCR-NUMA on top of 24 locks provided by LiTL. A cell at row X and column Y represents the throughput achieved with Y threads when GCR (GCR-NUMA, respectively) is used on top of lock X divided by throughput achieved when the lock X itself is used (i.e., without GCR or GCR-NUMA). The shades of red colors represent slowdown (speedup below 1, which in virtually all cases falls in the range of [0.8..1), i.e., less than 20% slowdown), while the shades of green colors represent positive speedup; the intensity of the color represents how slowdown/speedup are substantial. Both GCR and GCR-NUMA deliver robust gains (at times, over x1000), and those gains start for virtually all locks even before the machine becomes oversubscribed.

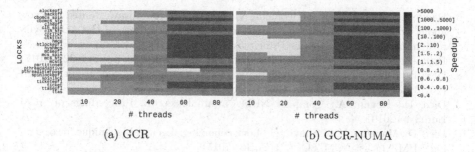

(a) GCR   (b) GCR-NUMA

Fig. 6. Speedup achieved by GCR and GCR-NUMA over various locks (Kyoto).

In the longer version of the paper [8], we also present results for LevelDB, an open-source key-value storage library [18]. The LevelDB results largely echo the results for Kyoto, and lead to the same high-level conclusion as in the other benchmarks—increased lock contention leads to increased speedups achieved by GCR and GCR-NUMA.

7   Conclusion

We have presented GCR, a generic concurrency restriction mechanism, and GCR-NUMA, the extension of GCR to the NUMA settings. GCR wraps any underlying lock and controls which threads are allowed to compete for its acquisition. The idea is to keep the lock saturated by as few threads as possible, while parking all other excessive threads that would otherwise compete for the lock, create contention and consume valuable system resources. Extensive evaluation with more than two dozen locks shows substantial speedup achieved by GCR on various systems and benchmarks; the speedup grows even larger when GCR-NUMA is used.

References

1. Afek, Y., Dice, D., Morrison, A.: Cache index-aware memory allocation. In: Proceedings of ACM ISMM, pp. 55–64 (2011)
2. Boyd-Wickizer, S., Kaashoek, M., Morris, R., Zeldovich, N.: Non-scalable locks are dangerous. In: Proceedings of the Linux Symposium (2012)
3. Chabbi, M., Fagan, M., Mellor-Crummey, J.: High performance locks for multi-level NUMA systems. In: Proceedings of the ACM PPoPP (2015)
4. Chadha, G., Mahlke, S., Narayanasamy, S.: When less is more (LIMO): controlled parallelism for improved efficiency. In: Conference on Compilers, Architectures and Synthesis for Embedded Systems (CASES) (2012)
5. Craig, T.: Building FIFO and priority-queueing spin locks from atomic swap. Technical report TR 93–02–02, University of Washington, Department of Computer Science (1993)

6. David, T., Guerraoui, R., Trigonakis, V.: Everything you always wanted to know about synchronization but were afraid to ask. In: Proceedings of the ACM Symposium on Operating Systems Principles (SOSP), pp. 33–48 (2013)
7. Dice, D.: Malthusian locks. In: Proceedings of ACM EuroSys, pp. 314–327 (2017)
8. Dice, D., Kogan, A.: Avoiding scalability collapse by restricting concurrency. CoRR (2019). https://arxiv.org/abs/1905.10818
9. Dice, D., Kogan, A.: Compact NUMA-aware locks. In: Proceedings of ACM EuroSys (2019)
10. Dice, D., Marathe, V.J., Shavit, N.: Lock cohorting: a general technique for designing NUMA locks. ACM TOPC 1(2), 13 (2015)
11. Eyerman, S., Eeckhout, L.: Modeling critical sections in Amdahl's law and its implications for multicore design. In: Proceedings of ACM ISCA, pp. 362–370 (2010)
12. Kyoto Cabinet. http://fallabs.com/kyotocabinet
13. Guiroux, H., Lachaize, R., Quéma, V.: Multicore locks: the case is not closed yet. In: Proceedings of USENIX ATC, pp. 649–662 (2016)
14. He, B., Scherer, W.N., Scott, M.L.: Preemption adaptivity in time-published queue-based spin locks. In: Proceedings of High Performance Computing (HiPC), pp. 7–18 (2005)
15. Heirman, W., Carlson, T., Van Craeynest, K., Hur, I., Jaleel, A., Eeckhout, L.: Undersubscribed threading on clustered cache architectures. In: Proceedings of IEEE HPCA (2014)
16. Johnson, R., Athanassoulis, M., Stoica, R., Ailamaki, A.: A new look at the roles of spinning and blocking. In: Proceedings of the International Workshop on Data Management on New Hardware (DaMoN). ACM (2009)
17. Johnson, R., Stoica, R., Ailamaki, A., Mowry, T.C.: Decoupling contention management from scheduling. In: Proceedings of ACM ASPLOS, pp. 117–128 (2010)
18. Leveldb. https://github.com/google/leveldb
19. Lim, B.H., Agarwal, A.: Waiting algorithms for synchronization in large-scale multiprocessors. ACM Trans. Comput. Syst. 11, 253–294 (1993)
20. LiTL: Library for Transparent Lock interposition. https://github.com/multicore-locks/litl
21. Mellor-Crummey, J.M., Scott, M.L.: Algorithms for scalable synchronization on shared-memory multiprocessors. ACM Trans. Comp. Syst. 9(1), 21–65 (1991)
22. Pusukuri, K.K., Gupta, R., Bhuyan, L.N.: Thread reinforcer: dynamically determining number of threads via OS level monitoring. In: Proceedings of IEEE IISWC (2011)
23. Radovic, Z., Hagersten, E.: Hierarchical backoff locks for nonuniform communication architectures. In: Proceedings of EEE HPCA, pp. 241–252 (2003)
24. Raman, A., Kim, H., Oh, T., Lee, J.W., August, D.I.: Parallelism orchestration using DoPE: the degree of parallelism executive. In: Proceedings of ACM PLDI (2011)
25. Yoo, R.M., Lee, H.H.S.: Adaptive transaction scheduling for transactional memory systems. In: Proceedings of ACM SPAA (2008)

Graph Coloring Using GPUs

Meghana Aparna Sistla and V. Krishna Nandivada[(✉)]

Department of CSE, IIT Madras, Chennai, India
sistla.meghana@gmail.com, nvk@iitm.ac.in

Abstract. Graph coloring is a widely studied problem that is used in a variety of applications, such as task scheduling, register allocation, eigenvalue computations, social network analysis, and so on. Many of the modern day applications deal with large graphs (with millions of vertices and edges) and researchers have exploited the parallelism provided by multicore systems to efficiently color such large graphs. GPUs provide a promising parallel infrastructure to run large applications. In this paper, we present new schemes to efficiently color large graphs on GPUs.

We extend the algorithm of Rokos et al. [21] to efficiently color graphs using GPUs. Their approach has to continually resolve conflicts for color assignment. We present a data driven variation of their algorithm and use an improved scheme for conflict resolution. We also propose two optimizations for our algorithm to reduce both the execution time and memory requirements. We have evaluated our scheme (called SIRG) against the NVIDIA cuSPARSE library and the work of Chen et al. [13], and show that SIRG runs significantly faster: geomean 3.42× and 1.76×, respectively. We have also compared SIRG against the scheme of Rokos et al. [21] for CPUs and show that SIRG performs faster on most input graphs: geomean 10.37×.

1 Introduction

Graph Coloring, widely studied as vertex coloring in an undirected graph, refers to the assignment of colors to the vertices of a graph such that no two adjacent vertices are assigned the same color. It is used in various applications such as scheduling of tasks [16], register allocation [3], eigenvalue computations [15], social network analysis [5], sparse matrix computations [12], and so on. The problem of optimal graph coloring and even that of finding the *chromatic number* of a graph (minimum number of colors needed to color the graph) are NP-Hard. Hence, various heuristics have been proposed to solve the graph coloring problem. As many modern applications deal with graphs containing millions of vertices and edges, coloring of such large graphs sequentially leads to prohibitively high execution times. To address this issue, various parallel graph coloring algorithms have been designed for multi-core and many-core systems.

Though graph coloring as a problem has been solved using many heuristics [1,7,17,20], parallel graph coloring algorithms have mostly been extensions

© Springer Nature Switzerland AG 2019
R. Yahyapour (Ed.): Euro-Par 2019, LNCS 11725, pp. 377–390, 2019.
https://doi.org/10.1007/978-3-030-29400-7_27

of two main approaches: (1) Maximal Independent Set (MIS) approach that finds maximal independent sets of a graph and assigns a unique color to each independent set. (2) Greedy approach that assigns each vertex v the smallest color that has not been assigned to any adjacent vertices of v.

Luby [14] proposed one of the first parallel graph coloring algorithms by computing MIS in parallel. The algorithm was later extended by Jones and Plassmann [11]. Compared to the MIS based algorithms, owing to the simplicity in implementation and ease of parallelization of greedy algorithms, many researchers have proposed the greedy approach based parallel graph coloring algorithms. For example, Gebremedhin and Manne [8] proposed a three-step approach as the initial parallelization of the sequential greedy algorithm. In Step1, the algorithm colors all the vertices in parallel with the minimum available color (that smallest color that has not been used to color any of the adjacent vertices). This may lead to conflicts between adjacent vertices. In Step2, conflicts are detected and for each conflict one of the vertices retains the color and the other vertex loses its color. After resolving conflicts, in Step3, all the remaining uncolored vertices are colored with the minimum available colors, sequentially. The Step3 was parallelized by Çatalyürek et al. [2], by invoking Step1 and Step2 on the remaining uncolored vertices, repeatedly. The process continues until there are no conflicts. After each invocation of Step1 and Step2, a barrier is inserted to synchronize among the threads.

Rokos et al. [21] improved the algorithm of Çatalyürek et al. [2] by reducing the synchronization overheads among the threads. In case of conflicts, instead of uncoloring and recoloring, the algorithm recolors the conflicting-vertex in the same iteration with the minimum available color. We refer to this improvised algorithm as RIG (Rokos Improvised Greedy).

As GPUs provide massive amounts of parallelism and are widely being used to run algorithms on large datasets, there also have been efforts to design parallel algorithms that can run efficiently on GPUs. For example, the csrcolor function, in the cuSPARSE library [19] of NVIDIA, implements the parallel MIS algorithm for GPUs. Grosset et al. [9] presented the first implementation of the greedy algorithm of Gebremedhin and Manne [8] on GPUs. Recently, Chen et al. [13] extended the work of Çatalyürek et al. [2] on to GPUs with a few optimizations; we refer to their work as ChenGC. One main drawback of their work is that their algorithm needs a pre-set value of the maximum color required ($maxColor$) to color the graph and the algorithm does not terminate if the value of $maxColor$ is too low. In contrast, setting $maxColor$ to a very high value leads to very high execution times and memory usage. Though the NVIDIA's cuSPARSE library does not suffer from any such limitations, it uses a large number of colors for producing a valid coloring of the graph. And also it runs slower (55% [13]) than ChenGC. In this paper, we present a solution to address these limitations.

We extend the algorithm of Rokos et al. [21] to efficiently color graphs using GPUs. We provide a data-driven extension of their algorithm, along with new heuristics for faster executions. We propose two optimizations for improving both the execution time and memory requirements. We have evaluated our optimized

```
 1  Function RIG (G) // G = (V, E)
 2  begin
 3  │  U = V;
 4  │  foreach v ∈ U do // parallel loop        ⎫
 5  │  │  C = {colors of u ∈ adj(v)};           ⎬ Coloring Phase
 6  │  └  color(v) = minimum color c ∉ C;       ⎭
 7  │  barrier();
 8  │  while |U| > 0 do                         ⎫
 9  │  │  L = φ;                                │
10  │  │  foreach v ∈ U do // parallel loop     │
11  │  │  │  if ∃ v' ∈ adj(v), v' > v: color(v) == color(v') then    ⎬ Conflict Re-
12  │  │  │  │  C = {colors of u ∈ adj(v)};     │  solve and
13  │  │  │  │  color(v) = minimum color c ∉ C; │  Recolor Phase
14  │  │  │  └  L = L ∪ {v};                    │
15  │  │  barrier();                            │
16  │  └  U = L;                                ⎭
```

Fig. 1. Improvised Greedy Algorithm of Rokos et al. [21].

algorithm (referred to as SIRG – Scalable and Improved RIG Algorithm for GPUs) and found that SIRG runs 3.42× and 1.76× faster than csrcolor and ChenGC, respectively. We have also compared SIRG (on GPUs) against RIG on CPUs and found that SIRG runs 10.37× (geomean) faster than RIG. We have also studied the impact of our proposed optimizations and the various design decisions and found them to be effective.

2   Background

Algorithm of Rokos et al. For the sake of completeness, we briefly present the improvised greedy algorithm of Rokos et al. [21]·(Fig. 1). We refer to it as the RIG (Rokos Improvised Greedy) algorithm. It consists of two phases: the `Coloring` phase (lines 4–6) and the `ConflictResolveAndRecolor` phase (lines 8–16) with a barrier in between, for synchronization. The `Coloring` phase tentatively assigns (in parallel) every vertex a color based on the *minimum available color* (the smallest color that is not assigned to any of its neighbouring vertices). After every vertex has been processed, the `ConflictResolveAndRecolor` phase starts, where every vertex v is checked for conflict of colors with its neighbouring vertices that have vertex-number higher than that of v. If a conflict is detected, the vertex with higher vertex number retains the color. The vertex with a lower vertex number is recolored by checking for colors of its neighbours and assigning the minimum available color. Once all the vertices have been processed (enforced by a barrier), the phase continues with the recolored vertices. The algorithm terminates when no vertices have to be recolored. This, in turn, indicates that the graph vertices have a valid coloring.

Parallelization on GPU. In CUDA programs, the computation is typically divided between the host (CPU) and device (GPU). The host side computation includes the allocation of the required memory on the device and copying of data required by the program from the host to the device. The host also launches the device code using a command like $\ll M, N \gg$kernelFunc(), to launch N number of threads on each of the M thread-blocks; the values of M and N are set by the programmer. After the parallel execution of the kernels, the control returns to the host. The required data is copied back to the host from the device.

3   Graph Coloring for GPUs

In this section, we present our novel graph coloring algorithm that can be run efficiently on GPUs. We derive this algorithm from the insightful work of Rokos et al. [21] (described in Sect. 2). We first show why their argument about the non-termination of their algorithm (for GPUs) does not hold. Then we extend their algorithm with a few heuristics for efficient execution on GPUs.

3.1   Non-termination of the RIG Algorithm

Rokos et al. [21, Section 5] discuss that the algorithm in Fig. 1 goes into an infinite loop due to SIMT-style execution of GPU threads. However, the algorithm will not lead to an infinite loop if the comparison at Line 11 is based on some unique ids (such as vertex numbers), which ensures that no two adjacent vertices will keep flipping their colors forever (as alluded by Rokos et al.). In this paper, we maintain and use unique vertex ids for such conflict resolution.

3.2   Improvements to RIG

We now list two improvements to the RIG algorithm (Sect. 2). The first one improves the conflict resolution criteria, and the second one is an efficient mechanism to implement the algorithm for GPUs.

Conflict Resolution. For the ease of presentation, for each vertex v, we use $S(v)$ to denote the set of neighbouring vertices that need to be checked for conflicts in every iteration (Line 11, Fig. 1). Figure 1 resolves the conflicts by giving priority to the higher number vertex (Line 11) and uses $S(v) = \{u | u \in adj(v), u > v\}$. While this works as a fine criterion for avoiding infinite loops, it can be improved by using the degree of the nodes as the first criteria for conflict resolution. We set $S(v) = \{u | u \in adj(v), degree(u) > degree(v)) || (degree(u) == degree(v) \&\& u > v)\}$. Thus, $S(v)$ includes the set of adjacent vertices of v, such that either their degree is greater than that of v, or they have the same degree as v, but have higher vertex-number than v. The intuition of setting $S(v)$ by using a prioritization scheme based on the degree is that it will lead to fewer conflicts, as the vertices with higher degrees will be removed from contention early. Note that we still include the vertex number based check to ensure that the algorithm does not go into an infinite loop.

```
1 Function GraphColoring (G) // G = (V, E)
2 begin
3      ≪M, N≫Coloring(G);
4      barrier();
5      Wᵢₙ = V;
6      while Wᵢₙ ≠ φ do
7          ≪M, N≫ConflictResolveAndRecolorKernel(G, Wᵢₙ);
8          barrier();
9          swap(Wᵢₙ, Wₒᵤₜ);
```

$$\left.\begin{array}{l}\\\\\\\end{array}\right\}\begin{array}{l}\text{Conflict Re-}\\\text{solve and}\\\text{Recolor Phase}\end{array}$$

Fig. 2. Data driven implementation - CPU

```
1 Function Coloring (G) // G = (V, E)
2 begin
3      for vertex v ∈ V | myThread do
4          C = {colors of u ∈ adj(v)};
5          color(v) = minimum color c ∉ C
6      return color
```

Fig. 3. Data driven implementation. Coloring phase on GPU

Data-Driven Implementation. We use the data-driven method proposed by Nasre et al. [18] to realize an efficient implementation of the RIG algorithm (Fig. 1) for GPUs. In the data-driven method, only vertices that do not have valid colors are processed in every iteration unlike the topology-driven method, where all vertices are processed in every iteration. The original algorithm has two parts: (i) the coloring phase (lines 4–6) and (ii) the conflict-resolve-and-recolor phase (lines 8–16). Our data-driven implementation mainly improves the second part.

Figure 2 shows the main pseudocode to be executed on the host (CPU). The initial Coloring phase (see Fig. 3) is similar to the RIG algorithm, except that $M \times N$ GPU threads are launched; see Sect. 5, for a discussion on the optimal choice of M and N. Each GPU thread is assigned a set of vertices to be colored (shown by the projection $V | myThread$). In our implementation, we have used a cyclic distribution.

The next phase (conflict-resolve-and-recolor) maintains two shared worklists W_{in} and W_{out}, where W_{in} represents the vertices that still need to be recolored. Initially, W_{in} contains the list of all the vertices. In every iteration, the host launches the GPU kernel on a set of GPU threads. Each of the GPU threads runs the code shown in the function ConflictResolveAndRecolorKernel (Fig. 4).

Each thread picks a vertex from the list of vertices (from W_{in}) that are assigned to it (represented by the projection $W_{in}|myThread$). In our implementation, we have used a cyclic distribution. Each vertex is checked for conflicts based on the conflict-resolution heuristic discussed above. In case a conflict is detected, the vertex is recolored with the minimum available color, and the

```
1  Function ConflictResolveAndRecolorKernel (G, W_in)
2  begin
3  │  W_out = φ;
4  │  for v ∈ W_in | myThread do
5  │  │  if ∃ v' ∈ adj(v), v' ∈ S(v): color(v) == color(v') then
6  │  │  │  C = {colors of u ∈ adj(v)};
7  │  │  │  color(v) = minimum color c ∉ C ;
8  │  │  │  W_out = W_out ∪ {v};                    // Atomic operation
```

Fig. 4. Conflict resolution and recoloring phase on GPU.

vertex is added to W_{out}. Since W_{out} is a shared list across the GPU threads, this operation has to be done atomically. See Sect. 5 on how we implement it efficiently. If no conflict is detected for a vertex, then the vertex retains its color and is not considered for (re)coloring in the subsequent iterations.

On the host, at the end of every iteration of the while-loop, W_{in} and W_{out} are swapped (double buffering [18]) and the process continues. The algorithm terminates when W_{in} does not contain any more vertices; that is, all the vertices have been colored without any conflicts. Thus, the graph finally has a valid coloring at the end of the algorithm.

4 Optimizations

We now list two optimizations for the baseline algorithm discussed in Sect. 3. Both these optimizations are related to the efficient implementation of the data structure that holds the set of colors of the adjacent vertices. We denote the baseline algorithm of Sect. 3 along with the optimizations discussed in this section, as SIRG (Scalable and Improved RIG Algorithm for GPUs).

In the GPU algorithm shown in Figs. 3 and 4, every thread colors/recolors a vertex with the minimum available color. For this, a naive way of implementation would be to use, for each vertex, an integer array adjColors to hold one bit for each of the colors that might be required to color the graph. Hence, the size of adjColors $= \lceil (maxColor \div 32) \rceil$, where $maxColor$ is the estimated maximum number of colors required to color the graph. As a quick and conservative estimate, we use the following equation as the estimate for $maxColor$.

$$maxColor = 2^{\lceil (\log_2 (1+\text{maximum-degree-of-the-graph})) \rceil} \tag{1}$$

For every vertex v, initially, every bit of the array adjColors is set to 1. For every adjacent vertex of v, the bit corresponding to the color of that adjacent vertex is unset in adjColors. Then, the color corresponding to the first bit in adjColors that is set to 1, is assigned to v.

Considering the overheads of maintaining, for each vertex, an individual adjColors array, and the scalability issues thereof, we allocate one adjColors array for each thread on the GPU device. An important point to note is that every thread may loop over all the elements of the `adjColors` array twice, for every vertex in every iteration – finding the first set bit (to find the min color, line 7, Fig. 4) and for resetting the array (to all 1s, at the end of processing each vertex, after line 8, Fig. 4). Hence, the size of the `adjColors` has a significant impact on the execution time of the individual threads and consequently the overall kernel. We now discuss two optimizations to address this challenge.

4.1 Use of `long long int` and CUDA `__ffsll` Instruction

CUDA provides a hardware instruction `__ffsll` to find the first set bit in a `long long int` number. Hence, we can use a `long long int adjColors` array (instead of an `int` array), where each element of the array can hold 64 bits – corresponding to 64 colors. The size of the array would be reduced to $maxColor \div 64$, from $maxColor \div 32$. As the size of the array decreases by half, every thread needs to loop a fewer number of times over the `adjColors` array, for every vertex thereby improving the performance.

Considering that this optimization is useful only when the initial number of colors is > 32, we use two versions of the code (one using `__ffsll` and one without); one of them is invoked at runtime, depending on the maximum degree of the input graph.

4.2 Stepwise Doubling of Maximum Colors Required

As discussed before, we use $maxColor$ to compute the estimate for the size of `adjColors`. However many of the web graphs are usually sparse graphs, with a small number of vertices having large degrees and the rest having low degrees. Consequently, using Eq. (1), we end up setting $maxColor$ to a unnecessarily high value, even though the actual number of colors required to color the graph is relatively very small. Such high values for $maxColor$ increase the size of the `adjColors` array, thereby increasing the execution time (and increasing the memory requirements). We now present a scheme to reduce these overheads.

We set the initial value of $maxColor$ to be a small number K_0. Consequently, the initial size of the `adjColors` array will be small, but may not be enough to color the graph without any conflicts. This insufficiency in the number of colors can be detected when there is no bit set (color available) in the `adjColors` array in an iteration (line 5 in Fig. 3 and line 7 in Fig. 4). In such a case, we double the value of $maxColor$ and resize the `adjColors` array, and continue the coloring process for the remaining vertices. Such a resizing can happen till the $maxColor$ value is sufficient to color the graph without any conflicts.

By doubling the value of $maxColor$ when required and not setting it to a large value conservatively, the size of the `adjColors` array can be significantly reduced. In our evaluation, we use $K_0 = min\left(256, 2^{\lceil(\log_2(1+\text{maximum-degree-of-the-graph}))\rceil}\right)$. Thus, this optimization is impactful only for graphs whose maximum degree is > 256.

5 Discussion

We now present some of the salient points in the implementation of SIRG.

Compressed Sparse Row. We represent the graph using the standard compressed sparse row (csr) format, that uses two arrays (ColIndices and Offset) to represent the graphs. In addition, we maintain another array (called nextVertices) to efficiently find, for each vertex v, the set of neighboring vertices that need to be checked for conflicts, (given by $S(v)$, see Sect. 3). The element nextVertices[i] points to the index in ColIndices such that the vertices in adjacency list of v_i from nextVertices[i] to Offset[i+1] belong to $S(v_i)$. The ColIndices array is arranged such that, for each vertex v_i, the vertices in the adjacency list of v_i are ordered by the vertex number, or the vertex degree, depending on whether vertex number or degree is used for conflict resolution (see Sect. 3). Maintaining this additional array nextVertices can provide access to the elements of $S(v_i)$ in $\mathcal{O}(1)$ time during the conflict resolution phase.

Adding Elements to Worklist. In Fig. 4 (Line 8), every thread updates a shared worklist (W_{out}) and this has to be done atomically. This leads to the invocation of a large number of atomic operations, which can be potentially inefficient. To address this issue we use the popular idea of using parallel prefix sum [10] to find the appropriate indices where each thread of a warp can write (in parallel) to the shared worklist, independently of each other. This leads to execution of one atomic operation per warp (in contrast to one atomic operation per thread) and hence reduces the number of atomic operations by a factor of up to 32 (warp size).

Distribution of Worklist Elements Among GPU Threads. The elements of the worklist W_{in} have to be divided among GPU threads in a data-driven implementation. For efficiency, we implemented the worklists (W_{in} and W_{out}) as global arrays and these elements are distributed among the GPU threads in a cyclic order. Therefore, a thread with id $= t$, accesses the vertices from W_{in} such that the index i of the vertex in W_{in} satisfies the equation $t = i\%totalNumThreads$. Note that we have also tried using the blocked distribution, but found the cyclic distribution to be more efficient.

Number of Threads. The optimal number of blocks per SM (*maximum residency*) to be launched depend on many factors, such as the blocksize, number of registers, shared memory size, and so on. We set the total number of blocks launched to be equal to maximum residency × number of SMs. On experimentation, we found that setting blocksize = 1024 threads gave the best performance, on our NVIDIA P100 system.

Topology-Driven Implementation. In addition to the data-driven implementation discussed in Sect. 3, we also implemented the coloring algorithm of Rokos et al. [21] using the topology-driven method [18]. We observed that the topology-driven implementation was significantly slower than the data-driven implementation and hence not elaborated on, in this manuscript.

Difference in Memory Requirements Between SIRG and ChenGC.
Both SIRG and ChenGC [13] follow the greedy approach and the memory usage
is similar. Compared to ChenGC, SIRG uses only an extra of 16 bytes overall
to maintain some additional meta-data information.

6 Implementation and Evaluation

We have compiled our codes using the CUDA 9.1 compiler and executed them on
a Tesla P100 GPU, with 12 GB memory. We have evaluated our codes using eight
different graph inputs (details shown in Fig. 5), with vertices varying between
0.4M to 50M, edges varying between 57M to 903M. These inputs span both
real-world graphs like road networks and scale-free networks that follow power-
law, and synthetic graphs (last three). While the first six are obtained from
the Florida Sparse Matrix Collection [6], the last two are created using the R-
MAT [4] graph generator (using the parameters shown in Fig. 5). We now present
our evaluation to understand (i) the performance improvements realized by SIRG
(uses the schemes discussed in Sects. 3 and 4) over the existing graph coloring
algorithm of Chen et al. [13] that is targeted to GPUs (abbreviated ChenGC),
and NVIDIA's cuSPARSE library. (ii) the effect of the proposed optimizations,
and (iii) the impact of some of the design decisions. All these codes (different
versions of SIRG, ChenGC, and the code using the cuSPARSE library) used for
the comparative evaluation can be found on GitHub [22].

Network	Nodes (10^6)	Edges (10^6)	Avg degree	Type
EUROPE_OSM	50.9	108.1	2.12	Road Network
ROAD_USA	23.9	57.7	2.41	Road Network
ORKUT	3.1	234.3	76.28	Scale Free Network
LIVEJOURNAL	3.9	69.4	17.35	Scale Free Network
TWITTER7	41.6	323.3	7.76	Scale Free Network
MYCIELSKIAN19	0.4	903.2	2296.95	General Network
RMAT_1	10.0	199.9	20.00	Synthetic (0.5,0.5,0.5,0.5)
RMAT_2	20.0	809.9	40.49	Synthetic (0.1,0.3,0.4,0.2)

Fig. 5. Graphs used in our experiments

6.1 Comparison of SIRG vs ChenGC and csrcolor

To perform a comparative evaluation of SIRG, we used ChenGC and the
NVIDIA's cuSPARSE library (csrcolor function) to color the input graphs. While
csrcolor was general enough to color any given graph, we found that ChenGC
did not terminate for four of the eight input graphs. We found that the issue was
because ChenGC uses a fixed value for the maximum number of the required
colors ($maxColor$) – the value for this variable is hardcoded in their algorithm,
unlike in SIRG, where no such restriction is present. We found that in ChenGC,

while setting *maxColor* to a very large number, made the programs run success-fully on all the inputs, but it had a drawback – the programs took a very long time to run. On experimentation, we found the minimum value for the variable *maxColor*, in order for ChenGC to run successfully on all the input graphs was 1024; hence, we set *maxColor*=1024 in ChenGC.

Figure 6a shows the speedup of SIRG with respect to ChenGC in terms of execution time. We can observe that across all the input graphs, SIRG performs better than ChenGC (between 1.15× to 5.68×, geomean 1.76×).

We find that in the real-world graphs the gains are much more than that in the synthetic graphs. In general, we found that the stepwise-doubling optimiza-tion was most effective in these real-world graphs in improving the performance. And this impact was much higher in power-law graphs (for example, TWITTER7).

Figure 6a shows the speedup of SIRG over csrcolor. In contrast to ChenGC, we did not have to make any changes to csrcolor, for it to run. Figure 6b shows that SIRG performs significantly better than csrcolor (1.15× to 21.38×, geomean 3.42×). We see that except for RMAT_1 and RMAT_2, SIRG performs leads to remarkably higher performance across both power-law and non-power-law graphs. We believe the very high speedups obtained in MYCIELSKIAN19 is because of the specific nature of the input graph (higher density, total number of nodes = 0.4 million, average degree ≈ 2300), which is making the csrcolor perform poorly.

We have also compared the coloring quality (number of colors used) by the three algorithms under consideration. While SIRG uses significantly fewer num-ber of colors (geomean 77% less) than csrcolor, the number is comparable to that of ChenGC (geomean difference < 6%). We have observed that even this minor difference is mainly related to the order in which the threads process the vertices. Further the main contributor for the increased geomean for SIRG (compared to ChenGC) is the MYCIELSKIAN19 input, where SIRG takes 29% more colors. This is mainly because the specific structure of MYCIELSKIAN19 where the increase in the number of threads is leading to more conflicts and more number of colors.

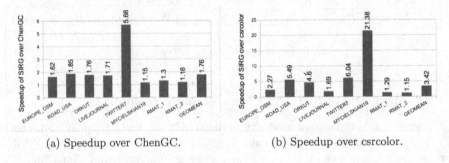

(a) Speedup over ChenGC.   (b) Speedup over csrcolor.

Fig. 6. Speedup of SIRG over ChenGC and csrcolor.

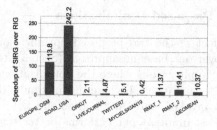

Fig. 7. Speedup of SIRG over RIG

Summary. We see that SIRG performs significantly better than csrcolor. It even performs better than ChenGC, which has to be tuned manually in order to run successfully on various graph inputs.

6.2 Comparison of SIRG vs RIG

We performed an comparative study of SIRG (on GPUs) over RIG (on CPUs) (see Sect. 2). We evaluated RIG on a CPU with 40 cores. Similar to ChenGC, we observed that RIG did not terminate for two of the eight input graphs, because of hardcoding the maximum number of required colors ($maxColor$) to 256. On experimentation, we found that the minimum value of $maxColor$ variable required for RIG to successfully run on all the input graphs was 512; hence, we set $maxColor = 512$ in RIG and performed the evaluations.

Figure 7 shows the speedup of SIRG over RIG. We can observe that SIRG performs better than RIG (geomean 10.37×) on almost all the input graphs except MYCIELSKIAN19. This is due to the specific structure of MYCIELSKIAN19 graph, where the gains due to increased parallelism are getting overshadowed by the overheads due to increased color conflicts, especially for large number of threads.

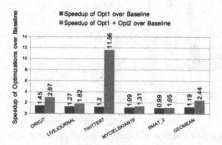

Fig. 8. Effect of the optimizations.

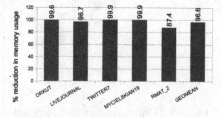

Fig. 9. Effect on memory usage due to stepwise-doubling optimization.

6.3   Impact of the Proposed Optimizations

Figure 8 shows the effect of the two proposed optimizations (Opt1: Sect. 4.1, and Opt2: Sect. 4.2) over our baseline approach (Sect. 3); the graph shows the achieved speedup over input graphs where the optimizations were invoked. For EUROPE_OSM, ROAD_USA and RMAT_1 where the maximum degree was not more than 32, Opt1 was not invoked, and Opt2 had no effect.

We see that, for most inputs, Opt1 performs better than the Baseline and Opt2 adds to the performance improvements much more. We also observe that in the power-law graphs, the effect of Opt2 is high and led to large gains (up to 11.56×).

In Sect. 4.2, we discuss that Opt2 (stepwise-doubling optimization) can also help reduce memory consumption. We show this impact in Fig. 9. The figure compares the memory consumption of SIRG, against SIRG without Opt2, for the inputs on which Opt2 had some impact. It shows that the impact of Opt2 on the memory requirements is high: leads to geomean 96.59% reduction in memory.

Summary. Our evaluation shows that the proposed optimizations lead to significant gains and attests to the importance of these optimizations.

6.4   Impact of Maintaining adjColors array per thread

In Sect. 4, we have discussed that due to the memory overheads and scalability issues, we allocate adjColors array for each thread instead of each vertex. We now discuss the impact of such a choice. We show the impact (in Fig. 10) in terms of total time and memory usage for two configurations: (i) SIRG with adjColors array allocated for each vertex, and (ii) default SIRG: with adjColors array allocated for each thread.

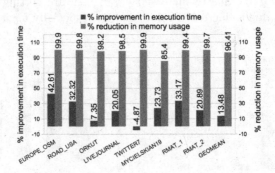

Fig. 10. %Improvement due to per-thread Vs per-vertex allocation of adjColors.

The figure shows that allocating adjColors for each vertex can increase the memory requirements significantly, which is avoided by doing per thread allocation (Geomean 96.41%). While a per-vertex scheme may lead to some minor gains for some inputs (for example, 4.87% for TWITTER7), overall we find that per-thread allocation of `adjColors` led to better execution times (geomean 13.48%).

We found that allocating `adjColors` per vertex increases the memory requirement so much that in the absence of Opt2 (which reduces the memory consumption significantly), the program runs out of memory for many inputs (for example, ORKUT, TWITTER7, MYCIELSKIAN19). This further shows the importance of our choice of per-thread allocation of the `adjColors` array.

Overall summary. Our evaluation shows that SIRG performs better than both csrcolor and ChenGC. We found our optimizations and design choices lead to efficient executions (both in terms of execution time and memory usage).

7 Conclusion

In this paper, we presented a fast and scalable graph coloring algorithm for GPUs. We extended the algorithm by Rokos et al. [21] to efficiently color graphs for GPUs using a data parallel implementation, with a better heuristics for color-conflict resolution. We also proposed two optimization techniques to improve both the execution time and memory requirements. We showed that compared to the NVIDIA's cuSPARSE library and the work of Chen et al. [13], our implementation runs significantly faster (geomean 3.42× and 1.76×, respectively). We also showed that our algorithm (on GPUs) performs geomean 10.37× faster than the scheme of Rokos et al. [21] (on CPUs).

References

1. Biggs, N.: Some heuristics for graph colouring. In: Nelson, R., Wilson, R.J. (eds.) Graph Colourings, pp. 87–96 (1990)
2. Çatalyürek, Ü.V., Feo, J., Gebremedhin, A.H., Halappanavar, M., Pothen, A.: Graph coloring algorithms for multi-core and massively multithreaded architectures. Parallel Comput. **38**(10–11), 576–594 (2012)
3. Chaitin, G.J.: Register allocation & spilling via graph coloring. ACM SIGPLAN Not. **17**, 98–105 (1982)
4. Chakrabarti, D., Zhan, Y., Faloutsos, C.: R-MAT: a recursive model for graph mining. In: ICDM, pp. 442–446. SIAM (2004)
5. Chalupa, D.: On the ability of graph coloring heuristics to find substructures in social networks. Inf. Sci. Technol. Bull. ACM Slovak. **3**(2), 51–54 (2011)
6. Davis, T.A., Hu, Y.: The University of Florida sparse matrix collection. ACM TOMS **38**(1), 1 (2011)
7. Dorne, R.É., Hao, J.-K.: A new genetic local search algorithm for graph coloring. In: Eiben, A.E., Bäck, T., Schoenauer, M., Schwefel, H.-P. (eds.) PPSN 1998. LNCS, vol. 1498, pp. 745–754. Springer, Heidelberg (1998). https://doi.org/10.1007/BFb0056916
8. Gebremedhin, A.H., Manne, F.: Scalable parallel graph coloring algorithms. Concurr. Pract. Exp. **12**(12), 1131–1146 (2000)
9. Grosset, A.V.P., Zhu, P., Liu, S., Venkatasubramanian, S., Hall, M.: Evaluating graph coloring on GPUs. ACM SIGPLAN Not. **46**(8), 297–298 (2011)

10. Harris, M., Sengupta, S., Owens, J.D.: Parallel prefix sum (scan) with CUDA. GPU gems **3**(39), 851–876 (2007)
11. Jones, M.T., Plassmann, P.E.: A parallel graph coloring heuristic. SIAM J. Sci. Comput. **14**(3), 654–669 (1993)
12. Jones, M.T., Plassmann, P.E.: Scalable iterative solution of sparse linear systems. Parallel Comput. **20**(5), 753–773 (1994)
13. Li, P., et al.: High performance parallel graph coloring on GPGPUs. In: IPDPS Workshops, pp. 845–854. IEEE (2016)
14. Luby, M.: A simple parallel algorithm for the maximal independent set problem. J. Comput. **15**(4), 1036–1053 (1986)
15. Manne, F.: A parallel algorithm for computing the extremal eigenvalues of very large sparse matrices. In: Kågström, B., Dongarra, J., Elmroth, E., Waśniewski, J. (eds.) PARA 1998. LNCS, vol. 1541, pp. 332–336. Springer, Heidelberg (1998). https://doi.org/10.1007/BFb0095354
16. Marx, D.: Graph colouring problems and their applications in scheduling. Period. Polytech. Electr. Eng. **48**(1–2), 11–16 (2004)
17. Mehrotra, A., Trick, M.A.: A column generation approach for graph coloring. INFORMS J. Comput. **8**(4), 344–354 (1996)
18. Nasre, R., Burtscher, M., Pingali, K.: Data-driven versus topology-driven irregular computations on GPUs. In: IPDPS, pp. 463–474. IEEE (2013)
19. Nvidia, C.: CuSPARSE Library. NVIDIA Corporation, Santa Clara (2014)
20. Philipsen, W., Stok, L.: Graph coloring using neural networks. In: IEEE International Sympoisum on Circuits and Systems, pp. 1597–1600. IEEE (1991)
21. Rokos, G., Gorman, G., Kelly, P.H.J.: A fast and scalable graph coloring algorithm for multi-core and many-core architectures. In: Träff, J.L., Hunold, S., Versaci, F. (eds.) Euro-Par 2015. LNCS, vol. 9233, pp. 414–425. Springer, Heidelberg (2015). https://doi.org/10.1007/978-3-662-48096-0_32
22. Sistla, M.A., Nandivada, V.K.: Artifact for Graph Coloring using GPUs (2019). https://doi.org/10.6084/m9.figshare.8486123

Featherlight Speculative Task Parallelism

Vivek Kumar(✉)

IIIT-Delhi, New Delhi, India
vivekk@iiitd.ac.in

Abstract. Speculative task parallelism is a widely used technique for solving search based irregular computations such as graph algorithms. Here, tasks are created speculatively to traverse different search spaces in parallel. Only a few of these tasks succeed in finding the solution, after which the remaining tasks are canceled. For ensuring timely cancellation of tasks, existing frameworks either require programmer introduced cancellation checks inside every method in the call chain, thereby hurting the productivity, or provide limited parallel performance.

In this paper we propose *Featherlight*, a new programming model for speculative task parallelism that satisfies the serial elision property and doesn't require any task cancellation checks. We show that Featherlight improves productivity through a classroom-based study. Further, to support Featherlight, we present the design and implementation of a task cancellation technique that exploits runtime mechanisms already available within managed runtimes and achieves a geometric mean speedup of 1.6× over the popular Java ForkJoin framework on a 20 core machine.

Keywords: Speculative parallelism · Async-finish programming ·
Task cancellation · Managed runtimes · Work-stealing

1 Introduction

With the advent of multicore processors, variants of tasks based parallel programming models [1,3,9,10,12,18,20,22] have gained a lot of popularity. They are extremely well suited for parallelizing irregular computations such as graph search algorithms. Some well-known examples are route planning in navigation and guidance systems, searching for entities on social networking sites like people and places, and finding the winning move in a game tree. Programmers using these parallel programming frameworks expose a parallel task and rely on an underlying work-stealing [10] runtime for dynamic load balancing. These frameworks often satisfy the serial elision for basic tasking support, the property that is eliding all parallel constructs results in a valid sequential program [10]. While serial elision improves programmer's productivity, using an underlying work-stealing runtime improves the parallel performance over multicore processors. However, this is not the case when using these frameworks for applications requiring speculative task parallelism, where only a few tasks could provide desirable results, as all remaining tasks should terminate after the goal is found.

© Springer Nature Switzerland AG 2019
R. Yahyapour (Ed.): Euro-Par 2019, LNCS 11725, pp. 391–404, 2019.
https://doi.org/10.1007/978-3-030-29400-7_28

Productivity becomes a first-order concern as several frameworks such as Intel TBB [22], C# [1], X10 [9] and TryCatchWS [18], require programmer inserted task cancellation checks inside every method in the call chain for timely cancellation of speculative tasks. Cilk [10] provides special support for task cancellation but the programmer has to implement an *inlet* that is essentially a C function internal to a Cilk procedure. The Java *fork/join* framework [20] does not support serial elision but provides a *shutdownNow* API for global task cancellation. OpenMP 4.0 [3] tasking pragmas and Eureka programming in HJlib [13] provide task cancellation checks, but the programmer must ensure optimal granularity for calling these checks to avoid performance degradation.

In this paper, we introduce a new programming model, *Featherlight*, for speculative task parallelism that doesn't require any form of task cancellation checks, and improves the productivity by satisfying the property of serial elision. For achieving high performance, Featherlight exploits runtime mechanisms already available within managed runtimes, namely: (a) yieldpoint mechanism [21], (b) ability to walk the execution stack of a running thread, and (c) support for exception delivery. We use six well-know search based micro-benchmarks and one real-world application from Dacapo benchmark suite [8] to compare the productivity and performance of Featherlight with the ForkJoin framework, and also with an approach that uses hand-coded implementation of the task cancellation policy. We use lines of code and time to code based empirical analysis to demonstrate high productivity in Featherlight. We show that Featherlight is highly competitive. It achieves performance comparable to the hand-coded implementation and significantly better than the ForkJoin implementation.

In summary, this paper makes the following contributions:

- *Featherlight*, a new task-based parallel programming model for speculative parallelism that satisfies serial elision property.
- A lightweight runtime implementation that supports Featherlight by exploiting existing managed runtime techniques.
- Productivity analysis of Featherlight by using it in a classroom-based study.
- Performance evaluation of Featherlight as compared to Java ForkJoin framework and a hand-coded implementation of task cancellation policy by using seven popular search based problems on a 20 core machine.

2 Background

2.1 Async-Finish Programming Model

Cilk language [10] popularized task parallelism by using *spawn* and *sync* keywords for creating and joining a parallel task. For scheduling these tasks, an underlying work-stealing runtime is employed that maintains a pool of *worker* threads, each of which maintains a double-ended queue (*deque*) of

```
1  void baz() {
2    finish {
3      async S1();
4      S2();
5    }
6    S3();
7  }
```

Fig. 1. An async-finish program

tasks. When the local deque becomes empty, the worker becomes a *thief* and seeks a *victim* thread from which to *steal* work. Likewise, Java supports a ForkJoin framework [20], and X10 language [9] introduced **async–finish** constructs for task parallelism. This **async–finish** construct satisfy serial elision and have been adopted by other frameworks such as Habanero Java library (HJlib) [12], Habanero C library (HClib) [19], and TryCatchWS [18]. Featherlight is built on top of TryCatchWS and supports **async–finish**. Figure 1 shows a sample TryCatchWS program that uses **async–finish** constructs. The **async** clause at Line 3 creates a task *S1*, which can run in parallel with the continuation *S2*. An **async** can be used to enable any statement to execute as a parallel task, including statement blocks, *for* loop iterations, and function calls. A **finish** is a generalized join operation. Lines 2–5 encloses a **finish** scope and ensures that both the parallel tasks *S1* and *S2* has completed before starting the computation *S3* at Line 6. Both **async** and **finish** can be arbitrarily nested.

2.2 Managed Runtime Services

Managed runtimes gained popularity with the advent of the Java language and have been a very active research area since then. Some of the key features of managed runtimes exploited in Featherlight are (a) yieldpoint mechanism, (b) ability to walk the execution stack of a running thread and (c) support for exception delivery. Yieldpoints are the program locations where it is *safe* to run a garbage collector and implement services such as adaptive optimization. The compiler generates yieldpoints as program points where a running thread checks a dedicated bit in a machine control register to determine whether it should yield. The compiler generates precise stack maps at each yieldpoint. If the bit is set, the yieldpoint is taken and some action is performed. If the bit is not set, no action is taken and the next instruction after the yieldpoint is executed. In JikesRVM virtual machine [7], yieldpoints are inserted in method prologues and on loop back edges.

Exception handling is also an important feature that is well supported by many modern programming languages like C++, Java, and C#. An exception is an event that can occur during the execution of the program and disrupts the program's control flow. Handlers are subroutines where the exceptions are resolved, and they may allow resuming the execution from the original location of the exception. Java uses *try* and *catch* blocks for exception handling. Exception delivery mechanism and other runtime services such as garbage collection are supported in a managed runtime with the ability to walk the execution stack of any thread. For walking the stack of a running thread (victim), the victim is first stopped by using yieldpoint mechanism. The victim saves all its registers and live program states before stopping. The thread requesting the stack walk can then easily go over each frame on victim's execution stack and can manipulate them as well. The garbage collector uses a stack walk to identify live and dead objects in the application thread.

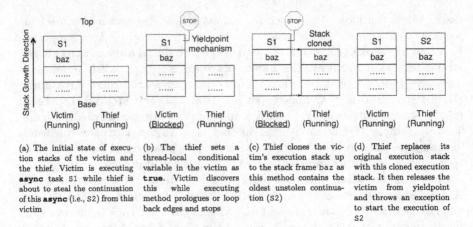

(a) The initial state of execution stacks of the victim and the thief. Victim is executing **async** task S1 while thief is about to steal the continuation of this **async** (i.e., S2) from this victim

(b) The thief sets a thread-local conditional variable in the victim as **true**. Victim discovers this while executing method prologues or loop back edges and stops

(c) Thief clones the victim's execution stack up to the stack frame baz as this method contains the oldest unstolen continuation (S2)

(d) Thief replaces its original execution stack with this cloned execution stack. It then releases the victim from yieldpoint and throws an exception to start the execution of S2

Fig. 2. TryCatchWS work-stealing implementation for executing the **async-finish** program shown in Fig. 1

2.3   TryCatchWS Work-Stealing Runtime

We have implemented the runtime support for Featherlight by modifying Java TryCatchWS work-stealing runtime developed by Kumar et al. [18]. TryCatchWS is implemented directly inside JikesRVM [7] Java Virtual Machine, and as demonstrated by Kumar et al. [16,18], it helps in achieving both good scalability and good absolute performance. Figure 2 illustrates the TryCatchWS work-stealing implementation for executing the **async-finish** program shown in Fig. 1 by using two workers. The user code written by using **async-finish** is first translated to plain Java code by using AJWS compiler [17]. TryCatchWS follows the work-first principle for task scheduling. The generated code exploits the semantics Java offers for exception handling, which is very efficiently implemented in most modern JVMs. The result is that the runtime does not need to maintain *explicit* deques. It uses the Java thread (execution) stack of both the victim and thief as their *implicit* deque. The thief can directly walk a victim's execution stack and identify all **async** and **finish** contexts, resulting in a significant reduction in overheads. This allows the programmer to expose fine granular tasks without worrying about the task creation overheads. For a detailed overview of TryCatchWS we refer readers to [18].

3   Featherlight Programming Model

Featherlight extends **async-finish** programming supported by TryCatchWS with two new constructs:

- **finish_abort**: This is the regular **finish** with an added responsibility to ensure graceful cancellation of speculative **async** tasks without having any cancellation condition checking code. Both **async** and **finish** can be

```
1  class UTS {
2   boolean found=false;
3   void search(){
4    finish_abort recurse(root);
5   }
6   void recurse(Node n){
7    if(n.equals(goal)){
8     found=true;
9     abort;
10    return;
11   }
12   for(int i=0;i<n.nChild;i++){
13    async recurse(n.child[i]);
14   }
15  }
16 }
```
(a) Featherlight

```
1  class UTS {
2   /*atomic cancelation token*/
3   AtomicBoolean found=new AtomicBoolean();
4   void search(){
5    finish recurse(root);
6   }
7   void recurse(Node n){
8    if(found.get()) return; /*check*/
9    if(n.equals(goal)){
10    found.set(true);
11    return;
12   }
13   for(int i=0;i<n.nChild;i++){
14    if(found.get()) return; /*check*/
15    async recurse(n.child[i]);
16   }
17  }
18 }
```
(b) ManualAbort obtained by hand-coding
task cancellation checks in TryCatchWS

```
1  class UTS { boolean found=false;
2   ForkJoinPool pool=new ForkJoinPool(2);
3   void search(){
4    try {
5     pool.invoke(new RecursiveAction(){
6      public void compute() {
7       new Recurse(root).fork();
8       helpQuiesce();
9      }
10    });
11   } catch(CancellationException e){}
12  }
13  class Recurse extends RecursiveAction{
14   Node n;
15   public Recurse(Node _n) {n=_n;}
16   public void compute() {
17    if(n.equals(goal)){
18     found=true;
19     pool.shutdownNow();
20    }
21    for(int i=0;i<n.nChild;i++){
22     new Recurse(n.child[i]).fork();
23    }
24   }/*compute*/ }/*Recurse*/
25 }
```
(c) Java ForkJoin framework

Fig. 3. Searching a unique node in the UTS tree by using three different implementations of speculative task parallelism. Only Featherlight supports serial elision as erasing the keywords *finish_ abort*, *async*, and *abort* will fetch the original sequential UTS.

nested inside a **finish_abort**. A **finish_abort** cannot be nested but can be called in parallel by placing it inside an **async** within a **finish** scope.

- **abort**: This construct cancels all speculative **async** tasks once the goal is found. Cilk also supports a variant of **abort** but the semantics are very different (Sect. 6). An **abort** can be called inside a Featherlight program only if there is an encapsulating **finish_abort** in the method call stack. If a worker encounters an **abort** statement, it will cancel only those **async** that are (or yet to be) spawned inside a **finish_abort** scope in this worker's method call stack. For example, in the statement "**finish{async{finish_abort{S1;}} async{finish_abort{S2;}}}**", calling an **abort** inside *S1* will only cancel task *S1* and its children (both pending and running) but will not affect the execution of *S2*.

```
1  class UTS {
2  boolean found=false;
3  void search() {
4  try {
5    Runtime.allocateNewFinishAbort();
6    try {
7      recurse(root);
8      Runtime.finish();
9    } catch(ExceptionFinish f) { }
10 } catch(ExceptionSuccessAbort sa) {
11   Runtime.updateFinishScope();
12   Object currentFA = Runtime.getFinishAbort();
13   currentFA.waitForExpectedExceptionFailAborts();
14   Runtime.allowWorkStealingAtAllWorkers();
15 } catch(ExceptionFailAbort fa) {
16   Object currentFA = Runtime.getFinishAbort();
17   currentFA.notifyExceptionFailAbort();
18   Runtime.restartAsThief();
19 }
20 }
```

```
22 void recurse(Node n) {
23 if(n.equals(goal){ found=true;
24   Object currentFA = Runtime.getFinishAbort();
25   if(currentFA.abortAlreadyInitiated()) return;
26   Runtime.pauseWorkStealingAtAllWorkers();
27   for(int w=0; w<Runtime.numWorkers(); w++) {
28     if(w == Runtime.getMyWorkerID()) continue;
29     Runtime.forceWorkerToEnterYieldpoint(w);
30     if(currentFA.equals(Runtime.getFinishAbort(w))){
31       Runtime.worker[w].throwExceptionFailAbort=true;
32       currentFA.incrementExpectedExceptionFailAborts();
33     }/*if*/ Runtime.releaseWorkerFromYieldpoint(w);
34   }/*for*/throw new ExceptionSuccessAbort();}/*If*/
35   for(int i=0;i<n.nChild;i++){
36     try { Runtime.continuationAvailable();
37       recurse(n.child[i]);
38       Runtime.checkContinuationAvailability();
39     } catch(ExceptionEntryThief e) {/*thief entry*/
40   }/*catch*/ }/*for*/ }/*recurse*/ } /*UTS*/
```

Fig. 4. Source-to-source translation of the code shown in Fig. 3(a) to vanilla Java. Underlined code is the default code generated by the compiler to support **async–finish**.

To further motivate Featherlight, in Fig. 3, we show three different implementations of UTS program (Sect. 5) as a motivating example. These implementations use speculative task parallelism for searching a unique node in the tree. Figure 3(a) shows Featherlight, Fig. 3(b) shows ManualAbort obtained by hand-coding task cancellation checks in TryCatchWS, and Fig. 3(c) shows Java ForkJoin implementation. Out of all these three implementations, only Featherlight supports serial elision. Calling an **abort** at Line 9 in Featherlight will cancel all **async** (as all **async** are inside single **finish_abort** scope), and resume the execution right after **finish_abort** (i.e., Line 5). ManualAbort requires an atomic cancellation token (Line 3), checking this cancellation token before executing the task (Line 8), and also checking before creating any new task (Line 14). These checks are prone to data races if not used properly. It could also delay task cancellation if not used inside every method in the call chain. Moreover, having multiple search criteria in the program can make it difficult to identify the program points where the code for cancellation checks should be added. Although Java ForkJoin does not require manual cancellation checks, it does not supports serial elision and requires extensive changes to the sequential program.

4   Design and Implementation

In this section, we briefly describe our implementation of Featherlight that builds on Java TryCatchWS work-stealing runtime (Sect. 2.3). Our implementation and the benchmarks are released open source online on GitHub [15].

For implementing Featherlight we exploit runtime mechanisms already available within managed runtimes, namely: (a) yieldpoint mechanism, (b) support for exception delivery, and (c) ability to stack walk the execution stack of a running thread. When a worker encounters an **abort** call in a Featherlight program, it will *pause* the execution of other workers by using yieldpoint mechanism. It will then identify the subset of workers that are executing **async** spawned from the same **finish_abort** scope as this worker. These shortlisted workers would then relinquish all pending and currently running **async**, and throw special exceptions to start the computation from another program point. The insight is that the cost of canceling the speculatively spawned **async** should not be incurred in the common case and should occur only once when the goal has been found. Our contribution is to design and implement Featherlight, a novel-programming model for speculative task parallelism that implements our above insight.

4.1 Source Code Translation of Featherlight to Java

Kumar et al. implemented the AJWS compiler [17] that could translate an **async-finish** program into a plain Java program capable of running using TryCatchWS runtime. We have extended their AJWS compiler to support Featherlight by translating the two new constructs **finish_abort** and **abort** into plain Java code. Figure 4 shows this generated Java code for Featherlight's implementation of UTS, shown in Fig. 3(a). All underlined code is the default code generated by the AJWS compiler to support TryCatchWS. For details on this default code, we refer readers to [18].

4.2 Canceling Speculative **async** Once the Goal Is Found

In Featherlight's implementation, the worker (victim) who started the computation (Line 3) will first create an object for this new **finish_abort** scope at Line 5 and then continue its execution. Any thief who attempts to steal from this victim will use default TryCatchWS, where it will stop this victim in yield-point and perform a stack walk of victim's execution stack to find out the oldest unstolen continuation. To support Featherlight, we extended this victim's stack walk such that now the thief also searches the reachability to any *catch* block for handling *ExceptionFailAbort* (Line 15). The thief will then verify if this *catch* block is still reachable from the program point where this thief has to resume the stolen computation (Line 39). If it is still reachable, this thief will copy the object corresponding to **finish_abort** scope stored at the victim (created at Line 5). Note that the thief will overwrite its copy of this scope object if it enters another **finish_abort**.

Assume a worker *W1* has found the goal (Line 23). *W1* has to decide which other workers should cancel their **async** tasks. Essentially, these should be the workers having the same **finish_abort** scope object as with *W1*. This will ensure that if there were **async** created from another **finish_abort** scope, then they would not be canceled. *W1* will first ensure that no other worker has initiated **abort** inside this same **finish_abort** scope (Lines 24–25). W1 will then temporarily pause the work-stealing on all workers, including itself (Line 26) to avoid deadlock. As thief also relies on the yieldpoint mechanism to steal from a victim, there could be a deadlock when the thief is attempting to steal from a victim that is, in turn, trying to yield that same thief from **abort** call. After pausing work-stealing globally, W1 will force all other workers to execute yieldpoint one by one (Line 29). Note that at this point, if any worker is executing a critical section by taking a mutual exclusion lock, W1 will wait inside the call at Line 29 until this worker has released the mutual exclusion lock. After a worker has paused its execution at yieldpoint, W1 will compare its **finish_abort** scope object with that of this worker (Line 30). If it matches, it will set a flag at this worker for throwing *ExceptionFailAbort* (Line 31) and increment the join counter at this **finish_abort** scope object (Line 32). It will then release this worker from yieldpoint (Line 33). Finally, W1 will throw ExceptionSuccessAbort (Line 34) to resume its execution from Line 11.

4.3 **ExceptionFailureAbort** and **ExceptionSuccessAbort**

Recall that W1 paused the execution of all other workers inside yieldpoint (Line 29) and released them after setting the flag throwExceptionFailureAbort (Line 31) in some of them. After resuming the execution inside yieldpoint, every worker will first check and reset their flag throwExceptionFailureAbort. Those who found throwExceptionFailureAbort set to **true** will throw ExceptionFailureAbort from yieldpoint to resume their execution from Line 16. They will first decrement the join counter at this **finish_abort** scope object (Line 17), and if the counter value reaches zero, this information is broadcasted to W1 who is currently waiting at Line 13.

After setting the flag in relevant workers (Line 31), worker W1 will throw ExceptionSuccessAbort at Line 34 and resume its execution from Line 11. It will first update its immediate **finish** scope at Line 11 (if any) and then wait until all the other relevant workers have resumed their execution inside **catch** block for ExceptionFailureAbort. Finally, W1 will allow all workers to resume their work-stealing (Line 14). After this, it will continue the execution of user code from Line 19 onward.

5 Experimental Evaluation

We have used six well-known search based micro-benchmarks and one application from Java DaCapo benchmark suite [8] for our experimental evaluation:

UTS. Variant of Unbalanced Tree Search [24] where it searches for a specific goal node in the tree. We used T1 configuration (geometric tree) with a maximum height of 10. Applications that fit in this category include many search and optimization problems that must enumerate an ample state space of the unknown or unpredictable structure.

LinearSearch. It searches for 10 items in a 2D array of size 1000×20000.

NQueens. Goal is to find 20% of total possible solutions for placing 14 queens on a 14×14 board such that no two queens can attack each other [18]. This benchmark uses a backtracking algorithm that is also used for solving constraint satisfaction and combinatorial optimization based problems.

SLP. It adds edge weights in UTS and then finds shortest and longest path from the root to goal nodes within a given range of 1058–7563 [13]. We used T3 configuration (binomial tree) with a maximum height of 10 and a total of 254 goal nodes. This algorithm is also used for a large variety of optimization problems in network and transportation analysis.

Sudoku. This solves a Sudoku puzzle by exploring a game tree [13]. Board size was 16×16 and a total of 148 unsolved entries.

TSP. Traveling salesman problem [13] for 20 cities that searches for a path ≤ 156. Similar to SLP, TSP is used in complex optimization problems such as planning and scheduling.

lusearch. Variant of lusearch-fix from Java DaCapo benchmark suite [8]. It uses Apache Lucene [23] for text search of keywords over a corpus of data comprising the works of Shakespeare and the King James Bible. In this variant, the search terminates when 80% of total search queries are completed.

To ensure serial elision we did not control task granularity in any of the above benchmarks. We implemented four different versions for each benchmark: (a) *Featherlight* that uses **async**, **finish_abort**, and **abort** constructs; (b) *ManualAbort* that replaces **finish_abort** with **finish** in Featherlight, removes **abort**, and uses token-based cancellation checks to cancel speculatively spawned **async**; (c) *ForkJoin* based on Java **ForkJoinPool** that uses **shutdownNow** library call for task cancellation; and (d) *Sequential* Java that is the serial elision of Featherlight.

The benchmarks were run on a dual socket 10 core Intel Xeon E5-2650 v3 processor running at 2.3 GHz and with a total of 96 GB of RAM. The operating system was Ubuntu 16.04.3 LTS. We have ported Kumar et al.'s TryCatchWS runtime on JikesRVM GitHub version 087d300. This version of TryCatchWS was used for the evaluation of ManualAbort. Sequential Java version of each benchmark was run directly on the above version of unmodified JikesRVM. Featherlight was implemented and evaluated on the above mentioned TryCatchWS version. For all evaluations, we used the production build of JikesRVM. Fixed heap size of 3 GB and single garbage collector thread was used across all experiments. We bound work-stealing worker threads to individual CPU cores and did not use hyper-threading. Other than this, we preserved the default settings of JikesRVM. AJWS compiler version bd5535f on GitHub was extended to support code generation for Featherlight. For each benchmark, we ran 30 invocations, with 15 iterations per invocation where each iteration performed the kernel of the benchmark. In each invocation, we report the mean of the final five iterations, along with a 95% confidence interval based on a Student t-test. We report the total execution time in all experiments (including time for garbage collection).

5.1   Productivity Analysis

Program size or Lines of Code (LoC) is a widely used metric for measuring software productivity [13,17]. Table 1 shows this number for each benchmark and its corresponding four variants. A support code is the common code across

Table 1. Productivity metrics in terms of LoC in actual implementations and time spent by students in classroom [6] for implementing speculative task parallelism.

Benchmark	Lines of Code (LoC) generated using David A. Wheeler's 'SLOCCount' [26]					Time (minutes) spent by students					
	Common code	Sequential	Featherlight	ManualAbort	ForkJoin	Featherlight			ForkJoin		
						Subjects	Mean	St.Dev.	Subjects	Mean	St.Dev.
UTS	545	39	39	45	58	9	8.6	6.1	9	52.2	13.5
LinearSearch	88	44	44	46	75	-	-	-	-	-	-
NQueens	75	48	48	53	68	7	13.6	10.2	8	61	17.2
SLP	558	54	54	60	76	6	11.7	4.1	8	43.4	16.6
Sudoku	469	48	48	54	66	6	6	2.6	8	58.8	11.6
TSP	158	55	55	61	84	7	10.4	4	8	53.1	24.8
lusearch	>126K	222	222	242	239	-	-	-	-	-	-

all four variants of a benchmark. It is highest for lusearch as it uses Apache Lucene for text search. Featherlight supports serial elision and has same LoC as in Sequential. ManualAbort has more LoC than Sequential as it has hand-coded task cancellation checks. ForkJoin requires significant modifications to the Sequential and hence has the maximum LoC.

We also conducted an empirical study [6] to quantify programming effort based on the time required for programming Featherlight and ForkJoin implementations. This classroom study was of 90 min and involved 41 senior undergraduate and postgraduate students from an introductory parallel programming course at IIIT Delhi (CSE502, Spring 2019 semester). These students were first taught about speculative task parallelism and were provided with working copies of both Featherlight and ForkJoin implementations of LinearSearch benchmark as a reference. For this study, each student was provided with two different Sequential benchmarks (except lusearch due to its cumbersome setup). They were then asked to implement ForkJoin version of one of these two Sequential benchmarks and Featherlight version of the other one. We recorded the time taken by students for both these implementations and report the average time along with the standard deviation in Table 1. Average time required for Featherlight implementation ranged between 6–13.6 min verses 43.4–61 min for ForkJoin. Support for serial elision and lesser time to code demonstrate that Featherlight is extremely effective in enhancing programmer's productivity, an important consideration given the current hardware trend and the plethora of real-world search based problems existing today.

5.2   Performance Analysis

Figure 5(a) shows the speedup of Featherlight relative to ManualAbort for all benchmarks by using 20 workers. Except for Sudoku, both Featherlight and ManualAbort perform within 5% of each other. This shows that Featherlight implementation does not add significant runtime overheads. Figures 5(b)–(g) shows the speedup of both Featherlight and ForkJoin relative to Sequential implementation for each of the benchmarks. We can observe that Featherlight can achieve significant speedup over the Sequential counterpart. Featherlight was also able to

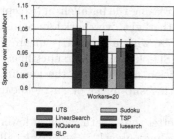

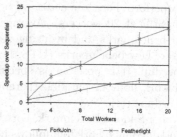

(a) Speedup of Featherlight over ManualAbort by using 20 workers

(b) UTS speedup over Sequential

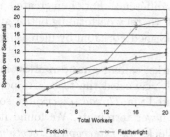

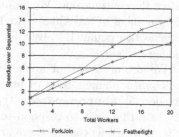

(c) LinearSearch speedup over Sequential

(d) NQueens speedup over Sequential

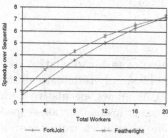

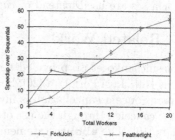

(e) SLP speedup over Sequential

(f) Sudoku speedup over Sequential

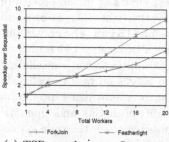

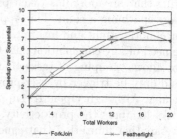

(g) TSP speedup over Sequential

(h) lusearch speedup over Sequential

Fig. 5. Performance analysis of Featherlight and ForkJoin on a 20 core machine. Some benchmarks achieve super-linear speedup, which is possible in speculative parallel programming.

outperform ForkJoin across all benchmarks by increasing the parallelism (except for SLP at 20 workers). Average speedup of Featherlight over ForkJoin across all benchmarks and by using 20 workers was 1.7× with a geometric mean of 1.6×. Few benchmarks (UTS, LinearSearch, and Sudoku) achieved super-linear speedup. It is possible as speculative decomposition may change the amount of work done in parallel, thereby resulting in either sub-linear or super-linear speedups [11].

For Sudoku benchmark, ForkJoin performed better than Featherlight at lower worker counts. ForkJoin follows help-first work-stealing policy [27], i.e., **fork** call merely pushes the task on the deque, and the continuation is executed before the task. Featherlight follows work-first work-stealing policy, i.e., **async** is executed before the continuation. We found that due to this difference, ForkJoin created a lesser number of tasks in Sudoku than Featherlight, thereby performing better at lower worker count. However, Featherlight outperformed ForkJoin by increasing the parallelism.

We also noticed that unlike all other benchmarks, calling **shutdownNow** in ForkJoin implementation of lusearch only partially canceled the tasks. As per Javadoc [5], **shutdownNow** is typically implemented via *Thread.interrupt()*, so any task that fails to respond to interrupts may never terminate. We found it to be true in this case as there are several *catch* blocks for *InterruptedException* inside Apache Lucene codebase over which lusearch is implemented. This is a limitation that Featherlight does not suffer as long as appropriate *Exception* subclasses are used instead of *catch(Exception e){}* blocks.

6 Related Work

Kolesnichenko et al. provided a detailed classification of task cancellation patterns [14]. Java ForkJoin [20], Scala [4] and Python [2] simply terminate all the threads once a cancellation is invoked by the user. Cilk allows speculative work to be canceled through the use of Cilk's **abort** statement inside function-scoped inlets [10]. The **abort** statement, when executed inside an inlet, causes cancellation of only the extant children but not the future children. For preventing future children from being spawned, users should set a flag in the inlet indicating that an abort has taken place, and then test that flag in the procedure before spawning a child. This approach differs in Featherlight as an **abort** will cancel both extant and future tasks inside the scope of **finish_abort** without the need of any cancellation flag. OpenMP supports a task cancellation pragma that allows grouping of tasks that could be canceled [3]. However, cancellation could only be trigger by user-provided cancellation checks on task cancellation pragma. Although OpenMP supports serial elision, user provided cancellation checks hampers the productivity. Unlike Featherlight, both Cilk and OpenMP have another limitation that cancellation is not possible when the code is executing in a nested function call (long running tasks). TBB users must use either cancellation tokens or interrupt checking for task cancellation [22,25]. C# supports cooperative cancellation by using cancellation token checking and throwing an exception once the result is found [1]. Eureka programming in HJlib [13] allows the user to identify the program points where the task could be canceled by using the runtime provided cancellation check call. A drawback is that the programmer has to determine the frequency (granularity) of the check calls to avoid overheads.

Featherlight radically differs from all existing approaches in following ways: (a) it improves the productivity by satisfying serial elision, (b) it doesn't require any cancellation checks inside **async** tasks, and (c) it uses managed runtime techniques to gracefully and safely cancel all speculatively spawned **async** when **abort** is called.

7   Conclusion

Several modern real-world applications are comprised of search based problems that perform best by using speculative parallelism. This parallel programming technique often requires programmer inserted cancellation checks inside speculatively spawned parallel tasks to terminate them once the search result has been found. In this paper, we designed and implemented a new programming model for speculative task parallelism that improves the programmer productivity by removing the need for any cancellation checking code and by satisfying serial elision. It uses existing mechanisms in modern managed runtimes to cancel all ongoing and pending computations once the search result is found. Our empirical results demonstrate that we can achieve better productivity and performance compared to traditional approaches for speculative task parallelism.

Acknowledgments. The author is grateful to the anonymous reviewers for their suggestions on improving the presentation of the paper, and to Imam et al. for open-sourcing HJlib micro-benchmarks for speculative task parallelism [13].

References

1. Destroying threads in C#. https://docs.microsoft.com/en-us/dotnet/standard/threading/destroying-threads. Accessed Feb 2019
2. Documentation on The Python standard library. https://docs.python.org/3/library/concurrent.futures.html. Accessed Feb 2019
3. OpenMP API, version 4.5. http://www.openmp.org/wp-content/uploads/openmp-4.5.pdf. Accessed Feb 2019
4. Scala scheduler. https://doc.akka.io/docs/akka/snapshot/scheduler.html?language=scala. Accessed Feb 2019
5. Oracle docs, February 2019. https://docs.oracle.com/javase/7/docs/api/java/util/concurrent/ExecutorService.html
6. Productivity analysis, February 2019. https://www.usebackpack.com/iiitd/m2018/cse000
7. Alpern, B., et al.: The Jalapeño virtual machine. IBM Syst. J. **39**(1), 211–238 (2000). https://doi.org/10.1147/sj.391.0211
8. Blackburn, S.M., et al.: The DaCapo benchmarks: Java benchmarking development and analysis. In: OOPSLA, pp. 169–190 (2006). https://doi.org/10.1145/1167473.1167488

9. Charles, P., et al.: X10: an object-oriented approach to non-uniform cluster comput-ing. In: OOPSLA, pp. 519–538 (2005). https://doi.org/10.1145/1094811.1094852
10. Frigo, M., Leiserson, C.E., Randall, K.H.: The implementation of the Cilk-5 multi-threaded language. In: PLDI, pp. 212–223 (1998). https://doi.org/10.1145/277650.277725
11. Grama, A., Kumar, V., Gupta, A., Karypis, G.: Introduction to Parallel Comput-ing. Pearson Education, Upper Saddle River (2003)
12. Imam, S., Sarkar, V.: Habanero-Java library: a Java 8 framework for multicore pro-gramming. In: PPPJ, pp. 75–86 (2014). https://doi.org/10.1145/2647508.2647514
13. Imam, S., Sarkar, V.: The Eureka programming model for speculative task paral-lelism. In: ECOOP, vol. 37, pp. 421–444 (2015). https://doi.org/10.4230/LIPIcs.ECOOP.2015.421
14. Kolesnichenko, A., Nanz, S., Meyer, B.: How to cancel a task. In: Lourenço, J.M., Farchi, E. (eds.) MUSEPAT 2013. LNCS, vol. 8063, pp. 61–72. Springer, Heidelberg (2013). https://doi.org/10.1007/978-3-642-39955-8_6
15. Kumar, V.: Featherlight implementation (2019). https://github.com/hipec/featherlight/archive/d60047a.tar.gz
16. Kumar, V., Blackburn, S.M., Grove, D.: Friendly barriers: efficient work-stealing with return barriers. In: VEE, pp. 165–176 (2014). https://doi.org/10.1145/2576195.2576207
17. Kumar, V., Dolby, J., Blackburn, S.M.: Integrating asynchronous task parallelism and data-centric atomicity. In: PPPJ, pp. 7:1–7:10 (2016). https://doi.org/10.1145/2972206.2972214
18. Kumar, V., Frampton, D., Blackburn, S.M., Grove, D., Tardieu, O.: Work-stealing without the baggage. In: OOPSLA, pp. 297–314 (2012). https://doi.org/10.1145/2398857.2384639
19. Kumar, V., Zheng, Y., Cavé, V., Budimlić, Z., Sarkar, V.: HabaneroUPC++: a compiler-free PGAS library. In: PGAS, pp. 5:1–5:10 (2014). https://doi.org/10.1145/2676870.2676879
20. Lea, D.: A Java fork/join framework. In: JAVA, pp. 36–43 (2000). https://doi.org/10.1145/337449.337465
21. Lin, Y., Wang, K., Blackburn, S.M., Hosking, A.L., Norrish, M.: Stop and go: understanding yieldpoint behavior. In: ISMM, pp. 70–80 (2015). https://doi.org/10.1145/2754169.2754187
22. Marochko, A.: Exception handling and cancellation in TBB–Part II (2008)
23. McCandless, M., Hatcher, E., Gospodnetic, O.: Lucene in Action, Second Edition: Covers Apache Lucene 3.0. Manning Publications Co., Greenwich (2010)
24. Olivier, S., et al.: UTS: an unbalanced tree search benchmark. In: LCPC, pp. 235–250 (2007). http://dl.acm.org/citation.cfm?id=1757112.1757137
25. Peierls, T., Goetz, B., Bloch, J., Bowbeer, J., Lea, D., Holmes, D.: Java Concur-rency in Practice. Addison-Wesley Professional, Reading (2005)
26. Wheeler, D.A.: SLOCCount (2001). http://www.dwheeler.com/sloccount/
27. Guo, Y., Barik, R., Raman, R., Sarkar, V.: Work-first and help-first scheduling policies for Async-finish task parallelism. In: IPDPS, pp. 1–12 (2009). https://doi.org/10.1109/IPDPS.2009.5161079

One Table to Count Them All: Parallel Frequency Estimation on Single-Board Computers

Fatih Taşyaran, Kerem Yıldırır, Mustafa Kemal Taş$^{(\boxtimes)}$, and Kamer Kaya

Sabancı University, Istanbul, Turkey
{fatihtasyaran,keremyildirir,mkemaltas,kaya}@sabanciuniv.edu

Abstract. Sketches are probabilistic data structures that can provide approximate results within mathematically proven error bounds while using orders of magnitude less memory than traditional approaches. They are tailored for streaming data analysis on architectures even with limited memory such as single-board computers that are widely exploited for IoT and edge computing. Since these devices offer multiple cores, with efficient parallel sketching schemes, they are able to manage high volumes of data streams. However, since their caches are relatively small, a careful parallelization is required.

In this work, we focus on the frequency estimation problem and evaluate the performance of a high-end server, a 4-core Raspberry Pi and an 8-core Odroid. As a sketch, we employed the widely used Count-Min Sketch. To hash the stream in parallel and in a cache-friendly way, we applied a novel tabulation approach and rearranged the auxiliary tables into a single one. To parallelize the process with performance, we modified the workflow and applied a form of buffering between hash computations and sketch updates.

Today, many single-board computers have heterogeneous processors in which slow and fast cores are equipped together. To utilize all these cores to their full potential, we proposed a dynamic load-balancing mechanism which significantly increased the performance of frequency estimation.

Keywords: Parallel algorithms · Streaming data ·
Single board computers

1 Introduction

Although querying streaming data with 100% accuracy may be possible by using cutting edge servers equipped with a large memory and powerful processor(s), enabling power efficient devices such as single-board computers (SBCs), e.g., Arduino, Raspberry Pi, Odroid, with smarter algorithms and data structures yields cost and energy efficient solutions. These devices are indeed cheap, are equipped with multicore processors, and portable enough to be located at the edge of a data ecosystem, which is where the data is actually generated.

© Springer Nature Switzerland AG 2019
R. Yahyapour (Ed.): Euro-Par 2019, LNCS 11725, pp. 405–418, 2019.
https://doi.org/10.1007/978-3-030-29400-7_29

Furthermore, SBCs can be enhanced with various hardware such as cameras, sensors, and software such as network sniffers. Hence, exploiting their superior price/performance ratio for data streams is a promising approach. A comprehensive survey of data stream applications can be found in [12].

Sketches can be defined as data summaries and there exist various sketches in the literature tailored for different applications. These structures help us to process a query on a massive dataset with small, usually sub-linear amount of memory [1,3,9,10]. Furthermore, each data stream can be independently sketched and these sketches can then be combined to obtain the final sketch. Due to the implicit compression, there is almost always a trade-off between the accuracy of the final result and the sketch size.

Count-Min Sketch (CMS) is a probabilistic sketch that helps to estimate the frequencies, i.e., the number of occurrences, of the items in a stream [6]. The frequency information is crucial to find heavy-hitters or rare items and detecting anomalies [4,6]. A CMS stores a small counter table to keep the track of the frequencies. The accesses to the sketch are decided based on the hashes of the items and the corresponding counters are incremented. Intuitively, the frequencies of the items are not exact due to the hash collisions. An important property of a CMS is that the error is always one sided; that is, the sketch never underestimates the frequencies.

Since independent sketches can be combined, even for a single data stream, generating a sketch in parallel is considered to be a straightforward task; each processor can independently consume a different part of a stream and build a partial sketch. However, with τ threads, this straightforward approach uses τ times more memory. Although this may not a problem for a high-end server, when the cache sizes are small, using more memory can be an important burden. In this work, we focus on the frequency estimation problem on single-board multicore computers. Our contributions can be summarized as follows:

1. We propose a parallel algorithm to generate a CMS and evaluate its performance on a high-end server and two multicore SBCs; Raspberry Pi 3 Model B+ and Odroid-XU4. We restructure the sketch construction phase while avoiding possible race-conditions on a *single* CMS table. With a single table, a careful synchronization is necessary, since race-conditions not only degrade the performance but also increase the amount of error on estimation. Although we use CMS in this work, the techniques proposed in this paper can easily be extended to other table-based frequency estimation sketches such as Count-Sketch and Count Min-Min Sketch.
2. Today, many SBCs have fast and slow cores to reduce the energy consumption. However, the performance difference of these heterogenous cores differ for different devices. Under this heterogeneity, a manual optimization is required for each SBC. As our second contribution, we propose a load-balancing mechanism that distributes the work evenly to all the available cores and uses them as efficiently as possible. The proposed CMS generation technique is dynamic; it is not specialized for a single device and can be employed on various devices having heterogeneous cores.

3. As the hashing function, we use *tabulation hashing* which is recently proven to provide strong statistical guarantees [16] and faster than many hashing algorithms available; a recent comparison can be found in [7]. For some sketches including CMS, to reduce the estimation error, the same item is hashed multiple times with a different function from the same family. As our final contribution, we propose a cache-friendly tabulation scheme to compute multiple hashes at a time. The scheme can also be used for other applications employing multiple hashes.

2   Notation and Background

Let $\mathcal{U} = \{1, \cdots, n\}$ be the universal set where the elements in the stream are coming from. Let N be size of the stream $\mathbf{s}[.]$ where $\mathbf{s}[i]$ denotes the ith element in the stream. We will use f_x to denote the frequency of an item. Hence,

$$f_x = |\{x = \mathbf{s}[i] : 1 \leq i \leq N\}|.$$

Given two parameters ϵ and δ, a Count-Min Sketch is constructed as a two-dimensional counter table with $d = \lceil \ln(1/\delta) \rceil$ rows and $w = \lceil e/\epsilon \rceil$ columns. Initially, all the counters inside the sketch are set to 0.

There are two fundamental operations for a CMS; the first one is *insert(x)* which updates internal sketch counters to process the items in the stream. To insert $x \in \mathcal{U}$, the counters $\mathtt{cms}[i][h_i(x)]$ are incremented for $1 \leq i \leq d$, i.e., a counter from each row is incremented where the column IDs are obtained from the hash values. Algorithm 1 gives the pseudocode to sequentially process $\mathbf{s}[.]$ of size N and construct a CMS.

The second operation for CMS is *query(x)* to estimate the frequency of $x \in \mathcal{U}$ as

$$f'_x = min_{1 \leq i \leq d}\{\mathtt{cms}[i][h_i(x)]\}.$$

With $d \times w$ memory, the sketch satisfies that $f_x \leq f'_x$ and $\Pr\left(f'_x \geq f_x + \epsilon N\right) \leq \delta$. Hence, the error is additive and always one-sided. Furthermore, for ϵ and δ small enough, the error is also bounded with high probability. Hence, especially for frequent items with large f_x, the ratio of the estimation to the actual frequency approaches to one.

Tabulation Hash: CMS requires pairwise independent hash functions to provide the desired properties stated above. A separate hash function is used for each row of the CMS with a range equal to the range of columns. In this work, we use tabulation hashing [18] which has been recently analyzed by Patrascu and Thorup et al. [13,16] and shown to provide strong statistical guarantees despite of its simplicity. Furthermore, it is even as fast as the classic multiply-mod-prime scheme, i.e., $(ax + b) \bmod p$.

ALGORITHM 1. CMS-CONSTRUCTION

Input: ϵ: error factor, δ: error probability
   s[.]: a stream with N elements from n distinct elements
   $h_i(.)$: pairwise independent hash functions where for
      $1 \leq i \leq d$, h_i: $\mathcal{U} \rightarrow \{1, \cdots, w\}$ and $w = \lceil e/\epsilon \rceil$
Output: cms[.][.]: a $d \times w$ counter sketch where $d = \lceil 1/\delta \rceil$
for $i \leftarrow 1$ to d do
   for $j \leftarrow 1$ to w do
      | cms[i][j] $\leftarrow 0$
for $i \leftarrow 1$ to N do
   $x \leftarrow s[i]$ for $j \leftarrow 1$ to d do
      | $col \leftarrow h_j(x)$
      | cms[j][col] $\leftarrow$ cms[j][col] +1

Assuming each element in $\mathcal{U}$ is represented in 32 bits (the hash function can also be used to hash 64-bit stream items [16]) and the desired output is also 32 bits, tabulation hashing works as follows: first a 4×256 table is generated and filled with random 32-bit values. Given a 32-bit input x, each character, i.e., 8-bit value, of x is used as an index for the corresponding row. Hence, four 32-bit values, one from each row, are extracted from the table. The bitwise XOR of these 32-bit values are returned as the hash value.

3   Merged Tabulation with a Single Table

Hashing the same item with different members of a hash family is a common technique in sketching applied to reduce the error of the estimation. One can use a single row for CMS, i.e., set $d = 1$ and answer the query by reporting the value of the counter corresponding to the hash value. However, using multiple rows reduces the probability of having large estimation errors.

Although the auxiliary data used in tabulation hashing are small and can fit into a cache, the spatial locality of the accessed table elements, i.e., their distance in memory, is deteriorating since each access is performed to a different table row (of length 256). A naive, cache-friendly rearrangement of the entries in the tables is also not possible for applications performing a single hash per item; the indices for each table row are obtained from adjacent chunks in the binary representation of the hashed item which are usually not correlated. Hence, there is no relation whatsoever among them to help us to fix the access pattern for all possible stream elements.

For many sketches, the same item is hashed more than once. When tabulation hashing is used, this yields an interesting optimization; there exist multiple hash functions and hence, more than one hash table. Although, the entries in a single table is accessed in a somehow irregular fashion, the accessed coordinates in all the tables are the same for different tables as can be observed on the left side of Fig. 1. Hence, the columns of the tables can be combined in an alternating fashion as shown in the right side of the figure. In this approach, when only a single thread is responsible from computing the hash values for a single item to CMS, the cache can be utilized in a better way since the memory locations accessed by that thread are adjacent. Hence, the computation will pay the penalty for a cache-miss only once for each 8-bit character of a 32-bit item. This proposed scheme is called *merged tabulation*. The pseudocode is given in Algorithm 2.

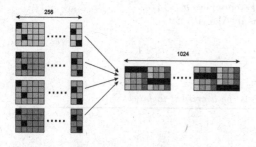

Fig. 1. Memory access patterns for naive and merged tabulation for four hashes. The hash tables are colored with different colors. The accessed locations are shown in black. (Color figure online)

ALGORITHM 2. MERGED-HASH

Input: *data*: 32-bit data to be hashed
Output: res[4]: filled with hash values
$mask \leftarrow 0x000000ff$
$x \leftarrow data$
$c \leftarrow 4 * (x \& mask)$
for $i \leftarrow 0$ **to** 4 **do**
    res[i] $\leftarrow$ tbl[0][c + i]
$x \leftarrow x >> 8$
for $i \leftarrow 1$ **to** 4 **do**
    $c \leftarrow 4 * (x \& mask)$
    res[0] $\leftarrow$ res[0] $\oplus$ tbl[i][c]
    res[1] $\leftarrow$ res[1] $\oplus$ tbl[i][c + 1]
    res[2] $\leftarrow$ res[2] $\oplus$ tbl[i][c + 2]
    res[3] $\leftarrow$ res[3] $\oplus$ tbl[i][c + 3]
    $x \leftarrow x >> 8$

---

4   Parallel Count-Min Sketch Construction

Since multiple CMS sketches can be combined, on a multicore hardware, each thread can process a different part of the data (with the same hash functions) to construct a partial CMS. These partial sketches can then be combined by adding the counter values in the same locations. Although this approach has been already proposed in the literature and requires no synchronization, the amount of the memory it requires increases with increasing number of threads. We included this *one sketch to one core* approach in the experiments as one of the baselines.

Constructing a single CMS sketch in parallel is not a straightforward task. One can assign an item to a single thread and let it perform all the updates (i.e., increment operations) on CMS counters. The pseudocode of this parallel CMS construction is given in Algorithm 3. However, to compute the counter values correctly, this approach requires a significant synchronization overhead; when a thread processes a single data item, it accesses an arbitrary column of each CMS row. Hence, race conditions may reduce the estimation accuracy. In addition, these memory accesses are probable causes of false sharing. To avoid the pitfalls stated above, one can allocate locks on the counters before every increment operation. However, such a synchronization mechanism is too costly to be applied in practice.

In this work, we propose a *buffered parallel* execution to alleviate the above mentioned issues; we (1) divide the data into batches and (2) process a single batch in parallel in two phases; (a) merged-hashing and (b) CMS counter updates. In the proposed approach, the threads synchronize after each batch and

---

ALGORITHM 3. NAIVE-PARALLEL-CMS

Input: ϵ: error factor, δ: error probability
       s[.]: a stream with N elements from n distinct elements
       $h_i(.)$: pairwise independent hash functions where for
              $1 \leq i \leq d$, $h_i: \mathcal{U} \to \{1, \cdots, w\}$ and $w = \lceil e/\epsilon \rceil$
       τ: no threads
Output: cms[.][.]: a $d \times w$ counter sketch where $d = \lceil 1/\delta \rceil$
Reset all the cms[.][.] counters to 0 (as in Algorithm 1).
for $i \leftarrow 1$ **to** N **in parallel do**
    $x \leftarrow s[i]$
    hashes[.] $\leftarrow$ MERGEDHASH(x)
    for $j \leftarrow 1$ **to** d **do**
        $col \leftarrow$ hashes[j]
        cms[j][col] $\leftarrow$ cms[j][col] $+1$ *(must be a critical update)*

---

process the next one. For batches with b elements, the first phase requires a buffer of size $b \times d$ to store the hash values, i.e., column ids, which then will be used in the second phase to update corresponding CMS counters. Such a buffer allows us to use merged tabulation effectively during the first phase. In our implementation, the counters in a row are updated by the same thread hence, there will be no race conditions and probably much less false sharing. Algorithm 4 gives the pseudocode of the proposed buffered CMS construction approach.

ALGORITHM 4. BUFFERED-PARALLEL-CMS

Input: ϵ: error factor, δ: error probability
       s[.]: a stream with N elements from n distinct elements
       $h_i(.)$: pairwise independent hash functions where for
              $1 \leq i \leq d$, $h_i: \mathcal{U} \to \{1, \cdots, w\}$ and $w = \lceil e/\epsilon \rceil$
       b: batch size (assumption: divides N)
       τ: no threads (assumption: divides d)
Output: cms[.][.]: a $d \times w$ counter sketch where $d = \lceil 1/\delta \rceil$
Reset all the cms[.][.] counters to 0 (as in Algorithm 1)

for $i \leftarrow 1$ **to** N/b **do**
    $j_{end} \leftarrow i \times b$ $j_{start} \leftarrow j_{end} - b + 1$
    for $j \leftarrow j_{start}$ **to** j_{end} **in parallel do**
        $x \leftarrow$ s[j]
        $\ell_{end} \leftarrow j \times d$
        $\ell_{start} \leftarrow \ell_{end} - d + 1$
        buf[$\ell_{start}, \cdots, \ell_{end}$] $\leftarrow$ MERGEDHASH(x)
    Synchronize the threads, e.g., with a *barrier*
    for $t_{id} \leftarrow 1$ **to** τ **in parallel do**
        for $j \leftarrow 1$ **to** b **do**
            $nrows \leftarrow d/\tau$
            $r_{end} \leftarrow t_{id} \times nrows$
            $r_{start} \leftarrow r_{end} - nrows + 1$
            for $r \leftarrow r_{start}$ **to** r_{end} **do**
                $col \leftarrow$ buf[$((j-1) \times d) + r$]
                cms[r][col] $\leftarrow$ cms[r][col] $+ 1$

5 Managing Heterogeneous Cores

A recent trend on SBC design is heterogeneous multiprocessing which had been widely adopted by mobile devices. Recently, some ARM-based devices including SBCs use the *big.LITTLE* architecture equipped with power hungry but faster cores, as well as battery-saving but slower cores. The faster cores are suitable for compute-intensive, time-critical tasks where the slower ones perform the rest of the tasks and save more energy. In addition, tasks can be dynamically swapped between these cores on the fly. One of the SBCs we experiment in this study has an 8-core Exynos 5422 Cortex processor having four fast and four relatively slow cores.

Assume that we have d rows in CMS and d cores on the processor; when the cores are homogeneous, Algorithm 4 works efficiently with static scheduling since, each thread performs the same amount of merged hashes and counter updates. When the cores are heterogeneous, the first inner loop (for merged hashing) can be dynamically scheduled: that is a batch can be divided into smaller, independent chunks and the faster cores can hash more chunks. However, the same technique is not applicable to the (more time consuming) second inner loop where the counter updates are performed: in the proposed buffered approach, Algorithm 4 divides the workload among the threads by assigning each row to a different one. When the fast cores are done with the updates, the slow cores will still be working. Furthermore, faster cores cannot help to the slower ones by stealing a portion of their remaining jobs since when two threads work on the same CMS row, race conditions will increase the error.

To alleviate these problems, we propose to pair a slow core with a fast one and make them update two rows in an alternating fashion. The batch is processed in two stages as shown in Fig. 2; in the first stage, the items on the batch are processed in a way that the threads running on faster cores update the counters on even numbered CMS rows whereas the ones running on slower cores update the counters on odd numbered CMS rows. When the first stage is

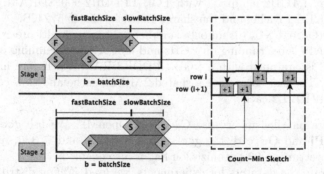

Fig. 2. For a single batch, rows i and $i + 1$ of CMS are updated by a fast and a slow core pair in two stages. In the first stage, the fast core performs row i updates and the slow core processes row $i + 1$ updates. In the second stage, they exchange the rows and complete the remaining updates on the counters for the current batch.

done, the thread/core pairs exchange their row ids and resume from the item their mate stopped in the first stage. In both stages, the faster threads process $fastBatchSize$ items and the slower ones process $slowBatchSize$ items where $b = fastBatchSize + slowBatchSize$.

To avoid the overhead of dynamic scheduling and propose a generic solution, we start with $fastBatchSize = b/2$ and $slowBatchSize = b/2$ and by measuring the time spent by the cores, we dynamically adjust them to distribute the workload among all the cores as fairly as possible. Let t_F and t_S be the times spent by a fast and slow core, respectively, on average. Let $s_F = \frac{fastBatchSize}{t_F}$ and $s_S = \frac{slowBatchSize}{t_S}$ be the speed of these cores for the same operation, e.g., hashing, CMS update etc. We then solve the equation $\frac{fastBatchSize+x}{s_F} = \frac{slowBatchSize-x}{s_S}$ for x and update the values as

$$fastBatchSize = fastBatchSize + x$$
$$slowBatchSize = slowBatchSize - x$$

for the next batch. One can apply this method iteratively for a few batches and use the average values to obtain a generic and dynamic solution for such computations. To observe the relative performances, we applied this technique both for hashing and counter update phases of the proposed buffered CMS generation algorithm.

6   Experimental Results

We perform experiments on the following three architectures:

- **Xeon** is a server running on 64 bit CentOS 6.5 equipped with 64 GB RAM and an Intel Xeon E7-4870 v2 clocked at 2.30 GHz and having 15 cores. Each core has a 32 KB L1 and a 256 KB L2 cache, and the size of L3 cache is 30 MB.
- **Pi** (Raspberry Pi 3 Model B+) is a quad-core 64-bit ARM Cortex A-53 clocked at 1.4 GHz equipped with 1 GB LPDDR2-900 SDRAM. Each core has a 32 KB L1 cache, and the shared L2 cache size is 512 KB.
- **Odroid** (Odroid XU4) is an octa-core heterogeneous multi-processor. There are four A15 cores running on 2 GHz and four A7 cores running on 1.4 GHz. The SBC is equipped with a 2 GB LPDDR3 RAM. Each core has a 32 KB L1 cache. The fast cores have a shared 2 MB L2 cache and slow cores have a shared 512 KB L2 cache.

For multicore parallelism, we use C++ and OpenMP. We use gcc 5.3.0 on **Xeon**. On **Pi** and **Odroid**, the gcc version is 6.3.0 and 7.3.0, respectively. For all architectures, -O3 optimization flag is also enabled.

To generate the datasets for experiments, we used *Zipfian* distribution [17]. Many data in real world such as number of paper citations, file transfer sizes, word frequencies etc. fit to a Zipfian distribution with the shape parameter around $\alpha = 1$. Furthermore, the distribution is a common choice for the studies in the literature to benchmark the estimation accuracy of data sketches. To cover the real-life better, we used the shape parameter $\alpha \in \{1.1, 1.5\}$. Although they seem to be unrelated at first, an interesting outcome of our experiments is that the sketch generation performance depends not only the number of items but also the frequency distribution; when the frequent items become more dominant in the stream, some counters are touched much more than the others. This happens with increasing α and is expected to increase the performance since most of the times, the counters will already be in the cache. To see the other end of the spectrum, we also used *Uniform* distribution to measure the performance where all counters are expected to be touched the same number of times.

We use $\epsilon \in \{10^{-3}, 10^{-4}, 10^{-5}\}$ and $\delta = 0.003$ to generate small, medium and large $d \times w$ sketches where the number of columns is chosen as the first prime after $2/\epsilon$. Hence, the sketches have $w = \{2003, 20071, 200003\}$ columns and $d = \lceil \log_2(1/\delta) \rceil = 8$ rows. For the experiments on **Xeon**, we choose $N = 2^{30}$ elements from a universal set $\mathcal{U}$ of cardinality $n = 2^{25}$. For **Pi** and **Odroid**, we use $N = 2^{25}$ and $n = 2^{20}$. For all architectures, we used $b = 1024$ as the batch size. Each data point in the tables and charts given below is obtained by averaging ten runs.

6.1 Multi Table vs. Single Table

Although *one-sketch-per-core* parallelization, i.e., using partial, multiple sketches, is straightforward, it may not be a good approach for memory/cache restricted devices such as SBCs. The memory/cache space might be required by other applications running on the same hardware and/or other types of sketches being maintained at the same time for the same or a different data stream. Overall, this approach uses $(d \times w \times \tau)$ counters where each counter can have a value as large as N; i.e., the memory consumption is $(d \times w \times \tau \times \log N)$ bits. On the other hand, a single sketch with buffering consumes

$$(d \times ((w \times \log N) + (b \times \log w)))$$

bits since there are $(d \times b)$ entries in the buffer and each entry is a column ID on CMS. For instance, with $\tau = 8$ threads, $\epsilon = 0.001$ and $\delta = 0.003$, the one-sketch-per-core approach requires $(8 \times 2003 \times 8 \times 30) = 3.85$ Mbits whereas using single sketch requires $(8 \times ((2003 \times 30) + (1024 \times 11))) = 0.57$ Mbits. Hence, in terms of memory footprint, using a single table pays off well. Figure 3 shows the case for execution time.

In Fig. 3(a), the performance of the single-table (ST+) and multi-table (MT and MT+) approaches are presented on **Xeon**. Although ST+ uses much less memory, its performance is not good due to all the time spent while buffering and synchronization. The last level cache size on **Xeon** is 30 MB; considering the largest sketch we have is 6.4 MB (with 4-byte counters), **Xeon** does not suffer from its cache size and MT+ indeed performs much better than ST+. However, as Fig. 3(b) shows for **Pi**, with a 512 KB last-level cache, the proposed technique significantly improves the performance, and while doing that, it uses significantly much less memory. As Fig. 3(c) shows, a similar performance

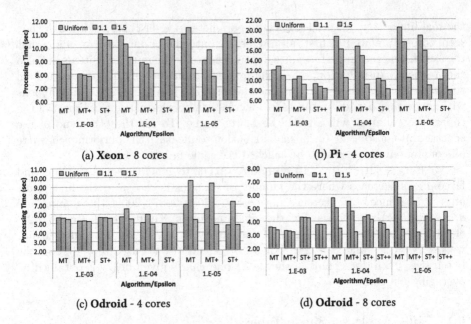

(a) **Xeon** - 8 cores

(b) **Pi** - 4 cores

(c) **Odroid** - 4 cores

(d) **Odroid** - 8 cores

Fig. 3. Performance comparison for multi-table (MT) and single table (ST) approaches. MT uses the one-sketch-per-core approach as suggested in the literature, MT+ is the MT-variant with merged tabulation. In all the figures, ST+ is the proposed scheme (as in Algorithm 4), where in the last figure, ST++ is the ST+ variant using the load-balancing scheme for heterogeneous cores as described in Sect. 5. For all the figures, the x-axis shows the algorithm and $\epsilon \in \{10^{-3}, 10^{-4}, 10^{-5}\}$ pair. The y-axis shows the runtimes in seconds; it does not start from 0 for a better visibility of performance differences. The first bar of each group shows the case when the data is generated using uniform distribution. The second and the third bars show the case for Zipfian distribution with the shape parameter $\alpha = 1.1$ and 1.5, respectively.

improvement on **Odroid** is also visible for medium (640 KB) and especially large (6.4 MB) sketches when only the fast cores with a 2 MB last-level cache are used.

Figure 3 shows that the performance of the algorithms vary with respect to the distribution. As mentioned above, the variance on the frequencies increases with increasing α. For uniform and Zipfian(1.1), the execution times tend to increase with sketch sizes. Nevertheless, for $\alpha = 1.5$, sketch size does not have a huge impact on the performance, since only the *hot* counters of the most frequent items are frequently updated. Although each counter has the same chance to be a hot counter, the effective sketch size reduces significantly especially for large sketches. This is also why the runtimes for many configurations are less for $\alpha = 1.5$.

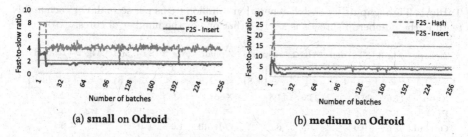

(a) **small** on **Odroid**   (b) **medium** on **Odroid**

Fig. 4. Plots of fast-to-slow ratio $F2S = \frac{fastBatchSize}{slowBatchSize}$ of hashing and CMS update phases for consecutive batches and for small (left) and medium (right) sketches.

6.2 Managing Heterogeneous Cores

To utilize the heterogeneous cores on **Odroid**, we applied the smart load distribution described in Sect. 5. We pair each slow core with a fast one, virtually divide each batch into two parts, and make the slow core always run on smaller part. As mentioned before, for each batch, we dynamically adjust the load distribution based on the previous runtimes. Figure 4 shows the ratio $F2S = \frac{fastBatchSize}{slowBatchSize}$ for the first 256 batches of small and medium sketches. The best F2S changes w.r.t. the computation performed; for hashing, a 4-to-1 division of workload yields a balanced distribution. However, for CMS updates, a 1.8-to-1 division is the best. As the figure shows, the F2S ratio becomes stable after a few batches for both phases. Hence, one can stop the update process after ∼30 batches and use a constant F2S for the later ones. As Fig. 3(d) shows, ST++, the single-table approach both with merged tabulation and load balancing, is always better than ST+. Furthermore, when $\tau = 8$, with the small 512 KB last-level cache for slower cores, the ST++ improves MT+ much better (e.g., when the medium sketch performance in Figs. 3(c) and (d) are compared). Overall, smart load distribution increases the efficiency by 15%–30% for $\tau = 8$ threads.

6.3 Single Table vs. Single Table

For completeness, we compare the performance of the proposed single-table approach, i.e., ST+ and ST++, with that of Algorithm 3. However, we observed that using *atomic* updates drastically reduces its performance. Hence, we use the algorithm in a *relaxed* form, i.e., with non-atomic updates. Note that in this form, the estimations can be different than the CMS due to race conditions. As Table 1 shows, with a single thread, the algorithms perform almost the same except for **Xeon** for which Algorithm 3 is faster. However, when the number of threads is set to number of cores, the proposed algorithm is much better due to the negative impact of false sharing generated by concurrent updates on the same cache line. In its current form, the proposed algorithm can process approximately 60 M, 4 M, and 9 M items on **Xeon**, **Pi** and **Odroid**, respectively.

Table 1. Throughputs for sketch generation - million items per second. For each architecture, the number of threads is set to either one or the number of cores.

Zipfian	Alg 3 (ST+ and ST++)		Alg 2 - relaxed		Zipfian	Alg 3 (ST+ and ST++)		Alg 2 - relaxed	
$\alpha = 1.1$	$\tau = 1$	$\tau \in \{4,8\}$	$\tau = 1$	$\tau \in \{4,8\}$	$\alpha = 1.5$	$\tau = 1$	$\tau \in \{4,8\}$	$\tau = 1$	$\tau \in \{4,8\}$
Xeon	17.6	60.0	22.6	17.8	Xeon	17.9	57.6	22.6	12.9
Pi	1.3	3.9	1.3	3.3	Pi	1.3	4.1	1.2	3.2
Odroid	1.6	9.0	1.6	6.6	Odroid	1.6	9.0	1.7	6.1

7   Related Work

CMS is proposed by Cormode and Muthukrishnan to summarize data streams [6]. Later, they comment on its parallelization [5] and briefly mention the single-table and multi-table approaches. There are studies in the literature employing synchronization primitives such as atomic operations for frequency counting [8]. However, synchronization free approaches are more popular; Cafaro et al. propose an augmented frequency sketch for time-faded heavy hitters [2]. They divided the stream into sub-streams and generated multiple sketches instead of a single one. A similar approach using multiple sketches is also taken by Mandal et al. [11]. CMS has also been used as an underlying structure to design advanced sketches. Recently, Roy et al. developed ASketch which filters high frequent items first and handles the remaining with a sketch such as CMS which they used for implementation [14]. However, their parallelization also employs multiple filters/sketches. Another advanced sketch employing multiple CMSs for parallelization is FCM [15].

Although other hash functions can also be used, we employ tabular hashing which is recently shown to provide good statistical properties and reported to be fast [7,16]. When multiple hashes on the same item are required, which is the case for many sketches, our merging technique will be useful for algorithms using tabular hashing.

To the best of our knowledge, our work is the first cache-focused, synchronization-free, single-table CMS generation algorithm specifically tuned for limited-memory multicore architectures such as SBCs. Our techniques can also be employed for other table-based sketches such as Count Sketch [3] and CMS with conservative updates.

8   Conclusion and Future Work

In this work, we investigated the parallelization of Count-Min Sketch on SBCs. We proposed three main techniques: The first one, merged tabulation, is useful when a single is item needs to be hashed multiple times and can be used for different sketches. The second technique buffers the intermediate results to correctly synchronize the computation and regularize the memory accesses. The third one helps to utilize heterogeneous cores which is a recent trend on today's smaller devices. The experiments we performed show that the propose techniques improve the performance of CMS construction on multicore devices especially with smaller caches.

As a future work, we are planning to analyze the options on the SBCs to configure how much data/instruction cache they use, and how they handle coherency. We also want to extend the architecture spectrum with other accelerators such as FPGAs, GPUs, and more SBCs with different processor types. We believe that similar techniques we develop here can also be used for other sketches.

References

1. Alon, N., Matias, Y., Szegedy, M.: The space complexity of approximating the frequency moments. In: Proceedings of the Twenty-Eighth Annual ACM Symposium on Theory of Computing, STOC 1996, pp. 20–29. ACM, New York (1996)
2. Cafaro, M., Pulimeno, M., Epicoco, I.: Parallel mining of time-faded heavy hitters. Expert Syst. Appl. **96**, 115–128 (2018)
3. Charikar, M., Chen, K., Farach-Colton, M.: Finding frequent items in data streams. In: Widmayer, P., Eidenbenz, S., Triguero, F., Morales, R., Conejo, R., Hennessy, M. (eds.) ICALP 2002. LNCS, vol. 2380, pp. 693–703. Springer, Heidelberg (2002). https://doi.org/10.1007/3-540-45465-9_59
4. Cormode, G., Korn, F., Muthukrishnan, S., Srivastava, D.: Finding hierarchical heavy hitters in data streams. In: Proceedings of the 29th International Conference on Very Large Data Bases, VLDB 2003, pp. 464–475 (2003)
5. Cormode, G., Muthukrishnan, M.: Approximating data with the count-min sketch. IEEE Softw. **29**(1), 64–69 (2012)
6. Cormode, G., Muthukrishnan, S.: An improved data stream summary: the count-min sketch and its applications. J. Algorithms **55**(1), 58–75 (2005)
7. Dahlgaard, S., Knudsen, M.B.T., Thorup, M.: Practical hash functions for similarity estimation and dimensionality reduction. In: Advances in Neural Information Processing Systems (NIPS), pp. 6618–6628 (2017)
8. Das, S., Antony, S., Agrawal, D., El Abbadi, A.: Thread cooperation in multicore architectures for frequency counting over multiple data streams. VLDB Endow. **2**(1), 217–228 (2009)
9. Dobra, A., Garofalakis, M., Gehrke, J., Rastogi, R.: Processing complex aggregate queries over data streams. In: Proceedings of the 2002 ACM SIGMOD International Conference on Management of Data, SIGMOD 2002, pp. 61–72. ACM, New York (2002)
10. Gilbert, A.C., Kotidis, Y., Muthukrishnan, S., Strauss, M.J.: How to summarize the universe: dynamic maintenance of quantiles. In: Proceedings of the 28th International Conference on Very Large Data Bases, VLDB 2002, pp. 454–465. VLDB Endowment (2002)
11. Mandal, A., Jiang, H., Shrivastava, A., Sarkar, V.: Topkapi: parallel and fast sketches for finding top-K frequent elements. In: NeurIPS 2018, Montréal, Canada, pp. 10921–10931 (2018)
12. Muthukrishnan, S.: Data streams: algorithms and applications. Found. Trends Theor. Comput. Sci. **1**(2), 117–236 (2005)
13. Pătrașcu, M., Thorup, M.: The power of simple tabulation hashing. J. ACM **59**(3), 14:1–14:50 (2012)

14. Roy, P., Khan, A., Alonso, G.: Augmented sketch: faster and more accurate stream processing. In: Proceedings of the 2016 International Conference on Management of Data, SIGMOD 2016, pp. 1449–1463. ACM, New York (2016)

15. Thomas, D., Bordawekar, R., Aggarwal, C., Yu, P.S.: A Frequency-aware Parallel Algorithm for Counting Stream Items on Multicore Processors. Technical report, IBM (2007)

16. Thorup, M.: Fast and powerful hashing using tabulation. Commun. ACM **60**(7), 94–101 (2017)

17. Zipf, G.: The Psychobiology of Language: An Introduction to Dynamic Philology. MIT Press, Cambridge (1935)

18. Zobrist, A.L.: A new hashing method with application for game playing. Technical report 88, University of Wisconsin, Madison, Wisconsin (1970)

Fine-Grained MPI+OpenMP Plasma Simulations: Communication Overlap with Dependent Tasks

Jérôme Richard[1,2(✉)], Guillaume Latu[1(✉)], Julien Bigot[3(✉)], and Thierry Gautier[4(✉)]

[1] CEA/IRFM, St-Paul lez Durance 13108, France
`guillaume.latu@cea.fr`
[2] Zébrys, Toulouse, France
`jerome.richard@zebrys.fr`
[3] Maison de la Simulation, CEA, CNRS, Univ. Paris-Sud, UVSQ, Université Paris-Saclay, Gif-sur-Yvette, France
`julien.bigot@cea.fr`
[4] Univ. Lyon, Inria, CNRS, ENS de Lyon, Univ. Claude-Bernard Lyon 1, LIP, Lyon, France
`thierry.gautier@inrialpes.fr`

Abstract. This paper demonstrates how OpenMP 4.5 tasks can be used to efficiently overlap computations and MPI communications based on a case-study conducted on multi-core and many-core architectures. It focuses on task granularity, dependencies and priorities, and also identifies some limitations of OpenMP. Results on 64 Skylake nodes show that while 64% of the wall-clock time is spent in MPI communications, 60% of the cores are busy in computations, which is a good result. Indeed, the chosen dataset is small enough to be a challenging case in terms of overlap and thus useful to assess worst-case scenarios in future simulations.

Two key features were identified: by using task priority we improved the performance by 5.7% (mainly due to an improved overlap), and with recursive tasks we shortened the execution time by 9.7%. We also illustrate the need to have access to tools for task tracing and task visualization. These tools allowed a fine understanding and a performance increase for this task-based OpenMP+MPI code.

Keywords: Dependent tasks · OpenMP 4.5 · MPI · Many-core

1 Introduction

The MPI and OpenMP programming models are widely used in numerical HPC applications [8]. While combining both models is commonplace, several challenges must be addressed to obtain improved performance. One of them is the efficient overlapping of communication with computation since communications are often a major source of overhead. This is critical for future exascale machines expected to interconnect a very large number of computing units.

© Springer Nature Switzerland AG 2019
R. Yahyapour (Ed.): Euro-Par 2019, LNCS 11725, pp. 419–433, 2019.
https://doi.org/10.1007/978-3-030-29400-7_30

With the recent shift of HPC platforms from multi-core to many-core architectures, the cumulated communication time can prevail over the computation time [3]. Meanwhile, it can be difficult to keep all cores busy when dealing with fine-grained computations since communication latencies and synchronization costs are possibly an issue at large scale. It is especially challenging as it would be preferable for parallel applications to provide portable performance on multiple platforms (with reduced development efforts).

Task-based programming is a promising approach to address these problems [5,16]. The introduction of this approach in the version 3.0 of OpenMP has significantly improved the way of expressing parallelism in numerical applications. Especially data dependencies in OpenMP 4.0 (*i.e.* the depend clause), and both task priorities and task loops in the version 4.5 of the norm [11].

As a first contribution, this paper demonstrates that OpenMP tasks can be used to efficiently overlap computations and MPI communications based on a specific case-study on many-core and multi-core architectures. A second contribution is the identification of three specific task parameters that should be carefully tuned to reach this goal: granularity, dependencies and priorities[1]. A third contribution is the proposal of a method based on visualization to understand and guide the tuning of these parameters. Finally, the paper identifies features absent from OpenMP 4.5 that could improve the situation; some of which are already present in OpenMP 5.0 [12].

Section 2 describes the use-case studied in this paper: a hybrid MPI + OpenMP 2D Vlasov-Poisson application while Sect. 3 discusses its implementation and specifically how we designed algorithms and tasks with communication/computation overlap in mind. Section 4 evaluates and discusses the performance in terms of efficiency, scalability, overlapping; it identifies important task parameters (granularity, dependencies, priorities) and presents a way to adjust these parameters based on tasks visualization. Section 5 discusses related work while Sect. 6 concludes the paper and presents some future work.

2   Use-Case Description

2.1   Overview and Numerical Approach

Overview. We consider an application that solves the Vlasov-Poisson equations[2] to model the dynamics of a system of charged particles under the effects of a self-consistent electric field. The unknown f is a distribution function of particles in the phase space which depends on the time, the physical space, and the velocity. This approach is useful to model kinetically different kinds of plasmas.

---

[1] See [10] for an advanced tutorial about these points.

[2] In practice, Poisson-Ampere [7] are solved instead of Poisson. But for sake of clarity, Poisson-Ampere is not detailed here as the algorithm and performance are very close.

Equations. The evolution of the distribution function of particles $f(t, x, v)$ in phase space $(x, v) \in \mathbb{R} \times \mathbb{R}$ is given by the Vlasov equation

$$\frac{\partial f}{\partial t} + v \cdot \nabla_x f + E(t, x) \cdot \nabla_v f = 0 \tag{1}$$

In this equation, time is denoted t and the electric field $E(t, x)$ is coupled to the distribution function f. Considering the Vlasov-Poisson system, Poisson is solved in the following way:

$$E(t, x) = -\nabla_x \phi(t, x), \quad -\Delta_x \phi(t, x) = \rho(t, x) - 1, \tag{2}$$
$$\text{with } \rho(t, x) = \int_\mathbb{R} f(t, x, v)\, dv$$

where ρ is typically the ionic density, ϕ is the electric potential. One can express the characteristic curves of the Vlasov-Poisson Eqs. (1)–(2) as the solutions of a first-order differential system. It is proven that the distribution function f is constant along the characteristic curves which are the basis of the semi-Lagrangian method we employ to solve the Vlasov equation [17].

Numerical Method. The semi-Lagrangian method [17] consists in evaluating the distribution function directly on a Cartesian grid in phase space. The driving force of this explicit scheme is to integrate the characteristic curves backward in time at each timestep and to interpolate the value at the feet of the characteristics. The chosen interpolation technique relies on Lagrange polynomials [4] of degree 5. To perform 2D interpolations, we use a tensor product on a fixed-size square region of the 2D grid surrounding the feet of the characteristics.

2.2   Distributed Algorithm and Data Structures

Algorithms. Algorithm 1 presents one timestep of the application. It is divided in two parts: the solving of the Poisson equation (lines 1–2) and the Vlasov solver (lines 4–10). The Vlasov solver operates on a 2D regular mesh with ghost areas (data structures are presented in the next paragraph). In the following, we will denote by Δt the time step, by $\rho^n = \rho(n\,\Delta t, x)$ the ionic density at time step n (the superscript notation $.^n$ will be used also for E and f). Ghost exchange is done through MPI_isend/irecv between surrounding processes so they can be available for the next iteration. The number of ghost cells in both direction is denoted G. In the upcoming Sect. 4 we will set $G = 8$.

Algorithm 1. One timestep
Input : f^n, ρ^n_{loc} **Output**: f^{n+1}, ρ^{n+1}_{loc}
1 $\rho^n = AllReduce(\rho^n_{loc})$ 2 $E^n = Field\_solver(\rho^n)$ 3 Perform diagnostics & outputs (E^n, ρ^n) 4 *Launch all isend/irecv for ghost zones f^n* 5 2D advections for interior points (Algo. 2) 6 *Receive wait for ghost zones f^n* 7 2D advections for border points (Algo. 3) 8 *Send wait for ghost zones f^n* 9 $\rho^n_{loc} = Local\_integral(f^n)$ 10 Buffer swap between timestep n and $n+1$

Algorithm 2. Interior points advection
Input : Set of local tiles T_* (representing f^n) and E^n **Output**: Set of local tiles T_*
1 **for** $k=$ *[indices of local tiles]* **do** 2   **for** $j = [vstart(k) + G : vend(k) - G]$ **do** 3   **for** $i = [xstart(k) + G : xend(k) - G]$ **do** 4   Compute the foot (x^*_i, v^*_j) ending at (x_i, v_j);   // All needed f values belong to T_k 5 $f^{n+1}_k(x_i, v_j) \leftarrow$ interpolate $f^n(x^*_i, v^*_j)$;

Algorithm 3. Border points advection
Input : Set of local tiles T_* (representing f^n) and E^n **Output**: Set of local tiles T_*
1 $D_J = [vstart(k):vstart(k)+G[\cup]vend(k)-G:vend(k)]$; 2 $D_I = [xstart(k):xstart(k)+G[\cup]xend(k)-G:xend(k)]$; 3 **for** $k=$ *[indices of local tiles]* **do** 4   **for** $j \in D_J$ **do** 5   **for** $i \in D_I$ **do** 6   Compute the foot (x^*_i, v^*_j) ending at (x_i, v_j);   // All needed f values belong to T_k 7 $f^{n+1}_k(x_i, v_j) \leftarrow$ interpolate $f^n(x^*_i, v^*_j)$;

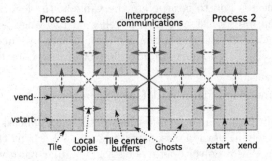

Fig. 1. Tiles and exchange of ghost buffers of the algorithm.

Data Structures. The whole (x, v) grid is split into uniform rectangular tiles. Within a tile, two internal buffers are used for double buffering, each buffer corresponding to a timestep. We have also two additional buffers to store ghosts required for the interpolation stencil (virtually surrounding the internal buffers): one for sending data to other tiles and one for receiving data. The ghost area of each tile is split into 8 parts for the 8 neighbor tiles. The tile set is distributed among processes using a 2D decomposition. The points (x, v) of a tile T_k are defined in the domain: $x \in [xstart(k); xend(k)[$ and $v \in [vstart(k); vend(k)[$. The structure of a tile is illustrated in Fig. 1 wherein orange areas are ghost zones while light-green areas are internal buffers updated by Vlasov 2D advections.

Computations and Dependencies. In Algorithm 1, Poisson computation is composed of two sub-steps. First (line l. 1), data is reduced to compute the integral in velocity space (computing ρ as in Eq. 2). Then (l. 2), a local computation is performed in each process. The reduction acts as a synchronization requiring all advection data to be computed before solving Poisson and starting a new step. Thus, most computations of the Vlasov advection and Poisson cannot be overlapped.

Between two advection steps, ghost cells are exchanged with the 8 surrounding tiles (l. 4); data is copied between buffers for tiles that lie in the same process and MPI is used otherwise. The interior points advection (l. 5) can start as soon as Poisson is finished since their interpolation does not depend on ghosts. We assume small displacements (*i.e.* $|v.\Delta t| < \Delta x$ and $|E.\Delta t| < \Delta v$), thus all interpolations can be done locally [7]. Once all ghosts are received for one tile (l. 6), its border points can be computed as well (l. 7).

When the advection of all points of a tile is done, the local part of the integral (needed for the next Poisson computation) is computed (l. 9). Finally, when they are not needed anymore by `MPI_Isend` (l. 8) internal buffers are swapped (l. 10).

Figure 1 displays the communication pattern of the ghost exchange for two MPI processes. Red solid arrows are MPI communications while green dashed arrows are in-process ghost buffers copies. Sent buffers and received buffers are distinct. For sake of clarity, communications/copies providing periodicity along dimensions x and v are not shown here.

3   Implementation Design

We have implemented Algorithm 1 in C with OpenMP and MPI so as to evaluate the use of OpenMP tasks, priorities and task loops (see Footnote 1) for communication/computation overlap. We have used the OpenMP Tool Interfaces (OMPT) [12] (from OpenMP 5.0) combined to tracing capabilities of the KOMP [5] runtime to analyze the behavior and performance of the code.

Overall Design. Except where specified otherwise, we use a *flat OpenMP task model* where the *master thread* submits all tasks that are then executed either by *worker threads* or by the master thread itself. This is the only way to create dependencies between sibling tasks [12]. We assign MPI calls and computations to distinct tasks to improve the flexibility of the scheduling and rely on task priorities to guide it. We submit all the tasks of each iteration in batch to provide enough work to feed all workers during a single iteration (critical on many-core systems). The tasks graph is similar on each MPI process.

On the MPI side, we use the `MPI_THREAD_SERIALIZED` mode where all threads can access MPI, but only one at a time. Most MPI implementations use locks to serialize communications in the `MPI_THREAD_MULTIPLE` mode which would interfere with the task model. We instead serialize MPI calls using additional tasks dependencies so that only one MPI task is active at a time. We use non-blocking MPI calls with wait calls in distinct tasks for a fine control of dependencies.

The tasks are submitted with the `omp task` directive and `depend` OpenMP clauses are used to specify the dependencies between them (unless explicitly stated). We decide to prune redundant data dependencies to mitigate submission and scheduling costs (which can be several time higher than the execution if the submission is so slow that workers are starving). For the same reason, we aggregated successive short calculations into single tasks, and consider the whole ghost zone of each tile as a single atomic memory area to achieve coarser granularity.

Algorithm Implementation. Poisson is implemented by two tasks. The first one communicates (`MPI_AllReduce`) the density field. The second task depends on the first one and solves Poisson for a local subdomain along space dimension. Once Poisson is solved, a task performs diagnostics: the output of the code.

Ghost buffers management is implemented by two tasks. The first one recursively submits two groups of independent sub-tasks (using synchronous *task loop* construct[3]). Sub-tasks of the first group copy data into ghost buffers and swap tile buffers; those from the second group exchange ghost buffers between local tiles, this avoids MPI transfers that would occur within each MPI process. The second task depends on the first one (and also on the `MPI_AllReduce` task due to MPI tasks serialization) and performs all the `isend`/`irecv` required for tiles whose neighbors are in a different MPI process.

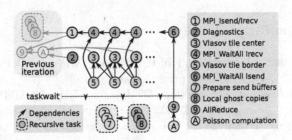

Fig. 2. Submitted task graph of one iteration with the advection (top) and Poisson (bottom) within the implementation.

Finally, the advection is implemented by four groups of tasks. Tasks in the first group compute the advected values of internal points of the tiles; each depends only on its own tile both as input and output. Tasks of the second group wait for the reception of ghosts sent in the ghost buffer management tasks. Tasks of the third group compute the advected values of border points and the density integrals ρ; each depends on its own tile both as input and output and on the associated ghost buffer as input. One last task waits for all buffers to be sent.

---

[3] This construct specifies to execute iterations of one or multiple loops in parallel using (independent) tasks. Unless specified by the user, it lets the runtime choose the best granularity and perform a final synchronization.

Finally, a `taskwait` directive is performed before moving back to the Poisson phase that depends on the completion of all tasks. MPI tasks have the highest *priority*, then come tile internal point tasks and border point tasks; other tasks have a default lower priority.

Figure 2 summarizes the scheduled OpenMP task graph of one timestep on one MPI process (similar on each process). Firstly, all MPI tasks (top and left) are serialized using an `inout` fake variable. Moreover, while the `MPI_Isend/Irecv` task perform all the Isend/Irecv, each `MPI_WaitAll Irecv` waits only for all ghost buffers of a single tile to be received. For each tile, one task of each of the three following types is submitted: `MPI_WaitAll Irecv`, `Tile center` and `Tile border`. The dependency pattern between the `Tile center` and `Tile border` tasks is a 2D stencil (simplified view on Fig. 2).

4   Performance Evaluation

4.1   Experimental Setup

System Configuration. The experiments have been performed on the Skylake (SKL) and Xeon Phi (KNL) partitions of the Marconi supercomputer[4]. SKL nodes include two sockets Xeon 8160 with 24 cores. KNL nodes contain a Xeon Phi KNL 7250 processor with 68 cores. The Xeon Phi is configured with the quadrant clustering and cache memory modes[5]. Hyper-threading is disabled on SKL and we chose to disable it on KNL. The network is an Intel Omni-Path 100 Gb/s (fat-tree). Experiments use one process per NUMA node (two processes per socket for SKL and four processes per socket for KNL) to prevent in-process NUMA effects which are out of the scope of this paper (the numactl tool was used so that each process is bound to a unique quadrant and access to its own memory). The code has been compiled with ICC 2018.0.1 and IntelMPI 2018.1.163[6]. The used OpenMP runtime is KOMP [5] (commit 32781b6), a fork of the LLVM/Intel OpenMP runtime. This runtime helps us to produce and visualize runtime traces in order to finely profile and track performance problems and behaviors. It also implements tasks priorities and provides good performance with fine-grained tasks [9].

Method. The median completion time is retrieved from a set of 10 runs. Each run performs 1000 iterations for the scaling and granularity experiments and 100 for the trace-based results (to reduce the trace size). Unless explicitly stated, each run works with a (small) tile size of 64×64 over a 2D dataset of 8192×8192. We choose a quite-small dataset for practical reasons: it exhibit issues that usually occur with much more nodes on bigger datasets, but actually takes less time and energy.

---

[4] http://www.hpc.cineca.it/hardware/marconi.
[5] The mode cannot be configured by the user on the selected computing machines.
[6] The latest available versions on the computing machines during the experiments.

4.2   Experimental Results

This Section presents and discusses the performance obtained on the considered use-case. First, the overall scalability is analyzed and performance issues are further investigated. Then, the benefits of using priorities is studied. After that, the amount of overlapping is quantified. Finally, task overheads are analyzed: the cost of the submission, the dependencies, and the impact of the task granularity.

Scalability. Figure 3a displays the completion time plotted against the number of cores on both KNL and SKL nodes. It shows the hybrid application scales well up to 64 nodes (respectively 4352 and 3072 cores) despite the small amount of data to process. However, some scalability issues appear on 128 nodes (respectively 8704 and 6144 cores).

Breakdown. Figure 3b shows the fraction of parallel time (cumulated sum of the duration of the tasks) taken by each part of the application plotted against the number of nodes used. First, we can see that the advection and the ghost exchange needed by the advection take most of the time, while the Poisson part seems negligible at first glance. However, from 32 to 128 nodes, the idle time and the runtime overhead[7] is increasing to the point of becoming dominant, and this growth is mainly due to Poisson solver as we shall see.

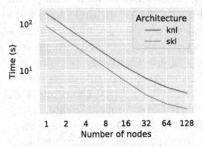
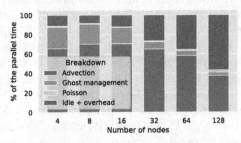

(a) Completion time over the number of nodes on each architecture.

(b) Breakdown of the parallel time plotted against the number of SKL nodes.

Fig. 3. Scalability and performance results.

Figure 4 displays the task scheduling of one iteration on one MPI process of 64 SKL nodes (the work is uniformly balanced on each process). Let us focus on Fig. 4a for the moment.

---

[7] The idle time includes periods where threads are busy waiting for ready tasks to be executed and thread synchronization periods, and the runtime overhead includes scheduling and task submission costs.

Schedule Analysis. Overall, the schedule is quite good since tasks related to the advection and ghost exchanges (left side) are feeding almost all cores. The overlap of communication is almost perfect in the Vlasov solver with `MPI_isend/irecv` triggered early in the timestep and the associated `MPI_Wait` do not slow down tiles computations. However, we can see that the Poisson solver (right side) is less effective: the AllReduce does not scale well and the overlapping exists but is dropping along with the number of cores. Indeed, it takes around 30% of the overall execution time on 64 SKL nodes there (and 47% with 128 KNL nodes), with a small fraction overlapped with computation. Please note that this operation only consists in performing communications and can hardly be well overlapped with computations at scale due to the actual dependencies between the steps of Algorithm 1 itself.

It demonstrates the need of overlapping. But, the dependencies of the algorithm prevent any additional overlap with computation in the Poisson solver. Though, the results from all tiles are required to perform the global collective, the result of which is used to solve Poisson, that finally leads to the next timestep.

At the beginning of the timestep, we can note that the master thread takes a while before executing tasks. This delay is spent to submit all the tasks for the current timestep and takes a non-negligible part of the time[8].

Task Priorities. Figure 4b displays the task scheduling with task priorities disabled, as opposed to Fig. 4a. This schedule is less efficient since `MPI_Wait` tasks are executed lately reducing the throughput of ready tasks that compute the border points, and at a later stage is delaying the start of Poisson. Please note that the AllReduce is slightly faster. We assume the management of traces by the runtime causes network transfers that perturbs the AllReduce operation. Overall, this version is 5.7% slower than the version with priorities. Thus, it shows the effectiveness of using task priorities. However, one can note that some OpenMP implementations do not currently support priorities. Indeed, the LLVM/Intel runtime does not yet, but KOMP and GOMP do.

Note that while GOMP could be used in the experiments of this paper, we encountered some limitation when we tried to use it. Indeed, OMPT implemented in GOMP that enable tracing capabilities is still in an early state and we did not succeed to make it work on the tested computing environment (with GCC 8.2.0). Studying results without such information was proven to be tricky.

Quantifying the Overlap. To measure the amount of overlapping more precisely on the overall execution time, we have designed and used two metrics: r_{comm} and r_{act}. Let us define $r_{comm} = \frac{t_{comm}}{t_{all}}$ where t_{comm} is the cumulated time of MPI-only tasks (which are serialized) and the t_{all} is the overall completion time. r_{comm} gives hints on whether the application is compute-bound ($r_{comm} \approx 0$) or rather communication-bound ($r_{comm} \approx 1$ with a small r_{act}). $r_{act} = \frac{t_{compute}}{t_{all} \times n_{cores}}$ where $t_{compute}$ is the cumulated sum of all computational task duration (parallel

---

[8] This time could be shortened, if only one could store and resubmit the task graph from one timestep to another such as in [2].

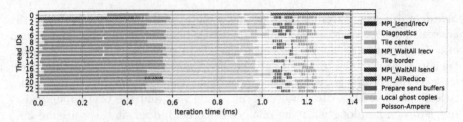

(a) Task scheduling with priorities enabled and task loops.

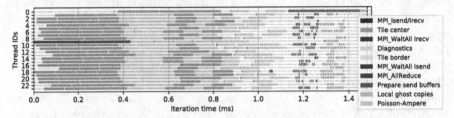

(b) Task scheduling without priorities enabled and with task loops.

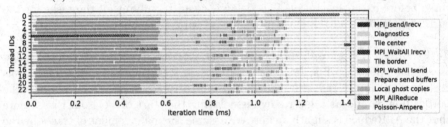

(c) Task scheduling with priorities enabled and without task loops.

Fig. 4. Task scheduling of one iteration within one MPI process using 64 SKL nodes. White areas are idle time and runtime overheads. Dashed lines are the completion time of the selected iterations.

time) and n_{cores} the number of cores. r_{act} represents the amount of activity of all the cores without including communications and runtime overheads.

On Fig. 4a, r_{comm} represent the ratio of serialized hatched areas (MPI calls) over the overall completion time and r_{act} is the fraction of non-hatched colored area (OpenMP computing tasks) over the overall two dimensional plotting area (parallel time).

Results show that $r_{comm} = 0.09$ and $r_{act} = 0.96$ on 1 SKL node and $r_{comm} = 0.64$ and $r_{act} = 0.60$ on 64 SKL nodes. It means the application is clearly compute-bound on 1 node as 9% of the overall execution time is spent in MPI calls and cores are busy to perform computation 96% of the time. On 64 nodes, the application spent a major part of its time in MPI calls (64%), but·cores are still busy 60% of the time, which indicates a good overlap. This is quite consistent with the schedule of the selected iteration displayed in Fig. 4a as serialized MPI calls take a significant portion of the sequential time and the idle time is not predominant although it is clearly significant.

Cost of the Dependencies. While synchronizations are known to cause load imbalance between threads and could be costly on many-cores systems; the cost of task dependencies can sometimes exceed them. Figure 4c displays the schedule of non-recursive tasks with fine-grained dependencies rather than task loops in recursive tasks of Fig. 4a. The task submission takes around 3 times as long as the first version. This large overhead is due to the high number of dependencies (9 per task) compared to the task granularity [9]. Still, the AllReduce is postponed and the master thread is busy at submitting tasks rather than executing them. As a result, the overall completion time of this variant is 9.7% slower than the first one. This justifies the use of task loops in recursive tasks. The overheads are expected to increase with more worker threads or a finer granularity.

More generally, the number of dependencies per task should be minimized[9]. Sometimes, it should be done at the expense of the code maintainability (*e.g.* indirect dependencies, over-synchronizations, control-based dependencies). An analysis of this kind of trade-offs is done in [9].

Impact of the Tile Granularity. Figure 5 displays the overhead coming from the choice of the tile size regarding the number of KNL nodes used. Such overhead includes the management of ghosts, runtime costs (*e.g.* task scheduling), scheduling effect (*e.g.* load balancing), hardware effects (*e.g.* cache effects). A ratio equal to 1 means that the selected tile size provides the best completion time of all evaluated tile sizes for a given number of nodes. A ratio greater than 1 means that the completion time sub-optimal since another tile size that results in a smaller completion time can be picked.

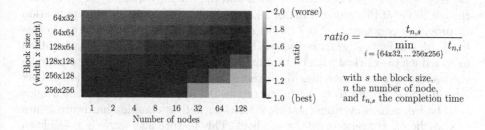

$$ratio = \frac{t_{n,s}}{\min\limits_{i=\{64x32,\ldots 256x256\}} t_{n,i}}$$

with s the block size,
n the number of node,
and $t_{n,s}$ the completion time

Fig. 5. Relative time (ratio) of the application plotted against both the tile size and the number of nodes of KNL. For each set of nodes, the time is normalized to the best tile size. For clarity, ratios greater than 2 are capped.

On one hand, a coarse tile granularity on a lot of nodes (under-decomposition) results in worker starvation since there is not enough tasks to feed them (bottom-right of the Figure). On the other hand, a small tile size on a few nodes (over-decomposition) introduces prohibitive runtime costs due to the number of tasks

---

[9] The management cost of dependencies could also be lowered by the runtime if dedicated studies are done along this line.

to schedule proportionally to the overall execution time (top-left of the Figure). Thus, the most efficient tile size is related to the number of nodes.

Strategies to Set the Tile Size. We can emphasize that the cost of an under-decomposition of the domain causes more problems than an over-decomposition. Thus, it is better to perform a slight over-decomposition, it provides more flexibility to the runtime to ensure a decent load balance. Finally, choosing 64×64 tiles (see Sect. 4.1) is not always the best but is an adequate trade-off to ensure the scalability of this code up to 128 nodes.

Discussion on the Granularity. The tile size, and more generally the granularity of tasks is a matter of concerns to reach good performances. This problem is usually addressed using recursive tasking in OpenMP: tasks can be submitted from different threads and from other tasks recursively to lower the cost of scheduling. However, in OpenMP dependencies can only be defined between sibling tasks of the same parent task, this is a pitfall to avoid on this use-case. Weak-dependencies proposal [14] would overcome the restriction if well integrated in OpenMP. Since MPI tasks are serialized, they must be submitted from the same thread or parent task and the same rule apply for the advection tasks since they depend on MPI tasks. An alternative is to work at a coarser grain using dependencies on recursive tasks. But, this approach mitigates the submission overhead at the cost of an increased complexity and introduces over-synchronizations that can harm overlapping. Practically, auto-tuning approaches can be used to find the best granularity, especially for more complex use-case.

Leveraging Task Graph Tracing. OMPT and the tracing capability of KOMP are the backbone of this paper. First of all, it has guided us to design the application by providing constant feedback on the runtime scheduling and the source of over-heads (dependencies, granularity, synchronizations). For example, it has enabled us to reduce the critical path by tuning the submitted task graph and to improve the overlapping at large scale. Moreover, it also enables the visualization of task scheduling. It proves to be useful to profile the application or even track bugs (*e.g.* bad dependency, abnormal slow task) as well as complex hardware issues (*e.g.* cache effects relative to the locality). This feature also made it possible to draw Fig. 4. However, there is no free lunch: tracing introduces an additional overhead which can be significant at fine granularity. That being said, it is still well-suited to analyze the complex behavior of OpenMP task-based applications provided that performance measures are close enough with or without tracing.

Combining Tasks and MPI. The serialization of MPI communications tasks is more a bypass to prevent issues related to MPI implementations than a definitive solution. Indeed, the developer nor the user are not in the best position to: adjust the number of threads allocated to MPI communications, pin them, deal with issues related to `MPI_THREAD_MULTIPLE`. Indeed, the tuning strongly depends on the MPI implementation, the runtime, the hardware. Moreover, it raises another problem: in which order MPI tasks should be executed to minimize the overall execution time? While we have chosen to force a static schedule of such tasks in the considered use-case, it may not be optimal in general. Indeed, the time of MPI primitives varies regarding the node architectures, the network hardware, the bindings of threads, as well as the actual use of the shared network infrastructure. Moreover, regarding the dependencies and the critical path, it may be worthwhile to start communications before others. OpenMP currently provides no way to deal with such a constrained multi-objective optimization with communication.

5   Related Work

Many studies have been previously conducted on building OpenMP+MPI applications, especially for loop-based applications. But, to our knowledge, no previous work have studied the use of OpenMP 4.5 task-based features on CPU-based many-core systems, especially fine-grained dependencies coupled with MPI.

The MultiProcessor Communications environment (MPC) [13] try to fill in the gap between OpenMP and MPI. While this approach address problems pertaining to the overlapping in hybrid applications, it mainly focuses on loop-based applications. So far, MPC only supports OpenMP 3.1 and thus features like data dependencies, task loops and priorities are not supported. Authors [15] consider to signal blocking MPI calls to OpenMP for better scheduling. The grain of their solution seems to be order of magnitude bigger than considered in our target simulation.

Some task-based runtimes that support OpenMP also support extension relative to MPI. StarPU [1], for example, supports asynchronous and task-based send/receive point-to-point communications, and more recently MPI collectives. The runtime is based on a pooling thread to handle the asynchronous MPI communications. It provides two main APIs: a C-extension based on pragma directives and a low-level C API. The first targets only GCC, and as far as we know, it does not support MPI-related features. The last is flexible, but also more intrusive as a lot of code is needed to submit and manage tasks. OmpSs [6] is another runtime supporting MPI in a similar way. It extends OpenMP with new directives so it can be used by end-users. However, OmpSs relies on its own compiler. These approaches can be a good starting point to create a standard interface between OpenMP and MPI or even an OpenMP extension that could be supported by multiple runtimes as well as MPI implementations.

Although, as of today, designing practical hybrid applications is still challenging for developers adopting both MPI and OpenMP task-based constructs to target recent and upcoming many-core systems. This is an active field of research and the state-of-the-art is moving quickly.

6   Conclusion

This paper evaluated the use of the OpenMP task-related features like priorities and task loops (introduced in the version 4.5 of the norm) in the context of a

MPI+OpenMP application that solves the Vlasov-Poisson equations on many-core architectures. It emphasized the impact of using tasks on the overlapping and the overall performance. A specific focus has been put on the tracing and visualization tools. The paper has also highlighted limits specific to OpenMP and provided feedback.

Experiments have been conducted on systems with Skylake and Xeon Phi processors from 1 up to 128 nodes. Results show that OpenMP tasks enable achieving a good overlapping. Task priorities are proven to be effective, especially to schedule MPI communications. The overhead due to tasks submission and due to dependencies management revealed to be quite high. We managed to reduce this overhead by using: less dependencies, task loops constructs and recursive tasks. Finally, OMPT and runtime tracing capabilities have enabled a fine analysis of the behavior and performance of the code, and thus have been essential.

We think that specific points should be mainly addressed in the future. First, the interaction between OpenMP and MPI should be improved in a way the runtime can reorder opportunistically the scheduling of tasks that embed MPI communications. Second, fine-grained dependencies between siblings of recursive tasks should be made possible. Indeed, it is difficult for the user to express all the available parallelism with the existing task features.

Acknowledgments. This work was supported by the EoCoE and EoCoE2 projects, grant agreement numbers 676629 & 824158, funded within the EU's H2020 program. We also acknowledge CEA for the support provided by *Programme Transversal de Compétences – Simulation Numérique*.

References

1. Augonnet, C., Aumage, O., Furmento, N., Namyst, R., Thibault, S.: StarPU-MPI: task programming over clusters of machines enhanced with accelerators. In: Träff, J.L., Benkner, S., Dongarra, J.J. (eds.) EuroMPI 2012. LNCS, vol. 7490, pp. 298–299. Springer, Heidelberg (2012). https://doi.org/10.1007/978-3-642-33518-1_40
2. Besseron, X., Gautier, T.: Impact of over-decomposition on coordinated checkpoint/rollback protocol. In: Alexander, M., et al. (eds.) Euro-Par 2011. LNCS, vol. 7156, pp. 322–332. Springer, Heidelberg (2012). https://doi.org/10.1007/978-3-642-29740-3_36
3. Bouzat, N., Rozar, F., Latu, G., Roman, J.: A new parallelization scheme for the Hermite interpolation based gyroaverage operator. In: 2017 16th ISPDC (2017)
4. Bouzat, N., et al.: Targeting realistic geometry in Tokamak code Gysela. ESAIM Proc. Surv. **63**, 179–207 (2018)
5. Broquedis, F., Gautier, T., Danjean, V.: LIBKOMP, an efficient OpenMP runtime system for both fork-join and data flow paradigms. In: Chapman, B.M., Massaioli, F., Müller, M.S., Rorro, M. (eds.) IWOMP 2012. LNCS, vol. 7312, pp. 102–115. Springer, Heidelberg (2012). https://doi.org/10.1007/978-3-642-30961-8_8
6. Bueno, J., et al.: Productive cluster programming with OmpSs. In: Jeannot, E., Namyst, R., Roman, J. (eds.) Euro-Par 2011. LNCS, vol. 6852, pp. 555–566. Springer, Heidelberg (2011). https://doi.org/10.1007/978-3-642-23400-2_52

7. Crouseilles, N., Latu, G., Sonnendrücker, E.: Hermite spline interpolationon patches for parallelly solving the Vlasov-Poisson equation. IJAMCS **17**(3), 335–349 (2007)
8. Diaz, J., Muñoz-Caro, C., Niño, A.: A survey of parallel programming modelsand tools in the multi and many-core era. IEEE TPDS **23**(8), 1369–1386 (2012)
9. Gautier, T., Pérez, C., Richard, J.: On the impact of OpenMP task granularity. In: de Supinski, B.R., Valero-Lara, P., Martorell, X., Mateo Bellido, S., Labarta, J. (eds.) IWOMP 2018. LNCS, vol. 11128, pp. 205–221. Springer, Cham (2018). https://doi.org/10.1007/978-3-319-98521-3_14
10. Martorell, X., Teruel, X., Klemm, M.: Advanced OpenMP Tutorial (2018). https://openmpcon.org/wp-content/uploads/2018_Tutorial3_Martorell_Teruel_Klemm.pdf
11. OpenMP Architecture Review Board: OpenMP Application Programming Interface Version 4.5, November 2015. http://www.openmp.org
12. OpenMP Architecture Review Board: OpenMP Application Programming Interface Version 5.0, November 2018. http://www.openmp.org
13. Pérache, M., Jourdren, H., Namyst, R.: MPC: a unified parallel runtime for clusters of NUMA machines. In: Luque, E., Margalef, T., Benítez, D. (eds.) Euro-Par 2008. LNCS, vol. 5168, pp. 78–88. Springer, Heidelberg (2008). https://doi.org/10.1007/978-3-540-85451-7_9
14. Perez, J.M., Beltran, V., Labarta, J., Ayguadé, E.: Improving the integration of task nesting and dependencies in OpenMP. In: IPDPS 2017. IEEE (2017)
15. Sala, K., et al.: Improving the interoperability between MPI and task-based programming models. In: Proceedings of EuroMPI 2018, pp. 6:1–6:11. ACM (2018)
16. Song, F., YarKhan, A., Dongarra, J.: Dynamic task scheduling for linear algebra algorithms on distributed-memory multicore systems. In: Proceedings of the Conference on HPC Networking, Storage and Analysis, SC 2009. ACM (2009)
17. Sonnendrücker, E., et al.: The semi-Lagrangian method for the numerical resolution of the Vlasov equation. J. Comput. Phys. **149**(2), 201–220 (1999)

Parallel Adaptive Sampling with Almost No Synchronization

Alexander van der Grinten$^{(\boxtimes)}$, Eugenio Angriman, and Henning Meyerhenke

Department of Computer Science, Humboldt-Universität zu Berlin, Berlin, Germany
{avdgrinten,angrimae,meyerhenke}@hu-berlin.de

Abstract. Approximation via sampling is a widespread technique whenever exact solutions are too expensive. In this paper, we present techniques for an efficient parallelization of adaptive (a.k.a. progressive) sampling algorithms on multi-threaded shared-memory machines. Our basic algorithmic technique requires no synchronization except for atomic `load-acquire` and `store-release` operations. It does, however, require $\mathcal{O}(n)$ memory per thread, where n is the size of the sampling state. We present variants of the algorithm that either reduce this memory consumption to $\mathcal{O}(1)$ or ensure that deterministic results are obtained.

Using the KADABRA algorithm for betweenness centrality (a popular measure in network analysis) approximation as a case study, we demonstrate the empirical performance of our techniques. In particular, on a 32-core machine, our best algorithm is 2.9× faster than what we could achieve using a straightforward OpenMP-based parallelization and 65.3× faster than the existing implementation of KADABRA.

Keywords: Parallel approximation algorithms · Adaptive sampling · Wait-free algorithms · Betweenness centrality

1 Introduction

When a computational problem cannot be solved exactly within the desired time budget, a frequent solution is to employ approximation algorithms [12]. With large data sets being the rule and not the exception today, approximation is frequently applied, even to polynomial-time problems [6]. We focus on a particular subclass of approximation algorithms: *sampling algorithms*. They sample data according to some (usually algorithm-specific) probability distribution, perform some computation on the sample and induce a result for the full data set.

More specifically, we consider *adaptive* sampling (ADS) algorithms (also called *progressive* sampling algorithms). Here, the number of samples that are required is not statically computed (e.g., from the input instance) but also depends on the data that has been sampled so far. While non-adaptive sampling algorithms can often be parallelized trivially by drawing multiple samples

Partially supported by grant ME 3619/3-2 within German Research Foundation (DFG) Priority Programme 1736 *Algorithms for Big Data*.

in parallel, adaptive sampling constitutes a challenge for parallelization: checking the stopping condition of an ADS algorithm requires access to all the data generated so far and thus mandates some form of synchronization.

Motivation and Contribution. Our initial motivation was a parallel implementation of the sequential state-of-the-art approximation algorithm KADABRA [6] for betweenness centrality (BC) approximation. BC is a very popular centrality measure in network analysis, see Sect. 2.2 for more details. To the best of our knowledge, parallel adaptive sampling has not received a generic treatment yet. Hence, we propose techniques to parallelize ADS algorithms in a generic way, while scaling to large numbers of threads. While we turn to KADABRA to demonstrate the effectiveness of the proposed algorithms, our techniques can be adjusted easily to other ADS algorithms.

We introduce two new parallel ADS algorithms, which we call *local-frame* and *shared-frame*. Both algorithms try to avoid extensive synchronization when checking the stopping condition. This is done by maintaining multiple copies of the sampling state and ensuring that the stopping condition is never checked on a copy of the state that is currently being written to. *Local-frame* is designed to use the least amount of synchronization possible – at the cost of an additional memory footprint of $\Theta(n)$ per thread, where n denotes the size of the sampling state. This algorithm performs only atomic `load-acquire` and `store-release` operations for synchronization, but no expensive read-modify-write operations (like `CAS` or `fetch-add`). *Shared-frame*, in turn, aims instead at meeting a desired trade-off between memory footprint and synchronization overhead. In contrast to *local-frame*, it requires only $\Theta(1)$ additional memory per thread, but uses atomic read-modify-write operations (e.g., `fetch-add`) to accumulate samples. We also propose the deterministic *indexed-frame* algorithm; it guarantees that the results of two different executions is the same for a fixed random seed, regardless of the number of threads.

Our experimental results show that local-frame, shared-frame and indexed-frame achieve parallel speedups of $15.9\times$, $18.1\times$, and $10.8\times$ on 32 cores, respectively. Using the same number of cores, our OpenMP-based parallelization (functioning as a baseline) only yields a speedup of $6.3\times$; thus our algorithms are up to $2.9\times$ faster. Moreover, also due to implementation improvements and parameter tuning, our best algorithm performs adaptive sampling $65.3\times$ faster than the existing implementation of KADABRA (when all implementations use 32 cores).

A full-length version of this paper (including an Appendix) is available from https://arxiv.org/abs/1903.09422 [13].

Algorithm 1. Generic Adaptive Sampling

Variable initialization:	Main loop:
$d \leftarrow$ new sampling state structure	**while not** CHECKFORSTOP(d) **do**
$d.\text{data} \leftarrow (0,\dots,0)$ ▷ Sampled data.	$\quad d.\text{data} \leftarrow d.\text{data} \circ \text{SAMPLE}()$
$d.\text{num} \leftarrow 0$ ▷ Number of samples.	$\quad d.\text{num} \leftarrow d.\text{num} + 1$

2   Preliminaries and Baseline for Parallelization

2.1   Basic Definitions

Memory Model. Throughout this paper, we target a multi-threaded shared-memory machine with T threads. We work in the C11 memory model [15] (more details in Appendix A of our full-length paper [13]); in particular, we assume the existence of the usual atomic operations, as well as `load-acquire` and `store-release` barriers.

Adaptive Sampling. For our techniques to be applicable, we expect that an ADS algorithm behaves as depicted in Algorithm 1: it iteratively samples data (in SAMPLE) and aggregates it (using some operator ∘), until a stopping condition (CHECKFORSTOP) determines that the data sampled so far is sufficient to return an approximate solution within the required accuracy. This condition does not only consider the number of samples (d.num), but also the sampled data (d.data). Throughout this paper, we denote the size of that data (i.e., the number of elements of d.data) by n. We assume that the stopping condition needs to be checked on a *consistent* state, i.e., a state of d that can occur in a sequential execution.[1] Furthermore, to make parallelization feasible at all, we need to assume that ∘ is associative. For concrete examples of stopping conditions, we refer to Sect. 2.3 and Appendix A.

2.2   Betweenness Centrality and Its Approximation

Betweenness Centrality (BC) is one of the most popular vertex centrality measures in the field of network analysis. Such measures indicate the importance of a vertex based on its position in the network [4] (we use the terms *graph* and *network* interchangeably). Being a centrality measure, BC constitutes a function $\mathbf{b} : V \rightarrow \mathbb{R}$ that maps each vertex of a graph $G = (V, E)$ to a real number – higher numbers represent higher importance. To be precise, the BC of $u \in V$ is defined as $\mathbf{b}(u) = \sum_{s \neq t \in V \setminus \{u\}} \frac{\sigma_{st}(u)}{\sigma_{st}}$, where σ_{st} is the number of shortest s-t-paths and $\sigma_{st}(u)$ is the number of shortest s-t-paths that contain u. Betweenness is extensively used to identify the key vertices in large networks, e.g., cities in a transportation network [14], or lethality in protein networks [16].

Unfortunately, BC is rather expensive to compute: the standard exact algorithm [8] has time complexity $\Theta(|V||E|)$ for unweighted graphs. Moreover, unless the Strong Exponential Time Hypothesis fails, this asymptotic running time cannot be improved [5]. Numerous approximation algorithms for BC have thus been developed (we refer to Sect. 5 for an overview). The state of the art of these approximation algorithms is the KADABRA algorithm [6] of Borassi and Natale, which happens to be an ADS algorithm. With probability $(1 - \delta)$, KADABRA approximates the BC values of the vertices within an additive error of ϵ in nearly-linear time complexity, where ϵ and δ are user-specified constants.

---

[1] That is, d.num and all entries of d.data must result from an integral sequence of samples; otherwise, parallelization would be trivial.

While our techniques apply to any ADS algorithm, we recall that, as a case study, we focus on scaling the KADABRA algorithm to a large number of threads.

2.3   The KADABRA algorithm

KADABRA samples vertex pairs (s, t) of $G = (V, E)$ uniformly at random and then selects a shortest s-t-path uniformly at random (in SAMPLE in Algorithm 1). After τ iterations, this results in a sequence of randomly selected shortest paths $\pi_1, \pi_2, \ldots, \pi_\tau$; from those paths, BC is estimated as:

$$\widetilde{\mathbf{b}}(v) = \frac{1}{\tau} \sum_{i=1}^{\tau} x_i(v), \quad x_i(v) = \begin{cases} 1 & \text{if } v \in \pi_i \\ 0 & \text{otherwise.} \end{cases}$$

$\sum_{i=1}^{\tau} x_i$ is exactly the sampled data (d.data) that the algorithm has to store (i.e., the accumulation $\circ$ in Algorithm 1 sums x_i over i). To compute the stopping condition (CHECKFORSTOP in Algorithm 1), KADABRA maintains the invariants

$$\Pr(\mathbf{b}(v) \le \widetilde{\mathbf{b}}(v) - f) \le \delta_L(v) \text{ and } \Pr(\mathbf{b}(v) \ge \widetilde{\mathbf{b}}(v) + g) \le \delta_U(v) \qquad (1)$$

for two functions $f = f(\widetilde{\mathbf{b}}(v), \delta_L(v), \omega, \tau)$ and $g = g(\widetilde{\mathbf{b}}(v), \delta_U(v), \omega, \tau)$ depending on a maximal number ω of samples and per-vertex probability constants δ_L and δ_U (more details in the original paper [6]). The values of those constants are computed in a preprocessing phase (mostly consisting of computing an upper bound on the diameter of the graph). δ_L and δ_U satisfy $\sum_{v \in V} \delta_L(v) + \delta_U(v) \le \delta$ for a user-specified parameter $\delta \in (0, 1)$. Thus, the algorithm terminates once $f, g < \epsilon$; the result is correct with an absolute error of $\pm \epsilon$ and probability $(1 - \delta)$. We note that checking the stopping condition of KADABRA on an inconsistent state leads to incorrect results. For example, this can be seen from the fact that g is increasing with $\widetilde{\mathbf{b}}$ and decreasing with τ, see Appendix B of our full-length paper [13].

2.4   First Attempts at KADABRA Parallelization

In the original KADABRA implementation[2], a lock is used to synchronize concurrent access to the sampling state. As a first attempt to improve the scalability,

```
int  epoch    ← e
int  num      ← 0
int  data[n]  ← (0,...,0)
```

(a) Structure of a state frame (SF) for epoch e. num: Number of samples, data: Sampled data

```
bool  stop          ← false
int   epochToRead   ← 0
SF *  sfFin[T]       ← (null,...,null)
```

(b) Shared variables

Fig. 1. Data structures used in epoch-based algorithms, including initial values

---

[2] Available at: https://github.com/natema/kadabra.

we consider an algorithm that iteratively computes a fixed number of samples in parallel (e.g., using an OpenMP `parallel for` loop), then issues a synchronization barrier (as implied by the `parallel for` loop) and checks the stopping condition afterwards. While sampling, atomic increments are used to update the global sampling data. This algorithm is arguably the "natural" OpenMP-based parallelization of an ADS algorithm and can be implemented in a few extra lines of code. Moreover, it already improves upon the original parallelization. However, as shown by the experiments in Sect. 4, further significant improvements in performance are possible by switching to more lightweight synchronization.

3   Scalable Parallelization Techniques

To improve upon the OpenMP parallelization from Sect. 2.4, we have to avoid the synchronization barrier before the stopping condition can be checked. This is the objective of our *epoch-based* algorithms that constitute the main contribution of this paper. In Sect. 3.1, we formulate the main idea of our algorithms as a general framework and prove its correctness. The subsequent subsections present specific algorithms based on this framework and discuss trade-offs between them.

3.1   Epoch-Based Framework

In our epoch-based algorithms, the execution of each thread is subdivided into a sequence of discrete *epochs*. During an epoch, each thread iteratively collects samples; the stopping condition is only checked at the end of an epoch. The crucial advantage of this approach is that the end of an epoch *does not* require global synchronization. Instead, our framework guarantees the consistency of the sampled data by maintaining multiple copies of the sampling state.

As an invariant, it is guaranteed that no thread writes to a copy of the state that is currently being read by another thread. This is achieved as follows: each copy of the sampling state is labeled by an epoch *number* e, i.e., a monotonically increasing integer that identifies the epoch in which the data was generated. When the stopping condition has to be checked, all threads advance to a new epoch $e + 1$ and start writing to a new copy of the sampling state. The stopping condition is only verified after all threads have finished this transition and it only takes the sampling state of epoch e into account.

More precisely, the main data structure that we use to store the sampling state is called a *state frame* (SF). Each SF f (depicted in Fig. 1(a)) consists of (i) an epoch number (f.epoch), (ii) a number of samples (f.num) and (iii) the sampled data (f.data). The latter two symbols directly correspond to d.num and d.data in our generic formulation of an adaptive sampling algorithm (Algorithm 1). Aside from the SF structures, our framework maintains three global variables that are shared among all threads (depicted in Fig. 1(b)): (i) a simple Boolean flag stop to determine if the algorithm should terminate, (ii) a variable epochToRead that stores the number of the epoch that we want to check the stopping condition on and (iii) a pointer sfFin[t] for each thread t that

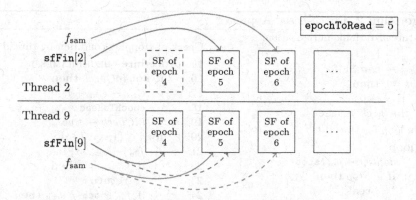

Fig. 2. Transition after `epochToRead` is set to 5. Thread 2 already writes to the SF of epoch 6 (using the f_{sam} pointer). Thread 9 still writes to the SF of epoch 5 but advances to epoch 6 once it checks `epochToRead` (dashed orange line). Afterwards, thread 9 publishes its SF of epoch 5 to `sfFin` (dashed blue line). Finally, the stopping condition is checked using both SFs of epoch 5 (i.e., the SFs now pointed to by `sfFin`). (Color figure online)

points to a SF finished by thread t. Incrementing `epochToRead` is our synchronization mechanism to notify all threads that they should advance to a new epoch. Figure 2 visualizes such an epoch transition. In particular, it depicts the update of the `sfFin` pointers after an epoch transition is initiated by incrementing `epochToRead`.

Algorithm 2 states the pseudocode of our framework. By $\leftarrow_{relaxed}$, $\leftarrow_{acquire}$ and $\leftarrow_{release}$, we denote relaxed memory access, **load-acquire** and **store-release**, respectively (see Sects. 2.1 and Appendix A of our full-length paper [13]). In the algorithm, each thread maintains an epoch number e_{sam}. To be able to check the stopping condition, thread 0 maintains another epoch number e_{chk}. Indeed, thread 0 is the only thread that evaluates the stopping condition (in CHECK-FRAMES) after accumulating the SFs from all threads. CHECKFRAMES determines whether there is an ongoing check for the stopping condition (*inCheck* is true; line 16). If that is not the case, a check is initiated (by incrementing e_{chk}) and all threads are signaled to advance to the next epoch (by updating `epochToRead`). Note that *inCheck* is needed to prevent thread 0 from repeatedly incrementing e_{chk} without processing data from the other threads. Afterwards, CHECKFRAMES only continues if all threads t have published their SFs for checking (i.e., `sfFin[t]` points to a SF of epoch e_{chk}; line 20). Once that happens, those SFs are accumulated (line 27) and the stopping condition is checked on the accumulated data (line 31). Eventually, the termination flag (`stop`; line 32) signals to all threads that they should stop sampling. The main algorithm, on the other hand, performs a loops until this flag is set (line 2). Each iteration collects one sample and writes the results to the current SF (f_{sam}). If a thread needs to advance to a new epoch (because an incremented `epochToRead` is read in line 7), it publishes its current SF to `sfFin` and starts writing to a new

Algorithm 2. Epoch-based Approach

Per-thread variable initialization:

$e_{\text{sam}} \leftarrow 1$

$f_{\text{sam}} \leftarrow$ new SF for $e_{\text{sam}} = 1$

if $t = 0$ then

$\quad e_{\text{chk}} \leftarrow 0$

$\quad inCheck \leftarrow$ false

Main loop for thread t:

1: **loop**
2: $\quad doStop \leftarrow_{\text{relaxed}}$ **stop**
3: $\quad$ **if** $doStop$ **then**
4: $\quad\quad$ **break**
5: $\quad f_{\text{sam}}.\text{data} \leftarrow f_{\text{sam}}.\text{data} \circ \text{SAMPLE}()$
6: $\quad f_{\text{sam}}.\text{num} \leftarrow f_{\text{sam}}.\text{num} + 1$
7: $\quad r \leftarrow_{\text{relaxed}}$ **epochToRead**
8: $\quad$ **if** $r = e_{\text{sam}}$ **then**
9: $\quad\quad$ reclaim SF of epoch $e_{\text{sam}} - 1$
10: $\quad\quad$ **sfFin**$[t] \leftarrow_{\text{release}} f_{\text{sam}}$
11: $\quad\quad e_{\text{sam}} \leftarrow e_{\text{sam}} + 1$
12: $\quad\quad f_{\text{sam}} \leftarrow$ new SF for e_{sam}
13: $\quad$ **if** $t = 0$ **then**
14: $\quad\quad$ CHECKFRAMES()

Check of stopping condition by thread 0:

15: **procedure** CHECKFRAMES()
16: $\quad$ **if not** $inCheck$ **then**
17: $\quad\quad e_{\text{chk}} \leftarrow e_{\text{chk}} + 1$
18: $\quad\quad$ epochToRead $\leftarrow_{\text{relaxed}} e_{\text{chk}}$
19: $\quad\quad inCheck \leftarrow$ true
20: $\quad$ **for** $i \in \{1, \ldots, T\}$ **do**
21: $\quad\quad f_{\text{fin}} \leftarrow_{\text{acquire}}$ **sfFin**$[i]$
22: $\quad\quad$ **if** $f_{\text{fin}} = $ null **then**
23: $\quad\quad\quad$ **return**
24: $\quad\quad$ **if** $f_{\text{fin}}.\text{epoch} \neq e_{\text{chk}}$ **then**
25: $\quad\quad\quad$ **return**
26: $\quad d \leftarrow$ new SF for accumulation
27: $\quad$ **for** $i \in \{1, \ldots, T\}$ **do**
28: $\quad\quad f_{\text{fin}} \leftarrow_{\text{relaxed}}$ **sfFin**$[i]$
29: $\quad\quad d.\text{data} \leftarrow d.\text{data} \circ f_{\text{fin}}.\text{data}$
30: $\quad\quad d.\text{num} \leftarrow d.\text{num} + f_{\text{fin}}.\text{num}$
31: $\quad$ **if** CHECKFORSTOP(d) **then**
32: $\quad\quad$ **stop** $\leftarrow_{\text{relaxed}}$ true
33: $\quad inCheck \leftarrow$ false

SF (f_{sam}; line 12). Note that the memory used by old SFs can be reclaimed (line 9; however, note that there is no SF for epoch 0). How exactly that is done is left to the algorithms described in later subsections. In the remainder of this subsection, we prove the correctness of our approach.

Proposition 1. *Algorithm 2 always checks the stopping condition on a consistent state; in particular, the epoch-based approach is correct.*

Proof. The order of lines 10 and 12 implies that no thread t issues a store to a SF f which it already published to $\text{sfFin}[t]$. Nevertheless, we need to prove that all stores by thread t are visible to CHECKFRAMES before the frames are accumulated. CHECKFRAMES only accumulates $f.\text{data}$ after f has been published to $\text{sfFin}[t]$ via the **store-relase** in line 10. Furthermore, in line 21, CHECKFRAMES performs at least one **load-acquire** on $\text{sfFin}[t]$ to read the pointer to f. Thus, all stores to f are visible to CHECKFRAMES before the accumulation in line 27. The proposition now follows from the fact that $\circ$ is associative, so that line 27 indeed produces a SF that occurs in some sequential execution. $\square$

3.2 Local-Frame and Shared-Frame Algorithm

We present two epoch-based algorithms relying on the general framework from the previous section: namely, the *local-frame* and the *shared-frame* algorithm. Furthermore, in Appendix D.2 of our full-length paper [13], we present the deterministic indexed-frame algorithm (as both local-frame and shared-frame are non-deterministic). Local-frame and shared-frame are both based on the pseudocode in Algorithm 2. They differ, however, in their allocation and reuse (in line 9 of the code) of SFs. The local frame algorithm allocates one pair of SFs per thread and cycles through both SFs of that pair (i.e., epochs with even numbers are assigned the first SF while odd epochs use the second SF). This yields a per-thread memory requirement of $\mathcal{O}(n)$; as before, n denotes the size of the sampling state. The shared-frame algorithm reduces this memory requirement to $\mathcal{O}(1)$ by only allocating F pairs of SFs in total, for a constant number F. Thus, T/F threads share a SF in each epoch and atomic `fetch-add` operations need to be used to write to the SF. The parameter F can be used to balance the memory bandwidth and synchronization costs – a smaller value of F lowers the memory bandwidth required during aggregation but leads to more cache contention due to atomic operations.

3.3   Synchronization Costs

In Algorithm 2, all synchronization of threads $t > 0$ is done wait-free in the sense that the threads only have to stop sampling for $\Theta(1)$ instructions to communicate with other threads (i.e., to check `epochToRead`, update per-thread state and write to `sfFin[t]`). At the same time, thread $t = 0$ generally needs to check all `sfFin` pointers. Taken together, this yields the following statement:

Proposition 2. *In each iteration of the main loop, threads $t > 0$ of local-frame and shared-frame algorithms spend $\Theta(1)$ time to wait for other threads. Thread $t = 0$ spends up to $\mathcal{O}(T)$ time to wait for other threads.*

In particular, the synchronization cost does not depend on the problem instance – this is in contrast to the OpenMP parallelization in which threads can idle for $\mathcal{O}(S)$ time, where S denotes the time complexity of a sampling operation (e.g., $S = \mathcal{O}(|V| + |E|)$ in the case of KADABRA).

Nevertheless, this advantage in synchronization costs comes at a price: the accumulation of the sampling data requires additional evaluations of $\circ$. $\mathcal{O}(Tn)$ evaluations are required in the local-frame algorithm, whereas shared-frame requires $\mathcal{O}(Fn)$. No accumulation is necessary in the OpenMP baseline. As can be seen in Algorithm 2, we perform the accumulation in a single thread (i.e., thread 0). Compared to a parallel implementation (e.g., using parallel reductions), this strategy requires no additional synchronization and has a favorable memory access pattern (as the SFs are read linearly). A disadvantage, however, is that there is a higher latency (depending on T) until the algorithm detects that it is able to stop. Appendix C.3 discusses how a constant latency can be achieved heuristically.

4   Experiments

The platform we use for our experiments is a Linux server equipped with 1.5 TB RAM and two Intel Xeon Gold 6154 CPUs with 18 cores (for a total of 36 cores) at 3.00 GHz. Each thread of the algorithm is pinned to a unique core; hyper-threading is disabled. Our implementation is written in C++ building upon the NetworKit toolkit [29].[3] We use 27 undirected real-world graphs in the experiments (see Appendix E of our full-length paper [13] for more details). The largest instances take tens of minutes for our OpenMP baseline and multiple hours for the original implementation of KADABRA. The error probability for KADABRA is set to $\delta = 0.1$ for all experiments. Absolute running times of our experiments are reported in Appendix F. The deviation in running time among different runs of the same algorithm turned out to be small (e.g., around 3% for our local-frame algorithm using 36-cores, in geom. mean running time over all instances). As it is specifically small compared to our speedups, we report data on a single run per instance.

In a first experiment, we compare our OpenMP baseline against the original implementation of KADABRA (see Sect. 2.4 for these two approaches). We set the absolute approximation error to $\epsilon = 0.01$. The overall speedup (i.e., both pre-processing and ADS) is reported in Fig. 3a. The results show that our OpenMP baseline outperforms the original implementation considerably (i.e., by a factor of 6.9×), even in a single-core setting. This is mainly due to implementation tricks (see Appendix C.1) and parameter tuning (as discussed in Appendix C.2). Furthermore, for 32 cores, our OpenMP baseline performs 13.5× better than the original implementation of KADABRA – or 22.7× if only the ADS phase is considered. Hence, for the remaining experiments, we discard the original implementation as a competitor and focus on the parallel speedup of our algorithms.

To understand the relation between the preprocessing and ADS phases of KADABRA, we break down the running times of the OpenMP baseline in Fig. 3b. In this figure, we present the fraction of time that is spent in ADS on three exemplary instances and for different values of ϵ. Especially if ϵ is small, the ADS running time dominates the overall performance of the algorithm. Thus, improving the scalability of the ADS phase is of critical importance. For this reason, we neglect the preprocessing phase and only consider ADS when comparing to our local-frame and shared-frame algorithms.

In Fig. 4a, we report the parallel speedup of the ADS phase of our epoch-based algorithms relative to the OpenMP baseline. All algorithms are configured to check the stopping condition after a fixed number of samples (see Appendix C.3 for details). The number F of SF pairs of shared-frame has been configured to 2, which we found to be a good setting for $T = 32$. On 32 cores, local-frame and shared-frame achieve parallel speedups of 15.9× and 18.1; they both significantly improve upon the OpenMP baseline, which can only achieve a parallel speedup of 6.3× (i.e., local-frame and shared-frame are 2.5× and 2.9× faster, respectively; they also outperform the original implementation by factors of 57.3 and 65.3, respectively). The difference between local-frame and shared-frame is insignificant for lower numbers of cores; this is explained by the fact that

---

[3] The algorithms of this paper have been integrated into NetworKit, in the KadabraBetweenness class. NetworKit is publicly available at https://github.com/kit-parco/networkit.

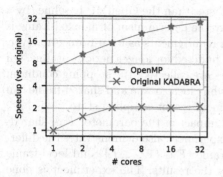

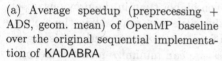

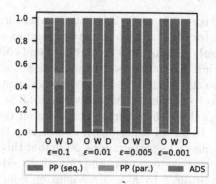

(a) Average speedup (preprecessing + ADS, geom. mean) of OpenMP baseline over the original sequential implementation of KADABRA

(b) Breakdown of sequential KADABRA running times into preprocessing and ADS (in percent) on instances orkut-links (O), wikipedia_link_de (W), and dimacs9-COL (D)

Fig. 3. Performance of OpenMP baseline

the reduced memory footprint of shared-frame only improves performance once memory bandwidth becomes a bottleneck. For the same reason, both algorithms scale very well until 16 cores; due to memory bandwidth limitations, this nearly ideal scalability does not extend to 32 cores. This bandwidth issue is known to affect graph traversal algorithms in general [2,18].

The indexed-frame algorithm is not as fast as local-frame and shared-frame on the instances depicted in Fig. 4a: it achieves a parallel speedup of 10.8× on

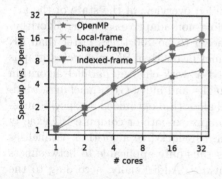

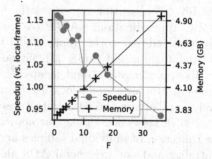

(a) Average ADS speedup (geom. mean) of epoch-based algorithms over sequential OpenMP baseline

(b) Average ADS speedup (over 36-core local-frame, geom. mean) and memory consumption of shared-frame, depending on the number of SFs

Fig. 4. Performance of epoch-based algorithms

32 cores. However, it is still considerably faster than the OpenMP baseline (by a factor of $1.7\times$). There are two reasons why the determinism of indexed-frame is costly: index-frame has similar bandwidth requirements as local-frame; however, it has to allocate more memory as SFs are buffered for longer periods of time. On the other hand, even when enough samples are collected, the stopping condition has to be checked on older samples first, while local-frame and shared-frame can just check the stopping condition on the most recent sampling state.

In a final experiment, we evaluate the impact of the parameter F of shared-frame on its performance. Note that this experiment also demonstrates the difference in memory consumption of shared-frame ($F \in \{1, \ldots, T\}$) and local-frame (equivalent to $F = T$). Figure 4b depicts the results. The experiment is done with 36 cores; hence memory pressure is even higher than in the previous experiments. The figure demonstrates that in this situation, minimizing the memory bandwidth requirements at the expense of synchronization overhead is a good strategy. Hence for larger numbers of cores, we can minimize memory footprint and maximize performance at the same time.

5   Related Work

Our parallelization strategy can be applied to arbitrary ADS algorithms. ADS was first introduced by Lipton and Naughton to estimate the size of the transitive closure of a digraph [17]. It is used in a variety of fields, e.g., in statistical learning [26]. In the context of BC, ADS has been used to approximate distances between pairs of vertices of a graph [25], to approximate the BC values of a graph [3,6,28] and to approximate the BC value of a single vertex [9]. An analogous strategy is exploited by Mumtaz and Wang [24] to find approximate solutions to the group betweenness maximization problem.

Regarding more general (i.e., not necessarily ADS) algorithms for BC, a survey from Matta et al. [20] provides a detailed overview of the state of the art. The RK [27] algorithm represents the leading non-adaptive sampling algorithm for BC approximation; KADABRA was shown to be 100 times faster than RK in undirected real-world graphs, and 70 times faster than RK in directed graphs [6]. McLaughlin and Bader [22] introduced a work-efficient parallel algorithm for BC approximation, implemented for single- and multi-GPU machines. Madduri et al. [19] presented a lock-free parallel algorithm optimized for specific massively parallel non-x86_64 architectures to approximate or compute BC exactly in massive networks. Unlike our approach, this lock-free algorithm parallelizes the collection of individual samples and is thus only applicable to betweenness centrality and not to general ADS algorithms. Additionally, according to the authors of [19], this approach hits performance bottlenecks on x86_64 even for 4 cores.

The SFs used by our algorithms are concurrent data structures that enable us to minimize the synchronization latencies in multithread environments. Devising concurrent (lock-free) data structures that scale over multiple cores is not trivial and much effort has been devoted to this goal [7,23]. A well-known solution is the Read-Copy-Update mechanism (RCU); it was introduced to achieve high multicore scalability on read-mostly data structures [21], and was leveraged by several applications [1,10]. Concurrent hash tables [11] are another popular example.

6 Conclusions and Future Work

In this paper, we found that previous techniques to parallelize ADS algorithms are insufficient to scale to large numbers of threads. However, significant speedups can be achieved by employing adequate concurrent data structures. Using such data structures and our epoch mechanism, we were able to devise parallel ADS algorithms that consistently outperform the state of the art but also achieve different trade-offs between synchronization costs, memory footprint and determinism of the results.

Regarding future work, a promising direction for our algorithms is parallel computing with distributed memory; here, the stopping condition could be checked via (asynchronous) reduction of the SFs. In the case of BC this, might yield a way to avoid bottlenecks for memory bandwidth on shared-memory systems.

References

1. Arbel, M., Attiya, H.: Concurrent updates with RCU: search tree as an example. In: Proceedings of the 2014 ACM Symposium on Principles of Distributed Computing, pp. 196–205. ACM (2014)
2. Bader, D.A., Cong, G., Feo, J.: On the architectural requirements for efficient execution of graph algorithms. In: 2005 International Conference on Parallel Processing, ICPP 2005, pp. 547–556. IEEE (2005)
3. Bader, D.A., Kintali, S., Madduri, K., Mihail, M.: Approximating betweenness centrality. In: Bonato, A., Chung, F.R.K. (eds.) WAW 2007. LNCS, vol. 4863, pp. 124–137. Springer, Heidelberg (2007). https://doi.org/10.1007/978-3-540-77004-6_10
4. Boldi, P., Vigna, S.: Axioms for centrality. Internet Math. **10**(3–4), 222–262 (2014). https://doi.org/10.1080/15427951.2013.865686
5. Borassi, M., Crescenzi, P., Habib, M.: Into the square: on the complexity of some quadratic-time solvable problems. Electr. Notes Theor. Comput. Sci. **322**, 51–67 (2016). https://doi.org/10.1016/j.entcs.2016.03.005
6. Borassi, M., Natale, E.: KADABRA is an adaptive algorithm for betweenness via random approximation. In: 24th Annual European Symposium on Algorithms, ESA 2016, Aarhus, Denmark, 22–24 August 2016, pp. 20:1–20:18 (2016). https://doi.org/10.4230/LIPIcs.ESA.2016.20
7. Boyd-Wickizer, S., et al.: An analysis of Linux scalability to many cores. In: OSDI, vol. 10, pp. 86–93 (2010)
8. Brandes, U.: A faster algorithm for betweenness centrality. J. Math. Sociol. **25**(2), 163–177 (2001)
9. Chehreghani, M.H., Bifet, A., Abdessalem, T.: Novel adaptive algorithms for estimating betweenness, coverage and k-path centralities. CoRR abs/1810.10094 (2018). http://arxiv.org/abs/1810.10094

10. Clements, A.T., Kaashoek, M.F., Zeldovich, N.: Scalable address spaces using RCU balanced trees. ACM SIGPLAN Not. **47**(4), 199–210 (2012)

11. David, T., Guerraoui, R., Trigonakis, V.: Everything you always wanted to know about synchronization but were afraid to ask. In: ACM SIGOPS 24th Symposium on Operating Systems Principles, SOSP 2013, Farmington, PA, USA, 3–6 November 2013, pp. 33–48 (2013). https://doi.org/10.1145/2517349.2522714

12. Gonzalez, T.F.: Handbook of Approximation Algorithms and Metaheuristics (Chapman & Hall/Crc Computer & Information Science Series). Chapman & Hall/CRC, Boca Raton (2007)

13. van der Grinten, A., Angriman, E., Meyerhenke, H.: Parallel adaptive sampling with almost no synchronization. CoRR abs/1903.09422 (2019). https://arxiv.org/abs/1903.09422

14. Guimera, R., Mossa, S., Turtschi, A., Amaral, L.N.: The worldwide air transportation network: anomalous centrality, community structure, and cities' global roles. Proc. Natl. Acad. Sci. **102**(22), 7794–7799 (2005)

15. ISO: ISO/IEC 14882:2011 Information technology – Programming languages – C++. International Organization for Standardization, Geneva, Switzerland, February 2012. http://www.iso.org/iso/iso_catalogue/catalogue_tc/catalogue_detail.htm?csnumber=50372

16. Jeong, H., Mason, S.P., Barabási, A.L., Oltvai, Z.N.: Lethality and centrality in protein networks. Nature **411**(6833), 41 (2001)

17. Lipton, R.J., Naughton, J.F.: Estimating the size of generalized transitive closures. In: Proceedings of the 15th International Conference on Very Large Data Bases (1989)

18. Lumsdaine, A., Gregor, D., Hendrickson, B., Berry, J.: Challenges in parallel graph processing. Parallel Process. Lett. **17**(01), 5–20 (2007)

19. Madduri, K., Ediger, D., Jiang, K., Bader, D.A., Chavarria-Miranda, D.: A faster parallel algorithm and efficient multithreaded implementations for evaluating betweenness centrality on massive datasets. In: IEEE International Symposium on Parallel & Distributed Processing, IPDPS 2009, pp. 1–8. IEEE (2009)

20. Matta, J., Ercal, G., Sinha, K.: Comparing the speed and accuracy of approaches to betweenness centrality approximation. Comput. Soc. Netw. **6**(1), 2 (2019)

21. McKenney, P.E., Slingwine, J.D.: Read-copy update: using execution history to solve concurrency problems. In: Parallel and Distributed Computing and Systems, pp. 509–518 (1998)

22. McLaughlin, A., Bader, D.A.: Scalable and high performance betweenness centrality on the GPU. In: Proceedings of the International Conference for High Performance Computing, Networking, Storage and Analysis, pp. 572–583. IEEE Press (2014)

23. Michael, M.M.: Hazard pointers: safe memory reclamation for lock-free objects. IEEE Trans. Parallel Distrib. Syst. **6**, 491–504 (2004)

24. Mumtaz, S., Wang, X.: Identifying top-k influential nodes in networks. In: Proceedings of the 2017 ACM on Conference on Information and Knowledge Management, pp. 2219–2222. ACM (2017)

25. Oktay, H., Balkir, A.S., Foster, I., Jensen, D.D.: Distance estimation for very large networks using mapreduce and network structure indices. In: Workshop on Information Networks (2011)

26. Provost, F., Jensen, D., Oates, T.: Efficient progressive sampling. In: Proceedings of the Fifth ACM SIGKDD International Conference on Knowledge Discovery and Data Mining, pp. 23–32. ACM (1999)

27. Riondato, M., Kornaropoulos, E.M.: Fast approximation of betweenness centrality through sampling. Data Min. Knowl. Discov. **30**(2), 438–475 (2016)
28. Riondato, M., Upfal, E.: ABRA: approximating betweenness centrality in static and dynamic graphs with rademacher averages. ACM Trans. Knowl. Discov. Data (TKDD) **12**(5), 61 (2018)
29. Staudt, C.L., Sazonovs, A., Meyerhenke, H.: NetworKit: a tool suite for large-scale complex network analysis. Netw. Sci. **4**(4), 508–530 (2016)

Theory and Algorithms for Parallel Computation and Networking

Parallel Streaming Random Sampling

Kanat Tangwongsan[1]([⊠]) and Srikanta Tirthapura[2]

[1] CS Program, Mahidol University International College, Nakhon Pathom, Thailand
kanat.tan@mahidol.edu
[2] Department of Electrical and Computer Engineering, Iowa State University,
Ames, USA
snt@iastate.edu

Abstract. This paper investigates parallel random sampling from a potentially-unending data stream whose elements are revealed in a series of element sequences (minibatches). While sampling from a stream was extensively studied sequentially, not much has been explored in the parallel context, with prior parallel random-sampling algorithms focusing on the static batch model. We present parallel algorithms for minibatch-stream sampling in two settings: (1) sliding window, which draws samples from a prespecified number of most-recently observed elements, and (2) infinite window, which draws samples from all the elements received. Our algorithms are computationally and memory efficient: their work matches the fastest sequential counterpart, their parallel depth is small (polylogarithmic), and their memory usage matches the best known.

1 Introduction

Consider a model of data processing where data is revealed to the processor in a series of element sequences (minibatches) of varying sizes. A minibatch must be processed soon after it arrives. However, the data is too large for all the minibatches to be stored within memory, though the current minibatch is available in memory until it is processed.

Such a minibatch streaming model is a generalization of the traditional data stream model, where data arrives as a sequence of elements. If each minibatch is of size 1, our model reduces to the streaming model. Use of minibatches is common. For instance, in a *data stream warehousing system* [13], data is collected for a specified period (such as an hour) into a minibatch and then ingested while statistics and properties need to be maintained continuously. Minibatches may be relatively large, potentially of the order of Gigabytes or more, and could leverage parallelism (e.g., a distributed memory cluster or a shared-memory multicore machine) to achieve the desired throughput. Furthermore, this model matches the needs of modern "big data" stream processing systems such as Apache Spark Streaming [22], where newly-arrived data is stored as a distributed data set (an "RDD" in Spark) that is processed in parallel. Queries are posed on all the data received up to the most recent minibatch.

© Springer Nature Switzerland AG 2019
R. Yahyapour (Ed.): Euro-Par 2019, LNCS 11725, pp. 451–465, 2019.
https://doi.org/10.1007/978-3-030-29400-7_32

This paper investigates the foundational aggregation task of random sampling in the minibatch streaming model. Algorithms in this model observe a (possibly infinite) sequence of minibatches $B_1, B_2, \ldots, B_t, \ldots$. We consider the following variants of random sampling, all of which are well studied in the context of sequential streaming algorithms. In the **infinite window** model, a random sample is chosen from all the minibatches seen so far. Thus, after observing B_t, a random sample is drawn from $\cup_{i=1}^{t} B_i$. In the **sliding window** model with window size w, the sample after observing B_t is chosen from the w most-recent elements. Typically, the window size w is much larger than a minibatch size.[1] In this work, the window size w is provided at query time, but an upper bound W on w is known beforehand.

We focus on optimizing the work and parallel depth of our algorithms. This is a point of departure from the traditional streaming algorithms literature, which has mostly focused on optimizing the memory consumed. Like in previous work, we consider memory to be a scarce resource and design for scenarios where the size of the stream is very large—and the stream, or even a sliding window of the stream, does not fit in memory. But in addition to memory efficiency, this work strives for parallel computational efficiency.

Our Contributions. We present parallel random-sampling algorithms for the minibatch streaming model, in both infinite-window and sliding-window settings. These algorithms can use the power of shared-memory parallelism to speedup the processing of a new minibatch as well as a query for random samples.

▷ *Efficient Parallel Algorithms.* Our algorithms are provably efficient in parallel processing. We analyze them in the work-depth model, showing (1) they are work-efficient, i.e., total work across all processors is of the same order as an efficient sequential algorithm, and (2) their parallel depth is logarithmic in the target sample size, which implies that they can use processors nearly linear in the input size while not substantially increasing the total work performed. In the infinite-window case, the algorithm is work-optimal since the total work across all processors matches a lower bound on work, which we prove in this paper, up to constant factors. Interestingly, for all our algorithms, the work of the parallel algorithm is sublinear in the size of the minibatch.

▷ *Small Memory.* While the emphasis of this work is on improving processing time and throughput, our algorithms retain the property of having a small memory footprint, matching the best sequential algorithms from prior work.

Designing such parallel algorithms requires overcoming several challenges. Sliding-window sampling is typically implemented with PRIORITY SAMPLING [1,3], whose work performed (per minibatch) is linear in the size of the minibatch. Parallelizing it reduces depth but does not reduce work. Generating skip offsets, à la Algorithm Z [20] (reservoir sampling), can significantly reduce work but offers no parallelism. Prior algorithms, such as in [20], seem inherently sequential, since the next location to sample from is derived as a function of the previously

---

[1] One could also consider a window to be the w most recent minibatches, and similar techniques are expected to work.

chosen location. This work introduces a new technique called R^3 sampling, which combines _r_eversed _r_eservoir sampling with _r_ejection sampling. R^3 sampling is a new perspective on PRIORITY SAMPLING that mimics the sampling distribution of PRIORITY SAMPLING but is simpler and has less computational dependency, making it amendable to parallelization. To enable parallelism, we draw samples simultaneously from different areas of the stream using a close approximation of the distribution. This leads to slight oversampling, which is later corrected by rejection sampling. We show that all these steps can be implemented in parallel. In addition, we develop a data layout that permits convenient update and fast queries. As far as we know, this is the first efficient parallelization of the popular reservoir-sampling-style algorithms.

Related Work. Reservoir sampling (attributed to Waterman) was known since the 1960s. There has been much follow-up work, including methods for speeding up reservoir sampling by "skipping past elements" [20], weighted reservoir sampling [9], and sampling over a sliding window [1,3,10,21].

The difference between the distributed streams model [5–7,11] considered earlier, and the parallel stream model considered here is that in the distributed streams model, the focus is on minimizing the communication between processors while in our model, processors can coordinate using shared memory, and the focus is on work-efficiency of the parallel algorithm. Prior work on shared-memory parallel streaming has considered frequency counting [8,19] and aggregates on graph streams [17], but to our knowledge, there is none so far on random sampling. Prior work on warehousing of sample data [4] has considered methods for sampling under minibatch arrival, where disjoint partitions of new data are handled in parallel. Our work also considers how to sample from a single partition in parallel, and can be used in conjunction with a method such as [4].

2   Preliminaries and Notation

A *stream* S is a potentially infinite sequence of minibatches $B_1 B_2, \ldots$, where each minibatch consists of one or more elements. Let S_t denote the stream so far until time t, consisting of all elements in minibatches $B_1, B_2, \ldots, B_t$. Let $n_i = |B_i|$ and $N_t = \sum_{i=1}^{t} n_i$, so N_t is the size of S_t. The size of a minibatch is not known until the minibatch is received, and the minibatch is received as an array in memory. A *stream segment* is a finite sequence of consecutive elements of a stream. For example, a minibatch is a stream segment. A *window* of size w is the stream segment consisting of the w most recent elements.

A sample of size s drawn *without replacement* from a set B with at least s elements is defined as a random set whose distribution matches S, the result of the following process. (1) Initialize S to empty. (2) Repeat s times: draw a uniform random element e from B, add e to S and delete e from B. A sample of size s drawn *with replacement* from a non-empty set B is defined as a random set whose distribution matches T, the result of the following process. (1) Initialize T to empty. (2) Repeat s times: draw a uniform random element e from B, add e to T and do not delete e from B.

Let $[n]$ denote the set $\{1, \ldots, n\}$. For sequence $X = \langle x_1, x_2, \ldots, x_{|X|} \rangle$, the i-th element is denoted by X_i or $X[i]$. For convenience, negative index $-i$, written $X[-i]$ or X_{-i}, refers to the i-th index from the right end—i.e., $X[|X| - i + 1]$. Following common array slicing notation, let $X[a:]$ be the subsequence of X starting from index a onward. An event happens with high probability (**whp**) if it happens with probability at least $1 - n^{-c}$ for some constant $c \geq 1$. Let $\texttt{UniformSample}(a, b)$, $a \leq b$, be a function that returns an element from $\{a, a + 1, \ldots, b\}$ chosen uniformly at random. For $0 < p \leq 1$, $\texttt{coin}(p) \in \{H, T\}$ returns heads (H) with probability p and tails (T) with probability $1 - p$. For $m \leq n$, an m-permutation of a set S, $|S| = n$, is an ordering of m distinct elements from S.

We analyze algorithms in the work-depth model assuming concurrent reads and arbitrary-winner concurrent writes. The *work* of an algorithm is the total operation count, and *depth* (also called parallel time or span) is the length of the longest chain of dependencies within that algorithm. The gold standard in this model is for an algorithm to perform the same amount of work as the best sequential counterpart (work-efficient) and to have polylogarithmic depth. This setting has been fertile ground for research and experimentation on parallel algorithms. Moreover, results in this model are readily portable to other related models, e.g., exclusive read and exclusive write, with a modest increase in cost (see, e.g., [2]).

We measure the space complexity of our algorithms in terms of the number of elements stored. Our space bounds do not represent bit complexity. Often, the space used by the algorithm is a random variable, so we present bounds on the expected space complexity.

3   Parallel Sampling from a Sliding Window

This section presents parallel algorithms for sampling without replacement from a sliding window (SWOR-SLIWIN). Specifically, for target sample size s and maximum window size W, SWOR-SLIWIN is to maintain a data structure $\mathcal{R}$ supporting two operations: (i) $\texttt{insert}(B_i)$ incorporates a minibatch B_i of new elements arriving at time i into $\mathcal{R}$ and (ii) For parameters $q \leq s$ and $w \leq W$, $\texttt{sample}(q, w)$ when posed at time i returns a random sample of q elements chosen uniformly without replacement from the w most recent elements in $\mathcal{S}_i$.

In our implementation, $\texttt{sample}(q, w)$ does something stronger and returns a q-permutation (not only a set) chosen uniformly at random from the w newest elements from $\mathcal{R}$—this can be used to generate a sample of any size j from 1 till q by only considering the first j elements of the permutation.

One popular approach to sampling from a sliding window in the sequential setting [1,3] is the PRIORITY SAMPLING algorithm: Assign a random priority to each stream element, and in response to $\texttt{sample}(s, w)$, return the s elements with the smallest priorities among the latest w arrivals. To reduce the space consumption to be sublinear in the window size, the idea is to store only those elements that can potentially be included in the set of s smallest priorities for any window size w. A stream element e can be discarded if there are s or more elements with a smaller priority than e that are more recent than e. Doing so systematically leads to an expected space bound of $O(s + s\log(W/s))$ [1][2].

As stated, this approach expends work linear in the stream length to examine/assign priorities, but ends up choosing only a small fraction of the elements examined. This motivates the question: *How can one determine which elements to choose, ideally in parallel, without expending linear work to generate or look at random priorities?* We assume $W \gg n_i \geq s$, where n_i is the size of minibatch i. The main result of this section is as follows:

Theorem 1. *There is a data structure for* SWOR-SLIWIN *that uses* $O(s + s\log(W/s))$ *expected space and supports the following operations:*

(i) insert(B) *for a new minibatch B uses* $O(s + s\log(\frac{W}{s}))$ *work and* $O(\log W)$ *parallel depth; and*

(ii) sample(q, w) *for sample size $q \leq s$ and window size $w \leq W$ uses* $O(q)$ *work and* $O(\log W)$ *parallel depth.*

Note that the work of the data structure for inserting a new minibatch is only logarithmic in the maximum window size W and independent of the size of the minibatch. To prove this theorem, we introduce R^3 sampling, which brings together reversed reservoir sampling and rejection sampling. We begin by describing reversed reservoir sampling, a new perspective on priority sampling that offers more parallelism opportunities. After that, we show how to implement this sampling process efficiently in parallel with the help of rejection sampling.

3.1 Simple Reversed Reservoir Algorithm

We now describe *reversed reservoir* (RR) sampling, which mimics the behavior of priority sampling but provides more independence and more parallelism opportunities. This process will be refined and expanded in subsequent sections. After observing sequence X, SIMPLE-RR (Algorithm 1) yields uniform sampling without replacement of up-to s elements for any suffix of X.

We say the i-th most-recent element has age i; this position/element will be called age i when the context is clear. The algorithm examines the input sequence X in reverse, $X_{-1}, X_{-2}, \ldots$, and stores selected elements in a data structure A, recording the age of an element in X as well as a slot (from $[s]$) into which the element is mapped. Multiple elements may be mapped to the same slot. The slot numbers are used to generate a permutation. The probability of selecting an age-i element into A decreases as i increases.

For maximum sample size $s > 0$ and integer $i > 0$, define $p_{-i}^{(s)} = \min\left(1, \frac{s}{i}\right)$, which is exactly the probability age-i element is retained in standard priority sampling when drawing s samples.

Let A denote the result of SIMPLE-RR. Using this, sampling s elements without replacement from any suffix of X is pretty straightforward. Define

$$\chi(A) = (\nu_A(1), \nu_A(2), \ldots, \nu_A(s))$$

---

[2] The original algorithm stores the largest priorities but is equivalent to our view.

Algorithm 1. SIMPLE-RR(X, s) — Naïve reversed reservoir sampling

    Input: a stream segment $X = \langle x_1, \ldots, x_{|X|} \rangle$ and a parameter $s > 0$, $s \leq |X|$.
    Output: a set $\{(k_i, \ell_i)\}$, where k_i is an index into X and $\ell_i \in [s]$
1 $\pi \leftarrow$ Random permutation of $[s]$, $A_0 = \emptyset$
2 **for** $i = 1, 2, \ldots, s$ **do** $A_i = A_{i-1} \cup \{(i, \pi_i)\}$
3 **for** $i = s+1, s+2, \ldots, |X|$ **do**
4   **if** $\texttt{coin}(p_{-i}^{(s)}) == H$ **then**
5         $\ell \leftarrow \texttt{UniformSample}(1, s)$
6         $A_i = A_{i-1} \cup \{(i, \ell)\}$
7   **else** $A_i = A_{i-1}$
8 **return** $A_{|X|}$

---

where $\nu_A(\ell) = \arg\max_{k \geq 1}\{(k, \ell) \in A\}$ is[3] the oldest element assigned to slot ℓ. Given A, we can derive $\bar{A}_i$ for any $i \leq |X|$ by considering the appropriate subset of A. We have that $\chi(A_i)$ is an s-permutation of the i most recent elements of X. This is stated in the following lemma:

Lemma 1. *If R is any s-permutation of $X[-i:]$, then* $\mathbf{Pr}[R = \chi(A_i)] = \frac{(i-s)!}{i!}$

Proof. We proceed by induction on i. The base case of $i = s$ is easy to verify since π is a random permutation of $[s]$ and $\chi(A_s)$ is a permutation of $X[-s:]$ according to π. For the inductive step, assume that the relationship holds for any R that is an s-permutation of $X[-i:]$. Now let R' be an s-permutation of $X[-(i+1):]$. Let $x_{-(i+1)}$ denote $X[-(i+1):]$. Consider two cases:

Case I: $x_{-(i+1)}$ appears in R', say at R'_ℓ. For $R' = \chi(A_{i+1})$, it must be the case that $x_{-(i+1)}$ was chosen and was assigned to slot ℓ. Furthermore, $\chi(A_i)$ must be identical to R' except in position ℓ, where it could have been any of the $i - (s-1)$ choices. This occurs w.p. $(i - [s-1]) \cdot \frac{(i-s)!}{i!} \cdot p_{-(i+1)}^{(s)} \cdot \frac{1}{s} = \frac{(i+1-s)!}{(i+1)!}$.

Case II: $x_{-(i+1)}$ does not appear in R'. Therefore, R' must be an s-permutation of $X[-i:]$ and $x_{-(i+1)}$ was not sampled. This happens with probability $\frac{(i-s)!}{i!} \cdot (1 - p_{-(i+1)}) = \frac{(i+1-s)!}{(i+1)!}$.

In either case, this gives the desired probability.   □

Note that the space taken by this algorithm (the size of $A_{|X|}$) is $O(s + s\log(|X|/s))$, which is optimal [10]. The steps are easily parallelizable but still need $O(|X|)$ work, which can be much larger than the $(s + s\log(|X|/s))$ bound on the number of elements the algorithm must sample. We improve on this next.

---

[3] Because $|X| \geq s$, the function ν is always defined.

3.2 Improved Single-Element Sampler

This section addresses the special case of $s = 1$. Our key ingredient is the ability to compute the next index that will be sampled, without touching the elements that are not sampled.

Let X_{-i} be an element just sampled. We can now define a random variable SKIP(i) that indicates how many elements past X_{-i} will be skipped over before selecting index $-(i+\text{SKIP}(i))$ according to the distribution given by SIMPLE-RR. Conveniently, this random variable can be efficiently generated in $O(1)$ time using the inverse transformation method [15] because its cumulative distribution function (CDF) has a simple, efficiently-solvable form: $\mathbf{Pr}[\text{SKIP}(i) \leq k] = 1 - \prod_{t=i+1}^{i+k}(1-p_{-t}) = 1 - \frac{i}{i+k} = \frac{k}{i+k}$. This leads to the following improved algorithm:

Algorithm 2. FAST-SINGLE-RR(X) — Fast RR sampling for $s = 1$

---
1 $i \leftarrow 1$
2 **while** $i < |X|$ **do**
3 $\quad$ $A \leftarrow A \cup \{(i, 1)\}$
4 $\quad$ $i \leftarrow i + \text{SKIP}(i)$
5 **return** A

This improvement significantly reduces the number of iterations:

Lemma 2. *Let $T_{\text{FSR}}(n)$ be the number of times the **while**-loop in the FAST-SINGLE-RR algorithm is executed on input X with $n = |X|$. Then, $\mathbf{E}[T_{\text{FSR}}(n)] = O(1 + \log(n))$. Also, for $m \geq n$ and $c \geq 4$, $\mathbf{Pr}[T_{\text{FSR}}(n) \geq 1 + c \cdot \log(m)] \leq m^{-c}$.*

Proof. Let Z_i be an indicator variable for whether x_{-i} contributes to an iteration of the **while**-loop. Hence, $T_{\text{FSR}}(n) = 1 + Z$, where $Z = \sum_{i=2}^{|X|} Z_i$. But $\mathbf{Pr}[Z_i = 1] = 1/i$, so $\mathbf{E}[Z] = \frac{1}{2} + \frac{1}{3} + \cdots + \frac{1}{n} \leq \ln n$. This proves the expectation bound. The concentration bound follows from a Chernoff bound. $\square$

Immediately, this means that if $A = \text{FAST-SINGLE-RR}(X)$ is kept as a simple sequence (e.g., an array), the running time—as well as the length of A—will be $O(1 + \log(|X|))$ in expectation. Moreover, FAST-SINGLE-RR(X) produces the same distribution as SIMPLE-RR with $s = 1$, only more efficiently computed.

3.3 Improved Multiple-Element Sampler

In the general case of reversed reservoir sampling, generating skip offsets from the distribution for $s > 1$ turns out to be significantly more involved than for $s = 1$. While this is still possible, e.g., using a variant of Vitter's Algorithm Z [20], prior algorithms appear inherently sequential.

458 K. Tangwongsan and S. Tirthapura

This section describes a new parallel algorithm that builds on FAST-SINGLE-RR. In broad strokes, it first "oversamples" using a simpler distribution and subsequently, "downsamples" to correct the sampling probability. To create parallelism, we logically divide the stream segment into s "tracks" of roughly the same size and have the single-element algorithm work on each track in parallel.

Track View. Define CREATE-VIEW(X, k) to return a view corresponding to track k on X: if $Y = $ CREATE-VIEW(X, k), then Y_{-i} is $X[-\alpha_s^{(k)}(i)]$, where $\alpha_s^{(k)}(i) = i \cdot s + k$. That is, track k contains, in reverse order, indices $-(s + k), -(2s + k), -(3s + k), \ldots$ Importantly, these views never have to be materialized.

Algorithm 3 combines the ideas developed so far. We now argue that FAST-RR yields the same distribution as SIMPLE-RR:

Algorithm 3. FAST-RR(X, s) — Fast reversed reservoir sampling

---

Input: a stream segment $X = \langle x_1, \ldots, x_{|X|} \rangle$ and a parameter $s > 0$, $s \leq |X|$.
Output: a set $\{(k_i, \ell_i)\}$, where k_i is an index into X and $\ell_i \in [s]$

1   $\pi \leftarrow$ draw a random permutation of $[s]$
2   $T_0 \leftarrow \{(i, \pi_i) \mid i = 1, 2, \ldots, s\}$
3   **for** $\tau = 1, 2, \ldots, s$ **in parallel do**
4      $X_\bullet^{(\tau)} \leftarrow$ CREATE-VIEW(X, τ)
5      $T_\tau \leftarrow$ FAST-SINGLE-RR$(X_\bullet^{(\tau)})$
6      $T_\tau' \leftarrow \{(i, \ell) \in T_\tau \mid \text{coin}(i \cdot s / \alpha_s^{(\tau)}(i)) = H\}$ // filter, keep if coin shows heads
7      $T_\tau'' \leftarrow \{(i, \text{UniformSample}(1, s)) \mid (i, \_) \in T_\tau'\}$ // map

8   **return** $T_0 \cup T_1'' \cup T_2'' \cup \cdots \cup T_s''$

Lemma 3. *Let A be a return result of* FAST-RR(X, s)*. Then, for $j = 1, \ldots, |X|$ and $\ell \in [s]$, $\mathbf{Pr}[(j, \ell) \in A] = \frac{1}{s} \cdot p_{-j}^{(s)}$.*

Proof. For $j \leq s$, age j is paired with a slot ℓ drawn from a random permutation of $[s]$, so $\mathbf{Pr}[(j, \ell) \in A] = \frac{1}{s} = \frac{1}{s} \cdot 1 = \frac{1}{s} \cdot p_{-j}^{(s)}$. For $j > s$, write j as $j = s \cdot i + \tau$, so age j appears as age i in view $X_\bullet^{(\tau)}$. Now age j appears in A if both of these events happen: (1) age i was chosen into T_τ and (2) the coin turned up heads so it was retained in T_τ'. These two independent events happen together with probability $p_{-i}^{(1)} \cdot \frac{i \cdot s}{\alpha_s^{(\tau)}(i)} = \frac{1}{i} \cdot \frac{i \cdot s}{s \cdot i + \tau} = \frac{s}{j} = p_{-j}^{(s)}$. Once age j is chosen, it goes to slot ℓ with probability $1/s$. Hence, $\mathbf{Pr}[(j, \ell) \in A] = \frac{1}{s} \cdot p_{-j}^{(s)}$. $\qquad\square$

3.4 Storing and Retrieving Reserved Samples

How Should We Store the Sampled Elements? An important design goal is for samples of any size $q \leq s$ to be generated without first generating s samples. To this end, observe that restricting $\chi(A)$ to its first $q \leq s$ coordinates yields a q-permutation over the input. This motivates a data structure that stores the contents of different slots separately.

Denote by $\mathcal{R}(A)$, or simply $\mathcal{R}$ in clear context, the *binned-sample* data structure for storing reserved samples A. The samples are organized by their slot numbers $(\mathcal{R}_i)_{i=1}^s$, with $\mathcal{R}_i$ storing slot i's samples. Within each slot, samples are binned by their ages. In particular, each $\mathcal{R}_i$ contains $\lceil \log_2(\lceil |X|/s \rceil) \rceil + 1$ bins, numbered $0, 1, 2, \ldots, \lceil \log_2(\lceil |X|/s \rceil) \rceil$—with bin k storing ages j in the range $2^{k-1} < \lceil j/s \rceil \leq 2^k$. Below, bin t of slot i will be denoted by $\mathcal{R}_i[t]$.

Additional information is kept in each bin for fast queries: every bin k stores $\phi(k)$, defined to be the age of the oldest element in bin k and all younger bins for the same slot number.

Below is an example. Use $s = 3$ and $|X| = 16$. Let the result from FAST-RR be $A = \{(1,2), (2,3), (3,1), (7,1), (10,3), (11,3), (14,2)\}$. Then, $\mathcal{R}$ keeps the following bins, together with ϕ values:

Bin:	$\mathcal{R}_i[0]$	$\mathcal{R}_i[1]$	$\mathcal{R}_i[2]$	$\mathcal{R}_i[3]$
Slot $i = 1$	$\{3\}_{\phi=3}$	$\emptyset_{\phi=3}$	$\{7\}_{\phi=7}$	$\emptyset_{\phi=7}$
Slot $i = 2$	$\{1\}_{\phi=1}$	$\emptyset_{\phi=1}$	$\emptyset_{\phi=1}$	$\{14\}_{\phi=14}$
Slot $i = 3$	$\{2\}_{\phi=2}$	$\emptyset_{\phi=2}$	$\{10,11\}_{\phi=11}$	$\emptyset_{\phi=11}$

From this construction, the following claims can be made:

Lemma 4. *(i) The expected size of the bin $\mathcal{R}_i[t]$ is $\mathbf{E}[|\mathcal{R}_i[t]|] \leq 1$.*
(ii) The size of slot $\mathcal{R}_i$ is expected $O(1 + \log(|X|/s))$. Furthermore, for $c \geq 4$,
$\mathbf{Pr}[|\mathcal{R}_i| \leq 1 + c \log_2(|X|)] \geq 1 - |X|^{-c}$.

Proof. Bin t of $\mathcal{R}_i$ is responsible for elements wit age j in the range $2^{t-1} < \lceil j/s \rceil \leq 2^t$, for a total of $s(2^t - 2^{t-1}) = s \cdot 2^{t-1}$ indices. Among them, the age that has the highest probability of being sampled is $(s2^{t-1} + 1)$, which is sampled into slot i with probability $\frac{1}{s} \cdot \frac{s}{s2^{t-1}+1} \leq \frac{1}{s \cdot 2^{t-1}}$. Therefore, $\mathbf{E}[|\mathcal{R}_i[t]|] \leq s \cdot 2^{t-1} \cdot \frac{1}{s \cdot 2^{t-1}} = 1$.

Moreover, let $Y_t = \mathbf{1}_{\{x_{-t} \text{ is chosen into slot } i\}}$, so $|\mathcal{R}_i| = \sum_{t=1}^{|X|} Y_t$. Since $\mathbf{E}[Y_t] = p_{-t}^{(s)}/s = \frac{1}{s} \min(1, s/t)$, we have

$$\mathbf{E}[|\mathcal{R}_i|] = \sum_{t=1}^{|X|} \mathbf{E}[Y_t] = 1 + \sum_{t=s+1}^{|X|} \frac{1}{t} \leq 1 + \int_{t=s}^{|X|} \frac{dt}{t} = 1 + \ln\left(\frac{|X|}{s}\right),$$

which proves the expectation bound. Because Y_t's are independent, using an argument similar to the proof of Lemma 2, we have the probability bound. $\square$

Data Structuring Operations. Algorithm 4 shows algorithms for constructing a binned-sample data structure and answering queries. To CONSTRUCT a binned-sample data structure, the algorithm first arranges the entries into groups by slot number, using a parallel semisorting algorithm, which reorders an input sequence of keys so that like sorting, equal keys are arranged contiguously, but unlike sorting, different keys are not necessarily in sorted order. Parallel semisorting of

n elements can be achieved using $O(n)$ expected work and space, and $O(\log n)$ depth [12]. The algorithm then, in parallel, processes each slot, putting every entry into the right bin. Moreover, it computes a min-prefix, yielding $\phi(\cdot)$ for all bins. There is not much computation within a slot, so we do it sequentially but the different slots are done in parallel. To answer a SAMPLE query, the algorithm computes, for each slot i, the oldest age within $X[-w:]$ that was assigned to slot i. This can be found quickly by figuring out the bin k where w should be. Once this is known, it simply has to look at ϕ of bin $k-1$ and go through the entries in bin k. This means a query touches at most two bins per slot.

Cost Analysis. We now analyze FAST-RR, CONSTRUCT, and SAMPLE for their work and parallel depth. More concretely:

Lemma 5. *(i) By storing T_0, T_i's, and T_i''s as simple arrays, FAST-RR(X,s) runs in expected $O(s + s\log\frac{|X|}{s})$ work and $O(\log|X|)$ parallel depth.*

(ii) CONSTRUCT(A,n,s) runs in $O(s+s\log\frac{n}{s})$ work and $O(\log n)$ parallel depth.

(iii) SAMPLE$(\mathcal{R},q,t)$ runs in $O(q)$ work and $O(\log n)$ parallel depth, where n is the length of X on which $\mathcal{R}$ was built.

For detailed analysis, see the full paper [18]. In brief, generating the initial length-s permutation in parallel takes $O(s)$ work and $O(\log s)$ depth [14]. The dominant cost stems from running s parallel instances of FAST-SINGLE-RR, which takes

---

Algorithm 4. Construction of binned-sample data structure and query

```
    // Below, use the convention that max ∅ = −∞
 1  CONSTRUCT(A, n, s):
        Input: A is a sequence of reserved samples, n is the length of the underlying stream
               segment X, and s is the target sample size used to generate A.
        Output: an instance of binned-sample structure R(A)
 2      Use semisorting to arrange A into G₁, G₂, ..., Gₛ by slot number
 3      for i = 1, ..., s in parallel do
 4          Create bins Rᵢ[0], ..., Rᵢ[β], β = ⌈log₂(⌈n/s⌉)⌉
 5          foreach (j, _) ∈ Gᵢ do
 6              Write j into Rᵢ[k], where 2^{k−1} < ⌈j/s⌉ ≤ 2^k
 7          Let φ(Rᵢ[0]) = max Rᵢ[0]
            // prefix max
 8          for k = 1, ..., β do
 9              φ(Rᵢ[k]) ← max(φ(Rᵢ[k − 1]), max Rᵢ[k])
10      return R
11  SAMPLE(R, q, w):
        Input: R is a binned-sample structure, q is the number of samples desired, w tells the
               algorithm to draw sample from X[−w :].
        Output: a q-permutation of X[−w :]
12      for i = 1, ..., q in parallel do
13          Let k be such that 2^{k−1} < ⌈w/s⌉ ≤ 2^k
14          γ ← max{j ∈ Rᵢ[k] | j ≤ w} // The oldest that is at least as young as w
15          rᵢ ← max(γ, φ(Rᵢ[k − 1]))
16      return (r₁, r₂, ..., r_q)
```

$O(1 + \log(|X|/s))$ work and depth each by Lemma 2. Furthermore, aside from the cost of semisorting, the cost of CONSTRUCT follows from Lemma 4(i)–(ii) and standard analysis. Finally, the cost of SAMPLE follows from Lemma 4, together with the fact that each query looks at q slots and only 2 bins per slot.

3.5 Handling Minibatch Arrival

This section describes how to incorporate a minibatch into our data structure to maintain a sliding window of size W. Assume that the minibatch size is $n_i \leq W$. If not, we can only consider its W most recent elements. When a minibatch arrives, retired sampled elements must be removed and the remaining sampled elements are "downsampled" to maintain the correct distribution.

Remember that the number of selected elements is $O(s + s \log(W/s))$ in expectation, so we have enough budget in the work bound to make a pass over them to filter out retired elements. Instead of revisiting every element of the window, we apply the process below to the selected elements to maintain the correct distribution. Notice that an element at age i was sampled into slot ℓ with probability $\frac{1}{s} p_{-i}^{(s)}$. A new minibatch will cause this element to shift to age j, $j > i$, in the window. At age j, an element is sampled into slot ℓ with probability $\frac{1}{s} p_{-j}^{(s)}$. To correct for this, we flip a coin that turns up heads with probability $p_{-j}^{(s)} / p_{-i}^{(s)} \leq 1$ and retain this sample only if the coin comes up heads.

Therefore, $\texttt{insert}(B_i)$, $|B_i| = n_i$ handles a minibatch arrival as follows:

Step i: Discard and downsample elements in $\mathcal{R}$; the index shifts by n_i.
Step ii: Apply FAST-RR on B_i, truncated to the last W elements if $n_i > W$.
Step iii: Run CONSTRUCT on the result of FAST-RR with a modification where it appends to an existing $\mathcal{R}$ as opposed to creating a new structure.

Overall, this leads to the following cost bound for $\texttt{insert}$:

Lemma 6. $\texttt{insert}$ *takes* $O(s + s \log(W/s))$ *work and* $O(\log W)$ *depth.*

4 Parallel Sampling from an Infinite Window

This section addresses sampling without replacement from an infinite window, consisting of all elements seen so far in the stream. This is formulated as the SWOR-INFWIN task: For each time $i = 1, \ldots, t$, maintain a random sample of size $\min\{s, N_i\}$ chosen uniformly without replacement from $\mathcal{S}_i$. We present a work-efficient algorithm for SWOR-INFWIN and further show it to be work optimal, up to constant factors.

For $p, q \in [r]$, let $\mathcal{H}(p, q, r)$ be the *hypergeometric random variable*, which can take an integer value from 0 to $\min\{p, q\}$. Suppose there are q balls of type 1 and $(r - q)$ balls of type 2 in an urn. Then, $\mathcal{H}(p, q, r)$ is the number of balls of type 1 drawn in p trials, where in each trial, a ball is drawn at random from the urn without replacement. It is known that $\mathbf{E}[\mathcal{H}(p, q, r)] = \frac{pq}{r}$.

Work Lower Bound. We first show a lower bound on the work of any algorithm for SWOR-INFWIN, sequential or parallel, by considering the expected change in the sample output after a new minibatch is received.

Lemma 7. *Any algorithm that solves* SWOR-INFWIN *must have expected work at least* $\Omega\left(t + \sum_{i=1}^{t}\min\{n_i, \frac{sn_i}{N_i}\}\right)$ *over minibatches* $B_1 \ldots B_t$.

Proof. First consider the number of elements that are sampled from each minibatch. If $N_i \leq s$, then the entire minibatch is sampled, resulting in a work of $\Omega(n_i)$. Otherwise, the number of elements sampled from the new minibatch B_i is $\mathcal{H}(s, n_i, N_i)$. The expectation is $\mathbf{E}[\mathcal{H}(s, n_i, N_i)] = \frac{s \cdot n_i}{N_i}$, which is a lower bound on the expected cost of processing the minibatch. Next, note that any algorithm must pay $\Omega(1)$ for examining minibatch B_i, since in our model the size of the minibatch is not known in advance. If an algorithm does not examine a minibatch, then the size of the minibatch may be as large as $\Omega(N_i)$, causing $\Omega(1)$ elements to be sampled from it. The algorithm needs to pay at least $\Omega(t)$ over t minibatches. Hence, the total expected work of any algorithm for SWOR-INFWIN after t steps must be $\Omega\left(t + \sum_{i=1}^{t}\min\{n_i, \frac{sn_i}{N_i}\}\right)$. $\square$

Parallel Algorithm for SWOR-INFWIN. Our solution is presented in Algorithm 5. The main idea is as follows: When a minibatch B_i arrives, generate a random variable κ according to the hypergeometric distribution to determine how many of the s samples will be chosen from B_i, as opposed to prior minibatches. Then, choose a random sample of size κ without replacement from B_i and update the sample S accordingly. We leverage Sanders et al. [16]'s recent algorithm for parallel sampling without replacement (from static data), restated below in the work-depth model:

Observation 2 ([16]). *There is a parallel algorithm to draw s elements at random without replacement from N elements using $O(s)$ work and $O(\log s)$ depth.*

Our algorithm uses static parallel sampling without replacement in two places: once to sample new elements from the new minibatch, and then again to update the current sample. In more detail, when a minibatch arrives, the algorithm **(i)** chooses κ, the number of elements to be sampled from B_i, in $O(1)$ time; **(ii)** samples κ elements without replacement from B_i in parallel; and **(iii)** replaces κ randomly chosen elements in S with the new samples using a two-step process, by first choosing the locations in S to be replaced, followed by writing the new samples to the chosen locations. Details appear in Algorithm 5.

Theorem 3. *Algorithm 5 is a work-efficient algorithm for* SWOR-INFWIN. *The total work to process t minibatches $B_1, \ldots, B_t$ is $O\left(t + \sum_{i=1}^{t}\min\{n_i, \frac{sn_i}{N_i}\}\right)$ and the parallel depth of the algorithm for processing a single minibatch is $O(\log s)$. This work is optimal up to constant factors, given the lower bound from Lemma 7.*

Algorithm 5. Parallel Algorithm for SWOR-INFWIN.

---

1   Initialization: Sample $S \leftarrow \emptyset$
2   **if** *minibatch B_i is received* **then**
     // Recall $n_i = |B_i|$ and $N_i = \sum_{j=1}^{i} n_i$
3   **if** $N_i \leq s$ **then** Copy B_i into S in parallel
4   **else**
5   Let κ be a random number generated by $\mathcal{H}(s, n_i, N_i)$
6       $S_i \leftarrow \kappa$ elements sampled without replacement from B_i (Obs. 2)
7       $R_i \leftarrow \kappa$ elements sampled without replacement from $\{1, \ldots, s\}$ (Obs. 2)
8   **for** $j = 1$ *to* κ **do** Replace $S[R_i[j]] \leftarrow S_i[j]$

Proof. When a new minibatch B_i arrives, for the case $N_i \leq s$, copying n_i elements from B_i to S can be done in parallel in $O(n_i)$ work and $O(1)$ depth, by organizing array S so that the empty locations in the array are all contiguous, so that the destination for writing an element can be computed in $O(1)$ time.

For the case $N_i > s$, random variable κ can be generated in $O(1)$ work. The next two steps of sampling κ elements from B_i and from $\{1, \ldots, n\}$ can each be done using $O(\kappa)$ work and $O(\log \kappa)$ depth, using Observation 2. The final for loop of copying data can be performed in $O(\kappa)$ work and $O(1)$ depth. Hence, the expected total work for processing B_i is $1 + \min\{n_i, \frac{sn_i}{N_i}\}$, and the depth is $O(\log \kappa)$. Summing over all t minibatches, we get our result. Since $\kappa \leq s$, the parallel depth is $O(\log s)$. $\square$

5   Parallel Sampling with Replacement

We now consider parallel algorithms for SWR-INFWIN, sampling with replacement. A simple solution, which uses $O(s)$ work per minibatch and has $O(1)$ parallel depth, is to run s independent parallel copies of a single element stream sampler, which is clearly correct. When minibatch B_i is received, each single element sampler decides whether or not to replace its sample, with probability n_i/N_i, which can be done in $O(1)$ time. We show that it is possible to do better than this by noting that when n_i/N_i is small, a single element sampler is unlikely to change its sample, and hence the operation of all the samplers can be efficiently simulated using less work. The main results are below (proof omitted):

Theorem 4. *There is a parallel algorithm for SWR-INFWIN such that for a target sample size s, the total work to process minibatches $B_1, \ldots, B_t$ is $O(t + \sum_{i=1}^{t} sn_i/N_i)$, and the depth for processing any one minibatch B_i is $O(\log s)$. This work is optimal, up to constant factors.*

This work bound is optimal, since the expected number of elements in the sample that change due to a new minibatch is sn_i/N_i.

6   Conclusion

We presented low-depth, work-efficient parallel algorithms for the fundamental data streaming problem of streaming sampling. Both the sliding-window and infinite-window cases were addressed. Interesting directions for future work include the parallelization of other types of streaming sampling problems, such as weighted sampling and stratified sampling.

References

1. Babcock, B., Datar, M., Motwani, R.: Sampling from a moving window over streaming data. In: Proceedings of the Annual ACM-SIAM Symposium on Discrete algorithms (SODA), pp. 633–634 (2002)
2. Blelloch, G.E., Maggs, B.M.: Chapter 10: parallel algorithms. In: The Computer Science and Engineering Handbook, 2nd edn. Chapman and Hall/CRC (2004)
3. Braverman, V., Ostrovsky, R., Zaniolo, C.: Optimal sampling from sliding windows. In: Proceedings of the ACM SIGMOD-SIGACT-SIGART Symposium on Principles of Database Systems (PODS), pp. 147–156 (2009)
4. Brown, P.G., Haas, P.J.: Techniques for warehousing of sample data. In: Proceedings of the International Conference on Data Engineering (ICDE), p. 6 (2006)
5. Chung, Y., Tirthapura, S., Woodruff, D.P.: A simple message-optimal algorithm for random sampling from a distributed stream. IEEE Trans. Knowl. Data Eng. (TKDE) **28**(6), 1356–1368 (2016)
6. Cormode, G.: The continuous distributed monitoring model. SIGMOD Rec. **42**(1), 5–14 (2013)
7. Cormode, G., Muthukrishnan, S., Yi, K., Zhang, Q.: Continuous sampling from distributed streams. J. ACM **59**(2), 10:1–10:25 (2012)
8. Das, S., Antony, S., Agrawal, D., El Abbadi, A.: Thread cooperation in multicore architectures for frequency counting over multiple data streams. Proc. VLDB Endow. (PVLDB) **2**(1), 217–228 (2009)
9. Efraimidis, P.S., Spirakis, P.G.: Weighted random sampling with a reservoir. Inf. Process. Lett. **97**(5), 181–185 (2006)
10. Gemulla, R., Lehner, W.: Sampling time-based sliding windows in bounded space. In: Proceedings of the International Conference on Management of Data (SIGMOD), pp. 379–392 (2008)
11. Gibbons, P., Tirthapura, S.: Estimating simple functions on the union of data streams. In: Proceedings of the ACM Symposium on Parallelism in Algorithms and Architectures (SPAA), pp. 281–291 (2001)
12. Gu, Y., Shun, J., Sun, Y., Blelloch, G.E.: A top-down parallel semisort. In: Proceedings of the ACM Symposium on Parallelism in Algorithms and Architectures (SPAA), pp. 24–34 (2015)
13. Johnson, T., Shkapenyuk, V.: Data stream warehousing in tidalrace. In: Proceedingsof the Conference on Innovative Data Systems Research (CIDR) (2015)
14. Reif, J.H.: An optimal parallel algorithm for integer sorting. In: Proceedings of the IEEE Annual Symposium on Foundations of Computer Science (FOCS), pp. 496–504 (1985)
15. Ross, S.M.: Introduction to Probability Models, 10th edn. Academic Press, Cambridge (2009)

16. Sanders, P., Lamm, S., Hübschle-Schneider, L., Schrade, E., Dachsbacher, C.: Efficient parallel random sampling - vectorized, cache-efficient, and online. ACM Trans. Math. Softw. **44**(3), 29:1–29:14 (2018)
17. Tangwongsan, K., Pavan, A., Tirthapura, S.: Parallel triangle counting in massive streaming graphs. In: Proceedings of the ACM International Conference on Information and Knowledge Management (CIKM), pp. 781–786 (2013)
18. Tangwongsan, K., Tirthapura, S.: Parallel streaming random sampling. arXiv:1906.04120 [cs.DS], https://arxiv.org/abs/1906.04120, June 2019
19. Tangwongsan, K., Tirthapura, S., Wu, K.: Parallel streaming frequency-based aggregates. In: Proceedings of the ACM Symposium on Parallelism in Algorithms and Architectures (SPAA), pp. 236–245 (2014)
20. Vitter, J.S.: Random sampling with a reservoir. ACM Trans. Math. Softw. **11**(1), 37–57 (1985)
21. Xu, B., Tirthapura, S., Busch, C.: Sketching asynchronous data streams over sliding windows. Distrib. Comput. **20**(5), 359–374 (2008)
22. Zaharia, M., Das, T., Li, H., Hunter, T., Shenker, S., Stoica, I.: Discretized streams: fault-tolerant streaming computation at scale. In: Proceedings of the ACM Symposium on Operating Systems Principles (SOSP), pp. 423–438 (2013)

Parallel Numerical Methods and Applications

Cholesky and Gram-Schmidt Orthogonalization for Tall-and-Skinny QR Factorizations on Graphics Processors

Andrés E. Tomás[1,2]([✉]) and Enrique S. Quintana-Ortí[3]

[1] Dept. d'Enginyeria i Ciència dels Computadors, Universitat Jaume I,
12.071 Castelló de la Plana, Spain
tomasan@uji.es

[2] Dept. de Sistemes Informàtics i Computació, Universitat Politècnica de València,
46.022 València, Spain
antodo@upv.es

[3] Dept. d'Informàtica de Sistemes i Computadors,
Universitat Politècnica de València, 46.022 València, Spain
quintana@disca.upv.es

Abstract. We present a method for the QR factorization of large tall-and-skinny matrices that combines block Gram-Schmidt and the Cholesky decomposition to factorize the input matrix column panels, overcoming the sequential nature of this operation. This method uses re-orthogonalization to obtain a satisfactory level of orthogonality both in the Gram-Schmidt process and the Cholesky QR.

Our approach has the additional benefit of enabling the introduction of a static look-ahead technique for computing the Cholesky decomposition on the CPU while the remaining operations (all Level-3 BLAS) are performed on the GPU.

In contrast with other specific factorizations for tall-skinny matrices, the novel method has the key advantage of not requiring any custom GPU kernels. This simplifies the implementation and favours portability to future GPU architectures.

Our experiments show that, for tall-skinny matrices, the new approach outperforms the code in MAGMA by a large margin, while it is very competitive for square matrices when the memory transfers and CPU computations are the bottleneck of Householder QR.

Keywords: QR factorization · Tall-and-skinny matrices ·
Graphics processing unit · Gram-Schmidt · Cholesky factorization ·
Look-ahead · High-performance

1 Introduction

There exist several relevant applications that require the computation of an orthonormal basis for a relatively small set of very long vectors. This problem is

© Springer Nature Switzerland AG 2019
R. Yahyapour (Ed.): Euro-Par 2019, LNCS 11725, pp. 469–480, 2019.
https://doi.org/10.1007/978-3-030-29400-7_33

often tackled via a "tall-and-skinny" QR factorization (TSRQ), named for the form of the matrix containing the vectors. This type of decomposition can be leveraged, among others, for orthogonalization in Krylov subspace methods [11]; the analysis of big data applications characterized with a few descriptors only (e.g., large datasets with a few variables produced by long data acquisitions of several sensors) [2,9]; and as a preprocessing step when computing the singular value decomposition (SVD) of a matrix [8] with many more row than columns.

It is well known that the blocked QR factorization based on Householder reflectors [8], hereafter QRF-H, is not efficient for the factorization of tall-and-skinny (TS) matrices on modern parallel processors; see, e.g., [4]. The reason is that, for matrices that have few columns but a large number of rows, the fraction of work of QRF-H that can be cast in terms of kernels from the Level-3 of BLAS (basic linear algebra subprograms [5]), as part of the highly parallel and efficient trailing update, cannot compensate the high cost of the panel factorization, which is performed via the much slower Level-1 and Level-2 BLAS.

TSQR-H [4] is an algorithm specifically designed for the factorization of TS matrices. In this approach, the matrix is split into small "square-like" blocks, and a QRF-H is computed for each block. These small QRF-H are then merged by pairs, using a structure-aware version of QRF-H. This procedure can follow a linear scheme [9] or, in parallel machines, a recursion tree [4], yielding a communication-reduction scheme.

The Cholesky QR factorization [12] (QRF-C) is an alternative that reduces the amount of communications but, unfortunately, often suffers from high orthogonality loss. The use of mixed precision (in particular, the introduction of extended precision) in [15] can improve the accuracy of QRF-C, but its implementation cannot benefit from standard BLAS libraries. A simpler solution is to perform a second step of QRF-C, to improve the orthogonality [6,14]. This result connects neatly with the classical "twice is enough" rule for Gram-Schmidt re-orthogonalization [7]. However, as the number of vectors grows, the cost of QRF-C increases cubically. In addition, for very large problems the conditioning of the Gram matrix can become too large and a second "pass" may not be sufficient.

In this paper we follow the approach in [16] to combine QRF-C and block Gram-Schmidt (BGS) [10], but propose to perform two steps of QRF-C and Gram-Schmidt instead of mixed (extended) precision. Furthermore, from the implementation side, when the target platform is equipped with a graphics processing unit (GPU), we propose to introduce a static look-ahead strategy [13] to overlap computations on CPU, GPU, and CPU-GPU data transfers. At this point we note that the formulation of a hybrid look-ahead variant of the algorithm demonstrates that it is also possible to develop either a static implementation or a runtime-based version, for multicore architectures, where the cost of the panel factorization can be practically amortized; see, e.g., [3] and the references therein.

The rest of the paper is organized as follows. Section 2 presents the details of our "two-pass" algorithm for the QR factorization of TS matrices. Next,

Sects. 3 and 4 respectively provide numerical and performance evaluations of the new method in comparison with a state-of-the-art hybrid library for CPU-GPU platforms. Finally, Sect. 5 summarizes the contributions of this work and suggests future lines of research.

2   The QRF-CBGS Algorithm

The QRF-C and BGS algorithms can be combined in several manners, depending on the specific order of the operations. Although these variants are mathematically equivalent, they have different numerical properties. In our work, we follow [12] to interlace the steps of QRF-C and BGS, in order to reduce the problems due to crossover orthogonality loss.

In particular, consider a TS matrix $A \in \mathbb{R}^{m \times n}$, with $m \gg n$, and the compact QRF given by

$$A = QR, \tag{1}$$

where $Q \in \mathbb{R}^{m \times n}$ has orthonormal columns and $R \in \mathbb{R}^{n \times n}$ is upper triangular. Furthermore, consider the partitionings

$$A = [A_1, \ A_2, \dots, A_k], \qquad R = \begin{bmatrix} R_{1,1} & R_{1,2} & \dots & R_{1,k} \\ 0 & R_{2,2} & \dots & R_{2,k} \\ \vdots & \vdots & \ddots & \vdots \\ 0 & 0 & \dots & R_{k,k} \end{bmatrix}, \tag{2}$$

where, for simplicity, we assume that n is an integer multiple of the algorithmic block size b, so that all block columns A_j consist of $b = n/k$ columns each, and all blocks $R_{i,j}$ contain $b \times b$ elements each.

Our approach QRF-CBGS, combining the Cholesky QR factorization with the block Gram-Schmidt method, is then described in Algorithm 1.

Algorithm 1. *QRF-C with Block Gram-Schmidt (QRF-CBGS)*

> **Input:** A
> **Output:** A, R
> 1 **for** $j = 1, 2, \dots, k$
> 2 $B := A_j^T A_j$
> 3   Compute the Cholesky factorization $B = U^T U$
> 4 $A_j := A_j U^{-1}$
> 5 $R_{j,j} := U$
> 6 $W := A_j^T [A_{j+1}, A_{j+2}, \dots, A_k]$
> 7 $[A_{j+1}, A_{j+2}, \dots, A_k] := [A_{j+1}, A_{j+2}, \dots, A_k] - A_j W$
> 8 $[R_{j,j+1}, R_{j,j+2}, \dots, R_{j,k}] := W$
> 9 **end**

In this formulation of the QRF-CBGS algorithm, upon completion, the input matrix A is replaced by the output matrix Q, which contains the first n orthonormal vectors of the factorization. Furthermore, in this algorithm, the block size b is a key parameter that should be set to a large value, with the specific value depending on the target platform, among other factors, to attain high performance. However, a block size that is "too large" can result in a considerable condition number of the Gram matrix $A_j^T A_j$, which could cause numerical issues for the Cholesky decomposition.

All the operations in QRF-CBGS, except for one in line 2, can be realized using direct calls to the efficient Level-3 BLAS, such as the symmetric rank-k update (xSYRK), the triangular solve with multiple right-hand sides (xTRSM), the triangular matrix-matrix multiplication (xTRMM), and the general matrix-matrix multiplication (xGEMM). The Cholesky factorization in line 2 can be realized via a call to the LAPACK routine for the corresponding decomposition (xPOTRF), which is then internally decomposed into Level-3 BLAS routines. However, the Cholesky factorization contributes a minor factor to the total cost, as $B \in \mathbb{R}^{b \times b}$ and, in practice, $b \ll n$.

The Cholesky factorization can fail if the condition number of the matrix $A_j^T A_j$ is too large. Fortunately, this failure is easy to detect thanks to the error value returned by xPOTRF or, more safely, it can be explicitly (and cheaply) identified by using a condition number estimator on $A_j^T A_j$ [8]. This breakdown is not critical for QRF-CBGS as none of the original data has been modified, and the algorithm can continue by just switching to QRF-H for the ill-conditioned block A_j.

The QRF-CBGS algorithm is a row variant of BGS where the vectors are updated several times during the orthogonalization process, similarly to what is done in the modified Gram-Schmidt method for single vectors. However, the orthogonality level attained by QRF-CBGS, measured as

$$\|Q^T Q - I\|, \tag{3}$$

(where I denotes the identity matrix,) will often fail short of the maximum attainable accuracy given the floating-point representation. This effect is due to both the in-block QRF-C and the Gram-Schmidt among blocks.

The classical solution to the lack of orthogonality in Gram-Schmidt is to re-apply the procedure yielding a re-orthogonalization. Naturally, this technique is also a solution for the possible lack of orthogonality in the QRF-C procedure. Therefore, it seems logical to perform twice QRF-CBGS, applying re-orthogonalization to both and QRF-C and BGS, *albeit in an interlaced manner*. Algorithm 2 (QRF-CBGS2) is a simple solution that applies two steps of QRF-CBGS. Note that an efficient implementation should perform the update of R in line 3 as the algorithm advances without storing the full matrices R_1 and R_2.

Algorithm 2. *QRF-CBGS2*

    Input: A
    Output: A, R
1 QRF-CBGS(A, R_1)
2 QRF-CBGS(A, R_2)
3 $R := R_2 \cdot R_1$

An additional advantage of the row variant of BGS is that this algorithm can overlap the orthogonalization inside a block with the orthogonalization of the subsequent blocks. This look-ahead technique can be introduced into the algorithm by a careful reordering of the operations. Concretely, Algorithm 3 is equivalent to QRF-CBGS but, in the new version, the Cholesky decomposition in line 8 can be performed simultaneously with the trailing update in lines 9–13.

Algorithm 3. *QRF-CBGS2 with look-ahead*

    Input: A
    Output: A, R
1 **for** $j = 1, 2, \ldots, k$
2   **if** $j > 1$
3      $R_{j-1,j} := A_{j-1}^T A_j$
4      $A_j := A_j - A_{j-1} R_{j-1,j}$
6   **end**
7    $B := A_j^T A_j$
8   Compute the Cholesky decomposition $U^T U = B$
9   **if** $j > 1$
10      $W := A_{j-1}^T [A_{j+1}, A_{j+2}, \ldots, A_k]$
11      $[A_{j+1}, A_{j+2}, \ldots, A_k] := [A_{j+1}, A_{j+2}, \ldots, A_k] - A_{j-1} W$
12      $[R_{j-1,j+1}, R_{j-1,j+2}, \ldots, R_{j-1,k}] := W$
13   **end**
14    $A_j := A_j U^{-1}$
15    $R_{j,j} := U$
16 **end**

The introduction of (a static) look-ahead is of paramount importance to obtain an efficient hybrid CPU-GPU implementation. Concretely, in this version the Cholesky factorization can be computed on the CPU while the GPU proceeds with the trailing updates with respect to the factorization of previous panel(s). Furthermore, this technique also allows that the necessary memory transfers between CPU and GPU can be overlapped with computations in the GPU. The look-ahead strategy also reduces the impact of any Cholesky breakdown, as the QRF-H of the offending block can be performed while updating the rest of the matrix.

The implementation of both variants of algorithm QRF-CBGS on a GPU from NVIDIA is direct, as all operations are available in the cuBLAS GPU-specific implementation of the BLAS. Therefore, compared with other algorithms, an appealing property of QRF-CBGS2 is that no custom GPU kernels are required, as all major building blocks are available as part of cuBLAS. (Note that xPOTRF is computed on the CPU.) This greatly simplifies the implementation as well as favours high performance on present as well as future GPU architectures.

Table 1. Numerical comparison of QRF-H and QRF-CBGS2

ρ	QRF-H		QRF-CBGS2	
	$\|Q^T Q - I\|_F$	$\dfrac{\|A - QR\|_F}{\|A\|_F}$	$\|Q^T Q - I\|_F$	$\dfrac{\|A - QR\|_F}{\|A\|_F}$
10^{-1}	6.41×10^{-15}	5.79×10^{-16}	5.13×10^{-15}	4.73×10^{-16}
10^{-2}	6.56×10^{-15}	5.80×10^{-16}	5.21×10^{-15}	4.74×10^{-16}
10^{-3}	6.62×10^{-15}	5.80×10^{-16}	5.16×10^{-15}	4.75×10^{-16}
10^{-4}	6.28×10^{-15}	5.79×10^{-16}	5.06×10^{-15}	4.74×10^{-16}
10^{-5}	6.36×10^{-15}	5.77×10^{-16}	5.18×10^{-15}	4.76×10^{-16}
10^{-6}	6.51×10^{-15}	5.79×10^{-16}	5.18×10^{-15}	4.78×10^{-16}
10^{-7}	6.39×10^{-15}	5.79×10^{-16}	5.35×10^{-15}	4.77×10^{-16}
10^{-8}	6.37×10^{-15}	5.78×10^{-16}	5.41×10^{-15}	4.76×10^{-16}
10^{-9}	6.48×10^{-15}	5.79×10^{-16}	5.21×10^{-15}	4.78×10^{-16}
10^{-10}	6.34×10^{-15}	5.79×10^{-16}	5.30×10^{-15}	4.77×10^{-16}
10^{-11}	6.29×10^{-15}	5.80×10^{-16}	5.26×10^{-15}	4.78×10^{-16}
10^{-12}	6.59×10^{-15}	5.81×10^{-16}	5.13×10^{-15}	4.76×10^{-16}
10^{-13}	6.69×10^{-15}	5.80×10^{-16}	5.34×10^{-15}	4.77×10^{-16}
10^{-14}	6.40×10^{-15}	5.78×10^{-16}	5.01×10^{-15}	4.77×10^{-16}
10^{-15}	6.55×10^{-15}	5.79×10^{-16}	5.03×10^{-15}	4.76×10^{-16}

3   Numerical Tests

In this section, we asses the numerical behaviour of the new algorithm QRF-CBGS2 by running some numerical experiments with TS matrices specifically designed to produce a breakdown of the Cholesky decomposition. This stress test is based on [1] and should allow a comparison of the reliability of QRF-CBGS2 with other alternative methods, as those in [1], whose implementation does not seem to be publicly available.

The test matrices are derived from the QR factorization of a $m \times n = 1000 \times 200$ matrix A with entries following a uniform random distribution in the interval $[0, 1)$. We then set $R_{100,100} = \rho$ in the upper triangular factor R, and multiply back Q and R to form $\tilde{A}$. The parameter ρ controls the condition number of the assembled matrix, which is given by $\kappa(\tilde{A}) \approx 1/\rho$ so that, varying $\rho \in [10^{-1}, 10^{-15}]$, we obtain matrices with a condition number of up to 10^{15}.

Table 1 compares the orthogonality loss

$$\|Q^T Q - I\|_F \qquad (4)$$

and relative residual,

$$\frac{\|A - QR\|_F}{\|A\|_F} \tag{5}$$

of the QR factorizations computed by QRF-H and QRF-CBGS2 for matrices with different values of ρ. All the tests were performed in a Intel Xeon E5-2630 v3 processor using IEEE double-precision arithmetic. The QRF-H implementation corresponds to that in Intel MKL 2017 and the block size of QRF-CBGS2 was set to $b = 16$.

Table 1 shows that QRF-CBGS2 offers orthogonality and relative residuals quite similar to those of QRF-H. This excellent numerical behaviour is partially due to the re-orthogonalization approach of QRF-CBGS2 and the Cholesky breakdown detection mechanism. Specifically, in this experiment the fail-safe detection on the Cholesky factorization only triggers once for each one of the matrices with $\rho \leq 10^{-8}$. This means that, among the $k(= \lceil n/b \rceil = \lceil 200/16 \rceil) = 13$ Cholesky decompositions that have to be computed for each matrix, only one had to be recomputed using QRF-H. We expect that, for real applications, the probability of a Cholesky breakdown will be even smaller.

4 Performance Evaluation

Hardware Setup. In this section we compare the performance of QRF-CBGS2 and QRF-H on two distinct platforms equipped with two representative GPUs: a high end NVIDIA Tesla P100 (Pascal) and a cost-effective NVIDIA GeForce Titan X (Pascal). The P100 is paired with two Intel Xeon E5-2620 v4 processors $(8 + 8$ cores) while the Titan X is paired with an Intel Core i7-3770K CPU (4 cores).

Software Setup. All codes are compiled with version 8.0 of the CUDA development environment. The optimized implementations of BLAS and LAPACK are those provided by NVIDIA cuBLAS 8.0 for the GPU and Intel MKL 2017 for the CPU. Hyper-threading is disabled in the Intel architectures as suggested by the MKL library documentation. To reduce the variance of execution times, the OpenMP and MKL number of threads is set to the number of physical cores and each thread is mapped statically to one core. The GNU C compiler is the default version provided by the Linux operating system installed on those computers. Nevertheless, the optimizations made by these compilers are not relevant for our study, because all the performance-sensitive code is implemented inside the cuBLAS and MKL libraries. To avoid noise caused by other processes activity on the systems, the execution times reported are the median values from 10 executions. Those times are similar with the exception of the first execution in a batch, which is significantly larger due to the dynamic loading of libraries.

Input Data. The input matrices are created following the same procedure described in the numerical tests in Sect. 3, with random elements in range $[0,1)$, and setting $\rho = 1$ so that the condition number is kept small. For brevity, we report results in (IEEE) double precision only for the P100; the comparison using single precision on this platform offers similar conclusions. Conversely, as the Titan X offers very low performance in double precision, we only employ single precision on that platform.

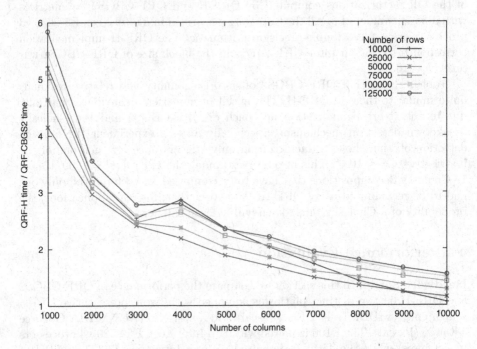

Fig. 1. Performance comparison of QRF-CBGS2 with look-ahead over QRF-H for TS matrices on an two Intel Xeon E5-2620 v4 CPUs and an NVIDIA P100 GPU (double precision).

QRF Implementations. The baseline GPU implementation QRF-H is provided by xGEQRF (QR factorization via Householder reflectors) and xORGQR (assembly of the $m \times n$ orthonormal matrix) available in the MAGMA library (version 2.2.0). Among the three variants of xGEQRF in MAGMA, we choose the first one as this is the only one with a corresponding implementation of xORGQR. To allow a fair comparison between QRF-H and QRF-CBGS2, as QRF-CBGS2 always produces the orthonormal matrix Q, the execution times of QRF-H reported next correspond to the combination of the runtimes for xGEQRF and xORGQR from MAGMA. We note that the implementation of xGEQRF in MAGMA employs look-ahead while xORGQR re-utilizes some intermediate factors computed in xGEQRF (in particular, the triangular factors for the blocked Householder reflectors) and it is much faster than xGEQRF. The block size in QRF-CBGS2 was set to 1,024 which we found optimal for both platforms.

Evaluation. Figures 1 and 2 compare the performance of QRF-H and QRF-CBGS2 with look-ahead on the P100 and the Titan X, respectively. The y-axis

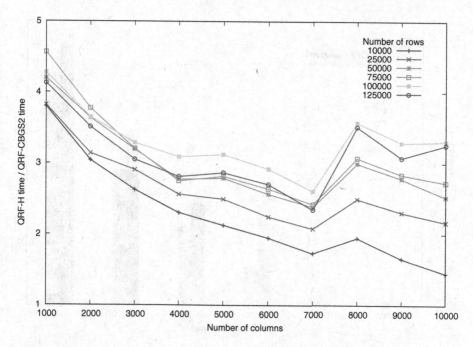

Fig. 2. Performance comparison of QRF-CBGS2 with look-ahead over QRF-H for TS matrices on an Intel Core i7-3770K and an NVIDIA Titan X GPU (single precision).

shows the ratio between the execution time of QRF-H divided by that of QRF-CBGS2. Each line corresponds to a group of matrices with the same number of rows n while the number of columns m is fixed as specified in the x-axis of the plot. The plots show a small performance gap in double precision for matrices with more than 3000 columns, and a larger gap in single precision for more than 7000 columns. Both cases are due to an increase of the block size internally employed by MAGMA (from 64 to 128 in double precision and from 128 to 256 in single precision). As expected, the performance of QRF-CBGS2 is much higher for TS matrices (up to 6 times) but this advantage diminishes as the difference between the number of columns and rows narrows. However, the performance drop is considerably less sharp in the Titan X platform, since (in part) the relative slow CPU on that machine drags the QRF-H performance down while QRF-CBGS2 benefits from the reduced communications. Quite unexpectedly, this effect allows QRF-CBGS2 to outperform QRF-H on the Titan X even for square matrices, as shown in Fig. 3.

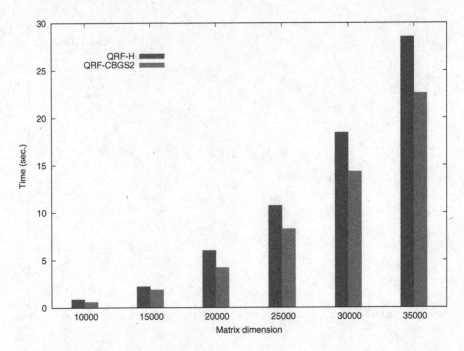

Fig. 3. Performance comparison of QRF-CBGS2 with look-ahead over QRF-H for square matrices on an Intel Core i7-3770K and an NVIDIA Titan X GPU (single precision).

5   Conclusions

The new algorithm presented in this work, QRF-CBGS2, is a variant of block Gram-Schmidt that uses the Cholesky decomposition to orthogonalize the columns inside a block. To obtain a satisfactory level of orthogonality, our proposal leverages re-orthogonalization and avoids Cholesky breakdowns by leveraging the standard QR factorization via Householder reflectors (QRF-H) in case of ill-conditioned blocks.

The QRF-CBGS2 algorithm computes the triangular factor by rows, allowing for an effective look-ahead technique that computes the Cholesky decomposition of the "current" block while Gram-Schmidt is applied to re-orthogonalize the remaining columns of the matrix with respect to "previous" blocks. Furthermore, this look-ahead alleviates the extra cost in case of a Cholesky breakdown.

The variant of QRF-CBGS2 with look-ahead can be efficiently implemented on a hybrid CPU-GPU system, with the CPU in charge of the Cholesky decomposition while the rest of operations (all BLAS level-3) are performed on the GPU. One advantage of this approach is the reduced volume of communications between CPU and GPU compared with the blocked Householder QR implementations available in MAGMA. An additional advantage of QRF-CBGS2 is that its implementation is much simpler than other methods specifically designed for tall-skinny matrices as no custom GPU kernels are required. This also favours portability to new GPU architectures or even different types of accelerators.

The performance of the new approach is very competitive for tall-skinny matrices, and even outperforms MAGMA for square matrices when the memory transfers and CPU computations are the bottleneck of the Householder-based QR.

The stability of QRF-CBGS2 has been analyzed with matrices that explicitly enforce Cholesky breakdowns. While this experiment shows that QRF-CBGS2 offers a level of orthogonality and relative error similar to those of the numerically-stable QRF-H, a numerical analysis may help to fully understand the behaviour of the algorithm and devise future strategies for improving the accuracy and reduce the re-orthogonalization cost.

Acknowledgment. This research was supported by the project TIN2017-82972-R from the *MINECO* (Spain), and the EU H2020 project 732631 "OPRECOMP. Open Transprecision Computing".

References

1. Ballard, G., Demmel, J., Grigori, L., Jacquelin, M., Knight, N., Nguyen, H.: Reconstructing Householder vectors from tall-skinny QR. J. Parallel Distrib. Comput. **85**, 3–31 (2015). https://doi.org/10.1016/j.jpdc.2015.06.003. iPDPS 2014 Selected Papers on Numerical and Combinatorial Algorithms
2. Benson, A.R., Gleich, D.F., Demmel, J.: Direct QR factorizations for tall-and-skinny matrices in MapReduce architectures. In: 2013 IEEE International Conference on Big Data, pp. 264–272, October 2013. https://doi.org/10.1109/BigData.2013.6691583
3. Catalán, S., Herrero, J.R., Quintana-Ortí, E.S., Rodríguez-Sánchez, R., Van De Geijn, R.: A case for malleable thread-level linear algebra libraries: the LU factorization with partial pivoting. IEEE Access **7**, 17617–17633 (2019). https://doi.org/10.1109/ACCESS.2019.2895541
4. Demmel, J., Grigori, L., Hoemmen, M., Langou, J.: Communication-optimal parallel and sequential QR and LU factorizations. SIAM J. Sci. Comput. **34**(1), 206–239 (2012). https://doi.org/10.1137/080731992
5. Dongarra, J.J., Du Croz, J., Hammarling, S., Duff, I.: A set of level 3 basic linear algebra subprograms. ACM Trans. Math. Softw. **16**(1), 1–17 (1990)
6. Fukaya, T., Nakatsukasa, Y., Yanagisawa, Y., Yamamoto, Y.: CholeskyQR2: a simple and communication-avoiding algorithm for computing a tall-skinny QR factorization on a large-scale parallel system. In: 2014 5th Workshop on Latest Advances in Scalable Algorithms for Large-Scale Systems, pp. 31–38, November 2014. https://doi.org/10.1109/ScalA.2014.11
7. Giraud, L., Langou, J., Rozložník, M., Eshof, J.v.d.: Rounding error analysis of the classical Gram-Schmidt orthogonalization process. Numerische Mathematik **101**(1), 87–100 (2005). https://doi.org/10.1007/s00211-005-0615-4
8. Golub, G., Van Loan, C.: Matrix Computations. Johns Hopkins Studies in the Mathematical Sciences. Johns Hopkins University Press, Baltimore (2013)
9. Gunter, B.C., van de Geijn, R.A.: Parallel out-of-core computation and updating the QR factorization. ACM Trans. Math. Softw. **31**(1), 60–78 (2005). https://doi.org/10.1145/1055531.1055534

10. Leon, S.J., Björck, Å., Gander, W.: Gram-Schmidt orthogonalization: 100 years and more. Numer. Linear Algebr. Appl. **20**(3), 492–532 (2013). https://doi.org/10.1002/nla.1839
11. Saad, Y.: Iterative Methods for Sparse Linear Systems, 3rd edn. Society for Industrial and Applied Mathematics, Philadelphia (2003)
12. Stathopoulos, A., Wu, K.: A block orthogonalization procedure with constant synchronization requirements. SIAM J. Sci. Comput. **23**(6), 2165–2182 (2001). https://doi.org/10.1137/S1064827500370883
13. Strazdins, P.: A comparison of lookahead and algorithmic blocking techniques for parallel matrix factorization. Technical report TR-CS-98-07, Department of Computer Science, The Australian National University, Canberra 0200 ACT, Australia (1998)
14. Yamamoto, Y., Nakatsukasa, Y., Yanagisawa, Y., Fukaya, T.: Roundoff error analysis of the Cholesky QR2 algorithm. Electron. Trans. Numer. Anal. **44**, 306–326 (2015)
15. Yamazaki, I., Tomov, S., Dongarra, J.: Mixed-precision Cholesky QR factorization and its case studies on multicore CPU with multiple GPUs. SIAM J. Sci. Comput. **37**(3), C307–C330 (2015). https://doi.org/10.1137/14M0973773
16. Yamazaki, I., Tomov, S., Kurzak, J., Dongarra, J., Barlow, J.: Mixed-precision block Gram Schmidt orthogonalization. In: Proceedings of the 6th Workshop on Latest Advances in Scalable Algorithms for Large-Scale Systems, ScalA 2015, pp. 2:1–2:8. ACM, New York (2015). https://doi.org/10.1145/2832080.2832082

Automatic Exploration of Reduced Floating-Point Representations in Iterative Methods

Yohan Chatelain[1,4]([✉]), Eric Petit[4,5], Pablo de Oliveira Castro[1,4], Ghislain Lartigue[3], and David Defour[2,4]

[1] Université de Versailles Saint-Quentin-en-Yvelines, Li-PaRAD, Versailles, France
yohan.chatelain@uvsq.fr
[2] Université de Perpignan Via Domitia, LAMPS, Perpignan, France
[3] Normandie Université, CORIA – CNRS, Caen, France
[4] Exascale Computing Research, ECR, Paris, France
[5] Intel Corporation, Paris, France

Abstract. With the ever-increasing need for computation of scientific applications, new application domains, and major energy constraints, the landscape of floating-point computation is changing. New floating-point representation formats are emerging and there is a need for tools to simulate their impact in legacy codes. In this paper, we propose an automatic tool to evaluate the effect of adapting the floating point precision for each operation over time, which is particularly useful in iterative schemes. We present a backend to emulate any IEEE-754 floating-point operation in lower precision. We tested the numerical errors resilience of our solutions thanks to Monte Carlo Arithmetic and demonstrated the effectiveness of this methodology on YALES2, a large Combustion-CFD HPC code, by achieving 28% to 67% reduction in communication volume by lowering precision.

1 Introduction

Representing infinite real numbers on a finite machine format exposes complex trade-off: IEEE-754 floating-point (FP) single and double are widely used standardized formats which have empirically proved their efficiency. Today's numerical algorithms conveniently rely on double precision FP format. Numerical formats outside IEEE-754 single and double FP are largely unexplored in hardware and software design for HPC.

With new application domains such as machine learning, FP arithmetic used in general purpose processor is entering a new burst of evolution as the IEEE-754 single and double FP are not necessarily the best choices for these problems. Novel hardware and software solutions are explored: variable precision formats (e.g. on FPGAs [15]), new vector instructions such (e.g. Intel Vector Neural Network Instruction), novel FP representations (e.g. BFloat [11], posits [18], fpanr [12]), and libraries for approximate computing [22].

© Springer Nature Switzerland AG 2019
R. Yahyapour (Ed.): Euro-Par 2019, LNCS 11725, pp. 481–494, 2019.
https://doi.org/10.1007/978-3-030-29400-7_34

In this paper we propose a methodology to explore alternative representations of hardware and software FP. Our first application is the widely used Computational Fluid Mechanics (CFD) solver YALES2 operated in many recent HPC simulations [3,4,6,17,25].

Variable precision can be harnessed at the application, compiler, and architecture levels. Our exploration goes beyond traditional mixed precision (single and double format). Due to hardware memory constraints of general purpose processors, the target format can only be represented with 8,16,32 or 64 bits. However, accuracy can be lowered to any given precision to limit the cost of computation and energy. Finally, to go further in the optimization, one may use architectural support, like FPGAs, where precision is fine-tuned up to the bit level [15].

The contributions of this paper are:

- An empirical methodology integrated in Verificarlo [7,14] to automatically lower precision in iterative algorithms while maintaining an user defined accuracy criterion.
- A VPREC backend to Verificarlo to emulate variable FP representations with a [1, 11]-bits exponent and [0, 52]-bits pseudo-mantissa.
- Integration of the temporal dimension in the exploration of FP precision. Precisions are not fixed for a variable or code section, but adapt as time passes.
- A validation step based on stochastic arithmetic [37] to increase robustness to rounding and cancellation errors.
- An evaluation of the validity and the performance gains of the proposed methodology on an actual implementation demonstrating runtime savings in an industrial use case.

2 Motivating Example

Let us consider as a simple example the Newton–Raphson method which finds the root $x^\star$ of a real-valued function f such that $f(x^\star) = 0$. Starting from an initial guess x_0, the method iteratively computes $x_{k+1} = x_k - f(x_k)/f'(x_k)$ until the relative error between two successive iterations is below a given threshold. At iteration k, the error ϵ_k and the number of significant digits s_k^β in base β are defined as:

$$\epsilon_k = \left| \frac{x^\star - x_{k+1}}{x^\star} \right| \qquad s_k^\beta = -\log_\beta(\epsilon_k)$$

The speed of convergence of this method is quadratic [20], which means that the number of significant digits doubles at each iteration. Table 1 shows the evolution of x_k and s_k when computing the inverse of π ($f(x) = 1/x - \pi$) with a stopping threshold set to 10^{-15}. The insignificant digits are highlighted in gray.

In the first iterations, most digits are incorrect, hinting that a low precision for the evaluation of f is enough. We used the methodology proposed in this

Table 1. (*left*)Convergence speed of Newton-Raphson for the computation of the inverse of π using the IEEE-754 `binary64` format (*right*). The stopping threshold is 10^{-15}. Highlighted digits in gray are non significant.

k	x_{k+1}	s_k^{10}	s_k^2
0	0.0690266447076745	0.11	0.37
1	0.1230846130203958	0.21	0.70
2	0.1985746566605835	0.43	1.43
3	0.2732703639721015	0.84	2.79
4	0.3119369815109966	1.79	5.95
5	0.3181822938100336	3.40	11.3
6	0.3183098350392471	6.79	22.6
7	0.3183098861837825	13.6	45.2
8	0.3183098861837907	15.6	51.8
9	0.3183098861837907	15.6	51.8

```
double newton(double x0) {
  double x_k, x_k1=x0, b=PI;
  do {
    x_k  = x_k1;
    x_k1 = x_k*(2-b*x_k);
  }while (fabs((x_k1-x_k)/x_k)
  >= 1e-15);
  return x_k1;
}
```

paper and described in Sect. 3 to explore the impact of lowering the precision with the VPREC backend for Verificarlo presented in Sect. 3.1.

Our methodology automatically finds for each iteration k, a reduced precision p_k; the p_k are chosen such that the overall convergence speed is not degraded. Figure 1 shows on the left the p_k's value found by VPREC. The plot at right compares the convergence speed of the standard `binary64` representation and the VPREC configuration. Both versions converge within the 10^{-15} threshold in nine iterations.

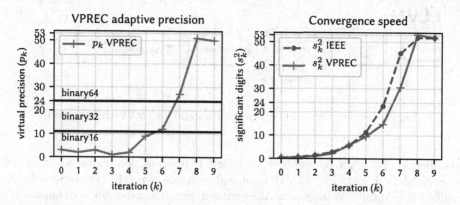

Fig. 1. (*left*) Precision found with VPREC for Newton-Raphson. (*right*) Both the standard IEEE-754 binary64 version and the VPREC low precision configuration converge to 10^{-15} in nine iterations.

Since the first seven iterations require less than 24 bits of precision, they can be executed in single precision (IEEE-754 `binary32`). To validate the solution found by VPREC, we run a mixed-precision version of the Newton-Raphson scheme where the first seven iterations use the `binary32` format. We note that the convergence speed and final result are almost identical to the full `binary64` version. While more efficient, the solution found by VPREC has only been validated for a given input data set and its resiliency has to be examined as discussed in Sect. 4.2.

3 Exploring Variable Precision

In large computational scientific codes, basic numerical computation functions are used many times in various places. Each call of the function may require a different numerical precision. Furthermore, as seen in Sect. 2, the same code section may require a different precision over time. To explore the temporal dimension of numerical precision, we use two components presented in the remaining of this section:

- A variable precision backend for Verificarlo: VPREC, detailed in Sect. 3.1;
- A heuristic optimizer to automatically minimize the precision configuration, while ensuring accuracy and convergence as described in Sect. 3.2.

3.1 Verificarlo and the VPREC Backend

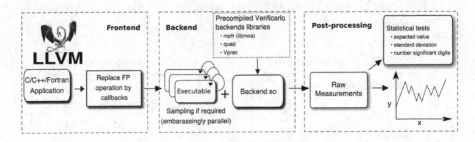

Fig. 2. General Verificarlo exploration workflow with VPREC backend

Verificarlo [14] is an open-source tool for FP interposition whose workflow is described in Fig. 2. The LLVM front-end replaces every FP operations by a call to the Verificarlo interface. After compilation, the program is dynamically linked against various backends [7,14]. Interposing FP operations at the compiler level allows to capture the compiler optimization effects on the generated FP operation flow. Furthermore, it reduces the interposition overhead by optimizing its integration with the original code.

The VPREC backend simulates FP formats that can fit into the IEEE-754 double precision format, avoiding the complex engineering process to implement a shadow memory [36].

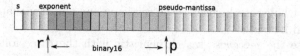

Fig. 3. By setting $r = 5$ and $p = 10$, VPREC simulates a *binary*16 embedded inside a *binary*32. Opaque bits represent the new exponent range and precision available. The sign remains the same.

As illustrated in Fig. 3, the current implementation of VPREC allows modifying the bit length of the exponent $r \in [1, 11]$ and the pseudo-mantissa $p \in [0, 52]$. The explored format can be converted back and forth to double without loss of precision. At each instrumented floating-point operation, VPREC rounds the operands in (r, p), converts them to double, performs the operation in double precision, rounds the result using the *Round Ties to Even* mode, and stores it as a 64-bit number. This process presents two advantages:

- VPREC operands can be converted to double to use hardware operators to perform VPREC operations with low overhead, including special values (subnormal numbers, NaN and $\pm\infty$) related to the user defined format (r, p)
- After rounding, converting the result back to double enables graceful degradation if some external libraries are not instrumented.

The user should note that in some rare cases, our implementation suffers from double rounding issue [5], when the first rounding done by the hardware at 53 bits impacts the second rounding to the required precision p. In practice, these cases, which occurs for numbers close to the midpoint of two p bits floating-point numbers, have no significant impact on our experiments.

The VPREC backend requires a single execution of the program and Verificarlo supports MPI. Therefore, we observe a reasonable overhead on full scale parallel applications ranging from $2.6\times$ to $16.8\times$ for very FP intensive codes.

3.2 Piecewise Constant Exploration Heuristic

Let consider an iterative program with n iterations. VPREC simulates the effect of using FP numbers represented on a p_k-bit mantissa and r_k-bit exponent at iteration k. From now on, the sequence of values $[(p_0, r_0), \dots, (p_n, r_n)]$ represents one VPREC run called a *configuration*.

When the precision is too low, the program execution fails: either it does not converge or it produces wrong results. We are only interested in *valid* configurations that preserve convergence and accuracy according to user knowledge. In our experiment (Sect. 4), the validation function checks that the number of iterations and the final results are within a threshold of some reference values.

Reducing the precision can be seen as introducing numerical errors terms in the computation. Determining how and where to distribute the errors across the iterations is an optimization problem with a large number of valid configurations.

486   Y. Chatelain et al.

Exploring the whole search-space is too costly on any non-trivial application, we have to rely on heuristics.

We propose the *piecewise* search heuristic with the three following design principles:

1. Configurations where the precision changes slowly over time are preferable to configurations which quickly oscillate between a low and high precision.
2. Precision lowering should be distributed among all iterations.
3. Early iterations are generally more robust to error. Therefore we foster configurations with lower precision in early iterations compared to late iterations.

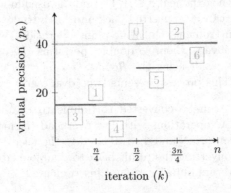

Fig. 4. First three steps of the piecewise constant search heuristic for the Newton-Raphson problem. The constant piecewise functions of step 0,1 and 2 are represented in green, blue and black. (Color figure online)

To enforce the first and second principles, we follow a top-down approach. The solution is modeled by a piecewise constant function that is progressively refined. Figure 4 illustrates the first three steps of the piecewise approach on the Newton-Raphson problem. For the sake of simplicity, we are solely focusing on lowering the mantissa size p_k. However, the method can simultaneously deals with the mantissa and exponent size. Initially, the piecewise constant function has a single domain (marked 0) that spawns all the iterations $[0, n)$. The valid lowest precision, corresponding to 40, is found by dichotomy on the precision domain between 1 and 53. In the second step, the domain is split in two subdomains (marked 1 and 2). To enforce the third principle, the precision in the left domain (marked 1) is lowered in a greedy manner, while keeping the maximal precision found in the previous step for the right domain (marked 2). Once the lowest precision for domain 1 is identified, we lower the precision in domain 2. This ends the second step and produces the blue piecewise function. This process continues recursively. This approach guarantees by construction that the piecewise function at step i is an upper bound of the function at step $i + 1$ and progressively refines the solution following the first principle. The exploration is breadth-first to evenly distribute the reduction in precision, according to the second principle.

4   Large Scale Study Validation on YALES2

YALES2 is a parallel CFD library that aims at solving the unsteady Navier-Stokes equations in the low-Mach number approximation for multiphase and reactive flows [28]. It efficiently handles unstructured meshes with several billions of elements, enabling the Direct Numerical Simulation of laboratory and industrial configurations. A projection method [8,32] enforces the mass-conservation constraint on the flow thanks to the resolution of a Poisson equation at each time-step. In the HPC context, this is usually achieved with Krylov methods and we focus here on the Deflated Preconditioned Conjugate Gradient (DPCG) [26,27,29] implemented in YALES2. In this algorithm, a coarse grid is built from the fine mesh by merging a fixed number of elements together in super-cells (this procedure is conceptually similar to the multi-grid approach [13]). The general principle of deflation is the following. The coarse grid is used to converge the low frequency eigenmodes of the solution which represent the long range interactions of the Poisson equation. This requires much less work than performing a classical CG on the fine mesh which is only used to obtain the remaining high frequencies in a small number of iterations.

Numerically, the deflated operator is solved in $iterdef$ iterations using a usual PCG method such that the convergence criteria $convcrit$ is met. The solution is then expanded and injected into the main PCG loop on the finer grid. This whole process is repeated until the $maxnorm$ of the fine grid residual is below a threshold. In both CG solvers (on coarse and fine grids), the system is preconditioned by the inverse of the diagonal. In all experiments, we constraint the total number of iterations performed, $\sum iterdef_k$, by the algorithm to be below 1% of additional iterations compared to the original.

The representative use-case we focus on is the PRECCINSTA burner [2,24]. It is a well-known lab-scale burner used to validate combustion CFD solvers. We use 3 different mesh sizes of 1.75 million, 40 million and 870 million of tetrahedral elements. For all configurations, the super-cell size in the coarse grid was set to 500 elements. We set the max norm of residual convergence criteria to 10^{-8}.

To reduce the search space, we consider two sets of functions. The first set, named $deflated$, is the set of functions used on the coarse grid to solve the deflated operator. The second set, named all, contained all the functions used to solve the fine grid operator.

4.1   Adaptive Precision Algorithm Experiment on DPCG

In this section, we apply our VPREC tool on the 1.75M mesh case to explore valid variable precision implementation. In order to use true single precision, we statically set the exponent range to 8-bits in VPREC exploration.

Figure 5 shows the result of the exploration. In both graphics the x-axis represents the number of iterations on the fine grid. In the top plot, the right y-axis represents, on the same scale, the norm $maxnorm$ of the residual between two successive iterations and the convergence criterion $convcrit$ of the deflated operator. The left y-axis represents $iterdef$, the number of iterations on the

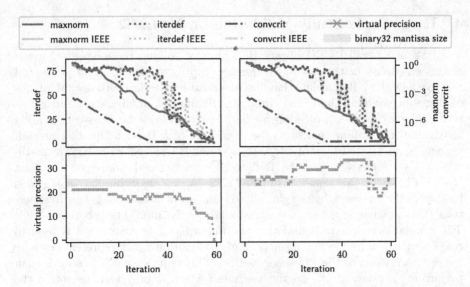

Fig. 5. Adaptive precision searching on YALES2's DPCG with the deflated part (*left*) and the entire code (*right*). On both plots, we can see that our reduced precision solution follows the reference IEEE convergence profile.

deflated operator. In the bottom plot, the y-axis represents the virtual precision used to compute the given iteration on x-axis.

Figure 5 (*left*) shows that less than 23 bits of precision are required for the deflated operator on the 1.75 million elements mesh, with an average precision of 18 bits. Therefore, the deflated operator can be computed with `binary32`, resulting in a mixed-precision implementation detailed in Sect. 4.3.

Figure 5 (*right*) shows the results of the proposed explorations on both coarse and fine grid at the same time. We notice that, contrary to the deflated experiment, the required precision increases over iterations. This is expected because the solver needs more and more precision to converge as it refines the solution. Surprisingly, the required precision drops at iteration 50 from 34 bits to 21 bits. We cannot yet explain this sudden drop, more investigations are needed.

4.2 Validating Resiliency to Round-Off Errors

In the previous sections, we demonstrated that YALES2's DPCG converges with a lower precision format. This result is only valid with the particular rounding mode used by VPREC and is sensitive to the input dataset. In a realistic setup, small rounding errors may occur when performing FP operations with a different software representation and/or hardware.

Monte Carlo Arithmetic (MCA) is a stochastic method to model round-off errors by artificially introducing noise within computations and performing Monte Carlo sampling. For the theoretical underpinnings, readers may refer to [14,31]. MCA is able to simulate rounding errors at a given virtual precision.

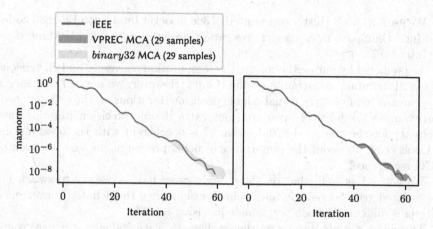

Fig. 6. Resiliency of VPREC and `binary32` configurations. In red the IEEE maxnorm convergence for reference. Blue envelop shows the 29 MCA samples for the previously found VPREC configuration. Green envelop shows the 29 MCA samples for the `binary32` configuration. All samples converge, showing the resiliency of both configurations.

We use MCA as a second step of our VPREC analysis to find a configuration that is resistant to round-off errors.

We model this process as a Bernoulli trial. We run 29 MCA samples to simulate the effect of rounding errors. If any one of the samples fail to converge, we conclude that the solution is not robust to round-off errors. On the other hand, if all the 29 samples converge we conclude, thanks to the confidence intervals introduced in [37], that the probability of convergence in the presence of round-off errors is 90% with a 0.95 confidence level.

Figure 6 shows that the VPREC solution found in the previous section is robust and converges for all the samples. Since the solution is very close to the `binary32` precision, our objective is to achieve a robust `binary32` configuration. The binary32 constant-precision configuration represented by the light red envelop in Fig. 6 converges in 57 to 63 iterations in the presence of round-off errors for all samples. This demonstrates that it is possible to safely rewrite the coarse grid operator of DPCG in `binary32`.

4.3   Evaluating Mixed-Precision Version

The deflated operator of DPCG can be computed within the `binary32` format for most iterations as shown in previous sections. To validate the results, we compiled a mixed-version of YALES2 where the deflated operator can be executed either in `binary32` or `binary64` format.

We evaluated the mixed precision version on the three different grids of PRECCINSTA and 10^{-9} convergence criteria. We limit the exploration algorithm to double and single precision since we are not running on variable precision hardware.

We use CRIANN cluster constituted of 366 bisocket Intel Xeon E5-2680 nodes and Intel Omnipath interconnect. We gather statistics using Intel IPM interface for Intel MPI.

As predicted by our methodology, the computation converges and all versions satisfy all accuracy constraints on the results. However, we noticed that larger experiments require extra initial double precision iterations on the deflated grid. For examples, respectively two and four extra double precision iterations are necessary for the 40M and 870M mesh. This is coherent with the observations of Cools et al. [9] about the importance of being precise in the first iteration of a CG recurrence:

We noticed as well, that on these larger cases it is necessary to switch for the deflated grid from single to double precision when the deflated convergence criteria is difficult to reach with single precision $\sim 10^{-8}$.

This effect did not appear on the smaller case with 500 elements per group. Our hypothesis is that the granularity difference between the two grids level is larger on the small mesh and therefore the small errors on the coarse grid iteration are less impacting on the fine grid iterations [26,27].

We measure a 28% to 67% reduction in the communication volume. The energy gain can be estimated to be linearly related to this volume gain with the simple model proposed in [1].

Since DPCG is mostly bounded by communication latency, the performance gain is limited when the number of processor grows for a given size falling from 28% speedup to −2% slowdown on critical strong scaling experiments. However, according to these results and end-user usage of the code, the expected speedup for daily usage will be in the 10% range.

5   Related Works and Background

Many tools and strategies have been developed for lowering precision in codes. For HPC purposes, the challenge is to have fast and scalable tools for addressing real world applications. A comparison with our methodology is presented in Table 2. Most of the tools focus on the spatial dimension while we investigate the temporal dimension as well. In addition, most of them focus on the mixed-precision exploration while we provide a more in-depth analysis by working at a bit level. Evaluating the resiliency to rounding errors is only proposed by Verificarlo and Promise although FlexFloat [21] and fpPrecisionTuning [38] propose statistic optimization according to input data ranges. However, they require the re-implementation of code to adopt the specific libraries.

Daisy [10], Herbie [30] and STOKE [35] are optimizing precision or accuracy by rewriting formulas. Most of them provides high level of guarantees, however they all face scalability issues.

Some authors propose adaptive schemes for specific linear algebra algorithms. Anzt et al. [1,19] propose an adaptive precision version of the Block-Jacobi preconditioner. Authors store data at low precision by truncating bits while computations remain in double precision. The change of format is guided by

Table 2. Comparisons of the different tools for exploring precision reduction.

Tool	Localization	Mixed prec.	Variable prec.	Round. error	Automatic
Precimonious [34]	Spatial	✓			✓
Blame-Analysis [33]	Spatial	✓	✓[1]		✓
Promise [16]	Spatial	✓		✓	✓
CRAFT [23]	Spatial	✓	✓[2]		✓
fpPrecisionTuning [21]	Spatial	✓	✓		
FlexFloat [38]	Spatial	✓	✓		
Verificarlo (this paper)	Temporal	✓	✓	✓	✓

the condition number and the data range. The authors estimate energy gains with predictive models with the underlying hypothesis that the cost depend linearly on the bit length of the data. These methods are interesting because they use mathematical properties of numerical schemes for adapting precision over iterations. However, the authors focused on small program sections based on their knowledge at high engineering cost. Therefore, their results are restricted to a class of specific algorithms unlike our method which provides a broader exploration tool. Of course, educated developers are still required to take the final decision to use lower precision provided by our VPREC tool.

6   Conclusion

Reducing communication volume and computation cost is important to reach exascale computing. Tailoring the precision to the requirements of the application offers consequent savings in performance and energy. We presented a methodology to automatically and finely adapt the precision over time for numerical iterative schemes. Our methodology goes beyond mixed-precision approaches by exploring precision configurations at bit level. The method explores the precision requirements over time, and therefore chooses an optimal precision for each application phase. To guarantee the accuracy of the results, we validate the robustness of our solutions to rounding errors with the help of stochastic arithmetic. Finally, our experiments show that the methodology handles large HPC codes like the Combustion-CFD solver YALES2. For YALES2, our approach shows that lowering the precision is viable and achieve 28% to 67% reduction in the communication volume, lowering the energy and runtime cost.

Acknowledgments. We thank Exascale Computing Research Lab supported by CEA, Intel, and UVSQ. This work has been granted access to the HPC resources of CINES under the allocation 20XX-A0031010295 made by GENCI and the computing resources of CRIANN (Normandy, France).

References

1. Anzt, H., Dongarra, J., et al.: Adaptive precision in block-Jacobi preconditioning for iterative sparse linear system solvers. Concurr. Comput. Pract. Exp. **31**, e4460 (2017)
2. Benard, P., Lartigue, G., et al.: Large-eddy simulation of the lean-premixed PREC-CINSTA burner with wall heat loss. Proc. Combust. Inst. **37**, 5233–5243 (2018)
3. Benard, P., Viré, A., et al.: Large-eddy simulation of wind turbines wakes including geometrical effects. Comput. Fluids **173**, 133–139 (2018). https://doi.org/10.1016/j.compfluid.2018.03.015. http://www.sciencedirect.com/science/article/pii/S0045793018301154
4. Benard, P., Balarac, G., et al.: Mesh adaptation for large-eddy simulations in complex geometries. Int. J. Numer. Methods Fluids **81**(12), 719–740 (2016). https://doi.org/10.1002/fld.4204. https://onlinelibrary.wiley.com/doi/abs/10.1002/fld.4204
5. Boldo, S., Melquiond, G.: When double rounding is odd. In: 17th IMACS World Congress, Paris, France, p. 11 (2005)
6. Boulet, L., Bénard, P., et al.: Modeling of conjugate heat transfer in a kerosene/air spray flame used for aeronautical fire resistance tests. Flow Turbul. Combust. **101**(2), 579–602 (2018). https://doi.org/10.1007/s10494-018-9965-8
7. Chatelain, Y., de Oliveira Castro, P., et al.: VeriTracer: context-enriched tracer for floating-point arithmetic analysis. In: 25th IEEE Symposium on Computer Arithmetic (ARITH), pp. 61–68 (2018)
8. Chorin, A.J.: Numerical solution of the Navier-Stokes equations. Math. Comput. **22**(104), 745–762 (1968)
9. Cools, S., Yetkin, E.F., et al.: Analysis of rounding error accumulation in Conjugate Gradients to improve the maximal attainable accuracy of pipelined CG. Research Report RR-8849, Inria Bordeaux Sud-Ouest, January 2016. https://hal.inria.fr/hal-01262716
10. Darulova, E., Horn, E., Sharma, S.: Sound mixed-precision optimization with rewriting. In: Proceedings of the 9th ACM/IEEE International Conference on Cyber-Physical Systems, pp. 208–219. IEEE Press (2018)
11. Das, D., Mellempudi, N., et al.: Mixed precision training of convolutional neural networks using integer operations. CoRR abs/1802.00930 (2018). http://arxiv.org/abs/1802.00930
12. Defour, D.: FP-ANR: a representation format to handle floating-point cancellation at run-time. In: 25th IEEE Symposium on Computer Arithmetic (ARITH), pp. 76–83 (2018)
13. Dendy, J.: Black box multigrid. J. Comput. Phys. **48**(3), 366–386 (1982). https://doi.org/10.1016/0021-9991(82)90057-2. http://www.sciencedirect.com/science/article/pii/0021999182900572
14. Denis, C., de Oliveira Castro, P., Petit, E.: Verificarlo: checking floating point accuracy through Monte Carlo arithmetic. In: 23nd IEEE Symposium on Computer Arithmetic (ARITH), pp. 55–62 (2016)
15. de Dinechin, F., Pasca, B.: Designing custom arithmetic data paths with FloPoCo. IEEE Des. Test Comput. **28**, 18–27 (2011)
16. Graillat, S., Jézéquel, F., et al.: PROMISE: floating-point precision tuning with stochastic arithmetic. In: Proceedings of the 17th International Symposium on Scientific Computing, Computer Arithmetics and Verified Numerics (SCAN), pp. 98–99 (2016)

17. Guedot, L., Lartigue, G., Moureau, V.: Design of implicit high-order filters on unstructured grids for the identification of large-scale features in large-eddy simulation and application to a swirl burner. Phys. Fluids **27**(4), 045107 (2015). https://doi.org/10.1063/1.4917280
18. Gustafson, Y.: Beating floating point at its own game: posit arithmetic. Supercomput. Front. Innov. Int. J. **4**(2), 71–86 (2017)
19. Haidar, A., Tomov, S., et al.: Harnessing GPU tensor cores for fast FP16 arithmetic to speed up mixed-precision iterative refinement solvers. In: Proceedings of the International Conference for High Performance Computing, Networking, Storage, and Analysis, SC 2018, Piscataway, NJ, USA, pp. 47:1–47:11. IEEE Press (2018)
20. Higham, N.J.: Accuracy and Stability of Numerical Algorithms. SIAM, Philadelphia (2002)
21. Ho, N.M., Manogaran, E., et al.: Efficient floating point precision tuning for approximate computing. In: 22nd Asia and South Pacific Design Automation Conference (ASP-DAC), pp. 63–68. IEEE (2017)
22. Intel Corp.: Intel VML (2018). https://software.intel.com/en-us/mkl-developer-reference-c-vector-mathematical-functions
23. Lam, M.O., Hollingsworth, J.K., et al.: Automatically adapting programs for mixed-precision floating-point computation. In: Proceedings of the 27th International conference on supercomputing, pp. 369–378. ACM (2013)
24. Lartigue, G., Meier, U., Bérat, C.: Experimental and numerical investigation of self-excited combustion oscillations in a scaled gas turbine combustor. Appl. Therm. Eng. **24**(11–12), 1583–1592 (2004)
25. Legrand, N., Lartigue, G., Moureau, V.: A multi-grid framework for the extraction of large-scale vortices in large-eddy simulation. J. Comput. Phys. **349**, 528–560 (2017). https://doi.org/10.1016/j.jcp.2017.08.030. http://www.sciencedirect.com/science/article/pii/S0021999117306010
26. Malandain, M.: Massively parallel simulation of low-Mach number turbulent flows. Theses, INSA de Rouen, January 2013. https://tel.archives-ouvertes.fr/tel-00801502
27. Malandain, M., Maheu, N., Moureau, V.: Optimization of the deflated conjugate gradient algorithm for the solving of elliptic equations on massively parallel machines. J. Comput. Phys. **238**, 32–47 (2013). https://doi.org/10.1016/j.jcp.2012.11.046. http://www.sciencedirect.com/science/article/pii/S0021999112007280
28. Moureau, V., Domingo, P., Vervisch, L.: Design of a massively parallel CFD code for complex geometries. Comptes Rendus Mécanique **339**, 141–148 (2011)
29. Nicolaides, R.A.: Deflation of conjugate gradients with applications to boundary value problems. SIAM J. Numer. Anal. **24**(2), 355–365 (1987)
30. Panchekha, P., Sanchez-Stern, A., et al.: Automatically improving accuracy for floating point expressions. In: Proceedings of the 36th ACM SIGPLAN Conference on Programming Language Design and Implementation, pp. 1–11. ACM (2015)
31. Parker, S.: Monte carlo arithmetic: exploiting randomness in floating-point arithmetic. Technical report CSD-970002, UCLA Computer Science Department (1997)
32. Pierce, C.D., Moin, P.: Progress-variable approach for large-eddy simulation of non-premixed turbulent combustion. J. Fluid Mech. **504**, 73–97 (2004). https://doi.org/10.1017/S0022112004008213
33. Rubio-González, C., Nguyen, C., et al.: Floating-point precision tuning using blame analysis. In: Proceedings of the 38th International Conference on Software Engineering, pp. 1074–1085. ACM (2016)

34. Rubio-González, C., Nguyen, C., et al.: Precimonious: tuning assistant for floating-point precision. In: International Conference for High Performance Computing, Networking, Storage and Analysis (SC), pp. 1–12. IEEE (2013)

35. Schkufza, E., Sharma, R., Aiken, A.: Stochastic optimization of floating-point programs with tunable precision. ACM SIGPLAN Not. **49**(6), 53–64 (2014)

36. Serebryany, K., Bruening, D., et al.: AddressSanitizer: a fast address sanity checker. In: USENIX ATC 2012 (2012)

37. Sohier, D., De Oliveira Castro, P., et al.: Confidence Intervals for Stochastic Arithmetic (2018). https://hal.archives-ouvertes.fr/hal-01827319, preprint

38. Tagliavini, G., Mach, S., et al.: A transprecision floating-point platform for ultra-low power computing. In: Design, Automation & Test in Europe Conference & Exhibition (DATE), pp. 1051–1056. IEEE (2018)

Linear Systems Solvers
for Distributed-Memory Machines
with GPU Accelerators

Jakub Kurzak[1]($\boxtimes$)(iD), Mark Gates[1](iD), Ali Charara[1](iD), Asim YarKhan[1](iD),
Ichitaro Yamazaki[1](iD), and Jack Dongarra[1,2,3](iD)

[1] University of Tennessee, Knoxville, TN 37996, USA
{kurzak,mgates3,charara,yarkhan,iyamazak,dongarra}@icl.utk.edu
[2] Oak Ridge National Laboratory, Oak Ridge, TN 37831, USA
[3] University of Manchester, Manchester M13 9PL, UK
https://www.icl.utk.edu/

Abstract. This work presents two implementations of linear solvers for distributed-memory machines with GPU accelerators—one based on the Cholesky factorization and one based on the LU factorization with partial pivoting. The routines are developed as part of the Software for Linear Algebra Targeting Exascale (SLATE) package, which represents a sharp departure from the traditional conventions established by legacy packages, such as LAPACK and ScaLAPACK. The article lays out the principles of the new approach, discusses the implementation details, and presents the performance results.

Keywords: Linear algebra · Distributed memory ·
Linear systems of equations · Cholesky factorization ·
LU factorization · GPU acceleration

1 Introduction

1.1 Linear Systems

Solving a system of linear equations $Ax = b$ is a fundamental capability in scientific and engineering computing. The most common approach is to apply the lower–upper (LU) decomposition, which factors the matrix A as the product of a lower triangular matrix L and an upper triangular matrix U. The procedure usually requires row permutations for numerical stability, referred to as partial pivoting. LU decomposition can be viewed as the matrix form of Gaussian elimination. It is also a key step in inverting a matrix or computing the determinant of a matrix. LU decomposition was introduced by Polish mathematician Tadeusz Banachiewicz.

This research was supported by the Exascale Computing Project (17-SC-20-SC), a collaborative effort of two U.S. Department of Energy organizations (Office of Science and the National Nuclear Security Administration).

© Springer Nature Switzerland AG 2019
R. Yahyapour (Ed.): Euro-Par 2019, LNCS 11725, pp. 495–506, 2019.
https://doi.org/10.1007/978-3-030-29400-7_35

The system of linear equations $Ax = b$ can be solved much faster when the matrix A is Hermitian, positive definite in complex arithmetic; or symmetric, positive definite in real arithmetics. Commonly, the Cholesky decomposition is used to factor the matrix A into the product of a lower triangular matrix L and its conjugate transpose. It was discovered by a French mathematician, André-Louis Cholesky, for real matrices. When it is applicable, the Cholesky decomposition is roughly twice as efficient as the LU decomposition for solving systems of linear equations.

1.2   SLATE Project

Software for Linear Algebra Targeting Exascale (SLATE)[1] is being developed as part of the Exascale Computing Project (ECP),[2] which is a collaborative effort between two US Department of Energy (DOE) organizations, the Office of Science and the National Nuclear Security Administration (NNSA). The objective of SLATE is to provide fundamental dense linear algebra capabilities to the US Department of Energy and to the high-performance computing (HPC) community at large.

The ultimate objective of SLATE is to replace the ScaLAPACK library [3], which has become the industry standard for dense linear algebra operations in distributed-memory environments. However, after two decades of operation, ScaLAPACK is past the end of its life cycle and is overdue for a replacement, as it can hardly be retrofitted to support hardware accelerators, which are an integral part of today's HPC hardware infrastructure.

Primarily, SLATE aims to extract the full performance potential and maximum scalability from modern, many-node HPC machines with large numbers of cores and multiple hardware accelerators per node. For typical dense linear algebra workloads, this means getting close to the theoretical peak performance and scaling to the full size of the machine (i.e., thousands to tens of thousands of nodes). This is to be accomplished in a portable manner by relying on standards like MPI and OpenMP. Figure 1 shows SLATE in the ECP software stack.

Fig. 1. SLATE in the ECP software stack.

---

[1] http://icl.utk.edu/slate/.
[2] https://www.exascaleproject.org.

2   Motivation

There is an urgent need for multi-GPU accelerated, distributed-memory software. Currently, the fastest machines in United States are the Summit[3] and Sierra[4] systems, at the Oak Ridge National Laboratory (ORNL) and the Lawrence Livermore National Laboratory (LLNL), respectively. As of today, they occupy positions #1 and #2 on the TOP500 list.

The urgency of the situation is underscored by the architectures of the aforementioned systems.[5] The Summit system contains three NVIDIA V100 GPUs per each POWER9 CPU. The peak double-precision floating-point performance of the CPU is $22\ (cores) \times 24.56\ gigaFLOP/s = 540.32\ gigaFLOP/s$. The peak performance of the GPUs is $3\ (devices) \times 7.8\ teraFLOP/s = 23.4\ teraFLOP/s$. I.e., 97.7% of performance is on the GPU side, and only 2.3% of performance is on the CPU side.

Also, the U.S. Department of Energy has recently announced plans for achieving exascale. The system, called Frontier, will be built at ORNL. It is planned to go online in 2021 and deliver 1.5 exaFLOP/s of theoretical peak performance. Frontier's nodes will contain one AMD EPYC CPU and four purpose-built AMD Radeon Instinct GPUs.[6]

3   Related Work

Due to the popularity of the Cholesky and LU factorizations, it would be difficult to survey all the related research efforts. Instead we opt for listing the most popular software packages that implement the two routines. Distributed-memory implementations are available in:

- ScaLAPACK (http://www.netlib.org/scalapack/),
- PLAPACK (http://www.cs.utexas.edu/users/plapack/),
- Elemental (http://libelemental.org),
- DPLASMA (http://icl.utk.edu/dplasma/).

While some efforts are being made to GPU-accelerate these packages, at this time we consider these developments experimental. On the other hand, accelerated implementations of the Cholesky and LU factorizations are available in:

- MAGMA (http://icl.cs.utk.edu/magma/),
- CULA (http://www.culatools.com/dense/),
- cuSOLVER (https://developer.nvidia.com/cusolver).

These packages, however, do not support distributed memory. In that respect, the SLATE project seems to be a unique effort in specifically targeting multi-GPU–accelerated distributed-memory systems.

---

[3] https://www.olcf.ornl.gov/summit/.
[4] https://hpc.llnl.gov/hardware/platforms/sierra.
[5] https://en.wikichip.org/wiki/supercomputers/summit.
[6] https://www.olcf.ornl.gov/frontier/.

4   Original Contribution

This is the only open-source implementation, that we know of, that targets Summit- and Sierra-class machines, i.e., large distributed-memory systems drawing virtually all of their computing power from GPU accelerators. Obviously, very efficient codes were written for the TOP500 runs for these machines. At this point, however, these codes remain proprietary and the details of their inner workings are not publicly available.

The implementations presented here are based on the infrastructure of the SLATE project, which is a radical departure from the established conventions, most notably from the legacy matrix layout of ScaLAPACK. Also, as far as we know, we produced a unique implementation of the LU panel factorization, which combines MPI messaging, OpenMP multithreading, internal blocking, and cache residency.

5   Implementation

5.1   SLATE Basics

Matrix Storage. Unlike legacy dense linear algebra packages, which store the matrix contiguously, by columns, SLATE stores the matrix as a collection of individual tiles. This offers numerous advantages, for example:

- The same structure can be used for holding many different matrix types,[7] e.g., general, symmetric, triangular, band, symmetric band, etc. No memory is wasted for storing parts of the matrix that hold no useful data, e.g., the upper triangle of a lower triangular matrix. There is no need for using complex matrix layouts, such as the Recursive Packed Format (RPF) [1,2,9] in order to save space.
- The matrix can be easily converted, in parallel, from one layout to another with $O(P)$ memory overhead, where P is the number of processors (cores/threads) used. Possible conversions include: changing the layout of tiles from column major to row major, "packing" of tiles for efficient execution of the gemm operation,[8] low-rank compression of tiles, re-tiling of the matrix (changing the tile size), etc. Notably, transposition of the matrix can be accomplished by transposition of each tile and remapping of the indices. There is no need for complex in-place layout translation and transposition algorithms [10].
- Tiles can easily be moved or copied among different memory spaces. Both inter-node communication and intra-node communication are vastly simplified. Tiles can easily and efficiently be transferred between nodes using MPI. Tiles can also be copied to one or more device memories in the case of GPU acceleration.

---

[7] http://www.netlib.org/lapack/lug/node24.html.

[8] https://software.intel.com/en-us/articles/introducing-the-new-packed-apis-for-gemm.

In practical terms, the SLATE matrix is implemented by the `std::map` container from the standard C++ library; that is, `std::map< std::tuple< int64_t, int64_t, int >, Tile<scalar_t>* >`

The key is a triplet consisting of the (i, j) position of the tile in the matrix and the device number where the tile is located, The value is a pointer to an object of a lightweight class that stores the tile's data and its properties. One issue that may require further attention is the logarithmic complexity of the default implementation of the container in the standard library. If it turns out to be a problem, the use of `std::unordered_map` may be required.

In addition to facilitating the storage of different types of matrices, this structure also readily accommodates partitioning of the matrix to the nodes of a distributed-memory system. Tile indexing is global, and each node stores only its local subset of tiles. Mapping of tiles to nodes is defined by a C++ lambda function, and set to 2D block cyclic mapping by default. Remote access is realized by mirroring remote tiles in the local matrix for the duration of the operation. In that respect, SLATE follows the single program, multiple data (SPMD) programming style. SLATE also has the potential to support matrices with non-uniform tile sizes in the future.

For offload to GPU accelerators, SLATE implements a custom memory consistency model, loosely based on the Modified/Owned/Shared/Invalid (MOSI) coherency protocol [13]. The distinguishing feature is that SLATE's model is symmetric; that is, there is no notion of the *main* memory—all memories (host, devices) are considered peers.

Matrix Class Hierarchy. SLATE has the matrix classes below. Inexpensive shallow copy conversions exist between the various matrix types. For instance, a general `Matrix` can be converted to a `TriangularMatrix` for doing a triangular solve (`trsm`).

BaseMatrix Abstract base class for all matrices.

> **Matrix** General, $m \times n$ matrix.
>
> **BaseTrapezoidMatrix** Abstract base class for all upper or lower trapezoid storage, $m \times n$ matrices. For upper, tiles $A(i, j)$ for $i \leq j$ are stored; for lower, tiles $A(i, j)$ for $i \geq j$ are stored.
>
>> **TrapezoidMatrix** Upper or lower trapezoid, $m \times n$ matrix; the opposite triangle is implicitly zero.
>>
>>> **TriangularMatrix** Upper or lower triangular, $n \times n$ matrix.
>>
>> **SymmetricMatrix** Symmetric, $n \times n$ matrix, stored by its upper or lower triangle; the opposite triangle is implicitly known by symmetry $(A_{j,i} = A_{i,j})$.
>>
>> **HermitianMatrix** Hermitian, $n \times n$ matrix, stored by its upper or lower triangle; the opposite triangle is implicitly known by symmetry $(A_{j,i} = \bar{A}_{i,j})$.

The `BaseMatrix` class stores the matrix dimensions; whether the matrix is upper, lower, or general; whether it is not transposed, transposed, or conjugate-transposed; how the matrix is distributed; and the set of tiles.

Handling of Multiple Precisions. SLATE handles multiple precisions by C++ templating, so there is only one precision-independent version of the code, which is then instantiated for the desired precisions. SLATE's LAPACK++ component [8] provides overloaded, precision-independent wrappers for all the underlying LAPACK routines, on which SLATE's least squares routines are built. For instance, `lapack::potrf` in LAPACK++ maps to `spotrf`, `dpotrf`, `cpotrf`, or `zpotrf` LAPACK routines, depending on the precision of its arguments.

Where a data type is always real, `blas::real_type<scalar_t>` is a C++ type trait to provide the real type associated with the type `scalar_t`, so `blas::real_type< std::complex<double> >` is `double`.

Currently, the SLATE library has explicit instantiations of the four main data types: `float`, `double`, `std::complex<float>`, and `std::complex<double>`. In the future, SLATE should be able to accommodate other data types, such as quadruple precision (double-double) or half precision (FP16), given appropriate implementations of the elemental operations.

5.2 Cholesky Implementation

SLATE provides routines for solving linear systems of equations, where the coefficient matrix is symmetric (Hermitian) positive definite. These routines compute the factorization $A = LL^T$ ($A = LL^H$) using the Cholesky decomposition, and follow with the steps of forward and backward substitution. The routines are mathematically equivalent to their ScaLAPACK counterparts [6].

Figure 2 (left picture) shows the basic mechanics of the Cholesky factorization in SLATE. Like most routines in SLATE, the implementation relies on nested tasking using the OpenMP standard, with the top level responsible for scheduling a small number of coarse-grained, interdependent tasks, and the nested level responsible for dispatching large numbers of fine-grained, independent tasks. In the case of GPU acceleration, the nested level is implemented using calls to batched Basic Linear Algebra Subprograms (BLAS) routines, to exploit the efficiency of processing large numbers of tiles in one call to a GPU kernel.

The Cholesky factorization in SLATE applies the technique of *lookahead* [5,11,14], where one or more columns, immediately following the panel, are prioritized for faster processing, to allow for speedier advancement along the critical path. Lookahead provides large performance improvements, as it allows for overlapping the panel factorization—which is usually inefficient—with updating of the trailing submatrix, which is usually very efficient and can be GPU-accelerated. Usually, the lookahead of one results in a large performance gain, while bigger values deliver diminishing returns.

5.3 LU Implementation

SLATE provides routines for solving linear systems of equations, where the coefficient matrix is a general (nonsymmetric) matrix. These routines compute the factorization $PA = LU$ using the process of Gaussian elimination with partial

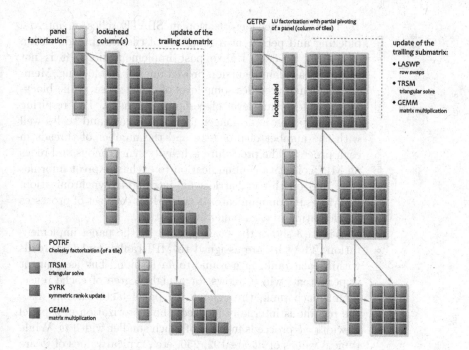

Fig. 2. Left: Cholesky factorization with lookahead of one. Right: LU factorization with lookahead of one.

(row) pivoting, and follow with the steps of forward and backward substitution. The routines are mathematically equivalent to their ScaLAPACK counterparts [6].

Figure 2 (right picture) shows the basic mechanics of the LU factorization in SLATE. While the parallelization is based on the same principles as the Cholesky factorization, the implementation is significantly more challenging, due to the application of row pivoting. The primary consequence of row pivoting is a fairly complex, and heavily synchronous, panel factorization procedure. The secondary effect is the communication overhead of swapping rows to the left and to the right of the panel. A further complication is introduced by GPU acceleration, which requires layout translation, as the row swapping operation is extremely inefficient in column major.

The critical component of the LU factorization is the step of factoring the panel, which in SLATE is an arbitrary selection of tiles from one column of the matrix. This operation is on the critical path of the algorithms and has to be optimized to the maximum. Resorting to a simple, memory-bound implementation could have profoundly negative consequences for performance. The current implementation of the LU panel factorization in SLATE is derived from the technique of *Parallel Cache Assignment* (PCA) by Castaldo et al. [4], and the work on parallel panel factorization by Dongarra et al. [7].

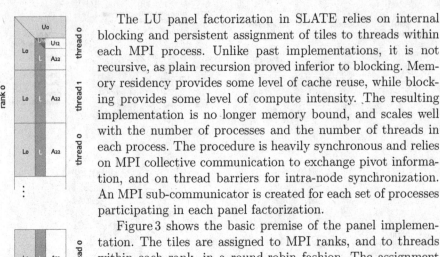
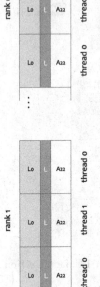
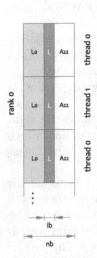

Fig. 3. LU panel.

The LU panel factorization in SLATE relies on internal blocking and persistent assignment of tiles to threads within each MPI process. Unlike past implementations, it is not recursive, as plain recursion proved inferior to blocking. Memory residency provides some level of cache reuse, while blocking provides some level of compute intensity. The resulting implementation is no longer memory bound, and scales well with the number of processes and the number of threads in each process. The procedure is heavily synchronous and relies on MPI collective communication to exchange pivot information, and on thread barriers for intra-node synchronization. An MPI sub-communicator is created for each set of processes participating in each panel factorization.

Figure 3 shows the basic premise of the panel implementation. The tiles are assigned to MPI ranks, and to threads within each rank, in a round-robin fashion. The assignment is persistent, which allows for a high degree of cache reuse, within each rank, throughout the panel factorization. Also, the routine is internally blocked: the factorization of a panel of width nb proceeds in steps of much smaller width ib. While typical values of nb are 192, 256, etc., typical values of ib are 8, 16, etc. The ib factorization contains mostly level 1 and 2 BLAS operations, but can benefit to some extent from cache residency, while the nb factorization contains mostly level 3 BLAS operations and can also benefit from cache residency.

At each step of the ib panel factorization, a stripe of the lower triangular matrix (L) is computed, along with a small part of the U factor (U_{11}). All this work is done one column at a time. What follows is application of the L transformations to the right, which includes updating the remaining A_{22} submatrix, and computing of a new horizontal stripe of the U factor (U_{12}). Most of this work is done using level 3 BLAS operations.

Each panel factorization is followed by an update of the trailing submatrix (Fig. 2), which involves: (1) applying row swaps (laswp), (2) triangular solve (trsm), and (3) matrix multiplication (gemm). This requires the following communication: (1) "horizontal" broadcasting of the panel to the right, (2) "vertical" exchanges of the rows being swapped, and (3) "vertical" broadcasting of the top row or tiles down the matrix.

This creates the extra complication of multiple OpenMP tasks issuing, possibly concurrently, independent communications. Specifically, the collective communication of the panel factorization may coincide with sends and receives of multiple simultaneous row swaps. This requires that the underlying MPI implementation be thread safe, and support the `MPI_THREAD_MULTIPLE` mode (i.e., multiple threads simultaneously issuing MPI communications). It also requires that the different communications be distinguished by different MPI tags.

6 Results

6.1 Setup

Performance numbers were collected using the SummitDev system[9] at the Oak Ridge Leadership Computing Facility (OLCF), which is intended to mimic the OLCF's much larger supercomputer, Summit. SummitDev is based on the IBM POWER8 processors and the NVIDIA P100 (Pascal) accelerators, and is one generation behind Summit, which is based on the IBM POWER9 processors and the NVIDIA V100 (Volta) accelerators.

The SummitDev system contains three racks, each with eighteen IBM POWER8 S822LC nodes, for a total of fifty-four nodes. Each node contains two POWER8 CPUs, ten cores each, and four P100 GPUs. Each node has 256 GB of DDR4 memory. Each GPU has 16 GB of HBM2 memory. The GPUs are connected by NVLink 1.0 at 80 GB/s. The nodes are connected with a fat-tree enhanced data rate (EDR) InfiniBand.

The software environment used for the experiments included GNU Compiler Collection (GCC) 7.1.0, CUDA 9.0.69, Engineering Scientific Subroutine Library (ESSL) 5.5.0, Spectrum MPI 10.1.0.4, Netlib LAPACK 3.6.1, and Netlib ScaLAPACK 2.0.2.

6.2 Performance

All runs were performed using sixteen nodes of the SummitDev system, which provides 16 *nodes* $\times$ 2 *sockets* $\times$ 10 *cores* = 320 IBM POWER8 cores and 16 *nodes* $\times$ 4 *devices* = 64 NVIDIA P100 accelerators. ScaLAPACK was run with one process per core, which is still the prevailing method of getting the best performance from ScaLAPACK. SLATE, on the other hand, was run using one process per GPU. While SLATE does provide multi-GPU support, the best performance was reached by assigning each GPU to one process and splitting the CPU cores evenly (i.e., five cores per process).

Figure 4 shows performance comparison of SLATE and ScaLAPACK for the Cholesky factorization. The left chart shows performance when using CPUs only for both SLATE and ScaLAPACK. The right chart compares CPU performance of ScaLAPACK with GPU performance of SLATE. At this point, we are not aware of an efficient way of GPU-accelerating ScaLAPACK.

---

[9] https://www.olcf.ornl.gov/kb_articles/summitdev-quickstart/.

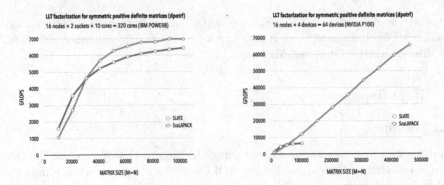

Fig. 4. Performance of `dpotrf` without acceleration (left) and with acceleration (right). The CPU peak is 8,960 gigaFLOPs, the GPU peak is 339,200 gigaFLOPs.

Similarly, Fig. 5 shows a performance comparison of SLATE and ScaLA-PACK for the LU factorization. The left chart shows performance when using CPUs only for both SLATE and ScaLAPACK. The right chart compares CPU performance of ScaLAPACK with GPU performance of SLATE.

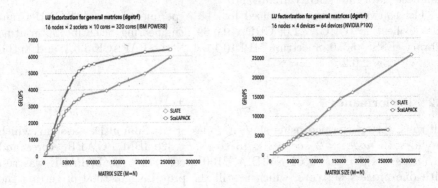

Fig. 5. Performance of `dgetrf` without acceleration (left) and with acceleration (right). The CPU peak is 8,960 gigaFLOPs, the GPU peak is 339,200 gigaFLOPs.

6.3   Discussion

For the Cholesky factorization, SLATE delivers superior performance compared to ScaLAPACK. The CPU performance of SLATE is higher than the CPU performance of ScaLAPACK, and SLATE delivers an order of magnitude speedup from GPU acceleration. For the LU factorization, the CPU performance of SLATE is lower than ScaLAPACK's for smaller matrix sizes, but catches up for larger sizes. GPU performance of LU is generally superior to ScaLAPACK's, although the gains of acceleration are smaller than for Cholesky.

While SLATE clearly benefits from GPU acceleration, it only achieves a small fraction of the GPU theoretical peak performance. This is mostly due to the fact that the computing power of the GPUs completely outmatches the communication capabilities of the interconnection, despite the fact that the network represents state-of-the-art technology. With this trend continuing, it will be necessary to seek new algorithms—algorithms that are even more compute-intensive than the traditional solutions to dense linear algebra problems. One such example is the QDWH algorithm [15] for computing the singular value decomposition (SVD).

Another problem is the one of mixing MPI messaging with OpenMP multi-threading. In SLATE, MPI messages are sent from inside OpenMP tasks, which requires the highest level of MPI thread safety (`MPI_THREAD_MULTIPLE`) and some other precautions to prevent deadlock. These measures have an adverse effect on performance. Ultimately, what is needed is an `MPI_TASK_MULTIPLE` mode of operation, as described by Sala et al. [12].

Finally, the biggest factor contributing to the poor performance of the LU factorization is the cost of pivoting (i.e., the operation of swapping rows). Currently, it is done in a sequential fashion, the same way it is done in LAPACK and ScaLAPACK. Moving to parallel pivoting, where all the rows can be swapped simultaneously, may improve the situation. Also, storing the matrix in column-major in the CPU memory has a significant impact on the performance of pivoting on the CPU side, and moving the CPU operations to row-major—same as was done for GPUs—may be necessary.

Acknowledgments. This research was supported by the Exascale Computing Project (17-SC-20-SC), a collaborative effort of two U.S. Department of Energy organizations (Office of Science and the National Nuclear Security Administration) responsible for the planning and preparation of a capable exascale ecosystem, including software, applications, hardware, advanced system engineering and early testbed platforms, in support of the nation's exascale computing imperative.

Software. The SLATE software if freely available at https://bitbucket.org/icl/slate. SLATE is distributed under the modified BSD license, imposing minimal restrictions on the use and distribution of the software.

References

1. Andersen, B.S., Gunnels, J.A., Gustavson, F., Wasniewski, J.: A recursive formulation of the inversion of symmetric positive definite matrices in packed storage data format. PARA **2**, 287–296 (2002)
2. Andersen, B.S., Waśniewski, J., Gustavson, F.G.: A recursive formulation of Cholesky factorization of a matrix in packed storage. ACM Trans. Math. Softw. (TOMS) **27**(2), 214–244 (2001)
3. Blackford, L.S., et al.: ScaLAPACK Users' Guide. SIAM, Philadelphia (1997)
4. Castaldo, A., Whaley, C.: Scaling LAPACK panel operations using parallel cache assignment. In: ACM Sigplan Notices, vol. 45, pp. 223–232. ACM (2010)

5. Chan, E., van de Geijn, R., Chapman, A.: Managing the complexity of lookahead for LU factorization with pivoting. In: Proceedings of the Twenty-second Annual ACM Symposium on Parallelism in Algorithms and Architectures, pp. 200–208. ACM (2010)
6. Choi, J., Dongarra, J., Ostrouchov, S., Petitet, A., Walker, D., Whaley, C.: Design and implementation of the ScaLAPACK LU, QR, and Cholesky factorization routines. Sci. Program. 5(3), 173–184 (1996)
7. Dongarra, J., Faverge, M., Ltaief, H., Luszczek, P.: Achieving numerical accuracy and high performance using recursive tile LU factorization with partial pivoting. Concurr. Comput. Pract. Exp. 26(7), 1408–1431 (2014)
8. Gates, M., et al.: SLATE working note 2: C++ API for BLAS and LAPACK. Technical report ICL-UT-17-03, Innovative Computing Laboratory, University of Tennessee, June 2017. Revision 03–2018
9. Gustavson, F., Henriksson, A., Jonsson, I., Kågström, B., Ling, P.: Recursive blocked data formats and BLAS's for dense linear algebra algorithms. In: Kågström, B., Dongarra, J., Elmroth, E., Waśniewski, J. (eds.) PARA 1998. LNCS, vol. 1541, pp. 195–206. Springer, Heidelberg (1998). https://doi.org/10.1007/BFb0095337
10. Gustavson, F., Karlsson, L., Kågström, B.: Parallel and cache-efficient in-place matrix storage format conversion. ACM Trans. Math. Softw. (TOMS) 38(3), 17 (2012)
11. Kurzak, J., Dongarra, J.: Implementing linear algebra routines on multi-core processors with pipelining and a look ahead. In: Kågström, B., Elmroth, E., Dongarra, J., Waśniewski, J. (eds.) PARA 2006. LNCS, vol. 4699, pp. 147–156. Springer, Heidelberg (2007). https://doi.org/10.1007/978-3-540-75755-9_18
12. Sala, K., Teruel, X., Perez, J.M., Peña, A.J., Beltran, V., Labarta, J.: Integrating blocking and non-blocking MPI primitives with task-based programming models. Parallel Comput. 85, 153–166 (2019)
13. Sorin, D.J., Hill, M.D., Wood, D.A.: A primer on memory consistency and cache coherence. Synth. Lect. Comput. Arch. 6(3), 1–212 (2011)
14. Strazdins, P., et al.: A comparison of lookahead and algorithmic blocking techniques for parallel matrix factorization (1998)
15. Sukkari, D., Ltaief, H., Keyes, D.: A high performance QDWH-SVD solver using hardware accelerators. ACM Trans. Math. Softw. (TOMS) 43(1), 6 (2016)

Accelerator Computing

Radio-Astronomical Imaging: FPGAs vs GPUs

Bram Veenboer[(✉)] and John W. Romein[(✉)]

ASTRON (Netherlands Institute for Radio Astronomy), Dwingeloo, The Netherlands
{veenboer,romein}@astron.nl

Abstract. FPGAs excel in performing simple operations on high-speed streaming data, at high (energy) efficiency. However, so far, their difficult programming model and poor floating-point support prevented a wide adoption for typical HPC applications. This is changing, due to recent FPGA technology developments: support for the high-level OpenCL programming language, hard floating-point units, and tight integration with CPU cores. Combined, these are game changers: they dramatically reduce development times and allow using FPGAs for applications that were previously deemed too complex.

In this paper, we show how we implemented and optimized a radio-astronomical imaging application on an Arria 10 FPGA. We compare architectures, programming models, optimizations, performance, energy efficiency, and programming effort to highly optimized GPU and CPU implementations. We show that we can efficiently optimize for FPGA resource usage, but also that optimizing for a high clock speed is difficult. All together, we demonstrate that OpenCL support for FPGAs is a leap forward in programmability and it enabled us to use an FPGA as a viable accelerator platform for a complex HPC application.

1 Introduction

Field-Programmable Gate Arrays (FPGAs) have long been favoured as energy-efficient platform for fixed-precision computations. Their floating-point performance used to be sub-par, because floating-point units (FPUs) had to be assembled from logic blocks, which is rather inefficient and consumes many FPGA resources. Recent FPGAs, such as the Intel Arria 10, have hardware support for floating-point operations, making them an interesting platform for high-performance floating-point computing.

FPGAs are traditionally programmed using hardware description languages, such as Verilog and VHDL, which is notoriously difficult, time-consuming, and error-prone. FPGA manufacturers such as Intel (formerly Altera) and Xilinx now support OpenCL as a high-level alternative. In this paper, we describe how we use the Intel FPGA SDK for OpenCL to implement and optimize a complex radio-astronomy imaging application for the Arria 10 FPGA, which would have been a daunting task when using a hardware description language. Radio-astronomical imaging is a computationally challenging problem and poses

© Springer Nature Switzerland AG 2019
R. Yahyapour (Ed.): Euro-Par 2019, LNCS 11725, pp. 509–521, 2019.
https://doi.org/10.1007/978-3-030-29400-7_36

strict performance and energy-efficiency requirements, especially for future exa-scale instruments such as the Square Kilometre Array (SKA). We previously demonstrated that imaging works particularly well on GPUs [11], so how does the FPGA perform in comparison?

The main contributions of this paper are: (1) We explain how we use the Intel FPGA SDK for OpenCL to build an efficient data-flow network for a complex radio-astronomy application; (2) We compare our implementation on the Arria 10 FPGA to highly optimized CPU and GPU implementations and evaluate performance and energy efficiency; (3) We discuss the differences and similarities between FPGAs and GPUs in terms of architecture, programming model, and implementation effort.

The rest of this paper is organized as follows: Sect. 2 provides background information on radio-astronomical imaging. Section 3 explains how we implemented and optimized the most critical parts of an astronomical imaging application. In Sect. 4 we analyze performance and show energy efficiency measurements. Section 5 describes the lessons that we learned while implementing and optimizing the same application for both FPGAs and GPUs. In Sect. 6 we discuss related work and we conclude in Sect. 7.

The source code of the FPGA implementations discussed in this paper is available online [1].

2   Radio-Astronomical Imaging

A radio telescope detects electromagnetic waves that originate from radio sources in the universe, which are used to construct a map of the sky containing the positions, intensity, and polarization of the sources. Radio telescopes (such as LOFAR and the future SKA-1 Low telescope) comprise many receivers of which the signals are combined using a technique called 'interferometry'. Figure 1 shows a simplified version of a radio-astronomical interferometer, where sky-images are created in three steps: correlation, calibration, and imaging. Every receiver measures two signals, corresponding to two orthogonal polarizations. The signals from a receiver pair (q, r) (called a *baseline*) are multiplied and integrated for a short period of time (correlated) such that the resulting sample $V_{(q,r)}$ (called a *visibility*) contains the 2×2 combinations of the (polarized) signals measured by receiver q and r, hence $V_{(q,r)} \in \mathbb{C}^{2 \times 2}$. Visibilities have associated (u, v, w)-coordinates that depend on the location of the receivers with respect to the observed sky. Due to earth rotation, (u, v, w)-coordinates change over time and every baseline contributes a track of measurements. During an observation, each baseline collects T_{Obs} integration periods, where every sample consists of C_{Obs} measurements in frequency. There exists a Fourier relation between the sampled data and the observed sky. Therefore, in the *imaging* step, visibilities are first placed onto a regular grid by an operation called *gridding*. This operation corresponds to applying a convolution to every visibility. After gridding, the grid is Fourier transformed to obtain a *sky image*. *Degridding* is the reverse operation where visibilities are computed taking a grid as input.

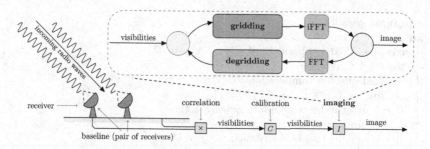

Fig. 1. In a radio-telescope, signals are received by pairs of *receivers*. The *correlator* combines the signal into *visibilities*. After *calibration* of the visibilities, the *imager* produces an image of the sky, using an *imaging pipeline*.

2.1 Image-Domain Gridding

Image-Domain Gridding (IDG [10,11]) is a novel imaging technique where neighbouring visibilities are first gridded onto so-called *subgrids*, after which the subgrids are Fourier transformed and added to the full grid. Subgrids are $N \times N$ pixels in size and are positioned such that they cover T integration periods (each with C frequency channels) and their corresponding convolution kernels. Algorithm 1 shows pseudocode for gridding.

By applying gridding in the *image-domain*, IDG avoids the use of convolution kernels in traditional gridding. Furthermore, the computation of one subgrid (one iteration of the loop on Line 2) is not dependent on the computation of another subgrid, making IDG very suitable for parallelization. We will refer to Line 4 through Line 15 as the *gridder*. After this step, a-term correction, tapering and a 2D FFT are applied. We will refer to these operations as *post-processing*.

Pixels of the subgrid are computed as a direct sum of phase-shifted visibilities [10]. This shift takes both the position of the subgrid (the *phase offset*, Line 5) and the position of the visibility in the subgrid (the *phase index*, Line 7) into account. Furthermore, the phase index is scaled according to frequency (Line 9).

The *phasor* term in Line 11 is a complex number that is computed by an evaluation of $cos(phase)$ and $sin(phase)$ or in more common terms $cis(phase)$ where $cis(x) = cos(x) + isin(x)$. *cmul* denotes a complex multiplication, which comprises four real-valued multiply-add operations. Since $P = 4$, the loop on Line 13 is typically unrolled. Thus for every iteration of the loop over frequency channels in line 8, one sine, one cosine, and 17 multiply-add operations are performed, one in the computation of *phase* in Line 10, and 16 in the complex multiplication of *phasor* with visibilities and addition to the subgrid in Line 15.

The operations outside this critical loop (the *offset* computation on Line 5, the index computation on Line 7, and post-processing steps) are described by van der Tol et al. [10]. The grid can be several tens of GBs in size and is therefore typically stored on a CPU-based system, while the computationally most challenging gridding step is preferably performed on an accelerator (such as a FPGA or a GPU).

```
 1   #pragma parallel
 2   for s = 1...S :
 3       complex<float> subgrid[P][N × N];
 4       for i = 1...N × N :
 5           float offset = compute_offset(s, i);
 6           for t = 1...T :
 7               float index = compute_index(s, i, t);
 8               for c = 1...C :
 9                   float scale = scales[c];
10                   float phase = offset - (index × scale);
11                   complex<float> phasor = {cos(phase), sin(phase)};
12                   #pragma unroll
13                   for p = 1...P : // 4 polarizations
14                       complex<float> visibility = visibilities[t][c][p];
15                       subgrid[p][i] += cmul(phasor, visibility);
16       apply_aterm(subgrid);
17       apply_taper(subgrid);
18       apply_ifft(subgrid);
19       store(subgrid);
```

Algorithm 1: Gridding pseudocode that is executed for every subgrid s of $N \times N$ pixels in size. $T \times C$ visibilities are associated with a subgrid, where T and C denote time and frequency channel, respectively. Typical values for these parameters are $N = 32$, $T = 128$ and $C = 16$.

3   Implementation

As we discuss in more detail later, FPGA applications are typically implemented as a data-flow pipeline. We show the data-flow pipeline that we created for the Image-Domain Gridding algorithm (Algorithm 1) in Fig. 2. The floating-point operations in this algorithm are implemented in hardware using DSP blocks. Our design is scalable and optimizes both the number of DSPs used and the occupancy of these DSPs such that every cycle, every DSP performs a useful computation. Although the computations in gridding and degridding are similar, the degridding data-flow network is different and not shown in Fig. 2.

To implement gridding on the FPGA, we applied the following changes to Algorithm 1: (1) we create a *gridder pipeline* that executes Line 5 through Line 15 to compute a single subgrid; (2) we move the computation of the *index* value (Line 7) and the computation of *offset* (Line 5) into separate kernels to avoid underutilization of the DSPs used to implement these computations; (3) we unroll the loop over pixels (Line 4) to increase reuse of input data; (4) we replicate the gridder pipeline by a factor ϕ to compute multiple subgrids in parallel; (5) input data (such as the visibilities, Line 14) is read from DRAM in bursts in separate kernels and forwarded to the gridder pipelines in a round-robin fashion.

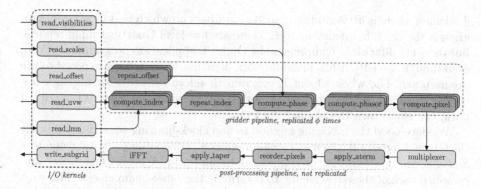

Fig. 2. All kernels in this design are single work-item kernels. The majority of the computation takes place in the gridder pipeline, which is replicated ϕ times to compute multiple subgrids in parallel. These subgrids are multiplexed and passed to the post-processing pipeline, which applies a-term correction, tapering and a 2D FFT.

The remaining steps are implemented in the form of a *post-processing pipeline* using as few resources as possible while still meeting throughput requirements imposed by the gridder pipelines. A-term correction (Line 16) is implemented as a series of two complex 2×2 matrix multiplications (one correction matrix per receiver). Tapering (Line 17) is implemented as a scalar multiplication to every pixel in the subgrid. The 2D FFT (Line 18) is based on the 1D Cooley-Tukey FFT algorithm, which is applied to the rows and columns of the subgrid to perform a 2D FFT.

3.1 The Sine/Cosine Computations

The Intel FPGA OpenCL compiler recognizes the sine and cosine pair and uses 8 memory blocks and 8 DSPs to implement it by creating a so-called *IP block* (cis_{ip}). In comparison, only a single DSP is used to compute the *phase* term on Line 10, and 16 DSPs are used to implement the computation on Line 15. To reduce resource usage for $cis(x)$, we investigated how lookup tables can be used as an alternative to the compiler-generated version. In the case of $cis(x)$ the input x is an angle and the output is given as a coordinate on the unit circle, which opens opportunities to exploit symmetry. Our lookup table implementation (cis_{lu}) contains precomputed values for $sin(x)$ in the range of $[0 : \frac{1}{2}\pi]$. We use one DSP to convert the input x to an integer index and then derive indices for $sin(x)$ and $cos(x)$ using *logic elements*. We analytically determined that a 1024-entry table provides sufficient accuracy.

3.2 Optimizing for Frequency

The OpenCL FPGA compiler gives feedback on resource usage by generating HTML reports, which is highly useful when optimizing for resource usage. Optimizing for high clock frequencies is difficult though: apart from a few general guidelines, there is little guidance, such as feedback on which part of a (large) program is the clock frequency limiter. There are low-level Quartus timing reports, but these are difficult to comprehend by OpenCL application programmers. Also, even though the FPGA has multiple clock domains, these are not exposed to the programmer. The whole OpenCL program therefore runs at a single clock frequency. Hence, a single problematic statement, possibly not even in the critical path, can slow down the whole FPGA design.

We developed the following method to find clock-limiting constructs: we split the OpenCL program into many small fragments, added dummy data generators and sink routines (so that the compiler does not optimize everything away), and compiled each of these fragments, to determine their maximum clocks. This way, we found for example that a single, inadvertently placed modulo 13 operation slowed down the whole application, something which was difficult to pinpoint but easy to fix.

4   Results

We compare our gridding and degridding design on an Arria 10 FPGA to a GPU in terms of performance and energy efficiency. We also add an optimized CPU implementation for comparison. We use contemporary devices with a similar theoretical peak performance and produced using a similar lithographical process, see Table 1 for details. The imaging parameters are set as follows: $N = 32$, $T = 128$ and $C = 16$. The FPGA designs are scaled up by increasing ϕ until the maximum number of DSPs is reached.

The Arria 10 GX 1150 FPGA (ARRIA) comes in the form of an PCIe accelerator card and has two banks of 4 GB DDR3 memory. The FPGA runs a so-called Board-Support Package (BSP) that is required to use the FPGA using the Intel FPGA SDK for OpenCL. We use the *min* BSP, which exposes all 1518 DSPs present on the FPGA to the application and uses only one DDR3 memory bank. We tested various combinations of the Intel FPGA SDK for OpenCL (versions 17.1, 18.0 and 18.1), recompiled each application with dozens of seeds, and report the results for the version that achieves the best clock frequency.

The CPU that we use is part of a dual-socket system, of which we use only a single processor (HASWELL) and the corresponding memory. We use an Intel compiler and the Intel Math Kernel Library (MKL) (both version 2019.0). The GPU (MAXWELL) uses the 396.26 GPU driver and CUDA version 9.2.88.

4.1   Resource Usage

We refer to designs that use cis_{ip} as GRIDDING-IP and DEGRIDDING-IP, while the GRIDDING-LU and DEGRIDDING-LU designs use our alternative implementation with lookup tables (cis_{lu}). We report resource usage and the highest achieved clock frequency (F_{max}) of all designs in Table 2. In all four designs the number of DSPs used is very close to the 1518 DSPs available and we run out of DSPs before we run out of any other resource (which is good). We provide a breakdown of DSP

Table 1. The Intel Haswell-EP CPU, Intel Arria 10 FPGA and NVIDIA Maxwell GPU used in our experiments. We refer to these devices as HASWELL, ARRIA and MAXWELL.

	# FPUs	Peak	Bandwidth	TDP	Process
Intel Xeon E5-2697v3	224[a]	1.39 TFlop/s	68 GB/s	145W	22 nm (TSMC)
Nallatech 385A	1518	1.37 TFlop/s	34 GB/s	75 W	20 nm (TSMC)
NVidia GTX 750 Ti	640	1.39 TFlop/s	88 GB/s	60 W	28 nm (TSMC)

[a] # cores × # vector units × vector length

Table 2. Resource usage of our gridding and degridding designs on ARRIA. Logic (ALUTs or FFs) is counted in terms of thousand elements. The ϕ parameter is used to scale up the design, see Fig. 2. The theoretical peak F_{max} of ARRIA is 450 MHz.

	ALUTs	FFs	RAMs	DSPs	MLABs	ϕ	F_{max}
GRIDDING-IP	334 (43%)	487 (31%)	1514 (64%)	1439 (95%)	5317 (71%)	14	258
DEGRIDDING-IP	364 (47%)	550 (35%)	1711 (72%)	1441 (95%)	6418 (78%)	14	254
GRIDDING-LU	207 (27%)	490 (32%)	1448 (61%)	1498 (99%)	5921 (57%)	20	256
DEGRIDDING-LU	252 (33%)	583 (38%)	1723 (73%)	1503 (99%)	7520 (69%)	20	253

resource usage in Fig. 3 where we distinguish between the DSPs used to implement various subparts of the algorithm. E.g. for gridding (Algorithm 1): DSP_{fma} (Line 15), DSP_{cis} (Line 11) and DSP_{misc} for the post-processing steps and miscellaneous computations, and similarly for degridding. The implementation of computations outside of the critical path consume few resources (DSP_{misc}). Since cis_{lu} uses fewer resources compared to cis_{ip} to implement the sine/cosine evaluation, we are able to scale up GRIDDING-LU and DEGRIDDING-LU further (by increasing ϕ from 14 to 20) than is possible with GRIDDING-IP and DEGRIDDING-IP.

4.2   Throughput and Energy Efficiency

We compare throughput, measured as the number of visibilities processed per second, in Fig. 4a. The designs that use a lookup table to implement the sine/cosine evaluation (cis_{lu}) achieve a higher throughput due to a larger number of parallel gridder or degridder pipelines. Both ARRIA and MAXWELL accelerate gridding and degridding compared to HASWELL by achieving more than double the throughput.

On both the FPGA and GPU the visibilities (and other data) are copied to and from the device using PCIe transfers. On MAXWELL, we can fully overlap PCIe transfers with computations, such that throughput is not affected by these transfers. On ARRIA, we found that PCIe transfers overlap only partially: the FPGA idles 9% of the total runtime waiting on PCIe transfers. This is probably a limitation in the OpenCL runtime or Board Support Package. We see no fundamental reason why PCIe transfers could not fully overlap on the FPGA. In Fig. 4a we therefore only include the kernel runtime to determine throughput.

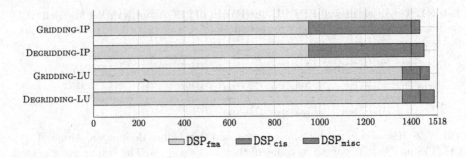

Fig. 3. Breakdown of DSP resource usage

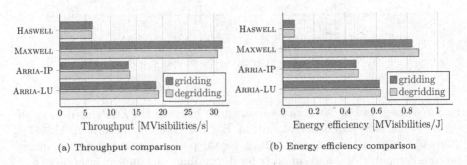

(a) Throughput comparison   (b) Energy efficiency comparison

Fig. 4. Throughput (the number of visibilities processed per second, MVis/s) and energy efficiency (the number of visibilities processed per Joule, MVis/J).

To asses energy-efficiency, we use PowerSensor [8] to measure energy consumption of the full PCIe device in case of ARRIA. On MAXWELL we use NVML and on HASWELL we use LIKWID [9]. Our measurements in Fig. 4b indicate that both accelerators are much more energy-efficient then HASWELL by processing about an order of magnitude more visibilities for every Joule consumed.

4.3 Performance Analysis

Despite their almost identical theoretical peak performance, there is quite a large disparity between the achieved throughput on the various devices. As we illustrate in Fig. 5, these differences are mainly caused by how sine/cosine ($cis(x)$) is implemented. On HASWELL we use MKL to evaluate $cis(x)$ in *software* by issuing instructions onto the FPUs. In the operations mix found in IDG (17 FMAs and one evaluation of $cis(x)$) 80% of the time is spent in the sine/cosine evaluation [11]. On MAXWELL, Special Function Units (SFUs) evaluate $cis(x)$ in hardware in a separate processing pipeline, such that FMAs and sine/cosine evaluations can be overlapped. Similarly, the distinct operations (fma, cis and $misc$) also overlap on ARRIA, since these are all implemented using dedicated DSPs. However, unlike MAXWELL, these operations compete for resources. On HASWELL and MAXWELL the miscellaneous operations contribute negligibly to

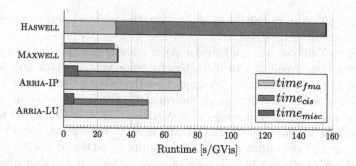

Fig. 5. Breakdown of gridding runtime for FMA operations ($time_{fma}$), sine/cosine evaluations ($time_{cis}$) and all other operations ($time_{misc}$). On HASWELL, 80% of the time is spend in sine/cosine evaluations. On MAXWELL and on ARRIA, the sine/cosine evaluations are performed concurrently with the FMA operations.

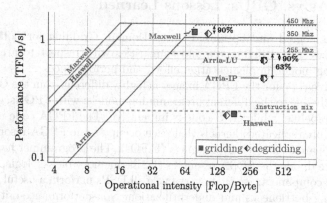

Fig. 6. The implementation of sine/cosine evaluations in software imposes an upper bound on performance on HASWELL. MAXWELL performs sine/cosine operations concurrently with FMA operations and performs close to the theoretical peak. On ARRIA, the performance is bound by the clock frequency.

the overall runtime. On ARRIA, the *misc* operations are implemented using as few DSPs as possible (and shared by multiple gridder pipelines) to minimize *underutilization*.

We analyze the achieved floating-point performance by applying the roofline model [12], see Fig. 6. In this analysis, we only include all $+$, $-$ and $\times$ floating-point operations in the operation count (e.g. $Flops_{fma} + Flops_{misc}$), while we exclude all $cis(x)$ operations (e.g. Ops_{cis}). According to the operational intensity, the performance of gridding and degridding is *compute bound* on all devices. As we illustrated in Fig. 5, on HASWELL the *Flops* and *Ops* are both executed on the FPUs and the performance is therefore bound by the performance of the $cis(x)$ implementation, e.g. Intel MKL (for which the bound is indicated with the blue dashed line). A lookup table does not improve performance over using the Intel

MKL library. Due to the SFUs, on MAXWELL the achieved performance is over 90% of the theoretical peak.

The dotted line on the roofline for ARRIA illustrates the theoretical peak, at the advertised frequency of 450 MHz. In practice, even with only a single DSP used, the maximum clock frequency that the compiler achieves is 350 MHz resulting in a lower practical peak indicated by the solid line. Our gridding and degridding designs on average achieve about 255 MHz (indicated with the red dashed line). The percentage of DSPs used to implement *Flops* (63% for GRIDDING-IP and DEGRIDDING-IP, 90% for GRIDDING-LU and DEGRIDDING-LU, see Fig. 3) provides upper bounds on attainable performance. The achieved performance is within 99% of these bounds, indicating that the designs are nearly stall-free.

5   FPGAs vs. GPUs: Lessons Learned

As we implemented and optimized Image-Domain Gridding for both FPGAs and GPUs, we found differences and similarities with respect to architecture, programming model, implementation effort, and performance.

The source code for the FPGA imager is highly different from the GPU code. This is mostly due to the different programming models: with FPGAs, one builds a dataflow pipeline, while GPU code is imperative. The FPGA code consists of many (possibly replicated) kernels that each occupy some FPGA resources, and these kernels are connected by *channels* (FIFOs). The programmer has to think about how to divide the FPGA resources (DSPs, memory blocks, logic, etc.) over the pipeline components, so that every cycle all DSPs perform a useful computation, avoiding bottlenecks and underutilization. Non-performance-critical operations, such as initialization routines, can consume many resources, while on GPUs, performance-insensitive operations are not an issue. On FPGAs, it is also much more important to think about timing (e.g., to avoid pipeline stalls), but being forced to think about it leads to high efficiency: in our gridding application, no less than 96% of all DSPs perform a useful operation 99% of the time.

FPGAs have typically less memory bandwidth than GPUs, but we found that with the FPGA dataflow model, where all kernels are concurrently active, it is less tempting to store intermediate results off-chip than with GPUs, where kernels are executed one after another. In fact, our FPGA designs use memory only for input and output data; we would not even have used FPGA device memory at all if the OpenCL Board-Support Package would have implemented the PCIe I/O channel extension. In contrast, the cuFFT GPU library even requires data to be in off-chip memory.

Both FPGAs and GPUs obtain parallelism through kernel replication and vectorization; FPGAs also by pipelining and loop unrolling. This is another reason why FPGA and GPU programs look differently. Surprisingly, many optimizations for FPGAs and GPUs are similar, at least at a high level. Maximizing FPU utilization, data reuse through caching, memory coalescing, memory latency hiding, and FPU latency hiding are necessary optimizations on both architectures. For example, an optimization that we implemented to reduce local memory bandwidth usage on the FPGA also turned out to improve performance on the GPU, but somehow, we did not think about this GPU optimization before we implemented the FPGA variant. However, optimizations like latency hiding are much more explicit in FPGA code than in GPU code, as the GPU model implicitly hides latencies by having many simultaneously instructions in flight. On top of that, architecture-specific optimizations are possible (e.g., the sin/cos lookup table; see Sect. 3.1).

Overall, we found it more difficult to implement and optimize for an FPGA than for a GPU, mostly because it is difficult to efficiently distribute the FPGA resources over the kernels in a complex dataflow pipeline. Yet, we consider the availability of a high-level programming language and hard FPUs on FPGAs an enormous step forward. The OpenCL FPGA tools have considerably improved during the past few years, but have not yet reached the maturity level of the GPU tools, which is quite natural, as the GPU tools have had much more time to mature.

6   Related Work, Discussion and Future Work

Licht et al. [4] present an overview of HLS FPGA code transformations such as transposing of the iteration space, replication and streaming dataflow that we also applied. However, they do not describe code transformation for overcoming underutilization of resources. Yang et al. [14] address underutilization of resources by using a consumer-producer model, which they implement using channel arbitrage. We also connect kernels running at different rates using channels, but we use channel depth to facilitate buffering and to avoid stalls.

Several studies compare energy efficiency between OpenCL applications for FPGAs and GPUs [3,5–7,15,16]. In most cases, they compare FPGAs and GPUs manufactured using a similar lithographical process and report higher energy-efficiency for FPGAs compared to GPUs. We compared contemporary and comparable devices (in terms of lithographical process and peak performance) and apply the roofline model to illustrate that our implementations perform close to optimal both on the FPGA and on the GPU. On Arria 10 we show that the performance of our designs are bound by clock frequency, something we can not improve with the current OpenCL compiler for FPGAs. We also explain that the GPU has an advantage, by computing sine/cosine using dedicated hardware. In contrast to what the related work suggests, our results indicate that FPGAs are not necessarily more energy-efficient than GPUs.

Intel claims that the Stratix 10 FPGA (produced at 14 nm) will be about 3.6× as energy-efficient compared to Arria 10 [13] and have a peak performance of up to 9 TFlop/s. In future work, we would like to extend our analysis to compare Stratix 10 and NVIDIA Turing GPUs.

7   Conclusion

In this paper we set out to implement a complex radio-astronomy application on an Arria 10 FPGA using the Intel FPGA SDK for OpenCL. Being able to implement such an application illustrates that having support for a high-level programming language is a major leap forwards in programmability, as we would not have been able to implement this application using a hardware description language. We show optimization techniques that make our implementation very scalable as it uses almost all DSPs available to perform useful floating-point computations while it stalls less than 1% of the time.

We compared optimized implementations of an astronomical imaging application on a GPU, FPGA, and a CPU. While the theoretical peak-performance for these devices is almost identical, the FPGA and GPU perform much better than the CPU and they consume significantly less power. In absolute terms, the GPU is the fastest and most energy-efficient device, mainly due to support for sine/cosine operations using dedicated hardware. On the FPGA, our implementation of a custom lookup-table for these operations is advantageous, but the maximum achieved clock frequency is only about 70% of the theoretical peak. Unfortunately, the Intel FPGA SDK for OpenCL (currently) provides few means to improve the clock frequency. This issue is non-existent on GPUs.

FPGAs are traditionally used for low-latency, fixed-point and streaming computations. With the addition of hardware support for floating-point computations and the OpenCL programming model, the FPGA has also entered the domain where GPUs are used: high-performance floating-point applications.

Acknowledgments. This work is funded by the Netherlands eScience Center (NLeSC), under grant no 027.016.G07 (Triple-A 2), the EU Horizon 2020 research and innovation programme under grant no 754304 (DEEP-EST) and by NWO (DAS-5 [2]). The European Commission is not liable for any use that might be made of the information contained in this paper. The authors would like to thank Atze van der Ploeg (NLeSC) and Suleyman S. Demirsoy (Intel) for their support.

References

1. ASTRON Netherlands Institute for Radio Astronomy: Image-Domain Gridding for FPGAs (2019). https://gitlab.com/astron-idg/idg-fpga
2. Bal, H., et al.: A medium-scale distributed system for computer science research: infrastructure for the long term. IEEE Comput. **49**(5), 54–63 (2016)
3. Cong, J., et al.: Understanding performance differences of FPGAs and GPUs. In: 2018 IEEE 26th International Symposium on Field-Programmable Custom Computing Machines, pp. 93–96 (2018)
4. de Fine Licht, J., et al.: Transformations of high-level synthesis codes for high-performance computing. Computing Research Repository (CoRR) (2018)
5. Jin, Z., Finkel, H.: Power and performance tradeoff of a floating-point intensive kernel on OpenCL FPGA platform, pp. 716–720 (2018)

6. Minhas, U.I., Woods, R., Karakonstantis, G.: Exploring functional acceleration of OpenCL on FPGAs and GPUs through platform-independent optimizations. In: Voros, N., Huebner, M., Keramidas, G., Goehringer, D., Antonopoulos, C., Diniz, P.C. (eds.) ARC 2018. LNCS, vol. 10824, pp. 551–563. Springer, Cham (2018). https://doi.org/10.1007/978-3-319-78890-6_44

7. Muslim, F.B., et al.: Efficient FPGA implementation of OpenCL high-performance computing applications via high-level synthesis. IEEE Access **5**, 2747–2762 (2017)

8. Romein, J.W., Veenboer, B.: PowerSensor 2: a fast power measurement tool. In: 2018 IEEE International Symposium on Performance Analysis of Systems and Software, pp. 111–113 (2018)

9. Treibig, J., Hager, G., Wellein, G.: LIKWID: a lightweight performance-oriented tool suite for x86 multicore environments. In: Proceedings of the International Conference on Parallel Processing, pp. 207–216 (2010)

10. van der Tol, S., Veenboer, B., Offringa, A.: Image domain gridding. Astron. Astrophys. **616**, A27 (2018)

11. Veenboer, B., Petschow, M., Romein, J.W.: Image-domain gridding on graphics processors. In: Proceedings of the International Parallel and Distributed Processing Symposium, IPDPS, pp. 545–554 (2017)

12. Williams, S., Waterman, A., Patterson, D.: Roofline: an insightful visual performance model for multicore architectures. Commun. ACM **52**, 65–76 (2009)

13. Won, M.S.: Meeting the performance and power imperative of the Zettabyte era with generation 10. Technical report, Intel Programmable Solutions Group (2013)

14. Yang, C., et al.: OpenCL for HPC with FPGAs: case study in molecular electrostatics. In: 2017 IEEE High Performance Extreme Computing Conference (HPEC), pp. 1–8 (2017)

15. Zohouri, H.R.: High performance computing with FPGAs and OpenCL. Ph.D. thesis, Tokyo Institute of Technology (2018)

16. Zohouri, H.R., et al.: Evaluating and optimizing OpenCL kernels for high performance computing with FPGAs. In: SC16: International Conference for High Performance Computing, Networking, Storage and Analysis, pp. 409–420 (2016)

Author Index

Printed in the United States
By Bookmasters